Finding
the
Winning Edge

Bill Walsh

with

Brian Billick

James A. Peterson

Sports Publishing Inc.
Champaign, IL

Book design: Michelle A. Summers
Dustjacket design and photo section layout: Michelle R. Dressen
Editor: Joseph J. Bannon Jr.

ISBN: 1-57164-172-2
Library of Congress Catalog Card Number: 97-80397

Unless otherwise noted all photos are from Bill Walsh's private collection.

Sports Publishing Inc.
804 N. Neil
Champaign, IL 61820
www.sagamorepub.com

Printed in the United States

DEDICATION

To my wife, Geri—my lifetime partner. Together, we shared the disappointments and frustrations of a struggling career and, ultimately, the euphoria of winning the world championship. The years of sacrifice finally proved worthwhile. I also dedicate this book to my children—Steve, Craig and Elizabeth. You've been great, even with a dad who wasn't always around.

BW

To Kim, Aubree and Keegan who gave up many nights and weekends, allowing me to pursue this endeavor.

BB

To Sue, my wife and best friend for thirty years.

JP

ACKNOWLEDGMENTS

I would like to recognize Owen Edwards who collaborated with me on our *Forbes Magazine* series. What a terrific person and gifted writer. Owen is an accomplished professional and a wonderful philosopher. I would also like to state my appreciation for the expert skills of Richard Van Rapaport, the writer who molded my thoughts into definable reading for our piece that appeared in the *Harvard Business Review*. Rich is a true intellectual, a marvelous writer and a great guy. I am quite proud of the body of work that the three of us produced. Owen and Rich were able to translate football into something of interest to the corporate environment.

I would also like to acknowledge the following individuals who have affected my life in meaningful ways: Martin Connelly—my lifetime friend and colleague—your insight and wisdom have meant so much; Jane Walsh—my friend and associate—your part in this project has been invaluable; Dr. Harry Edwards—your strength and professionalism have made a major impact on my life; newspaper columnist—Jim Murray—I am indepted for your support throughout the ebb and flow of my career; Eddie DeBartolo and Carmen Policy—we've shared every possible emotion; Coach Bob Bronzan—thanks for setting a standard for individuals like myself to emulate; Steven Kay—I am indebted to you for your counsel, advice and friendship; Dr. Glen Albaugh—your dedication and your commitment to society have given justification to sport; and Dick Vermeil and Mike White—what a run we've had.

BW

As is usually the case, the completion of this book was made possible though the help and guidance of a number of people. The authors would like to thank Erica Wieland, Mike Eyers, Frank Cooney, Jeff Walker, Darci Bransford and Colonel Charles F. "Casey" Brower for their assistance in compiling the information. We would also like to thank Bob Oates, Gordon Forbes, Andrea Kremer and Phil Simms for their input and counsel throughout the project.

Our gratitude is also expressed to the staff at Sagamore Publishing/Sports Publishing Inc. for their assistance with this project, particularly Michelle Summers, Joanna Wright and Laura Main.

Finally, we would like to acknowledge those in the coaching profession, too numerous to list, for their creative and devoted commitment to the industry and their collective contributions to the philosophies and structures outlined in this material.

BB

CONTENTS

PART IV: THE GAME

PART V: THE BUSINESS

APPENDICES

FOREWORD

We know that football teams, similar to organizations everywhere, improve by going through an evolutionary progression as they learn, apply, adapt, and learn again. Bill Walsh's *Finding the Winning Edge* provides readers with the first-ever systematic, practical guide to establishing and mastering the steps involved in that crucial process. In my personal opinion, no individual in the history of the game is more qualified to put forth such invaluable guidance.

During his illustrious career, Bill was more than a football coach. In a very real sense, he has been an exceptional visionary. Although he is widely renowned as the architect of the "West Coast" offense, his innovative approach to the game has extended far beyond his imaginative ideas on offense.

During the time he spent working with the San Francisco 49ers, he transformed San Francisco's game into an art form. To Bill, football is more than a physical contest, and success is more than a victory on the playing field.

Success is the progression of worthy ideas and goals. Such a progression involves at least two key cerebral factors—attention to detail and an absolute commitment to perfection.

To Bill's way of reasoning, no detail or situation is too unimportant to be overlooked. Every possible circumstance that might affect the performance of the team and the productivity of the organization should be addressed. In turn, a contingency plan to handle each situation should be developed.

Bill was no less adamant about the need to shoot for perfection. His convictions on the matter were illustrated vividly to me during an event that occurred one day in practice. As the 49ers' quarterback coach, I watched Joe Montana throw a pass slightly behind Jerry Rice, who nevertheless would catch such a pass 99 times out of 100.

Most coaches might be satisfied with this success ratio. Not Bill. He immediately came to me and explained in great detail why a pass involving that route had to be thrown twelve inches in front of the receiver, not six inches behind him.

Bill had a singular focus on perfection. Every day. Every practice. Every play. Every meeting. Every situation.

Finding the Winning Edge is destined to become the number one reference book in the library of every football coach in the game. Written in an easy-to-read, straight-forward style, this ground-breaking text can help coaches at all competitive levels.

In his more than four decades of involvement with the game as a player, a coach, and a top-level administrator, no individual has had a more worthy or meaningful impact on the players he coached or the coaches with whom he worked.

A list of the assistant coaches that served with Bill—and who subsequently went on to achieve remarkable success as head coaches on both the collegiate and professional levels—is quite extraordinary. As a result, his influence continues to be felt throughout all levels of the game today.

Finding the Winning Edge is Bill's detailed effort to share his ideas, principles, and programs for developing a winning program. The book offers every coach a game plan for success.

Mike Holmgren
Head Coach
Green Bay Packers

INTRODUCTION

Arguably, one of the most exciting and most closely contested games in the history of the Super Bowl occurred on January 22, 1989, in Joe Robbie Stadium in Miami, Florida. This game had everything—passion, drama, heroics and two highly competitive teams with comparable talent levels, the Cincinnati Bengals and the San Francisco 49ers.

Super Bowl XXIII also had one of the most defining three-minute periods in the history of football—a period which has come to be known over the years as simply, "The Drive." 92 yards. Twelve plays. Methodical efficiency. A 20-16 49ers' victory.

Trailing 16-13 with just over three minutes to play, the 49ers' offense began a fateful scoring drive that culminated with a 10-yard pass from Joe Montana to John Taylor for the winning score with 34 seconds left. As conceived and orchestrated, the drive was the definitive example of coaching proficiency.

In reality, the drive was simply an extension of "the man" and "the system." The man was Bill Walsh, and the system was the West Coast Offense (an offensive scheme that reflects the factors that Bill holds in the highest regard—preparation, planning, precision and poise).

Unbeknownst to the 75,000 people who were in the stands that day or the millions of individuals who were watching the intense gridiron struggle on television, Walsh had made the decision before the game to retire as head coach of the 49ers after Super Bowl XXIII. The four-point victory over the Bengals that earned both him and the 49ers their third Super Bowl victory in a decade only served to reinforce the validity of Bill's preoccupation with perfection.

When Bill approached me about helping him develop and write this book, it became immediately clear to me that one of Bill's main priorities with the project was to keep the focus and perspective of the material on a well-defined and practical level. Furthermore, he wanted this book to be an invaluable reference text for coaches at all competitive levels.

As you read this book, I believe that you will conclude that both of Bill's goals in this regard have been achieved. *Finding the Winning Edge* presents Bill's ideas, principles and concepts for developing a successful football program in a single volume.

This book is organized into five distinct sections: Part I—Experiences and Values; Part II—The Organization; Part III—The People; Part IV—The Game; and Part V—The Business. In addition, *Finding the Winning Edge* features an extensive Appendices section that includes several valuable segments (e.g., sample job description outlines, team lectures, employee lectures, etc.).

The section on *Experiences and Values* provides a brief summary of Coach Walsh's background and a review of some of the major influences on his personal and professional attitudes and values. In addition, an overview of the factors required for a focused philosophy is presented, with a particular emphasis on understanding the meaning of true *competition*.

The section on *The Organization* explains how and why a football organization must be structured to accomplish specific goals. How the head coach should recruit, develop and effectively utilize a competent staff is also examined. This section also includes a thoughtful discussion of what it means to be a head coach.

The section on *The People* discusses how the head coach should utilize the various methods of acquiring players to build a successful team. An overview of the steps involved and the criteria used to evaluate players is also presented.

Furthermore, this section includes a summary of what a head coach should do to ensure that the skills and talents of each player on the team are developed and utilized in an appropriate way, particularly those of the quarterback. In addition, the area of how the head coach should deal with relevant issues facing his athletes is reviewed.

The section on *The Game* looks at several of the critical factors that directly impact on the team's performance and success level, including game planning, practice structure and game-day management. In addition, a review of how the head coach can make sound decisions and how selected mental aspects can inhibit a player's performance is summarized.

This section also includes an extensive discussion of how the head coach should deal with specific circumstances. Among the seasonal situations that are examined are those instances involving a newly named coach, an extended losing streak, the last-second loss, an extended winning streak, rebounding from a losing season, the coach who leaves the job, and the off-season. Advice is also presented concerning how to handle different types of teams, including the inexperienced team, the down-and-out team, the talented team and the team with high expectations. The final part of the section covers how the head coach should deal with individual game circumstances (e.g., the last-second loss, key games, games as a big underdog or a lopsided favorite, games after a huge win, road games, preseason games, etc.).

The section on *The Business* discusses how the head coach should deal with specific financial issues, including interacting with the team's CFO and understanding the NFL salary cap. In addition, an overview of common sense recommendations and advice on how the head coach should deal with the media in a variety of circumstances is presented.

The book also includes almost 100 quotes that have inspired and have helped clarify and illuminate specific issues and factors for Bill over his career. Each of these quotes is boxed-in to highlight its importance.

Whenever the legacy of Bill Walsh is discussed, a number of factors will typically be considered—his lifetime commitment to excellence, his complete and total concentration on the task at hand, his ability to translate and apply his insightful concepts to offensive schemes, and his gift of inspiring and motivating others (as reflected by his three Super Bowl victories and the legion of former assistants and players who have gone on to make their marks in the coaching profession).

Hopefully, this book will also be one of his legacies to the game which he holds in such high regard. If *Finding the Winning Edge* provides coaches and administrators with a tool that enhances their ability to help their teams reach the next level of success, then the efforts to write this book will have been well worthwhile.

Brian Billick

PART I

EXPERIENCES AND VALUES

CHAPTER 1

PUTTING THINGS INTO HISTORICAL PERSPECTIVE

"Who knows what force gnaws at us, telling us that our accomplishments, no matter how sensational, are not enough, that we need to do more?"

—Arthur Ashe
Tennis Legend
Days of Grace

Finding the winning edge...

Perhaps the secret to effective action lies in how you interpret the length of the "day" in Carpe Diem. If it's a moment, or a day, you're cutting down on the odds for success. But if you recognize that in business as in sports (or any of life, for that matter), there's a "season" made up of several opportunities, those odds go up considerably.

The most successful business people are those who realize that they are going to take some hits in the process of searching out the big scores—those who know that performance over the long haul is what counts. If you can seize the day, great. But never forget that there are days yet to come.

—Bill Walsh, "Carpe Diem—Or the Diem After That," *Forbes*, October 25, 1993.

I was extremely fortunate to serve with John Ralston at Stanford. John assembled a fine staff that included Dick Vermeil, Mike White and me. All three of us were able to sustain recognition as head football coaches. Dick has distinguished himself at every level. He won championships at Hillside High School and Napa Community College, and led his UCLA team to victory in the Rose Bowl. As coach of the Philadelphia Eagles, he was twice awarded Coach of the Year honors.

For Dick, Mike and me, energy and enthusiasm marked the early stages of our careers and were followed by a period of learning to teach the tactical phases of the game. I believe we became outstanding teachers, both individually and collectively. In the latter stages of our careers, we each became well-grounded in organization and management.

Each period of development requires a blend of unrelenting energy and enthusiasm and a continual search for knowledge and expertise. All three of us had the ability to communicate and interact with others to establish an atmosphere of high motivation and a search for excellence.

History is our collective memory. It is our accumulated experiences. It is invoked constantly and unconsciously by every person, every day, to help them make decisions based, to some extent, on what has gone on before in their lives.

Accordingly, all factors considered, the more you know and understand your past, the better your insights regarding the present and the future. In that regard, past events and actual experiences in my life have had a tremendous influence on me personally.

Certainly, my own background and personal experiences have helped shape and orient my attitudes toward contemporary issues, values, goals, and behavior. The breadth of the personally significant occurrences in my life ranges from being able to observe firsthand my father's steadfast work ethic to having the opportunity to work with and learn from some of the finest individuals in the coaching profession.

SPRINGBOARD TO A CAREER IN COACHING

Not unlike many young people in my generation, I was born into an environment where every kid played sports in the streets and on the neighborhood lawns until we were kicked off. With no basketball courts in the neighborhood, playing football was our primary pursuit.

I grew up in an area of southwest Los Angeles—a location that is now known as south central—that was within two minutes of the campus of the University of Southern California. The atmosphere at USC only served to heighten my interest in football.

I can still vividly remember the first college football game I ever saw. Notre Dame—sparked by its Heisman Trophy-winning back Angelo Bertelli—beat USC 13-0.

In later years, I had the opportunity to hang around USC as a ball boy for the Trojan football team. In the process, I associated with several USC players who later became coaches.

In addition to sports, my father played a very influential role in my life as I was growing up. In particular, he ingrained in me the value of having a strong work ethic.

During the week, he was employed in a blue collar job in an auto plant. On the weekends, he ran a body and fender business in which I also worked. As my boss, he showed me that there was only one way to do a job—the right way.

Subsequently, my father decided to turn his weekend endeavor into a full-time business, so we moved to an area near Medford, Oregon. After discovering that Oregon did not exactly receive Californians with open arms, we then relocated to Hayward, California.

Because of my family's numerous travels, I had the opportunity to attend three different high schools. I played on the football team at each school—sometimes as a quarterback, but usually as a running back because I was always new to the program and the system. I then went to San Mateo Community College for two seasons, where I was finally able to play quarterback on a regular basis.

I then decided to complete my undergraduate education at San Jose State University, where I had the opportunity to play as an end on the Spartan football team under the direction of Bob Bronzan. Bronzan had a significant influence on me—both as a person and as a future coach.

He demanded high standards of performance at all times from everyone associated with the team. He stressed the fact that everyone needed to be willing to make sacrifices if the team was to succeed. And he was very creative offensively.

My interest in furthering my athletic career as a coach was sparked. The U.S. Army, however, had more immediate plans for me.

With the Korean War a recent memory, I was drafted into the Army. Fortunately for me, I spent my entire two-year tour of duty at Ft. Ord (CA), where I got to play on the post football team and box. I also began to take life much more seriously.

After my time on active duty, I returned to San Jose State to pursue a graduate degree and to serve on Bob Bronzan's staff as a graduate assistant coach. As my mentor, Bob spent countless hours working with me to develop the skills and abilities that I would need as a coach.

After I completed my graduate degree, I interviewed for only one coaching position—which I got. Despite the fact that at the age of 24 I was not quite ready to fully handle the responsibility, I was named head football coach at Washington High School in Fremont, California, where I stayed for three years.

Then, with Bronzan's support, Marv Levy hired me to be a member of his staff at UC-Berkeley. In my first year at Cal, my primary responsibility involved recruiting.

In my second year on Marv's staff, he appointed me as his defensive coordinator. Although I wasn't as completely prepared as I would like to have been for such a position, the job was a great experience. Unfortunately, Cal was not very talented at the time, so we struggled (a lot).

After three seasons with Marv and the Cal Bears, I then began an association with Stanford which I would come to treasure highly for the rest of my life. John Ralston hired me to be a member of the Cardinal's staff.

In my first year working for John, I served as his chief recruiter, administrative assistant, and freshman coach. I was then appointed as his defensive backs coach. Given the situation, I felt that I was making measurable strides toward achieving my ultimate goal—to become a head football coach at a major university.

FOLLOWING THE DREAM

When you actually sit down and try to summarize how you pursued the major goals in your life, it is relatively difficult to determine from which point you should begin. I imagine I should start by answering the question I am most often asked: "Where did I develop my professional philosophies and, in particular, when did the 'West Coast Offense' begin to take shape?"

All factors considered, the genealogy of the "West Coast Offense" started with the legendary Paul Brown, for whom I worked in Cincinnati from 1968-75, and with the offensive genius of Sid Gillman. Sid made his mark in 10 seasons with the San Diego Chargers, leading them to five championship appearances in the old American Football League.

I had the opportunity to learn Sid Gillman's offense when I was with the Oakland Raiders (1966). Being knowledgeable and gaining insights into Sid's offensive scheme was probably the biggest influence in my early career.

Gillman was, of course, just one of numerous pro coaches who I studied and from whom I borrowed along the way. I also gained a tremendous amount of insight into the game from individuals like Blanton Collier, Al Davis, Don Coryell and Clark Shaughnessy, the legendary Stanford coach and Chicago Bear assistant to George Halas, who brought the "T" Formation into college and professional football.

Having the chance to work at the college level at two great schools like Cal and Stanford was also particularly meaningful in my development as a coach. What many people don't realize is that I spent my first few years in college football on the defensive side of the ball. Working as Marv Levy's defensive coordinator at Cal, then later with John Ralston at Stanford as his defensive backs coach, were tremendous learning experiences for me.

It was the time I spent with the Cincinnati Bengals, however, that gave me a chance to fully develop my own coaching philosophies and to put them to practical application. Working for Paul Brown, the renowned coach from Ohio State and later the Cleveland Browns, and the founder of the Cincinnati Bengals, was a tremendous professional opportunity for me. To Paul's credit, he gave his coaches total autonomy. As a result, we were able to develop our own philosophies and systems.

At the time, Cincinnati was an expansion team that had Virgil Carter as its quarterback. Virgil was a quarterback who had a great collegiate career at Brigham Young. Virgil was only six feet tall and without much of a deep throwing arm, yet he was a good runner.

Because the Bengals weren't strong enough on the offensive line to be able to run the ball consistently, we decided that our best chance to win football games was to somehow control the ball. As a result, we devised a ball-control passing game in the hope that if we could make 25 first downs in a given game and if we also had good special teams play, we would have a reasonable chance to stay competitive in the ball game. In the process, hopefully something good would happen.

Over the eight-year period that I spent on the Bengals' staff, we were able to develop a system that is now known as the "West Coast Offense"—a term which I imagine sounds much more glamorous than the "Mid-West Offense." Ideally, I would like to say that what we developed and began in Cincinnati was done with a conscious eye to the future and the affirmation that we would be able to extend this system to historic levels of offensive production for years to come.

The truth of the matter, however, was that, at the time, we never really thought of it as being an all-encompassing system. As Paul would say, "This is just what we did." The concept of "scripting" an opening set of plays, which has generated a great deal of discussion over the years, is a perfect example of this.

Later chapters in this book present a more detailed discussion of how the practice of scripting began and what it encompasses. The point to remember is that we did not develop the innovative concept of scripting openers out of some overt, insightful recognition of the needs of the future. It was simply "what we did" to make ourselves as competitive as possible.

Subsequently, one particular event had a very significant impact on the path my coaching career was to take. When Coach Brown decided to retire, I was passed up for the head coaching position for a very fine coach in Bill Johnson. Not getting the Cincinnati job was at the time very devastating for me. I was particularly concerned that other people elsewhere would question my abilities to be a head coach if top management in Cincinnati did not see fit to make me the head coach.

Leaving Cincinnati was a very difficult time for my wife, Geri, and me. We had developed several valued friendships there and our children considered Cincinnati their home. These factors only added to my frustration.

Looking back, there are a number of things I wish I would have done differently. Most prominent among those disappointments was the way it affected how I dealt with people.

My final year in Cincinnati, leading up to Coach Brown's departure, was replete with a dispiriting atmosphere. I knew that the time had come for me to leave the Bengals.

Many people erroneously think they have only one chance to succeed in their life's work, and that if they miss that chance, they are doomed to failure. In fact, most people have several opportunities to succeed. If they learn from past mistakes, they will be better able to take full advantage of the next opportunity when it presents itself.

Certainly for me, this was the case when I was hired by Tommy Prothro to be his offensive coordinator with the San Diego Chargers. My new job opportunity in life turned out to be a very fortuitous situation for me on two counts.

Tommy was a great coach in his own right. He was one of the most honest, ethical men the game has ever seen.

Working for Tommy gave me a chance to further develop some of the philosophies we had established with the Bengals outside of the comfort zone that we had created in Cincinnati. Second, it gave me a chance to work with an exceptionally talented quarterback in Dan Fouts.

Dan was a brilliant performer, and one of the best competitors I have ever coached. It was a real thrill and honor to be inducted into the National Football League Hall of Fame with Dan in 1993. In reality, it is very unfortunate that Dan did not have a chance to play on a championship team.

So often, a quarterback is judged by whether he led his team to a Super Bowl victory. That single criteria, however, does not take into account the fact that the game of football is such a large dynamic, involving numerous different people and factors. Seldom, if ever, has there been another quarterback that was as pivotal to the success of a team as Dan was with the San Diego Chargers in the late 1970s and 80s.

THE DREAM COMES TRUE

At age 47, I got my first chance to be a head coach since my days at Washington High School in the late 1950s when I was named the head coach at Stanford University in 1977. This job was the opportunity of a lifetime—one that more than made up for the disappointment I suffered in Cincinnati.

This position afforded me the chance to take full control of an organization and field test the precepts and philosophies I had worked so hard to develop over the years just for this type of opportunity. It also gave me a chance to further develop an offensive system, but at a decidedly different level.

The time spent at Stanford during my first stint as the head coach of the Cardinal also enabled me to develop an appreciation for the overall attention to detail required for the daily preparation of a team. The college game presents as much challenge from a technical standpoint as pro football does.

There is more involved in college coaching because of the varying stages of development of your players. Teaching is more comprehensive in college because a dramatic range exists in the abilities of your players. Sometimes, you can depend on a player's inherent abilities. Other times, the coach's ability to teach and develop a player is more crucial.

At Stanford, we were challenged by powerhouses like Notre Dame, Texas A&M, USC and Washington. As with the Bengals, we had to employ an extra dimension to compensate for being physically outmanned. As I had been in earlier coaching assignments, I was fortunate to get to work with two excellent young quarterbacks in Guy Benjamin and Steve Dils. Guy had tremendous natural instincts, while Steve possessed surprising poise and presence.

For numerous reasons, not the least of which is the truly unique environment that exists on the Leland Stanford campus, I always think fondly of my time at Stanford. It was this affection which led me back to the "Farm" in 1992 for another three years as the Cardinal head coach.

The success we had at Stanford, culminating in a national ranking and a win in the 1978 Bluebonnet Bowl, gave me the chance to become the head coach of the San Francisco 49ers in 1979. That Bluebonnet Bowl game against the University of Georgia (much like "The Drive" that culminated my years with the 49ers) turned out to be a defining moment for me in my early career as a head coach.

In the Bluebonnet Bowl game, we had fallen behind to a point where we were facing what might have appeared to be an insurmountable lead by Georgia. To make matters worse, after what I thought was an inspiring half-time speech, the Bulldogs proceeded to take the second half kickoff and methodically marched the length of the field for another score to up their advantage to 22-0.

I can only imagine what Eddie DeBartolo was thinking at the time as he watched this debacle unfold (i.e., "This is the man I am turning my organization over to?"). It was a credit to the players and coaches that we were able to keep our composure.

Not quite panicking, we were finally able to adjust to their eight-man fronts and pressure package with our quick passes and "Hot" adjustments. Our come-from-behind, 25-22 win was an excellent springboard to the challenge of taking over the San Francisco 49ers.

The 49ers had been virtually dismembered in the late 70s by mismanagement and horrendous personnel decisions. The apathy in the Bay Area for the 49ers was at an all-time high, as evidenced by the fact that we had the lowest season ticket base in the NFL.

The 49ers had been through a tumultuous period with confluences of head coaches and general managers who constantly were at odds with one another. As a result, the organization had no single leadership and no meaningful direction. To make things even worse, the 49ers had few draft choices with which to rebuild due to some poor trades.

It was agreed that if I was going to be the coach, I would be in charge of all football operations. Being assigned that role was a major decision because I'd just been an NFL assistant and then a college head coach for two years.

It was a real challenge. My eight years with Paul Brown, however, had enabled me to observe firsthand the workings of a brilliant man. They also convinced me that I should have complete control of personnel matters.

I took a proactive approach to getting a top-flight person to assist me by talking to several of the top people in the profession about assuming the general manager's duties. It became obvious, however, that they were not interested in aligning themselves with the 49ers. Things had gotten so bleak in San Francisco—both on and off the field—that few saw much chance for improvement and all thought it too great a job security risk. John Ralston joined us and did an excellent job in the organization, but then departed.

For this reason, a decision was made that I should take on the additional duties of serving as the team's general manager. Everything I had learned and established throughout my entire career (particularly in the past 11 years) would be severely tested by my new challenge.

One of the most invaluable steps that I was able to take in this regard was being able to attract John McVay, who had recently departed as the head coach of the New York Giants, to join my administrative staff. We worked together as a team for ten years. John proved to be an invaluable part of our operation and was a key element in the 49er organization's continued success after I left.

This initial step proved to be very pivotal in the success that the 49ers eventually achieved. The players had been fragmented by the previous organizational structure, not truly knowing who was in charge and how much authority the people they worked directly with, via the coaches, really had.

Accordingly, it was vital to the organization that a single figure, with total control, emerge if there was any chance of correcting the melee that existed in the organization. The three world championships that we were able to experience with the 49ers over the next 10 years were made that much more exhilarating because of our relatively inglorious beginnings.

After we won our first Super Bowl in 1981 and began to establish ourselves as one of the dominant franchises in the League, some individuals began to attribute certain characteristics to me based on our accomplishments. Some people held the attitude that my abilities and the successes we experienced were presented to me like a "gift" or that I simply had the good fortune of being aligned with players such as Joe Montana, Jerry Rice and Ronnie Lott.

Other individuals suggested that my own abilities were somehow bestowed on me by some power from beyond and that these abilities were something that just came naturally with little effort. This contention belies the countless hours of study and sacrifice I spent developing my craft and the often-times painful process of trial and error that I endured.

Most of the methods that I developed I learned and enhanced from observing others. I'd like to think there's considerable originality in what I did with my career, and certainly a person has to have a particular predisposition toward a subject to experience any level of success. I would not endeavor, however, to be so bold as to conclude that the process involves either a totally unique discovery or a great revelation.

As a coach, the primary point to remember is that a knowledge or expertise of any subject must remain dynamic. As renowned organization theorist Abraham Kaplan has noted, "As knowledge of a particular subject matter grows, our conception of that subject matter changes. This paradox is resolved by a process of approximation: the better our concepts, the better the theory we can formulate with them, and in turn, the better the concepts for the next improved theory. It is only through this succession that (we) can hope ultimately to achieve success."

An excellent example of Kaplan's progression is the interaction of ideas and theories I have exchanged with the many fine coaches with whom I have had the pleasure of working over the years. As a result, my attempts to be more knowledgeable about the game and to continually expand my offensive concepts eventually led to the next step in the evolution of, for lack of a better term, the "West Coast Offense."

Whatever label, genuine or otherwise, others want to give it, the "West Coast Offense" still amounts to nothing more than a total attention to detail and an appreciation for every facet of offensive football and refinement of those things that are needed to provide an environment that allows people to perform at their maximum levels of self-actualization.

In 1996, I returned for a year to work with the San Francisco 49ers organization. It was very interesting making the transition to the role of consultant with the 49ers and trying to be effective in a new role without the authority I once had. Stepping away from the 49ers for a while enabled me to pinpoint what it was I did well and to identify those things I could do better.

As president and head coach of the team, I didn't have much chance to pay close attention to details. When I returned as a consultant with specific objectives centering on offensive strategy and quarterback performance, I didn't have to worry about the big picture.

This closer focus also allowed me to pay attention, in an unofficial way, to broader questions of the team's future considerations. That is not what I was hired to do, but for me it was a reward of being out from under the weight of leadership, a situation which only added to my overall effectiveness as a consultant.

Of all the accomplishments I may have achieved over the years, I value the relationships with my coaches and players above all else. The ability to help the people around me self-actualize their goals underlines the single aspect of my abilities and the label that I value most—*teacher*.

I suppose this experience in coaching had something to do with my own orientation to the university and to a teaching career. It also marked the beginning of my own style of management. I always have found that if I could create an environment around me in which everybody felt they were learning, I would have a hot group. I have always tried to include people in what I was doing, to encourage them to say what they think, to let them see the problems that were confronting us all, and to create an atmosphere in which everyone could feel at the end of the day, or the end of a week or a month, that he or she had learned something.

George P. Shultz
Former Secretary of State
from *Turmoil and Triumph*

CHAPTER 2

DOING WHAT COMES NATURALLY

"Duty is the sublimest word in our language. Do your duty in all things. You cannot do more. You should never wish to do more."

—Robert E. Lee
Commanding General
Army of the Confederacy

Finding the winning edge...

For men and women who are extremely good at what they do, nothing is more discouraging than discovering that the thing they do so well isn't what's needed to get the job done. When a successful manager confronts a situation in which a philosophy that has always worked—and he has every reason to believe is fundamentally sound—fails, he may have to face the hard fact that the ground rules have changed and that he and his way of doing things may be a problem.

In the world of fast companies, this kind of thing happens all the time. The true test of leadership is the adaptability and flexibility a manager brings to this type of situation. The challenge comes in having to leave your comfort zone—an area where you've been operating effectively, perhaps for years.

—Bill Walsh, "When Good Isn't Good Enough," *Forbes*, April 11, 1994.

A leader who has a focused philosophy is more likely to know what the "right" decision is and to have the courage to make it. This point has been made clear to me on a number of occasions in my coaching career.

At the end of the 1987 season, for example, San Francisco met the Minnesota Vikings in a playoff game. Minnesota was vastly underrated and San Francisco had tired and become stale during their two weeks of preparation.

During the game, we fell behind and were unable to move the ball. I sensed that, in addition to not having the protection he needed, Joe Montana was not at his best.

In the middle of the third quarter, I knew what I had to do. On one hand, it was one of the toughest decisions I have ever had to make, but on the other hand, it was also very easy. I decided to pull Joe and insert Steve Young at quarterback.

Because of the lack of pass protection, I believed Steve's incredible mobility as a quarterback might spark the team and turn the game around. But I was still pulling perhaps the greatest quarterback in the history of football out of a playoff game.

I knew that fans would be outraged and that the media would forever criticize and second-guess my decision if the 49ers lost. I also knew the experience would be traumatic for Joe.

Despite all the potential drawbacks, my decision was simple. I was the head coach and I was responsible for making appropriate decisions, even if I knew I would be condemned by others. I had no alternative. I was aware of the possibility that Steve might fare no better than Joe, but we were down to a "one-game season" and something had to be done quickly for us to have any chance of winning. I made the change.

When Joe came off the field, I put my arm around him, explained why I had replaced him, and told him I cared about him. Steve did spark the team, and we became more competitive but still lost. As the coach, I had to make the tough decision and then live with it.

As I expected, I was criticized for some time regarding that decision. It also fueled a quarterback controversy early the next season. If I had taken the easy way out, letting Joe stay in the game and then be criticized for not playing up to par, I would not have been fulfilling my responsibilities as the head coach.

Coaching is an enriching endeavor that can involve pronounced challenges. In order to handle those challenges successfully, the head coach must have the insight to know what needs to be done and must possess the capabilities and the conviction to do whatever is necessary.

Several factors impact his ability in this regard. Perhaps, none is more important than the dictates of his personal beliefs. Collectively, these beliefs comprise his philosophy.

His philosophy is the aggregate of his attitudes toward fundamental matters. It is derived from a process of consciously thinking about critical issues and developing rational reasons for holding one particular belief (position) rather than another.

A head coach's philosophy is shaped by a number of factors, including his background, experiences, work environment, education, aspirations, etc. By adhering to his philosophical tenets, he is provided with a systematic, yet practical, method of deciding what to do in a particular situation.

As such, his philosophy provides him with a conceptual blueprint for action (i.e., within reason, it increases his awareness of what should be done, when it should be done, and why it should be done). In other words, his philosophy is often the single most important guiding influence on how he coaches.

A head coach's philosophy also has a substantial effect on his ability to keep a proper perspective on critical matters. For example, while winning is certainly important (given the fact that an individual can lose his job if his team doesn't win on a regular basis), it's certainly not the only criteria for success. In fact, all factors considered, it should not even be the most essential factor.

To a point, a head coach should measure success in terms of how well he is able to carry out his responsibilities relative to what he feels coaching is all about. As such, he can place greater emphasis on developing his players to take advantage of their full potential, and on developing a proper foundation for the team to perform well in the future, than on whatever actions might otherwise emanate from a "win-now-or-else" approach.

Discipline is based on pride in the profession of arms, on meticulous attention to details, and on mutual respect and confidence. Discipline must be a habit so ingrained that it is stronger than the excitement of battle or the fear of death.

George S. Patton, Jr.
"Letter of Instruction Number 1"
from *War as I Knew It*

Although many of these factors are discussed in greater detail in subsequent chapters in this text, there are numerous precepts that should be the building blocks of a sound philosophy. As the head coach, you should consider embodying the following points of philosophical counsel:

- *Be yourself.* Throughout your career, you will have the opportunity to observe and work with other coaches. While it is important that you learn whatever you can from each one of them, you must recognize the fact that you can't be any one of them.

  You should work to take advantage of your strengths and to diminish your weaknesses. For example, you can become more knowledgeable. You can enhance your ability to apply that knowledge in the fulfillment of your professional responsibility. At any given moment in time, however, "you are who you are."

If you try to be someone you're not or act as someone you want to be, the effort will typically be perceived as phony—by both your assistants and your players. In the process, everyone may lose respect for you. As a result, your ability to lead effectively will be severely compromised.

Your approach to coaching football should be a natural extension of your personality and your philosophy. Some great coaches are extroverts, others are introverts. The important thing is to approach every task in a sincere and honest manner.

- *Be committed to excellence.* To a point, you must be willing to work extremely hard and make whatever reasonable sacrifices are necessary to achieve the organizational goals that have been established for the team. At the same time, you must ensure that every member of your staff and all of your players fully understand that the commitment to excellence can never willingly be compromised.

At all times, the focus must be on doing things properly. Every play. Every practice. Every meeting. Every situation. Every time.

In reality, the talent level of most NFL teams is relatively even. As such, one of the critical keys to success is execution. Players making plays is what wins football games. More often than not, the primary catalyst for the occurrence of such plays is an unwavering commitment to excellence.

- *Be positive.* One of the most important things a head coach can do is to adopt a positive attitude. Your staff and your players will respond better to a positive environment than to a negative one.

While it is often very easy to accentuate the negative aspects of a particular situation or set of circumstances, such an approach typically accomplishes little (if anything) other than to serve as a means to let you vent your feelings. In most instances, what it really achieves is to establish a mental barrier between you and your staff and your players that inhibits their ability to maintain the proper focus and to communicate effectively with you.

- *Be prepared.* No aspect of coaching is more important than preparation. While coaches cannot actually control which team wins a game, they can determine how their teams prepare to win.

Good fortune on the playing field (i.e., performing well, winning, etc.) is a product of design. Accordingly, you must develop a plan to ensure that your team is properly prepared to handle every contingency and possible situation.

Attention to detail is critical in this regard. You must address all aspects of your team's efforts to prepare mentally, physically, fundamentally and strategically in as thorough a manner as possible.

- *Be organized.* It is critical that you make the best possible use of the available time and resources. Being organized is the single best way to avoid wasting either.

Fortunately, the effort needed to be organized is not that extensive. The process of becoming organized essentially requires two qualities: a disciplined mind and the ability to think clearly. However much energy you spend on the process, it is time well invested.

Getting organized can provide substantial benefits (e.g., it frees up time; relieves stress and pressure; and helps engender confidence in your competence from other individuals). Given the axiom that "luck is merely preparation meeting opportunity," the more well organized you are, the more likely you will be "lucky."

- *Be accountable.* You must accept responsibility for those matters over which you are in charge. Deflecting blame, even if you are not responsible for a particular occurrence, is often viewed as a sign of weakness by both your staff and your players.

Whatever the situation, offering apparently well-reasoned excuses and plausible alibis to explain your failings is simply irresponsible. "Passing the buck" when times get tough will not enhance the level of respect you engender from others. If you expect loyalty from your staff and your players, you must show it to them first by being accountable for your own actions.

The factor that is most often at the heart of accountability issues is the team's win-loss record. However unfair it may seem that you are held responsible for something that is not totally within your control, the responsibility comes with the position. If the team wins, you get much of the credit; if it loses, you get most of the criticism.

You should remember that ultimately, you are responsible for the performance of your players. As such, fair or not, it is logical that you would be held accountable for whether their performances led to the requisite number of victories.

- *Be a leader.* From a leadership standpoint, an effective head coach is someone who is able to develop a vision on how the team should operate, is able to establish a strategy for achieving that plan, and is able to inspire everyone (staff and players) to carry it out successfully.

An effective leader is an expert in his field. His actions embolden confidence and respect for him by those with whom he works. He cares about people and treats them fairly. He demands that all staff members meet the highest possible standards. He prefers positive reinforcement, rather than the "big stick" approach.

He knows that results are what count—not the number of hours spent on a task. He does not second guess himself on decisions that were made with integrity, intelligence and a "team-first" attitude. He is able to identify appropriate priorities. He doesn't coach "caution"; he coaches to win.

In this regard, one of the more outstanding coaches in the history of the game was John Madden. John deserves to be in the Hall of Fame, not only for his coaching efforts with the Oakland Raiders, but also for his contributions to the game as a television commentator.

Another exceptional coach who was an outstanding leader was Tom Flores, who led the Oakland Raiders to two Super Bowl championships. During my first year on the Raiders' staff, I had the opportunity to learn a lot about quarterbacking from Tom, when he was still an active player.

- *Be focused.* You must be able to keep everything in the proper perspective and to concentrate on the appropriate task at hand. Everything should be viewed in terms of how it affects the team and the organization—not how it affects you.

  All factors considered, your focus must be results-oriented. To the extent possible, these results should be measurable. All efforts and plans should be considered not only in terms of their short-run effect, but also how they might impact the team and the organization in the long term.

  Several examples exist of NFL coaches who were unwilling or unable to maintain the proper focus. One of the better ones involved a coach who believed that by building the most intense, most physical, toughest, best conditioned squad, his team would have undeniable success—even to the extent of dominating and intimidating the opposition.

  Despite the fact that his team subsequently developed a well-deserved reputation for toughness and endured an incredible level of human sacrifice in both training camp and practice sessions during the season, the team proceeded to lose virtually every game badly. The losses were directly attributable to faulty strategies and poor game-to-game tactics. His team's unsophisticated, simplistic scheme of football was outsmarted and outmaneuvered week after week. Although physically they had the capability to hurt their opponents when they hit them, all too often they weren't able to get close enough to do any damage.

  The key point is that at least three elements must be present to build a winning team: talent; strategies and tactics; and conditioning and execution. As such, the head coach must not focus solely on one factor to the exclusion of the other two.

- *Be ethical.* You must have a strong value system. Your values serve as your moral compass. Morally sound values engender respect from others and enhance the likelihood that your decisions and your behavior will reflect high principles. Your values also help to determine what things you choose to pay attention to and how hard you will work at them. In that regard, the welfare of the organization and the well-being of the players and your assistants must be among your preeminent concerns.

  You must have the character to abide by a morally sound code of conduct regardless of the circumstances. In that regard, you must exhibit integrity in all of your dealings with others. Furthermore, you should believe that it is important that your team wins in a manner that is a credit to the organization.

- *Be flexible.* You must have the ability to respond and adapt to changing circumstances. While consistency is important, if the situation changes, you must change with it.

There is only one way to do anything: The right way.

> Golda Meir
> Prime Minister of Israel
> 1969-74
> from *My Life*

One of the most important areas of coaching in which flexibility is essential involves the need to give your team the tools to win. Within the specific framework of your system, you must be bold, creative and willing to take risks when necessary.

For example, in the 1960s, John Ralston, who was the head coach at Stanford, learned a pointed lesson in the value of flexibility. Although John had his teams play with great intensity, Stanford usually found itself outmanned by schools with faster, more athletic players.

Stanford simply had to do everything right during the game in order to have a chance to win. One bad break could wreck any chances that John's team had to win.

During the same period that John was at Stanford, USC, under the direction of the renowned John McKay, fielded one of the best teams in the nation, year in and year out. Even though John would implore the Cardinal players to play with more intensity when Stanford was competing against USC, the reality of the situation was simply that the Trojans had more and better players.

Even though the scores of these contests were usually relatively close after three quarters, Stanford often would end up losing by a substantial margin. Upon examination, Stanford's approach to playing USC and other nationally ranked teams had at least one inherent flaw.

John's offensive system was basically too limited and too conservative. All factors considered, it played right into the hands of opponents that had superior talent.

Over the years, John and his outstanding staff of assistants—who, over time, included individuals like Mike White, Jim Mora, Dick Vermeil, Bob Gambold, Rod Rust, Leon McLaughlin and Jack Christiansen, began to learn what it would take to compete against the USCs of the game. To be competitive, Stanford needed to install an NFL-type system of offense (a step that was prompted by Stanford's Athletic Director at the time, Chuck Taylor).

The philosophical underpinning of the proposed system was passing proficiency. Ultimately, the arrival of All-American (later to be a Heisman Trophy winner) Jim Plunkett and a battery of sure-handed receivers like Randy Vataha broke USC's stranglehold on Stanford's gridiron fortunes.

This situation illustrates two key points. First, athletes must be given the tools that best suit them and will give them their best chance to succeed. Second, the coach must be willing to change what he is doing if it obviously is destined to fail and if a feasible alternative exists.

- *Believe in yourself.* You must have confidence in yourself and your system. It is also important that you sell your program to your players. They must believe in you in order for them to be able to make the sacrifices that will be required of them.

  Everyone in the organization (e.g., your staff, the players, the athletic trainers, the team managers, etc.) must believe that your plan for success will be effective if it is carried out as directed. They must also feel that you have their best interests at heart.

Never take counsel of your fears.

General Thomas J. (Stonewall) Jackson
Renowned General
Army of the Confederacy

UNDERSTANDING THE MEANING OF TRUE COMPETITION

In the football arena, competition not only involves winners and losers, it also serves as a meaningful opportunity for the development, exercise and expression of human excellence. In that regard, trying to win means attempting to do the best you can at all facets of the game.

In other words, your focus should be on attempting to demonstrate excellence in all of the ways that the game calls for. Concurrently, your opponent's efforts to excel and to outperform you provide you with the opportunity to strive to do your best.

In order to ensure that you get as much as possible out of such an opportunity, you should take the time to carefully reflect on how you truly feel about competition. Your feelings can help you keep critical matters in the proper perspective and can enable you, depending on the circumstances, to be better prepared to handle adversity.

True Competition

One of the first issues you should consider in this regard is the relationship between "true" competition and the capability level of your opponent in a particular contest. Several reference points should guide you in this matter, including:

- True competition does not exist when you have measurably better personnel than your opponent. In this instance, the basic standard of performance of your team should dominate.

- True competition also does not exist when you are totally outmanned by your opponent. In this instance, the intensity of your team's play, the strategy you employ as an underdog, and the number of fortuitous breaks your team receives in the game can make the contest competitive.

- True competition is best achieved by meeting an opponent of comparable talent, or an opponent with better—but not dominating—talent.

- True competition can best be measured against an opponent that is very good, but whose style and tactics are difficult to understand or predict. Stepping into an arena against an opponent that has a number of "unknown" factors with which you must deal is the true test of competition.

- Your real test as a coach—as a competitor—will be how you deal with such competition. You can measure your performance against evenly matched opponents (or against those who might be considered as up to a six-point favorite).

- Provided you retain your poise and stick to your game plan, competing against an opponent that has an ominous mystique and a reputation for being an extremely formidable team is a challenge that will truly test your skills.

People acting together as a group can accomplish things which no individual acting alone could ever hope to bring about.

Franklin D. Roosevelt
32nd President of the United States

Inspirational Events

Two of the most inspirational individuals of my lifetime have been Sir Edmund Hillary and Arthur Ashe. Each, in his own way, led a singularly magnificent life. Both combined an indomitable spirit and physical toughness with a willingness to reach for the unknown to overcome tremendous challenges and to achieve great accomplishments.

Hillary, conqueror of Mt. Everest, Antarctic explorer and builder of schools, bridges and hospitals in the Himalayas, was an adventurer who was driven to discover the apparent limits of his body and mind and to push beyond them. Ashe, the first African American tennis player to win the Wimbledon Championship, was a gifted athlete, a talented author and a tireless worker who, with grace and dignity, championed the cause of racial tolerance and social injustice at every possible opportunity.

Every coach has been impacted, in a similar vein, over the years by observing great efforts made against incredible odds. Collectively, those experiences help shape a personal value system that is referred or related to when an individual is confronted with similar circumstances.

For me personally, several events have forever been imprinted onto my mindset. Each of these noteworthy occurrences involved a situation where someone or some group of individuals had to deal with a difficult challenge that involved unknown elements.

In some of these events, I have been personally involved. In a few, I was a spectator. Others, I explored through readings. Among the noteworthy circumstances that have had an inspirational impact on my life experiences have been the following:

- When the U.S. Marines on Guadalcanal displayed incredible courage and resolution to defeat the Japanese during a sixth-month battle that lasted from August 1942 to February 1943 despite the fact that their Japanese adversaries were better trained, more seasoned, and better equipped. In less than a month, these Marines became renowned as one of the greatest fighting forces of World War II.

- When Lauro Sallas upset the great Jimmy Carter in fifteen rounds to win the World Lightweight Boxing Championship in 1952. Although Sallas absorbed immense punishment, he won the title.

- When Confederate General Stonewall Jackson took his men on an incredible twenty-six mile forced march to attack Hooker's flank in 1863. This staggering task was accomplished in six hours.

- When thirteen U.S. Navy Dauntless Dive Bombers incredibly appeared over the Japanese fleet in the Battle of Midway, after all of the other U.S. planes had been decimated. Striking with a vengeance in this critical battle that occurred in June 1942, the U.S. fliers changed the fortunes of the war in the Pacific.

- When in 1944 thirteen non-combatant, U.S. Army engineers who were all that were left to hold off an elite German Panzer unit that was trying to capture St. Vith somehow held for one night before a patchwork of reinforcements arrived the next day. This incredibly courageous action afforded the Americans just enough time to change the course of the "Battle of the Bulge."

- When Harrison Dillard, the greatest high hurdler in the world at the time, failed to qualify for the 1948 London Olympics in his event after he hit two hurdles during qualifying trials. Subsequently, he rechanneled his energies and attempted to qualify in the 100-meter dash.

  Dillard earned the third and last position on the U.S. Olympic team. He then spent the next month working on the 100-meter dash, took on the best sprinters in the world in the Olympics, and won a gold medal in the event.

  In that same 100-meter dash final, Dillard's teammate, Mel Patton, faltered and finished seventh, despite the fact that he was generally recognized as the fastest man in the world at the time. Universally condemned as a quitter, Patton refocused his talents and came back to win the Olympic gold medal in the 200-meter dash.

- When the Jewish residents of the Warsaw ghetto in Poland held out for 28 days (April 19 to May 16, 1943) against the intense efforts of the German military. Seriously outmanned (the Jewish fighting force numbered about 1500 out of approximately 60,000 Jews who remained in the ghetto) and severely lacking in both supplies and resources, the ghetto inhabitants fought fiercely and bravely, and held off the Nazis for a much longer period than expected.

- When Erwin Rommel exhibited courage and brilliant personal leadership when commanding the Germans' famed North Afrika Korps during the period 1941-1943. Despite being almost always outnumbered by his adversaries, his tactics and military insights enabled him to achieve legendary victories.

- When the British in Burma, despite having relatively few survivors and having their backs to the wall, dug in for over two years (1943-1945) and stopped the Japanese who had been badly beating them for months.

- When Ken Venturi won the 1964 U.S. Open in debilitating heat by playing thirty-six holes of terrific golf on the final day of the tournament against the greatest golfers of his time.

- When Admiral Jim Stockdale was shot down in 1965 after flying fifty missions in Vietnam. Subsequently, he was beaten and tortured by his captors, chained and held in isolation for two years, and not allowed to speak to another American. Stockdale retained his indomitable spirit and his sense of personal discipline to survive his ordeal and become the dominant leader of the American POWs for eight years.

- When Evander Holyfield outboxed and outpunched Mike Tyson on his way to knocking out the previously feared Tyson in their first bout on November 9th, 1996. Facing one of the most explosive, powerful punchers in the history of boxing, Holyfield encountered an intimidating presence, which seemed virtually unbeatable. With a strategy that he followed throughout the bout, Holyfield displayed a blend of patience, skill, courage and an ultimate degree of confidence.

- Within the football arena, an inspiring event for me is not seeing a team win the Super Bowl or become the collegiate national champion. Rather, I am heartened by watching a team overcome an opponent that has superior talent or seeing a team with a history of failure or with an established tradition prevail.

On the college level, I have been inspired by the successes of Gary Barnett at Northwestern and Bill Snyder at Kansas State. Over the years, I have also been motivated by the efforts of Rich Brooks, who took his Oregon team to the 1995 Rose Bowl, and the accomplishments of Jack Elway, who led his San Jose State team to victories over both Stanford and California in the same (1981) season.

On the pro level, the Cincinnati Bengal team in my second season on Paul Brown's staff had a positive effect on my appreciation of the true meaning of competition. This team defeated two of the greatest teams of the era—the Oakland Raiders and the Kansas City Chiefs, the ultimate Super Bowl champions.

- For me personally as a head coach, two victories hold particular significance for me. The first was the 49ers' beautifully executed 45-14 win in 1981 over America's team—the Dallas Cowboys.

In the previous season, the Cowboys had poured it on against the 49ers in a 59-17 Dallas victory. This triumph became the launching point for San Francisco's subsequent NFL dynasty.

The second very meaningful win for me personally was Stanford's 1993 victory over Colorado during the regular season. At the time, the Buffaloes were fifth in the national rankings and were actively campaigning for the national championship. Although we were completely outmanned, we were able to combine nerve, focus, precision execution and a passing scheme that bewildered our opponent to score in the final moments and win the game.

Avoid having your ego so close to your position that when your position falls, your ego goes with it.

> Colin Powell
> Former Chairman, Joint Chiefs of Staff
> *My American Journey*

Overcoming Adversity

In each of the aforementioned, inspirational events, distinct elements exist that are the essence of "total" competition or confrontation (e.g., dealing with a deadly adversary; fighting for survival; competing when virtually no one else knows or cares; locking horns against an opponent when no one is there to "bail you out"; etc.).

The very nature of the game of American football exemplifies the extreme demands and sacrifices that are attendant to a situation where you're fighting or competing for your very existence. A total commitment on your part, a complete mobilization of your efforts and an unwavering level of concentration and focus are essential, not only to successfully compete, but to simply be competitive as you participate.

To deal with and overcome adversity, several personal attributes are required. By degree, you must possess all of the following elements:

- *An inner confidence that has been tested.* You must have a level of self-assurance that has been molded by defeat, has overcome obstacles, has been shaken, has absorbed punishment and has engendered a sober, steel-like toughness that results in a hardened sense of independence that will take on anything, yet survive and win.

- *Sound fundamentals and skills that have been firmly entrenched by weeks, months and years of training, practice, rehearsal and direct competition.* In order for these to be the appropriate tools for you to handle the situation, they must be an extension of your unique talents.

  Your fundamentals and skills must relate—one to the other—to form a complete inventory of useful capabilities at your disposal. Each of these areas must be continually refined and adapted as needed.

- *A functional intellect for the activity.* While a high IQ is not essential, you must possess the intuitive instincts that seem to thrive on the activity and that provide you with a sense of resourcefulness when frustration or paralyzing fear could otherwise consume an individual.

As a rule, the individuals at the two extremes of the intelligence continuum (i.e., most intelligent and least intelligent) are often unable to maintain an appropriate level of focus. As a result, these individuals are more likely to panic and to prematurely look for alternatives.

- *A belief—a conviction—that is able to effectively control your urge to "quit and run."* Within the confines of the activity, theoretically speaking, you must be willing to possibly perish before conceding. In the football arena, the issue does not involve mortal terms, but rather competing to your last ounce of energy or until the final whistle blows.

- *A willingness to sacrifice for others.* Situations may arise when it will be necessary for you to subordinate your own personal interests to the greater common good of the team or your teammates.

- *A refined sense of communication that enables you to have a realistic sense of what your teammates are thinking and how they will react and respond to a given situation.* When competition is in its most critical stages, you must have both a level of verbiage and points of reference that collectively provide you with a means of communicating concisely and precisely.

- *Trust in yourself and in your teammates.* This trust must have been nurtured through months and years of practicing, playing and sacrificing for a common goal.

- *A philosophy, a scheme, and a system that has evolved, matured and become established.* This system must be a complete entity that can function in every possible circumstance and that can account for unexpected circumstances.

- *Flexibility and adaptability that enable you to effectively deal with change.* Your approach to the game must evolve and transform itself when you meet new and different challenges. You must be able to recognize and adapt to markedly different styles, strategies and tactics.

- *A qualified support staff and system.* Your staff and system must provide you with the necessary tools, equipment, services and logistics for you to do your job. Both your staff and your system must reflect a high level of intensity and a comparable level of willingness to make critical sacrifices. Both elements must be well-organized and well-led.

- *Leadership.* Driven leadership that is decisive, thoughtful and calculating is critical. Such leadership ability should be developed through study, extensive preparation and a variety of experiences.

  Such leadership should be proactive and should exhibit an ability to effectively assess, analyze, and respond to circumstances as they occur. Your leadership should draw from the strengths and buttress the weaknesses of those who surround you.

- *A plan, a goal and a dominating thought process that motivates and inspires.*

- *A knowledge and understanding of your opponent—his strategies, tactics, system, personnel, attitudes and goals.*

- *A system of replacing and acquiring new players and staff members.*

PART II

THE ORGANIZATION

CHAPTER 3

UNDERSTANDING THE ROLE OF A HEAD COACH

"Extraordinary resourcefulness, his almost superhuman capacity for work, his hardiness and lack of concern for personal comfort, his disregard of danger; and despite his reputation for driving them remorselessly, despite his sharp tongue on occasion, despite his exacting standards, they were also speaking of his concern for them, of his fellow-feeling with them, of his utter lack of pretension or pomposity, of the fact that he was manifestly moved, and only moved, by the interests of the sufferings of his troops. He would, they said, do anything for them, and they knew it. Above all, they had come to know that with him they would win."

> —David Fraser
> from *Knight's Cross:*
> *A Life of Field Marshal Erwin Rommel*

Finding the winning edge...

The role of a leader is to deal with the one time in a hundred. Otherwise, when that one time comes, people are going to slip into the instinctual survival state of mind that can breed very unfortunate decisions. Constructing such grim possibilities is a whole lot less enjoyable than calculating the size of your bonus if the year goes well. But if you're willing to plan for a wide range of small and large disasters—thus reducing the potential for you and others to be caught off-guard—you can actually be more aggressive, and thus more likely to avert setbacks. Having planned for the worst, you can do a lot more than hope for the best.

> —Bill Walsh, "When Things Go
> Bad," *Forbes*, March 29, 1993.

Successful managers have a multitude of responsibilities. Perhaps, none is more important than how they make use of their organization's most valuable resource: their subordinates.

Over the years, I have always accepted the fact that one of the most critical roles a coach has is to utilize his players to their full potential. Against equal competition, great coaches are distinguished by their ability to fully utilize the talents of their individual players.

As a high school coach, I had an outstanding quarterback-receiver battery in Bob Hidalgo and Grady Hudson. Hudson would catch four or five passes a game and score once or twice. To this day, I wonder why I didn't have him catch 10-12 passes a game and score three or four touchdowns, but I believe I was too busy proving the theories I had concocted at the age of 24.

Another example of a player who was improperly used for part of his career was Craig Morton, later a great quarterback with the Dallas Cowboys. Morton spent his first three years of college in the Wing-T offense, in which the quarterback throws only when it is necessary or when the coach believes a receiver will be wide open. Finally, in his senior year at California, Morton was coupled with his high school teammate Jack Schraub. Both players broke numerous records that year and brought California great success.

There are hundreds of examples of coaches who were able to take full advantage of their players' talents: Buddy Ryan with middle linebacker Mike Singletary; Bill Parcells with outside linebacker Lawrence Taylor; and the 49ers of the 1980s with Joe Montana and Dwight Clark, who had an amazing ability to find openings in zone defenses. In each of these cases, the players went on to become All-Pro selections and potential Hall of Famers.

A recent example of this ability is Dom Capers of Carolina with his two outside linebackers, Micheal Barrow and Lamar Lathon. When he coached the Philadelphia Eagles, Dick Vermeil took his team to numerous division and conference championships with his unique way of utilizing Wilbert Montgomery, who many considered too small to be a regular player.

The role of a head coach is often very diverse and extraordinarily complex. As the individual in charge, you must fulfill a variety of responsibilities, including being a teacher, setting standards of performance and behavior, managing both people and time, establishing a communications policy involving the team and the other employees of the organization and keeping the big picture.

Although each of these duties can be somewhat challenging and demanding, performing these functions is not work as long as you keep everything in perspective. All factors considered, nothing is really work unless you would rather be doing something else.

But that was the day I realized I knew almost nothing about coaching football, much less about The Lombardi Sweep.

I listened to Lombardi talk about The Lombardi Sweep for eight hours. That's right, eight hours. He drew the play on the black board. He showed film. One by one, he pretended he was each of his eleven players and explained what each of them did on the play. Not only against one defense, but against several different defenses. And the first time he paused for questions, a guy in the first row raised his hand.

"Vince..." the guy began.

"Yes, Sid," Lombardi said.

Sid Gillman, then the coach of the San Diego Chargers who would win the AFL championship later that year, was asking the first question. Sid had a reputation as one of the most innovative offensive minds in football but he was not only here, he was sitting in the first row to make sure he didn't miss anything and he was asking a question.

John Madden/Dave Anderson
Former Football Coach/Renowned Sports Reporter
Oakland Raiders/*New York Times*
from *Run to Daylight*

BEING A TEACHER

No aspect of coaching is more important than teaching. While the actual teaching is often delegated to one of your assistant coaches, the primary responsibility for ensuring that it is done, and done well, is yours, and yours alone.

It is absolutely critical that you do not neglect your responsibility in this area. If you cannot or do not teach your players and staff the things they need to know, even performing the rest of your responsibilities well will not be enough to guarantee that the team will be successful.

The admonition "for the want of a nail in the wall" is as true in football as in any other situation. Without properly executed fundamentals, the entire system can break down. Accordingly, you must ensure that every player gets the information and hands-on instruction that he needs to develop and refine those skills that are required for his position.

In this regard, several steps are involved in the teaching process, including deciding how (i.e., preparing a plan) the material will be taught, explaining the information to the player, demonstrating (showing) the skill to the player, having the player practice the skill, critiquing the player's performance, and having the player continue to practice under your supervision.

You should recognize that individuals often have distinctly different responses to the learning process. As such, you must adjust your teaching approach and methods to account for individual differences.

Among the steps that you can take to ensure that the teaching process for the team is appropriate are the following:

- Use a straightforward, broad-based vocabulary that allows you to communicate in very specific, descriptive terms.
- Employ clear, concise language that ensures that your explanations to and exchanges with other individuals will be clearly understood.
- Ensure that the information you provide and the instruction you offer on a given topic accounts for a wide range of knowledge and comprehension among the members of your intended audience.
- Ensure that your approach to teaching a particular subject matter accounts for the fact that some members of the group to whom you are speaking may be more receptive and more ready to learn than others. The critical factor in this regard is how important an individual perceives the information to be, relatively speaking.
- Demonstrate enthusiasm and passion for the material you are presenting. What you say and how you say it can help display your steadfast concern for a particular subject.

As the head coach, one of your responsibilities is to generate interest in and excitement for a given matter among your players. The most effective way to accomplish such an objective is to utilize a high level of energy and show ardent enthusiasm for the subject when discussing it with your players.

For example, in 1996, staff presentations to the 49er players had become somewhat redundant. Although these presentations were thorough and detailed, they did not generate the desired level of energy and enthusiasm among the players.

Despite the fact that the team was playing well at the time, the presentations didn't appear to have the same aura they had had in the past. After reviewing the situation with the staff, the decision was made that I should address the team and discuss each player's assignments and techniques on each play.

I often ended my description of a particular play by pinpointing two or three key players and challenging them by reminding them that on Monday morning after the game, all their coaches and teammates would be able to judge how well they had carried out their duties. These challenges had to be tailored to each individual player.

On one hand, when talking to a less-experienced offensive guard, I might explain to him that he has the quickness and ability required to get the job done, and remind him what to do next if he loses his man, as every blocker will do on occasion.

For example, on a trapping route, I might tell him, "Step with your near foot. Don't let your pad raise above the level of your stance. Keep your head up and take an inside leg out from under your man. All we want to see is his cleats facing toward the sky. See if you can hit him so clean he does a forward somersault."

On the other hand, in the case of Jerry Rice, one of San Francisco's greatest players, I might state, "Jerry, you are the greatest blocker to ever play your position. This is a guy you've got to get. When we view the tapes Monday, I expect everyone to continue to say, 'This is the greatest blocker of all time at this position.'"

Wars may be fought with weapons but they are won by men. It is the spirit of the men who follow and the man who leads that gains the victory.

> General George S. Patton, Jr.
> Commander, United States Third Army
> World War II

- Observe the members of the group while you are speaking and determine whether they are paying attention. If, for any reason, the attention span of the group is not what it should be, take steps to remedy the situation.

- Emphasize to the group that note taking is strongly encouraged. This practice not only helps them to thoroughly recall the information that you presented, it enables them to be better prepared to connect the details of one point to another and one teaching session to another.

- Ensure that the teaching process for a given subject accounts for those individuals who may struggle or fail to keep up with the material or the expected schedule of learning.

- Make certain that any theory, concept or precept you initially offer to introduce a particular topic is thoroughly comprehended by your audience before you discuss more complex aspects of the subject matter.

- Be aware of and sensitive to the limitations of a group of individuals to learn a given task or subject.

- Employ a somewhat unpredictable presentation style. Varying your delivery can help enhance or at least maintain the attention level of your audience. It can also be used to place a specific level of emphasis on a given topic.

- Keep the length of your presentation an appropriate duration. Be alert for a loss of concentration by members of your audience. Speaking for too long can render your entire presentation ineffectual.

- Organize and give your presentation in sequential "building blocks." It is better to begin a discussion with an overview of basic factors and then to progressively develop the topic to more complex levels.

- Review your presentation of specific material constantly. Revise as necessary to keep your delivery current and fresh.

- Encourage audience participation in your presentation as long as such involvement is appropriate and timely. Audience participation should be limited to given situations.

- Employ visual aids to illustrate a point, to add variety to your presentation, to enhance the attention span of the audience, and to place specific emphasis as intended. Your presentations must be graphic and animated, yet detailed and thorough, to energize players and stimulate them to perform at their highest level. Some players are extremely motivated on their own, while others need more encouragement from you.

- Ensure that members of your audience have confidence in the material that you are presenting to a point where their desire to learn the material and to be better prepared to achieve their (individual or team) goals is enhanced.

- Educate your athletes to the highest levels possible. Far too often, the "art" of coaching is lost when coaches fail to realize the depth to which the game should be and must be taught. Keep in mind the thoughts of Sun-Tzu, the renowned military strategist, in his classic work—*The Art of War*—who concluded that with more sophistication comes more control. Furthermore, with sophistication occurs a visualization beyond common concepts and progress toward the path of perfection.

> *I learned how crucial a teacher can be in nurturing or ruining a student's passion. A teacher needs to find the trigger inside each student that will release his or her best work. Some students need to be pushed; others need space. Some need every detail explained, others work better on instinct.*
>
> Tara VanDerveer
> Head Women's Basketball Coach
> Stanford University
> from *Shooting from the Outside*

SETTING STANDARDS OF PERFORMANCE AND BEHAVIOR

Setting a standard of performance and play often comes down to an attention to detail. The focus on details cements the foundation that establishes a standard of play. The simplest execution of procedures symbolizes the commitment of the players to the organization and the organization to the players.

Details, such as shirt tails in, never being seated on the field, helmets in hands (when not participating), control of profanity, no smoking on premises, etc., all contribute (if only symbolically) to the commitment to high standards that is visible to everyone. The image of the 49ers as a first-class professional organization was nurtured and carefully developed in this way.

A commitment to high standards can influence how a team finishes a game—winning in a solid, cohesive, well coordinated manner or losing and keeping its poise, executing well and not becoming unraveled. Inappropriate acts of behavior (e.g., fighting, cheap shots, strutting and posturing, demonstrations attempting to attract individual attention, etc.) were far less visible with the 49ers because of each player's commitment to his teammates to adhere to a standard of behavior that was fostered at all times.

This "standard" relates to the respect and sensitivity shown to others and to an appreciation of the roles that each member of the organization fulfills. Each player is an extension of his teammates. When Jerry Rice catches a ball, he is an extension of several players—those who are blocking the pass rushers, the receivers who are precisely coordinating their routes with his and the quarterback who is taking a hit after throwing the ball. When Roger Craig broke through with a big run, it embodied the fierce execution of the offensive line, the timing of their blocks and the execution of the down-field blocks by the receivers.

One of the most important steps that you can undertake to make certain that a valid standard of performance exists is to ensure every practice session is conducted in an appropriate manner. (Note: A complete overview of how to organize and conduct practice sessions is presented in Chapter 11.)

Every player must have an appreciation for and take great pride in his performance during practice. He must concentrate fully and exert a maximum effort at all times.

Son, your potential is going to get me fired.

> Jerry Claiborne
> Former Head Football Coach
> University of Kentucky

In addition to teaching practical football issues, you should also teach your players about your philosophy—the team's big picture. In addition, you should take advantage of opportunities to teach and reinforce to your players the attitudes and values you believe are important in football and in life.

These beliefs—values such as respect, loyalty, responsibility, self-discipline and cooperation—should be an integral part of your philosophy. Football is not an individual sport; you must teach each of your players and staff members to work as a team.

Setting the standard for performance also begins with the expectations the head coach sets. It is crucial that you expect all individuals in the organization to possess the highest level of expertise in their particular area of responsibility, to continually refine their skills and to be physically and intellectually committed to do whatever is necessary to make the team successful.

Accordingly, you would not be fulfilling your responsibilities as the leader of the team if you did not attempt to make the people involved with the team give the "extra effort" needed to achieve the organization's most noteworthy goals. To do otherwise would simply be inappropriate on your part.

The key is to keep the bounds of "extra effort" in proper perspective. On one hand, you want to do everything possible to enable the team to reach its goals. On the other hand, you don't want to unduly exhaust individuals to a point where either their effectiveness is diminished or their health is impaired.

Whether you are a CEO or a football coach, finding a relative middle ground between the well-being of the people who work for you and the achievement of a goal is one of the most difficult aspects of leadership. We have all known leaders and managers who drove people mercilessly, simply to reassure themselves that they could do it.

If you have a staff that is always working on adrenaline, nothing may be left (energy-wise) for the extra effort necessary when a real emergency arises. Worrying too much about your staff is more humane than worrying too little, but that approach is burdened by its own load of problems.

The art of leadership requires knowing when it makes sense to take people over the top. No one will love you for failing because you asked too little.

One concept I continually addressed with my staff was taking observations or requests on my part to their logical conclusion. If I gave a project to an assistant, it was his duty to follow it up to a point where it was completely carried out. In this regard, this completion might mean something as immediate and simple as turning right around and suggesting another course of action at the time I issued the order.

In some cases, I might agree with the assistant's assessment of the situation and rescind my request. In this instance, he has taken the project to its logical conclusion.

If I decided that the problem needed further action, the assistant had to follow up on the request and take whatever time was available to either come up with a suggested plan or implement whatever course of action was needed. He also had to be willing to take the initiative in bringing the topic up with me again, even if a considerable amount of time had passed (i.e., weeks or months).

Use every means before and after combats to tell the troops what they are going to do and what they have done.

George S. Patton, Jr.,
Commander, United States Third Army
World War II
"Letter of Instruction Number 1,"
from *War as I Knew It*

MANAGING PEOPLE

You must establish a framework that structures the responsibilities and performance priorities of both your coaching staff and your support staff. In this regard, you should develop a work schedule that is realistic and manageable, yet produces the desired results.

It is also important that you establish clearly defined job profiles that are continually evolving and being revised, based on the demonstrated performance capacity of each individual. A more detailed discussion of these profiles is presented in Chapter 5.

You must ensure that all staff members understand their roles within the organization and your expectations of them. When I joined the 49ers, I recognized the critical need to clarify the responsibilities of everyone within the San Francisco organization.

Accordingly, I decided to address the employees of each area of the organization regarding the requirements and responsibilities of their positions. Subsequently, I established policies and procedures involving each individual's role and held meetings to discuss those roles with the various groups.

Each person was given an outline of my presentation. We then discussed each point. An effort was made to establish an atmosphere during the meetings where individuals could ask questions and lines of communication would be opened. Whenever appropriate, new guidelines and policies were discussed and set up. For meeting purposes, the organization was divided into ten groups:

- Squad (four one-hour sessions).
- Coaching staff (two one-hour sessions).
- Management team (two one-hour sessions).
- Team physicians (90 minutes).
- General secretarial pool (60 minutes).
- Training staff (90 minutes).
- Scouting and personnel staff (90 minutes).
- Public relations staff (90 minutes).
- Legal staff (60 minutes).
- Ownership (two four-hour sessions).

Most of these meetings were held in the spring before the draft. The coaches' meetings were scheduled just prior to training camp, while the meetings with the players were held the first week of training camp.

The ownership meetings were scheduled by the owner and his staff and were usually conducted in Youngstown, Ohio, where Eddie DeBartolo's headquarters are located. Several samples of the employee lectures I presented while I was with the San Francisco 49ers are included in Appendix B.

Working With Players

In order to manage your players in an appropriate manner, you need to act responsibly and professionally. In this regard, you should employ an approach that is based on the following steps:

- Have answers. The players look to you for direction, advice, and counsel. In order for them to have confidence in you, you must be knowledgeable and be able to apply that knowledge to address issues and situations as they arise.

- Be an expert in your specialized area. While your players don't expect you to be totally knowledgeable in all areas of the game, they do expect you to have a high level of expertise in the aspect of the game in which you have the greatest experience (i.e., offense or defense, line play vs. back play, etc.).

- Isolate the skills and the techniques that are essential to each position.

- Develop a plan on how best to teach these skills and techniques.

- Treat each player as a unique person.

- Demonstrate sincere interest in each player.

- Gain the players' confidence by working with each athlete to help him reach his full potential by enhancing his level of abilities.

- Determine how each player best responds to instruction (i.e., comprehends new information, maintains his attention span, learns new materials, etc.).

- Be sensitive to and flexible with the players' moods and demeanors while teaching and coaching.

- Search for and implement new ways to teach and impart information and to get and maintain the attention level of the players.

- Move on quickly to a different method of handling the situation if your current approach to dealing with and teaching your players is not eliciting the intended level of results.

- Exhibit strength and persistence in your dealings with your players. Hold your players to the highest expectations.

- Be personal with your players, but not too familiar. Excessive familiarity, in a misguided attempt to be socially accepted by your players, will prevent you from fully developing their performance potential.

- Avoid attempting to communicate with your players in their vernacular or their 1990s dialect. Be natural in all of your dealings. Anything else will be perceived as phony.

One of the great strengths of General George S. Patton, arguably one of the best general officers in the history of the U.S. military, was his ability to work with and lead those individuals under his command. In this regard, many of his insights can be applied to the way that coaches work with their players. For example, in his *Letter of Instruction Number 1*, which he addressed to the officers under his command in the United States Third Army, Patton offered six key dictates—each of which has application to coaching:

- Remember that praise is more valuable than blame. Remember too, that your primary mission as a leader is to see with your own eyes and be seen by your own troops while engaged in personal reconnaissance.
- Use every means before and after combat to tell the troops what they are going to do and what they have done.
- Discipline is based on pride in the profession of arms, on meticulous attention to details, and on mutual respect and confidence. Discipline must be a habit so ingrained that it is stronger than the excitement of battle or the fear of death.
- Officers must assert themselves by example and by voice. They must be preeminent in courage, deportment and dress.
- General officers must be seen in the front line during action.
- There is a tendency for the chain of command to overload junior officers by excessive requirements in the way of training and reports. You will alleviate this burden by eliminating non-essential demands.

MANAGING TIME

It is essential that your time is used efficiently and effectively. In that regard, you should develop a course of action for making decisions. Collectively, your procedures should feature a step-by-step process that allows for the following actions:

- Establishing issues, projects and needs that you should address.
- Examining these matters in detail.
- Gathering any necessary resources and the information from key personnel to make an appropriate decision.
- Developing a plan to implement the decision.
- Putting the plan into action.
- Following the plan to its conclusion.
- Dealing with out-of-the-ordinary developments concerning the plan and your decision. If necessary, be prepared to adopt contingency alternatives.

You should establish a system to move rapidly through the decision-making process, and then move on to deal with the next issue. You should keep in mind that you are likely to have a number of these situations in "motion" at one time. A more extensive overview of the decision-making process is presented in Chapter 14.

MANAGING THE COMMUNICATIONS PROCESS

Managing communications that involve the team in any way is another important responsibility of a head coach. For example, you must make it clear to everyone on your staff that you expect them to participate in the decision-making process by volunteering their thoughts, impressions and ideas. One of your primary goals in this regard is to create a channel of communications that allows for essential information to get to you from all levels of the team (i.e., from the bottom to the top).

Successful coaches realize that a winning team is not run by a single individual who dominates the work environment and reduces the rest of the group to marionettes. Winning teams are more like open forums in which everyone participates in the decision-making process—coaches and players alike—until a decision is made.

Although everyone must know who (i.e., the head coach) is in command, the head coach should behave democratically. Once a decision is made, the team must then be firmly committed to implementing the plan as intended.

During 49ers games, my coaches and I always tried to respond to what the players said. We knew we needed their input because often it made a difference.

An example occurred in a game against New Orleans in 1987. I told the team at half-time that we would call one particular pass play when we got inside the Saints' 30-yard line. For whatever reason, I simply didn't think of sending in the play when we got into that situation.

On the sideline, Steve Young, who at the time was our backup quarterback to Joe Montana, immediately reminded me of my half-time announcement. Fortunately, he wasn't a bit hesitant about doing so.

I called the play, and we scored. I couldn't worry about being embarrassed because I had forgotten what I said in the locker room. Only the result of the game mattered. We all wanted to win.

Communication is absolutely critical to this process. For example, if you are somewhat uncomfortable walking through your team's locker room, you may be losing your ability to communicate with the players. At the very least, you probably haven't developed or enhanced your ability to interact with the players as well as you should have.

Any discomfort you may experience in this situation may be because the conversations are different, the dialects are unconventional (to you), and you feel uncomfortable and uneasy about the new environment you've entered. In other words, you don't feel a part of it.

Addressing this factor was very important to me. As a result, I directed that each coach, at least one day a week, spend his lunch hour in the locker room with the team—in an unassuming way (i.e., having lunch next to some players). The goal was simple: Be there and be seen.

It is also important that you establish policies and procedures that require everyone in the organization to respond to any telephone calls, faxes or letters they receive. Any responsible contact that is made to the team's employees should receive a response.

A format should be established to categorize and process these contacts. Every response should be both timely and appropriate. Every employee must understand and adhere to this policy.

The organizational policy is most critical in those situations involving either the head coach or the Director of Football Operations. During the course of the season, both of these individuals may receive (literally) hundreds of telephone calls that result in messages being left on their answering machine.

Each message must receive a response. The secretary of either individual or the administrative assistant should establish a basic (simple) response that could either completely close off any further contact with the person who called or leave lines of communication open to the possibility of additional contact.

For example, if a "crank" message is received that includes a call-back number, a simple reply of "we have received your message" would suffice. Even though such a response may seem to be somewhat a waste of time, every correspondence—however trivial— requires some type of response, if only for basic public relation reasons (i.e., no matter or individual is too inconsequential or unimportant not to receive a reply).

Every contact of consequence should be logged. The point to remember is that proper protocol is an essential practice of a well-managed business.

Some contact will require research or sorne degree of deliberation by the individual involved before a response can be given. Accordingly, a step-by-step mechanism to handle this procedure should also be established.

As the head coach, you may decide to assign your assistant coach the responsibility of managing this on-going, sometimes overwhelming deluge of contacts. In turn, many of the contacts can be redirected to the team's public relations staff, which will have its own procedures for handling such communication.

Communicating With Your Players

You must also be able to communicate effectively with your players. I learned a lot about this area from Paul Brown when I coached for him at Cincinnati. Brown gave his annual lecture to the team on the first day of training camp.

He would begin by saying, "let's set the record straight," and then proceed to do just that. Step by step, he explained what was expected of each man, covering every aspect connected with the Cincinnati Bengals.

For example, Brown discussed how to wear your uniform, how to dress for meals, and how each player was expected to keep his locker. He instructed players on how to respond to coaching, how to take notes during lectures, how teaching would be done, and what to expect from each assistant coach.

Brown also covered such topics as punctuality, the training room, what would happen when players were waived, and the overall atmosphere he intended to create. Futhermore, he shared his policy of treating each player—stars, back-ups, veterans, rookies, free agents—equally, with the same respect and dignity.

Brown's lecture lasted four hours. When the Bengals' players left the meeting room, they were expected to enthusiastically adhere to every procedure, policy, and timetable.

Interacting With Other Individuals

Out of necessity, a head coach interacts with a variety of people. Accordingly, one group of people you should develop a positive relationship with is your fellow head coaches. As such, this relationship will improve communication with these individuals and will give you a fresh perspective on their words and actions.

Futhermore, when business contact with these individuals is necessary, you will be better able to understand them and better able to discuss your mutual needs more easily. Cultivating these relationships also builds a level of trust and a basis for sharing support. All factors considered, these relationships can be among the most positive and rewarding aspects of coaching.

You must also develop good relationships with members of your staff. Assistant coaches can make or break any large football organization. Your assistants should know you are available to discuss any problems or differences of opinion they may have with you.

They should also be aware that they must be absolutely loyal and stand behind whatever decision is made. This atmosphere is virtually impossible to create if you do not expend the time and energy necessary to cultivate good relationships with all your assistant coaches.

As you cultivate relationships with other individuals, you must also try to avoid making enemies and learn to co-exist with your adversaries. You should understand that even those people who do harm to you may be people with whom you have to do business at some point in the future.

As long as someone is a potential business contact, you should make every reasonable effort to keep the lines of communication open and maintain a civilized relationship.

You should be the one to initiate communication following a conflict, even if the other person misunderstood you or wrongfully ridiculed you. While it may certainly be appropriate (depending on circumstances) to confront those who purposely insult you or do you harm, you should avoid conflict.

You must be astute enough to avoid becoming the loser in such situations. By being sensitive to inherent hazards of a hostile relationship, you can give yourself a chance to win the person over to having at least a "neutral" association with you.

The reality of the situation is that regardless of the reason behind an extremely adversarial relationship, such a relationship can have negative consequences. In turn, by minimizing the forces working against you, you do away with resultant distractions and free your mind to focus on your work.

DEVELOPING A NETWORK OF PERSONAL COUNSEL AND SUPPORT

You should have a network of counsel and support. It is important to have someone besides your immediate family to talk to about matters of particular concern to you.

While your spouse and family can be extremely important as a source of support, you also need to have regular sessions with a mentor(s). You should realize that this type of assistance can enable you to be better prepared to work through difficulties, as well as successes.

Your mentor(s) can help you keep things in perspective, by reminding you that this kind of thing has happened before and will happen again. Furthermore, they can help you clarify and prioritize situations and responsibilities.

You should take care in selecting your mentors. On one hand, they should not be immediate family members. On the other hand, they should not be total strangers. It is, however, very important that they are people you respect.

Regardless of the format, you should be very selective and discreet about your use of counseling. You should take care that you don't talk to too many people or to the wrong people. In reality, if you openly tell others about what you're doing, they will often end up embellishing the story to a point where it may frustrate, hurt or embarrass you.

KEEPING THE BIG PICTURE

As you attempt to fulfill all your responsibilities as a head coach, you must learn how to maintain your perspective. You cannot do everything; if you could, you would not need assistants and support staff.

While you are ultimately in charge of many things, you do not necessarily have to oversee every day-to-day aspect of them. While trying to put out little fires, you may lose your perspective on more important issues which do demand your personal attention. You should keep in mind that you have a limited amount of time available. As such, you must learn to allot it wisely to the things that are most important.

For example, on occasion, it will be appropriate for you to pitch in to help by providing hands-on instruction and coaching. Ethically and practically, there's no better way to inspire hard work than by the example of your own work. In turn, the secret to managing well and motivating those you manage is to understand the fine line between losing sight of the big picture and letting others lose sight of you.

Keeping a proper balance between micro- and macro-managerial approaches to coaching is somewhat like appreciating a work of art. If you stand close to the piece, you may be able to appreciate the fine detail and texture of the material.

You do so, however, at the risk of being so close that you can not keep the entire scope of the work in proper perspective. If you stand too far back, you may have a better view of the "big picture," but you risk losing the appreciation of the attention to detail and the quality of the work.

Within the football arena, a position coach can and should "stand too close" to the work. It is his responsibility to keep the attention to detail and the proper perspective of the game plan as it pertains to his specific position.

The coordinators must step back a little further than the position coach. They should be close enough to keep the attention to detail, but also must maintain the bigger perspective to make sure that the varying components of their schemes (offense or defense) are working well together and don't become too compartmentalized. It is part of the coordinator's job to make sure that the position coaches don't get so focused on their own perspective that they lose sight of the overall main objective.

The head coach must pull back even a step further than the coordinators. You must have the encompassing perspective of all. It is your responsibility to make sure the offense, defense and special teams interact together to maintain the balance that is needed to achieve any type of sustained success in the NFL.

On occasion, you may have to constantly remind your coordinators that, in and of itself, finishing high in the league statistical standings has little or no value except as it pertains to the overall goal of winning and losing. The proper distance you need to accomplish this task is wholly subjective and hard to quantify.

It is also important that you keep things in perspective when considering whether to accept the advice and input of your assistant coaches. For example, if, for whatever reason, you are overanxious, desperate or not thinking calmly or clearly, you may be unduly susceptible to taking advice or directions from assistant coaches who are in a similar emotional upheaval as you.

The problem arises from the fact that your assistant coaches don't have anything to lose, relatively speaking. As the head coach, you are rightfully responsible and accountable for all decisions.

You must answer to the owner of the team, to the media, and to your staff. Most of all, however, you must answer to the team.

Denny Green, the successful head coach of the Minnesota Vikings, has developed a process of interacting with his coaches and players in a way that no other coach in the NFL does. In Minnesota, Denny runs both offensive and defensive scout teams during the week's preparation. This practice is an inventive way of accomplishing several tasks:

- Denny's approach enables him to interact daily with virtually every member of the squad. This practice creates a truly open door policy with the players in that they are more willing to go to the head coach and address an issue because they have already interacted with him during the day in a more informal setting.

- Denny's method gives the players a tangible way of seeing the head coach actively involved in preparations for the opponent. Many times, players will not be aware of the amount of time and effort a head coach puts into preparing for the week's opponent because he is not actively involved in the decision-making process. During the game, they have a more realistic sense that he has prepared as much as any of the coaches or players because they have seen the energy and effort that Denny has put in on a daily basis.

- Denny's way provides him with a very practical and working knowledge of what the coaching staff feels the opponent will try to do and what the team's actual plan is to counter it. On occasion, times exist when the offensive or defensive coordinator may "clinic" the head coach on what the plan is for the week. Then, after making a concerted effort to install and practice the game plan during the week, the coordinators might decide to not fully implement that plan.

MAKING A DIFFERENCE

At some point in every coach's career, he will question whether he is making a difference or not. A basic review of the won-loss records of NFL teams in the past few seasons suggests that an NFL head coach can make a difference.

In recent years, the NFL has become a very homogeneous entity. Factors such as the advent of free agency, the reduced number of draft choices that each team has and the salary cap have left the league as a whole drifting towards the middle (i.e., the middle being a .500 or 8-8 season).

Given the continuous mobility among players in the NFL, the W-L records suffer even for the most talented teams. The impact of this mobility is noticeable. Weaker teams can improve immeasurably in a given year, while better teams can erode toward the middle of the pack. As a result, the largest number of NFL teams have either a 7-9, an 8-8, or a 9-7 record.

Because of a team's inherent lack of depth, injuries can take a major toll on a team or on other teams in its division. As a consequence, circumstances can turn around dramatically in only one or two games.

For example, a team can start very poorly, find itself, gain momentum and become a playoff team (or even a Super Bowl champion) with a 9-7 or a 10-6 regular-season record. This situation puts added pressure on the head coach to bring his team back from losses that are bound to occur over the course of the season. The pressure is even worse when a team suffers consecutive losses.

The key for a team is to be fully mobilized and building momentum as the regular season closes and the playoffs begin. As such, when his team suffers a loss in the regular season, it is critical that the head coach has the ability to hold his team together and maintain his composure. He should remember that his opponents are suffering from similar disappointments and frustrations.

A Bell-Curve Distribution

The accompanying graphs illustrate that over the last three years (1994-96), the league has typically taken on a unique bell-curve distribution. The horizontal axis represents the total numbers of wins by team, while the vertical axis represents the total number of teams winning that number of games that year.

For example, five teams had nine wins in 1996. This statistic indicated that the majority of the League is bunched together within a relatively small margin of difference, with the outliers (those teams that separate themselves from the pack in a winning or losing profile) accounting for the same percentages each year.

In any given year in the NFL between 12-14 teams will be one game above or below .500 (8-8). These teams will account for between 40-45 percent of the entire League. Sixty to sixty-five percent will cluster between two games above or under .500. As a result, it has been hypothesized statistically that as few as 6-10 plays a year will separate a team from finishing one game over .500 to one game under 8-8. Typically, the two or three outliers with the most positive records will distinguish themselves from the 40-45 percent grouping with a 12-4 or 13-3 record.

Diametrically opposed to that group are the three or four teams that will finish the season with only two or three wins (sometimes even fewer). The reasons for these outliers are usually apparent. The positive teams possess a high number of talented players, experience and continuity, while the bottom-end teams experience a number of injuries, have a lack of skill at several key positions or are enduring a run of plain bad luck.

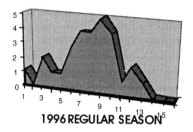

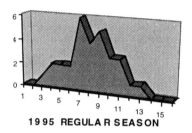

1996 REGULAR SEASON

Interestingly, the negative outliers tend to be the same teams year after year. This situation leaves the majority of teams in the homogeneous grouping to find a way to stay ahead of the curve and to strive to separate themselves from the curve and move up with the positive outliers.

1995 REGULAR SEASON

Any number of factors can contribute to a team staying ahead of the curve consistently. For example, I believe that coaching is a critical factor in maintaining your position as a team that continually finishes ahead of the curve. Typically, talent will vary from team to team, and one or two key acquisitions will be made in the off-season by each team. Continuity of coaching and maintaining a solid structure are the factors that usually differentiate the teams that stay consistently on the positive side of the curve, compared to the teams that drift

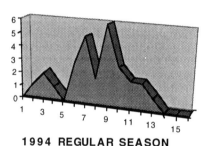

1994 REGULAR SEASON

back and fourth from the negative to positive side of the curve from year to year.

Three excellent examples of teams that have maintained a positive position on the curve year after year are Marty Schottenheimer's Kansas City Chiefs, Denny Green's Minnesota Vikings and Bill Cowher's Pittsburgh Steelers. Each of these teams is in a medium-market city with a limited financial base.

Yet, each team has maintained a winning profile, never falling below 8-8, and making the playoffs four of the last five years. In fact, the Steelers have reached the playoffs the last five years and made it into the Super Bowl in 1996.

The bottom line is that as the head coach, you must believe that your abilities can make a positive difference. When you lose that perspective and fall prey to the naysayers who have all the excuses as to why you can't win, then you have lost the winning edge.

In the process, you may panic, lose the "courage of your convictions" and just start pressing buttons in hopes that the situation will fix itself. You must regain the proper perspective.

In this scenario, the old adage may apply that a football coach has to be smart enough to bring all the abilities and the personalities on a team together into a solid single working unit, and dumb enough to think it is important to do so.

CHAPTER 4

DEVELOPING A SUCCESSFUL ORGANIZATIONAL STRUCTURE

"Without organization and leadership towards a realistic goal, there is no chance of realizing more than a small percentage of your potential."

—John Wooden
Hall-of-Fame Basketball Coach
UCLA

Finding the winning edge...

Once a leader establishes standards, top lieutenants have to be given the power to solve problems quickly and decisively. Success-ful delegation of major responsibilities is a sign of good leadership. It requires hiring people who can handle significant roles well, and letting them exercise that power independently while you still maintain control. This is why a mood change when you enter a room full of subordinates signals you've still got a way to go in creating an organization that reflects your leadership and yet is one in which that leadership is effectively shared. If, for instance, a staff doesn't seem fully mobilized until the boss arrives, the self-assurance that is the hallmark of a well-led company hasn't percolated down.

—Bill Walsh, "Holy Macro: Delegat-ing Requires a Sure Touch—Too Little and You Become a Figure-head, Too Much and You Squelch Creativity," *Forbes*, August 26, 1996.

At some point, an organization must have a single source of authority who can collect information and then make a decision. Organizations must take care, however, that they do not place a person in this position who does not have the capacity to fill that role. If the person in this role is overmatched by the position, he will often make incorrect decisions. Vince Lombardi, George Allen, Don Shula, Bill Parcells, Tom Coughlin and Jimmy Johnson are outstanding examples of single source authority. This individual does not necessarily have to be the head coach; Al Davis, Bobby Beathard, Bill Polian and Don Klosterman are examples of single source authority besides the head coach who have built an organization to championship levels. Examples also exist of teams who formed successful relationships between the head coach and administration: Tex Schramm and Tom Landry; George Young and Bill Parcells; Bobby Beathard and Joe Gibbs; Bill Polian and Marv Levy; and Pat Bowlen and Mike Shanahan. The key is to have a talented personnel man who can do business with other teams, as well as a strong football person (not just a good businessman).

Historically in sports, most organizations were run essentially by one person—an individual whose domineering presence enveloped the entire organization. All factors considered, this autocratic approach to management enabled the organization's employees to understand that their basic role in the scheme of things was to simply do whatever that person dictated.

To a point, the authoritarian-based style of overseeing an entire organization made it somewhat "easy" for everyone involved. The authority figure gave orders, and everyone else just followed them.

Over time, however, many of the factors that made a dictatorial style of organizational structure acceptable (i.e., "tolerable") have changed. Most NFL teams recognize the fact that getting to the Super Bowl involves a lot more than a leader with a firm, controlling hand and a wealth of football knowledge.

Rather, an organization needs to be structured in such a way that it can operate in the most efficient, effective and organized manner possible. To the extent that the way in which an organization is set up and managed can ensure that all necessary tasks are performed in a timely manner and can enhance accountability and eliminate ambiguity with regard to the club's chain of command, having the appropriate organizational structure is crucial.

The key point to remember is that different organizations are often best served by different structures. Deciding which structure is most appropriate for an organization can involve several factors, including the philosophy of the team's ownership, the team's specific goals and priorities, the value structure of the head coach, the competency level of the organization's key employees, the size of the organization, financial considerations, etc.

Not surprisingly, a variety of organizational structures currently exists in the NFL. Given the very complex and the multi-dimensional nature of the work environment in the NFL, different teams have taken different approaches over the years regarding which organizational setup enables them to best meet their own unique needs.

Some teams give virtually total control to a single individual (i.e., a person in the dual role of head coach/general manager). Other teams adopt a more decentralized structure by separating the duties of the general manager, the director of operations, and the head coach. The third major type of organizational structure involves a situation where ownership plays a prominent role in football matters. In a very few instances, regardless of how a team's managerial setup is configured on paper, the majority of the important decisions is made by ownership.

In this regard, four owners who brought new standards of professionalism, honesty and ethics to the NFL were Lamar Hunt, Wellington Mara, Dan Rooney and Ralph Wilson. The dignity and respect that these individuals engendered to the game lent credence to the NFL, not only as a business, but also as a sport.

It is important to keep in mind that no single "best" organizational structure exists. A team should adopt a structure that not only enables it to maximize its objectives both in the short-run and in the long-run, but also to adapt to changing circumstances.

ESTABLISHING A SINGLE SOURCE OF AUTHORITY

Whatever operational structure an organization establishes, it is absolutely critical that at some point, there must be a single source of authority. In that regard, it is also crucial that the individual who is assigned or assumes that role has the capacity to fill it.

Depending upon the circumstances, decisions can be made at varying paces once the information necessary to reach a decision has been collected. What cannot vary, however, is the need to have a well-qualified person make the final decision. The fact of the matter is that incompetent individuals will frequently make the wrong decisions on matters which they are "ill-equipped" to handle.

Over the years, the ultimate responsibility for final authority on an NFL team has generally been assumed by one of three entities: the head coach; a single individual other than the head coach (e.g., the general manager, the president of the team, the owner, etc.); or a combination of the head coach and someone in upper-level management (usually, the general manager).

Feeling that if they're going to be held accountable for the final "product" (i.e., the team's performance), many head coaches have concluded that they should have the final say on all of the factors that will impact on that product. As such, these individuals (particularly those head coaches who have the "clout" to receive it) have demanded single source authority. A list of those coaches who have capably filled such a role over the years in the NFL is impressive. Examples of individuals who have served in this capacity include Vince Lombardi, George Allen, Don Shula, Mike Ditka (with the New Orleans Saints), Jimmy Johnson, Dick Vermeil, and Bill Parcells (with the New York Jets). Tom Coughlin exemplifies the newer wave of outstanding coaches who are attempting to take a similar path to success.

Among the teams that have utilized someone other than the head coach as the compelling force in their decision-making process have been the Los Angeles Rams

(Don Klosterman), the Oakland Raiders (Al Davis), the Dallas Cowboys (Jerry Jones—in the post-Jimmy Johnson era), and the San Diego Chargers (Bobby Beathard).

A majority of the NFL teams employ a combination of the head coach working in close concert with a very competent administrator to get the job done properly. Historically, four of the tandem duos that best illustrate this particular approach to wielding authority have been Tom Landry-Tex Schramm (Dallas Cowboys), Bill Parcells-George Young (New York Giants), Joe Gibbs-Bobby Beathard (Washington Redskins), and Marv Levy-Bill Polian (Buffalo Bills).

Among the current groups of individuals who have successfully combined to lead their teams are Mike Holmgren-Ron Wolf (Green Bay Packers), Mike Shanahan-Pat Bowlen (Denver Broncos), Tony Dungy-Richard McKay (Tampa Bay Buccaneers), Bruce Coslet-Mike Brown (Cincinnati Bengals), and Dennis Green-Roger Headrick (Minnesota Vikings).

However authority is exercised, it is essential that a team has a talented individual in charge of personnel so that business can be conducted with other teams in a productive and professional manner. Every team must also have a strong football person who can lend his expertise and insights to the decision-making process.

RECOGNIZING THE INEVITABILITY OF CHANGE

The structure of an NFL organization is not an entity unto itself. All factors considered, no organization will be able to sustain any single type of structure indefinitely. Circumstances change. Things happen.

A natural evolution to the life of an organizational structure exists that at some point it must and will change. The extent and the swiftness of any changes will depend on the nature of the change in circumstances. For example, a minor change might involve a situation where an individual from within the organization is promoted or transferred to a position that becomes vacant for any reason. In this instance, the transition from having one employee in a particular position to filling that position with another could (and should) be relatively smooth.

Indeed, if top management (or ownership itself) anticipates and properly prepares for such changes in personnel, subsequent transitions can be made as seamless as possible. A more serious type of change occurs when an organization loses a key person. The NFL is replete with examples of teams that reached a certain level of success only to go tumbling back to relative mediocrity when one or two people left the organization. Another example of an occurrence that can greatly impact an organization's structure is a change in ownership.

The Dallas Cowboys, one of the preeminently successful teams in the world of professional sports in the 1960s and 1970s, exemplify a team that had a particularly difficult time adjusting to change for a while. The loss of a few key players, coupled with two ownership changes, had a devastating effect on the Cowboys' performance on the field. Even the presence of the renowned troika of Tex Schramm, Gil Brandt, and Tom Landry was virtually powerless to stop the Cowboys' slide from their winning ways. Eventually, the shift was reversed only after major changes were made in both the team's personnel (management and coaching) and the team's way of conducting business.

One of the difficulties in dealing with the inevitability of the evolution of circumstances is the multifaceted nature of change. Making changes in response to traumatic events, like a loss of key personnel, a switch in ownership, or something as detestable (and direct) as failing to win may not always be enjoyable, but it certainly is understandable.

Another kind of change—no less essential—also exists. This type of change is much more difficult to undertake. Sometimes it is appropriate to change for the sake of seeing matters—and doing things—in an entirely different, revitalized way.

What makes this kind of change so difficult is the fact that it's not the product of (or a reaction to) disaster. The need to make this kind of change occurs, as often as not, when everything is going relatively well.

The comfort of success in a known world is a powerful source of denial. Even though change can bring about a new situation where life is far less predictable, an organization must be structured in such a way that personnel are continually encouraged to look for "a better way."

He taught wherever he went, and at every level; his eye was sharp, his military instinct as sound in schooling a platoon commander as a general. He was, it was said, everyone's instructor.

David Fraser
from *Knight's Cross:
A Life of Field Marshal Erwin Rommel*

IDENTIFYING THE PARAMETERS OF
AN EFFECTIVE ORGANIZATIONAL STRUCTURE

Although no one single type of organizational structure has been found to be the most successful way for conducting business, three basic conditions must exist if a particular approach is to be effective:

- A primary figure who has an extensive knowledge and expertise in the game must be at the center of the decision-making process.
- A well-defined organizational structure with a distinct delineation of responsibility must be established.
- The purpose of that structure must be equally well-defined and documented.

It should be noted that the capabilities of the individual who is at the center of the decision-making process will be the relative "measuring stick" of the organization. His background, basic intellect, ability to approach his duties in a proactive manner, and ability to anticipate and react to changing circumstances will be the touchstone for top management and the group as a whole.

It is not necessary that the individual who fills this role be the top executive within the organization. If it is, however, that person must have access to someone who possesses an inclusive knowledge of the mechanics of the profession for advice and counsel.

A well-defined organizational structure that has a distinct delineation of responsibility is important for at least two reasons. Without such a structure, a duplication of effort may occur. This scenario often leads to conflict and frustration between the parties involved, a situation exacerbated by the subsequent waste of time and energy.

The absence of such an organizational setup can also lead to finger pointing when certain duties aren't performed. Without a distinct delineation of responsibilities, the crack that exists between broadly defined functions may widen into a chasm into which critical tasks and assignments may fall uncompleted.

It is also very important that the purpose of an organization's structure is spelled out, clarified, and documented. In many instances, individuals make assumptions regarding what this purpose is. Some of these assumptions are accurate, while others are not.

If the individuals within an organization are to be able to prioritize their professional obligations and decision-making processes, it is vital that at least at the top management level, a "prime directive" (i.e., the fundamental purpose of the organization) must be established. Accordingly, everyone within the organization would be able to position the "prime directive" over any other duty or action that might otherwise come into conflict with it.

Winning is the "prime directive" of many NFL organizations. Other clubs place a higher value on the bottom line (i.e., being profitable). At face value, these missions may seem entirely compatible. At some point, however, these two priorities will come into direct conflict with each other.

A notable example of this conflict involves the NFL's free agency process. All factors considered, it is not too difficult to identify those organizations that constantly let their developed talent leave via the free agent route, not because the teams don't recognize their free agent's skills and performance capabilities, but because they either can't or won't commit to the financial outlay it would take to keep a particular athlete in the organization.

In reality, it is far less expensive for a team to let its developed players get away, and then simply to fire the coaching staff for not winning enough games. For example, a team can often replace an entire coaching staff for less than the cost of keeping a single "key" free agent.

Surprisingly, teams that continually adhere to "profitability" as their "prime directive" have a somewhat difficult time recognizing why they are often at the bottom of the NFL curve (i.e., standings). From a performance standpoint, the axiom "penny wise and pound foolish" applies to these teams.

Regardless of the realities of the situation, the head coach must understand where "winning" is held by the organization relative to its other objectives. If the organization's commitment to winning is not preeminent, he needs to know it.

As such, it is absolutely essential that the organization must have clearly defined parameters that precisely spell out its "prime directive." If the head coach deludes himself into believing that the "prime directive" of his organization is winning, when in fact the ownership is most concerned with the team's financial spreadsheet, he won't be able to accurately anticipate the perceived needs of the organization and make appropriate decisions.

Accordingly, the head coach must fully comprehend the substance of the organization's "prime directive" if he is going to be able to make suitable decisions within the framework in which he has to function. A logical argument can be made that the only thing worse (relatively speaking) than being in an organization that will not or can not compete financially with other NFL clubs is not recognizing it.

ESTABLISHING A PLAN FOR STRUCTURING THE ORGANIZATION

The essential purpose of an NFL organization is to function in the NFL market place in such a way that will enable it to achieve its objective (i.e., "prime directive") in the most efficient and effective manner possible. Toward that end, a plan for structuring the organization must be established that ensures the organization will accomplish its primary purpose. Such a plan should consider a number of factors, including:

- An organization's structure should be designed in such a way that the strengths of the organization's employees are maximized and their weaknesses made irrelevant.

- An organization must be staffed at the top levels of management with capable and competent people in the field. If a top echelon manager is devoid of the necessary skills and acumen, a productivity vacuum may be created that negatively affects other aspects of the organization, possibly to the degree that the entire structure of the organization is rendered ineffective.

- The head coach must be placed as the central figure in the organization, regardless of whether he is the top executive or decision maker. The players must know that the head coach is in complete command of the team (and their destiny) or he and his assistants may have difficulties getting them to respond appropriately.

  For example, a head coach with only one year left on his contract who is "hung-out-to-dry" by an organization often finds it virtually impossible to govern the behavior of his players—particularly in those critical situations that always arise during the course of a season.

- An organization must not attempt to manage the team from the second-level administrative wing. Effective management must occur at the ground level by those (i.e., the coaching staff) who deal with the players on a day-to-day, face-to-face basis.

- Everyone in the organization must recognize the fact that an organization's structure is not static, but dynamic. Because circumstances and events change quickly in the NFL, no one can afford to get into a comfort zone of complacency (i.e., not being prepared for contingencies).

- The structure of an organization must have the flexibility and adaptability to meet unexpected obstacles, crises, or developments.

- An organization should take steps to prepare its employees to handle adversity in such a way that unexpected setbacks can be readily overcome. Such preparation should involve a systematic and ongoing effort.

- Top management in an organization must realize that planning for adversity is the key to overcoming adversity. Unfortunately, "bad things" sometimes do happen to "good companies." As such, contingency planning must be ongoing—as opposed to something that is pulled out of a drawer, dusted off, and used whenever a crisis occurs.

- One of the keys to effective leadership isn't so much in being decisive (even loose cannons can be decisive in some situations), but in being able to acknowledge that changes in circumstances are inevitable and to prepare to react appropriately to each changing situation.

  Organizations must ensure that changes in their circumstances have a minimal effect (i.e., cause as little—if any—damage as possible). This advice is particularly relevant in the age of free agency where a variety of potentially devastating personnel-related scenarios can occur.

  For example, a team may lose a key player to free agency. In the other extreme, a team may expend a sizable financial outlay to sign a particular free agent, only to subsequently discover that the player is not meeting the team's expectations from a performance standpoint.

  In either scenario, an organization must be structured in such a way to handle a mistake of this nature. Otherwise, a single mistake involving personnel matters can be further compounded by failing to undertake corrective measures.

- Crisis management requires anticipation, preparation, and practice (drills), as well as a cool-headed troubleshooting team. Practicing what to do in the event of a crisis can be an invaluable experience.

  An organization should not forego performing crisis drills just because it has an experienced and capable crisis management team. Members of this team must be individuals who can exhibit "grace under fire" (i.e., be able to handle pressure in all situations).

- An organization (especially top management) must never panic in a crisis situation, regardless of how circumstances turn out. For example, in numerous instances, an organization can bring on failure by the inappropriate way in which it reacts to pressure. On the other hand, an organization that exhibits both the nerve and the patience to stay with a particular program or endeavor is often rewarded with extraordinary results.

- A plan for structuring an organization should be put in writing to provide a documented source of reference and guidance for everyone involved, including ownership. Among the aspects of such a plan that should be written down are an operations manual, a personnel manual, a budget manual, and an overall set of job descriptions.

- In the face of massive (and often conflicting) pressures, an organization has to be resolute in its vision of the future and how it plans to get where it wants to go. Such a plan should include an overview of the team's goals and objectives, a detailed assessment of its current state of affairs, and a realistic projection of where it hopes to be within a predetermined timetable.

- The head coach must not allow himself to become "captive" to the agenda of other people (e.g., assistant coaches, operations personnel, league personnel, outside consultants, etc.). Despite the fact that most of these individuals are well-meaning and simply trying to do their job for the perceived benefit of the organization, the head coach must keep in perspective the fact that each of these individuals is only one of many voices.

Remember that praise is more valuable than blame. Remember too, that your primary mission as a leader is to see with your own eyes and be seen by your troops while engaged in personal reconnaissance.

George S. Patton, Jr.
Commander, United States Third Army
World War II
"Letter of Instruction Number 1,"
from *War as I Knew It*

MAKING PEOPLE THE HEART OF THE ORGANIZATION

One of the most strategically important and economically sound steps that an organization can take is to attract, develop, and retain a diverse group of the best and the brightest human talent in the market place. As such, assembling a "winning" group of employees requires thoughtful leadership and a comprehensive plan.

Among the factors that management should consider when developing a plan to effectively utilize an organization's most important resource (i.e., people) are the following:

- In order to develop and maintain an effective organization, management must be knowledgeable and competent when dealing with people.

- All factors considered, the organizations that have traditionally been the most successful are those that have demonstrated a pronounced commitment to their employees by providing a work environment that enables them to achieve at their maximum levels of productivity and potential.

- Management must recognize and acknowledge both the uniqueness of each individual employee and the bona fide need that individuals have for a reasonable degree of job security and self-actualization.

- The fact that some of the most talented people are individuals who are very independent-minded requires management to carefully consider how it can effectively communicate with this type of employee.

- Although a personalized approach should be employed when dealing with employees, undue familiarity should be avoided. Simply stated, the head coach should be cognizant of the capabilities of his players and the members of the organization's management team in order to help them to utilize and enhance their unique skills and talents.

  Furthermore, it is essential that the head coach helps his players and the employees of the organization to fully realize their potential. On the other hand, it is also important that the head coach gains a clear grasp of the shortcomings of these individuals and, to the extent possible, steers them clear of their deficiencies.

- On occasion, management will face a real "balancing act" between the specific interests of the organization and the unique interests of the individual when deciding the proper course of action in a particular situation. As a result, top management may frequently be forced to choose between the "good of the whole" versus the "good of the individual."

- In a best-case scenario, the organization and the individual must be made to understand that what is good for one must also be good for the other.

- Employees who are creative will sometimes require "special handling." Passionate about seeing their ideas implemented (all of their ideas, as soon as possible), creative people should be made to understand that every one of their ideas will not be appropriate and, as such, will not be used.

  Coming up with an idea, no matter how brilliant it may be, is just the beginning of the creative process. Initially, the utility of each idea must be assessed. If the idea is deemed suitable, a decision should then be reached regarding how to put the idea into effect. Finally, the idea is enacted.

- New ideas are important at every level of the organization. For example, coming up with a unique way to drill a particular technique or a fundamental skill may not be as exciting as reinventing the forward pass, yet it's very useful and a lot more likely to have a practical application on the football field.

- Although an organization should demonstrate a reasonable amount of flexibility in the work environment to accommodate the needs of its employees, top management must be totally inflexible with regard to its expectations of the performance of its employees. In this instance, the key step is to document those expectations.

- People are most comfortable in their working environment when their duties are laid out in specific detail and their performance can be gauged by distinct and measurable parameters. Employee accountability is facilitated when the responsibilities of the employees are spelled out in great detail.

- It is critical that employee expectation levels are both reasonable and attainable, as well as high.

- The process of establishing and documenting employee expectations must be done in a timely manner that enables the organization's "prime directive" to be accomplished.

- Once the employee expectations have been identified and documented, they must be continually monitored, revised, and refined (as either the situation or the personnel changes).

- A protocol detailing how various members of the organization should interact with each other should be established. In order to enhance the performance of the employees as a group, the role that each person is assigned in the organization and how each employee relates to the roles played by the other employees must be explicitly delineated and clearly understood by everyone involved.

  If such an awareness is not established, the organization (as a single entity) may become compartmentalized to a point where efficiency and productivity are severely compromised. The risk of individuals and departments becoming overly obsessed with protecting their own "turf" may also be heightened. The potential for a counterproductive situation occurring applies to all elements of the organization (e.g., the pro-personnel director to the college scouts, the equipment manager to the facility coordinator, the offensive line coach to the offensive coordinator, etc.).

ESTABLISHING ORGANIZATIONAL RESPONSIBILITIES

To a major degree, an organization is defined by how different work is done. In order to ensure that all work is performed in the most efficient and productive manner possible, an organizational structure is required that puts similar work into departments (e.g., accounting, marketing, scouting, etc.).

Basically, an organizational structure involves a pattern of task groupings, reporting relationships, and authority stipulations within an organization. Organizations are structured to accomplish one or more specific goals. As a rule, structuring an organization involves the following steps:

- Job design (i.e., grouping positions into units).
- Distribution of power.
- Determining the span of management (i.e., deciding how many subordinates report to a single manager).
- Establishing a chain of command.

Although the scope of responsibilities and the exact job titles may vary somewhat from one position to another between different organizations, it is important that all critical tasks be efficiently and competently performed within an organization, regardless of what structure exists or what job title is assigned. As a general rule, most NFL organizations are structured into at least two basic levels—a top management level and a professional support level. The top management level typically consists of a General Manager (i.e., President or CEO), a Director of

Operations, a Director of Pro Personnel, a Director of College Scouting and a Head Coach.

Depending upon how each position has been defined and what chain of command has been established, the professional support level is further subdivided. For example, the direct staff of the general manager normally includes the individuals in charge of finance, legal affairs, marketing, and public relations.

The professional support staff is also responsible for such diverse—yet important—functions as stadium operations, publications, equipment, security, suite management, athletic training, medical affairs, and facility management. In addition, the individuals in charge of specific departments or performing certain duties can be combined into "teams" to facilitate particular functions or projects of the organization (e.g., a negotiation team, a talent acquisition team, etc.).

In turn, the professional support staff is bolstered by an array of core employees who perform a variety of jobs (e.g., clerical, ticket staff, grounds-keeping, locker room attendants, etc.). Collectively, these employees play an important role in the daily operations of the organization.

At a minimum, a comprehensive plan for establishing a successful organizational structure must include an itemized list of the requisite qualifications for each of the principal positions within the organization and a detailed overview of the responsibilities for each of those employees. Among the positions that should be profiled are the following:

Impress upon the mind of every man, from first to the lowest, the importance of the cause and what it is they are contending for.

George Washington
1st President of the United States

- *General Manager (President/CEO).* The individual who fills this role should be well-educated, ideally with an advanced degree. He should have competitive sports experience—at the collegiate level if possible.

  Furthermore, he should have some background of involvement in activities outside of professional sports (for at least a brief period). This individual should be someone who has grown into the culture of the NFL through a series of diverse experiences, however briefly, in other facets of the game.

  It is important that this person should view his role within the organization as an executive administrator—not as a pseudo-coach. He must have organizational experience, as well as be someone who is committed to being fully knowledgeable about current (i.e., contemporary) management practices, innovations, and thinking.

This individual should be well-versed in the financial aspects of professional football, including those that affect an organization's agreements, policies, and directives. He should also be thoroughly knowledgeable about those NFL bylaws that are related directly or indirectly to the operation of an NFL franchise.

The person in this role should be able to function independently of ownership. He should not take on the role as someone who appeases ownership. Rather, he must perceive his role as an executive who has a broad level of expertise in management matters and extensive working knowledge of the business.

This individual must have a full appreciation of the effects that the media can have on the organization. If not, he may enable immense damage to be done to the organization if he is not alert to the negative consequences that can occur if interactions with the media are not handled properly. (Refer to Chapter 17 for a more complete discussion of how to work with the media.)

All factors considered, it would be an advantage to the organization if this person did not become a highly visible public figure. An individual who is a highly quotable personality who constantly is seeking a platform from which to editorialize, or who isn't sensitive to the numerous challenges imposed by working with the media, is simply not as qualified as he should be for this particular position.

Because the individual in this role will often need to reconcile (conciliate) disagreements within the organization among coaches, players, and management personnel, he must possess effective communication skills. He also should be sensitive to and capable of dealing with management matters where high levels of emotion are involved.

In both appearance and demeanor, this person should exemplify the professionalism, personality, and the sophistication that are commonly associated with individuals at the highest levels of corporate America. In reality, an individual with a stark, hard-hitting, insensitive persona does not generally epitomize the type of person who can best represent an organization.

In recent years, San Francisco has been very fortunate to have Carmen Policy fill this role for the 49ers. His legal background as a trial attorney, coupled with his resolute commitment to excellence, has enabled him to exhibit dynamic leadership as the President of the 49ers.

It is important that this individual is an integral part of the day-to-day operations of the organization. As such, he must be well-acquainted with employees at all levels of the organization (including the athletes) on a personal basis.

He should be someone who gets along well with other top management people throughout the League. As such, he should make every attempt to cultivate relationships with other club executives and with representatives of the NFL's hierarchy. All relationships should be executed in an engaging, positive and professional basis.

Within the structure of the organization, the general manager (president/CEO) should be directly accountable to the ownership. He should serve as the conduit between the owner and all activities, developments, and issues involving the organization.

He should directly oversee staffing and establish the method of operation and chain of command at the top management level. In addition, he should serve as the main spokesperson for the organization in all daily operations involving League matters. Furthermore, he should act as the primary conduit between the ownership and the League concerning the functional operation of the organization.

One of the most important responsibilities of the general manager is to establish the nature of the communication process within the organization's structure and to be a viable part of that process on an ongoing, day-to-day basis. As such, one of his major priorities must be to ensure that direct lines of communication between the various departments and within the organization as a whole are set up and maintained.

In other words, he must make sure that the appropriate people at appropriate levels have access to all the information they need to make informed decisions. He should also take steps to ensure that his key employees are not burdened with "information overload" (i.e., engulfed by analysis and levels of detail that are important to a few, interesting to some, and purposeless to most).

In order to be effective, communication must be timely and have an appropriate level of detail. Accordingly, the general manager must provide specific parameters to each section head within which his department is expected to function.

It is also important that the general manager and the CFO are kept fully abreast of all negotiations and relevant matters concerning the NFL's Collective Bargaining Agreement (CBA). To that end, a format must be in place to expeditiously make step-by-step revisions to the CBA as last-minute changes occur.

The general manager must also take steps to ensure that a definitive policy exists for the organization to work with the press. This policy should include the team's ownership. All factors considered, a single media spokesperson for the organization should be designated.

There is a tendency for the chain of command to overload junior officers by excessive requirements in the way of training and reports. You will alleviate this burden by eliminating non-essential demands.

> George S. Patton, Jr.
> Commander, United States Third Army
> World War II
> "Letter of Instruction Number 1,"
> from *War as I Knew It*

- *Director of Operations (DOO).* The individual who is best suited for this position is someone who has varied and extensive experience at all levels in the tasks involved in the operation of an NFL franchise. While a formal education can be useful, the training and hands-on experience this individual has been afforded are more important.

Because the duties of a DOO are so diverse and extensive, it is critical that this person has been a competitive athlete—even if only at the intercollegiate level. He must have an appreciation for and a working knowledge of all facets of the organization.

He must be a tireless, totally committed individual who approaches every project, issue, or negotiation in a thorough, detailed, well-organized manner. On one hand, he is expected to make independent decisions; on the other hand, he must be in close communication with ownership and other members of management.

Above all, he must have a keen appreciation for the role of the head coach. As such, he must be totally committed to providing the head coach with everything that is possible to build a successful football team.

The DOO should not be a high profile, highly visible, media-oriented person. His work is best accomplished in a relatively private environment—without fanfare and in a professional and ethical manner. Similar to all members of top management, he should have a demeanor that is personable, positive, and supportive of everyone, without becoming too familiar with the organization's employees.

Within the structure of the organization, the DOO must oversee any aspect of the organization that entails direct involvement with organizational efforts to acquire (i.e., trades, free agency, and the NFL draft) or interact with (i.e., training camp, security, travel arrangements, etc.) players.

Typically, the DOO and his department staff also oversee all operational matters involving the athletic trainers, the facilities, and the equipment room. Although the major department heads may not have to answer to the DOO, he is responsible for establishing the lines of communication between the organization's two personnel departments (college and pro) and the coaching staff.

In some instances, an organization may find it appropriate to combine the duties and the authority of the DOO and the head coach. In such a scenario, the head coach would employ and direct a separate staff to handle the DOO's functions.

He who requires much from himself and little from others, will keep himself from being the object of resentment.

Confucius
Chinese Philosopher and Political Theorist

- *Directors of Pro Personnel (DPP) and College Scouting (DCS).* The most important attribute for individuals who are appointed to these positions is basic intelligence. All too often, individuals are given these personnel jobs for an inappropriate reason.

  For example, some people have been assigned to these positions simply because of their past service to the organization, loyalty, or friendships with other members of the club. In this scenario, the organization has "rewarded" former players or former assistant coaches who were either retired or unemployed (i.e., available) at the time of their hiring.

  Regrettably, such a profile of the DPP or the DCS has traditionally been commonplace. Although some of the individuals who were hired in these circumstances have gone on to become outstanding personnel people, some have not.

  In recent years, it has become quite evident that the DPP and the DCS can figuratively hold the future of the organization in their hands. Accordingly, their evaluation of talent must be competent, credible and ultimately trusted.

  The importance of the departments of pro personnel and college scouting cannot be over-emphasized. On more than one occasion, an individual scout has been expected to make a decision that will have an extraordinary impact on the future of an NFL franchise that is worth more than 200 million dollars.

  Often such a decision has been deferred all the way from the owner through every level of top management to the head coach and his assistant coaches. Finally, an area scout is asked to make a critical evaluation that can define the future of the team.

  Accordingly, the ability to scout effectively and to evaluate players successfully requires an inquisitive mind, a formal education, and good organizational skills, as well as a sound sense of reasoning. As such, an organization cannot take a risk by awarding the DPP and DCS positions to good friends, loyal employees, or renowned former players.

  In the 1990s, a personnel staff person must also be computer proficient, extensively well-rehearsed and trained in the profile of an organization's specific requirements, and systematically organized. He must be willing and able to use all techniques and options available for studying and evaluating the abilities of an athlete.

  One of the major prerequisites for arriving at a personnel-related decision on a player is to obtain numerous evaluations of that particular athlete from a number of sources. The process of obtaining the evaluations and reaching a decision must be done in a very proactive and timely way.

  Becoming either a DPP or a DCS requires both experience and training. The ability to communicate effectively (both verbally and in writing) is also very important for both positions.

- *Chief Financial Officer (CFO).* The individual who is appointed to this position should have an advanced degree. He should also have had a variety of experiences involving financial matters prior to joining the organization.

   He should be able to effectively communicate at all levels of the organization on issues involving the club's financial policies and practices. He must be conversant with the CFOs of other NFL teams, and should be totally current and knowledgeable on financial matters (e.g., financial technology, tax laws, accounting methods, cash flow management, etc.).

   In a logical and sequential manner, the CFO must be able to convey and explain the financial implications of all organizational decisions. In order to be effective, he must be someone who is communicative, reasonable, and socially adept. As such, he must be able to interact smoothly with everyone at all levels of the organization and with all those individuals with whom the organization does business (e.g., agents, contractors, clients, etc.).

   As with every employee of the organization, this individual should exude energy and enthusiasm, be willing to expend whatever time it takes to accomplish a particular task, be available around the clock (i.e., 24 hours a day), and be someone who can be trusted in utter and complete confidence on all work-related matters.

   One of the truest measures of an effective CFO is how quickly he can make valid and reliable judgments in the extreme give-and-take environment attendant to player-agent negotiations. A broad-based, creative, solution-oriented (yet practical) CFO can have a major impact on player-acquisition efforts.

   Ultimately, he can make the difference in whether a particular player acquisition is profitable (from a financial standpoint). Some CFOs are clearly more gifted at handling these critical cases in an appropriate manner than others.

   Within the structure of the organization, the CFO serves as the primary facilitator for the general manager on all short- and long-term budgetary concerns. He also plays a major role in planning and implementing all salary cap-related matters.

   As such, it is critical that the CFO works closely with the organization's talent acquisition team. In addition, on (salary) contractual matters, he could either act as the organization's chief negotiator or help establish a separate branch of the organizational structure to handle such matters. A more detailed overview of the basic responsibilities of a CFO within an organization is presented in Chapter 18.

- *Public Relations Director.* The individual who holds this position must be one of the most capable people in the organization. Accordingly, this person must be extremely intelligent and be extraordinarily perceptive and people-oriented.

   This individual must also have outstanding communications skills (both written and verbal). Furthermore, the individual in this position must be able to deal with even the most sensitive and objectionable developments with true professionalism and social aplomb.

An advanced degree with extensive public relations experience is a primary prerequisite for this position. A variety of experiences in other fields of endeavor or with other organizations is also of immense value to this person.

This individual should also possess a high level of both maturity and trustworthiness. In addition, this person should be able to communicate effectively with even the most determined adversary. This position also requires a positive demeanor, a strong sense of professionalism, a polished appearance, and a pronounced sensitivity to others.

Rodney Knox of the San Francisco 49ers is a compelling example of someone who possesses the aforementioned attributes. One of the most competent public relations professionals in the NFL, he is thoroughly businesslike and decidedly results-oriented.

Erroneously, ownership, management, and the coaching staff sometimes take this position for granted. In reality, mismanagement of media relations can lead to severe difficulties for the organization.

If such relations are not handled properly, crisis after crisis can develop and can gain momentum. As a consequence, the public relations director position must be given the proper emphasis within an organization's upper management echelon. Accordingly, many NFL teams place the public relations director on the same management level as the general manager, the DOO, and the head coach.

ESTABLISHING SUB-GROUP, SPECIAL PROJECT UNITS

Organizations often combine department heads, directors, and group managers into sub-groups (i.e., teams, units, etc.) that undertake special projects or perform special functions. These unique units are made up of those individuals in the organization who can contribute to the goal of the sub-groups (i.e., provide vital information to the project; have the authority to make relevant decisions; etc.).

If the group is weighted down with a superfluous number of members who are not pertinent to its immediate task, its efficiency will be severely inhibited. Each team should have a specific purpose, an operations outline, and a chain of command to establish protocol within the group.

These units may be either temporary or relatively permanent. Two of the most important and ongoing sub-groups that exist in most organizations are the negotiation team and the acquisition team.

Negotiation Team

An organization's negotiation team should include the following representation: ownership, the CEO, the CFO, legal, and the individuals who perform hands-on negotiating. The negotiation team should be assisted by a special advisory "resource group" that would be comprised of the head coach, the team's NFL liaison, the particular assistant position coach of the player with whom the team is negotiating, an athletic trainer and a physician from the team's medical staff, personnel directors, and a management information (computer) specialist.

A systematic plan for conducting negotiations should be established. An integral part of that plan should be the development of a club negotiation manual that formalizes and documents the steps that should be followed during the negotiation process.

The manual should be as detailed and thorough as possible and should be revised, refined, and reapproved annually. Among the factors, considerations, and actions that should be addressed in the manual are the following:

- Outside sources should be employed to develop and enhance the negotiating skills of the members of the organization's negotiation team. For example, attendance at seminars designed to develop these skills should be an integral part of the ongoing process to develop an effective negotiating team.

- An intense workshop on negotiating should be held each year (even if only a relatively few individuals within the organization are involved in the negotiating process). Outside consultants and experts can be utilized to conduct the workshop and to provide relevant feedback on how attendees can improve their negotiating techniques.

- The negotiation team must have a complete and thorough understanding with regard to NFL directives and the CBA. At least one person in the organization must be an expert in both of these areas.

- One person should act as the sole spokesperson for the negotiating team. Multiple exchanges with the press are bound to create crossed signals and contradictions, which can be excellent ammunition for the player's agent. The negotiating team must keep in mind that every "statement" will be brought to the negotiation table.

- All contacts with a player or his representatives must be documented, with details of each contact being extensive enough to be easily understood by other members of the negotiating team. A format should be established for addressing each type of contact with the agent.

- Contract decisions are often based on other agreements.

- Information reliability is critical.

- A profile should be prepared on each agent which includes information on that agent's tactics and personality.

- A general dialogue should be held with other League management people regarding the agent's pattern of negotiation on behalf of other clients. The progress of other people's dealings with this particular agent should be monitored. The negotiation team should remain alert for rumors and misinformation regarding the agent, the player, or the status of negotiations.

- Contact between the organization and the agent should be frequent, but not regularly scheduled.

- The negotiating team should expect to be insulted by the agent. To a degree, the organization can almost anticipate when such insults will occur. Not responding is the best approach in such situations.

- The negotiating team should anticipate that the agent will inform his/her client of each remark the club makes concerning the player. Often, such remarks will be isolated and relayed out of context.

- The negotiating team should calculate its appraisal of the athlete. In most instances, distinctly positive or negative remarks will return to the table.

- The negotiating team should anticipate that the press will be contacted by the agent, either directly or covertly.

- The negotiating team should prepare a public stance that may be taken in the negotiation process if necessary. The organization should have "fall-back" responses ready when surprised or caught off-guard.

- Ego is a factor in the negotiating process. The impact of ego can be very subtle. Members of the negotiating team should expect theirs to be attacked or damaged.

- A business-like, formal setting must be at the core of serious negotiation.

- A definitive policy should be established with regard to the press, including the obligations of ownership.

- Public statements become "fact" even when taken out of context.

- Agent posturing with the press is to be expected as the negotiating process becomes more intense.

- An agreement of confidentiality, as the process starts, is necessary. However, the agent may still find a way through a third party or other sources to "pressure" concessions from the club.

- The press should be expected to slant their stories in favor of the athlete and the agent. The negotiating team should keep in mind that, while a verbal battle will normally make little difference to the player, it can damage management in several ways.

- Concise, defined statements are all that should be released from the designated club spokesperson regarding the negotiations. Anything stated must be factual.

- Reaching a final agreement can mean altering or revising other contractual negotiations. The CEO and the CFO must be on top of all final decisions. Unfortunately, last minute changes in these agreements sometimes occur. A systematic contingency format must be in place to make rapid revisions in an organization's contractual offers.

- Legal counsel must be continually updated concerning the process of negotiations. At no time should the negotiating team surprise the legal counsel with a proposed agreement that contains "new language."

- Financial counsel must be given time to research important issues and matters.

- Spontaneous, instantaneous communication may be necessary in "eleventh hour" negotiations. As such, the negotiator must know where everyone on the negotiation team is during this period. The negotiator must have access to the entire negotiation team 24 hours a day.

- An agreement is not an agreement until it is signed. An agent may attempt to "come back" at the last moment.

- Negotiators must report on an ongoing basis to the CEO.

- Although outsiders often compare sports negotiations with corporate or sales negotiations, significant differences exist between them. The leverage is dissimilar, but axioms of thorough professionalism are identical.

- When serious exchanges are made in the negotiating process, the chief negotiator should always have the CFO at his/her side.

- The negotiating team must know how and when to close down negotiations, when to shift to other candidates and how to terminate negotiations without undue "fallout."

- A personalized step-by-step plan for each "project" (contractual negotiation) should be formulated.

- A plausible set of responses to difficult actions or questions by the agent must be a part of a prepared, rehearsed policy of negotiation.

- Taking an honest, reasonable, seemingly fair approach to negotiation rarely has the desired impact on the process.

- In most instances, long, extended exchanges typically do not make progress until the "eleventh hour" because such negotiations normally lack direction and momentum until that point.

- Final prolonged negotiations often result in concessions not anticipated by the team.

- The negotiating team should plan, prepare and anticipate its meetings with the player's agent. Other individuals should be asked to provide "feedback" on the negotiator's specific remarks.

- A step-by-step presentation from a written agenda should be employed whether by phone or "in person."

- During the negotiating sessions, the negotiator should have all relevant research available and must understand it completely.

- Other resources should be utilized when the negotiator is cornered or in a tenuous position. The negotiator should not hesitate to leave the room when he/she feels "off-balance." The negotiator should have an explanation ready in each instance.

- Unless a response is appropriate, the negotiator should remain quiet; making no response can protect the negotiator's position.

- To a point, a certain amount of social talk tends to give the impression that the negotiator is at ease, not uptight, anxious or desperate.

- Anger is acceptable, but dangerous. It should be utilized in small, short doses.

- The negotiator should be careful of using examples or comparisons unless he/she has an "ironclad" case.

- The negotiator should have patience; being completely thorough must be the essence of the negotiation process.

- Alcohol should not be part of any social interaction with agents, not even when informally discussing the contract.

- Late hours often lead to fatigue. The negotiator's need for food and sleep can also affect his/her ability to function effectively in a formalized setting.

- Results should not be expected with every contact. The negotiator should understand that the player's agent may "double back." The same ground may have to be covered a number of times.

- The less experienced the agent, the more volatile the contacts can be. An agent can make snap judgments that can complete the process or momentarily cause frustration. The negotiator should not demean the agent's credibility. An inexperienced agent is usually in contact with a more experienced person. The negotiator should continue to communicate with the agent as he/she normally would. This situation is often one of the most difficult for the negotiator.

- The negotiating team must know exactly what they are negotiating for. A thorough appraisal of the proposed contract must be made—short-term and long-term—before negotiations begin. Every individual who can contribute meaningful feedback to the process (e.g., physician, trainer, conditioning coach, head coach, position coach, etc.) should be involved as resources when discussing the length of an agreement.

- Anything that is said, no matter how casually, will often be perceived as a commitment.

- Care must be taken with extensive exploration or creative exchanges. The agent may "double back," combining all categories as commitments in the process.

- A "confidential" contact with the athlete, in an attempt to use reason with him, is rarely effective. An athlete will always inform his agent, who will resist such an attempt. Any attempt to make a private deal with the athlete will almost always be negated by the player's agent. The agent will then establish that deal as a starting point.

- Contacting the friends or family of an athlete is also an extremely sensitive matter. To the agent, such an action infers "panic" on the part of the negotiator. In almost all instances, the agent will resist pressure applied from outside sources, unless the organization is extraordinarily "lucky."

- The use of other individuals in the organization as second party closers is a dubious step.

- If excesses develop, they should be with athletes who handle the ball or with a player who makes most of the defensive stops.

Acquisition Team (Free Agents)

A systematic plan for acquiring free agents should be developed by the organization. A detailed overview of the factors that should serve as the basis for such a plan is presented in Chapter 7.

To help ensure that its efforts to sign free agents are as successful as possible, the organization should develop an acquisition team. The primary focus of such a sub-group is to coordinate the team's acquisition process.

One of the essential steps that the acquisition team should undertake in this regard is to develop written procedures and guidelines that should be followed in the organization's attempts to sign free agents. Among the considerations, circumstances, and actions that should be addressed by such procedures and guidelines are the following:

- A complete file should be established on the negotiation strategies used by other NFL franchises, including their tactics concerning contractual negotiations, their historical financial limitations (i.e., bottom line restrictions), their philosophy, and their owner's mindset toward the acquisition process (i.e., mentality, responses, ego, etc.).

- An inclusive file on the "negotiation teams" of other clubs (i.e., personalities, strategies, tendencies, negotiating styles, background, experience, history, etc.) should be developed.

- While contractual (financial) commitments are the primary basis of an agreement, no assumptions should be made that other considerations will not be addressed.

- A distinct contractual meeting with an agent may be part of the athlete's visit. The acquisition team should not expect anything to be finalized except when the process involves a peripheral player. Because the agent will be "posturing," typically nothing much is accomplished.

- The athlete and his agent should be allowed moments of privacy, after which they may then ask for clarification of a particular contractual point, etc.

- The acquisition team should schedule and conduct an organizational meeting that includes everyone in the organization with whom the athlete will come in contact. Each person in attendance at the meeting should be given specific do's and don'ts concerning the acquisition process for this particular player.

- The positive selling points of the organization should be identified. The entire organization should serve as a "sounding board" regarding the validity of these points and whether any additional factors may have been overlooked.

- The acquisition team should find out, as accurately as possible, how each club will "sell" itself.

- The organization should learn as much as possible about the criteria a particular free agent will use to make his decision about which team to sign with and who will be a factor in his decision (i.e., wife, children, friends, agent, etc.).

- Those selling points that are compatible with the player's needs and interests should be emphasized.
- The organization should identify those who are best able to "sell" and introduce the club's position and opportunities.
- The acquisition team should find out if the athlete knows anyone on the squad and how well he knows them.
- Anyone in the organization in whom the athlete may want to confide (e.g., assistant coach, players, etc.) should be identified.
- Former players from the organization can often serve as good intermediaries between the team and the player.
- Gratuitous, frivolous selling of the organization can be extremely counterproductive. It "smacks of insincerity" and a "phony sale."
- The obvious should be avoided in attempting to persuade the free agent to sign.
- A step-by-step plan should be established to introduce the athlete to the organization, the adjacent community, his potential teammates, the team's facilities, local housing, etc.
- One person should be designated to escort the athlete through the entire introduction process.
- Before visiting, the athlete should be asked about his requests and expectations concerning his trip. His schedule should then be established. When the athlete arrives, the club's proposed schedule for his visit should be reviewed with him. He may choose to revise it.
- The organization must remain flexible during a visit by a free agent (e.g., schedule, points of emphasis, personnel involvement in the process, etc.). The team should try to get a sense of what the athlete is "looking for."
- The athlete should not be permitted to linger too long in meetings with peripheral staff members.
- The athlete must be "fresh" when important issues are addressed. Travel fatigue can affect his attention span and nullify or diminish the value of critical exchanges.
- If the athlete spends the night, everything possible should be done to minimize any partying he might otherwise do. If the organization is unsuccessful in this regard, the player won't be worth anything the next day, and the trip may become a waste of time.
- The organization should avoid allowing the athlete to do too much in one day, or the athlete may become unduly fatigued or bored.
- The organization's facilities should be at their best (i.e., clean office, locker room, weight room, etc.).
- All personnel should refer to the athlete by his name.

- A member of the coaching staff should be given ample time to "talk football" to the free agent, but not when the athlete is tired, bored, hungry, etc. The coach must have a thorough, updated knowledge of the athlete's career, talent, skills, injury history, etc. The athlete should not be asked ill-advised questions.

- The organization should be reasonably accurate and objective in discussing the proposed role the athlete will have on the team if he signs. In most instances, he can see through an overly optimistic (i.e., deceitful) appraisal.

- The athlete's demeanor is not always an indicator of his level of interest.

- A videotape of the athlete's play should be put together that demonstrates why he can "thrive" with the team. At a minimum, such an effort demonstrates sincere interest in the athlete by the organization.

- The player should have an opportunity to review a special video prepared by the organization (involving 10-15 plays) that indicates what the athlete would be doing if he signs with the team.

- The organization should not be too discouraged or frustrated over the athlete's initial response, indifference, or apparent lack of interest. These outward factors are not always clear indicators of the organization's likelihood of signing the athlete.

- A thorough effort must be made to know more about the athlete that is being recruited. A series of questions or remarks should be developed that reveals as much as possible about the player that the team is attempting to acquire. These kinds of player "inventories" can be developed in connection with sports psychologists.

- The organization's athletic training, conditioning and medical staffs should be a part of the team's acquisition process.

- An individual from top management (e.g., the head coach, the CEO or the owner) should provide the athlete with a ride to the airport. Whoever this individual is should know a lot about the athlete and should be ready to carry on a conversation with the player.

- All follow-up conversations with the athlete or visits by the athlete are critical. In both scenarios, the organization should continue to put its best foot forward (i.e., answer questions, continue to sell the benefits of the team, etc.).

Military organizations and success in battle depend upon discipline and a high sense of honor.

> General Omar N. Bradley
> 5-Star General of the Allied Armies
> World War II

KEEPING THE FOCUS ON THE PRODUCT

An organization is not just a tool. It bespeaks values. It reflects the personality of a business. It is defined by its results on the field.

In that regard, one of the most candid aspects of professional sports is that the bottom line is so identifiable—winning. Few professions have such defined accountability as simply looking at the scoreboard to ascertain the organization's bottom line.

Despite the tremendous economic prosperity of the NFL, true success must be achieved on the playing field. When everything is stripped to its barest essentials, there is the game.

Accordingly, the organization must always keep its fundamental focus on the game and on developing and sustaining a high level of quality in the product it puts on the playing field. As a rule, this area is where the priorities and the structure of the organization will be most severely tested, primarily by outside forces that have agendas that are at cross purposes to having a quality team.

Many of the problems in this regard have evolved from the fact that, in recent years, some organizations have placed individuals with little or no coaching background in the top leadership role in developing and managing the game. These people have no real sense of what is needed for the team to succeed.

Instead of seeking out people that began their careers or grew up in an environment of competitive sports, some organizations (on both the collegiate and professional levels) seek out and hire individuals who have extensive backgrounds in some other area of expertise (e.g., legal, financial, marketing, etc.) to run the operation.

Difficulties can occur, however, if the individual who is tapped to head the organization doesn't have a genuine sense for the game and doesn't accept the fact that, to a point, a competitive sports organization is not just like any other business. Rather, it has very distinct features and characteristics that must be addressed within its own unique environment.

In more than one instance, however, it can be very difficult to address these issues in an appropriate way if the individual controlling the decision-making process in an organization doesn't have a realistic perspective and feel for the game. For example, many people who are successful in one field mistakenly believe that they can recreate their success with a new product by using the same methods that were responsible for their former achievements.

In some cases they can; in other circumstances, they can't. Accordingly, while certain fundamental managerial principles apply to all situations, great flexibility needs to be shown in the way organizations approach the various tasks that need to be performed.

One of the greatest challenges facing the top management of an NFL organization is the need to be prepared to handle the demands of a rapidly changing environment. Without abandoning its basic principles, an organization must be able to adapt to changing circumstances. Each adjustment, however, must be made with the "product" in mind. That product does not necessarily mean winning every game at all costs.

An organization needs to be aware of the fact that each action it undertakes can have both a short-term and a long-term effect on its product. A professionally directed organization realizes the value of developing and sustaining a basic foundation for a successful product—an approach that requires a long-term perspective.

Effective leadership recognizes the fact real success requires patience and an unswerving commitment to developing a product that will be consistently successful—season after season. While taking such an approach may produce results that don't show up as quickly as the organization would like on its won-lost record, in the long haul, the primary focus of the organization will be where it should be—on establishing a quality product.

> *Beware of rashness, but with energy and sleepless vigilance go forward and give us victories.*
>
> Abraham Lincoln
> 16th President of the United States

MAINTAINING CONFIDENTIALITY WITHIN THE ORGANIZATION

The need for strict confidentiality concerning specific matters and circumstances within the organization is critical. Surprisingly, many clubs fail to place a sufficient amount of emphasis on this factor.

One organization which has addressed the issue in a serious way is the Oakland Raiders. Traditionally, the Raiders have had a reputation for an absolute (some individuals would claim—paranoiac) policy of extreme secrecy.

While many people have scoffed at and ridiculed this seemingly unnecessary organizational stance, the Raiders' approach makes much more business sense than the policies of the large majority of NFL franchises (indeed, of most professional sports organizations).

In reality, the layers of employees who have access to critical internal information is often far-reaching. Disturbingly, because many of these individuals would like to have others believe that they have a heightened degree of importance within the organization, they inherently can't control the urge to divulge sensitive information.

The net result is an almost complete loss of confidentiality in the organization. In the process, the organization's decision-makers are disarmed and severely compromised.

Even off-hand remarks gossiped from one second-level employee to another can have negative consequences. The employee who was the recipient of the gossip then proudly takes the information (often after embellishing it) to his/her decision maker.

The armchair warriors defuse world crises, wipe out budget deficits and solve the welfare mess, all before the commercial break: and it's all make-believe. They don't have to build coalitions or crunch numbers or live with the consequences of their errors. If they screw up, there's always next week's show to test-drive new theories...The old checks and balances are gone forever. It is up to the audience to sort it all out.

Howard Kurtz
Former New York Bureau Chief
Washington Post
from *Hot Air: All Talk All the Time*

Such a loose, apparently uncontrollable environment makes it very difficult to coordinate and successfully implement organizational strategies. When everybody knows everything that "might" occur within an organization, disturbing and disruptive scenarios can arise.

Accordingly, the organization's general manager (CEO), DOO and head coach must precisely define and institute a policy that makes a breach of confidentiality a "capital offense." Such a breach will result in the offending employee losing his/her job.

Because leaking information or personal assessments to the media or to another organization by a single employee can figuratively bring a club to its knees, a concerted effort must be made to minimize the likelihood of such a problem occurring.

In this regard, it is critical that the organization has a written policy on confidentiality, engages in an ongoing internal discussion of the importance of the matter, and is alert to potential sources that may violate organizational policy in this area. No exceptions should be allowed or tolerated toward the organization's policy on confidentiality.

CHAPTER 5

ORGANIZING THE STAFF

"A commander must accustom his staff to a high tempo from the outset, and continuously keep them up to it. If he once allows himself to be satisfied with norms, or anything less than an all-out effort, he gives up the race from the starting post, and will sooner or later be taught a bitter lesson."

—Erwin Rommel
Infamous German Combat General
World War II

Finding the winning edge...

The secret to managing well and motivating those you manage is to understand the fine line between losing sight of the big picture and letting others lose sight of you. If you're there when the action gets hot, the results can be spectacular. Stay in the rear echelon too long, peering through binoculars, and you'll find the competitors taking the high ground.

—Bill Walsh, "Let 'em See You
Sweat," *Forbes*, December 5, 1994.

Successful organizations establish a "winning" environment that allows dissenting feedback to occur while ensuring that key employees support and are aligned with the organization's overall mission. Ultimately, however, there are certain values so significant that they must not be compromised by the mission.

The inclination of some assistant coaches to focus solely on winning has been sorely obvious to me on a few occasions in my coaching career. One case involved an instance where the health (and future) of a player was improperly jeopardized by the actions of one of my assistants.

Going into one game, Eric Wright, who at the time was the premier cornerback in football, had a slightly-pulled groin muscle. We decided to play him. As the game progressed, however, the injury worsened. It became so severe that we had to remove him from the game. If he had remained on the sideline, he would have recovered and continued with his career, but we had a breakdown in command.

I assumed Eric would not return to the game, but I was mistaken. Without notifying me, the doctors told the defensive coaches that Eric would be okay. The coaches sent him back into the game, and he further aggravated the injury. It took him a year to recover, and he was never the same.

I had assumed that the people involved would make sound judgments. I continually reminded my coaches that the safety and well being of our players came first. In this case, the health of the player was apparently sacrificed in the hope of winning the game. We won the game even without Eric in the lineup. The head coach should never assume anything; he must make sure that his assistants communicate with him regarding key decisions.

Similar to the benefits afforded by an appropriate organizational structure, a well-qualified staff can have a positive impact on the organization in a number of ways. One of the most important effects is the influence that capable staff members have on an organization's level of productivity and efficiency.

Capable staff can also have an effect on an organization by improving overall morale and motivation. Furthermore, competent employees provide the head coach with the type of peace of mind that comes with knowing that critical tasks can be delegated to the staff and that everything will get done properly.

As the head coach, you face several critical issues in putting a qualified staff together and utilizing their talents to the fullest, including identifying the desired attributes of staff members, interviewing candidates for staff positions, determining the job assignment for each staff member, assessing the job performance of each staff member, facilitating staff transition, interacting with the staff, and dealing with staff members who perform poorly.

The coach must not only be dedicated to football, but he must be tough mentally.

> Paul "Bear" Bryant
> Hall-of-Fame Football Coach
> University of Alabama
> from *Building a Championship Football Team*

IDENTIFYING THE DESIRED QUALIFICATIONS OF STAFF MEMBERS

Putting a qualified staff together is somewhat similar to organizing a church choir. You need to recruit the right people, who can sing the right notes at the right time. The obvious key is to select the appropriate individuals (i.e., staff members who can do the job you need them to do, when you need them to do it).

In this regard, deciding what qualities staff members should possess is a multi-faceted task. On one hand, the staff must have the technical knowledge of the game that is necessary to ensure that every player performs up to the best of his natural abilities. On the other hand, the staff must be endowed with the personal attributes (e.g., the ability to work well with others, follow directions, handle stressful situations, accept challenges, keep things in the proper perspective, etc.) that enable them to collectively focus their energies on a common goal.

Most of the members of the head coach's staff serve as position coaches. Determining the precise qualities that a position coach should have, however, is not as simple as it may appear.

The extent to which he should possess a particular quality and the relative priority of one quality to another are issues that can complicate the task. Each individual is a mosaic of attributes. Each person offers a somewhat different combination of traits, capabilities and experiences.

As the head coach, even if you are able to prioritize the qualities you are looking for in a staff member, it would be a mistake to clone each of your assistant coaches in the same relative mold as the next. Diversity should be one of the key elements in the total make-up of your staff.

Among the qualities that you, as the head coach, should look for in an assistant coach (regardless of what position he coaches) are the following:

- *A fundamental knowledge of the mechanics of his position.* An assistant coach must be technically competent. His competence level must be such that he can work with each player on an individual basis as needed.

  In this regard, it is critical that you surround yourself with highly capable assistants. Not only will their capabilities help the team achieve its goals, they will also be a positive reflection on you.

If you hire an assistant who does not have the technical knowledge necessary to do his job properly (a fact that will soon become apparent to the players he coaches), you may create an environment where the players will begin to question your competency as well. Over time, you may lose some of the respect of your players if you repeatedly employ less-than-top-drawer assistant coaches.

- *Ability to communicate.* An assistant coach must be able to communicate with the players in a relaxed, yet authoritative, manner. Such a quality is the fundamental basis of an assistant's ability to effectively teach and interact with his players—perhaps the two key responsibilities of every assistant coach.

The assistant coach is the most direct link a player has with the game and learning how to play it well. Most of the efforts to mold the skills and abilities of a particular player are in the capable hands of his position coach.

Having served in that capacity for many years, most head coaches fully appreciate this often publicly overlooked role. As in any human endeavor, however, some assistant coaches are, by degree, more effective and achieve better results than others.

In many instances, career assistant coaches are individuals who would have been outstanding head coaches had they ever been given the opportunity. The nature of the NFL is such that on occasion, a less-than-fully-capable person has been appointed as a head coach.

These individuals have survived—even thrived—in these roles when they surrounded themselves with a group of top-flight assistant coaches. As such, the value of assistant coaches who are extraordinarily gifted teachers cannot be overstated.

Quite honestly, the San Francisco 49er teams during the period of 1979-1989 would never have come near reaching the heights of greatness that they did without the efforts of a group of brilliant technician-teacher assistant coaches. In the early years of this period, this group included such talented assistants as Chuck Studley, Sam Wyche, Billie Matthews, Milt Jackson, and Al Vermeil.

Subsequently, the list of outstanding 49er assistants in this time frame included Paul Hackett, Tommy Hart, Dwaine Board, Lynn Stiles, and Fred vonAppen. In later years of this period, Dennis Green, Ray Rhodes, Sherm Lewis, and Mike Holmgren became key factors in the success of the 49ers.

Two of the finest coaches in 49ers' history are Bobb McKittrick and Bill McPherson. Both individuals are renowned as being one of the best coaches in their field of specialty in the history of the game.

McKittrick is recognized as the premier offensive line coach of his time, while McPherson is widely acclaimed for his efforts as a defensive coordinator. Given their personal bearing, resolute regard to detail, and unwavering commitment to doing the task at hand, they could have served with distinction on the staff of either George S. Patton or Erwin Rommel—perhaps the two most skilled general officers in the history of the military.

Other assistant coaches who were able to make a major contribution to the 49ers' success, despite the fact that they only spent a single year on San Francisco's staff, were Bruce Coslet, Chip Myers, and Cas Banaszek. During this period, the 49ers were also aided by the coaching efforts of Tyrone Willingham, who served as an intern with the team.

- *Ability to evaluate and project talent.* Traditionally, assistant coaches have always been required to evaluate the abilities and the performance potential of those players with whom they are working. With the advent of free agency and the increased role that assistant coaches have been assigned in their team's NFL draft process, this responsibility has become even more crucial.

  Position coaches should also be assigned to keep abreast of the skill and ability levels of the players (at each coach's particular position) on the other teams in the League. If a key player is injured on his team, an assistant coach who is knowledgeable about possible replacement players from other teams can provide an invaluable service to the organization.

- *A relatively high level of energy.* Assistant coaches must exhibit an appropriate level of energy that enables them to be upbeat, motivated, and animated while in the presence of the players and their fellow employees. It is not unusual that a group of players will collectively take on the personality of their position coach.

  Such a scenario can be very worthwhile to a team if the assistant coach has an animated, high-powered persona. On the other hand, if a team has an assistant coach who is a negative, complaining type who sees inadequacies in everything around him, the situation can be quite downbeat.

- *Loyalty.* Assistant coaches must exhibit loyalty at all times, both to the head coach and to their fellow coaches. While a head coach always expects his assistants to display unconditional loyalty to him, their sense of loyalty should also extend to the other staff members.

  The staff must truly stick together during tough times. It is extremely divisive to the team, as a whole, if the assistant coaches are constantly chipping away at each other behind their backs to the players, other coaches, and other employees of the organization.

  No offense should be viewed more seriously than disloyalty, especially among coaches who should know better. An assistant coach who feels compelled to criticize or demean a staff member to others in the organization, media, or fans can be an extraordinarily disruptive force. Accordingly, the head coach must not tolerate disloyalty in any form.

  One of the important ways that the head coach can show that he has the well being of his staff at heart is to always be considerate of their wives and family. In every possible instance, he should treat family members with full respect and sincere concern. In addition, he should make every attempt to pay his coaches well—including compensating them on special merit whenever possible.

CONSIDERING FORMER PLAYERS AS ASSISTANT COACHES

As the head coach, you must not assume that a popular, serious-minded, energetic former player will naturally make a good coach. Many people mistakenly believe these individuals are always ideal candidates for coaching positions. Such a scenario is not always the case, however. Even if he possesses excellent social skills and was an outstanding player, he may not have the teaching skills necessary to be an effective coach.

The point you must keep in mind is that if you hire such an individual to be a position coach, you must establish procedures that enable the more experienced members of your staff to monitor this person's work. Even if your new assistant played for a number of years in the NFL (i.e., ten or more), his experiences will not immediately translate into coaching competence.

Except in very unusual circumstances, these individuals have not yet learned to organize their thoughts, teach in an appropriate sequence, and recognize and work with the shortcomings of less-gifted athletes. Former-players-turned-coaches often assume that a team's current players think and respond as they would. As such, these coaches do not always appreciate the importance of the long-term development of a less-talented player.

Former players who are new assistant coaches also tend to become too familiar with their players. As a result, they often establish relationships similar to those that they enjoyed with their former teammates. In addition, some of these individuals are often shocked by the daily work schedule expected of an assistant coach.

On the other hand, individuals who were back-up or short-term NFL players often possess innate teaching ability. Throughout the NFL, examples exist of outstanding coaches who never played a down in the NFL.

Men such as Marv Levy, Chuck Knox, Al Davis and Dick Vermeil were excellent college athletes who, for one reason or another, never became professional players. Enormously talented and successful head coaches like George Seifert, Don Coryell, Mike Holmgren and even Vince Lombardi molded their skills through years of experience as assistant coaches.

INTERVIEWING CANDIDATES FOR THE STAFF

To be able to sit down with an individual for a somewhat limited length of time and to determine whether the candidate has the requisite capabilities is one of the most ambiguous, subjective, and challenging tasks a general manager or a head coach will face. Whether the process involves the hiring of a head coach or a position coach, the individual interviewing the candidate must know what he is looking for and how it will be determined whether he finds it.

Even the most seasoned, veteran head coach can have a tough time determining if an individual has the abilities he is looking for in a position coach or has exemplary communication skills and gives good interviews. This dilemma is why head coaches often hire people with whom they have worked before or individuals who have been recommended by someone in whom they have a great deal of trust.

When developing a systematic plan for conducting interviews to hire staff members, the head coach or the general manager should consider the following factors:

- At some point, a single individual will have to make the choice of whom to hire (like most sound decisions).

- The more people who are included in the hiring process, the greater the likelihood that either a superfluous number of criteria will be added to the approach employed by the organization for decision making or the effectiveness of the undertaking will be diluted. This situation is particularly true when colleges look to hire a head football coach.

  Colleges typically utilize committees to coordinate and conduct the process of hiring a new head coach. In turn, the process gets bogged down with so many agendas that it becomes very difficult for a college to identify and hire a clear-cut candidate, no matter how ideally suited he may be for the job.

  Some collegiate athletic directors (ADs) appear to prefer the committee approach to hiring. If the head coach turns out to be relatively unsuccessful, the AD can easily protect his own interests by offering the not-so-veiled excuse of "Well, I didn't want to hire this guy in the first place, but the committee recommended him."

  One of the first things an individual seeking the head coach's position in such a scenario should do is to determine which individual is going to actually make the hiring decision and whether he has the authority and the autonomy to "pull the trigger."

  If the committee process seems too big or too involved, it may be a good indication that the AD does not have the control to make the final decision or will not be strong enough down the line to help the head coach get what he needs to do the job.

- The process of interviewing and hiring an assistant coach will be relatively easy if the individual conducting the interview (and making the hiring decision) has a history or a working relationship with a candidate who is well-suited for the position.

- If the situation, however, involves a candidate with whom the organization has little or no familiarity, it is imperative that a specific plan be established regarding what qualities the head coach wants in an assistant, how it will be determined whether a candidate has those attributes, and how the organization can make the process equitable for all the interviewees so that the procedures are not unknowingly biased toward one candidate.

- A precise set of criteria detailing what the position calls for must be established. If such criteria are not identified, the head coach (or whoever is conducting the process) may become distracted by the different skills and capabilities of the individuals who are being interviewed and may lose sight of the specific position he is trying to fill.

- With regard to hiring a head coach, ownership must determine the scope of the head coaching position within the organization. For example, such key issues as "will the head coach be able to exert a high level of influence over personnel decisions" and "will the head coach be expected to also serve as his own offensive coordinator" must be addressed.

  Furthermore, is ownership looking for a strong individual to head the entire organization? On the other hand, does ownership prefer hiring a head coach who can work well in a secondary role to the general manager, the DOO, or even the DPP?

- The basic qualifications of each candidate must be assessed. This step can be accomplished in several ways. For example, his background should be closely scrutinized to determine the level of success he has enjoyed as a coach, the caliber of competition the teams which he has coached have faced, the level and type of responsibility he has performed as a coach, etc.

  In many instances, one of the primary sources for information on a candidate's background will be recommendations from individuals for whom and with whom the applicant for an assistant's position has coached. An organization must be vigilant, however, to carefully consider these recommendations in light of any agenda the person giving the recommendation may have.

  For example, a head coach may downgrade his recommendation for a particular assistant in a dishonorable attempt to keep him with his organization. On the other hand, a head coach may give one of his assistants an unduly positive recommendation in an effort to get rid of him. In either case, the interviewer must be aware of a deceitful agenda and respond accordingly.

- An organization must make every effort to ensure that the different candidates are evaluated on an even field. For example, the unique qualities of a particularly talented candidate may be overlooked simply because the individual has been working for a team that has an inferior win-loss record compared to those of other candidates.

  The interviewer should keep in mind, however, that such a record may be the result of a team operating in a much tougher environment for succeeding than other organizations. At the college level, this consideration can help explain why assistant coaches at schools who don't always have the most physically gifted athletes because of stringent academic requirements (e.g., Stanford, California, USMA, etc.) are so sought after by other teams.

THE INTERVIEW PROCESS

Once an organization has been able to define what it needs in a candidate for a particular position and whether the candidate's background and experiences qualify him to be a finalist for the job, the next step is to ensure that the actual interview is conducted in a productive and meaningful way. Among the factors that the interview process should yield insight on are the following:

- The ability of the candidate to field questions. He does not need to have a prescribed right answer to a particular question, but he must show the ability to formulate an answer quickly while under pressure, and then articulate that answer in a concise and informative way.

- The candidate should have his own questions. To a point, he can be judged on the nature of how comprehensive and detailed his inquiries are. These questions may show how knowledgeable he is about the organization's situation and the degree to which he has the ability to size up the circumstances in a particular situation.

- The ability of the candidate to be a facilitator. In other words, does he show a grasp of how to properly approach a problem? Does he have a systematic way of going about solving that problem or does he just throw out a hodgepodge of ideas hoping one hits the right nerve?

- The candidate should have an appreciation of the dictates of the job and should have a specific plan to address those factors. For example, if the candidate is prone to making grandiose guarantees, it is usually indicative of a "clinic" coach who may have a certain flair for the communicative process but likely lacks the substance to back up his claims. In any instance, the interviewer should thoroughly question candidates who make seemingly unwarranted assurances to determine how they plan on accomplishing them.

DETERMINING STAFF ASSIGNMENTS

One of the most important and fundamental decisions a head coach must make involves hiring and assigning his assistant coaches. It is absolutely critical that no assignments or responsibilities be given to an assistant who is not capable of doing an excellent job.

As the head coach, you must make a realistic judgment regarding what an assistant coach can handle (i.e., in Paul Brown's parlance—"is the assignment too big for him?"). Simply assigning individuals to the various positions that typically exist on a staff just to fill out a job specification sheet is irresponsible.

Unless you plan to be continually involved in each area of responsibility (a scenario that is totally unrealistic on a sustained basis given the extensive demands on your time), taking such an approach is not in the team's best interests. Each assignment must be carefully considered—whatever the responsibility.

One of the areas that traditionally has not always received the amount of attention that it deserves is peripheral (supplementary) assignments. An overview of some of the more common supplemental assignments is provided in Appendix D. Although these duties are not part of an individual's basic on-the-field coaching responsibilities, the assistant coach must be made to understand that they are very important nonetheless.

For example, if you have an assistant who has an aptitude for computers or technical materials, he would be an appropriate choice to serve as the coaches' liaison with the team's video and/or computer game-analysis support staff. By the same token, if one of your coaches has a particularly keen interest in strength training, he should be considered as someone you could appoint to act as your liaison with the team's conditioning coaches.

Some of the supplemental assignments may be less obvious than others. For example, you should designate a member of your staff who is well-organized and possesses good writing skills to take notes at every staff meeting (unless you direct him otherwise). Such meeting notes can clarify and document any decisions that are made.

These notes provide an on-the-record verification of what key issues were addressed in a particular meeting, who participated in the meeting, how and why certain subjects were considered and what decisions were reached. Accordingly, these notes should be dated and taken in outline form.

> *Officers must assert themselves by example and by voice. They must be pre-eminent in courage, deportment, and dress.*
>
> George S. Patton, Jr.
> Commander, Unites States Third Army
> World War II
> "Letter of Instruction Number 1,"
> from *War as I Knew It*

PROFILES OF A WORKING STAFF

Players must be given as much hands-on coaching and assistance as they need to maximize their abilities and performance. In order to accomplish this goal, you must make certain that you are fully staffed with highly qualified assistants. As a rule, this situation requires that the following positions are established and basic responsibilities are assigned:

- *Defensive coordinator (with/without position).* This person must be the primary conduit between the head coach and the assistant coaches for establishing defensive staff assignments and procedures. He must oversee every aspect of situational and contingency planning as it pertains to the total defensive scheme. He must also oversee implementation of the defensive game plan in practice format by using scouting reports, scripting and carding. In addition, he makes the game-day defensive calls.

- *Defensive backfield.* This individual oversees the establishment, development and implementation of the game plan as it pertains to defensive secondary personnel. He must be an expert in both pass coverage and run support.

- *Linebackers (inside, outside).* This person oversees the establishment, development and implementation of the game plan as it pertains to linebacking personnel. Depending on the team's defensive scheme, this responsibility may be assigned to two position coaches—one for the inside linebackers and one to work with the outside linebackers.

- *Defensive line.* This individual oversees the establishment, development and implementation of the defensive game plan as it pertains to the defensive down (front) linemen. He must be knowledgable about pass-rush techniques and how to deal effectively with run-blocking combinations.

- *Offensive coordinator (with/without position).* This person must be the primary conduit between the head coach and the assistant coaches for establishing offensive staff assignments and procedures. He must oversee every aspect of situational and contingency planning as it pertains to the total offensive scheme. He also oversees implementation of the game plan in practice format using scouting reports, scripting and carding. In addition, he makes the game-day offensive calls.

- *Offensive line (with assistant).* This individual oversees the establishment, development and implementation of the game plan as it pertains to the interior offensive line personnel. He must have a high level of expertise in both run-blocking combinations and pass-protection schemes.

- *Receivers.* This person oversees the establishment, development and implementation of the game plan as it pertains to wide receivers. He must have a thorough knowledge of pass-route combinations and how to utilize multiple receiver combinations.

- *Tight ends.* This person oversees the establishment, development and implementation of the game plan as it pertains to tight ends. He works in association with the offensive line coach and the receivers coach. His primary responsibility is to work with the tight ends on their blocking techniques and skills.

- *Quarterbacks.* This individual oversees the establishment, development and implementation of the game plan as it pertains to quarterbacks. He must work in close association with the offensive coordinator.

- *Running backs.* This person oversees the establishment, development and implementation of the game plan as it pertains to running backs. He works in association with the offensive line coach to develop the blocking techniques and skills of the running backs.

- *Special teams (plus staff participation).* This individual oversees the establishment, development and implementation of a game plan for special team situations. He also works closely with individuals involved in the team's kicking game, including the punter, the kick-off specialist, the field goal kicker, and the long snapper. He must be the primary conduit between the head coach and the assistant coaches with regard to the special teams format. He makes game-day calls involving the special teams in conjunction with the head coach.

- *Special assistant.* This individual is an outside resource or advisory consultant with specific duties in assigned areas involving the team.

- *Conditioning coach.* This individual oversees all conditioning and physical training of team members. He works in conjunction with the team's athletic training and medical staffs with regard to dietary needs, rehabilitation and physical enhancement.

- *Quality control (general) assistant.* This person's primary responsibility is to coordinate taking game film of the opponent and providing support to the offensive and defensive staff in their efforts to prepare scouting reports and game plans. He also provides general administrative support.

- *Administrative assistant.* The responsibilities of an administrative assistant are generally handled in one of two ways. Either they are given to a single designated individual or they can be assigned separately to several members of the coaching staff.

  This position is particularly essential to a head coach who also holds additional key responsibilities for the organization (e.g., general manager, DOO, etc.) On the San Francisco 49ers, this position was assigned at various times to individuals serving either as the team's executive administrator or as the organization's executive assistant. A comprehensive overview of the job descriptions for these two positions on the 49ers' staff is included in Appendix C.

  When selecting an individual to serve as your administrative assistant, you should look for the following attributes and consider the following factors:

  — Depending on the circumstances, the administrative assistant (AA) can be one of the most valuable people in the organization. All factors considered, the more intelligent and the more energetic the individual in this position, the more valuable the AA will become.

  — The AA must be a responsible, totally loyal person who thrives on work.

  — A commitment to learn, to inquire, and to be as knowledgeable as possible about all relevant matters is a prerequisite. This person should be someone with potential executive abilities.

  — While it is not necessary that the AA have experience as a professional athlete, this individual should have experienced competitive athletics at least on the high school level, preferably on the college level. To have competed as an athlete and to have had the opportunity to see firsthand the fact that athletics involves sacrifices affords this person a better appreciation for the players and their needs.

  — The AA should not be considered as a coach, but rather as someone whose primary area of responsibility is to serve the needs of the coaching staff. Accordingly, he must confine his role to administrative duties.

  — Initially, the AA's role should be structured within the individual's abilities. As the AA gains experience and demonstrates an improved level of capabilities, his/her role can be broadened, thereby enabling the head coach to be relieved of many of the peripheral demands on his time.

  — The AA must be computer proficient. Eventually, the person in this position must become skilled at computer graphics.

  — The AA should be sufficiently knowledgeable about football to be able to understand an offensive play or a defensive scheme and to draw either accurately as requested by the staff.

— The AA must be completely trustworthy. In that regard, the head coach must be satisfied that the AA's level of maturity enables this person to deal with confidential and sensitive information.

— With each passing year, the individual in the position of AA should become even more valuable. One-year stays are not only disruptive to staff continuity, they also involve redundant and wasteful expenditures of time (e.g., introducing the new AA to people with whom his/her position must interact, teaching the new AA the nuances of the job, etc.).

— The duties of an AA can vary from organization to organization according to the needs of the head coach of a particular team.

— One of the more critical responsibilities of the AA is to work closely with the team's personnel staff. For example, the head coach will often require an hour-by-hour update from the AA concerning the status of contract negotiations or some other personnel transaction.

— The AA must demonstrate the maturity necessary not to become too familiar with the players on the team. Because his age may be closer to the players than to the members of the coaching staff, the AA may tend to gravitate toward the players in social settings. Accordingly, the AA can be in a difficult role in this regard, especially if he is a recent NFL player.

— In order to fully serve the head coach and the team, the AA must exhibit the poise, demeanor, and maturity required to interact in an appropriate way with individuals of the same professional status as the head coach. On numerous occasions, the AA will be required to be involved with such individuals (i.e., give or receive messages, arrange appointments or contact times, etc.).

During training camp, your staff may be augmented by several additional coaches. For example, someone from the minority coaches intern program may join your staff for a few weeks if your team participates in that program. Most teams also use the services of a kicking coach during this period to help train those players involved in the kicking game.

MONITORING THE ASSISTANT COACHES

As the head coach, you must establish clear parameters for your assistant coaches regarding the overall method by which you expect things to be done. Your assistants must be in complete agreement with you on philosophy, teaching methods and standards, style and system, strategies and game-day tactics.

Any philosophical differences between you and one of your assistants must be identified and subsequently addressed by you in a private meeting with that assistant. Accordingly, you must establish policies and procedures to continually monitor what is being installed, covered, presented and implemented from the top down. Among the factors which your policies must consider are the following:

• On occasion, an assistant coach may quite naturally revert to his own personal philosophies, techniques and coaching style when he is alone with his particular group of position players. This situation occurs most often with experienced assistants who have their own established beliefs, especially if they have a long-time affiliation with a team whose philosophy or system was distinctly different from yours.

- The impact of these beliefs may surface in teaching fundamentals, in response to the pressures of game day or in making key decisions that the head coach will mistakenly (but naturally) believe will be made according to the dictates of his own philosophy.

- Sometimes, an assistant coach will be teaching a concept different from the one the head coach wants and may not be aware of it. The point to keep in mind is that such an assistant is not necessarily being insubordinate (although such an attitude also exists on occasion). The lack of continuity resulting from such a situation, however, can go on indefinitely if left unchecked.

- It is the head coach's responsibility to monitor his assistant coaches concerning what is being addressed and how. The problem of different philosophies is most dangerous when the team's coordinators present personal philosophies that conflict with his.

- At times, the head coach may be so relieved to find an experienced coordinator that he concedes a great deal of his power and control to the coordinator by assigning complete responsibility for a large segment of the squad without establishing appropriate philosophical parameters. The differences in philosophy can subsequently become entrenched in the players without the head coach recognizing it. As a result, the staff and the squad may be split into two or more distinct factions.

- To help ensure unanimity throughout the coaching staff, the head coach must regularly visit team meetings (both announced and unannounced). Over the years, there have been a number of coaches who did not appreciate the importance of this step. Eventually, many of these coaches, in a sense, lost their teams to powerful coordinators and were subjugated to simply "servicing" the demands and the interests of their coordinators.

- The head coach must keep in mind that if he does not fully embrace his responsibility to keep track of what his assistants are teaching and planning, it may take very little time before he finds himself out of touch with both the squad and the game plan. Many coaches who find themselves in this situation as the regular season begins are afraid to reinject themselves into the process.

Instead, they turn their backs on their dilemma and hope for the best. Such a strategy can only cause their situation to deteriorate further as the season progresses. The importance of a head coach employing a hands-on approach with his assistant coaches was succinctly summarized by Mike Ditka, who coached the Chicago Bears to a Super Bowl victory, when he observed, "Personal contact is part of hands-on management. Go to the other guy's office; tell him what you have in mind so there is no misunderstanding."

- Another danger of allowing your assistants to espouse their own personal beliefs instead of subscribing to the philosophy established by you is the breakdown it can cause among the staff. What may have begun as positive staff chemistry can deteriorate over a period of weeks, months or even years as each position coach or coordinator becomes more powerful within his own territory.

- As an individual's sense of power increases, the natural need for control may become more and more pronounced until the assistants are concerned only with "their offensive line" or "their wide receivers." Eventually, the players may begin to take sides as well. Such a divisive situation can destroy a team.

- A head coach must also be alert for those assistant coaches who seek personal gratification by using their authority to teach and express their personal beliefs and philosophies. Such assistants may also be involved in creating their own agenda in an attempt to prove a theory or evaluation.

  In the first instance, the assistant coach can easily breed disloyalty and dissatisfaction among his players. In the second scenario, his efforts are usually a waste of time and energy that he should otherwise be dedicating to legitimate tasks or objectives. Instead, he is seeking to prove himself on a particular point or seeking to embellish his own reputation.

- Assistants who continue teaching faulty techniques or strategies as the only option can undermine a team's efforts to be successful. The most appropriate approach for the head coach in this scenario is to keep everyone "on the same page."

- The head coach must take proactive steps to diminish the likelihood of discord between him and his assistants. For example, he should participate and be visible in all possible settings involving either players or coaches (e.g., staff and player interactions, developmental and training programs, staff meetings, etc.).

GIVING YOUNGER COACHES AN OPPORTUNITY

As the head coach, you should not restrict yourself to hiring only seasoned, veteran assistant coaches with proven expertise in particular areas. You should view the insertion of new and young coaches into the profession as a genuine and practical responsibility on your part.

The extraordinary success of many of the individuals who served as assistant coaches on the staff of the San Francisco 49ers during the period 1979-1989 is dramatic evidence of the value of such an attitude. Being put in an environment where they had an opportunity to succeed and where, if necessary, they could gain invaluable experience and guidance allowed individuals like George Seifert, Mike Holmgren, Ray Rhodes, Denny Green, Sam Wyche, Mike Shanahan, Pete Carroll and Bruce Coslet to expand and refine their skills and to subsequently go on and make their marks as head coaches.

A specific step that the San Francisco 49ers took to give younger coaches an opportunity involved the establishment of the minority coaches program in the mid-1980s. The primary focus of the program was to develop an effective link to the pool of minority coaches in the college ranks.

This program was designed to give minority coaches access to professional teams (as active participants in assigned coaching roles) for two weeks during training camp. Not only did the program provide these minority coaches with hands-on, NFL coaching experience, it also introduced these individuals to NFL management and ownership.

In addition to the previously mentioned Tyrone Willingham, three other individuals also participated in the 49ers' minority intern fellowship program—Jerry Brown, Marvin Lewis and Bobby Turner. All of these individuals currently hold key coaching positions in the NFL.

By affording these minority coaches the opportunity to develop social and working relationships with NFL coaches and administrators, it was hoped that it would enhance and help promote career opportunities for African-Americans in the NFL. Although the program has proven to be a definite (albeit limited) success, much more needs to be done in this area.

For example, the same type of intern program for minority individuals should be established to provide these individuals with an opportunity to serve as active participants in the decision-making and administrative management levels of the NFL. Similar to the program for coaches, such experience can only serve to increase the number of minorities who are taking active roles in top management.

What is required of an officer is a certain power of discrimination, which only knowledge of men and things and good judgment can give.

> Carl von Clausewitz
> Director of General War Academy
> Prussia
> from *On War*

Assigning Specific Coaching Duties

The distribution of duties to the position coaches and the coordinators can vary a great deal from one staff to another. The key factor is to make sure that each essential responsibility is covered by a qualified staff member. Tables 5-1 and 5-2 provide examples of how these duties might be assigned to the team's defensive coaches and offensive coaches, respectively.

As the head coach, you should recognize that your coordinators may work in different ways, using approaches that may differ substantially from yours. All factors considered, such differences can be relatively inconsequential as long as you and your coordinators are philosophically compatible on the key issues (e.g., the system, the emphasis on teaching, the attention to detail, etc.).

You should also recognize that, as a rule, of the two coordinators, it takes longer to prepare the offense. Generally speaking, defense is a matter of establishing a defensive plan and reacting properly to what happens on the field.

As Joe Gibbs—three-time Super Bowl champion coach—observed in the book, *Game Plans for Success,* offense is usually far more complicated (e.g., blocking schemes, pass protections, blitz pickups, pass patterns, reads, adjustments, etc.) than defense.

Accordingly, in most circumstances, a majority of your game-day decisions will involve the offense (i.e., do you settle for a field goal or go for it on 4th down; do you punt or go for a first down; do you kick the extra point or try for two points; do you run your two-minute offense at the end of the half or run the clock out; etc.).

If your background and experience are on the offensive side of the ball, you should consider hiring an offensive coordinator who has a firm grasp of an effective passing attack and support him with offensive line and running back coaches who would concentrate on developing a strong running game. In turn, you assign responsibility for the team's defense to a coordinator with impressive credentials in this area.

Table 5-1. An example of a defensive coach's assignment chart.

POSITION	DEF COORDINATOR	SECONDARY	LINEBACKERS	DEFENSIVE LINE
GAME ANALYSIS	All situations	Formations Coverages	Adjustments Points of attack	Blocking schemes Computer reports Opponent analysis
SCOUT REPORT	Game plan outline Tendency breakdown	Sets, motion, two-minute and four-minute breakdown and route sheet	Run blocking schemes Cover sheet	Pass pro scheme Red-zone breakdown and personnel
WEEK	Script Two-minute defense Goal line defense	Routes, special category cards, formation cards, and 7-on-7 cards	Compile cards Group run cards Scout run formations	Pass pro cards All-running game cards Walk-through cards
GAME	Play calling	Secondary adjustments Secondary substitution	Point of attack	Call chart
LOCATION	Pressbox	Field	Pressbox	Field
HALF-TIME	Coordinate half List 2nd half calls Address defense	Compile formation and coverage reports Meet with secondary	Compile run game reports Review coverage Meet with linebackers	Review blocking scheme reports Meet with defensive line

Table 5-2. An example of an offensive coach's assignment chart.						
POSITION	OFF COORD	QB COACH	WR COACH	RB COACH	TE COACH	OL COACH
GAME ANALYSIS	All situations	Nickel pass Blitz	RZ pass	Gen run SY-GL RZ run 4-minute	Computer reports Self scout Opp analysis	Gen run SY-GL Blitz 4-minute
SCOUT REPORT	Game plan outline Route sheets	Coverages	Personnel Cover sheet	Fronts Run sheet Pro sheets	Tendencies	Stunts Blitz
WEEK	Scripts	Team cards Blitz period	Coverages Scout team coverages 7-on-7 cards	Compile cards Group run cards 9-on-7 cards Short yrdg	Walk-through cards Spec cat cards Scout fronts Goal line	Team cards Blitz cards 2-point tape
GAME	Play calling	Secondary	Substitution DB match-up	Call chart Backfield	Fronts	POA
LOCATION	Field	Booth	Field	Field	Booth	Field
HALF-TIME	Coordinate half List 2nd half calls Address offense	Compile pass rec Isolate cov Meet with QB	Meet with WR	Situation chart Compile run rec Meet with RB	Meet with TE	Isolate front Meet with OL

An excellent example of a situation where the head coach's background is primarily on the defensive side of the ball is Ray Rhodes of the Philadelphia Eagles. Previously, Rhodes served as the defensive coordinator with the San Francisco 49ers for George Seifert.

In Philadelphia, Rhodes has established a system similar to the one that was employed in San Francisco when he was on the 49ers' staff. The major difference between what he does with the Eagles and what he experienced in San Francisco is that his involvement is primarily with the defense. He has turned the offense over to his offensive coordinator, Jon Gruden, with whom he coached with the 49ers.

The Responsibilities of the Offensive Coaching Staff

Assigning specific coaching duties to the various members of the staff requires a thorough analysis of the tasks that must be performed in any given situation (offensive or defensive) and a systematic determination of who should accomplish these responsibilities and how. The complexity of such an undertaking can be better understood by examining the process involved in assigning duties to the offensive coaching staff.

The individual in charge of the offensive staff is the offensive coordinator. His most critical responsibility is to develop and implement the offensive game plan.

By definition, one of the key duties of the offensive coordinator is to do just that—coordinate. When a team has a diverse offensive staff, it would be foolhardy not to fully utilize the knowledge and capabilities of these staff members by excluding them from the process of creating and implementing the offensive game plan.

The feedback and ideas that can be provided by the offensive staff should be encouraged and given a platform. It is then the job of the offensive coordinator to blend and focus everyone's input into a single, cohesive game plan that adheres to the basic parameters of the team's offensive system.

The process of developing a game plan for a particular opponent is initiated by the offensive coordinator, who breaks down the specific responsibilities of each coach for helping prepare that game plan. He identifies what he wants each coach to focus on when the assistant coach analyzes the opponent for the upcoming week.

With the limited time that a staff has to prepare for an opponent in any given week (usually a little more than a day), the offensive coordinator simply does not have enough time to personally address in an adequate manner all of the areas that have to be accounted for in a game plan with the necessary attention to detail.

Accordingly, the various key elements that must be accounted for in an offensive game plan are assigned to the offensive position coaches who are able to devote more time to identifying, analyzing and developing suggestions for attacking an opponent's defensive tendencies. Table 5-2a illustrates how these basic areas could be distributed among the offensive coaches.

On a few areas, several coaches may need to work together to develop a plan for handling a particular element of the offense. For example, Table 5-2a shows that the offensive coordinator wants the quarterback and the offensive line coaches to combine their efforts to isolate the needs of the offense to counteract the blitz.

Table 5-2a. Distribution of the coaches' responsibilities for game analysis.

POSITION	OFF COORD	QB COACH	WR COACH	RB COACH	TE COACH	OL COACH
GAME ANALYSIS	All situations	Nickel pass Blitz	RZ pass	Gen run SY-GL RZ run 4-minute	Computer reports Self scout Opp analysis	Gen run SY-GL Blitz 4-minute

These two coaches are responsible for the two positions that most often have to account for the blitz. Accordingly, it is natural that they work together to analyze this area of the game plan.

Another example of this approach involves a situation where the wide receiver and the running backs coaches work in concert to analyze and suggest an offensive plan of attack in the red zone. This alliance of coaches enhances the likelihood that the run/pass perspective can be kept in an appropriate balance.

In the example illustrated by Table 5-2a, the tight ends coach is in charge of compiling the computer reports that most teams use to analyze their opponents and to self scout. In recent years, data and data processing have become an integral part of the infrastructure of NFL organizations.

The key for the offensive coordinator is to establish specific priorities about what information he needs, when he needs it, when it should be introduced into the decision-making process, and most importantly, when he has enough. Accordingly, one of the most basic questions the offensive coordinator should ask with regard to the need for a specific report is, "Will this information affect the play selection?"

Once the offensive game plan starts to take a tangible form, each position coach is then assigned specific aspects of the scouting report. Table 5-2b shows how these responsibilities could be allocated among the offensive coaches.

Table 5-2b. Allocation of the coaches' responsibilities for the scouting report.						
POSITION	OFF COORD	QB COACH	WR COACH	RB COACH	TE COACH	OL COACH
SCOUT REPORT	Game plan outline Route sheets	Coverages	Personnel Cover sheet	Fronts Run sheet Pro sheets	Tendencies	Stunts Blitz

The next step in the process of developing and implementing the offensive game plan for a particular opponent involves having the offensive staff address the issues required to prepare for the meetings and practices with the players during which the game plan will be explained and put into effect. Even the most brilliant game plan is relatively useless unless it can be readily learned and executed by the team's players.

In this regard, how the offensive game plan is installed and practiced is almost as important, if not more, than the selection of plays included in the plan. Table 5-2c illustrates how the specific preparation periods during the practice week could be earmarked to members of the offensive staff. Practice week duties also include making sure that the script and the practice cards are coordinated.

Table 5-2c also attests to the emphasis that is placed on two videotapes that are prepared by several of the position coaches. The quarterbacks coach puts together a blitz video, while the front-seven coaches develop a tape that addresses three special situations (short yardage, goal line, and two-point plays).

Table 5-2c. Designation of the coaches' responsibilities for the weekly preparation periods.

POSITION	OFF COORD	QB COACH	WR COACH	RB COACH	TE COACH	OL COACH
WEEK	Scripts	Team cards Blitz period	Coverages Scout team coverages 7-on-7 cards	Compile cards Group run cards 9-on-7 cards Short yrdg	Walk- through cards Spec cat cards Scout fronts Goal line	Team cards Blitz cards 2-point tape

> *He who has never learned to obey cannot be a good commander.*
>
> Aristotle
> Greek Philosopher

Both of these videos are special tapes. They are made in addition to the breakdown tapes that the team's video support staff normally produces.

Under normal circumstances, a team will use an opponent's last three or four games as the basis on which it develops its offensive game plan. Certain aspects of an opponent's play, however, must be examined in even more detail.

For example, it is critical that a team's offensive preparation efforts include assigning a coach (in this instance, the quarterback coach) the responsibility of compiling a complete inventory of what pressure each opponent presents during the course of the entire year. For other factors (i.e., the two-point play), it may be necessary to go back to the beginning of the season—perhaps to the previous season in some instances—to get enough "looks" on which to base the game plan.

Another important aspect of the game-planning process involves the game day assignments and locations of the offensive staff. Table 5-2d shows how these assignments and locations could be designated to the offensive staff. A basic overview of the responsibilities of the various members of the coaching staff to make half-time adjustments is presented in Chapter 12.

Table 5-2d. Game-day assignment of the coaches' responsibilities and locations.

POSITION	OFF COORD	QB COACH	WR COACH	RB COACH	TE COACH	OL COACH
GAME	Play calling	Secondary	Substitution DB match-up	Call chart Backfield	Fronts	POA
LOCATION	Field	Booth	Field	Field	Booth	Field

> *There are only three things you should do when you make a mistake:*
> *1) admit it, 2) learn from it, and 3) don't repeat it.*
>
> Paul "Bear" Bryant
> Hall-of-Fame Football Coach
> University of Alabama

The Size of the Coaching Staff

In the last few years, the size of coaching staffs has grown. Some individuals feel that such growth is unwarranted. While some validity may exist in the observation that "it didn't used to take this many people to organize and manage the entire team," clearly the times have changed to a point where it is crucial that a team has as many competent coaches as it can helping (servicing) its players.

Not only is it necessary that the players receive extensive hands-on training and instruction, it is also important that the players have a sense that the organization values them highly. They also want to feel that someone is directly responsible for meeting their developmental needs and enhancing their level of preparation (i.e., someone to act as their personal trainer).

This scenario is particularly true for the quarterback coach. Given the fact that so much is at stake and riding on this position, every effort must be undertaken to make the quarterback feel that his abilities are being enhanced by his environment. Although the traditional role of having the offensive coordinator serve as his own quarterback coach has long been a functional arrangement, separating the jobs into two positions has some clear-cut advantages, including:

- It allows the offensive coordinator the freedom to give the proper attention to detail that the game plan demands without feeling like this is being done at the expense of spending extra time with his quarterbacks, especially any young player who could use the extra time.

- While the offensive coordinator may be preoccupied with the entire offensive scheme during any given practice, he can be assured that the quarterbacks are being coached on every single play.

- It is human nature for an individual to be protective of his position. For example, if the coordinator serves as his own quarterback coach, he may be inclined to blame a lack of production on anything but "his quarterback."

  This tendency can cause a problem with the other players who perceive the quarterback as being above criticism. Separating the job into two coaching positions allows the offensive coordinator to make more objective comments when critiquing the quarterback.

- If the offensive coordinator also serves as the quarterback coach, the quarterback is only exposed to a single perspective. Such a scenario may have a negative impact on the quarterback's learning curve.

In this situation, the quarterbacks have no respite from dealing with the same individual all day long. Depending on the individuals involved, these circumstances could have adverse consequences.

For example, if all of a student's classes are with the same professor, regardless of how good that professor may be, it does not heighten the learning curve the way multiple perspectives do. In his interactions with the quarterback, the quarterback coach may redefine or reemphasize a point in just enough of a different way that it heightens the awareness of the player.

General officers must be seen in the front line during action.

George S. Patton, Jr.,
Commander, United States Third Army
World War II
"Letter of Instruction Number 1,"
from *War as I Knew It*

A fundamental factor that must be considered when deciding who will be responsible for coaching the quarterbacks is the need for the offensive coordinator and the quarterback coach to be clearly on the same page. Not only must the quarterback coach be philosophically compatible with the offensive coordinator, he must also be completely comfortable with the intrusive relationship the offensive coordinator must have with the quarterbacks.

In some instances, this relationship may have to be dictated by the head coach. If the positions are separated and a quarterback coach is added, the offensive coordinator may become very territorial and feel threatened by the presence of an additional coach in an area that he has traditionally handled himself. The head coach will essentially have two options if such an attitude exists.

On one hand, he can try to educate the parties involved about the advantages that an additional perspective will add to the situation and how such a delegation of coaching responsibilities can help to optimize the time and energy of the offensive coordinator. On the other hand, he may assess the level of discomfort his offensive coordinator has with this new reassignment (usually due to the coordinator's ego) and determine that such a realignment of duties is simply not worth the divisiveness and disharmony it will cause. Above all else, he must assign only men who can teach to these positions.

All Coaches Are Not Equally Talented

As the head coach, you should not assume that every member of your coaching staff is equally competent. In reality, some are more talented than others.

All factors considered, in normal circumstances, you will discover that approximately 40 percent of your staff will be extremely capable. In turn, the most talented individuals will end up being assigned the majority of the team's supplementary responsibilities.

While it is certainly in your best interests to utilize your most gifted staff members to the fullest extent, you should also endeavor to achieve an appropriate degree of balance within your staff by coupling coaching assistants who are more driving and intense with your more solid, dutiful coaches.

The interdependence of the staff is extremely important in these pairings. Grouping creative, assertive, hyperactive, independent-thinking individuals with other assistant coaches of a similar profile can easily lead to staff confrontation and chaos.

It is also important that you recognize the fact that depending on the circumstances, you can in fact have too many staff members. For example, you should not add a person as a coach or as an administrator simply to show that an area is covered.

If that individual is not fully capable of contributing to the position in a meaningful way, adding such a staff member could create a problem, rather than solve one. For example, if you decide that you want to actively run your team's offense, hiring both an offensive coordinator and a quarterback coach may be an unnecessary action on your part that could subsequently lead to staff confusion and difficulties.

It is also essential for you to keep in mind that as the structure of the coaching staff takes shape, it can be relatively easy for a head coach to compartmentalize and delegate responsibility to the point where he is figuratively left with "nothing to do but hide in his office and wait for the next crisis to appear." Accordingly, the head coach must always structure the staff process in such a way to include identifiable mechanisms for interacting with each coordinator and position coach.

> *The man who commands efficiently must have obeyed others in the past, and the man who obeys dutifully is worthy of some day a commander.*
>
> Marcus Tullius Cicero
> Roman Statesman and Orator

TAKING FUTURE STAFFING NEEDS INTO ACCOUNT

All factors considered (e.g., staff morale, continuity, motivation, etc.), it is almost always easier if a team fills its coaching vacancies and selects its coordinators from within its staff. Accordingly, the head coach must keep a larger perspective in mind when completing his staff.

In that regard, he should anticipate that over time—particularly if his team is relatively successful—he will suffer attrition among his staff when members of his coaching staff take positions with other teams that advance them professionally. As such, a head coach must not become so dependent on his coordinators that if one of them were to leave the organization, that entire aspect of the team's system would go with him.

Subsequently, in such a situation, the head coach then becomes a casualty of the constant changes in his team's system or style of play. Despite his efforts to the contrary, it will be very difficult for his team to maintain the continuity needed to remain successful over a long period of time.

Hiring a coach from the outside (e.g., a new coordinator) is not without possible benefits. For example, a fresh hire can bring a slightly different perspective and experience to his new job. In the process, he may certainly inject new ideas and concepts into his new team's system.

The best way to maintain the continuity of an already winning profile, however, is to hire from within. As a rule, any time a head coach fills a key position on his staff from within shortly after the vacancy occurs, his actions are usually the result of the fact that he probably took the future staffing needs of his team into account when he initially put his staff together.

As the head coach, if you are primarily involved on the offensive side of the ball, your hirings on defense become especially critical because of the relative level of autonomy they likely will have. All factors considered in this regard, a pass defense specialist is preferred over a run defense specialist because pass coverage is the most critical aspect of defense in the NFL.

Defensive line coaches (and in some instances linebacker coaches) tend to focus on and to be more concerned about the running game than the passing game. In the process, they often become overly preoccupied with 4- and 5-yard gains, while huge chunks of yardage are being given up in the passing game.

During the period of 1979-1989, the San Francisco 49ers' focus on pass defense was realized when George Seifert was promoted in 1983 to coordinate the 49ers' defense after serving as the team's defensive backs coach. The leadership backbone of the 49ers was then completed when equally talented Bill McPherson was assigned to focus on the team's run defense.

ESTABLISHING THE HEAD COACH'S MEETING SCHEDULE

Because of the substantial pressures and stresses that a head coach faces, he may be predisposed to delegate as much responsibility as possible and to spend a considerable amount of time in his office. In the extreme, such an emotional overload can cause him to become almost dysfunctional.

By falling out of touch with the various aspects of the team dynamic, he may lose some of his ability to effectively participate in the effort to make the team successful. In order to avoid such a situation, as the head coach, you must develop and adhere to a systematic schedule that will require you to interact with every level of the team on a regular basis.

Among the steps that you should undertake to ensure that your schedule addresses your needs in this regard are the following:

• Hold strategy meetings several times a week with both of your coordinators (e.g., early in the week, mid-week, and prior to the game) to specifically discuss your opponent's strengths and weaknesses. You should coordinate and determine the total, overall game plan and communicate that perspective with your coordinators. You should also hold discussions with your entire staff on their impressions, determinations and recommendations regarding the game plan.

- Hold a specific meeting (usually by Wednesday) in order to have a firm, complete grip on contingency decisions and who will participate directly in extreme circumstances (e.g., backed up offense, 4th down decisions, 3rd down on goal line, etc.).

- Hold two scheduled weekly meetings with the special teams coach, who should present his initials plans during the first meeting and his final plans during the second session.

- Establish a format for the practice week in which you will sit in on selected position meetings, both announced and unannounced.

- Establish and maintain appointed meeting times with the athletic trainer, conditioning coach and team physicians.

- Hold at least one weekly meeting where the offensive, defensive and special teams coordinators meet together to more fully appreciate each other's plans of attack and how they might affect their individual plans. This meeting is also an excellent time to bring these specific coaches up to speed on what you have learned from your meetings with the athletic training and medical staffs.

- Hold regularly scheduled meetings with ownership, the CEO and/or the DOO to outline and review ongoing processes involving the team.

Coaches who can outline plays on a blackboard are a dime a dozen. The ones who win get inside their players and motivate.

Vince Lombardi
Hall-of-Fame Football Coach
Green Bay Packers

CREATING AN EFFECTIVE STAFF COMMUNICATIONS NETWORK

As the head coach, your ability to communicate with your staff is of vital importance. The operative word here is "communicate," not "dictate." If you determine that all you are doing is handing down directives for your coaches to follow with little room for give and take on their part, you may have hired the wrong staff.

In order for you to communicate effectively with your staff, you must first account for a factor which can disrupt the communications process—your ego. Over the years, the word "ego" has taken on a broad spectrum of perceived meanings, including self-confidence, self-assurance, and assertiveness. These attributes are generally viewed in a positive sense by most people.

On the other hand, another interpretation of the word "ego" exists. This type of ego can wreak havoc on a team or an organization. In this definition, "ego" is defined as "being distracted by your own importance."

This type of ego can emanate from a variety of factors. It can come from an individual's basic sense of insecurity in working with others. It can spring from a person's need to draw attention to himself in the public arena. Furthermore, it can originate from a feeling that other individuals are a threat to his own territory.

Collectively, these negative manifestations of ego can eventually lead to possibly the most negative impact of this aspect of ego—the fact that ego can make people insensitive to how they interact with others. As a result, this type of ego can end up interfering with and building barriers to the meaningful goals of any group effort.

As the head coach, you must do everything possible to ensure that no ego barriers exist that can hinder the effective exchange of information and ideas between members of your staff. People have to be able to communicate without fear.

Your staff must feel comfortable about expressing their opinions. They must be made aware of the fact that if—for any reason—they change their opinion about something, you will not demean them for it.

It is not uncommon for an assistant coach to make a definitive comment regarding a particular aspect of his team's game plan or a certain player. It is inexcusable, however, for that coach to hold to his original statements for fear of appearing wrong if he receives additional information or facts that contradict his initial opinions.

In fact, the head coach should make a point of reminding his staff that he expects them to change their impressions and opinions over time. All-in-all, the process is quite natural—the more information that an individual has available, the faster things can change.

Assistants should also know that they will not be ridiculed if their comments turn out to be mistaken or if their ideas are not compatible with those of their superior. In reality, legitimate differences of opinion are to be expected and encouraged to stimulate the free flow of opinions.

The point that should be emphasized is that when an assistant coach makes a relatively serious mistake, it is rarely necessary for the head coach to say anything to him. In most instances, the assistant is usually fully aware of his mistakes and is far more critical and self-deprecating about his shortcomings than the head coach would be with him.

The fact that an assistant coach readily admits his missteps is an indication that a real high-water mark in the effort to establish a quality staff has been reached. It is a very positive sign when the head coach surrounds himself with staff members whose self-expectations exceed his expectations for them.

One of the most valuable tools a head coach has at his disposal to motivate his assistants is praise and acknowledgment. While the importance of recognizing a talented, productive staff member may seem quite obvious, a surprisingly high number of head coaches find face-to-face, highly personal, public recognition of their assistants to be very difficult.

Knowing when to bestow praise on others is another issue that some head coaches find somewhat bewildering. For example, an emotional boost is obviously needed when someone is down, but what about a situation when morale is relatively high?

In that regard, many coaches erroneously reason that no one needs a psychological lift when morale is high. However, that's a situation when recognizing the efforts and achievements of staff members can be quite valuable.

Subsequently, when times get tough, the "investment" of infusing positive reinforcement into the staff environment when times were good can function somewhat like a cash contingency fund. The greater the investment, the larger the amount of positive feelings (support) that will be available when it is needed.

Similar to other essential management techniques, offering personal recognition to others is a skill that requires both planning and training. For example, giving the same impersonal compliments to every assistant for a job well done can render the process almost useless.

By the same token, the head coach who overdoes his complimentary remarks or confers his favorable comments on someone who obviously did not deserve them will undoubtedly not achieve the desired morale boost in his staff.

The head coach must keep in mind that he can be damned by faint praise; he can sabotage himself with effusive praise. Or, he can master the art of high praise.

There are times, however, when circumstances justify the head coach being harshly direct. Given the speed and tempo of the game and the ongoing time pressures that accompany the decision and the communicative processes during the intense competitive environment, the ability of the head coach to communicate in a direct manner is absolutely critical.

In this situation, the recipient (i.e., the assistant coach) of this type of communication must be responsive to and must handle in an appropriate manner what otherwise might seem to be an unduly harsh or abusive interchange with his head coach. For the moment, the assistant must subjugate his own ego and emotions and understand and appreciate the fact that the situation may not have allowed the head coach to employ a more subtle approach.

It is incumbent on the staff to be able to properly deal with the passions of the moment. Under no circumstances should they allow such instances either to become too personal or to interfere with the way that they perform their jobs.

On occasion, a situation may arise when the head coach feels the need to critique or criticize one of his assistants. The process utilized to give such feedback must be carefully considered.

It is important that the head coach assess the intent of his criticism to make sure that its sole purpose is to improve the performance of the individuals involved and not just a way to vent his frustration and disappointment that otherwise serves no valid purpose. The head coach must also ensure that his comments are both honest and accurate.

Furthermore, he must consider the fact that the impact of his message will depend, to a degree, on who's receiving it and the ability of that person to understand and respond to the feedback at that particular moment in time.

In most instances, this type of evaluation is usually best conducted in a private environment. The desired effect of such comments may be greatly diminished if they are made in front of other coaches or in a staff meeting.

The head coach should remember that, all factors considered, when an individual is backed into a corner by a potentially embarrassing matter, he usually will embrace and hold onto an indefensible position—even though he knows in his heart that the head coach's comments or criticisms are valid.

It is also very important for the head coach to carefully consider the venue for any critical comments he may want to direct to his players. For example, one of the more effective ways to ensure that he doesn't embarrass a player or put the player unduly on the defensive is to criticize that individual via his position coach.

Accordingly, the head coach must take steps to ensure that his staff know that on occasion he might direct somewhat harsh comments to them in front of the team that would, in reality, be designed to make a point to a particular player without embarrassing or demeaning the athlete in front of his peers. The assistant has to be able to absorb and handle such an orchestrated criticism or outburst.

A typical situation in this regard might involve the head coach's concern over the ineffective blocking of the team's wide receivers. Instead of criticizing the wide receivers directly, he would point his comments to the wide receivers' position coach by asking him "why he can't get his receivers to block anybody."

In this scenario, the head coach's remarks might help bond the assistant to his players. Furthermore, these players might conceivably respond (i.e., attempt to be better blockers) to the coach's criticism because they don't want to let their position coach down.

At the proper time and in the appropriate place, however, the head coach must redefine and expound on the reasons for his comments. In effect, he is expressing his regrets (i.e., apologizing) for his statements in the given circumstances.

His approach, however, enables him to accomplish his desired objective. He is able to deal with matters and issues in a harsh and direct manner (if need be), without dragging personalities into it.

Another possible technique (tool) that the head coach can use to defuse a possible volatile moment is humor. A good-natured demeanor can help neutralize a particularly unsettled moment and keep it from becoming too personal. All factors considered, self-effacing or self-deprecating humor is usually an excellent way to return a situation to a point where it is relatively normal and to create a "we-are-in-this-together"-type of atmosphere.

One final issue involving communication between various members of a team's coaching staff is the role of anger in the process. The point to consider in this matter is that bad tempers are not always bad news.

As a rule, highly competitive workplaces often produce highly charged emotional situations. In these circumstances, the more talented and dedicated people are, the more likely that they may spontaneously engage in passionate behavior, such as showing anger.

Depending upon the situation, restraining anger is not always the best course of action, especially when the alternative is to let the anger simmer. In reality, one of

the likely consequences of avoiding angry confrontations is a degree of a grudging undercurrent of unresolved hard feelings. Under normal circumstances, an occasional show of emotional fireworks by typically upbeat individuals can serve positive ends (e.g., relieve tension, shake up everyone's thought processes, help establish a more creative edge, etc.).

> *When sending a message, it is not enough to be honest and accurate. The impact of the message will hinge on who's receiving it and what they're willing to take in at the time.*
>
> Bill Parcells
> Head Football Coach
> New York Jets
> from *Finding a Way to Win*

FACILITATING STAFF TRANSITION

As the head coach, you must be able to project the future staffing needs of the organization, not unlike the way you have to constantly plan for the player needs of your team. Over time, openings for assistant coaches will occur for any number of reasons (e.g., individuals take a position with another team, someone retires, a coach is fired, the size of your staff increases, etc.).

Each time an opening exists and is filled, a certain level of transition among the previous staff members typically transpires. If this transition is not handled properly, the situation can be very divisive and disruptive when individuals are passed over for a particular position they wanted or reassigned from a job they preferred.

When explaining the situation to a disgruntled member of your staff, it is important that you are sensitive to the feelings of that individual. Although being honest and direct with the person sounds good, it may not be the best approach.

If such directness and honesty give rise to insensitive, hammer-like comments, serious damage can be done to the relationship between both parties. Subsequently, the harm that results may end up reverberating throughout the entire organization.

For example, over time, people may lose the sense of bonding they need to work together effectively. Furthermore, your directness may isolate you somewhat from the individuals with whom you work. To a point, honesty (other than in fact) is often only a manifestation of someone's subjective interpretation of a particular matter.

Staff Self-Esteem

One of your key responsibilities involving your staff is to lead them through troubled times and to help them maintain as much of their self-esteem as possible when they are demoted, find themselves passed over, or are practically at the end of their coaching careers. One of the most productive steps you can take in this regard is to give each staff member a constructive opportunity to enhance his level of marketability in the job market (i.e., perform selected supplemental duties, take coursework, learn new skills, represent the team at selected functions, increase his visibility, etc.).

If properly executed, this step will help mitigate or eliminate the potential corrosive effects of uncertainty that a staff member may otherwise face. In turn, the staff's energy level will be refocused on more productive issues or matters.

Although it may only be on a very short-term basis, getting your assistants to "give a damn" can work to your advantage. For example, helping a staff member deal with disappointing circumstances involving his career can also help enhance his sense of loyalty to you and the team, even while he is very concerned about his own future.

The drawing power of the workplace is no longer the testimonial dinner and the tribute plaque in honor of someone's extended period of service. Rather, the attraction and the promise of a particular assistant coaching job for many individuals is essentially to have an opportunity to reach their own goals and to gain support and guidance in achieving these objectives.

Anti-Tampering

In recent years, the NFL has established three tiers of coaching levels in an attempt to better define and prevent teams from tampering with the coaching staffs of other teams: level #1—the head coach; level #2—two supervisory coaches; and level #3—all other assistant coaches.

Traditionally, professional ethics and protocol dictated that a team would not approach someone on the coaching staff of another team about making a lateral move. For example, an individual with the title of coordinator used to be assumed to be someone in a supervisory role.

No more. Teams have become very creative in their efforts to justify their efforts to obtain (i.e., "steal") a coach off of the staff of another team by establishing such job titles as associate head coach, assistant head coach, offensive coordinator in charge of the running game, offensive coordinator in charge of the passing game, etc.

According to League rules, every team must designate two coaches as having a supervisory role, regardless of what titles are assigned to them. In turn, every other assistant coach must have his team's permission to talk to another team about accepting a lateral transfer.

In other words, if a team is interested in discussing an assistant coaching position with an assistant who is contractually obligated to another club, and the prospective new position involves moving from one non-supervisory assistant coaching job to another or from one supervisory assistant coaching position to another, it would be considered a lateral move. As such, the team currently employing the assistant considering moving is under no obligation to grant the coach the opportunity to even discuss a position with another club.

The NFL's anti-tampering structure presents an interesting dilemma to the head coach. In most instances, the supervisory title is accorded to the team's two primary coordinators.

In a few cases, however, some head coaches have placed the supervisory title on assistant coaches other than their coordinators in order to retain key assistants that they don't want to lose to other teams. In taking this approach, however, they run the risk of allowing one of their coordinators to leave for a better offer.

In 1996, for example, two NFL teams lost their coordinator for exactly that reason. Accordingly, it is relatively easy to determine whom the head coach or the organization values most among its assistant coaches by checking to see which two coaches have been given the supervisory title.

The NFL's anti-tampering structure is not without a major flaw, however. The primary inequity of the system involves the fact that the various teams are under no obligation (whatsoever) to financially augment the income of the coaches with supervisory titles, simply because of the title. On the other hand, an assistant who has the supervisory title literally does not have the option to seek a better deal in the open market, even if he isn't his team's top paid assistant coach.

DEALING WITH A POORLY PERFORMING STAFF MEMBER

Ideally, every staff member would perform at the desired level of competence. In reality, however, circumstances dictate otherwise.

For whatever reason, some assistant coaches simply don't satisfactorily meet the job requirements for their positions. In these instances, two things are absolutely crucial with regard to you (as the head coach) dealing with a staff member who is not performing at an acceptable level:

- You must have established specific criteria as to what is expected in the assistant's position.

- You must have identified specific shortcomings in the performance of the individual.

As such, you must establish a plan and procedures for handling members of your staff who are not meeting the standards you have set for them. Among the factors and the points that must be considered when developing such a plan are the following:

- Every member of your coaching staff must be made aware of the specific needs and expectations of his position. If, for any reason, he does not know what is expected of him, he has considerable latitude to question your critique of his performance.

- When questioning a staff member's performance, you must be very careful to state that his lack of productivity is the primary basis of your dissatisfaction, as opposed to attempting to explain your opinions regarding why he has not been productive. In other words, if you try to be an "armchair diagnostician," you can open up a Pandora's box of potential problems that you may not be able to adequately address (e.g., open yourself up to some form of litigation that might arise from any misunderstanding of your comments).

- When dealing with a staff member who is not performing up to your expectations, you should be firm, but not confrontational.

- In such situations, you should be ready to cope with the staffer's resistance, defensiveness, and even hostility. One of the most effective methods for overcoming a defensive attitude of such an individual is to explain to the person how the situation makes you feel—without moralizing.

  After you've shared your feelings, you should then move to a discussion of the specifics of your concerns about his inadequate job performance. You should never talk about how he is doing his job first. If you do, you increase the likelihood of him having an unduly antagonistic attitude towards you.

- You should attempt to get the staffer to identify and admit that he has a problem, for whatever reason. He should understand the fact that his performance has not been up to your expectations.

- You should not accept his excuses for failure. If you go along with his explanations regarding why his performance has been less than satisfactory in an ill-advised attempt to placate the situation, you have simply compromised the authority of your position in two significant ways.

  First, you demonstrate that his lack of productivity is acceptable. Second, you show that you have no interest in helping the staffer improve his situation.

  Such an approach on your part can either create additional anxiety in the staffer who already knows that you are about to make a change in his position or further enhance the assistant's misguided sense of self-importance.

- If the staffer offers excuses, you should refocus the discussion on the specific job criteria for his position and attempt to have him identify (i.e., explain) how each of his specific excuses relates to his particular lack of performance.

  In this scenario, one of two situations may occur. Either the staffer will be forced to accept responsibility for his failures or a problem may be identified that in reality is not the fault of the individual in question.

- It is important that you do not allow the staffer to attribute his problems to other individuals or to other aspects of the organization. You must hold fast to your conviction that it is his responsibility to improve his job performance.

- After you have identified the problems of a staffer, you must set up an improvement plan for the assistant that enables both you and the individual to know if he's making meaningful progress in his efforts to improve. More importantly, you must provide the staffer with a quantitative objective on which both of you can base future assessments of his performance.

- At the very least, you must take the responsibility to intervene in a situation where a staffer is not performing at an acceptable level. In all likelihood, a troubled staffer's performance and actions (both on and off the job) will improve if he is confronted frequently in a constructive manner. In reality, his performance will probably get worse if his actions are ignored or if he is just warned occasionally about his lack of commitment to doing the job expected of him.

- If the staffer's performance continues to be lacking and you decide that you have to make a change in his position, it is critical that you don't transfer the problems imposed by this individual to another area of the organization. All this step would accomplish would be to pass the same problems to someone else.

  Eventually, the individual's inability (or unwillingness) to be a productive employee would have a similar negative effect on another part of the organization. While it may be easier to avoid a confrontation with the staffer by simply convincing yourself that he would be more effective in another position, this is rarely the situation.

- If you decide that you have to terminate the staffer, you must take painstaking care in detailing and documenting his lack of production. If, for any reason, your documented reasons for letting the staffer go are not both accurate and measurable, you face the risk of the litigation that inevitably ensues in the 1990s when anyone, however inept, is fired.

- If the source of the problems exhibited by the staffer involves his personal life (e.g., alcohol, drugs, domestic violence, gambling, etc.), you should remember that you have a moral obligation to help the staffer address the source of his difficulties. Such assistance can be very precarious, however, if not handled properly.

  Your first step in this matter must be to recognize that you personally may not have the expertise and the skills necessary to deal with the staffer's problems other than giving him advice about his need to get professional counsel. You should not moralize or attempt to transpose your ethical standards on the staffer. If you do, you may only cause more problems.

- Your primary objective in the process of dealing with a staffer (at least initially) must be to determine if the individual does indeed recognize that he has a problem and, more importantly, whether he is receptive to change. As harsh as it may appear on the surface, if the staffer does not have either perspective, you may be doing unforeseen damage to the organization, and possibly to the individual himself, by not terminating the person.

PART III

THE
PEOPLE

CHAPTER 6

EVALUATING PLAYERS

"The greatest leader in the world could never win a campaign
unless he understood the men he had to lead."

—General Omar N. Bradley
5-Star General of the Allied Armies
World War II

Finding the winning edge...

*Probably the toughest thing a manager has to do with a winning
team is to assess the strengths of those who got you there.
Ironically, some of the best performers may not be the ones
destined to continue to achieve. They may be coming off a career
season. Everyone loves them. Making changes with people like
these, at a time when loyalty might seem the natural human
response, can appear almost incomprehensible to close-knit staffs
and to the outside world. But they are part of the hard task of
adapting to and confronting the success syndrome.*

—Bill Walsh, "Succeeding Despite
Success," *Forbes*, September 13,
1993.

When I took over the 49ers, we had what appeared to be a good young quarterback in Steve DeBerg. Unfortunately, Steve was the only quarterback we had. He had done well the previous year but was injured, and I needed a quarterback who could be a back-up for Steve and, conceivably, replace him if the new player had enough potential.

Sam Wyche, our quarterback coach, canvassed the country to see which quarterbacks could be had in the mid-rounds. In addition to our second round pick, we had Dallas' third round pick. It was understood that several quarterbacks would be picked in the first round.

I chartered a plane and flew to Kentucky to see Phil Simms at Morehead State. The rural airport had a very short runway surrounded by trees, and the weather was lousy. The pilot circled several times, dodging clouds and squalls, before finally landing. The airport terminal was an old house trailer.

The woman inside, a housewife with a number of children running around the trailer, did not even hear my plane land. I waited 45 minutes for the cab from Morehead, met with Phil, spent the afternoon analyzing film, and joined him for a burger and fries for dinner, dreading the flight out. I left feeling that Phil was our man, but it soon became evident that other teams were looking at Phil, and he would likely be drafted early, despite his team's losing record.

I was also looking for a big receiver and a speed receiver as I was searching for a quarterback. When I looked at Steve Fuller, I also looked at Dwight Clark, who had caught only 12 passes his senior year. We had few draft choices because of the O.J. Simpson and Jim Plunkett trades, and had to choose carefully. Clark was much faster and quicker than I had expected, and had an outgoing personality. We had enjoyed considerable success with a similar player when I was with the Cincinnati Bengals, Chip Myers—a very fine 6'5" receiver.

We looked at 14 quarterbacks and arranged them in priority order. We finally tracked down Joe Montana, who was living in southern California, and Sam Wyche and I went to see him a few days before the draft. When I saw Joe, I knew immediately that he was our man. He was quick, agile and fluid in his movements, almost like a ballet dancer, and reminded me of Joe Namath.

His throwing was also good, though not as good as Terry Bradshaw's. We were also looking closely at James Owens, the NCAA high hurdles champion, and were impressed by his speed and intelligence. On our flight home, Sam and I decided that Joe and Owens were our choices.

As the draft neared, we did all the research we could and decided that Joe would not be taken before the fifth round if at all. Everyone knew he had poise, but they were put off by his slight appearance, inconsistent performance at Notre Dame, and, some believed, relatively weak arm. We selected Owens in the second round, Joe in the third, and Clark in the eleventh. The rest is history.

Simms became one of the game's great quarterbacks, and Fuller had a good career with the Bears. Clark became a consensus All-Pro choice in 1981. Joe became arguably the greatest quarterback of all time. Unfortunately, Owens never reached our highest expectations because of repeated hamstring pulls and the fact that his hands were merely adequate, but he became a great kickoff return specialist. Just as *it appeared he was reaching his full potential, he suffered a severe hamstring pull on a kickoff he returned for a touchdown against Detroit. We later traded him to Tampa Bay, where he had a few good seasons as a running back.*

Without question, one of the primary factors affecting success in the National Football League is having talented players. While acquiring those players is a multifaceted issue that every team addresses in its own way (see Chapter 7 in this book), the most important step in securing the players a team needs is evaluating the available talent pool (both collegiate and professional players).

Several factors have resulted in an even higher value being placed on the ability to evaluate and assimilate talent into the organization, including the advent of the salary cap and free agency, and the reduction in the number of rounds conducted in the annual NFL draft. In addition, free agency has also affected the need for a team to have a systematic process for evaluating the players who are already on its roster. Decisions relating to how much of a team's resources (i.e., salary cap) should be devoted to retaining a particular player who is eligible for free agency will be based—to a great extent—on a detailed evaluation of his capability to perform.

Each team has its own criteria and procedures for evaluating players. Over the years, these criteria have changed as the game has evolved. They differ from team to team, depending upon the needs and the particular system of each team. On the other hand, certain basic requirements will always exist for players at each position. Despite this situation, evaluating players is not an exact science. The process must take into account a number of factors. In the final analysis, one critical question must be answered: "Can this individual make a meaningful contribution to the team?"

EVALUATING PLAYERS WHO ARE CURRENTLY ON THE ROSTER

As the head coach, you must ensure that a process is established to evaluate your players on an on-going basis even after they have joined your team. This evaluation is typically performed by members of your coaching staff as part of their responsibility to help develop a projection of the team's needs for the upcoming year. Among the steps that you can take to make sure that such an evaluation is conducted in an appropriate way are the following:

- Make sure that the evaluation is completed with both a short-term and a long-range appraisal in mind.
- Project the maturation of younger players—how their skills and abilities may improve and how those capabilities will affect the make-up and overall production of your team. As part of this effort, individual and collective talent must be continually reassessed, with projections three to five years in the future.
- Develop a plan for dealing with free agency as it affects your team's roster. Such a plan is critical, given the high priority that many teams place on maintaining the continuity of their existing rosters and the fact that most players are eligible for free agency in a relatively brief period of time (i.e., if otherwise unrestricted, five years or four years with a capped year).

USING COACHES AS TALENT EVALUATORS

Members of the coaching staff should be given a substantial role in the scouting and evaluation processes of their teams. Typically hired because of their expertise and experience in working with players at a particular position, these individuals have a wealth of knowledge that can be used in the evaluation process.

Most of these men have either been in the league for a relatively long period of time or have moved up from the college ranks, where one of their duties often was to evaluate athletes who were at a much younger and more difficult age for projecting their potential abilities. In either instance, it is very likely that your coaches have the ability to systematically evaluate and project their players' attributes with respect to athletes' current and future status on the team.

The observations and feedback provided by your coaching staff must be kept in proper perspective with the information and opinions offered by your team's scouting staff. It is highly unlikely, for example, that a position coach would have had the opportunity to see the wide array of players that a regular scout has watched.

Accordingly, the position coach would not be able to objectively compare the potential worth of a player at one position, relative to that of a player in another position. Such judgments must be made by the existing team hierarchy of head coach, director of college and pro personnel, etc. or whatever structure has been established by the organization.

The value of utilizing your coaches in the player evaluation process can be further supported if you consider a situation where a coach is given the assignment of evaluating the top ten players at the position he coaches. It is very likely that his approach to the task will include reviewing all available game films involving those players, traveling to the players' schools to work the athletes out, visiting with the players' coaches, and interviewing the players. After completing such an assignment, the coach obviously has much to offer to a team's efforts for evaluating players— particularly his opinions regarding the relative ranking of the specific players he was asked to size up.

An excellent example of how the coaching staff can make a positive contribution to a team's player evaluation process involves the quarterback position. Although all teams have a very competent scouting department, almost every team also has an offensive coordinator and/or a quarterback coach who is one of the top people in the game in evaluating, developing, and quantifying the mechanics required by a professional-level quarterback. Accordingly, it is logical that coaches, in conjunction with a team's head coach and director of scouting, should have a substantial amount of input into the final ranking and the selection of players for this position.

IDENTIFYING WORKOUT CRITERIA FOR THE SCOUTING PROCESS

It is critical that a distinct format is established and utilized when one of your team's scouts or coaches works out a potential squad member. A detailed checklist of the suggested workout criteria for selected positions is presented in Appendix F.

The uniformity afforded by a checklist assures that every essential criteria for a particular position is evaluated during a specific workout. In turn, regardless of whether the individual being evaluated is a potential draft choice, a veteran free agent, a free agent who has only been in the League for a year or two or an undrafted college free agent, the use of such an information-gathering tool ensures that every candidate is given a comparable opportunity to be evaluated.

As such, a standardized scouting format and checklist makes certain that nothing is overlooked when a candidate is evaluated. Ideally, the same scout or coach would administer the workout session for all candidates for a particular position (preferably their own).

In addition, it is also preferable to include one or more athletes who play the same position as the candidate being evaluated in the workout. This step allows demonstrations to be conducted and relative comparisons (between the candidate and the other player) to be made.

Involving a veteran player currently on the team in the workout can also be beneficial. Not only can the skills and abilities of the candidate be directly compared to the veteran, the seasoned player can provide a specific demonstration of what is being taught or required.

ESTABLISHING EVALUATION TOOLS

In February each year, coaches, scouts and personnel department members from every National Football League team gather in Indianapolis for a pre-draft NFL-style ritual of sorts—to watch the top collegiate football draft prospects in the nation take a series of tests designed to evaluate the potential of these individuals to play at the pro level. Each prospect is evaluated on a diverse array of measures, including the 40-yard dash, the vertical jump, the standing long jump, the bench press, an intelligence test, a personal interview and several position-related skill tests (e.g., passing, catching, agility, runs, etc.).

The scores and marks that the prospects achieve on these measures are subsequently recorded, scrutinized, and used as input in each team's evaluation process. In a few instances, players are sometimes linked with their "Indy" results for the rest of their careers. Astute teams, however, keep the results of these evaluative measures in perspective, using them as reference guidelines, rather than as absolute criteria.

For example, a player's time in the 40-yard dash doesn't really tell you how fast he will be in a game. His scores on either the vertical jump or the long jump may only indicate that he is out of shape (rather than lacking leg power). Even a player's marks on an intelligence test may have limited value. They may have less to do with an individual's innate instincts that enable him to play "smart" in the game than with his ability to take written tests.

On the other hand, value exists in the process, if you keep the results in perspective and you know how to properly utilize the collected data. It is important to remember that functionality is the most important indicator of a player's ability to perform.

No matter how fast an athlete runs, how high he jumps, or how well he scores on a written test, his value can only be related to how functional he is on the field. In reality, functionality is usually something that cannot be precisely measured any place except on the practice field or in a game situation.

Many teams feel that the most valuable evaluative measure is not the one that yields precise marks, but rather one that must be evaluated with a great deal of subjectivity: the personal interview. It seems ironic that, after going through all the existing intricate tests and procedures, teams often reach their final judgment on a player based on a good, old-fashioned face-to-face discussion. The 49ers utilized the accomplished services of Dr. Harry Edwards, a renowned expert in the interview process, to help in this area.

Another issue that has increasingly become a problematic factor in assessing the usefulness of the Indy testing results involves the fact that many coaches and scouts use the Indy data to inject a self-protective mechanism into the evaluative equation. "This player has good size, speed and plays with lots of heart, *but* he only had a 28-inch vertical jump at the combine." This type of qualifier is often put in the evaluation report to cover one's backside if the evaluation proves inaccurate and the player does not pan out (i.e., "I told you he didn't have a good vertical jump.").

Eventually, each team must decide for itself how to use the information obtained at the Indy combine. One of the initial steps in deciding what to do with the Indy results should be to thoroughly review each testing measure for its application to the team's needs and interests. How well teams perform this task will have an impact not only on the effectiveness of their process for evaluating players, but also on their ability to be successful where it counts—on the field.

40-Yard Sprint

The 40-yard dash is one of the most universally adopted and most commonly accepted aptitude measures for football players. On the other hand, however, the relatively high value placed on this measure is open to question.

As an evaluative measure, a player's time in the 40-yard dash has at least two deficiencies. First, the conditions under which the event was conducted (e.g., weather, type of running surface, etc.) can make a substantial difference in the resulting times. Second, and more important, the game of football requires functional speed, not pure track (foot) speed. Functional speed is related to playing the game and responding to external stimulis (e.g., another moving object, etc.).

The problems with using the 40-yard dash time are illustrated by Jerry Rice— unquestionably, the greatest wide receiver in the history of the NFL. Rice's combine time in the 40 was 4.59 seconds.

As such, Rice was considered to have marginal speed for a starting NFL wide receiver by virtually every team in the NFL. The only exceptions were the New York Jets, the Dallas Cowboys and the San Francisco 49ers, who ultimately drafted him. Had other teams considered Rice's functional speed (which is probably among the very best in the history of the game), instead of his foot speed, Rice's draft day status would have improved immeasurably and his potential for greatness recognized.

Every year, a number of players with extraordinary 40-yard dash times (e.g., 4.3 seconds or faster) try out for the NFL. Although highly talented because of their foot speed, these individuals are often out of football in a year or two.

Despite the fact that the 40-yard dash time is a commonly accepted measuring "stick," in reality, it's only a viable evaluative measure at either extreme of the time continuum. A player with a 4.4 time is obviously very fast, while a 5.4 time means that the athlete is very, very slow. As indicated by the Jerry Rice example, those times in the middle of the continuum are less useful.

Another problem with using the 40-yard dash time as an evaluative measure involves its lack of application to certain positions. For example, timing offensive linemen in the 40-yard dash is of questionable value. Knowing how fast he is and what kind of body mechanics a 300-pounder has in the 40-yard dash provides information of dubious utility.

Because of its historical roots and its normative reference, timing players in the 40-yard dash can furnish useful data. Coaches should remind themselves, however, that 40-yard dash times involve tenth-of-a-second differentials that can be significantly affected by the conditions of the running surface on which the test is conducted and by the amount of training the athlete has had with a track start.

The limits of using the 40-yard dash time as an evaluative measure are illustrated even further when the 40-yard dash times of the 1970s are considered. Twenty years ago, the times in the 40s were relatively slow. The testing was often conducted on less-than-ideal surfaces.

Athletes just ran anywhere anyone directed them to—on grass or any type of field. Hardly anyone practiced his starting techniques. The individual to be tested simply got into his football stance and ran the 40...no rehearsal, no work on starting technique, etc. Although the 40-yard dash times have improved considerably over the years, in some ways, they have become less reliable as an evaluative measure.

A more valid test of speed for a wide receiver would be the speed involved when he is running at full stride with a defensive back in hot pursuit. This speed would be comparable to an individual running the last 40 meters in a 100-meter race.

Vertical Jump

Considered by many individuals to be the best measure of explosiveness (a critical factor in a player's performance), the vertical jump test is designed to measure leg power (and, to a limited extent, coordination). The test involves having an athlete jump straight up as high as he can from a flat-footed start. The test score achieved is the measured distance between his reach while standing flat-footed and the highest point he can touch on his jump. No running starts are permitted.

Although the vertical jump is a reliable indicator of explosive leg power, this test has a few limitations as an evaluative tool. For example, vertical jump scores are affected by body weight. All factors considered, a 260-pound offensive lineman, who would be considered light by NFL standards for his position, would normally be able to jump higher than his 300-pound teammate. Even if both players were in comparable physical condition, the 300-pounder has to do more work than the 260-pound player because he has to move more weight over the same distance.

Vertical jump scores are also affected by training. The athlete who trains for this test will achieve scores substantially closer to his actual potential than an individual who doesn't train. Finally, vertical jump scores are generally affected by age. Most athletes reach a point in their lives, age-wise, where (all factors considered) their strength levels start to decline somewhat. As a consequence, their vertical jump scores decline.

Bench Press

The bench press is a weight lifting exercise which is designed to measure upper body muscular fitness. At the Indianapolis combine, the test involves having an athlete perform one set of as many repetitions of the bench press as he can with 225 pounds.

Similar to other evaluative measures, the bench press has some limitations. All factors considered, a larger individual can lift more weight than a smaller one. Given the absolute relationship between strength (force exerted one time) and endurance (the ability of a muscle or a muscle group to engage in repeated bouts of a task), it follows that a larger player can generally perform more repetitions of a 225-pound bench press than an athlete who is lighter.

The ability to perform a bench press is also affected to a substantial degree by the length of the arms of the lifter. The athlete with shorter arms can perform more repetitions of a bench press (when all other factors are comparable) than an individual with relatively long arms because he has to move the weight less distance (i.e., perform less work). Finally, like other evaluative measures which involve physical work, training will have an effect on results. An athlete who has been working out regularly in the weight room will almost always perform better on the bench press test than someone who hasn't.

Although upper body strength and endurance certainly can have a significant impact on an individual's performance on the football field, the value of using the bench press scores for evaluation purposes appears to lie primarily at the extremes of a results continuum. For example, if an athlete is only able to perform half as many repetitions of the bench press as comparable players at his position, a problem may exist (i.e., he hasn't been working out regularly, he's too embarrassed to strength train, his work ethic is lacking, he doesn't have the muscular fitness appropriate for doing the job on the field, etc.). On the other hand, even if an athlete can perform substantially more repetitions of the bench press than average, a question still exists as to how much his bench press performance relates to functional football strength.

One final consideration involving the use of bench press results as an evaluative measure concerns the value of bone girth to offensive linemen. Bone girth helps give a player ballast to keep his balance. Ballast helps make it difficult for a defender to move an offensive lineman out of the way, or if the offensive lineman gets moving in a certain direction, ballast makes it more difficult to stop him.

As such, an offensive lineman's bone girth is probably more important than the number of bench press repetitions he can perform with 225 pounds. An offensive lineman could have ballast (heavy bone girth) and be a comparably poor performer on the bench press test, yet be a very effective football player because he has functional strength.

A team may have a player who has dedicated himself to the weight room and, in the process, has broken several weight lifting records. However, if he has a relatively small skeletal structure, he is vulnerable to being unduly moved around (against his wishes) by his opponent. Jesse Sapolu, an ex-offensive lineman who formerly played for the San Francisco 49ers, provides an excellent example of this factor. Jesse had great bone girth. Regardless of how he was able to perform in the weight room, he was a great performer on the field.

Because of its application as a comparable reference point and its size-related limitations, bench press results are normally evaluated by position (i.e., wide receivers versus other wide receivers, defensive linemen versus other defensive linemen, etc.). Players who play the same position typically utilize the same skills and are of comparable height and weight, etc.

The Wunderlich

The Wunderlich is a written test that is administered to all prospects at the Indianapolis combine. Technically not an IQ test, this evaluative measure is designed to show innate intelligence (i.e., the ability to reason).

All factors considered, the Wunderlich holds more significance for some positions than others. For example, a team might be more interested in the Wunderlich test results of an offensive lineman than a defensive lineman because of the amount of mental processing that playing the position of offensive lineman requires.

Similar to many of the other tests conducted at the Indianapolis combine, the question of the direct application of the Wunderlich test results is a factor that must be considered. The issue is innate intelligence versus functional intelligence (i.e., there is take-written-test "smarts," and there is on-the-field "smarts"). Some successful players have both types of intelligence, while others tend to be more inclined toward functional intelligence.

Steve Young, the talented quarterback for the San Francisco 49ers, is an example of a player who possesses both innate and functional intelligence. Young is extremely bright, has a law degree, and is an exceptional performer on the field. On the other hand, there have been Hall-of-Fame quarterbacks who were great football players, intense competitors, and insightful decision makers on the field, yet would not have scored in the highest percentile on a written test like the Wunderlich.

An example of an individual who did not have the highest score on this particular measure, yet exhibited extraordinary functional intelligence on the football field was Phil Simms. Anyone who has ever dealt with Simms, however, knows that his intelligence is extremely high.

Perhaps the most appropriate way to use the results of the Wunderlich test for evaluation purposes is to look for extremes. The fact that a prospective player received a single-digit score on the test (i.e., way below the norm) would certainly have to be considered. For example, would that player have the capacity to handle the intricacies of a complex offensive (or defensive) scheme?

Medical History

A player's medical history is another type of information collected, in varying degrees, at the Indianapolis combine workouts. Because of each team's need to expend available resources wisely and the demands of the NFL's salary cap, obtaining and thoroughly analyzing the medical history of each prospective player the team is considering is extremely critical. Any unusual factor uncovered in the analysis should be systematically scrutinized.

It is very important that a team conducts extensive research on a player's health, including his past injuries. Unfortunately, it's not uncommon for a college to mask the injury history of one of its athletes. The athletic trainers and coaching staff members of some colleges are so loyal to their athletes that they are very reluctant to share or release any information on those athletes which might be perceived as damaging to the athletes.

As a result, in some situations it is often difficult for a team to get a complete medical history on a particular player. This reluctance appears to be even more of a factor when drugs and/or alcohol are involved. It is important to understand that a player's school may feel an ethical, as well as legal, obligation to withhold that type of information.

Several medical-related factors (especially when considered collectively) can indicate that a potential problem exists with a prospective player. For example, if a player has been in and out of the training room, even with minor injuries, and has been unable to practice on given days and is missing parts of games or missing a whole game here and there, those circumstances have to be a serious factor when a team is thinking about committing a high draft pick.

While it wouldn't eliminate a player, it definitely would be a consideration. Certain types of injuries often become chronic. Joint injuries, for example, have a history of recurring and then developing into arthritic problems. This type of consideration must be factored in when evaluating a prospect.

Personal Interview

Perhaps the most valuable evaluative tool at the Indianapolis combine is the personal interview. The more shrewd organizations in the NFL go through the tedious and laborious process of interviewing virtually every prospect in attendance. At the least, they interview players in whom they might have interest.

Conducted by a professional who is thoroughly knowledgeable in the process, the personal interview involves a series of questions that are addressed to each candidate.

The answers to these questions provide a common denominator that can be used to make comparisons between candidates. Dr. Harry Edwards, the eminent sociologist, directed this program for the 49ers.

These interviews often yield useful information or an insightful perspective on a player. More often than not, if the interview goes on long enough, the player will reveal a lot about himself, including some of his more discordant personality traits. A few of these traits may be less than desirable.

The interview may also reveal that the player has a history of problems socially or that he had difficulties in his relationships with his coaches. In addition, the interview might provide an indication of a prospect's willingness, desire or ability to learn. Furthermore, by examining a player's college transcript (i.e., what courses he took, what kind of grades he earned, etc.), a coach can get an idea of how serious this individual was as a student or what he might have learned and retained.

Over the years, the personal interview has become a more and more important part of the evaluative process. Character has become a distinctive factor in the process. As a result, player evaluation has become much more personalized than it once was.

For example, a coach might ask a series of questions that are designed to get a player to open up a little and reveal a side of his personality that might otherwise not be seen. For example, "What was the toughest class you took in college?"; "Why did you choose the major you're in?"; "What class outside of your major did you enjoy the most/least? (Why?)"; etc.

Given the nature of the NFL in the 1990s (i.e., free agency; salary cap; ownership expectations that a team must win sooner, rather than later; etc.) it is critical that a drafted player (particularly someone chosen in the high rounds) make the team and quickly contribute to the team in a meaningful way. The value of a personal interview is enhanced by the fact that most teams simply don't have the luxury of waiting until after a player is drafted to find out if he has recurring (chronic) problems with studying, learning, or relating to coaches and teammates.

All men are frightened. The more intelligent they are, the more they are frightened. The courageous man is the man who forces himself, in spite of his fear, to carry on.

General George S. Patton, Jr.
Commander, United States Third Army
World War II

EVALUATING PLAYERS BY POSITION

The requirements to play a position effectively vary greatly by position. The factors each organization employs in this regard also vary somewhat from team to team. This section of the book discusses the criteria and considerations that many NFL teams use when evaluating players at a particular position. The description of each position includes a statement of what constitutes an "ideal size" for an individual who plays that position.

The "ideal size" represents an average of what size player a team might expect and want at that position. The height and weight of the NFC's 1997 Pro Bowl players at that position are also listed (except for the center, fullback and weak safety positions, where both the NFC and AFC players are listed). The actual sizes of the Pro Bowlers underscore the variation that occurs between players, even at the same position.

All too often, great players do not meet recognized height and weight standards established by personnel people. On occasion, they are measurably below the requirements that scouts embrace as necessary.

WIDE RECEIVERS

Ideal size, 6-3, 210

1997 NFC Pro Bowlers	Team	Ht	Wt
Isaac Bruce	St. Louis Rams	6.00	200
Cris Carter	Minnesota Vikings	6.03	206
Herman Moore	Detroit Lions	6.04	210
Jerry Rice	San Francisco 49ers	6.02	200
average		6.02	204

To play effectively, a wide receiver must possess several traits and characteristics. For example, a wide receiver should have a high level of agility. The ability to change his body position (sometimes while off the ground) is essential if a wide receiver is to be able to get his hips turned and his hands in position to catch a ball that was not perfectly thrown. Body control is particularly critical for a wide receiver who wants to get to the highest tier of play (e.g., Jerry Rice, Cris Carter, etc.).

Wide receivers must also be relatively strong. Strength can help wide receivers in several ways. For example, strength plays a role in a wide receiver being able to maintain his balance after a collision with his defenders.

Strength also affects a receiver's ability to go up for the ball (i.e., vertical jumping) and his ability to maintain his performance level as the game progresses (i.e., delay the onset of muscular fatigue). Finally, all factors considered, the stronger a player is, the less likely he is to be injured (a relationship that exists for all players— particularly those involved in violent contact).

Soft hands are also vital. It's a given that to have a legitimate chance to play in the NFL, a receiver must have outstanding hands. The key is to be able to catch the ball in a crowded situation, while on the move.

Almost all potential receivers can run under the ball and catch it in the open. In reality, however, most catches in the NFL must be made with the ball and the defender closing at the same instant. In such a situation, the receiver must get his body in position to catch the ball, actually catch the ball and be hit—all at the same moment.

Wide receivers must also have the ability to focus. They must be able to "find" the ball, focus on it, and isolate it from everything else that is happening around them. When a coach is evaluating videotapes on a particular wide receiver, he looks for and evaluates those plays that demonstrate situations where the player must be focused.

Speed also plays a role. While pure (track) speed may be desirable, the ability to increase his foot speed as needed (i.e., explosiveness) and his full-stride speed are more important factors for a wide receiver. Acceleration has a number of obvious applications for a wide receiver.

Full-stride speed enables a receiver who has the ball in the open field to be able to keep the separation with the closing defenders until he crosses the goal line. He doesn't have to out-run the defenders or gain ground on them—just get to the goal line before the defenders do. This situation requires full-stride speed, rather than track speed. For example, Mike Quick, when he was with the Philadelphia Eagles, had just an average 40-yard dash time, but once in the open field, his long strides gave him the functional speed to stay away or get away from defenders in the open field.

The NFL has also had a few wide receivers with Olympic-level sprinting speed who lacked full-stride speed. As a result, they weren't able to score whenever they got tangled up with a defender and weren't able to get back into full stride quickly enough.

"Coachability" is another factor that is important that wide receivers have (as it is for all players). Coaching can help enhance a receiver's ability to evade a defender at the line of scrimmage, to read the form of coverage, and to change a pattern accordingly.

Wide receivers must also be durable. Durability is a factor because receivers get hit a lot. Often, they're hit when they're in a vulnerable position (i.e., being hit by a much larger opponent after running a hooking pattern against a linebacker).

Wide receivers are finely tuned athletes who need to be in top condition to perform well. If they are hurt or injured, it can be very difficult for them to function at a high level. Unlike a few other positions (e.g., offensive lineman), wide receivers must be almost totally injury free to perform well.

During my career, I had the opportunity to coach a number of great wide receivers, including Chip Myers, Charlie Joiner, James Lofton, Ken Margerum, Isaac Curtis, Dwight Clark, John Taylor and the incomparable Jerry Rice. At one time or another, all of them were either Pro Bowl players or All-Americans in college.

Each, however, was uniquely qualified and different from the others. For example, Chip Myers was 6'5", while Charlie Joiner was only 5'10"; Isaac Curtis was an NCAA sprint champion; Dwight Clark ran a 4.6 40-yard dash, etc. The one thing that they had in common, however, was that they were all brilliant performers.

It is important to remember that not everyone is fortunate enough to play out their complete career. For example, Bill Kellar, a very talented wide receiver who played for me at Stanford, was an outstanding collegiate performer who had his NFL career shortened by injuries.

TIGHT END

Ideal size 6-4 ½, 245

1997 NFC Pro Bowlers	Team	Ht	Wt
Keith Jackson	Green Bay Packers	6.02	258
Wesley Walls	New Orleans Saints	6.05	250
average		6.04	254

The requirements for playing tight end depend primarily on the system a team deploys. Accordingly, each team must find the athlete who best fits the team's approach to offensive football.

Some teams want a tight end who has girth, ballast and strength. For these teams, the tight end is one of the primary keys to their offensive system because he has the size and physical tools to secure the point of attack. If the tight end is able to block a defensive lineman who is positioned on the edge of the offense, then a team automatically has an increased likelihood of having a running game with just that single feature.

In many of the defensive alignments of the 1990s, defensive linemen are lining up adjacent to or across from the tight end, whereas years ago they weren't. If the tight end can block those defensive linemen, then the entire offense has a focal point from which to work.

This type of tight end can be a dominating factor. He is bigger and stronger, though less quick and agile, than the other type of tight end. Teams tend to fashion their passing game with him in the vicinity of the linebackers. Accordingly, he must have both the ability to absorb a ball as he is being hit and soft hands. On virtually every pass thrown to him, he is going to be hit almost simultaneously with the catch.

This type of tight end also does not need to possess great speed—a 5.0 time on the 40-yard dash will get the job done. The major shortcoming attendant to his lack of extraordinary speed is the fact that he is not going to be able to clear defenders on certain pass patterns to help other receivers. All in all, that limitation is not that significant compared to all the blocking capabilities he provides.

The other extreme would be a Brent Jones-type tight end, who can be a major factor all over the field. This type of tight end has the ability and the foot speed to go anywhere on the field quickly—across the field, to the outside, down the field, etc.

In the process, he will be able to either bring defenders with him or find openings in the defenses. This kind of tight end needs the body control, the great hands and a lot of the skills of wide receiver, although more girth (size) than a wide receiver because many of the passes he catches will be in the vicinity of linebackers and even defensive linemen.

The quicker and faster type of tight end will utilize an all-technique (rather than bulk) approach when blocking. It is essential that he learns and develops those blocking techniques that he can use with a reasonable level of effectiveness against defensive linemen and linebackers. Unlike the stronger, bigger type of tight end, he will not be able to use a mass-against-mass approach to blocking.

A third kind of tight end also exists—the great all-around type. This type of tight end is so gifted (athletically) that he can do all of the things both of the other types of tight ends would normally be expected to do. With Hall of Fame-level skills, this type of player makes the tight end position truly valuable in the NFL.

A multi-talented, all-around tight end who is both a great blocker and a great receiver gives his team multiple offensive options. In the history of the NFL, only a few of these individuals have existed. Possibly, the two best examples of an all-around type of tight end are Mike Ditka and John Mackey, both of whom have been inducted into Pro Football's Hall of Fame.

I was very fortunate to have coached several outstanding tight ends in my career, including Bob Trumpy, Charle Young, Russ Francis and Brent Jones. At some point in their NFL playing days, each was named to the All-NFL team.

Each individual had measurably different physical characteristics. All of them, however, were great champions.

OFFENSIVE TACKLE

Ideal size: 6-4, 310

1997 NFC Pro Bowlers	Team	Ht	Wt
Lomas Brown	Arizona Cardinals	6.04	275
Willie Roaf	New Orleans Saints	6.05	300
Erik Williams	Dallas Cowboys	6.06	324
average		6.05	300

The NFL has a number of highly skilled offensive tackles who weigh 330 pounds or so. In reality, these athletes play well in spite of weighing 330, not because of it. The only apparent benefit of weighing that much is to attract the attention of the television camera crew. While most of them might enhance their playing skills and performance if they lost a substantial amount of weight (i.e., get down to 300 pounds), the fact is that they play pretty well at their current weight.

The one absolute essential trait for all offensive linemen is natural body girth. In addition to girth, offensive tackles must be very strong and have a high level of agility (body control).

Because an offensive tackle tends to function most of the time in the game in a two-yard square area, the ability of this individual to move his feet quickly and purposefully within this area is absolutely critical. A substantial part of this ability can be developed and enhanced to a degree. On the other hand, if an offensive tackle has "slow feet," he may improve somewhat, but he will always be limited.

An offensive tackle should also have strong, long arms to facilitate those blocking tasks involving leverage. From a blocking perspective, however, the timing of the block itself (i.e., the timing of the extension) is the critical factor. In addition, the offensive tackle must have an intuitive sense of feeling or knowing where to intersect defenders.

In NFL football in the 1990s, the offensive tackle must also be able to anticipate and be ready to handle any one of three to four different situations that might occur. Historically, the offensive tackle only had to deal with one or two possible scenarios. Over the years, however, as NFL defenses have become more complex, the possible adjustments the offensive tackle must make have become more diverse.

For example, the offensive tackle must be able to adapt to a situation where a linebacker blitzes from the outside and the defender he was expecting to block drops back into pass coverage. As a result, the offensive tackle must be sharp enough to quickly identify the scenario and be able to move and adjust to the circumstances as needed. He must also be extremely well-versed and prepared in the skills and the techniques required to handle a variety of situations.

The nature of the position of offensive tackle also requires that athletes who play this position possess a level of inner-confidence and natural self-control that enables them to deal with frustration (e.g., the defender head slaps him, the play is stopped for no gain, etc.) and, on some occasions in a football-sense, disaster (e.g., his man sacks the quarterback). Regardless of the circumstances, the offensive tackle must be able to regain his focus and function at a high level of performance within 30-40 seconds or less. In reality, some athletes appear to have a better disposition to deal with potentially disruptive elements than others.

During my career, I had the opportunity to work with a number of Pro Bowl-talented offensive tackles, including Harris Barton, Keith Fahnhorst, Bubba Paris and Steve Wallace. Similar to great players at the other positions, each individual exhibited unique physical characteristics.

Each of these great players, however, was an excellent technician. More importantly, all of them exhibited the poise and the patience to take on the challenge each week of dealing with some of the best pass rushers in football.

OFFENSIVE GUARD

Ideal size: 6-3, 300

1997 NFC Pro Bowlers	Team	Ht	Wt
Larry Allen	Dallas Cowboys	6.03	326
Randall McDaniel	Minnesota Vikings	6.03	277
Nate Newton	Dallas Cowboys	6.03	320
average		6.03	308

Similar to some of the other positions, the requirements for playing guard depend to a great extent on the type of offensive system in which he plays. In this regard, two obvious options exist: either the offensive guard has to be selected based on his capacity to contribute to a team's existing system of offense or a team has to style its offense according to who its guards are. Typically, the latter option prevails. A team adapts its offensive style to the abilities of its guards.

An example of how a team adapts its offensive system to its guards occurs when a particular offensive guard can or cannot do something to his right or left. If the left guard can pull and trap, then the team is more likely to run plays to the right with the left guard pulling (and vice versa). The guard positions are "personalized" according to what they can do. Typically, one or the other offensive guard on a team is stronger or weaker in a particular technique or the ability to get the job done.

As a rule, great offensive guards possess several traits, including quickness, agility, explosiveness, the ability to pull and trap, and the ability to go inside-out on a linebacker. Randall McDaniel of the Minnesota Vikings is an excellent example of this type of offensive guard. Although he only weighs approximately 280 pounds, he is an outstanding player in every sense.

Offensive guards must also be able to pass block. Generally speaking, girth, stability and body balance are essential factors in this skill. Because the offensive guard can usually get help as a pass protector, he just has to have enough power to avoid being knocked back. Just the sheer number of people inside will help the guard pass block. As a result, the guard can have some limitations as a pass blocker as long as he has enough girth to keep the defensive tackle from picking him up and moving him.

The offensive guard position requires less technique for pass protecting than is essential for an offensive tackle. On the other hand, the offensive guard position requires more blocking and movement skills. For example, the guard is used on numerous blocking combinations where he must get from point "A" to point "B," pulling through a hole, trapping, pulling on sweeps, coming inside-out on a blitzing linebacker, etc. Collectively, this capability requires that the offensive guard has agility, mobility, and a refined level of techniques.

I was fortunate to have worked with three outstanding guards while I was coaching the 49ers—Randy Cross, John Ayers and Guy McIntyre. Each had mobility, strength and explosiveness.

All factors considered, they are most notably recognized for their almost aesthetic level of grace as pulling guards on the 49ers' "Bob" sweep. Each earned All-Pro honors.

While I was at Stanford, I had two other exceptionally talented offensive guards—Jeff Buckey and Brad Badger. Both are currently starting on NFL teams.

CENTER

Ideal size: 6-2, 290

1997 Pro Bowlers	Team	Ht	Wt
Ray Donaldson	Dallas Cowboys	6.03	311
Dermontti Dawson	Pittsburgh Steelers	6.02	288
average		6.03	300

The offensive center has a critical role in the team's offensive system. Not only must he start every play with a flawlessly executed snap, he is typically the key man in making line calls. These calls are vital, and there is no way a team can do without them.

For example, with the constant defensive changes that occur during a game, the offensive line must react to those changes if an adjustment in the blocking scheme is required. Because he is literally at the "center" of the action (i.e., in the middle of things), the center is the obvious member of the offensive line to identify and communicate to the other offensive linemen what blocking adjustment must be made.

As a result, the center must have a thorough command of the offensive line blocking system, the game plan, and individual defensive players his team is facing. In a few isolated instances, some teams use an offensive guard to make line calls because the guard is either more experienced or more adept at making them.

As a general rule, the center doesn't have to be an exceptional blocker. The center usually doesn't have to block the nose tackle one-on-one, although if he can, it provides a considerable advantage to his team. The center who can isolate one-on-one with a nose tackle will take tremendous pressure off of the offensive line, particularly the guards.

Most teams typically find a way to help the center with the nose tackle (e.g., slide a line). If the other team is in alignment that doesn't have a nose tackle (e.g., the 4-3 defense) or has the nose tackle stunt away from the center, the center helps a teammate with his blocking responsibilities.

One additional factor related to the center that some teams address is his height. Although there have been successful centers in the NFL who were relatively tall, many teams feel that, all factors considered, a shorter center is better. Not only does a shorter center have lower center of gravity (thereby facilitating body balance), he also tends to be more mobile—a trait that offers significant benefits to an individual who must operate in a relatively small area.

A large body can be a hindrance in a small area (somewhat analogous to the limitations imposed on a jockey who weighs more than 150 pounds). Most teams prefer a center who is able to quickly move in between people. In most cases, a shorter center can do that better than a tall, rangy one.

At San Francisco, I had two outstanding Pro Bowl centers, Fred Quillan and Jesse Sapolu. Jesse was an equally fine guard. Both players were intelligent, communicative performers. Physically, both were extremely nimble athletes who could adjust and adapt simultaneously as needed.

Chris Dalman, who was a very fine player at Stanford, inherited Jesse's spot with the 49ers and has since played very well. Chris has that low center of gravity that is so vital for the center position.

QUARTERBACK

Ideal Size: 6-3, 210

1997 NFC Pro Bowlers	Team	Ht	Wt
Troy Aikman	Dallas Cowboys	6.04	223
Brett Favre	Green Bay Packers	6.02	220
Steve Young	San Francisco 49ers	6.02	205
average		6.03	216

A logical argument can be made that no position on an NFL team is more important than the quarterback. Playing quarterback requires several skills and traits—some of which can be developed through practice and sound coaching, and others which are inherited (i.e., genetic "gifts").

One of the most obvious requirements for a quarterback is the ability to pass. If an individual can't pass, he won't have any chance to play as a quarterback in the NFL. The days that a "flinger" or "slinger" (i.e., someone with a Joe Kapp-type arm) would be given a legitimate opportunity to make an NFL roster as a quarterback are history. It is important to realize that arm strength and being able to pass are not synonymous. Some players can throw a football 80 yards, but they aren't good passers. Good passing involves accuracy, timing, and throwing a ball with enough touch so that it is catchable.

Good passing also requires understanding both the offensive system and the receivers in the system, and having a great sense of anticipation. While it is certainly admirable to be able to throw a ball on a line for 35 yards, if the ball is off target or arrives in such a way that it is difficult to catch, such an ability is of dubious value. The fundamental goal of passing a ball is to make sure it's caught...by the intended receiver.

One of the more important criteria for assessing the pro potential of a quarterback is to what extent does he have the ability to throw a "complete inventory" of passes—from screen passes to times, short passes to medium-range passes and down-the-field throws. Not having a "complete inventory" of passes in his arsenal does not eliminate a quarterback from a team's considerations, but it can be a meaningful factor. While a number of extraordinarily talented quarterbacks have played in the NFL who were not able to throw a complete array of passes, having such an individual quarterback the team would limit the type of offense that the team could run effectively.

Several other factors involving how well a quarterback can perform in the passing game segment of a team's offense should also be considered, including a quick delivery, touch, the ability to read defenses, mobility, and an ability to avoid a pass rush. A quick delivery is essentially the ability to get the ball "up and gone" with no wasted motion.

While a quick delivery can be acquired to some degree by learning and practicing the proper techniques for passing a ball, such a release is primarily related to an inherited motor skill—the quarterback's reaction time (i.e., how long it takes between when the quarterback spots his receiver and when he actually throws the ball). Particularly when it's not telegraphed in such a way that helps the defense, a quick delivery is an advantage for the quarterback once he "sees" his receiver. The faster he releases the ball, the less time the defense has to react to the situation.

The ability of a quarterback to throw a pass with the proper touch is also important, especially in a medium-range passing game. The right touch on a throw enables a pass to be more easily caught by a receiver without having to break his stride. One of the best "touch" passers in the history of the NFL was Joe Montana of the San Francisco 49ers.

Successful quarterbacks also have the ability to read defenses. Such a skill is not something that most quarterbacks have learned to a high degree coming out of college. Even if they have, they face very different defenses in the NFL. Regardless of whether quarterbacks are required to read defenses in college, most intercollegiate offensive systems require quarterbacks to look at their primary and secondary receivers, usually based on the defense confronting him.

If a review of game films indicates that the quarterback is able to locate his secondary receiver (or even an emergency-outlet receiver on occasion) with ease, or with a sense of urgency, this player has a chance to be a consistent performer in the NFL. The quarterback, however, must be able to handle such situations in a composed, systematic manner (i.e., initially, look for his primary receivers; then, immediately see his secondary receivers). Mobility and the ability to avoid a pass rush are also essential criteria for quarterbacks. Quarterbacks must be mobile enough to avoid a pass rush when they feel pressure in the pocket.

If throwing a ball was the only aspect of playing quarterback, evaluating the position of quarterback would be a relatively easy task. Because of the dynamic role that a quarterback plays on a team, he must have physical, mental, emotional and instinctive traits that go well beyond his ability to pass the football. A quarterback, for example, must be courageous and intensely competitive. Because he is the individual who is leading the team on the field, his teammates must have confidence in both his skills and his ability to withstand the pressure-packed situations he will face. His intestinal fortitude must be unquestioned. In this regard, two of the best in the history of the NFL were Bart Starr and Bob Griese.

A great quarterback also has excellent instincts and intuition. He has a "feel" for the game that goes well beyond knowing the playbook and his teammates, and understanding the nuances of the defensive schemes his team's offense must face. All factors considered, quarterbacks are born with such instincts and intuition. As a rule, there is not much that coaches can do to develop this area.

The ability to make superior, spontaneous decisions (especially at crucial times) is another trait that great quarterbacks possess. By combining his experience, vision, and what might be termed "instinctive genius," a great quarterback almost always seems to be able to make the "right call" at the "right time."

Finally, quarterbacks must have the ability to function at an appropriate level while injured. The pro season is almost twice as long as the college season. The level of intensity and punishment quarterbacks must endure is also considerably higher. Every time a quarterback goes back to pass, he is vulnerable to being hit hard. He must have the ability to withstand the hitting, to avoid being rattled, and to continue to exert a high level of leadership.

I have been extremely fortunate in the number of very talented quarterbacks whom I had the opportunity to coach. This group that includes Greg Cook, Virgil Carter, Ken Anderson, Guy Benjamin, Steve Dils, Dan Fouts, Joe Montana and Steve Young (two All-Americans, four NFL most valuable players, and three NFL Hall-of-Fame performers) makes me realize how really fortunate I was to work with them.

FULLBACK

Ideal size: 6-1, 245

1997 Pro Bowlers	Team	Ht	Wt
Larry Centers	Arizona Cardinals	5.11	215
Kimble Anders	Kansas City Chiefs	5.11	230
average		5.11	223

In many ways, the fullback position parallels the tight end position. The traits a team should look for in a fullback will depend on the offensive system run by the team and the type of fullback that is available to the team.

If a team has a fullback who is a devastating blocker, he can be the focal point of the offense (similar to the way that a great-blocking tight end is used). Such a fullback can be directed at any defender near the line of scrimmage. In a high percentage of situations, he will be able to effectively block the defender. In such a scenario, a team will be able to implement a wide array of running combinations in its running game.

Fullbacks can also play a critical role in pass-protection situations. If the fullback is stout (and skilled) enough, he can take on a charging pass rusher if necessary, either with a replacement block or a clean-up block.

He must be able to focus on a specific defender, find him (i.e., read the play), and take him on successfully. This skill requires functional intelligence. He must be able to process the array of variables that occur on a particular play and respond to them in such a way that he is a consistently effective blocker.

For a blocking-type fullback, speed is not a major consideration. Ideally, a fullback will be able to run 40 yards in 5.0 seconds or less. He must, however, have ballast, girth, and a high level of strength.

Fullbacks who are devastating blockers must also be very durable. A high level of durability is important because fullbacks probably endure more intense contact than anyone else on the field, considering the velocity of the hits they experience—often, play after play.

Blocking-type fullbacks should also be adequate receivers. If his receiving skills are satisfactory, he can serve as an outlet receiver. Often, as the last person who releases out of the backfield, the fullback gets the ball clear of defenders (thereby, providing him with a good opportunity to gain yardage).

The other kind of fullback is more of a halfback-type fullback. Compared to the blocking-type of fullback, this individual is more skilled. Although he may be only an adequate blocker, he is usually an extraordinary receiver and a terrific ball carrier.

This type of athlete is typically the focal point of his team's offensive attack because, from his position on the field, he can go anywhere and can provide so many offensive weapons. Roger Craig, who played on many of the San Francisco 49ers' greatest teams, is an excellent example of a halfback-type fullback.

In a limited number of instances, fullbacks may be great blockers, as well as great receivers and ball carriers. On those occasions, the fortunate teams for whom they play have multiple offensive options.

The 49ers managed to win several Super Bowls with two distinctly different styles of fullbacks. Roger Craig was a brilliant performer at the position, when coupled with Wendell Tyler. Both players shared blocking and running duties, with Roger as the featured pass receiver. In actuality, it was a two-halfback offense.

Later, I maneuvered in the draft to select Tom Rathman—a great blocking fullback from Nebraska. Subsequently, Tom developed into the best pure fullback in football as a blocker for Craig.

HALFBACK

Ideal size: Large enough to take punishment and retain stamina

1997 NFC Pro Bowlers	Team	Ht	Wt
Terry Allen	Washington Redskins	5.10	208
Barry Sanders	Detroit Lions	5.08	203
Ricky Watters	Philadelphia Eagles	6.01	217
average		5.40	209

A talented halfback typically possesses a number of traits, including durability, stamina, pure running instincts, blocking skills, receiving skills, and discipline. Size requirements for the position vary. Some relatively smaller halfbacks "play big." Due to their size (i.e., which enhances their body's ability to absorb physical punishment), larger halfbacks are somewhat more durable and more likely to possess the ability to fall forward when hit by a defender.

Durability is, perhaps, the most overlooked requirement for effective halfback play. As a general rule, a halfback is going to be hit a lot during the game. As a result, he must be able not only to withstand the physical abuse, he must also be able to maintain his focus and concentrate on doing his job well on every play. His team must be able to count on him if the halfback is a key part of his team's offensive philosophy. If a halfback isn't durable, all of his other talents diminish in value.

Stamina is an important factor because a halfback must be nearly as effective in the fourth quarter as he was in the first. Such a goal will be impossible if his performance is limited by physical fatigue.

All talented halfbacks also have pure running instincts. Every talented running back has his own intuitive style (which differs from running back to running back). This style enables him to do the "little" things on the field that make him successful—knowing when to cut back or change directions, knowing how to avoid being hit at full force by a defender, knowing when to change his running speed, being able to break poorly executed tackles, etc. Without such instincts, an individual will not be able to play the halfback position at an acceptable level in the NFL.

Ideally, a halfback will also possess an adequate level of both blocking and receiving skills. If he can block, his team's offense will have many more dimensions. As a receiver, he should at least be adept at screen passes. By degree, the further down the field he can go and catch the ball, the more dimensional his team's offense can become.

Finally, a halfback must have the discipline to get the first four yards within his team's offensive scheme, and then must be able to rely on his instincts to take the play beyond that point. Although times occur when an instinctive halfback has to occasionally do things on his own early in a play, he will not be able to gain the yardage that his team needs consistently if he leaves the designated play too early too often.

Great running backs come in all sizes. Many of the best performers, however, have been under six feet and have weighed approximately two hundred pounds. In my experience, the best I've worked with have been Darrin Nelson (180 lbs.), Paul Hofer (195 lbs.), Wendell Tyler (200 lbs.) and Roger Craig (220 lbs.).

This profile is at odds with the great talents and extraordinary careers of several relatively large halfbacks, for example, Franco Harris, John Riggins and Eric Dickerson. On the other hand, the profile is reinforced when the abilities and careers of players like Walter Payton, Tony Dorsett, Barry Sanders and Emmitt Smith are considered.

DEFENSIVE TACKLES

Idea size: 6-2, 290

1997 NFC Pro Bowlers	Team	Ht	Wt
John Randle	Minnesota Vikings	6.01	277
Eric Swann	Arizona Cardinals	6.05	295
Bryant Young	San Francisco 49ers	6.02	276
average		6.03	283

A defensive tackle must have several qualities to consistently play well. It is essential that he has enough girth (ballast) to hold off an offensive guard, or to step into an offensive tackle's block without being knocked off the line of scrimmage.

It is also critical that a defensive tackle has quick, strong hands and quick feet. Great defensive tackles have the physical tools (upper body strength and quick, strong hands) to control (grab and pull) and ward off possible blockers. They also have quick feet that enable them to take advantage of a moving man (i.e., getting him off balance).

NFL teams place particular value on defensive tackles who can demonstrate lateral quickness in a relatively small area. Such defenders are able to get moving quickly—over and through people. If necessary, they have the ability to move down the line of scrimmage while pursuing the ball carrier and make the tackle.

An individual who gets knocked off the line of scrimmage, or gets moved sideways, or gets knocked off-balance cannot play the position of defensive tackle effectively. Because they must be able to "work their way" through blockers to get to the ball, they must have above-average, total body strength.

The best defensive tackles are able to move the offensive guard back into the quarterback. While they may not have as many quarterback sacks as some of their teammates, defensive tackles who can move individuals by blocking them backwards have an essential skill. This scenario creates a disruptive situation where the quarterback has to avoid his own (backtracking) lineman as if he were an oncoming pass rusher before he throws the pass.

When I reflect back on the great defensive tackles that I was associated with over the years (e.g., Jeff Stover, Pierce Holt, Mike Reid, Michael Carter and Bryant Young, among others), I can't help but think about the fact that each of these extraordinary athletes possessed great closing speed, quickness and explosiveness.

In order to dominate on the inside, a player must have this dimension. Early in my coaching career with the Bengals, I had the opportunity to work with one of the quickest athletes ever to play this position—Mike Reid.

Steady, solid performers are an integral part of a championship team. Among the defensive linemen who fulfilled this role for the 49ers were Pete Kugler, Archie Reese and Jim Stuckey.

DEFENSIVE ENDS

Ideal size: 6-5, 275

1997 NFC Pro Bowlers	Team	Ht	Wt
William Fuller	Philadelphia Eagles	6.03	280
Tony Tolbert	Dallas Cowboys	6.06	263
Reggie White	Green Bay Packers	6.05	300
average		6.05	281

Talented defensive ends typically possess several important characteristics, including the ability to move in an explosive manner, extraordinary upper body strength, and quickness. Collectively, these traits enable defensive ends to achieve their primary purpose on the field—put pressure on the quarterback.

In order to be a good pass rusher, a defensive end must have the ability to cover ground quickly in three to five yards of space. He must have the quickness to get his shoulder past the shoulder of the offensive tackle.

Upper body strength is also an important factor for a defensive end. Such strength enables him to execute any one of a number of counter-moves when an offensive blocker reacts to the defensive end's initial moves. For example, a defensive end starts the play by taking a step in one direction and when the offensive blocker makes an appropriate response to that particular move, the defensive end (if he is quick enough) can arm over him or slug past him and come underneath him.

It is imperative that a defensive end does not allow himself to be turned out (i.e., turned to the outside, away from the play) on a consistent basis. He must have enough girth and skill to avoid being knocked off-balance and being turned out. If he does not, he will not be able to recover back inside to defend against running plays when they come his way.

The application of upper body strength in the play of a defensive end is somewhat different than in the play of a defensive tackle. While a defensive tackle comes into immediate contact with a blocker on the snap of the ball, a defensive end usually doesn't make contact with a blocker (i.e., the offensive tackle) until after the defensive end has determined the tactical situation, or after he has set up the blocker. A defensive tackle tends to rely on brute force, while a defensive end uses his hands and skills to get past a blocker.

Similar to the more talented defensive tackles, some defensive ends also have the ability to force the man blocking them back into the quarterback. This ability makes a defensive end just as effective (and perhaps even more so) as a defensive player who sacks the passer once or twice a game. A quarterback who has to avoid one of his own men being pushed into his pathway will have his rhythm broken.

In my career with the 49ers, we had several great defensive ends, including Fred Dean, Dwaine Board, Kevin Fagan and Charles Haley. As battering pass rushers, they were extraordinarily talented.

Gifted pass rushers are a critical element in building a championship-caliber team. You must have a *great* (not just a solid or a better than average) pass rush. To win an NFL championship, one or both of your defensive ends must be the best in the League at their position.

OUTSIDE LINEBACKERS

Ideal size: 6-3, 245

1997 NFC Pro Bowlers	Team	Ht	Wt
Kevin Greene	Carolina Panthers	6.03	247
Ken Harvey	Washington Redskins	6.02	245
Lamar Lathon	Carolina Panthers	6.03	260
average		6.03	251

Several types of outside linebackers exist in the NFL. In general, these types can be grouped into two categories—weak (side) outside linebackers and strong (side) outside linebackers.

The weak side category is further broken into two additional sub-groupings—the pass rusher linebacker and the pursuit-coverage linebacker. Very few linebackers are effective at both roles (Lawrence Taylor of the New York Giants and Derrick Thomas of the Kansas City Chiefs are two of the limited number of players who have such all-around skills).

The pass-rush type of weak side outside linebacker has taken the place of the defensive end in the 3-4 defensive scheme. Although many teams have shied away from using the 3-4 defense in the past few years, it is important to remember that the popularity of a particular defensive scheme tends to be cyclical (more often than not, a team's regard for a defense is directly related to the skills and capabilities of the personnel on the team).

In a 3-4 defense, the pass-rush type of weak side outside linebacker can go all-out on the pass rush because he has inside help right next to him. As a result, he can use his quickness to work that much harder at beating the offensive tackle at the line of scrimmage.

The pass-rush type of weak side outside linebacker is a pass rusher first and then a run defender. In some instances, he has a role in coverage situations as a game drop defender. He rarely is asked to help provide man-to-man coverage. He must have the size, foot speed, and quickness necessary to rush the passer. In that regard, he can "sell out" as long as he coordinates his efforts with the defensive end on his side.

In addition to having quickness, pass-rushing weak side outside linebackers should possess natural instincts for handling offensive tackles who may be up to 100 pounds heavier. For example, they must know how to use leverage, how to get underneath the larger man's pads, and how to work back toward the quickness. They must also be strong enough to bounce off attempted blocks and still make the play.

The other type of weak side outside linebacker requires a combination of the skills needed to employ lateral pursuit against running plays and to provide man-to-man or zone pass coverage. An athlete who is highly proficient at both pass coverage and pursuit should play this position.

Because he plays on the weak side and is not primarily a pass rusher, he must be able to function in the open space. On the other hand, he must have enough strength to avoid being knocked around by blockers when he pursues a ball carrier (i.e., he goes across the face of an offensive lineman to get to the ball).

The second general category of outside linebackers is the strong side linebacker. Aligned opposite the tight end, the strong side linebacker should be stronger and larger (approximately 6-4, 250) than the weak side linebacker. He typically plays on the side of the tight end. His primary responsibility is to hold the edge of the defense.

Playing the position of strong side linebacker requires specific skills and abilities. He must have the strength, the hands, and the range to hold up the tight end and to get through the fullback (or whoever is blocking) to make contact with the ball carrier. He must be able to meet the off-tackle play of either the fullback or the pulling guard. He should be able to blitz effectively against an attempt by a running back to pass block him.

The strong side linebacker position is not as common as it once was. Many NFL teams have revised their defensive alignments by shifting the line so that a defensive lineman is positioned over the tight end. The strong side linebacker is then stacked behind the defensive lineman.

All factors considered, however, the same type of athlete (stronger, bigger) is still required to play strong side linebacker. The primary change in this regard is that when the strong side linebacker is stacked (and protected) behind a defensive lineman, he is assigned important coverage responsibilities. Previously, the strong side linebacker did not have a key coverage role.

Even with the philosophical changes that have occurred in recent years, teams still flop their outside linebackers. According to the defensive situation, they have a pursuit linebacker and a run-defender linebacker.

Any discussion of great outside linebackers tends to include mention of extraordinarily talented players like Lawrence Taylor, Jack Ham and Bobby Bell. The 49ers also had several very good outside linebackers, including Willie Harper and Dan Bunz.

During my time with San Francisco, however, the best player we had at this position was Keena Turner. He was the ultimate athlete at outside linebacker. Possessing remarkable all-around skills and abilities, at 6'3" and 220 lbs, he could cover, pass rush, meet blockers and pursue and was a great open-field tackler.

At Stanford, I had the opportunity to coach three very talented outside linebackers—Milt McColl, Ron George and Dave Garnett. Nicknamed "the Bird" because of his gangly frame, McColl did an outstanding job for the Cardinal. Drafted by San Francisco, McColl also played very well for the 49ers. McColl, who later became a physician, could rush the passer with great effect. At 6'6", he had great range and natural instincts.

George and Garnett (both of whom were 6'0", 215 lbs.) provided Stanford with the quickest outside linebacker combination in the country. Each was a very skilled player and a tireless worker, who played with great intensity.

INSIDE/MIDDLE LINEBACKER

Ideal size: 6-2 1/2, 250

1997 NFC Pro Bowlers	Team	Ht	Wt
Sam Mills	Carolina Panthers	5.09	232
Hardy Nickerson	Tampa Bay Bucs	6.02	229
average		5.11	231

An inside (middle) linebacker must have several qualities. It is very important that he is big enough and strong enough to meet blockers coming from any angle and to not be easily knocked from his position. He must be able to get off a block, shed the blocker, and then move to the ball, almost without wasting a step.

He cannot attempt to avoid a lot of blockers while going for the ballcarrier. If he does, he won't be able to do his job properly. If he goes around someone to avoid being blocked, he has, in effect, been blocked.

An inside linebacker must also have quickness. Quickness can help him get a "jump" on someone attempting to block him, by enabling him to meet (and shed) the blocker before the blocker was fully ready to engage him.

Instinct is another essential trait for an inside linebacker. An inside linebacker must be able to watch the ball to read the blocking. Instinct cannot be taught. Players who have it are those who almost always find a way to get to the ballcarrier and make the tackle.

An inside linebacker must also have a relatively indestructible body. Given the level of intense, aggressive contact that the position involves, it is not surprising that over the years, a number of NFL middle linebackers have suffered debilitating injuries. Such injuries not only prevent some athletes from being in the game when they're needed, they also diminish the effectiveness of those individuals who continue to play despite being injured.

An inside linebacker does not have to have great coverage skills. Teams have the option of designing their pass coverage around their middle linebackers. While it is desirable that an inside linebacker has the ability to help in coverage situations, he can be protected by a team's defensive scheme if he does not.

If the middle linebacker is a great natural pursuer and a clean tackler, is someone who can work right through pass blockers, and is able to move instantaneously when he makes his reads, then a team is usually willing to overlook (i.e., make concessions for) any limitations in his pass coverage skills. Such limitations are more than compensated for by such rare instincts. Possibly, the two greatest middle linebackers of all time were Dick Butkus of the Chicago Bears and Mike Curtis of the (then) Baltimore Colts.

The 49ers were blessed to have a prototype player like Jack Reynolds at the inside linebacker position. Possessing a powerful girth, he could stun a blocking lineman, pursue the ball and then make the tackle. He was a tireless competitor, with great stamina, and was a true student of the game, whose work ethic inspired his teammates.

Over the years, however, the requirements of the position have changed. Explosive, quick, ground-covering players have come to dominate the position. Given the pass-oriented offenses in the NFL in the 1990s, athletes with a fully dimensional game are best suited for inside linebacker (e.g., Mike Singletary, Chicago Bears; Junior Seau, San Diego Chargers; Hardy Nickerson, Tampa Bay Buccaneers; etc.).

CORNERBACK

Ideal size: 6-2, 195 (good ones, however, come in all sizes)

1997 NFC Pro Bowlers	Team	Ht	Wt
Eric Davis	Carolina Panthers	5.11	185
Deion Sanders	Dallas Cowboys	6.01	190
Aeneas Williams	Arizona Cardinals	5.10	190
average		5.11	188

Most teams tend to prefer a good-sized cornerback (to be better able to cover over-sized receivers). In reality, however, talented cornerbacks come in all sizes. Although some of the best coverage men in the NFL have been relatively small and have been dwarfed by some of the receivers they were asked to cover, they were still able to do their job because they had quickness, explosiveness, and the ability to anticipate.

Regardless of their size, great cornerbacks have the ability to play a physical game with receivers. They have the capability of bumping a receiver on his release from the line of scrimmage. More importantly, however, they have the ability to go up for a ball and not be overwhelmed or knocked off the pass by the receiver.

It is essential that a cornerback has both quickness and explosiveness. Both attributes are important, particularly in pass coverage situations. Ideally, a cornerback should be able to run 40 yards in under 4.5 seconds. While having sprint (track) speed is beneficial, a number of cornerbacks have played at a Pro Bowl-level of performance in the NFL over the years who lacked great straight-ahead speed. What they lacked in footspeed, they more than made up for in other traits.

Not only are talented cornerbacks highly effective in pass coverage situations, they are also very good against the run. As a general rule, cornerbacks serve a support role on running plays. They have the ability to take the ball carrier one-on-one after all of the blockers have committed themselves.

In a few instances, some cornerbacks also have the ability (and courage) to cut down an approaching pulling guard by going underneath him. The resulting pile-up of players obstructs the ball carrier who is following the guard.

Those cornerbacks who don't have extraordinary levels of quickness, explosiveness, and sense of anticipation can make adjustments in their game to compensate. For example, this type of cornerback can tighten up on the receiver he is covering and can be as physical as possible in order to inhibit the receiver's quickness. Such a cornerback is particularly suited for bump and run coverage (and somewhat less so for man-to-man coverage).

In addition to the physical qualities required to play cornerback, the cornerback must be emotionally resilient. He must be able to maintain his composure, even when he has allowed a pass to be completed in a critical situation or allowed a touchdown pass to be thrown to his man. He must have an inner confidence that enables him to continue to function at a high level of performance regardless of what has occurred in the game.

One of the primary reasons that the 49ers won five Super Bowls during a 14-year period was because of greatness at the cornerback position. Talented athletes like Ronnie Lott, Eric Wright, Don Griffin, Marquez Pope and Deion Sanders allowed San Francisco to use its full package defensive tools. For example, we could blitz; we could zone; and we could isolate individual receivers in a one-on-one coverage. As a result, our great pass rushers could unload on the rush.

Just as important, however, were the tackling skills of cornerbacks such as Lott and Wright. Their extraordinary skills enabled them to beat the blockers and stop the sweep. In recognition of the great talent in the 49ers' defensive backfield, all four of our starters were named to the Pro Bowl in 1985—the first and only time this has occurred in the history of the NFL.

SAFETIES

Ideal size: Weak: 6-2, 200

1997 Pro Bowlers	Team	Ht	Wt
Merton Hanks	San Francisco 49ers	6.02	185
Steve Atwater	Denver Broncos	6.03	217
average		6.03	201

Ideal size: Strong: 6-3, 215

1997 NFC Pro Bowlers	Team	Ht	Wt
LeRoy Butler	Green Bay Packers	6.00	200
Darren Woodson	Dallas Cowboys	6.01	216
average		6.01	208

Depending on the system that a team plays, a distinct difference can exist between the roles and responsibilities of a weak (free) safety and a strong safety. In some systems, however, no differences exist. In this situation, players are assigned dual responsibilities to play both positions according to the defensive formation called.

Most teams, if they had the right personnel, would prefer to have a strong safety who can provide run support and a weak safety who can cover ground, see the entire field, make a play on a ball thrown high in the air while moving to his left or his right, and make all of the audible calls for the secondary. Because more audibilizing frequently occurs in the secondary than on the line of scrimmage by the quarterback, the weak safety is often the most important field general in the game.

The talented free safety has the range of a center fielder in baseball, natural instincts, the skills to make the great catch and the ability to make the big hit. Typically, such a safety is relatively tall (i.e., 6-2 to 6-3) and weighs 190-200 pounds. He has excellent range and speed—much like a hurdler in track.

Because he has the speed and quickness to go for a ball and has excellent hands, he can be a major factor defensively from sideline to sideline. If he can cover ground in full stride to the extent that he can "work" either sideline when the ball is in the air, his potential value to the defense is immeasurable.

An all-pro weak safety is much like a star running back. He has the natural instincts to play the game. He is not easily fooled. He has the inherent ability to respond (in a non-verbal sense), react, and see the entire field.

An effective free safety also has the ability to make the big, pulverizing hit. He can meet the ball carrier in the hole and stop the play. He can finish off the ball carrier.

Historically, the strong safety is the run support player. Typically, he must have several of the traits found in a talented linebacker. He can hit and stop people, respond spontaneously to the play as it unfolds, and go to the ball. Often, he is fearless. If he isn't the type of player who will physically commit himself on every play, his team must undertake specific defensive adjustments.

The better his coverage skills, the more he can be lined up on any receiver. Occasionally, an NFL team will have a strong safety who is as big as a linebacker, yet possesses an extraordinary ability to cover all types of receivers.

Some teams employ a defensive system where both safeties play a two-deep coverage and only occasionally come out of the middle of the field to support the run. In this type of system, both safeties play the ball in the air, in the middle of the field, and on the sidelines. In this situation, the emphasis is then on the cornerbacks to be the support men.

Teams should keep in mind the various defensive philosophies when considering what types of cornerbacks and safeties they want to put together to form their defensive secondary. Obviously, their abilities should be complementary. They should also attempt to match their players to the system they want to employ. If their players don't suit their desired system exactly, teams should adjust their systems and assign their personnel accordingly.

With Carlton Williamson and Dwight Hicks at the safety position and Ronnie Lott and Eric Wright at the corners, the 49ers had a secondary unit comparable to the talented defensive backfield groups of the Raiders, Steelers and Dolphins during their dynasty years.

Hicks was a great leader and a smart, heads-up ball hawk. He directed the unit with great competence via audible adjustments and coverage calls.

Williamson, on the other hand, was an outstanding downfield hitter. He served as an exemplary support man, who often came up with critical interceptions.

Another very talented safety who played for the 49ers was Jeff Fuller. Fuller had everything—size (6'3", 220 lbs.), speed (4.5 in the 40-yd dash), agility and competitive intensity. He had a Hall-of-Fame future before being injured.

During the time I coached at Stanford, one of the best safeties I had the opportunity to work with was John Lynch, who is currently starting for the Tampa Bay Buccaneers. Lynch was a great hitter and an outstanding athlete. His hits on Jerome Bettis of Notre Dame were instrumental in our victory over the Fighting Irish.

This is what happens whenever people on a team decide not to trust: everyone will gear down their effort until they're doing just enough to get by. They want, subconsciously, to enroll everyone else in their cycle of disappointment.

Pat Riley
Head Baseketball Coach
Miami Heat
from *The Winner Within*

DETERMINING THE FUTURE DYNAMICS OF PLAYER PROFILES IN THE NFL

Over the years, the profile of the typical NFL player has changed dramatically. As physical training methods have improved, as individuals have been more knowledgeable about how to properly take care of themselves, and as each succeeding generation has generally grown in size (i.e., taller and heavier), this profile has been affected accordingly. As such, the future dynamics of player profiles may be reflected in the following attributes and circumstances:

- Players will have more natural ability.
- Players will be bigger, faster, and stronger.
- Players will have a higher level of skills and techniques (many of which they will learn and master on their own).
- Players will receive better coaching on an individual basis, beginning in high school.

- Players' careers will last longer (i.e., more seasons).
- Players will be more durable.
- Sports medicine techniques and methods will continue to improve. As such, players will take advantage of these services, and their injuries will be treated more effectively.
- Sound nutrition will be even more important to a dedicated athlete.
- Teams will give even more latitude to individual athletes in decisions and tactics.
- Players will work together to an even greater degree to develop their skills and techniques. Players will attempt to emulate great performers even more than they have in the past.
- Teams will highlight individual players and their skills to an even greater degree.
- Teams will have even more gifted players—particularly at the skilled positions.

CHAPTER 7

ACQUIRING TALENTED PLAYERS

"When I was selected to lead the first mission I was responsible to name who would fly with me. Very simply, I picked the best flyers, men I could trust in the heat of deadly combat. This was serious. Rank, credentials, efficiency reports didn't mean a thing. It would be the guys who could fly and shoot."

—Admiral Jim Stockdale, U.S. Navy
Prisoner of War, 1965-73
Vietnam Conflict

Finding the winning edge...

It is always a combination of factors that add up to the right person. It's his level of natural ability. It's his competitive instincts. It's also the history of that athlete; his ability to learn, retain, and apply what he has learned; and his ability to work under stress with other people. Then you have to be able to project those qualities into the slot or role that athlete would play for your team.

—Bill Walsh, "To Build a Winning Team," *Harvard Business Review*, January-February 1993.

The most surprising and unexpected trade that occurred while I was with the 49ers was the acquisition of Wendell Tyler of the Los Angeles Rams. Los Angeles was looking for a smooth transition to Eric Dickerson. San Francisco had replaced the Rams as the top team in the division and Los Angeles wanted to make changes quickly.

Many organizations are encumbered with a committee-type decision-making process and are unable to move quickly, especially if questions exist about a player, but our structure made it possible for us to act quickly. Los Angeles called John McVay, the 49ers' general manager whose duties included serving as the contact man for other teams in the League. McVay and I moved quickly and decided to acquire Tyler. The trade was extraordinarily advantageous to San Francisco. Tyler was one of the quickest, most explosive running backs in the League, and paired with Roger Craig, he gave us a great combination that led the way to our championship in 1984.

Our strategies were successful because of our smooth, professional approach. McVay was non-confrontational and nonabrasive. He did not attempt to upstage the other person.

When acquiring players, an organization must be decisive. In my case, I had authority to make decisions and the full confidence of Eddie DeBartolo. This trade was the last step that made us one of the four or five greatest NFL teams of all time.

Another important trade was the trade for Fred Dean. At the time, he was considered the best pass rusher in all of football and was the mainstay of the San Diego Chargers' defensive unit. He was difficult to communicate with, however, and had acquired an agent with whom it was difficult to negotiate.

Dean was under contract but was also underpaid. His agent hammered San Diego owner Gene Klein to renegotiate his contract. Gene was a tough owner who believed that "a deal was a deal," and instead of renegotiating, he decided that Dean could be traded.

His agent wanted a new contract before the trade occurred. Because San Francisco could meet this requirement and Eddie DeBartolo was determined to improve the team, the decision was made that Dean was worth the money.

I was playing tennis when I received the call about the proposed trade: we would give San Diego our second round draft pick and switch first round picks. In the process, we acquired a premier player who could change the team's fortunes. In fact, San Francisco reached the Super Bowl that year, and the loss of Dean may have kept the Chargers out of the championship.

In this instance, an owner compromised his team's talent for a higher principle: he refused to be outmaneuvered by a player. While I strongly believe that an organization must adhere to its fundamental values and moral order, I also feel that at some point an organization should weight the importance of each possible decision against the "big picture."

A third key acquisition was that of Jack "Hacksaw" Reynolds in early 1981. The Los Angeles Rams had an outstanding team organized and put together by Don Klosterman, one of the game's brilliant administrators. Don had a unique ability to identify athletes, negotiate with other clubs and get what he needed.

The Rams released Reynolds because he was highly paid and they had someone to replace him. The release came as a surprise because many teams would have traded for Reynolds, but it meant that he was able to select where he played next. The herd mentality in the NFL was such that many teams felt if Klosterman released someone, that player was of dubious value.

At the time, San Francisco needed mature leadership. We admired Reynolds' dedication to the game, and our defensive unit needed someone who would assume a leadership role, so we began competing with other teams for his services. Fortunately, the 49ers organization was structured in such a way that a critical decision could be made relatively quickly without the problems of decision-making by committee.

Reynolds was impressed by our offense, which was only a few key players away from success. I pointed out to him that his leadership could turn the team around, and that Chuck Studley, our defensive coordinator, was extremely enthusiastic about his experience and ability.

Reynolds exceeded all of our expectations. In addition to being a great player, he established a work ethic and true commitment throughout the team. His attention to detail and his tedious study of his opponent created an atmosphere in which the defensive unit thrived. Jack Reynolds is the "ultimate warrior."

The three primary methods for acquiring talented players are the NFL Draft, free agency, and trades. The more adept a team is at each of these three methods, the more likely it will have players who can make a meaningful difference in the team's performance.

If the competition has laptop computers and you're still using yellow legal pads, it won't matter how long and hard you work, they're going to pass you by.

> Bill Parcells
> Head Football Coach
> New York Jets
> from *Finding a Way to Win*

THE NFL DRAFT

Once a year in April, the National Football League draft is conducted in a hotel ballroom in mid-town New York City. The process involves seven rounds, held over a two-day period. Provided a team has not gained or lost draft choices through trades, each team has one selection per round. Every round, all teams select in inverse order to their win-loss record the previous season. Each team then selects a player from the available pool of players who are eligible for the draft when its turn to choose comes up.

In recent years, the drafting process has changed dramatically. The advent of several factors, including the salary cap, free agency, and a major reduction in the number of rounds (seven) in the draft, has created an environment where little allowance exists for a team to consider taking chances, to undertake gambles, or to put up with "projects."

The changed nature of the NFL draft in the 1990s is illustrated by the comments of Bill Polian, the highly regarded general manager for the Carolina Panthers, who observed: "At this stage of free agency, teams have spent themselves to the very edge of the limit. From now on, going into the draft you'll have to look at where each team stands in relation to the cap, which ones will spend the $6 million bonus on a top draft choice and which ones will trade out or down in the top rounds."

Polian goes on to point out, "I count four things that go into the trade-down mentality: One, the first guy drafted probably will hold out, which means he won't be able to help you right away. Two, people want to draft more for need now than with the old best-available-athlete outlook. Three, you're going to have a player for a limited number of seasons, and then you'll lose him (to free agency). Finally, you can pick up a veteran and plug him into a spot, and he'll be a lot cheaper than a top draft pick."

Given the divergent factors affecting the NFL draft, it would not be impossible to envision a draft in which players such as Joe Montana and Dwight Clark (both of whom were drafted by and went on to star for the San Francisco 49ers) might not be considered. At the time, Montana (who was taken in the third round of the 1979 draft) had not established himself as a consistent starter in college (Notre Dame).

In a similar vein, Clark was considered far too slow for the NFL. Although he had good size at 6-4, 215, Clark had caught only 12 passes in his senior year at Clemson. As a result, he was a virtual unknown, who was taken as somewhat of a "gamble"—also in the 1979 draft.

History shows that both players were extraordinary selections. Montana became a Hall-of-Fame player, who is widely considered one of the best quarterbacks in the history of the NFL. Clark went on to set receiving records with the 49ers and was named *Sports Illustrated's* NFL Player of the Year in 1982 when he made one of pro football's most memorable plays, which will be forever known as "The Catch."

The seemingly absurd scenario where Montana and Clark would not be drafted shows how demanding the requirements can be for NFL draft prospects. Teams must identify and draft players who can contribute immediately and quickly, and can fulfill a solid role on the field.

This factor is important for both the player and the team because in approximately four or five years, that player will be eligible for free agency. If questions concerning the ability of a particular player to make a substantial contribution to the team still exist after the player's initial contract expires, the whole free agency issue becomes even more difficult for the team to evaluate.

For the most part, teams can't afford to take a chance on a draft prospect who might otherwise be considered a "project." Given an environment where teams are expected to win sooner, rather than later (i.e., as reflected by the fact that eleven NFL teams had new coaches to start the 1997 season), most teams don't have the luxury of making a draft-day gamble, even on an intriguing prospect.

Because of free agency, the draft is no longer perceived by most teams as the primary means for stocking their rosters, particularly with the higher rounds. It is vital that the high draft picks be projected to play early in their careers.

Athletes who are not projected to be drafted in the higher rounds also have a certain degree of appeal to many teams. Not only can players drafted in the lower rounds have potential and abilities that, for whatever reason, have been heretofore unfulfilled, the viability of such players to a particular team can be enhanced because they have salaries that tend to be relatively stable (and more cap-friendly) from year-to-year.

Regardless of where he is drafted, a player entering the draft in the 1990s is expected to be further along in his skills, further along in the level of competition that he has faced, and further along physically. That additional maturity will be needed. In most instances, a draft prospect must be able to demonstrate that he already has the natural instincts and abilities necessary to play in the NFL. Upon joining a team, he's expected to have some degree of specialized skills that can be of immediate value. If he doesn't, his chances of making the squad are greatly diminished.

All factors considered, an individual selected in the draft is going to have a relatively short trial period to demonstrate that he should survive the final squad cut. At best, the August training camp and four-game pre-season schedule provide only a limited amount of time for an organization to make decisions regarding which players will make the team.

Players drafted in the lower rounds and individuals trying to make the team as undrafted prospects will have stiff competition in their efforts to be on the roster. At the start of the season, along with the team's high draft choices, their competition will come from aging veterans who may be willing to take a salary reduction to remain on the squad as backups and from adept journeymen who have learned over the years to adapt to their circumstances by identifying someplace where they fit in and, subsequently, moving from team to team.

Because teams, as a rule, don't have the latitude to consider young prospects as long-term projects (i.e., adopt an attitude that proclaims "ultimately, a young player will be better than an aging veteran or better than a journeyman who has played in the League for several years"), most prospects must overcome their competition almost immediately. Their ability to prevail will depend on several factors, including the level of coaching they received and the competition they faced at the collegiate level.

Free agency, the shortened draft, and the heightened urgency to win may affect the type of player selected and the ability of a particular player to make the team in other ways, including:

- Compared to the past, players from smaller colleges will be less likely to make NFL rosters. The shortened draft (seven rounds—down from its historical high of seventeen rounds) and the reduced number of players invited to training camp combine to increase the possibility that teams will overlook such players.

- The gravity of the situation facing small college players is illustrated by the fact that under the circumstances of the 1990s, small college players such as NFL greats Terry Bradshaw (Louisiana Tech), Ken Anderson (Augustana), and Jackie Smith (Northwestern State), may not have been drafted. The obstacles facing small college players may be even more acute for athletes from the predominately black colleges. Historically, black colleges have provided some of the most talented players in the NFL, including such Hall-of-Fame members as Willie Brown (Grambling), Art Shell (Maryland-Eastern Shore), and Willie Lanier (Morgan State).

- More will be expected from backup players. One of the basic elements of the NFL's labor agreement with the NFL Players Association involves a restriction on the size of a team's roster (i.e., the number of active duty and practice squad players a team is permitted to carry). A "limited" roster necessitates that a team must maximize its use of its personnel. As a result, backup players are expected to be able to contribute more than just serving on special teams. These players must be able to step in and play well in the event of an injury to a starter.

- The fact that drafted players cannot come in and work full-time with the team that drafted them until after the 1st of June will make the challenge of earning a roster spot even tougher, except for those athletes who have exceptional skills. Previously, drafted players had the option of spending their time working with their new team and fulfilling their school obligations as they saw fit. The change in rules that eliminated this critical learning period further encumbers a drafted player's ability to assimilate into the pro game.

- Depending upon the position they play, some players will have a better opportunity to overcome the draft-related limitations of the 1990s. For example, because receivers and defensive backs are able to demonstrate their skills in the open field, their potential to contribute can be more easily evaluated. By the nature of the position they play, they can be at least part-time players in their rookie season. For example, a newly drafted receiver may get the opportunity to play in situations that involve three or four receivers on the field at a time. Conversely, such situations may enable a rookie defensive back to get into the game as a fifth or sixth defensive back, in what are commonly referred to as nickel or dime defenses.

- Evaluating the potential of offensive and defensive linemen is a more difficult task. The primary problem involves the fact that what offensive and defensive linemen are required to do in college can often be quite different than what they will be expected to do in pro-style offenses and defenses. The difficulties are further compounded by the fact that the sense of urgency that demands that these players come in and be first-line backups (or starters in some cases) does not permit these players to have a couple of seasons to learn the nuances of how to play the pro game. As a result, an organization must be more astute and have a clearer insight into what it will take for an offensive or defensive lineman to step in and make a contribution to the team.

Identifying a "Good" Draft Choice

Deciding whether an individual is a "good" draft choice is a subjective matter. Different people use different criteria when addressing this issue.

For example, many sports writers tend to believe that if an individual is selected in the first or second round of the draft, then that athlete should meet Pro Bowl standards. In reality, such a perception is neither warranted nor reasonable.

Personally, I believe a more objective, realistic approach to assessing the value of a particular draft choice involves looking at his specific effect on the team. In that regard, if a drafted player contributes to the team in a measurable way for at least two years, he should be considered a "good" draft choice.

During the time I spent as the head coach of the 49ers, we drafted several players whom I considered to be "good" draft choices, including Jim Stuckey, Earl Cooper, Todd Shell, Dan Stubbs, Larry Roberts, and Craig Puki. Although these individuals were instrumental in the 49ers' three Super Bowl victories during the period, they were never Pro Bowl selections. These athletes were the "guts" of our teams, yet were never acknowledged by the media as meaningful draft choices.

Accordingly, the best approach for determining a "good" draft choice is not how the media rates a particular selection, but rather how well the athlete performs up to the standards of the organization. And yes, there were some draft choices who simply couldn't cut it as an NFL player. Thank goodness, there weren't too many— otherwise I wouldn't be writing this book.

Deciding When Enough is Enough

As the head coach, you should be aware of the fact on occasion you will select a talented player in the draft who just isn't able to do his job at an acceptable level in the game for whatever reason. The point to keep in mind is that no matter how long and hard you practice, no matter how thorough and detailed your teaching, if a player is dysfunctional during the game, it's a waste of everyone's time.

A player who simply can't compete or perform with poise (regardless of his physical skills and potential) will not only disappoint you, he can literally destroy everything everyone else is accomplishing. This situation is especially true at the quarterback position.

A recent event brought this point home vividly to me. A good friend of mine (one of the great coaches in the NFL) committed himself to a young quarterback who did not have the poise and competitive zeal to compete against top-level teams. The athlete possessed all of the physical tools to be outstanding, but when playing against top-flight opposition, he self destructed.

Upon accepting the duo-role position as head coach and general manager, my colleague "inherited" this young quarterback, who had failed to achieve the great things expected of him, despite his obviously high level of talent. Subsequently, in extreme confidence and to demonstrate good faith in this young man, my colleague publicly announced that this particular athlete would be his team's quarterback of the future.

Upon reviewing the situation, my friend decided that through good coaching, detailed attention to the proper techniques and a vocal demonstration of his support, he could mold this young quarterback into the accomplished performer that many individuals felt was the athlete's destiny.

Hundreds of hours were spent working with the player during the mini-camps and training camp. In turn, he had several very good performances in the team's preseason games. He continued to show promise as a performer in the first game of the regular season, although against a very weak opponent.

In the second game, however, his fortunes changed dramatically when he faced one of the top defenses in the NFL. The contest was a home game, against a traditional rival that had been badly weakened by injuries.

Everything was in place for a decisive victory—one that was expected to launch his team to a terrific season that would culminate in being in the playoffs for the first time in several years. Under the stress and demands of formidable competition, however, this quarterback failed miserably.

If some other quarterback, even an aging journeyman, had been given the opportunity to lead the team, my colleague would have received a better "return" on the investment . To me, the obvious point was that despite the fact that my friend is renowned as one of the finest coaches in the history of the game, he miscalculated miserably.

Not knowing when to conclude that "enough is enough" with a player on the team who is not performing at an acceptable level is a slow, but sure, road to catastrophe. If after a reasonable opportunity a player fails to meet your expectations, he must be replaced and released to try elsewhere.

Coaches are ultimately fired and franchises suffer a setback that may last for years if they are unable or unwilling (for whatever reason) to take such an action. You must keep in mind that functional instincts and competitive poise must be present for a player to be of value. Neither element can be fabricated.

The critic is one who knows the price of everything and the value of nothing.

Oscar Wilde
Author and Playwright

FREE AGENCY

Free agency is a process by which a player is eligible to sign with any team he wants after his contract has expired. An integral part of the NFL's agreement with the NFL Players Association, free agency is designed to provide players with the opportunity to market their abilities to the highest bidder.

In some instances, the free agency process has been very fruitful for both the free agent player and the team that acquired him. In many other cases, however, free agency has only served as a catalyst for teams to waste (valuable salary cap) money on over-priced veterans who are being paid more for their past performances than they are for a realistic assessment of their ability to contribute to their new teams in the future.

Several examples exist that show that free agency has worked in the way that it was intended. At a minimum, it has caused a substantial redistribution in player salaries; for example, money that previously might have been given to a veteran backup quarterback is now being paid to first-line offensive and defensive linemen.

Free agency has also helped several players gain a new lease on life and revitalize their careers by enabling them to go to a different team. In a similar vein, the free agency process has been of significant help to those NFL teams who have used it to acquire players who fulfilled a special need or to obtain veteran players who were available (for whatever reasons) at bargain basement (fixed cost) prices.

In reality, however, for every instance where the free agency process has worked for both the player and the team that acquired him, there have been many more cases where the process didn't work out (e.g., the player didn't fit in with his new team; the acquired free agent was unable to make the contribution expected of him; the player proved to be a major distraction; relatively speaking, the "cap" funds given to a particular player could have been better spent; etc.).

As a result, every NFL team must have a comprehensive and systematic plan for participating in the free agency process. An organization that is considering adding one or more free agent veterans to its team must address at least two key issues: first, "Will a particular free agent fit the dynamics of the team?" and, second, "How can the team identify such a free agent?"

Several factors are involved when deciding whether a particular free agent will be suitable to the dynamics of a team. For example, will the player fit into the offensive/defensive scheme of the team and what role will the prospective signee play? Are his style of play, his skills, and his personality in accord with the needs of the team? Will he be able to make a meaningful contribution to his new club?

Teams acquiring free agents should realize that veteran players who have been in the league for a number of years (i.e., six or more) will probably not experience any dramatic changes in the way they play the game, their skills, or their performance level—even with intense coaching. As such, a team cannot realistically expect to rebuild or reinvent the "game" of a veteran player. While some adjustment in an athlete's "game" may be possible, the key for a team who acquires a veteran free agent is to identify those things that the athlete does best and take advantage of them.

On occasion, a younger free agent (i.e., a player who has been in the League less than five years) whose full playing potential has yet to be fulfilled or even recognized during his relatively brief NFL career will become a free agent. Such a player is often someone who is relatively unknown because he has been playing behind a well-known front-line player, or who is an individual who has been limited to playing strictly on special teams.

Regardless of a free agent's level of experience or notoriety, the head coach should establish realistic and well-defined expectations regarding how well the acquired player should perform. If an organization develops unrealistic performance standards for an acquired free agent, an atmosphere will be created where discord and disharmony will eventually occur between the team and the player. To preclude such a situation, the performance expectations for an acquired free agent must be based on the considered judgments and seasoned insights of an experienced staff.

As a general rule, most teams tend to set their expectations for such a player somewhere in the middle of a continuum that ranges from the minimum level of performance that would be reasonably expected of a particular free agent (i.e., the lower end of the continuum) to the level of performance that might result from a player's overly generous infusion of optimism that arises from being in a new working environment (i.e., the higher boundary of the continuum). More often than not, the lower range of the continuum provides a more realistic benchmark for establishing expectations for a free agent.

As a member of the team's top management, it is reasonable for you to expect that a veteran free agent who signs a sizable contract will have something to prove and, within a reasonable period of time, will set about learning the system of his new team. Such an understanding should be established before the contract is signed. Nothing should be taken for granted, however.

Every free agent your team signs must be placed in an intense indoctrination program, regardless of how many years he has played in the League. This program should address several factors, including a schedule of required sessions for conditioning, skill development, and a thorough introduction to the system your team employs. A rigorous timetable for him to study, train, and work out over the course of the entire off-season should be established.

Your team should be on alert and cautious about a free agent who has a history of a poor work ethic. For example, if a player has previously exhibited a behavior pattern of missing required workouts, it would not be all that surprising if his lack of self-discipline were to continue. Even if the coaching staff makes an extra effort (i.e., resources, attention, time, etc.) with that free agent, he may still revert to his old habits—even at the most critical times. All this must be taken into consideration before a team acquires a veteran player.

To a point, the team that acquires a free agent must demonstrate patience and be willing to initially accept the shortcomings of that player. Eventually, however, the team must make a concerted effort to get the acquired free agent to understand why his behavior must change. Although such an assignment may be somewhat of a challenge for you, it is a critical function that you must be willing to undertake in the NFL in the 1990s.

It is also important for you to make an acquired free agent understand that he may have a distinctively different role on his new team than he had on his previous team. The change in roles will impact most on those individuals who go from being a second-line player to being a starter or on those players who go from one system to a drastically different one.

Regardless of the number of years a player has spent in the League, the process of a free agent adapting to a new role will involve growing pains—particularly at the quarterback position. For example, learning a new system, developing a critical sense of timing with his receivers, getting a feel for the protection capabilities of his offensive line, and establishing a leadership role all take time for a quarterback. Accordingly, a step-by-step plan must be established that enables a quarterback to systematically meet the requirements of his new role.

Understanding what criteria a free agent must satisfy to ensure that he will be appropriate to the dynamics of a team is one thing; finding such a player is yet another critical issue that a team must address. As a general rule, the decision to attempt to acquire a free agent is typically based on several factors, including subjective evaluations of his skills and his potential to contribute to the team, his salary cap cost, etc. Most teams consider the opinions of their assistant coaches as the most reliable source for determining a free agent's potential value within a specific system. On occasion, however, such evaluations are made by the team's director of operations or by members of a team's scouting staff.

Coaches often have a unique and more inclusive insight into the "actual" value of a free agent. For example, by following an athlete's career through college and into the NFL, personnel staff members and coaches can develop an appreciation for the athlete over a "complete body" of work. After a team loses a player in the draft, that athlete may become available as a free agent any number of years later. (This factor illustrates another reason why coaches should be used in a team's evaluation process for the draft.) By the nature of their position, coaches may continue to "track" a player through the League that they initially became familiar with during the draft process. Subsequently, as a result of competing against that player and interacting with other coaches in the League, assistant coaches often possess the most reliable data base to use in the process of evaluating free agents.

Not only must a team identify free agents whom it wishes to pursue, it must also take steps to ensure that every free agent acquisition makes financial sense under the salary cap. An organization must avoid getting into an undue bidding war with other clubs over the services of a veteran player.

When another team escalates the price for a particular free agent, your team may get drawn into a situation where it spends more for the player than he is worth to your team. Your team must not let the evaluation process or the salary cap situation of another club dictate the value of a specific player to your team. To a point, your organization should establish a certain value (both monetary and practical) on the services of a free agent and abide by the financial guidelines which your team has set.

The only circumstances that would justify a team spending more on a particular free agent than its initial allotted budget are if a team feels its initial projections were too low or if a team deems that player to be worth the elevated price. More often than not, however, an organization that lets another team force it into extending its resources because the organization thinks the other club knows something about the free agent it doesn't is usually setting itself up for a major disappointment.

Another underlying premise to which a team participating in the free agency process must adhere is the old adage, "let the buyer beware." To that end, every prospective free agent acquisition must undergo a thorough medical exam. A sound medical appraisal will help a team address the issue of whether it is pursuing a "significant asset" or a player who will have constant medical problems. If such chronic problems exist, a team should not expect the athlete or his agent to reveal their presence.

As a rule, free agent players with chronic joint problems should undergo intense medical scrutiny. At the least, such problems should be accounted for fully. A team's medical staff should have input into the evaluation process for free agent players who have potentially debilitating medical conditions. If necessary, relevant accommodations can be established for a particular free agent prior to that player being signed (e.g., planned recovery time, reduced practice time, scheduled rehab sessions with the medical staff, etc.).

Teams should also be aware that some free agents may be available whose careers are on the decline. Such players have already had their "best" years, and may only have value as either spot players with greatly reduced roles or as temporary (i.e., one-year) stop-gap measures.

A veteran player may also come available as a free agent because of a set of circumstances unrelated to his performance on the field. An organization should caution itself about going after a free agent who seems "too good to be true." Chances are, he is. There may be underlying circumstances that the organization should, at the very least, be aware of that have contributed to the player's apparent "devaluation" on the free agent market. For example, a talented player may be a disruptive force in the locker room, may have a history of spousal abuse, may use drugs, may have an alcohol problem, etc.

While a new "lease on life" or being "reborn" is theoretically possible, it is foolish for a team to acquire a free agent whose circumstances are contemptible—regardless of how well he performs on the field. A team should evaluate every situation on a case-by-case basis and determine whether a free agent burdened by destructive circumstances could change and to what extent would such a change make the player an appropriate acquisition. A disagreeable finding in either instance should cause a team to divert its attention in the free agent market to other possible acquisitions.

TRADES

Many of the factors that are involved in the free agency process should be considered when making a trade. It is essential that a team must ensure that any player it is interested in obtaining in a trade must be compatible with the dynamics of the team.

A thorough evaluation of the skills and abilities of such a player should also be factored into any decision to trade for a particular player. Furthermore, the "price" of the player (i.e., players, draft choices, money, etc.) must be appropriate to the team's short-term and long-term goals and plans and must fit within a team's salary cap circumstances.

It is essential that every organization has a system in place for tracking the players on other NFL rosters. If the situation warrants it, a team must be prepared to make a trade on relatively short notice that is in its best interests. For example, during the season, a team may lose a key player to injury who can best be replaced through a trade. Another scenario may involve a situation where, for one reason or another, another team wants to get "rid of" a player your team covets.

An organization which has a knowledgeable general manager or a director of operations who is well respected and gets along well with his counterparts on other teams has a distinct advantage when making trades. The San Francisco 49ers were particularly fortunate to have the astute John McVay in this role for a number of years.

All factors considered, the period of significant player trades in the NFL has passed because of free agency. In the history of the game, one general manager stands out as being perhaps the best person ever at making trades—Don Klosterman with the then-Los Angeles Rams.

Table 7-1 provides an overview of the major trades that Don was able to complete in just a six-year period. Because of Don's efforts, the Rams were able to continuously stockpile draft choices and then turn some of those choices into outstanding players (acquired through the draft). Eventually, some of those players were subsequently traded for more draft choices, and the cycle continued.

Of course, the most unbelievable trade in the history of the NFL occurred when General Manager Mike Lynn gave up much of his Minnesota Vikings team for Herschel Walker. In the process, he devastated the future of the Vikings franchise and almost single handedly gave the Dallas Cowboys the players and draft choices they needed to become world champions.

THE TWENTY PERCENT FAILURE FACTOR

If a personnel department is doing an outstanding job of evaluating and acquiring talent through the draft and free agency, its failure rate (i.e., the number of players who don't "pan out" for whatever reason) can be expected to be around twenty percent. In other words, regardless of how capable and efficient your scouts and coaches are in identifying, researching and projecting the potential value of a particular player, a fall out of approximately twenty percent will occur.

Over the years, every team in the NFL has experienced some degree of disappointment in its acquisitions. Top draft choices have turned out to be "busts," and expensive free agent signings have not lived up to their expectations.

The point to be emphasized is that no matter how much time and effort a team puts into the acquisitions process (i.e., no matter how thoroughly a team "studies" a given athlete), some miscalculations will happen. The process simply involves too many variables to be able to accurately account for every factor.

On the other hand, if the percentage of a team's acquisitions failures climbs to over twenty percent, then shortcomings exist in the team's system of evaluating and acquiring players. If disappointment after disappointment occurs, they can't all be related to "bad luck."

All factors considered, a failure rate of approximately twenty percent in this regard is about all a franchise can absorb and continue to be competitive. Capable, experienced management will have a firm grasp of this reality.

Table 7-1. An example of major trades completed by Don Klosterman of the Los Angeles Rams during the period 1973-78.

June 8, 1973: Rams trade quarterback Roman Gabriel to Philadelphia for WR Harold Jackson, RB Tony Baker, the Eagles' first-round selection in 1974 and the Eagles' first-and third-round selections in 1975.

Choice	Rams Selected
Eagles 1st 1974:	John Cappelletti RB Penn State (#11)
Eagles 1st 1975:	Dennis Harrah T Miami (#11)
Eagles 3rd 1975:	Dan Nugent G Auburn (#67)

October 22, 1974: Rams trade quarterback John Hadl to Green Bay for the Packers' first-round selection in 1975, Baltimore's second-round selection in 1975, the Packers' third-round selection in 1975, and the Packers' first- and second-round selections in 1976.

Choice	Rams Selected
Packers 1st 1975:	Mike Fanning DT Notre Dame (#9)
Colts 2nd 1975:	Monte Jackson DB San Diego State (#28)
Packers 3rd 1975:*	Geoff Reece C Washington State (#61)
Packers 1st 1976:	Compensation for signing WR Ron Jessie
Packers 2nd 1976:	Pat Thomas DB Texas A&M (#39)

August 22, 1978: Rams trade defensive back Monte Jackson to Oakland for the Raiders' first-round selection in 1979, third-round selection in 1980, and second-round selection in 1981.

Choice	Rams Selected
Raiders 1st 1979:	George Andrews LB Nebraska (#19)
Raiders 3rd 1980:	LeRoy Irvin DB Kansas (#70)
Raiders 2nd 1981:	Traded Miami LB Bob Brudzinski for the Dolphins' second- and third-round selections in 1981 and Tampa Bay's second-round selection in 1982 (4/28/81).

* '76 Traded Reece and swapped 2nd's with Seattle to get Nolan Cromwell.

A player who fails to perform at an acceptable level, after being given a reasonable opportunity to establish himself, must be moved on (i.e., released, traded, etc.). On occasion, you will have an athlete who will fall short of expectations, but may still be of some value to the team.

This player may be an athlete who can contribute to some degree in a meaningful way to the team, yet—all factors considered—be overpaid for the role he's fulfilling. Logically, he will be criticized by the media.

The point to remember, however, is that if this player can help the team and is not a major distraction, then it is the responsibility of the coaching staff to assimilate that player into the squad and to take advantage of his skills and abilities (however limited they may be).

A potentially serious problem in the acquisition system can occur when someone integrally involved in the process (e.g., a scout, a coach, the DPP, even the president of the organization) refuses to come to terms with the fact that his/her decision had to be mistaken with regard to acquiring a particular player. In this regard, the ego factor, or even internal competition over talent decisions, can be a very difficult obstacle when trying to make a considered decision whether to retain a specific player.

On occasion, a few individuals will refuse to admit (concede) that they made a mistake in their evaluations of a given athlete. More often than not, these people will try to place blame for the player's failure to perform as expected on some other factor (e.g., poor coaching, a change in the system or style of play, minor injuries suffered by the athlete, etc.).

As such, the individual within the organization who makes the final decision on personnel matters involving the team must account for the "failure factor" and, with some patience and thorough deliberation, must determine whether the athlete is "going to make it." Once a decision is made that a player is not worth retaining, you must not look back. Such decisions are simply part of the game.

DETERMINING THE FUTURE DYNAMICS OF PLAYER ACQUISITIONS

In the future, the process of determining which players to retain and which athletes to acquire for a team will continue to be substantially affected by such factors as the salary cap, higher salaries, free agency, etc. As such, the make-up of the roster of NFL teams will be affected by several of the changing circumstances that must be considered when acquiring players, including:

- More player movement (team to team) will occur.
- Because of the salary cap, more contracts will be renegotiated.
- Teams will have less depth because of the salary cap.
- Because of the constant level of player movement (resulting in new players on the roster), more teaching will be done in mini-camps.
- Teams will devote more time and energy to team play in their training camps in order to develop cohesiveness with new players that have either been signed since last season or have been elevated to starting roles within the squad.
- More emphasis will be placed on evaluating new players (their skills and particular talents) and on determining how they would be most effective.
- More older players will remain in the game, but at reduced salaries as back-ups.
- First-year players will be expected to play a more active role on the team immediately.
- The degree to which a team will be able to expand either its offensive or its defensive system will be limited annually by the level of the squad's development.

- Spontaneous changes will occur in team personnel. The coaching staff must have patience and must exhibit flexibility when dealing with the rather shocking loss of front-line players.

- As a team begins to experience a losing season, soon-to-be free agents may lose their intensity to compete (particularly once their teams are out of the playoff picture).

- Because of free agency, a team's win-loss record will tend to gravitate toward the middle (i.e., an 8-8 record). As a consequence, a team must be aware that it needs to generate momentum in its last four games.

- Player character will become extremely important, especially at the lower end of the roster. Although players in this situation are paid dramatically lower salaries than their teammates, they may, on occasion, be starting because of injuries. It is important that they sustain their intensity and their efforts in the later stages of the season.

- Teams will have a significant number of free agents who remain on the squad for only a brief period of time (i.e., one or two years). For example, a team signs a 32-year old offensive lineman to a four-year contract. In his first year, he starts and plays well, but begins to exhibit some evidence of declining skills. He continues to start in his second year, but performs only at an adequate level. At that point, the team must consider moving him.

CHAPTER 8

DEVELOPING PLAYERS

"Football is like life—it requires perseverance, self-denial, hard work, sacrifice, dedication, and respect for authority."

—Vince Lombardi
Hall-of-Fame Football Coach
Green Bay Packers

Finding the winning edge...

To keep people focused when the company anthem doesn't inspire them anymore, narrow the focus of loyalty. Military leaders have long known that the smaller the unit, the easier it is to feel allegiance to it; the regiment, the platoon, even the squad, can arouse deeper fidelity than more abstract concepts like cause and country. Just the goal itself may be enough. Give people the chance to win a championship or design the widget that changes the world, and you'll get all the loyalty you need.

Getting people to "give a damn" means harnessing their concern about the future to your advantage. The promise of the workplace is no longer the testimonial dinner and the plaque, but the chance to improve skills and become more valuable in the marketplace. I've coached short-term players who knew they were going to be around only one or two seasons. But they realized they had an opportunity to leave the team better players than when they arrived and made real contributions.

—Bill Walsh, "Insecurity Complex: Managers Must Figure Out New Ways to Generate Staff Loyalty When Pink Slips are in the Air," *Forbes*, April 8, 1996.

The need for organizations to have a process and procedure in place that ensure that the skills and talents of each member of the organization are refined and utilized in an appropriate way has been demonstrated to me several times over the years. For example, when I arrived at Stanford in 1977, the quarterback at the time was a young man named Guy Benjamin. Guy had been portrayed as a very undisciplined, scrambling quarterback who depended completely on his innate passing abilities.

When I arrived, I began teaching my system of football, the "West Coast Offense." I paid particular attention to Guy's footwork, mechanics and techniques. Throughout spring practice, I gave him drills to work on his techniques and concentrated on making him be concerned about fundamentals. Guy was a Stanford-type student. He picked things up quickly and appreciated the extra attention I gave him.

I wanted the receivers to run their patterns properly and Guy to time out on every pass he threw. He made progress throughout spring practice. Even though he went to his outlet receiver too early, he was learning to go through the proper sequence (primary, alternate, secondary) and use the proper footwork. We also developed a receiver battery of Bill Kellar and James Lofton.

As the season began we played number one-ranked Colorado in Boulder. Although we lost 27-21, we were on our way to a very respectable season. We capped the year with a 24-14 victory over LSU. Guy improved so much that he led the NCAA in passing and at the end of the season was named a consensus All-American. James Lofton, who had previously been ignored, was given the opportunity to play and became an All-American and, eventually, an NFL Hall-of-Famer.

While Guy was receiving personal attention from Rod Dowhower and me, Steve Dils, the back-up quarterback, was learning by osmosis. Just prior to the UCLA game, Guy was injured. In his first game, Steve led Stanford to a 31-29 victory over UCLA.

As a coach, I had to understand the skills that were required in my system of football and then develop a method for teaching those skills that would help the athlete develop to his full potential. In 1978, Steve led the NCAA in passing, making the most of his opportunities to first learn from Guy and then take over the team himself. Steve's season was capped by a come-from-behind bowl victory over Georgia. Steve played several years in the NFL. Guy became a back-up to Joe Montana during San Francisco's Super Bowl years. Guy, Steve, and Turk Schonert learned from the opportunity to play a complete system of football.

A team should do everything possible to ensure that the skills and talents of each player on its roster are developed, refined, and utilized in an appropriate way. A team's players are obviously the core building blocks (i.e., human capital) for a successful organization. One of the best investments a team can make in those "building blocks" is to establish a systematic plan to train and develop its players to their fullest potential.

The essence of such a plan is to create an environment where meaningful learning can occur. Several steps can be taken to facilitate learning, including ensuring that all players receive hands-on instruction designed to develop their skills and techniques. Such instruction should be provided on a regular basis by members of the coaching staff.

Steps should be undertaken periodically to follow-up on all instructional efforts. The progress of each player should be measured. All instructive procedures and programs should be reevaluated and changed, as appropriate. Constructive feedback and encouragement should be provided to each player.

A team must have a strategy for providing systematic training and development for its players. The factors affecting such a strategy will be different for draft choices than for veteran players.

There is no greater waste of a resource than that of unrealized talent.

Theodore Roosevelt
26th President of the United States

DEVELOPING DRAFT CHOICES

Although organizations need first-year players (particularly high draft choices) to contribute to their team's success, in most instances, first-year players encounter too many obstacles which must be overcome for them to make a significant contribution. Several factors can influence the degree to which a player has a limited role in his first year on the team, including his lack of physical maturity, whether he is prone to injuries, the fact that he may be in a survival mode in training camp, his possible lack of focus, the lack of attention he will receive in training camp, and the major changes in his lifestyle.

As the head coach, it is important that you consider the fact that most first-year players are still maturing physically. Such a point may be somewhat difficult to grasp when the player "under the team's microscope" is a twenty-one or twenty-two year old athlete with a highly muscular body and a reputation for being a "physical" player.

In reality, even if a first-year player is considered to be the prototype physical specimen, that athlete may have difficulty adapting to the physical demands of the month-long training camp and the upcoming extended season (i.e., twenty games over the course of the preseason and the regular season—even more if his team is involved in post-season play). The lack of physical maturity is even more likely to be a problem for those underclassmen who enter the draft.

The fact that a first-year player may not have the physical maturity of a veteran can lead to several possible problems. For example, all factors considered, a first-year player is more likely to suffer a muscle pull than a veteran player. Many players participating in their first training camp tend to expend more energy than is necessary, while they learn what being a professional football player involves. In addition, these players often do not have a complete appreciation for the value of using the team's athletic training staff over the course of a long, arduous season—the way that veteran players do.

The coaching staff can take several steps to lessen the possible problems that may arise from a lack of physical maturity in its newly signed draft choices. At the least, every rookie player must be made aware of the resources the team has available to assist his development and to ensure the well-being of every member of the team. Such resources include the team's physical conditioning staff, the team's medical staff (i.e., the team physician, orthopedists, athletic trainers, etc.), the training facilities, and a coaching staff capable and willing to provide advice, insights, and instruction as needed.

Upon signing, first-year players must also be required to participate in a regularly scheduled, individualized physical development program. Such a program should be prescribed and closely supervised by the team's physical conditioning staff. The prescription for each individual should be based on a comprehensive assessment of that player's physical abilities and motor skills.

Another issue that may affect a first-year player is the fact that during training camp, such a player often feels like he is in somewhat of a survival mode. This attitude may limit his focus to a point where he just concentrates on getting through each "new" task (e.g., reporting to camp, getting past the first preseason game, dealing with the substantial increase in media attention he receives, etc.). His resulting mental reference point may also limit his ability to concentrate well in team meetings. As a consequence, he may occasionally seem to be somewhat confused or appear to be unable to grasp and retain essential material.

The development of first-year players is also affected by the fact that they normally receive much more individual attention during mini-camps[1] than they do during training camp. One of the major focal points of mini-camps is to provide an environment where the coaching staff can address the inexperience and the lack of preparation of the team's first-year players. All factors considered, the coaching staff has relatively low expectations for the performance of first-year players in mini-camps. Whatever opinions the staff has in this environment are often based solely on the athletic ability of each player.

In contrast, the primary focus at training camp is to prepare the entire team for the upcoming season. With the preseason and the first game of the regular season rapidly approaching, the patience and tolerance of the coaching staff for the typical mistakes and learning difficulties of first-year players are diminished.

In fact, the performance of a first-year player may be a disappointment to the coaching staff for some time—possibly for the entire season. Eventually, a rookie player may lose his poise and his ability to focus in some competitive situations. At some point, he may even appear to have forgotten everything he has supposedly learned.

Another significant factor that can affect the development of first-year players is the overwhelming change that typically occurs in their personal lives. For example, if an athlete is a high draft choice, he probably will have more money than at any time in his life. Possibly for the first time in his life, he will be living on his own, in an environment drastically different from the one he lived in during his college days.

An athlete's new environment may expose him to a variety of "characters" and circumstances of dubious value. In an unfortunate number of situations, a first-year player will attract an array of "predators" who are drawn to him by his newly acquired affluence and his celebrity "status" as a pro football player. The "baggage" that these predators bring to their relationship with rookies often involves drugs, excessive alcohol consumption, attempts to financially defraud their new-found "friends," etc.

As a consequence, it is important that each team take systematic steps to acclimate its rookie players to the NFL. Every player should be thoroughly counseled on financial matters (i.e., how to manage money, how to choose a financial advisor, etc.), behavior matters (i.e., off-the-field comportment, avoiding individuals of low character, etc.), and the dangers of substance abuse (i.e., drugs, alcohol, steroids, etc.).

One of the most positive factors for a player in his first year in the NFL occurs when the team establishes a specific role for him on the team. By earning an active role on the field as a pass-rush specialist, a special teams player, or an extra receiver in a 3-or-4-receiver formation, a first-year player gains a measure of self-respect because his contribution to the team has been "isolated."

By establishing his role on the team and taking pride in the fact that he is contributing in a tangible way, a rookie can achieve a sense of control in his professional life. Not only is he able to earn his "keep," he also is able to acquire the acceptance of his teammates.

In reality, it is unrealistic for a team to expect a first-year player to experience much improvement as a result of practice during his rookie season. The only area in which substantial development will occur is in the skills the athlete needs to fulfill his specific role on the team.

Too much is happening during the regular season for coaches or his teammates to give much detailed coaching to a second-line back-up player. A first-year player who is not ready to be thrust into a starting position may only have a minimal sense of "urgency" to learn. As a result, his skills and level of preparedness may actually erode over the course of the season. Consequently, most of the development of first-year players occurs in training camp and the subsequent off-season.

On every team, there is a core group that sets the tone for everyone else. If the tone is positive, you have half the battle won. If it is negative, you are beaten before you ever walk on the field.

Chuck Noll
Hall-of-Fame Football Coach
Pittsburgh Steelers
from *Game Plans for Success*

COMING OF AGE AS A PROFESSIONAL

The second year of training camp is a much more realistic measuring stick for evaluating the development and the abilities of most NFL players. By this point in their careers, these athletes should have a relatively clear understanding of the sequencing of practicing, what is expected of them during practice, and what is involved in playing in the NFL.

Several factors can contribute to such an understanding. For example, between the end of his first season in the NFL and the start of his second training camp, every player undergoes an intense off-season program of teaching and training. This program is designed to provide each player with a thorough understanding of the team's system and the skills required of him to perform his job effectively within that system.

Players are also changed physically before the start of their second training camp. Not only have they undergone a natural "spurt" of physical maturation that tends to occur in most individuals between the ages of twenty-two and twenty-three, they have also participated in a rigorous off-season strength development program, supervised by the team's conditioning staff.

In addition, in his second training camp, a player does not have to deal with the paralyzing sense of anxiety arising from unfamiliar surroundings. By their second year, most players have familiarized themselves with their environment enough to enable the coaching staff to realistically assess their abilities to perform at a professional level.

Developmentally, the coaching staff should place a major emphasis on cultivating and refining the skills of every rookie player who has just completed his initial season in the NFL. The focus of such an effort must be to totally prepare each player for his second training camp. Each athlete should be a "special" project for his position coach. In this regard, the job of the position coach is to establish what skills and abilities are essential for the position and to take steps to progressively develop those traits in those players for which he is responsible.

Among the factors that a position coach should consider when working with second-year players during the off-season are the following:

- Every position coach must be totally versed in the specific skills a particular player needs to function within the team's system.

- The conditioning program prescribed for each player must enhance his efforts to develop the skills required to play his position.

- Every player should be given information regarding what constitutes sound nutrition, how nutrition can affect his on-the-field performance, and what steps can be taken to safely control (manage) his weight.

- Every athlete must be made to understand how he should prepare each week to maximize his continued development over the course of the season.

- During this (off-season) period, the position coach should attempt to determine the commitment level of each of the athletes he is coaching to football.

- Both the player and his position coach must learn to communicate effectively with each other. Using the vernacular (language) of the team's system, it is essential that they are able to provide each other with the critical information that each needs to do his job under the pressure and demands of the game.

- Every player must be made to understand how his skills and responsibilities dovetail with the other positions on the team with which he must interact.

- Every player must begin to develop a detailed understanding of the capabilities, strengths, and weaknesses of the other teams in the NFL—particularly those in his team's division.

- Every player must learn to conduct himself properly within the social environment that exists for a professional athlete.

When all the engineers and designers were finished speculating what should happen it was the experienced test pilots who took hold of the rudder and gave practical application to what was at that time just theory.

Chuck Yeager
Brigadier General, retired
United States Air Force

DEVELOPING THE QUARTERBACK

Developing the quarterback is at the heart of a team's ability to compete in the NFL. As such, the quarterback position should receive a substantial amount of attention from the coaching staff. This attention should be well-planned and should focus on sequential learning.

The need for a comprehensive and well thought-out plan for developing the quarterback has been heightened by the fact that the "process" of developing players in the NFL has changed more for the quarterback position than for any other position since the advent of free agency. The traditional approach of a team drafting a quarterback, developing him over a period of three to four years, and positioning him to be that team's eventual starter is no longer consistent with the philosophy of many teams.

This change in philosophy is illustrated by the fact that during the four-year period of 1994-97, only one quarterback was selected per round in each of the first three rounds of the NFL draft. Some NFL observers believe that such a situation is primarily an outgrowth of the lack of talented quarterbacks coming out of the collegiate ranks. Many other individuals feel that most clubs simply don't want to expend a high draft choice on someone who probably won't play for them because he'll be lost to the team that drafted him via the free agency process.

Not surprisingly, most talented, young quarterbacks who are eligible for free agency want to go to a situation where they have a reasonable chance to play (now).

A unique set of circumstances is required for a team to systematically project, coordinate and arrange for its existing starting (veteran) quarterback to exit the team at just the "right" time for the backup (younger) quarterback to replace him.

At least two factors compound the difficulties facing a team in this situation. First, the development of the backup quarterback may not have progressed as much as expected or needed. Second, during the period when the switch-over was contemplated, it may become quite apparent that the experienced quarterback has several productive years left in his career.

As a result, a growing sentiment among many NFL teams is to use the free agency process to obtain a "new" quarterback at the point when he's actually needed. The prevailing attitude is to let another organization spend the time, money, and resources on developing a young quarterback.

The statistics bear out the relatively transient nature of NFL quarterbacks. For example, at the beginning of the 1997 NFL season, of the 103 quarterbacks drafted from 1989 to 1996, only six are starting for the franchises that picked them in the draft, and only 25 percent remain in the city where they were chosen. Of the 71 selected from 1989-1993, only five are even on the rosters of their original franchise.

In fact, two of the last three Super Bowl Champions acquired their starting quarterbacks by methods other than the draft. Furthermore, of the top-ten rated quarterbacks during the 1996 season (based on efficiency ratings computed by the League), only four are with their original team. Four were acquired by free agency, while Steve Young (Tampa Bay to San Francisco) and Brett Favre (Atlanta to Green Bay) came by way of trades, both of which occurred prior to the advent of free agency.

If you are the quarterback, one of the realisms that very quickly hits you in the face is that it's not going to be all cheers. There'll be boos when things aren't going well. You'll be called a great leader when your team is winning and a lousy leader when it isn't, though you still are the same person trying to do the same things. I don't know of any quarterback who hasn't experienced this kind of roller-coaster existence at one time or another, and that includes those who are in the Hall of Fame.

Ken Anderson
Former Quarterback
Cincinnati Bengals
from *The Art of Quarterbacking*

UNDERSTANDING WHAT IT TAKES TO BE A GREAT QUARTERBACK

No single "blueprint" exists for specifying what skills and traits a quarterback should possess and how much of each characteristic a quarterback should have. The veracity of such a point is reinforced when the playing abilities of several of the great quarterbacks in the history of the NFL are considered.

For example, it is very difficult (if not impossible) to compare and rank the agile efficiency of Joe Montana, to the courage and throwing touch of Dan Fouts, to the pure mechanics of Ken Anderson, to the sheer athletic ability of Steve Young, etc. In his own unique way, each great quarterback has a wide range of qualities that are reflected in varying levels of specific abilities.

The issue is further compounded by the fact that although some quarterbacks appear, at face value, to have every quality that would be necessary for that position, they never developed into productive players—for whatever reason. In these situations, the sum of the parts did not equal the whole, because for the quarterback position, the whole is normally greater than the sum of the parts.

On the other hand, several examples exist of players who otherwise might seem to be somewhat deficient in some of the quantifiable measures deemed essential for a quarterback who excelled on the playing field—for whatever combination of reasons. Unquestionably, the illustration of this situation is Joe Montana—quite possibly the best quarterback to ever play in the NFL.

A number of factors diminished Montana in the eyes of the NFL talent evaluators. He lacked the ideal size and arm strength. He seemed a bit too shy and reserved in his demeanor. He also did not have a particularly significant playing career at Notre Dame (i.e., he did not have a body of work from which definitive conclusions regarding his playing potential could be drawn).

As a result, Montana was drafted in the third round—by all reasonable standards, an extraordinary "bargain" for the San Francisco 49ers. Given the opportunity to play, he became the embodiment of the ultimate competitor whose agility, efficient footwork, uncanny instincts, and marvelous touch and timing, coupled with his amazing level of spontaneity and sense of anticipation, combined to make him the winningest and most productive quarterback in the history of the game.

IDENTIFYING THE KEY QUALITIES OF A QUARTERBACK

Collectively, effective quarterbacks exhibit a number of traits, including the fact that they are courageous, competitive, spontaneous, adaptable, poised, and mentally and physically tough. They also tend to possess the following critical qualities:

- *Functional intelligence.* The ability of a player to organize and isolate different categories of tasks that he must perform in a particular situation is commonly referred to as functional intelligence. Involving more than strictly his innate IQ level, this characteristic reflects the fact that a quarterback has the ability to quickly break things down (e.g., events, situations, circumstances, etc.) to a point of understanding where he does not overly complicate his response to them. This ability is the key to being able to instantly process information in highly stressful situations.

- *Ability to learn.* A quarterback must have the ability to develop and adhere to the proper mechanics for playing quarterback. For some athletes, the learning process will be intuitive—almost natural—requiring minimal effort on their part. For other individuals, the steps to understand and to ingrain these abilities will require more time and hands-on instruction.

  On the other hand, some quarterbacks will never be able to develop the mechanics required for their position to an acceptable degree, regardless of how much energy they expend trying. In reality, if they aren't able to acquire the proper attributes for playing quarterback within a reasonable period of time, it's quite likely they never will.

- *Willingness to improve.* An inherent willingness to improve and learn is vital to the developmental progression of a quarterback. With regard to the learning process, a quarterback must have a reasonable level of compatibility with the coaching staff and his teammates.

- *Good work ethic.* Not only should a quarterback understand the proper mechanics for his position, he must also spend an appropriate amount of time working on them. The most effective approach in this regard is frequent repetitive practice.

  For example, it is essential that a quarterback has efficient footwork. In fact, working on a quarterback's footwork is one of the most helpful steps that the coaching staff can take to improve the quarterback's skills and playing abilities.

  Many coaches have discovered the fact that effective quarterbacking involves much more than having the mechanical ability to sit, unencumbered, in the pocket and efficiently set the feet, transfer weight from the back foot to the front foot, and efficiently follow-through with the arm and shoulder. While many individuals may have this capability, few throws are made in such a rarefied atmosphere— outside of quarterback exercises during warm-ups and 7-on-7 drills.

  In reality, during the game, the quarterback must have the physical skills and the proper mechanics to be able to deliver the ball effectively to his intended receiver, while moving in the pocket, throwing off his back foot, or scrambling for his "life." In other words, a quarterback must have the ability to accurately, quickly, and with a sufficient amount of arm strength throw a pass no matter what position his feet are in.

- *Proper throwing action.* A quarterback must master the basic mechanics of the throwing action. Accordingly, he must regularly work on maintaining his natural, normal throwing motion.

  Two coaching points are particularly critical in this regard. First, during his delivery, he must never allow the tip of the ball to drop below his waist. Second, he must always release the ball above his shoulders.

  On the other hand, coaches should be aware of the fact that, for the most part, an athlete either has the ability to throw the ball properly or he doesn't. In reality, coaching usually has only minimal effect on this skill (i.e., "if an individual can't throw, he can't throw").

It is also important to note that, all factors considered, arm strength is not a major factor in proper throwing action. While an appropriate level of arm strength is a necessary attribute for a quarterback, other considerations are even more important (e.g., touch, the ability to deliver the ball in a smooth and efficient manner, etc.).

* *Emotional stability.* A quarterback must have the ability to handle the stress and pressures that occur during the game. He must be able to control his emotions to a point where he can think clearly, evaluate his options, and act rationally, regardless of the situation. Similar to other aspects of quarterbacking, within a reasonable period of time, an athlete will either show that he can deal with his emotions properly within the framework of the game or demonstrate to the coaching staff (by his actions) that further effort in this regard is a waste of time.

* *Leadership abilities.* A quarterback should lead by example. In this regard, his performance during the game is crucial. While different quarterbacks will have different leadership styles, ranging from somewhat casual, not particularly demonstrative (e.g., Joe Montana) to vocal and very demanding (e.g., Brett Favre), all successful quarterbacks exhibit the proper mind set, the necessary poise, and the absolute focus required for the position while on the field—characteristics which are often subsequently emulated by their teammates.

So much of what you do physically happens because you've thought about it and mentally prepared for it.

Dan Fouts
Hall-of-Fame Quarterback
San Diego Chargers

DETERMINING A TEACHING PROGRESSION

Establishing and implementing a comprehensive plan for ensuring that the quarterback acquires and maintains the requisite abilities for his position are absolutely critical. Not only must the plan encompass detailed steps for developing the basic fundamentals for the quarterback position, it must also address how the entire sequential learning package will be implemented with regard to *when* such instruction will occur (in-season versus off-season) and *where* such instruction will take place (classroom versus on-the-field).

The Basic Fundamentals of the Quarterback Position

The quarterback position involves several aspects which are central to effective performance. Among the factors which must be addressed at every opportunity are stance, hand position, drop-step footwork, movement in the pocket, throwing action, and drop and read progressions.

- *Stance.* The basic elements of a proper stance remain constant from quarterback to quarterback. Each of the following elements should be emphasized as often as is feasible:

  - The quarterback's feet should be shoulder width apart.
  - His weight should be on the balls of his feet.
  - His knees should be bent, but not crouched down under the center.

  In many instances, much of the focus of the coaching staff on a quarterback's stance will involve eliminating a false step that many quarterbacks develop at one point or another in their playing careers. Two methods are commonly employed to eliminate such a false step.

  One approach is to have the quarterback stagger one foot slightly in front of the other. The second technique involves having the quarterback place his weight on the inside of the balls of his feet in a pigeon-toe type of alignment.

  As a rule, one of these methods will enable a quarterback to get rid of a false step, thereby making his drop more efficient. It is important, however, that a quarterback does not overly focus on his stance to a point where he is thinking about it too much, instead of more critical matters (e.g., coverage rotation, protection concerns, etc.).

  An important point to remember can be made using a receiver who uses his body to catch the ball. While the coaching staff would prefer that a team's receivers extend their arms and catch everything thrown to them with their hands, the bottom line is whatever it takes for a player to get the job done, the staff should just let the athlete (including the quarterback) do it.

- *Hand position.* Similar to the stance, the fundamental considerations of hand position also remain constant from quarterback to quarterback. The following factors should be stressed at every opportunity:

  - The quarterback should exert pressure with his upper hand against the butt of the center.
  - He must be careful not to apply so much pressure that he disturbs the center's balance. Too much pressure can also cause the quarterback's hands to separate when the ball is snapped into his upper hand.
  - He should have a slight bend in his elbow in order to ride and follow the center.
  - He should maintain two hands on the ball whenever possible.
  - The ball should be held chest high (at a point just above the quarterback's nipples) when he is dropping back.
  - His elbows should be kept in close to his body when he's dropping back. If his elbows flare out, the balance of his drop will be thrown off. As a result, he will lower the ball relative to his body. At no point should the quarterback allow the ball to drop below his waist.

- *Drop-step footwork.* The critical factor in the quarterback drop is to get immediate separation between the blocking offensive linemen and the men that they are blocking. A quarterback's drop involves three primary components: Drive (separation) steps away from the center, throttle steps taken prior to setting up to slow his drop, and a balance (hitch) step to bring his body into the proper position for throwing.

Quarterbacks use three different types of drops in a game: the 3-step drop, the 5-step drop, and the 7-step drop. Each of these drop techniques employs a different variation of the three kinds of drop-steps:

— 3-step drop
    Step #1.   Initially, an aggressive drive step.
    Step #2.   Then, a quick crossover/throttle step.
    Step #3.   Finally, a balance step which must be made quickly.
        √   The third step of the quarterback must land on the ball of his foot.
        √   His heel never touches the ground.
        √   He must be ready to pivot and throw.
        √   He should keep his vision down the field in order not to tip a quick throw.
        √   On passes involving inside breaks (the slant, the shoot, etc.), three big steps are used for clearance and timing. On outside breaks (the quick out or hitch), three short quick steps are employed for timing.

— 5-step drop
    Step #1-3.   Initially, three smooth drive steps.
    Step #4.   Then, a crossover/throttle step.
    Step #5.   Finally, a slight hitch to a 5th balance step.
        √   He should keep his weight on the ball of his back foot.
        √   He must attempt to maintain his throwing balance in the pocket.
        √   He should be prepared to hitch step up into the pocket.
        √   Outbreaks call for five quick steps (e.g., outs, etc.), and then throwing off the back foot. Inbreaks (e.g., hooks, etc.) involve five big steps, and then either throwing off the back foot or taking a hitch step and bouncing forward.

— 7-step drop
    Steps #1-3. Initially, three smooth drive steps.
    Steps #4-7. Then, four quick steps to slow his drop.
        √   The sixth step should be a crossover/throttle step.
        √   He should take a slight hitch to execute the seventh step, which is for balance.
        √   He should keep his weight on the ball of his back foot.
        √   He must attempt to maintain his throwing balance in the pocket.
        √   He should adjust his footwork for those routes which require a designed, multiple-hitch step for timing purposes.
        √   A concise coaching point is to have the quarterback take the three biggest steps, followed by the four shortest. The quarterback then takes a hitch step and bounces forward.

Regardless of what kind of drop is employed, the quarterback should adhere to certain factors with regard to his body position. Among the key coaching points relating to a quarterback's body position while dropping are the following:

— The quarterback's back foot should always be under his hips when the throwing motion is initiated.
— He should keep the need for this balance step in mind during all of his drops and while scrambling.
— He should keep his hips and shoulders perpendicular to the line of scrimmage.
— He should not overextend his last (balance) step, thereby forcing unneeded hitch steps.

• *Movement in the pocket.* During a game, the quarterback has to make some type of movement in the pocket before he throws about half of the time. Such movement usually involves a skillful attempt to avoid the rush, rather than a full-blown scramble.

The quarterback must constantly work on being able to move smoothly and efficiently in the pocket, all the while attempting to perform a balance step after every movement he makes. One of the more common errors a quarterback makes is to raise up while moving forward in the pocket, thereby causing him to lose his throwing profile. To prevent such a problem from occurring, he must not open his hips and shoulders if he's forced to move up in the pocket.

• *Throwing action.* Proper throwing action involves several factors. Among the points which should be stressed are the following:

— The quarterback should create momentum for the ball to carry to the receiver as much with his throwing motion and his follow-through as with his arm.
— He should use his whole body, push off his back foot, and rotate his hips and shoulders.
— He should bring the elbow on his throwing arm up and follow-through with it, while his throwing hand follows through to his opposite hip after the ball is released.
— The elbow on his non-throwing arm should be driven down and back.
— He must not lock out his front leg or his follow through will be halted. It is important to remember that for most sports involving a ball (football included), accuracy in throwing is established by properly following through.
— He should try to get into a balanced position before throwing. In this regard, passing while moving is very much like passing from a drop-back position.
— If running, the quarterback should gain depth on his drop to enable him to have a downhill motion before releasing the ball.
— He should not raise up too high on the throw.
— Because most quarterbacks have a tendency to overpower the throw, he should use more wrist while throwing—somewhat similar to the wrist action in throwing a dart.

The coaching staff should also emphasize the following additional instructions to the quarterback regarding his throwing action:

— He should maintain both hands on the ball to enhance his level of balance and to help him secure the ball, thereby keeping him from fumbling in the pocket.
— He should never allow the tip of the ball to drop below his waist.
— He should use a hitch (balance) step to help him maintain his back foot under his hips.
— He should retain this throwing position even when forced to move around in the pocket.
— His movements in the pocket should be distinct and clear.
— He should settle and relax before throwing if he is forced to scramble.
— He should not overgrip the ball in order to keep his upper body loose and should be ready to throw the ball at any time.
— His aiming point for the ball should always allow the receiver to catch the ball in stride and run with it.

• *Drop and read progressions.* Every pass varies from every other pass according to the depth and width of the receiver's route. To better understand how each pass is different, a baseball analogy can be used to illustrate the point.

For example, a throw from a third baseman to first base is different from a throw to first by a second baseman. In turn, both throws are different than a throw from an outfielder to the infield.

Each quarterback drop involves a progressive read. The quarterback first looks at his primary read. If the quarterback decides that the timing and the movement required for throwing to the primary read are less than suitable, he then turns his attention to the alternate receivers in the progression.

The progression then goes to a third alternative—the outlet receiver. He should look for this receiver to come open late, near the line of scrimmage. Typically, this man gets the ball late against a zone if the quarterback gets in trouble. A fourth option should come into play if the quarterback is required to make a "hot" throw based on his protection scheme.

The coaching staff should emphasize to the quarterback how important it is for him to keep his helmet (as opposed to his eyes) positioned down field on his "hot" throws. The quarterback should never throw blindly to any route—particularly a "hot" route. By keeping his helmet positioned down field, the quarterback will NOT tip the "hot" throw to the defender, thereby giving him a "jump" on the receiver.

Each drop and read action involves different mechanics by the quarterback. As such, each sequence should be identified and practiced within the framework of the route progressions. Establishing a drill and response sequence for each route entails several steps that the coaching staff should undertake, including:

— Install the route in a classroom situation. The process should involve outlining the specific type of drop to be used, identifying the "hot" receiver based on the quarterback's protection needs, and describing the progression of reads from the primary to the alternate receivers. Cut-ups should be available that illustrate each of the possible alternatives (i.e., "hot," to primary, to alternate and, if possible, for a scramble).

— Work on the mechanics of each particular drop with the quarterback on the practice field; verbally take the quarterback through the different steps and mechanics for each throw.

— Have the quarterback practice the different types of throws with an appropriate receiver during a route period; stress the need for the quarterback to adhere to the proper mechanics at all times in this "perfect" practice environment where no defense exists.

— Place a stationary receiver at each of the possible points the quarterback might throw to based on his read. As the quarterback works through his drop and reads, signal which receiver should raise his hands to indicate to the quarterback to whom he should throw.

If no receiver raises his hand, it is a signal for the quarterback to scramble. When forced to scramble, the quarterback and the receivers should practice what the receivers should do based on the direction of the quarterback's scramble and the location of each receiver on each route.

— Include a "hot" throw option in the progression that can be employed in those applicable situations where the quarterback is under intense pressure (i.e., when he is forced to extend off his back leg and use a high delivery).

— Have the quarterback repeat the progression, if time and personnel permit, with defenders dictating the progression read.

— In a 7-on-7 period, make a regular habit of forcing the quarterback to move and adjust his balance step, based on the actions of an inside rusher. Using a handbag (or some similar item), a ball boy or a coach can be employed as the pass rusher.

After the quarterback has thrown the ball, the pass rusher can "tap" the quarterback with the bag (while being very careful not to get in the way of the quarterback's throwing action). A quarterback will not get as much out of a 15 minute 7-on-7 period if he is free to sit back in a no-rush "comfort zone" and work unimpeded against the secondary.

In this step, the coach should have the option of yelling "scramble" at any time to signal the quarterback to break contain. On the signal for the quarterback to scramble, the receivers should run their predetermined "scramble routes."

Habit gives strength to the body in great exertion, to the mind in great danger, and to judgment against first impression.

Carl von Clausewitz
Director of General War Academy
Prussia
from *On War*

Developing the Quarterback in the Classroom

Some coaches mistakenly believe that they can improve a quarterback strictly in a classroom environment. They are erroneously convinced that if a quarterback is shown enough video and talked through enough situations, he can be prepared for everything that might happen during the game.

In reality, classroom meetings between the quarterback and appropriate members of the coaching staff (e.g., the head coach, the offensive coordinator, etc.) tend to have two primary objectives—to clarify communication and exchange information.

It is very important that the quarterback and those coaches with whom he must interact clarify how they will communicate with each other during the game. Given the stress and pressure that can occur during the game, they must be able to communicate with each other in a meaningful—yet succinct—way. As a result, they will be better prepared to provide each other with the information they need to base their decisions on in the "heat of battle."

Classroom meetings also provide a useful forum for informing the quarterback what is expected of him. For example, it is critical that when the developmental process is moved from the classroom to the practice field, the quarterback must have a clear and definitive idea of what each drill and instructional period represents and what the coaching staff is looking for in each teaching segment.

As the head coach, it is important that you carefully consider what learning points you want to make to the quarterback in a classroom situation. You should not attempt to cover all aspects of his play.

If you attempt to emphasize everything, you have—in essence—emphasized "nothing." Accordingly, every point you share (review) with the quarterback should have a specific purpose (e.g., to reduce the uncertainty he faces in any given situation).

Developing the Quarterback on the Practice Field

It can be argued that true learning occurs when there is a need to know, a concrete understanding of how to learn exists, and both coaches and players realize that a particular goal can be achieved. For the quarterback, the single most compelling learning environment is the practice field.

While it is basically true that "there is no experience like game experience," actually playing the game does not provide the quarterback with the repetitive practice he needs for developing and refining his skills and techniques. Such essential repetitions can easily be arranged in a well-designed practice (refer to Chapter 11 for a detailed overview of how to organize practice sessions).

Several factors need to be considered when designing a practice to ensure that the quarterback is exposed to an appropriate learning environment on the field, including properly warming up, developmental drills, the off-season schedule and in-season matters.

- *Warm-up.* As many different and viable methods for properly warming up exist as there are different types of quarterbacks. The one constant feature of all such warm-up routines is that they emphasize total body stretching prior to every workout.

  A sound stretching program for a quarterback focuses on the major muscle groups in both the upper body and the lower body—not just the musculature in his throwing arm and shoulder. Because his calves, hamstrings, hips, lower back, abdominals, and torso are an integral part of his throwing action, a quarterback must warm-up these key areas also.

  Stretching properly helps to prepare the various muscle groups for action by warming up the muscles and eliminating any tightness in them. Combined with the fact that, over time, stretching enhances the range of motion that a particular muscle can go through, such preparation serves to protect the quarterback from suffering a muscle-related injury (e.g., pull, strain, etc.).

  One of the most pivotal characteristics of a sound stretching routine is the fact that it, indeed, stays routine. As the head coach, you should be aware of what steps your quarterbacks are undertaking to properly warm-up before each practice and game, and then follow-up to make sure that each athlete maintains his warm-up routine over the course of the (long) season.

  It is also critical that every practice be closely monitored by the coaching staff so that a quarterback is not put into a situation where he is idle for an extended period before he has to resume throwing without rewarming up. For example, if the practice session includes a lull in circumstances where the quarterback has to throw the ball, he should be alerted when the non-throwing period is about to end and allowed time to re-warm up.

  Another important point involving the warm-up period is to ensure that the quarterback adheres to the proper mechanics of his drop, even if he is just engaged in a casual game of catch before practice. He must always use a final crossover and a balance step in throwing.

  He should never stand flat-footed and throw the ball. Instead, he should take advantage of every opportunity to practice the last two steps in the mechanics of his drop.

- *Developmental drills.* One of the most useful tools for developing and refining the skills and techniques of a quarterback are properly designed drills. As such, a comprehensive plan for developing a quarterback must include a substantial amount of drill work.

  Drill work provides a tangible opportunity for invaluable repetitive practice. Such practice should be conducted on a year-round basis—particularly during the off-season in the spring. Tables 8-1 and 8-2 present a list of 25 drills for developing a quarterback's mechanics that could be incorporated into a practice session and a slate of possible steps that could possibly be used to vary each drill, respectively.

Table 8-1. Sample drills for developing a quarterback's mechanics.

THREE QUICK—Hitch—Quick Out.

THREE QUICK—To Alternate (TE-BKS)—Move Feet.

THREE BIG—Slant—HB Flat.

THREE BIG—HOLD—Slant (vs. coverages)—Stick—Fade—Fly—Colorado.

THREE BIG—HOLD—To Alternate—Move Feet—Run.

FIVE QUICK—Square Out—Seam Post.

FIVE QUICK—MOVE FEET—To Alternate—Outlet.

FIVE BIG—Pivot Hook—Basic Cross—Read.

FIVE BIG—HOLD—"Y" Out—Alternate.

FIVE BIG—HOLD—MOVE FEET—Alternate—Outlet—Run.

FIVE BIG—HITCH STEP—Square In—Hook.

FIVE BIG—MULTIPLE HITCH STEPS—WAITING—Alternates—Outlets—Run.

SEVEN STEPS—HITCH STEP—Comeback—Dig—Deep Over—Go.

SEVEN STEPS—MULTIPLE HITCH STEPS—WAITING—Alternates—Outlets—Run.

SEVEN STEP—Screen.

FIVE STEP—Screen.

THREE STEP—PLAY PASS—(e.g., 331-H 200, etc.) Primary—Alternate—Run.

FIVE QUICK STEPS—PLAY PASS—(e.g., FOX 2-3) Primary—Alternate—Outlet—Run.

FIVE BIG—PLAY PASS—(e.g., P42-43-H 2-3) Primary—Alternate—Outlet—Run.

SEVEN STEP—PLAY PASS—(e.g., H 2-3) Deep Over—Comeback etc.—Primary—Secondary—Outlet—Run.

ACTION PASS—WAGGLE ACTION (SPRINT) (Pull Up—Or Continue, Five Step Or Moving)—Primary—Alternate—Run.

ACTION PASS—PEEL (Pull Up or Moving)—Primary—Alternate—Run.

ACTION PASS—DRIFT (Five Step—Move)—Primary—Alternate—Outlet—Run.

ACTION PASS—ROLL (LAG) PULL UP (Continue)—Primary—Alternate—Run.

OTHER—Goal Line Boot, etc.

Table 8-2. Possible options to add variety to the drills designed to develop the mechanics of a quarterback.

- Talk the quarterback through his drops. Call the receiver's pattern. Call the alternates (e.g., outlets, runs, etc.).

- "Call" off the primary timed pass. Then call the alternates (e.g., outlet, runs, etc.).

- Call "move" (having given directions) as the quarterback is working through his receiver selection.

- Station receivers at specific points (e.g., primary, alternate, outlet, etc.). Then signal to the receiver to whom the ball should be thrown in proper sequence. If none of these receivers is signaled, then the quarterback should run the ball.

- Have the receiver run a timed pattern. The receiver then remains at his designated point for more throws.

- Employ defenders to take specific drops versus each individual receiver (for example, the middle linebacker versus the tight end).

- Add a late pass rusher to the basic drills. Either the quarterback must avoid the pass rusher, throw quickly to the alternate, throw the ball away, or run.

- Add "scramble" to the call; the receiver makes an appropriate adjustment to the scramble.

- Run a "hot" receiver drill (where the quarterback extends off back leg and uses a high delivery); the defender rushes or drops off.

- Add an "audible" to the drill (i.e., the quarterback changes the play). For example, the quarterback switches from a square out to a "Denver" call.

- Practice "outlet" options (e.g., while moving, either throwing to an outlet receiver who is signaling or running the ball).

- Employ action passes—containment, etc.

- Employ play passes—faking, faking and throwing, etc.

- Have the quarterback execute his drop movement in the pocket upon a signal from the coach, who is facing him. The number of steps in the drop (5-7) is indicated by the coach, who then signals which direction the quarterback should move (i.e., to avoid the pressure) in the pocket. The quarterback then throws to a stationary receiver.

- Add a signal that scrambles the quarterback in a particular direction. The quarterback then throws to the receiver who is signaling.

- Have the quarterback attempt to thwart the attention of the defenders (e.g., look away from his receiver before throwing, pump throw, etc.).

The coaching staff should emphasize at least seven key points to the quarterback regarding proper drop mechanics when he is engaged in drill work:

- Bounce while dropping back (i.e., don't move flat-footed).
- Maintain two hands on the ball while dropping back.
- Retain the proper throwing position while dropping back.
- Move (get clear of pressure, using distinct movements).
- Keep "cool" if forced to scramble (relax before throwing).
- Have the ability to throw the ball at any time (use wrist action).
- Use a high release when throwing the ball (the receiver should catch all balls at chest height or higher).

Depending on the drill being run, certain personnel are required to perform each drill. A quarterback, a receiver and two service people are necessary for all drills. Additional personnel involvement varies according to the primary developmental focus of the drill:

- *Tight end work.* A tight end and one or more inside linebackers are needed. Subsequently, a strong safety and one or more outside linebackers can also be employed in the drill.
- *Wide receiver work.* A wide receiver, a cornerback, and a safety are necessary. Subsequently, an outside linebacker can be added to the drill.
- *Running back work.* Two running backs and two outside linebackers are required. Subsequently, an inside linebacker can also be utilized in the drill.

> *We stress the point frequently that coaching is teaching of the highest degree, and a good coach is a good teacher.*
>
> Paul "Bear" Bryant
> Hall-of-Fame Football Coach
> University of Alabama
> from *Building a Championship Football Team*

Developing the Quarterback in the Off-Season

Proper planning can enable the off-season to be an extremely productive time in the developmental process for a quarterback. It is essential, however, that the coaching staff keeps in mind the fact that the mini-camps, the training camp, the four preseason games, and the 16-game regular season schedule collectively add up to a very long year (and that doesn't even include any post-season games in which the team may be involved).

The point that must be remembered is that a quarterback can be required to do too much in the off-season. If he is, his performance will suffer, and he may incur an arm or shoulder problem that does not manifest itself until training camp.

When those types of injuries occur, the rehabilitation process can involve several months. Often, shoulder and arm injuries (depending on the nature and extent of the injury) are not able to be treated successfully until after the season.

As a result, the number of throws a quarterback must take (or is allowed to make) during a given period of time should be closely monitored—particularly during a mini-camp. Quarterbacks should be encouraged to do some throwing before a mini-camp to "toughen" their arms and shoulders to the demands that will be placed on their bodies during the subsequent training sessions.

If they wait until the mini-camp and overextend themselves all at once, they heighten the likelihood of being injured. Their efforts to prepare themselves prior to a mini-camp (or the fall training camp) should be conducted over a reasonable period of time (i.e., three to four weeks) and should involve progressively increasing the number and types of throws being made. Their preparation schedules should also provide for an adequate amount of rest (i.e., no throwing at all).

Table 8-3 presents an off-season (springtime) workout program for quarterbacks. Involving ten workouts lasting for seventy minutes each, this inclusive program is designed to address all of the primary factors of quarterback play.

The particular actions and procedures worked on during each workout should be closely monitored by the coaching staff and should be recorded daily. Table 8-4 provides a sample of a chart that could be used to retain the schedule of events during a particular workout.

Table 8-3. Off-season workout program for quarterbacks.

- Ten on-the-field workouts
- 70 minutes per workout, not including time spent on warming up (700 minutes total).
- Daily program schedule (minutes per segment)

  10 min.   Warm-Up

  15 min.   Drop Mechanics
  1. 3 QUICK—Omaha, Thunder, Ind. Slant, Stick (322, 370), Lion
  2. 3 BIG—Drag Slant, HB Flat
  3. 3 BIG AND HOLD—Fade, Colorado, Sluggo
  4. 5 QUICK—Double Square Out, Spot, Arrow Flat, Hank, Break Out, Winston
  5. 5 BIG—Texas, Double Go, HB Read
  6. 5 BIG AND HOLD—In, HB Read
  7. 5 AND HITCH—In, All Go
  8. 5 AND 2 HITCH—In @ 2nd Hole, Short Cross
  9. 7 (3 BIG—4 SMALL AND HITCH)—Double, CB, Dig, Drive, FB Arrow, Deep Over, Delay "Y" Dino, Bingo Cross, Shallow Cross, Strike, Double Circus
  10. 7 (TURN AND RUN 3 BIG—4 SMALL)—vs. Blitz; Same Routes
  11. 7 AND 2 HITCH—Deep Over, Deep Cross

Table 8-3. Continued.

15 min.	Throwing
	With receivers spotted or running patterns
	(Above routes as planned per session)
15 min.	Special Categories

     1. ACTION (MOVEMENT) PASS—Waggle Solid "Z" Out, FK 18-19 QB, Keep FB Slide, FK 15-14 CTR QB Keep, Sprint Option

     2. PLAY PASS—Pass 316-317 Power "X" ("Z") Slant, Fox 2-3 DSO-CB-Go, Pass 43-42 "X" Deep Over (Deep Cross), Lag Pass "X" Dig, Lag Pass "Z" Deep Cross, Fox 2-3 Dino "Y" Out, Fox 2-3 "X" and "Y" Hook

     3. SCREENS

     4. HOT RECEIVER (HB-FB-Y-WR)

20 min.   Progression Work (Specific Plays—Receivers Spotted)

     1. Cover Pass Play on Board (Video)

     2. 4 Plays Per Session

     3. On Field—position 3 receivers in spots; throw all progressions; incorporate "run" skill

     4. Run Routes vs. Defenders

        Ex.—Cloud, Sky, Lber Drops, Blitzer (Hot)

5 min.   Movement Drill (Aerobic) (Skills)

     1. 5 Step:

        A. 5 Big—Hold—Hitch and Throw

        B. 5 Big—Hitch (rt-lt)—Throw—Run

        C. 5 Big—Hitch (rt-lt)—Move—Throw—Run

        D. 5 Big—Bail—Throw on Move/Settle

     2. 7 Step:

        Same as above

     3. Play Pass Fakes with Movement

     4. Wave Drill

     5. Scramble Drill with Receivers

- Continuing work with no huddle—audible calls
- Classroom—30 minutes as planned
  1. Reads
  2. 3-5-7 Step Cut-ups
  3. Front Tapes
  4. Coverage Tapes
- Monitor—Conditioning Program
- Totals

100 mins.	Drop Mechanics
150 mins	Throwing—with receivers spotted—or running patterns (as planned)
150 mins	Special Categories: Action Pass; Play Pass; Screen Technique; Hot Receiver (HB-FB-Y-WR)
200 mins	Progression Work (specific plays—receivers spotted)
100 mins	Movement—throw (in pocket—scramble)

Table 8-4. Daily chart of an off-season quarterback workout.

Date: _____   Practice: _____

QB SESSION		SUPPORT (PERSONNEL)	SELECTIONS (SPECIFIC ROUTES AND PASS PRINCIPLES)
15 Min	**Drops** (Mechanics)		
15 Min	**Patterns** (Spotted or Running)		
15 Min	**Categories** (Movement Plays) (Play Passes) (Screen Tech) (Hot Receiver) (Motion Patterns)		
20 Min	**Progression** (Primary) (Alternate) (Outlet) (Run)		
5 Min	**Movement** (In or Out of Pocket)		

Table 8-4. Continued.

Date: 3-17-97   Practice: _____

QB SESSION		SUPPORT (PERSONNEL)	SELECTIONS (SPECIFIC ROUTES AND PASS PRINCIPLES)
15 Min	**Drops** (Mechanics)	QB's	3 QK - OMAHA 5 BIG - RAZOR 7 - RENO BLADE
15 Min	**Patterns** (Spotted or Running)	WR'S - QK-OUT (FADE, RUN IT - IN VS. MAN - BLADE, POST TE'S - SHORT CROSS (& UNCOVER) - SHALLOW CROSS RB'S - SLOW FLAT, WIDE, CHECK THRU	324-325 OMAHA (VS. OFF, ROLL, BUMP) 22-23 RAZOR JET 2-3 BASIC 'X' RAZOR 96-97 RENO BLADE
15 Min	**Categories** (Movement Plays) (Play Passes) (Screen Tech) (Hot Receiver) (Motion Patterns)	HOT RECEIVER TE's - RB's	96-97 RENO BLADE 96-97 'X' SHALLOW CROSS 22-23 RAZOR
20 Min	**Progression** (Primary) (Alternate) (Outlet) (Run)	INCORPORATE "RUN" SKILL 3 CATCHERS	324-325 OMAHA 22-23 RAZOR JET 2-3 BASIC 'X' RAZOR 96-97 RENO BLADE
5 Min	**Movement** (In or Out of Pocket)	QB's	5 BIG - HOLD - HITCH & THROW

Table 8-4. Continued.

Date: 3-18-97   Practice: _____

QB SESSION		SUPPORT (PERSONNEL)	SELECTIONS (SPECIFIC ROUTES AND PASS PRINCIPLES)
15 Min	**Drops** (Mechanics)	QB's	3 BIG — DRAGON 5 BIG — TEXAS 7 — DOG
15 Min	**Patterns** (Spotted or Running)	WR's- SLANT vs. {OFF KICK PRESS PIVOT DOG TE's - DRAG LAZY BASIC DEEP MIDDLE CROSS RB's - CHECK THRU, TEXAS, FLAT	JET 200-300 DRAGON (392-393 DRAGON) 22-23 TEXAS (SCRAM) 28-29 DOG
15 Min	**Categories** (Movement Plays) (Play Passes) (Screen Tech) (Hot Receiver) (Motion Patterns)	WR's	SPRINT RT/LT 'Z' FLAT
20 Min	**Progression** (Primary) (Alternate) (Outlet) (Run)	3 CATCHERS	JET 200-300 DRAGON (392-393 DRAGON) 22-23 TEXAS (SCRAM) 28-29 DOG
5 Min	**Movement** (In or Out of Pocket)	QB's	5 BIG-HOLD-HITCH & THROW

Developing the Quarterback During the Season

The coaching staff should consider several factors concerning how much "work" a quarterback should be given each week during the season. One of the primary considerations is whether a quarterback is the starter or a backup.

The starter should get about 80 percent of the snaps during the week of a game, a percentage which should progressively tail off at the end of the week in order to keep his arm fresh. If a particular practice involves routine plays that the starter is already executing at a proficient level, this situation may be a good time to have the backup take the snaps, even if for just one play. These plays are often the type that will be called if the backup has to go into the game (for whatever reason), so it is a good time for him to work on them.

Similar to a classroom situation, the coaching staff should be specific as to what it is trying to address at any given time during the work week (e.g., working on the mechanics of his drop, developing the proper reads, etc.). If a coach attempts to correct too many facets of a quarterback's play at the same time, the learning effect will be greatly diminished.

The coaching staff should also not assume or expect that a quarterback will get a lot of serious work accomplished at home during the week of a game. If a quarterback is taking an entire game film home to look at after practice, he may arrive at some wrong conclusions or, at the very least, he may not gain any meaningful focus that can be applied to the game.

On the other hand, home study can be used in a beneficial way. For example, the coaching staff may want to give the quarterback a few specific film clips to look at, particularly aspects that need to be emphasized even though they may have already been covered in practice.

Developing the Quarterback in the World League

All factors considered, the World League is an excellent avenue for developing a young quarterback. The opportunity for a young quarterback to compete in a 10-game schedule of highly competitive contests is not an experience which can be duplicated in a practice environment. Such an experience can help identify (and develop when appropriate) the specific strengths or needs of a particular quarterback. In turn, that information can be used by the organization to evaluate the performance potential of that quarterback.

One of the most notable athletes to benefit from playing in the World League was Brad Johnson, the quarterback for the Minnesota Vikings. A 7th round draft choice from Florida State, where he had limited playing time as a starter, Johnson was able to enhance his skills and demonstrate his abilities to the Vikings by participating in the World League.

As a general rule, a team should consider at least three criteria to determine whether it wants to utilize the World League to help develop a particular quarterback:

- Would the time a particular player spends in the World League be better spent with the team's staff during the off season? For example, if a young quarterback is new to a team and does not fully understand its system, learning yet another system in the off-season may not be in his or the team's best interests.

- If the individual who is contemplating playing in the World League is a team's backup quarterback, the team has to consider what would it do to its program if he were injured playing in the World League. Under no circumstance does a team want to leave itself vulnerable at the backup spot going into the season.

- Are the system and the coaches a quarterback will be working with in the World League going to develop him in a manner and a style with which the team is comfortable?

Endnotes

[1]Based upon the NFL's agreement with the NFL Players Association, a team may hold an unlimited number of mini-camps for rookies and one mandatory mini-camp for veterans. If a team hires a new head coach after the regular season ends, the team may hold up to two additional voluntary mini-camps for veterans.

CHAPTER 9

HANDLING THE PRO ATHLETE

"My general rule, which I have followed throughout my coaching career, is that everyone doesn't necessarily get treated the same way, because I'm not sure that's possible. But everyone has to be treated fairly. Moreover, they have to know and trust that they will be treated fairly."

—Dennis Green
Head Football Coach
Minnesota Vikings
Game Plans for Success

Finding the winning edge...

It's the old message of moderation in all things—noble in theory, but often maddening when you face the challenges of competitive life. Whether you're a general, a CEO or a football coach, finding a middle ground between the well-being of the people who work for you and the achievement of a goal is one of the trickiest aspects of leadership. While there's no definitive solution—situations vary from one day to the next—some kind of personal standard on the question of people versus success is imperative. This applies not just to managers but to the managers of managers.

—Bill Walsh, "What Price Glory? Walking the Line Between Ruthless and Toothless," *Forbes*, February 26, 1996.

Effective leaders must have the ability, insight, and courage to deal with relevant issues involving their subordinates. The application of this point became particularly clear to me shortly after I had just completed my second season as the head coach of the San Francisco 49ers.

Although the 49ers had a difficult year in 1980 (finishing the season 2-14), our offensive line had great potential, especially Ron Singleton, our left tackle. During the season, Ron decided that he should be a marquee player, and subsequently sounded off in the locker room about how he should have been receiving credit and publicity. Ron had been a free agent acquisition off the streets. Reflecting his lack of foresight, Singleton was not willing to wait for what he believed was his due. He brought an agent in to negotiate and demanded a top salary from John McVay, the 49ers' director of operations at the time.

Ron's agent came to the locker room and verbally abused several people, including our equipment manager. He then claimed that I was unwilling to negotiate properly simply because Ron was African-American. I could tolerate neither the mistreatment of individuals in the organization nor the use of racial issues in an attempt to force concessions. I waived Ron immediately, and we went on to win several Super Bowls without him.

This incident made it clear to everyone in the organization that if a situation called for toughness, I would deliver. Our organization stood for honesty and fairness, and we would not tolerate being insulted. Ron never played in the NFL again. We were left with a gap at the left tackle position that we filled by signing Dan Audick, a 245-pound guard who was forced to play at the tackle position in 1981. Dan started every game that season and helped us achieve our first Super Bowl victory in Cincinnati.

———————————————

Effectively managing players requires more than just ensuring that everyone understands the game plan, practices hard, and plays well on game day. It must also include an acute appreciation of the fact that each player is an individual—with specific needs, interests, and perspectives.

The obvious challenge for you, as the head coach, is to develop a managerial approach that enables you to collectively mold a group of individuals into a well-functioning team. At the same time, to a point, you must recognize and respect each player's individuality.

One of the key points to keep in mind is that the primary issue that has to be addressed is what constitutes a sound managerial approach when working with players. The matter to be resolved is "managerial approach," not "managerial style."

Essentially, managerial style is a direct reflection of an individual's personality. Some coaches are more outwardly demonstrative and vocal, while others are somewhat more emotionally reserved. Regardless of where a coach falls on a personality continuum, however, he must employ a sound managerial approach when dealing with his players.

In reality, the kinds of approaches needed to make players productive and relatively stable (emotionally and behaviorally) have changed enormously in recent years. Much of the impetus for such change emanates from the fact the athletes of the 1990s are quite different from their predecessors.

> *The brave man, inattentive to his duty, is worth little more to his country than the coward who deserts her in the hour of danger.*
>
> General Andrew Jackson
> 7th President of the United States

UNDERSTANDING THE ATHLETE IN THE 1990S

For most professional football players, the time has long passed where an athlete will rigidly accept and adhere to a coach's command or advice simply because the coach "said so." Players in the 1990s not only are concerned about when, where, and how, they also want to know why.

Their heightened sense of inquisitiveness is not the result of a newly sparked sense of curiosity. Rather, the athletes of the 1990s are typically much more driven by the degree to which a particular action or issue is perceived to affect their own self interests.

Such an attitude is hardly surprising in light of the changes which have occurred in society over the years. For example, almost every player in the 1990s who plays with an unbounded level of enthusiasm and intensity and who openly is deemed to be the "consummate team player" is referred to as being from the "old school."

The "old school" represents such values as discipline, unquestioned authority, loyalty, accountability, and a willingness to sacrifice for the good of the team. The "new school," on the other hand, is more introspective. In other words, a "how-does-this-matter-affect-my-life" attitude has become a dominant factor in many issues.

Such a distinction is not meant to imply that most football players in the 1990s don't have immense personal pride and a pronounced "love" for the game. They do. They also tend to have different priorities in life and a different value structure than their predecessors.

For example, the economics of the game have virtually eliminated "team loyalty" as a factor in where an athlete plays. Not only are the players in the 1990s more talented, they're also much more well paid. As greed becomes more of a prevailing mind set, many players simply "follow the money."

Depending on the situation, the economic circumstances in the NFL can influence players in other ways also. Some effects are positive, while others are much less so.

For example, given the impact of the NFL's salary cap and the ever-growing need for a team to win sooner rather than later, coaches and players alike have a more short-term perspective on issues involving playing time. All factors considered, coaches are less patient with players who may not be able to make an immediate contribution to the team.

By the same token, the situation has heightened the commitment of many players to find some way that they can make the team (e.g., play on special teams; be a role player in certain situations; etc.). Given the potential economic upside (i.e., salary, pension, endorsement possibilities, etc.) such a reaction is hardly surprising.

The money has also affected the attitudes of many of the older players who are on the downside of their careers. For example, many veteran players do as much as possible to extend their tenure in the NFL an extra year or two.

The "new" economics has also had an affect on those individuals in close proximity to an athlete (e.g., his friends, agents, family, etc.). Operating under the perception that their opinions and actions are in the best interests of the athlete, these associates often engage in behavior that is detrimental to the player.

For example, some may try to foster an attitude in the player that he should distinguish himself from his team and his teammates. Accordingly, he should place a relatively high priority on "his" particular image, "his" personal statistics, and "his" general value in the professional marketplace.

Eventually, the player may develop a perception that personal sacrifice is proportional only to the potential benefits, as opposed to the collective needs of the team. In turn, the player's ability to act in a team-oriented manner may be seriously compromised.

For example, a player may face a situation at a particular point in time where he has a clear choice of acting in a manner that directly benefits the team (e.g., provide contain in an area, stop a blitzing defender, etc.) but offers no direct personal advantage or he can perform an act (e.g., a quarterback sack, an interception, a noteworthy pass reception, etc.) that will earn him a sizable bonus. In this instance, a self-centered player may not make the appropriate decision.

In addition, all factors considered, the more a player becomes self-centered, the more likely he may be affected by his external companions. In a worst case scenario, these associates will encourage him to engage in inappropriate behavior (e.g., drugs, steroid abuse, excessive drinking, etc.).

The lack of an appropriate team-oriented focus may be just one of a number of factors that complicates a head coach's working relationship with a particular player. For example, a given player may be less tolerant and respectful of a coaching staff that he believes is unable to recognize (and showcase accordingly) his true worth.

As a result, the player may seek coaching input from another source (e.g., a member of the coaching staff from his former team, a hired specialist, etc.). At the least, such a player may be excessively judgmental toward the opinions and advice offered by the coaches on his current team.

All in all, the environment in which coaches and players interact in the 1990s is multifaceted. To the extent that coaches accept the fact that certain factors exist that affect player-coach relationships and develop a carefully considered plan for dealing with each factor, they will be better prepared to handle the demands attendant to working with their team's players.

Sound player relations do not occur by accident. They take time, effort, planning and managerial skill. Perhaps no skill is more important than the ability to create a working environment where everyone (coaches and players alike) has a clear understanding, appreciation of, and respect for their own and each other's roles within the organization.

An excellent example of an NFL coach who is widely considered to have a very good working relationship with his players is Dennis Green, the head coach of the

Minnesota Vikings. In turn, Green's players have responded to his managerial approach by playing well and making the Vikings one of the most successful (and least problem-plagued) teams in the NFL during his tenure in Minnesota. Green has an excellent rapport with his players, yet does not lose his perspective as the man who has to make the decisions regarding their future.

Green's way of handling players points out the fact that a head coach should not take a "one-size-fits-all" approach with his athletes. A coach must be able to adapt his style of coaching or be creative in finding a solution to any unique problem one of his players may have.

When appropriate, a coach must be able to adjust his managerial approach to accommodate the intellectual, emotional, and, in some instances, the religious attitudes of his players. The coach who does not change with the times or the situation (as necessary) provides a relatively convenient excuse for a player who is looking for a scapegoat for his lack of success.

The point to keep in mind is that sound player relations typically involve several interrelated factors. Among the steps that you can take, as the head coach, to deal with these factors in an appropriate way are the following:

- Treat each player with dignity and respect.
- Spend time with each individual player on a regular basis. Discuss his performance, his role on the team, your expectations of him, his progress to date, and your specific concerns about matters involving him.
- Blend honesty and diplomacy at the appropriate time when dealing with each player.
- Take a personalized approach when dealing with each member of the regular squad. This step involves carefully considering each player's unique physical characteristics and the skills and techniques that are best suited for those traits.

Discipline is the soul of an Army. It makes small numbers formidable, procures success to the weak, and esteem to all.

George Washington, 1759
Ist President of the United States

In turn, you should ensure that an individualized "style" or "game" for each player is developed. This step should require each player to master techniques that involve more than basic fundamentals.

- Require each player to continue his efforts to enhance and improve those skills at which he is already adept. The goal for each player in this regard should be to improve his level of sophistication in skills each year. As a result, his level of efficiency and performance will be raised.

- Maintain a positive relationship on an individual basis with each player through the thoughtful use of encouragement, support, and critical evaluation.

- Maintain an uplifting atmosphere at work through the on-going use of positive, enthusiastic, energizing leadership.

- Allow a wide range of moods in the workplace environment, ranging from very serious to very relaxed. Set the tone by your demeanor. Realize that players will respond to your comportment. Take action to ensure that players understand when a dead, serious tone is necessary, and when a relatively light, easy-going climate is appropriate.

- Make the players very aware that their well-being has the highest priority of the organization. Reinforce this understanding by assembling a medical staff for the team that is characterized by a high level of quality, competence and professionalism.

  Such a sports medicine staff should not only be very skilled, it should also demonstrate an appreciation for the sacrifices made by the athletes. The staff should primarily be composed of a highly trained, experienced team of physicians who are highly respected in their medical area of specialization.

  Their primary focus and sense of dedication should be to serve the medical needs of the players. Staff members should not be overly consumed with their own level of visibility or with their being accepted socially by the team's players, coaches, and management.

- Demonstrate an even-handed approach to everyone. Realize that giving flagrant, "V.I.P." treatment to selected players will promote a stratified-class system that eventually will split the squad into two distinct groups—the "haves" and the "have nots."

- Make sure that all meals, lodging and transportation provided to the players are first class.

- Speak in positive terms about former players. Show respect for the efforts and sacrifices made by individuals who were once on your team, but who are now playing elsewhere. Display admiration for those athletes who have left the game, including men who completed their careers many years ago.

- Demonstrate interest and support for a player's extended family—spouse, children and parents.

- Communicate on a first-name basis with each player.

- Don't force the players to participate in "unnecessary" social activities with coaches and management.

- Be direct and honest with the media, but frame everything with a positive, supporting spin.

- Set standards that players should abide by and live up to at all times. Realize that players need structure within the organization. They have an appreciation for high standards and high expectations.

  While a few individuals may not respond appropriately to such standards, most players want a team environment that is characterized by structure, discipline and performance expectations. Those players who are too stubborn or foolish to adapt to their environment have a definitive choice—either adjust their mind-set and abide by the standards or become history.

- Stand by your decisions. Players are aware when you vacillate or hesitate regarding a particular issue or directive. Eventually, your wavering will erode player trust in your leadership.

- Maintain whatever policies that have been established. For example, a firm stance must be taken with any disciplinary action. Any fine system that is in place must be enforced. Exceptions should not be made. If you begin making allowances for the behavior of certain players, you run the very real risk of having everyone else consider the system to be a fraud.

- Address and resolve whatever differences may develop between coaches and players or just between players. Such differences must not be allowed to linger.

- Avoid "pleading" with your players. Such imploring is often viewed by players as a sign of weakness. Droning on in such a manner can easily be perceived as empty rhetoric by the players. In reality, players expect substantive remarks from you that they can apply to their immediate situation.

- Be yourself. For example, avoid trying to copy the vernacular of the players in a misplaced attempt to get close (i.e., relate) to the players. Your "style" evolves from your personality. Attempts to change it can readily be viewed as counterfeit behavior on your part.

Keep in mind that all factors considered, players always tend to respond best to a coach who demonstrates a definitive ability to help them achieve their particular goals and aspirations. Accordingly, your actions should reflect the fact that you are very knowledgeable in your area of expertise and should constantly reinforce the fact that your instructional advice is deeply rooted in the "cutting edge" of current techniques and procedures.

Without consistency there is no moral strength. The secret of success is constancy of purpose...It is no use saying, "We are doing our best." You have got to succeed in doing what is necessary.

Sir Winston Churchill
Former Prime Minister
Great Britain

PROMOTING SOUND PLAYER RELATIONS

While everyone in an organization should be concerned with sound player relations, as the head coach, you can take at least two significant steps to enhance the likelihood that players and coaches will interact in a responsible, appropriate manner. One step involves assigning direct responsibility for player relations to a particular staff member; the other entails establishing a committee of players to provide feedback to you on given issues.

It is vital that every organization appoints a specific staff member to direct, coordinate, and be responsible for the organization's structured efforts involving player relations. This individual must be given the resources (e.g., funding, assistance, etc.) and the support necessary to become a viable part of the organization's operating structure.

In the area of player relations, this staff member should be given a broad array of responsibilities, ranging from helping new players and their families get settled to providing a wide range of counseling on factors that can have a meaningful impact on players, during their playing days and beyond.

Typically, the staff member responsible for player relations is accorded departmental status. As such, his department is responsible for developing a comprehensive plan for offering counseling in a wide range of issues, including substance abuse, domestic violence, financial matters, career opportunities outside football, continuing education, and family assistance.

It is crucial that the organization address these types of issues in order to establish an all-encompassing, thoughtful work environment for the players. Although not every player will respond positively to such an environment for whatever reason (e.g., a player's agent may want to foster an "us-versus-them" mentality), a genuine effort to create a positive organizational atmosphere can be beneficial to almost all parties involved.

The second major step that you can take to improve your ability to deal with players in a sound manner is to develop a committee of players who will act as a two-way sounding board. On one hand, the committee can provide meaningful feedback on issues that you bring to them. On the other hand, it can make you aware of specific matters that are of concern to the players.

For example, if the head coach has a "problem" with a particular player, the coach can take the problem to the committee (e.g., behavior of a certain player, friction between two players, etc.) and solicit the members' opinions on how to deal with the troublesome matter. By the same token, the players on the team can present an issue they feel strongly about (e.g., the length of team meetings, the amount of scheduled practice, etc.) directly to the head coach via the committee.

One of the keys to making the "players' committee" work effectively is to pick an appropriate mix of individuals for the committee. Committee membership should reflect the entire makeup of the team's roster—veteran players, as well as younger ones; individuals from the defensive, offensive and special teams; star players, as well as journeymen, etc.

Dealing With Diversity in the Locker Room

One of the important issues facing a head coach in the 1990s is how to effectively deal with diversity in the locker room. As such, the head coach must possess the intellect, the training and the experience to appreciate and respect the differences between his players arising from such factors as the fact that, on occasion, individuals come from different "cultures," espouse different values and have totally different life experiences.

Over the years, I have had the opportunity to discuss this issue in depth with Dr. Harry Edwards, a noted sociologist and a valued colleague. Dr. Edwards feels (and I strongly concur) that the strong African-American influence in the NFL (i.e., approximately 66 percent of the players in the NFL are African-Americans) has distinctly altered coach-player relationships.

In order to handle the challenges imposed by diversity in an appropriate manner, the head coach should adhere to several guidelines, including:

- The head coach must set the tone for what is appropriate and what is not. For example, racially-biased humor or comments are never appropriate in the locker room.

- The head coach should hold all players to the same standard of behavior and performance. Valuing differences does not mean lowering standards or quality.

- The head coach should not appear to be trying "too hard" to relate to his players. Over the long term, such a cosmetic approach just doesn't work.

- The head coach should not assume that he can deal with the team along racial lines. The stereotypic Caucasian-African-American dichotomy is far too simplistic and can be completely ineffectual as a basis for understanding individual differences. It is a mistake for the head coach to assume that any individual will respond in an anticipated way.

- The head coach must look at each individual as a single entity who has his own needs, aspirations and values, and treat him as such.

- Both the head coach and the player must be willing to accommodate each other. While differences may exist (e.g., cultural, chronological, personal experiences, etc.), each person must adapt to the environment created by the coach. This approach is in the best interests of each athlete and coach and collectively the entire squad and organization.

A reflective reading of history will show that no man ever rose to military greatness who could not convince his troops that he put them first, above all else.

General Maxwell Taylor
Former Chairman
Joint Chiefs of Staff

DEALING WITH SUBSTANCE ABUSE

One of the most demanding aspects of dealing with athletes is how to handle substance abuse-related problems. Such problems basically tend to be manifested in two illegal practices: using performance enhancing drugs (e.g., steroids, growth hormones, etc.) and taking "recreational drugs"—for lack of a better term (e.g., marijuana, cocaine, etc.).

Another common type of substance abuse involves consuming an excessive amount of alcohol. Whatever the form, however, substance abuse can lead to several dire consequences.

First and foremost, substance abuse is illegal. Not only is it against local and state laws, it also is a violation of the NFL's substance abuse policy, one of the league's policies for players. Individuals who repeatedly abuse either drugs or alcohol are subject to specific punitive measures by the League.

Substance abuse can also have a negative impact in several other areas. For example, over time, it will diminish a player's performance. His reactions will slow. His ability to make sound judgments (decisions) during the game will be decreased. In addition, his level of depth perception will be impaired (which can be a particular problem for a receiver, for example). His ability to focus and concentrate will also be hindered.

Substance abuse can also have a negative affect on a player's health. Not only do drug usage and excessive alcohol consumption place undue demands on a player's bodily organs (e.g., liver, kidneys, etc.), they also overtax his body's systems (e.g., cardiorespiratory, neuromuscular, digestive, etc.).

For example, cocaine use has been shown to disrupt the electrical system of the heart. Eventually, repeated use of cocaine can lead to a massive coronary event (somewhat similar to the circumstances that allegedly led to the death of basketball star Len Bias).

The addictive nature of most forms of substance abuse can also be a major health problem. Research has found that substance dependency is responsible for a variety of debilitating emotional and physiological problems.

At a minimum, substance abuse can lead to aberrant behavior off the field. Not only will a player's ability to act rationally be impaired, the likelihood that he will associate with individuals of questionable character will also be increased. Together, the two factors can easily cause a player to engage in inappropriate behavior.

As the head coach, you should ensure that every player is informed about the potential dangers of substance abuse. You should also take steps to identify any individual who may have a problem with substance abuse as early as possible.

Realizing that a player has a substance abuse problem, however, can sometimes be a difficult task. For example, a substance abuser is often someone no one would ever readily conceive as having a problem.

The difficulty in identifying an individual who has a problem is compounded by the fact that the player is almost always someone who will not admit to having a problem. Table 9-1 illustrates a step-by-step cycle of the steps that were involved in a team recognizing and responding to substance abuse by one of its top players.

Table 9-1. A step-by step cycle of realizing that a pro bowl defensive player suffers from alcohol and drug abuse

1. The player is not getting off blocks.
2. He frequently is knocked off the line of scrimmage.
3. He is slow to pursue the play.
4. He is not diagnosing (i.e., reading) the play properly.
5. Initially, he began playing very poorly only in the second half.
6. Then he began playing the entire game in a lethargic manner.
7. Subsequently, he began to develop minor injuries.
8. He begins taking time off in practice.
9. He demonstrates a lack of concentration in the meeting room.
10. He is still saying the "right things."
11. Eventually, his position coach determines the player has a debilitating problem.
12. Around that time, his live-in girlfriend contacts the team and informs them he has not been home for the past two days.
13. She admits to physical abuse by the player.
14. She also tells the assistant coach the player is "running" with a former player who is using and dealing drugs.
15. The player performs poorly in the closing games of the regular season and in two playoff games. He distinctly affects the team's performance in its playoff loss.
16. The team's recognition of the pattern leading to severe abuse was delayed by sentiment and its confidence in the player.
17. It was extremely difficult to believe this problem was developing with a "good person" who had been so dedicated to the game of football; therefore, the coaches had accepted the player's early explanations for his declining performance.
18. When the team begins contacting the player's friends, they concede that he has been "out using" and that another woman is involved.
19. The player is finally located. His assistant coach speaks with him and tells him that the team is aware of his problem.
20. He returns home and indicates that he is going to quit.
21. In the meantime, the club contacts a counselor. She is to get in touch with the player to begin a counseling program.
22. When the contact is made, the player insists he can take care of his own problem.
23. He disappears again, and his girlfriend calls the team, citing more abuse.
24. The club decides to consider trading the player.

Once a problem has been detected, however, appropriate action should be taken by the team. In most instances, the initial step in treating such a problem is to require the individual to undergo professional counseling.

Under no circumstances should a substance abuse problem be overlooked. The scenario where a coach convinces himself that he has a moral obligation to help an athlete who has a substance abuse problem and decides, for whatever reason (e.g., extraordinary talent of the player, the coach's desire to be a "buddy," etc.), that the best way he can help the player is to let the problem take care of itself is never warranted.

Not only does it fail to address the "real needs" of the substance abuser, it also sends the wrong message to the team that, in some situations, such behavior will be tolerated. In reality, not dealing with the problem serves neither the player nor the organization well.

DEALING WITH DOMESTIC VIOLENCE AND SEXUAL ABUSE

Two other types of unacceptable behavior involving NFL players that have been on the rise in recent years are domestic violence and sexual abuse. It is extremely important that an organization has a well-considered plan to deal with such behavior.

Similar to the approach used for substance abuse, the plan for dealing with domestic violence and sexual abuse issues must involve at least two proactive steps. First, all players should be counseled about why such forms of behavior are inappropriate and will not be tolerated under any circumstances.

Second, every effort must be undertaken to identify as early as possible any individual who may have a problem with such behavior. Staff members should be fully aware of and able to detect the early warning signs that indicate an individual has difficulties in this area. Upon determining that a problem exists, the player involved must be placed in a program designed to prevent such behavior in the future.

DEVELOPING PLAYER ASSISTANCE PROGRAMS

In addition to having a plan for dealing with aberrant behavior, most teams recognize the fact that they also have an obligation to assist their players on personal matters, such as dealing with financial matters and preparing for a successful life after their football careers are completed.

Helping players on personal matters is not as easy as it might seems. Most players have a "natural" tendency not to trust the organization on personal issues. Accordingly, the club must demonstrate to its players that the organization's intentions in this area are well-placed.

Some teams, in conjunction with the cooperation of the National Football League, have undertaken efforts to develop structured player-assistance programs. Designed to help players and their families to meet the challenges of a professional sports career and to actively plan for the future, these programs normally focus on four general areas—financial education; continuing education; career internship; and family assistance.

- *Financial education.* Usually presented in a seminar format, the financial education program is designed to educate players on an array of money matters, including budgeting, personal finances, cash management, insurance planning, checkbook balancing, real estate taxes, securing a mortgage, and basic information on making investments.

  The emphasis of the program is on educating, not providing investment advice. Players typically are not required to attend every scheduled session in the program. If they prefer, they can attend only those sessions that interest them. Most teams also encourage the spouses of players to attend the seminar.

- *Continuing education.* This program is designed to enable players and their spouses to earn their undergraduate degrees in the cities in which their team is located (if possible). Currently, the Minnesota Vikings are an example of an NFL team that reimburses tuition to its players for completing their undergraduate education.

- *Career internship.* This program is designed to provide players with opportunities to develop skills in many career fields while each player is still active in the NFL. This program has three primary purposes: To explore the requirements of the job market as it exists outside of pro sports; to expand the employment experience of players outside of football in ways that will lead to meaningful employment when their football careers are over; and to network with companies participating in the internship program who are willing and relatively eager to extend temporary employment opportunities to players and spouses.

- *Family assistance.* This program is designed to help players and their families identify and manage a wide range of personal issues that, if left unattended, will interfere with the players' on-the-field performance and their personal and family lives. It involves efforts to provide players with the opportunity to work with a network of qualified professionals who can offer counseling on personal issues when needed.

For example, the family-assistance program can help newly acquired players and their families relocate and acclimate to their new communities. When appropriate, it can also help organize family self-help seminars. Whatever the focus of the program in a given situation, all personal matters involving problems with players and their families must be approached in total confidentiality by the team.

If they desire, teams can further expand their player-assistance programs by including structured efforts that focus on motivational counseling and performance enhancement. These efforts could deal with a diverse array of issues, including goal setting, time management, stress, concentration, fear of failure, relationships with coaches and staff, loss of confidence, transition and retirement.

Counseling injured players is another area that can be addressed by a team's player-assistance program. Such an endeavor can be designed to assist injured players to be able to handle such factors as player-trainer relationships, motivation for rehabilitation, loss of self-esteem, loneliness, and ostracism.

All aspects of a team's player-assistance program should be closely coordinated with other programs sponsored by the organization. For example, the decision of which player to use to make a player-appearance at a goodwill or charity function could be based, in part, on recommendations from the player-assistance program.

DEALING WITH PLAYERS WHO LEAVE THE GAME

The same dynamics that affect a head coach who retires (refer to Chapter 16 for a detailed overview of how such a situation can impact on the life of a head coach) also exist for players who leave the game for whatever reason (e.g., retirement, being released, etc.). The loss of recognition and praise once an athlete "hangs up his cleats" unquestionably occurs in the life cycle of a player.

One of the most important steps that you, as the head coach, can take to be better prepared to handle issues arising with a player who has left the game is to develop an understanding of how the situation may be affecting him. Once you have determined the nature of the impact that the situation is having on a particular individual, you can devise a plan to deal with relevant matters (i.e., provide counseling, career advice, educational opportunities, etc.).

Among the factors and the circumstances that may affect a player who has left the game that a coach should consider are the following:

- The most common problem with players who leave the game is that most of these individuals have almost forty productive years ahead of them (or as Paul Brown would say… "their life's work") and have no idea what to do with those years. Unfortunately, many of these individuals spend a number of years aimlessly trying to find themselves and trying to decide on doing something that is of real interest to them. They subsequently realize, however, that nothing excites them as much as playing in the NFL.

- The shock of being an integral part of something one day and completely out of the NFL the next day can have a traumatic affect on a former player. Suddenly, his life changes dramatically (e.g., the phones stop ringing, invitations to social gatherings aren't received, etc.). In reality, an individual who leaves the game is basically excluded from his former NFL life-style.

- Such an exclusion often affects the spouse of a former player also. She may feel the loss of NFL-related social opportunities even more than her husband.

- The wife of a former player may also find her husband's response to his situation to be very disturbing (i.e., severely depressed). The former player misses the crowded cubicle in the locker room—to a point where he feels completely alone in his spacious, well-appointed home.

  She probably has never seen her husband in such a state of mind before. Often, the shock arising from their situation to both the ex-athlete and his wife will lead to severe domestic difficulties between the two.

- Upon looking into the job market, the ex-player (e.g., a 34-year-old individual) may find that he has to compete with a 24-year-old, recent college graduate for the same position. The somewhat desperate situation for the former player is further compounded by the fact that the younger job candidate exudes a level of energy and enthusiasm that the ex-athlete hasn't exhibited since his days as a rookie in the NFL (a decade earlier).

- The key to resolving such a situation for most former players is reeducation and formal training for a new career. Without returning to the classroom or entering an extensive training program, a smooth and productive career change is virtually impossible for most ex-athletes.

- The ex-player's former head coach should realize that, all too often, a level of deep bitterness begins to build up toward him by the athlete. The athlete perceives his former coach to be the single person who had the greatest role in the player's ultimate destiny.

   Accordingly, the coach becomes the symbol that serves as a conduit for all of the depression and sadness that overtakes the athlete's life. In all too many instances, an ex-athlete believes that he could have continued to play.

   The player may also feel that other NFL organizations were not interested in him because the former coach ruined his chances by stating that his career should be over. Rarely is this the case. Coaches seldom (if ever) disparage a player in this manner to other teams.

   On the other hand, even if a coach were to publicly proclaim his opinions about whether a player should retire, most organizations are astute enough to make their own judgment on whether an available player has the ability to make a meaningful contribution to their teams.

   And yet, an ex-player may harbor harsh feelings toward his former head coach for years. Often, these feelings may last until the former player reaches a point in his life where a new-found maturity enables him to become more objective and realistic about why his career really ended.

- An even more deplorable situation may occur if the athlete tries to hang on too long to his playing career. For example, some athletes have been subjected to utter humiliation when attempting to extend their careers by joining another team.

   His new team holds little or no respect for him, other than having him serve as another "body" or as a convenient, short-term way to sell tickets. Unfortunately, the scenario for the academy award-winning movie, "Requiem for a Heavyweight," (which told the story of a formerly great boxer who stayed in the fight game far too long) has been revisited far too many times in the NFL.

DETERMINING THE FUTURE DYNAMICS OF PLAYER RELATIONS

Similar to other successful organizations, the NFL is constantly evolving in response to such factors as changing conditions, new guideline principles, and new priorities. In reality, many of the future dynamics of the NFL will have an impact on player relations.

Among the circumstances and factors that may affect player relations in the future are the following:

- Players will be even more preoccupied with "self."
- Agents will become even more dominating factors in the lives of the players they represent; these agents will provide counsel on all matters involving their clients and will act in a self-serving manner.
- The personal commitment of players to the organization, coaching staff, and team will diminish.
- Only the most informed (i.e. knowledgeable) and most talented (i.e., demonstrated ability to teach) coaches will gain the respect of the players.
- Because of the high salary structure for players, the time, thought and values of athletes will be taken up by outside forces.
- Because of the money involved, players will be even more concerned with their current situation, as opposed to having a long-term perspective.
- Players will be less willing to make a sacrifice by playing when injured.
- Players will make earning money their number one priority; their agents will foster and reinforce such an attitude, even though it is seldom in the long-term, best interests of the athletes.
- Players will give even more attention to their "unique image"; as such, the media will become even more of a major factor in a player's life.
- As they earn and accumulate wealth, players will be even more susceptible to the "lure" of an unacceptable life-style.
- Players will be even more likely to compare their salaries with other players and to lose their commitment to performing well at all times.
- Players will reprioritize their sense of loyalty; their allegiance will be given to their agents first, then to their friends, and next to the media. In this regard, the team will not fare well.
- Players will place an even more undue emphasis on their personal statistics. These statistics will be perceived by a player to be a major indicator of his worth, visibility, and rightful financial status.
- Given a player's relative wealth, instituting fines as a form of disciplinary action to discourage unacceptable behavior will have even less impact on him.
- Players will be even more inclined to engage in histrionics on the field during the game. Such attention-seeking demonstrations will continue to be an outgrowth of a player's attempt to achieve notoriety by drawing attention to himself.
- The salary disparity between the "haves" and "have-nots" on a team will become a major disruptive factor in the locker room.
- The changes in a team's coaching staff and the system the new staff plans to employ will be a major factor in the collective development of the entire team.

PART IV

THE
GAME

CHAPTER 10

DESIGNING A
WINNING GAME PLAN

"Admiral Nelson did not fight in order to carry out a plan;
instead, he planned in order to carry out a fight."

—J.F.C. Fuller
British Military Corespondent
The Decisive Battles of the Western World

Finding the winning edge...

*The goal of planning is to remove from a tough situation the panic
element of "What the hell are we going to do now?" The less thinking
people have to do under adverse circumstances, the better. When
you're under pressure, the mind can play tricks on you. It's a terrible
mistake to let outside forces influence you more than the pragmatic
realities of the situation already are. For instance, if I'm on the
sideline and the wind-chill factor is 10 degrees, I may decide,
"Damn, it's too cold, nobody could catch a pass." So I'll depart from
my plan and not call a pass, even though the players out on the field
are feeling a lot warmer than I am.*

*Better to reduce the effect of outside variables and revert to some-
thing you've practiced and practiced. When things get tense in a
football game, I want to be able to make decisions clinically, because
I've thought them through beforehand, rather than take an ad-libbed,
seat-of-the-pants approach. Sometimes this works, but more often
than not, these kinds of reactive decisions will be wrong. Being able
to go with a well-rehearsed plan is far better than depending on
heroics, which work better in fiction than in real life.*

—Bill Walsh, "When Things Go Bad,"
Forbes, March 29, 1993.

The literature is filled with volumes of information and theories concerning what it takes for an organization to be successful. Unquestionably, no factor affecting success is more important than preparation.

I have always believed in the absolute necessity of having a comprehensive plan for achieving organizational goals. Such a plan must deal with and address every reasonably foreseen contingency. The value of such a plan became even more evident to me in 1987, the year the players went on strike early in the season.

That season, the San Francisco 49ers, along with two or three other teams, had prepared for the strike. Believing that games played during the strike would actually count, Neal Dahlen, our head of scouting, searched for prospective players who might join the 49ers if the strike occurred. We also kept in touch with those players whom we had cut during camp because they knew our system.

Once the players went on strike, we immediately contacted all of these potential replacement players. Subsequently, those players who agreed to play during the strike formed a formidable team. We won every strike game, catapulting us to a great season record. This success was possible because we did our homework and took the League's memos seriously. Other teams did not; they apparently felt that if it was not "real NFL football," they wanted nothing to do with it. We took a strictly business approach, assembling a team without regard to sentiment. Other organizations became too emotionally involved with the issue. Because these organizations didn't see a clear bottom line, they were at cross-purposes to reality. In San Francisco, we treated our interim players with dignity and respect and tried to make the situation as interesting as possible. We even went to a wishbone-style attack for a game or two to add interest to practices and games.

When what is now known as the "West Coast Offense" was being developed, it was summarily dismissed by many people as nothing more than "nickel and dime" football. They argued that, as an offensive system, the "West Coast Offense" was developed out of a "desperate" attempt by a team to counteract its lack of overpowering personnel. History has shown that these individuals were glaringly mistaken.

All factors considered, this system of offensive play has proven to be very effective. Its success is reflected in a number of ways, including the fact that various forms of the "West Coast Offense" proliferated throughout the NFL. In a very literal sense, the "nickels and dimes" that the developers of the "West Coast Offense" brought to the game have become the current "coin of the realm."

The formula for the success of the offense was a highly disciplined, very structured form of utilizing the forward pass. To make our system work for the 49ers, Joe Montana had to master the disciplines to know which receiver to throw to, when and why. The success of the team depended on Joe's ability to work within that framework. Consequently, the job of the coach was to use drills and repetition so that Joe developed almost automatic moves and decision-making ability.

Teams which attempt to adopt the "West Coast Offense" and to duplicate its success solely by copying the schematics and the blocking schemes are taking a fragmented approach to installing such a system. In order to fully understand the

"West Coast Offense," a number of factors concerning the parameters of the system must be considered, including:

- *The type of offense needed.* The general rule is that the lower the level of play, the more basic the needs of the offensive system. The basic issue which should be addressed is whether the "West Coast" offensive system fits a team's personnel and whether this offensive system is the best system for facilitating success on the field.
- *The amount of total offense required.* Because every level of play involves a certain amount of demands being placed upon a team's offensive structure, teams should decide whether the "West Coast Offense" fits within a scope of offensive philosophy which is appropriate to their level of play.
- *The requirements for installing and implementing the system.* In this regard, the primary point that needs to be addressed is what is involved in properly installing the "West Coast Offense" and implementing its concept.

  For example, what are the time requirements for installation of the "West Coast Offense"? What is the proper sequencing for installing the components of the "West Coast Offense"? What additional factors (e.g., teaching progressions, mastering the fundamental concepts, etc.) should be considered when implementing the offense?

- *The practical application of the "West Coast Offense" on game day.* Applying the components of an offensive system against a particular opponent involves addressing five basic queries: Who, When, Where, Why, and How. For example, at a minimum, the following questions should be asked:
  - Who will be the key personnel at the point of attack?
  - When is the best time to run a particular play or initiate a specific sequence?
  - Where on the field does a particular play or play-sequence have the best chance for success?
  - Why will a particular play or play-sequence be productive versus this particular opponent or this specific defense?
  - How often may a particular play or play-sequence be repeated with relative assurance of its success and how should it be adjusted if it is to be repeated?
  - How do the environmental conditions (e.g., field conditions, weather conditions, etc.) affect the potential for the quality of play?

  In turn, an offensive system designed with these parameters in mind will "naturally" provide the head coach with insight into the all-important question— "what should be done." A team must know what to do in a given situation. For example, asking the following types of questions can enable a coach to be better prepared to handle specific contingencies as they arise.

- What adjustments in assignments, techniques, or schemes should a coach anticipate will be needed to improve a play or expand a play-sequence? And will these adjustments set up a complementary run or play pass?
- What defensive alignments or schemes does a particular play or play-sequence most effectively attack? To what defense is a play best suited? This point must

be considered when developing an audible package for a game and setting the conditions for its use.

- What players are indispensable to the success of a play or play-sequence? Which player or players, if lost to injury, would cause a particular play to be dropped from (or at the very least dropped down) the play-calling list.

- What risks are involved in running a particular play or play series? What is the cost-benefit ratio? On one hand, a particular play may have a relatively low-percentage chance of success; while on the other hand, it may provide substantial benefits.

   For example, a deep pass down the field may be a low-percentage throw (i.e., 3 of 10). If two of the three completions result in touchdowns and the third produces a 40-yard gain on the play, that kind of pass would typically be viewed as involving an acceptable risk.

   To some degree, most (if not all) of the issues involving what to do in a given situation are addressed in a properly designed offensive system. On the other hand, a coach must not allow the somewhat mundane routine of practicing a particular system to cause him to overlook the need to consider how the system applies to each different opponent. Neglecting to assess how the team's offensive system will be affected by a particular opponent can be a costly mistake.

No defensive coach will admit it, but it takes longer to prepare on offense. Now that I am out of football I can say so. With defense, it is a matter of setting a plan and reacting to what happens on the field. It is far more complicated on offense. You have so many details: blocking schemes, pass protections, blitz pickups, pass patterns, reads, adjustments, and so on.

Joe Gibbs
Hall-of-Fame Football Coach
Washington Redskins
from *Game Plans for Success*

IDENTIFYING AND IMPLEMENTING ESSENTIAL SKILLS

A critical part of the game-planning process is to identify the skills each player needs to perform the steps (tasks) involved in a particular play or play-sequence. After identifying the skills needed by the player, a team must have a process in place for ensuring that their players develop these skills so that each play or play-sequence is productive. Taking steps to develop these skills in every player occurs in two stages: isolating the skills and teaching the skills.

- *Isolate the skills.* The first step in the game-planning process should be to analyze the tasks involved in the assignment of every player. Next, a decision must be made regarding whether the players have the ability to master the necessary skills. If it is determined that the ability of the players does not mesh with the skills required for a specific task. If they do not, the head coach must either discard this part of his offensive plan or alter the play or play-sequence to fit the level of talent.

Whatever the head coach's decision, his decision can be made easier if he strictly adheres to one of the cardinal principles of training—specificity. Specificity refers to the fact that "an individual gets what he trains for." All factors considered, the more specific his players' preparation for a particular game, the better their performance.

* *Teach the skills.* Collectively, teaching players the skills they need involves an evolutional process of promoting, enhancing, practicing and refining each facet of the capacity being developed. In this regard, the rudimentary teaching progression of "hear it—see it—do it" is as applicable as it ever was.

Employing the proper teaching sequence is possibly the most viable way a coach can impact the game, certainly at the position level. Accordingly, as the head coach, you must make a decision as to what level of the teaching hierarchy you wish to utilize.

For example, with regard to teaching skills to your players, you must decide whether to rely on having the players learn by rote memorization or to require them to utilize critical thinking skills and acquire a more comprehensive knowledge of the offensive system. You should keep in mind that the more players are taught to critically analyze their responsibilities and to understand the relationship of these responsibilities to the total structure of the offense, the more productive the system will be.

By grasping a better understanding of the structural dynamics of the system and how one aspect of the offense interacts with another, the players will be better prepared to function as a "team" rather than simply a collection of eleven bodies following a prescribed action which they learned through rote memorization.

As the head coach, you should always endeavor to teach with a broad stroke (i.e., keep the "big picture" in mind). At all times, however, you must remain aware of the fact that some players are "better learners" than others. For those who have learning limitations (for whatever reason), you must be able to find a teaching vehicle that enables them to reach their full potential, despite their learning difficulties.

Success on the field does not occur by accident. Simply put, preparation precedes performance. The most brilliantly designed scheme and game plan is virtually worthless unless a well-orchestrated method of presenting, installing and practicing that scheme and plan exists.

As a rule, such a plan is implemented in two formats: meetings and practice. In each format, a very specific, definable and finite amount of time is allotted to accomplish what is required. A critical part of this triad (presentation, installation, and practice) is the realization that a physical and mental limit exists regarding the amount of time a player or group of players should be expected to function efficiently.

For example, an experienced coach is normally aware of the fact that there is a specific "time window" for maximum learning. In most instances, a coach cannot adequately cover a subject in less than ten minutes.

On the other hand, many players have difficulty maintaining their focus and giving their undivided attention to a particular subject for longer than twenty minutes at a time. As a result, coaches must make optimal use of the ten-minute window of opportunity that exists for effective teaching and learning.

As a teacher, the coach has an obligation to be tireless in his efforts to heighten the learning curve of his players. All the latest technological developments (e.g., video, digital filming, computers, etc.) must be used to facilitate optimal learning.

In reality, however, one of the best ways for a coach to enhance the learning process for his players is by being organized. Wasting time during the week not only can drain the physical and mental energy of the players and coaching staff, it can result in a lack of concentration and a lack of a central focus.

Players should always be informed about what they will be doing in practice and why they will be doing it. For example, the purpose of any drill conducted in practice, as well as the techniques or skills the drill is intended to develop, should be communicated to the players. Particularly on the professional level, an effort must be made to make the purpose of drills clear to the players.

DEVELOPING A STANDARD OF PERFORMANCE

The old adage that a team doesn't win on game day but in the meeting rooms and on the practice field during the week leading up to the game may be overly simplistic, but it does underscore a critical point. As the head coach, you have the greatest opportunity to impact the outcome of a game prior to game day.

While the standard of performance that you, as the head coach, are held accountable for is manifested on game day, this standard is established during the off-season, training camp and weekly preparation times. The process begins with you insisting that your players exhibit an uncompromising work ethic.

The players must be made to understand that football should involve a business-like atmosphere—one in which the players must conduct themselves accordingly. In this regard, there are several steps you can take to help facilitate a proper training atmosphere, including:

- Enlist and utilize the support of the veteran players.
- Convince the players of the value of a strong work ethic.
- Make the players understand the value of time (i.e., because a limited amount of time to prepare exists, it must not be wasted).
- Convince the players of the need for professionalism in their work and behavior.
- Make the players feel at ease with the direction of the team's leadership.
- Appreciate the value of using humor and an easy-going manner in the learning process, as long as such an approach doesn't divert the present level of focus and concentration of the players on the task at hand.
- Ensure that the assistant coaches maintain the continuity of the program.

Demanding a high standard of performance requires the coaching staff to be very sensitive to the need to use the players' time wisely. The coaching staff has an obligation to the players to keep the process for installing the game plan meaningful and vibrant.

Toward that end, the coaching staff should not waste the players' time with superfluous meetings or pointless practice sessions. It is also important that all coaches continually demonstrate the highest standards of coaching.

Perhaps, the key factor in establishing a proper work environment is the fact that coaches and players must have a professional respect for the value of each other's role in the process. Coaches prepare the team to play; players make a commitment to learning and to applying what they have learned in the game.

Getting the team ready to play requires the coaching staff to put the players in a learning environment that is designed to condition and prepare them for every possible contingency they might face in a game situation. In other words, the primary responsibility of the coaching staff involves "the reduction of uncertainty"—a simple, but eloquent, description of the absolute essence of teaching.

The critical point that the coaching staff should keep in mind is that if the information that has been provided to the players does not in some measurable way reduce their level of uncertainty or hesitation with regard to their basic understanding then it is information that either is not needed or has been presented in an ineffective manner.

As the head coach, you can undertake several steps to optimize the players' learning curve and to reduce their level of uncertainty, including:

- Drive the players to concentrate. Be assertive in your insistence that they focus on the task at hand.

- Individualize your teaching approach to fit certain individuals, when necessary. Give extra time to those players who need it.

- Be as precise as possible when teaching. Always use the system's terminology as a common language.

- Be patient, but demanding. Require your players to adhere to proper techniques at all times.

- Teach the skills progressively. Adhere to a systematic methodology of teaching that allows the players to improve and enhances their level of confidence in your competence and professionalism.

- Keep your finger on the pulse of the situation. Be alert to the intensity level of the players. Be sensitive to signs of those factors which can affect the learning curve (e.g., fatigue, enthusiasm of coaches, etc.). Never overlook the fundamental reality of the teaching axiom, "quality repetitions are the mother of all learning."

- Keep the meetings quality, not quantity, oriented. Use a variety of learning tools to enhance the learning environment and to help stimulate the players' level of concentration and focus (e.g., computer graphics, overhead projection, videotape, etc.).

- Demonstrate the highest level of knowledge about the subject matter being taught (e.g., position techniques, game strategy, the opponent, etc.).

- Teach the players in a professional manner. Unless you're trying to elicit a specific emotional response from your players, refrain from screaming and demonstrative behavior. Keep in mind that such behavior seldom, if ever, enhances the learning curve—particularly if the subject matter involves technical information.

- Evaluate the players' performance on a daily basis to ensure that they are progressively mastering the techniques required to perform the tasks they are assigned in an effective and efficient manner.

Rapidity is the essence of war; take advantage of the enemy's unreadiness, make your way by unexpected routes, and attack unguarded spots.

Sun-Tzu
Chinese Military Strategist
from *The Art of War*

Another teaching technique that has proven to be very effective is to have players emulate the techniques and actions of other athletes. For example, if players watch video showing Jerry Rice run a particular pattern in a certain way, you (as the head coach) can single out and stress particular coaching points, by using Rice as the case in point.

All factors considered, players tend to respond more favorably to an actual visual representation of a particular teaching point than to an abstract illustration of that point drawn up on a chalkboard or written up in a playbook. This learning technique is typically referred to as "modeling."

As such, modeling has been shown to have a positive effect on the learning process. With video as its primary medium, modeling is a "natural" teaching tool for most athletes. Very few competitive athletes cannot recall their boyhood experiences of watching a favorite sports hero perform some Herculean act on television (e.g., throwing a game-winning touchdown pass, making a key interception, etc.), and then going to their local playground with their friend to play and imagining that they were equally heroic while imitating the hero's every move.

An example of using multiple settings to make a point might involve a situation where you want to address your belief that engaging in histrionics (i.e., undue demonstrations) after a score produces an unacceptable distraction to both the players participating in the theatrics and their teammates. Initially, you might cover the subject in a team meeting.

Realizing that more needs to be done in this area, you might then follow-up that effort in the next few days by going into the individual position meetings and reinforcing your message on histrionics. Finally, while walking off the field after a practice, you might emphasize the point individually to some of those players who are most prone to that kind of behavior.

Whatever the sequence and the selection of settings, you should vary your message somewhat every year. For example, if you give the same speech year after year, the players who have been associated with you for any length of time may arbitrarily tune you out.

If you don't periodically alter your talk, you may, in this situation, be greeted with a collective sigh of "oh no, here goes the no-demonstrations-in-the-end zone speech again." Accordingly, it is incumbent on you to constantly find new ways to present the same material.

If there is a point you feel particularly strongly about, you must include your assistant coaches in the process of reinforcing your message. For example, if your staff is made aware of a particular theme or topic that you are going to address with the team, your assistant coaches can prepare materials to facilitate the objectives of your talk.

At the very least, your assistants can give some thought as to how they might reemphasize some of the basic concepts attendant to the fundamental point you want made in their daily meetings and interactions with the players. Having both the head coach and his staff emphasize a particular point will give the players a real sense of the importance of a given topic and will prevent your players from misconstruing your message as something that just occurred to you.

An example of using both the head coach and his staff to communicate, fortify and support a particular message might involve a situation where the head coach wants to make a theme such as "beat the opponent to the punch" a major team focus. Early in the planned effort to make the theme an integral part of the team's thought processes, the point could be covered by the head coach on numerous occasions during mini-camps and training camps.

The head coach's message could be conveyed in several ways (e.g., pre-lecture comments; video clips from other sports, such as boxing; etc.). The assistant coaches could then reinforce the theme, not only in their daily meetings with the players, but also verbally on the field in their teaching progressions.

At every opportunity, the importance and the practical application of the theme should be accentuated by every member of the coaching staff. Eventually, the "beat them to the punch" theme should be stressed to a point where it becomes an integral part of every player's mindset during the game.

Firm reliance on self must make him proof against the seeming pressure of the moment; his first conviction will in the end prove true.

Carl von Clausewitz
Director of General War Academy
Prussia
from *On War*

ACCOUNTING FOR SITUATION, CONTINGENCY AND REACTIVE OFFENSE

One of the most difficult tasks a head coach faces is making crucial judgments under severely stressful conditions. The better prepared the head coach is, the more capable he will be of acting under pressure.

Because preparation is based on probability rather than certainty, as the head coach, you must account for every situation and contingency that can be reasonably anticipated. Anticipating the factors which may cause you to experience severe stress during the game can be helpful in several ways, including:

- Reduces the likelihood that you will have to do too much guessing under the stress of the game.
- Enhances your ability to make adjustments during the game.
- Provides the players with a preview of what to expect in critical situations.
- Takes tremendous pressure off the signal caller.
- Gives confidence to the players and the staff in knowing that you are prepared for all possible circumstances.
- Allows you to believe in and stay with your game plan.

Preparing for potential problems doesn't mean you are taking a negative outlook. For example, practicing your goal line defense doesn't necessarily reflect the fact that you think your defense will be soft and allow the opponent on the goal line.

By the same token, practicing the "scramble drill" doesn't mean you feel that your quarterback will probably be under pressure all day. Rather, practicing for every reasonable situation and contingency means that you are upholding your primary responsibility to the team—reducing the level of uncertainty by thoroughly preparing the team.

Situational Offense

The term "situational offense" refers to the specific situations which have to be addressed, in varying degrees, during the game. Each of these involves very specific conditions (e.g., down, distance, field position, etc.). At least nine different categories of the situational offense exist:

- *Normal down and distance in the open field.* This situation offers the head coach the most latitude to establish his preferred style and tempo of play. As a rule, fifty percent of the offensive play calls during a game will occur within the parameters of normal down and distance in the open field. On first and second down, the normal down-and-distance situation in the open field should be attacked with three main objectives in mind: get a first down or a series of first downs; position the offensive unit in a favorable third-down situation (e.g., 3rd-and-4, 3rd-and-2, etc.); and score or run an explosive play (i.e., make a big gain that establishes dominant field position).

Moving the chains on first and second down is a hallmark of a good offense. Most of a team's attention in a 1st-and-10 situation should be focused on positioning the offense in a favorable down-and-distance situation (i.e., keeping the distance convertible).

Statistics demonstrate, however, that only 25-35 percent of a team's first downs are generated on third-down conversions. The remaining 65-75 percent of the team's first downs are generated on first and second down. Consequently, a team's third-down conversion ratio, while an important factor, is typically not a primary factor in winning the game.

As the head coach, you should not only consider the best method for converting the necessary third down, you should also attempt to obtain the most favorable third-down field position possible. To ensure a favorable third-down situation, your play selection should emphasize calls with a high probability of at least 4+ yards efficiency on both first and second down.

An efficient first-down level of success is defined by the ratio of the number of gains of 4+ yards on first down to the total number of first-down opportunities. Statistically, the first-down ratio has been shown to be one of the major determinants affecting the outcome of the game.

A team's third objective in a normal down-and-distance situation in the open field should be to strike with an explosive play. First and second down are normally the best downs for calling an explosive play because of the multiple concerns that a defense must prepare for on these downs.

The NFL defines an explosive play as a play that results in a gain of 20 yards or more. Statistics show that a team which achieves a +2 advantage in explosive plays (i.e., has at least two more explosive plays than its opponent) wins the game 80-85 percent of the time.

Explosive plays may either be by design or take the form of a broken play which results in a score or a big gain. If you determine that your offense is being controlled to the point where it has been unable to successfully execute explosive plays, you must change the situation by injecting a higher degree of explosiveness into your offense through planned plays that have been specifically designed to strike a "decisive blow."

You should keep in mind that even the top NFL teams demonstrate the ability to sustain drives of ten plays or more only 15-20 percent of the time. As a result, the inclusion of explosive plays is a critical step when planning a situational offense.

- *Backed-up.* The most critical situation to consider when developing a situational offensive plan is when a team is backed-up (i.e., when the offense takes possession of the ball inside of its own ten-yard line). The critical nature of a backed-up situation is even greater when the offense takes possession inside its own five-yard line.

Among the priorities which you should consider when your team is operating within the confines of the backed-up situation are:

— Moving the ball past at least the five-yard line.
— Selecting core plays which are low-risk.
— Reducing the chances of fumbling by limiting the ball-handling to key players.
— Selecting plays from the short-yardage section of your game-plan.
— Cutting off defensive penetration with a double tight-end formation.
— Utilizing a close flanker to block the blitzing strong safety.
— Selecting passes that emphasize ball control.
— Selecting ball-control passes which are thrown to the outside (i.e., passes thrown over the middle are more likely to result in either an interception or a fumble caused by a forceful hit on a relatively exposed receiver by a defender).
— Throwing the ball deep to change the momentum and keep the defense off the field.
— Throwing passes only to the strong-hand side of the quarterback (i.e., a right-handed quarterback should pass to his right).
— Avoiding plays in which both guards pull.
— Attacking the defense between the ends.
— Deciding if taking a safety is an acceptable option.

• *Third down.* One of the less complicated situations during a game for which a team has to prepare is third down. Most teams have very specific tendencies with regard to their defensive package and strategy on third down. Most NFL teams typically face an average of twelve to fourteen third-down situations a game.

Statistics show that ten of these third-down situations will occur in the open field. As a rule, the "better" NFL teams convert on 3rd-down situations at the following rates:

— 3rd-and-long (7+ yards)   20-25 percent
— 3rd-and-medium (2-6 yards)   45-50 percent
— 3rd-and-short (one yard or less) 80-85 percent

A statistical analysis of the more successful teams in the NFL reveals the necessity of focusing on getting the offense into a favorable third-down situation (e.g., either 3rd-and-medium or 3rd-and-short). For example, a 3rd-and-medium yardage situation is converted at twice the rate of the third-and-long situation.

The importance of this factor is further underscored by the previously discussed first-down ratio. A productive first-down ratio in the open field directly affects the number of favorable third-down situations attained.

• *Fourth down.* Although the average NFL team rarely attempts to convert on a fourth-down situation, the critical nature of this type of situation demands that a team's planning efforts for fourth-down situations be given a high priority. A team should plan for three distinct types of fourth-down situations: 4th-and-inches, 4th-and-short, and 4th-and-long.

Factors such as the caliber of the opponent, whether a team is at home or on the road and the defensive style of a team's opponent are examples of circumstances which should be considered when a team is calculating its chances of success in this situation and is developing an appropriate fourth-down conversion strategy. The situation in which a fourth-down conversion attempt will be made should be well-defined prior to the game.

- *Red zone.* In the 1990s, NFL teams have averaged three red-zone (i.e. a situation where a team is on or is within 20 yards of its opponent's goal line) possessions a game and scored 80-85 percent of the time. A recent defensive trend toward the use of a four-across zone coverage in the red zone has greatly reduced the level of effectiveness of the traditional offensive strategy of attacking favorable man-to-man matchups in the passing game. When you are establishing the priorities of your red-zone offense, the following steps should be considered:
  — Run the ball if possible.
  — Use motion to isolate the desired matchups.
  — Run plays which are designed to beat the blitz and man-to-man coverage.
  — Pass the ball to the underneath routes.
  — Run plays that do not risk losing yardage; the offense should not be taken out of field-goal range.
  — Group your play-calling with regard to the ten-yard divisions of the red zone (e.g., 30-yard line, 20-yard line, 10-yard line). Once inside the 20-yard line, the passing game should normally be opened up since the depth of the drop is less likely to result in a sack which could take your team out of field goal range. In addition, since defenses tend to base their red-zone strategy according to the location of the ball with regard to the ten-yard divisions, considering these defensive tendencies when establishing a red-zone offense can produce positive results. Keep in mind that the red zone is an excellent area of the field to run different plays from formations previously shown in the open field.
  — Anticipate the blitz and run a package designed to take advantage of the blitz when your team is positioned somewhere between the 15- and 25-yard lines. As a general rule, the defense is unlikely to blitz on back-to-back plays in this area. Throw the ball into the end zone. Use motion to isolate the desired matchup with your best receiver.
  — Select rushing plays, because in most instances, the defense tends to stay in a base front when the offense is positioned between the 10- and 15-yard lines. Alert the quarterback to audible if the defense jumps into a goal line front.

- *First and goal.* Statistics indicate that, on the average, a team should plan on having about two 1st-and-goal opportunities in a game. A first-and-goal offensive package should include two or three runs and one or two passes off of those formations.

Don't hesitate to give serious consideration to throwing the ball on the goal line, particularly from awkward situations (e.g., 1st-and-goal from the 9-yard line, 2nd-and-goal from the 7-yard line, etc.). Since virtually every pass this close to the goal line involves a throw into the end zone, the quarterback must be very focused on what he expects to see before he throws the ball.

In this area of the field, it is very difficult to account for every defender. As a result, the quarterback is vulnerable to being intercepted. You should keep in mind that nothing tends to demoralize an offense more than moving the ball the length of the field and then turning it over so close to the goal line.

- *Goal line.* Similar to the first-and-goal situational offense, the offensive package for those situations where a team is within three yards of its opponent's goal line should be carefully planned. The average NFL team will encounter the goal line situation approximately three times a game.

   Accordingly, a team should decide exactly which goal-line plays it plans to use during a game and how much yardage it expects to gain on each play. Furthermore, for its running plays on the goal line, it is desirable to distinguish between those running plays which will be used from the three-yard line and those that will be called when the team is within a yard of the goal line.

   You should plan to run a play in only one direction, either to the right or to the left. Plays should not be flipped from side to side.

   This approach will eliminate some of the guess work that may occur during the pressure situations of a game and will help bring more focus to a team's weekly preparation. When running the ball, a team should call a play that gives the ball to the back who runs most effectively behind the team's best blockers.

   Because it is often extremely tough to run the ball well in a goal-line situation, a team should plan to have passes as 50 percent of its goal-line offense. Furthermore a team should have a plan for what play it will call (run or pass) when it only needs to gain inches.

- *2-point play.* In the NFL, the average team runs only one or two 2-point conversion attempts a year. Because a team will typically (at best) face only two third-down calls a game inside its opponent's 10-yard line, it may be sensible for a team to combine these two situational elements of the offense into a three-to-four play package that encompasses both its first-and-goal calls and its 2-point conversion plays.

   Deciding what to call in this situation is compounded by the tactical circumstances. On one hand, the three-yard distance makes rushing for a 2-point conversion a challenging assignment. On the other hand, the relatively compact area of the field (i.e., a working depth of 13 yards) makes it somewhat difficult to pass.

   The major coaching point for your quarterback is to recognize that an interception cannot be returned for points. This rule applies only to the NFL. Accordingly, if the quarterback is about to be sacked on a two-point conversion, he should go down fighting and take his chances by throwing the ball up for "grabs."

   This advice is obviously confined solely to 2-point conversion attempts in the NFL. It certainly differs from a situation involving a 3rd-down attempt from the same area on the field where the option of kicking a field goal still exists. It is also different from a 4th-down situation where an errant pass attempt can be returned for points.

- *Blitz.* Most teams normally carry two or three "blitz- beaters" in their offensive game plan. Blitz beaters are specific plays and protections that can be called or audibled to in order to enable a team to take advantage of a defensive blitz.

All factors considered, the best way to discourage a team from blitzing is to "hurt it" and to "hurt it big" (i.e., either score or gain substantial yardage on a particular play). The reality of the situation is that conservative measures will not stop an opponent from blitzing.

One of the best ways to "hurt" a defensive team that blitzes is to exercise the "hot" option of a basic pass play. The "hot" option involves a situation where the quarterback has the choice of dropping the ball off to a designated receiver for which the defense cannot account when blitzing.

For example, a sight read of the blitz may enable the quarterback to hit a quick slant that occurs as a result of a route adjustment by his receiver. By the same token, the quarterback may audible to an eight-man protection scheme that enables his receivers to push their routes further downfield against the one-on-one coverage that occurs during a blitz.

Both of these scenarios are examples of situations where the countermeasures to a blitz are likely to result in a big gain. In either instance, it is important that your team understands why you are using this play and when you expect to employ it.

It is also important that a team does not rely on an eight-man protection scheme as the foundation of its blitz beaters. Some teams often spend an inordinate amount of time on practicing the eight-man protection scheme, yet employ it only a few times a year.

The point to consider in this regard is that if a scheme is only going to be used on a very infrequent basis (i.e., a team audibles to it only in extreme situations), it is not likely to be something that the team is going to be able to execute with a great degree of confidence.

A more desirable approach would be to develop a viable offensive package to counter the blitz that is more a part of your team's base offense. As a result, because this element of the offense would be something that a team would perform on a more regular basis, the team's chances for success would be increased substantially.

Finally, it is very important that you address the emotional and mental circumstances of a blitzing situation. You should take the approach that the blitz is an "opportunity," rather than a foreboding event. Accordingly, a blitzing situation offers an excellent chance for the offense to make a big gain (i.e., achieve an explosive play).

One reason I so seldom reacted to a big Cowboys' play was because I hardly ever saw any of our offensive plays. I always knew what play we had called. I didn't have to watch it. The only uncertainty was how the opposition reacted; it was their defense I needed to watch and analyze so I would know best how to counter it. Once a play ended, I never had time to react, immediately shifting focus to my game plan to decide what play I should send in next.

Tom Landry
Hall-of-Fame Football Coach
Dallas Cowboys
from *Tom Landry, An Autobiography*

Contingency Offense

The contingency component of a team's offense is designed to deal with those situations which are time-related. Contingency offensive situations may not even arise in a game.

When they do arise, however, they are critical to the success of your team. The two basic types of contingency offensive situations are the four-minute offense and the two-minute offense.

- *Four-minute offense.* The primary goal of the four-minute offense is to take as much time off the clock as possible, while enabling a team to protect its lead. This type of offense involves four basic objectives:
  - Moving the ball on the ground.
  - Making first downs.
  - Keeping the clock running.
  - Protecting the football.

  Every player should be aware of the fact that a play that does not go out of bounds normally will take a minimum of 35 seconds off the clock. As a result, every ball carrier should stay in bounds unless he has a very distinct opportunity to make a first down by going for the sideline.

  Other coaching points involving the four-minute offense that should be made to the players include:
  - The ball carrier should not struggle for extra yardage unless he is going for a first down. Struggling for "inches" may needlessly expose the ball to the defenders.
  - The ball carrier should anticipate that the defenders will attempt to strip the ball. Accordingly, downfield blockers should make every effort to keep additional defenders from taking a shot at the ball carrier.
  - The quarterback should follow the running play in a case of a fumble.
  - The quarterback should take a sack, rather than throw a risky pass.
  - The quarterback should run down the 30-second play clock whenever possible.

— The quarterback should be prepared to run the ball on any pass play.
— The receivers should be aware of the distance needed to get a first down and to keep the drive alive.
— The linemen should be alert for stunts and blitzes.
— Each first down made either takes at least 90 seconds off the running clock or forces the defense to use its time-outs.
— Poise is crucial late in the game when tempers often flare because of the frustration of the opponent. Players should not retaliate under any circumstances.
— Players must avoid penalties. An offensive penalty not only stops the clock (thereby giving an opponent 35 extra seconds), it can also have an impact on tactics (i.e., leads to a potential—clock-stopping—incomplete pass in an attempt by the team to make up the penalized yardage).

Among the strategic considerations that should be factored in when designing a four-minute offense are the following:

— Using tight formations (i.e., a close flanker, two tight ends, a tight wide receiver, etc.) to help protect against outside blitzing or penetration.
— Using a consistent and short snap count in order to avoid illegal procedure penalties.
— Using basic timing pass patterns when throwing the ball if the team is in a must-pass situation.
— Using play-passes.
— Avoiding reverses and other types of plays that involve extra ball handling.
— Avoiding special plays or untested plays.
— Reminding the players to keep the pace slow (i.e., use at least 30 seconds per play; get up slowly off the pile of players on a ball carrier; etc.).
— Avoiding the unnecessary shuffling of personnel into the game.
— Alerting the punter to punt the ball as high as possible and informing the punt team to cover but not down the ball outside of the red zone.
— Alerting the punt returner to either fair catch or avoid the ball.
— Deciding if taking a safety is appropriate when punting from a backed-up situation.
— Being prepared to attack the goal line defense as the clock winds down.
— Knowing when to call the "victory" formation and have the quarterback down the ball.

- *Two-minute offense.* The second type of time-related contingency offense is the two-minute offense. A two-minute offense is designed to enable a team to accomplish specific objectives within the limited amount of time available.

The offense must have the ability to activate the two-minute offense within the body of a drive. A two-minute offense is usually driven by the specific conditions of the game.

For example, a two-minute offense activated prior to the end of the first half is usually directed to get the team into position for a medium-range field goal. If the two-minute drill is employed near the end of the game, the objective is usually to secure whatever points are needed for a win or at least a tie.

If a field goal is necessary for a tie, a team should get within reasonable field-goal range (i.e., to the 20-yard line) before taking a shot at a winning touchdown. On the other hand, if a field goal will win the game, the team should just work to get as close as possible during the two-minute offense.

Among the coaching points involving the two-minute offense that should be emphasized to the players are the following:

— If the situation permits, the quarterback should be prepared to discuss strategies and make plans for dealing with the immediate circumstances. In addition, the entire offensive unit should gather together to discuss the parameters of what the offense is planning to do and to be reminded of the tactical situation (i.e., review the expected defensive scheme).
— The quarterback should alert the referee that he will be calling a quick time-out if the ball stays in play.
— The quarterback should be alert to have the team line up at the line of scrimmage as soon as possible if the clock is running.
— The quarterback should call out the formation as soon as possible.
— The quarterback should call the play without a huddle if the clock is running or if there is confusion on a play call.
— The quarterback should kill the clock by spiking the ball if necessary.
— The quarterback should be sure to use a distinct move when downing the ball.
— The quarterback should play with poise and avoid all desperate acts.
— The quarterback should remember that, depending on the situation, an incomplete pass may be better than a completed pass involving a short gain.
— The quarterback should employ high-risk throws only in the waning seconds of the game (half).
— The wide receivers should be prepared to remain on the same side of the field as the previous play (i.e., X stays on left, Z on right, etc.), unless the quarterback directs them to move.
— The wide receivers and the offensive linemen should be prepared to react to the quarterback scrambling.
— The running back should knock down the "meaningless" catch (i.e., a catch that could result in a loss and the clock continuing to move).
— The running back should be prepared to receive a lateral downfield from the receiver if the clock is winding down.
— The running back should not struggle for extra yards; it's a waste of valuable time.
— The linemen should avoid any suspicion of holding.
— The linemen should hustle to the line of scrimmage.
— Everyone should be alert to a no-huddle call by the quarterback.
— Hustle back across the line of scrimmage after each play; everyone should assume that the next play is a no-huddle call and line-up immediately.

- The entire unit should establish a rhythm as practiced; no one should panic or act in a hysterical manner.
- Everyone should maintain his poise (i.e., concentrate) before the ball is snapped; each player should remember that it is better to initiate his movement somewhat late than to move too early.
- Every offensive player should assume that the defense will blitz on the play; no one must be surprised by a blitz.
- A ball carrier (or receiver) who is going out of bounds should get completely across the sideline, on his feet.
- The team should get a first down on a third-down pass (and certainly gain one on fourth down).
- No one should be provoked or distracted by the defenders; such a reaction is a waste of time.
- Everyone (running backs, wide receivers, the quarterback) should protect the ball when running; this possession may be the last time the offense has the ball in the game.
- All running backs and receivers should catch the ball before running with it; once they catch the ball, they should run in a decisive manner and avoid desperate actions.
- If the clock is running, everyone should keep in mind that a field goal attempt takes approximately 15 seconds to get the field goal-kicking unit onto the field and to kick the ball.
- Every player should focus on the fact that the team's best chance for success is for everyone to properly execute their responsibilities as planned and practiced.

Among the steps that you, as the head coach, should take with regard to the two-minute offense are the following:

- Be aware of the two-minute warning; if possible, let the clock run down to the warning.
- Plan plays which may be used for conditions that may develop.
- Gather the offense on the sideline whenever possible; keep everyone else clear of the area.
- Make a decision to return a punt or to fair catch before the return team takes the field.
- Keep messengers ready to run messages into the game.
- Be sure that your key personnel are on the field.
- Have the ball snapped on "set," unless otherwise indicated in the huddle.
- Have plays called at the line of scrimmage in order to increase the pressure on the defense.
- Call a rushing play that is designed for a second-down situation against a nickel package.
- Avoid calling special plays or new plays because they have a limited chance of success because of the stressful nature of the situation.
- Alert the field goal team to be ready if called upon.

Depending upon how much time is left in the game (or half), a team should vary its offensive strategy as follows:

— Three minutes remaining.

√ Speed up the offense (i.e., get set up quickly).

√ Alternate using a huddle and running a no-huddle offense.

√ Stop the clock as often as possible by having the ball carrier go out of bounds on run and pass plays.

√ Consider taking a time-out when facing a critical third-down call (before punting).

√ Take advantage of the game clock being stopped at the two-minute mark.

√ Realize that a running play is appropriate if the game clock is approaching the two-minute mark (i.e., up to 2:10 left on the clock).

— Two minutes remaining.

√ Employ the no-huddle offense unless the clock is stopped.

√ Run your basic offense.

√ Utilize one of your three remaining time-outs.

√ Stop the clock with sideline passes or quarterback runs.

√ Utilize all four downs when calling plays at the end of the game.

— Ninety seconds remaining.

√ Utilize a no-huddle offense after a big gain, unless too much time will be taken; in that instance, spike the ball.

√ Must begin using time-outs with the clock running; save one time-out.

√ Be decisive in calling a time-out; must not waste precious seconds deciding whether to use a time-out; get immediately to the referee to call a time-out.

√ Be aware that using a time-out for a conference between the quarterback and the coaches can be very worthwhile.

√ Must be willing to use your time-outs; don't leave them on the board when the game ends.

— One minute remaining.

√ Throw downfield (to the sideline, if possible).

√ Realize that you can afford throwing one pass inside if you have one remaining time-out you can call or if the quarterback "spikes" the ball to kill the clock on the next snap of the ball; be aware that a spike typically takes 10-20 seconds to execute.

√ Use a time-out or spike the ball if the clock is running when the play ends.

— Fifteen seconds remaining.

√ Throw a pass and have the receiver go out-of-bounds after catching the ball or immediately call a time-out.

√ Run the pass package that you've planned for the last five seconds and hope for an interference call on the play.

√   Realize that the team must first get into position for a "rebound pass" on a ball thrown into the end zone (or into field-goal range if the tactical situation warrants it).

Depending upon a team's offensive game plan and the tactical situation, a team has several play-calling alternatives, including:

- Scenario #1: The clock is stopped—a single play is called from the press box.
    - If the clock is running after the play is completed, utilize a no-huddle offense (call a basic pass or run play).   .
    - If the clock is stopped after a play is run, start the play sequence again.
    - If the clock continues to run after the next play is completed, either call a time-out prior to third down or continue to use the no-huddle offense until the clock is stopped (either by the results of the play or by utilizing a time-out).
- Scenario #2: The clock is stopped—two plays are called from the press box.
    - Even if the clock is stopped after the first play is completed, continue on and run the second play that was called (unless such a play is inappropriate for the situation).
    - Then, go to a no-huddle offense unless it's a third-down situation; if it's third down, call a time-out.
    - In a four-down situation, you must call time-out immediately before the fourth down; this step enables calls to be made that are not part of a team's audible package or that require additional information (e.g., motion, formation, etc.) in the huddle.
- Scenario #3: A no-huddle offense is utilized regardless of whether the clock is stopped.
    - This approach puts more pressure on a defense by limiting the defense from making personnel changes (on the fly) or inhibiting the ability of the defense to make the proper defensive calls.
    - Because of the critical nature of the situation facing the offense, a team's offensive play calling may be somewhat hurried in the no-huddle offense and its options may be relatively limited.

If you make a mistake, admit it quickly and emphatically, and don't dwell on it.

John Madden
Former Football Coach
Oakland Raiders

Reactive Offense

Similar to their offensive counterparts, defensive coaches base much of their game plans on the offensive tendencies of their opponents. Such tendencies typically evolve from the offense's reaction to such fundamental factors as down, distance, field position, personnel, situational circumstances, and contingency plans.

In response, defenses often develop plans to counter a team's offensive tendencies. Accordingly, a team should include plays in its offensive attack that offset its own tendencies or take advantage of a defense's probable predisposition to act in a certain way in a particular situation.

Collectively, these special plays are commonly referred to as a team's "reactive offense." As the head coach, you should ensure that your team is properly prepared to react in all conventional reactive situations, including:

- A first-down call after getting a first down rushing.
- A first-down call after getting a first down passing.
- A first-down call after the completion of an explosive pass.
- A first-down call after an explosive run.
- A first-down call after a positive penalty (i.e., 1st-and-5).
- A second-down call after a sack.
- The next first-down call to start a series after your team has lost the ball on a fumble or interception.
- A first-down call to start a series after your opponent's loss of a possession due to a turnover.

Win the war, then fight the war.

Sun-Tzu
Chinese Military Strategist
from *The Art of War*

ESTABLISHING OPENERS

An integral part of many teams' offensive game plan is to script "openers." Openers are a prepared list of plays (i.e., 10-15 plays) that a team plans to use to start ("open") the game.

As a rule, players tend to like the use of openers because the procedure enables them to know ahead of time what they will be doing on their first one or two series. Scripting openers offers several other advantages, including:

- *Allows the head coach to make decisions in a detached and thoughtful manner.* This point recognizes the fact that even the best of game-day coaches must plan ahead for all possible contingencies if the circumstances that a team will inevitably face each week are going to be handled effectively.

- *Allows the head coach to determine an appropriate balance between running plays and passing plays on first down.* For example, most teams prefer to achieve a 50-50 balance between runs and passes on first downs. One of the best ways to maintain such a ratio is through the scripting of openers.

- *Allows the head coach to be more creative in his team's personnel groupings early in the game by having the offensive sequence planned ahead of time.* By controlling the sequencing of his team's openers, the head coach can take a much more detailed approach to establishing legitimate play-action and play passes based on the formations and the personnel groupings that will be employed early in the game plan. In addition, openers provide those players who have a limited role in the offense with an opportunity to see exactly where and how they will have a chance to contribute.

- *Enables the head coach to be able to quickly determine how the defense will react to specific formations and personnel groupings.* Openers are an excellent way to test the defense to see what its game plan is, based on the offense's formations and personnel. In turn, by anticipating what adjustments a defense will make, the offense can be designed to counter (and take advantage of) those adjustments.

- *Allows the head coach to give his assistant coaches an opportunity to check for defensive factors which might affect the effectiveness of a particular play or offensive sequence.* By knowing ahead of time what plays will be run, when such plays will be run and what they should watch for, the coaching staff will be better prepared to provide meaningful feedback (i.e., suggest alternative plays) concerning the defense's reaction to a team's openers.

- *Allows the players, especially the quarterback, to get into an appropriate rhythm.* All factors considered, when players have practiced a particular sequence of plays, they tend to derive a certain level of confidence in the sequence from the experience.

  This confidence increases the likelihood that these players can get into and maintain a sense of rhythm in the game. When an offense is in rhythm, a certain desirable level of pacing exists in the huddle, as well as on the line of scrimmage.

- *Allows the head coach to script specific "special" plays and increases the likelihood that they will actually be employed in the game.* Most teams have a couple of special plays that are part of their game plan (e.g., some type of reverse, a unique route combination, etc.).

  Frequently, teams practice these special plays, but don't use them in the game (for whatever reason). By scripting these plays as part of its openers, a team can guarantee that they will be run and can predetermine when and how they will be used.

- *Multiplies the confidence of a team when a scripted sequence results in a score.* The level of confidence that a team has in the game plan, the coaching staff and its own abilities will be substantially increased when a successful offensive sequence has been established ahead of time in the classroom and has been refined on the practice field.

- *Increases the versatility of the offense without having to run a large or unmanageable number of plays or having to use an excessive number of formations.* By scripting the proper sequence of openers, the offense can confuse and cause hesitation in the defense as the defenders try to adjust to a number of different looks and plays. In the process, the offense can take some of the aggressiveness out of the defense.

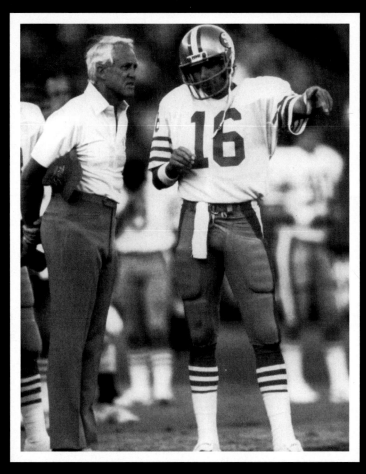

Making decisions—
Bill Walsh standing
next to his star pupil,
Joe Montana.

A young, impetuous group of men who decided to win the 1981 Super Bowl,

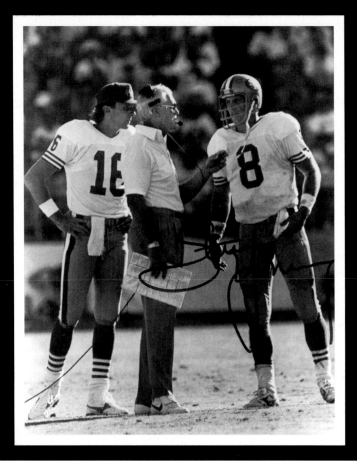

Bill Walsh in the
company of two
brilliant performers
with a total of five
Super Bowl victories
between them.

Four of the greatest, Ronnie Lott, Keith Fahnhorst, Keena Turner, and Joe Montana

Championship defense against the Raiders.

Bill Walsh with two great Hall of Famers from the San Diego Chargers —wide receiver Charlie Joiner and quarterback Dan Fouts.

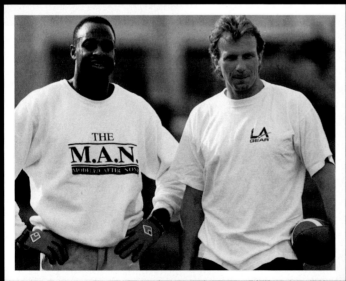

Jerry Rice and Joe Montana—the two greatest of all time. (photo by David Gonzales)

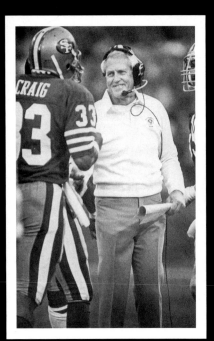

Bill Walsh congratulates Roger Craig after he surpassed 1,000 yards in both rushing and receiving in a single season. Craig's performance epitomized the success of the West Coast Offense. (photo courtesy of *San Francisco Examiner*)

While at Cincinnati, Bill Walsh employed the Pro Bowl talents of running back Essex Johnson and wide receiver Chip Myers to help fuel the Bengal's high-powered attack.

All Pro and League MVP Ken Anderson received his early tutelage from Bill Walsh when Walsh served as quarterback coach for the Cincinnati Bengals.

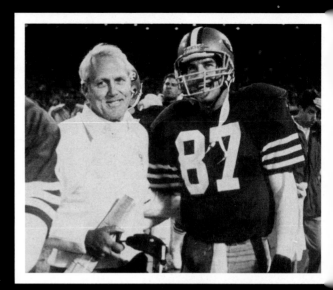

Not only did Dwight Clark make the most famous "Catch" in NFL history, but he went on to hold every 49er receiving record—until Jerry Rice rewrote the record book for the entire League.

Bill Walsh with his three Pro Bowl receivers in Cincinnati—Charlie Joiner, Bob Trumpy, and Isaac Curtis.

Bill Walsh's West Coast Offense has had a huge impact on modern football.

Bill Walsh standing next to two of the greatest coaches of all time— Don Shula and Chuck Noll.

A banquet for great quarterbacks. All are pupils of Bill Walsh—Virgil Carter, Dan Fouts, Greg Cook, Ken Anderson, Steve Dils, Guy Benjamin, Joe Montana, and Steve DeBerg.

Hall of Fame celebration July 31, 1993, Canton, Ohio.

The team of Bill Walsh and Eddie DeBartolo, Jr. developed a franchise that has brought five NFL championships to San Francisco.

A group of world champions who now just play golf—Ronnie Lott, Keena Turner, Bill Walsh, Joe Montana, Eric Wright, and John Taylor. (photo by Rod Searcey)

Dr. Harry
Edwards,
renowned
sociologist
and friend.
(photo by
David
Gonzales)

Bill and Geri
Walsh—a
championship
team.

CHAPTER 11

PREPARING TO WIN

"Once you have a plan, you must sell it to the players. It is not enough to put it on the blackboard and say, 'Okay, here it is.' You have to convince the players that the plan is a good one and show them, in specific ways, why it will work. If you do, you send them out to the practice field with more confidence."

—Joe Gibbs
Hall-of-Fame Football Coach
Washington Redskins

Finding the winning edge...

The bottom line in professional sports is winning. Everything has to focus on that product: winning football games. Other offshoots—the public relations, the merchandising, the high-sounding philosophical approach—mean little compared with being successful on the playing field.

But winning does not necessarily mean being a victor in every game. It's not winning every game at any cost. We have to remind ourselves that it's not just a single game that we are trying to win. It is a season and a series of seasons in which the team wins more games than it loses and each team member plays up to his potential. If you are continually developing your skills and refining your approach, then winning will be the final result.

Bill Walsh, "To Build a Winning Team," *Harvard Business Review*, January-February 1993.

When coaches are intent on having their teams at their best, they may take the team too far in preparation, extending them so much in practice that the players become stale or fatigued. Coaches may make their preparation too elaborate or tedious and their practices too arduous and time-consuming. In general, when you change your approach to prepare for an upcoming opponent, you can throw your own team out of sync.

I made this mistake at the conclusion of the 1987 season when we were preparing to meet Minnesota in the playoffs. The 49ers had become a great team, and we were destroying everyone we played. Our first playoff game was against the Vikings, who had "backed" into the playoffs. Similar to the Japanese at Midway, we felt we would demolish the opposition.

We had two weeks to prepare for the Vikings. I had not fully developed our deep passing game and therefore was not satisfied with this dimension of our offense, so we spent a lot of time practicing it. The practices tired my players and they became stale. I sensed too late that they were becoming fatigued. We hardly did anything the last two days of practice, but the damage was already done.

Minnesota was vastly underrated and had a great defense that included Keith Millard and Chris Doleman. It became evident early in the game that we were in for a battle. By the middle of the second quarter, I knew we were in deep trouble. Their defensive scheme made it difficult for us to run, and their offense had had several great plays.

As the game progressed, we were not sharp. We should have been easing up; instead we were having to double up. I had made the common mistake of losing sight of the need for players to be at their best both physically and mentally, and we lost the game 36-24.

No aspect of coaching has a more substantial or a more lasting effect on the players and their performance than the methods and techniques used to install and teach the team's system (e.g., offensive and defensive schemes, etc.). On the other hand, it is interesting to note that no procedure has more dramatic differences in philosophy and practical application from one team to the next than the approach a team utilizes to install and practice its system.

Whatever the offensive or defensive philosophy of the head coach, however, the core of any type of detailed preparation is the need for maximizing *meaningful* repetitions. Accordingly, as the head coach, you have to develop and implement a plan that ensures that every player gets the meaningful repetitions he needs to refine his skills and techniques.

INSTALLING THE SYSTEM IN TRAINING CAMP

Most of a team's efforts to install its (offensive/defensive) system occur in training camp. Accordingly, it is absolutely critical that all available time in this period is used purposefully and wisely. In this regard, as the head coach, one of your first steps must be to carefully review your team's preseason calendar of events in its entirety.

Subsequently, you have to make several important decisions regarding your team's preseason schedule of training, including what kinds of practices to have each day, what objectives to accomplish each practice, how much time to allot to each task, what steps to take to ensure that the goals of each practice are achieved, etc.

Before you can decide what the team should do during each practice, you have to determine how many hours the team should reasonably be expected to practice (work) each week. It is important that the schedule of required training does not place undue physiological demands on your players.

Although physical conditioning must obviously be an integral part of an athlete's efforts to prepare for the upcoming season, great care must be taken to avoid overtraining your players. Unfortunately, it appears that overtraining is a common occurrence at all competitive levels of football.

Overtraining can lead to several negative consequences. For example, it can result in excessive physical and emotional fatigue, thereby exposing a player to a higher risk of being injured and diminishing his capacity to master a particular skill or subject.

Training that does not provide adequate time for recovery can also bring on staleness and a decreased level of performance. Furthermore, this type of training can lead to a sense of apathy, irritability and an altered appetite in your players.

Somewhat surprisingly, several research studies have shown that the average football player is most fatigued prior to the first game of the season, not at the end of the season when most people might expect. These investigators attributed this factor to the toll of two-a-day practices and the amount of continual hitting that usually occurs in practices.

Once you understand the perils of overtraining and take specific measures to avoid it, your team will gain a significant advantage over your opponents who fail to adopt a similar approach. Accordingly, one of your top priorities must be to make sure that your team is as "fresh" as possible when the season's opener draws near.

After you have decided how many hours of practice will be conducted during a given week and how those practices will be divided among the various days of the week, your next task should be to determine how best to use the various time periods available during each practice.

By developing a comprehensive plan for training camp, you can decide the most effective way for installing and implementing each aspect of your team's system (e.g., fundamentals, techniques, situational and contingency offense, defensive blitz scheme, etc.). Allotting specific time periods to accomplish particular tasks helps to ensure that your practices are conducted in a systematic, goal-oriented manner.

As a general rule, NFL teams typically conduct three different types of practices during training camp. Each type of practice involves a different level of physical contact that is germane to what the team is trying to accomplish during a particular practice. Depending upon the degree of contact wanted, three distinct forms of practice dress (i.e., uniform) are worn—full pads (heavy contact), shells (controlled contact), and shorts (no contact).

A conventional practice schedule is outlined in Table 11-1. This schedule indicates that the typical practice is designed to enable the players to progress from

```
Typical Practice Outline
─────────────────────────────
AM: 90 minutes (pads)
    15 min      Individual
    15 min      Group
    10 min      9-on-7/3-on-4
    15 min      7-on-7
    20 min      Team
    15 min      Post Practice
```

Table 11-1.

working on their individual skills to working in combination with other players with whom they directly interact on the field.

Finally, the teaching progression advances to the 7-on-7 and team periods where the various sub-groups come together to practice the offense or the defense as an entire group. Every team and 7-on-7 period is usually identified in terms of relating to what type of situation (e.g., base, nickel, red zone, etc.) will be addressed during the period.

Teams also vary the way they approach their developmental training needs during two-a-day practices. As a rule, one of the steps they undertake in this regard involves mixing the various types of practices in a way that is designated to maximize learning and to minimize undue physical fatigue.

Table 11-2 illustrates examples of three different combinations of two-a-day practice schedules. Teams must carefully weigh the specific teaching objectives for a particular day against their choices of possible practice schedules.

Plan "A" is an example of a typical two-a-day practice format with the morning practice designed to be the most demanding. This session would be followed by a lighter afternoon practice in sweats that would be geared more toward a teaching sequence.

Plan "B" is a schedule that features a two-a-day practice format that involves a very physically demanding practice in the morning. This practice would then be combined with an afternoon session that could be used for either a strength training workout, a special teams walk-through, or classroom meetings.

Plan "C" is an example of a two-a-day practice format in which both the morning and the afternoon workouts involve a high level of physical contact. Other than enhancing the physical endurance level of the players, it is a schedule that may only be appropriate for testing the physical and mental toughness of your team.

On the other hand, the possible benefits of conducting two consecutive physically demanding practices should be carefully weighed against the loss of preparation time due to the additional time needed for the players to recuperate from the undue fatigue that may result from this type of schedule. Not surprisingly, most NFL teams employ plan "C" on an infrequent basis in this era of cap-limited rosters.

	Plan A		Plan C	
	One Padded—One Short Workout		Double Workout Day (pads)	
		7:15 am	Wake up call	
7:15 pm	Wake up call	7:15-8:00 am	Breakfast	
7:15-8:00 am	Breakfast	7:15-8:45 am	Tape schedule	
7:15-8:45 am	Tape schedule	9:00-11:30 am	Practice (pads)	
9:00-11:30 am	Practice (pads)	Noon	Lunch	
Noon	Lunch	1:30-2:45 pm	Tape schedule	
3:00-3:45 pm	Group meetings	3:00-3:46 pm	Group meetings	
4:15-5:15 pm	Practice (sweats)	4:15-5:15 pm	Practice (pads)	
6:00 pm	Dinner	6:00 pm	Dinner	
7:00 pm	Special teams meeting	7:00 pm	Special teams meeting	
9:30 pm	Staff meeting	9:30 pm	Staff meeting	
11:00 pm	Curfew	11:00 pm	Curfew	

	Plan B	
	One Pads—Afternoon Meetings	
7:15 am	Wake up call	
7:15-8:00 am	Breakfast	
7:15-8:45 am	Tape schedule	
9:00-11:30 am	Practice (pads)	
Noon	Lunch	
4:00-5:30 pm	Group meetings	
6:00 pm	Dinner	
Night off		
11:00 pm	Curfew	

Table 11-2.

INSTALLING THE OFFENSE

As the head coach, one of your prime objectives in training camp must be the installation of your team's basic offense. The foundation of whatever basic offense is installed in training camp must sustain the team throughout the season.

The team must be able to access the plays in its base offense at different times during the season (i.e., whenever they're needed). The key point that you should keep in mind is that a "new" play installed in a single week's time during the season doesn't stand a reasonable chance of succeeding.

Accordingly, you must take steps to ensure that your team develops an inclusive base offense in the time allowed in minicamps and training camp. It is important that your team masters a complete inventory of offensive plays prior to the start of the season.

By using a comprehensive training camp plan as a guideline, you can determine exactly how much time the offense can anticipate having for meetings, individual skill practice, group technique practice, etc. In turn, once the position coaches see the progression of how the offense will be installed and the allocation of practice time, they must compile the total number of minutes they will have during training camp, identify the skills and fundamentals that must be taught, and determine the optimum use of the available time.

Proper preseason planning also enables the coaching staff to schedule more productive cross-group training periods. A cross-group period involves a situation where the position coaches work their players against their counter-parts on the opposite side of the ball (e.g., tight ends versus outside linebackers, wide receivers versus defensive backs, etc.).

Table 11-3 provides an example of how I specifically organized the 49er practices one year. This table is noteworthy for both its attention to detail and the fact that the schedule is very thorough with regard to the team's needs.

Table 11-4 provides a more basic example of how practices could be broken down to cover a team's base offense. This specific example provides an overview of how time in the first 15 sessions leading up to a team's first preseason game should be allotted. This chart illustrates exactly how many minutes a position coach has for a particular drill or a particular subject (e.g., technique, situational factor, etc.).

In this instance, the training camp situation outline shows the position coaches that they are going to have a total of 120 minutes to work on individual skills and techniques in the first 15 practices. The coaches will also see that they will have a total of 60 minutes for both 1-on-1 (wide receivers versus defensive backs) and 3-on-4 (tight ends and running backs versus linebackers) work.

The same 15 practices can also be broken down according to the number of situational and contingency plays run. Table 11-5 illustrates how the offensive coordinator and his assistants can determine the size and the scope of the offensive inventory which will be covered prior to the first game by placing a particular emphasis on specific plays.

Table 11-5 indicates that a "mock game" is scheduled during the seventh practice. A "mock game" is a specialized scrimmage conducted in shorts. Its primary purpose is to take the entire team through as many different "administrative" situations as possible that collectively force both the coaches and the players to adjust quickly to the flow of the game.

The head coach serves as the "referee" for the mock game. In that capacity, you take both the offense and the defense through as many different scenarios as you can within a "semi-game" environment (e.g., arbitrarily institute a 10-yard penalty, dictate a huge gain by the offense, rule a change of possession, determine that a key player is injured and out of the game, etc.).

It is also important that a detailed schedule of meetings between the coaching staff and the players be an integral part of a team's comprehensive plan for training camp. Such a schedule will allow the assistant coaches to plan properly for their meetings with the players by deciding how to use the total time they will have available to them, given the amount of offense they need to cover.

Table 11-6 provides an example of a training camp meeting schedule. This schedule indicates the time of each meeting, what practice this meeting is designed to service, and the situations that will be covered in that particular practice.

The coordinators then identify the subject matter and the materials that will be dealt with during each meeting. Subsequently, each position coach is expected to fill out the teaching outlines in accordance with the coordinator's master meeting schedule.

Almost every professional educator should easily recognize the strong similarity between a coach completing his outlines for the master training camp meeting schedule and a teacher filling out lesson plans for the upcoming school year.

The key point to remember is that taking a detailed approach to practice scheduling is the best way a team can adequately prepare its coaches and players to take full advantage of the available practice time.

Certainly, circumstances may arise which may force a team to change the lesson plan it developed and refined in the preseason, but this type of scheduling has been proven to be very reliable (i.e., 80-85 percent) in past training camps. It should be noted that this practice format will provide a team with over 450 offensive snaps (not including live scrimmage plays) in its initial 15 training camp workouts. Because the average NFL team runs approximately a thousand plays during the regular season, the 450+ offensive snaps represents just under a half a season's worth of work.

Preparing in such a fashion allows a team's coaches to plan their training camp practices well in advance, during the relative calm of the week prior to when camp starts. Such an approach helps to prevent the need for coaches to stay up late during the long training-camp days to script the next day's practice.

All factors considered, coaches who get more rest (i.e., they don't have to burn "the midnight oil") will be fresher and more alert for the most important part of the training camp day—practice. Too often, many coaches mistakenly believe that late hours and "drop-dead" fatigue are directly correlated to hard work and personal commitment.

In reality, under normal circumstances, late hours and fatigue are not valid indicators of anything other than poor planning. Given the extended length of the season (i.e., it begins in mid-July and, hopefully, ends in late January), proper planning is the most effective method of ensuring that members of the coaching staff will be able to maintain reasonable levels of energy and attentiveness over the course of the season.

I am not a bit anxious about my battles. If I am anxious I don't fight them. I wait until I am ready.

> General Bernard Montgomery, Viscount of Alamein
> Commander, Allied Land Forces
> World War II

Table 11-3. An example of the 49ers' practice schedule.

	Sunday July 17th	Monday July 18th	Tuesday July 19th	Wednesday July 20th	Thursday July 21st	Friday July 22nd	Saturday July 23rd
	No Practice	2 Practices AM—Shorts—8:45 (2:00) PM—Shells—2:45 (1:30)	2 Practices AM—Shorts—8:45 (2:00) PM—Shells—2:45 (1:30)	2 Practices AM—Pads—8:45 (2:10) PM—Shorts—2:45 (1:30)	2 Practices AM—Pads—8:45 (2:10) PM—S.T.—2:30 (:45)	2 Practices AM—Pads—8:45 (2:10) PM—Shorts—2:45 (1:30)	2 Practices AM—Pads—8:45 (2:10) PM—Shorts—2:45 (1:30)
	7:00 PM—Team Mtg (2:00)	6:50 PM—ST Mtg (:40) 7:30 PM—Team Mtg (2:00)	6:50 PM—ST Mtg (:40) 7:30 PM—Team Mtg (2:00)	6:50 PM—ST Mtg (:40) 7:30 PM—Team Mtg (2:00)	4:00 PM—Team Mtg (1:00) 6:20 PM—ST Mtg (:40) 7:00 PM—Team Mtg (:30) Night Off (D.E.A.)	6:50 PM—ST Mtg (:40) 7:30 PM—Team Mtg (2:00)	6:50 PM—ST Mtg (:40) 7:30 PM—Team Mtg (2:00)
All Players report to Sierra College Lunch 1:00 PM Meet 3:00 PM General and Team		AM—Shorts (2:00) #1 15 IND/ADJ 15 IND/GRP 15 IND/GRP 15 1-on-1/9-on-7 30 7-on-7 30 Team ST-15 Post (SP)	AM—Shorts (2:00) #3 15 IND/ADJ 15 IND/GRP 15 IND/GRP 15 1-on-1/9-on-7 30 7-on-7 30 Team ST-15 Pre (SP) ST-15 Post (SP)	AM—Pads (2:10) #5 15 SLED/IND/ADJ 15 IND/GRP 15 IND/GRP 15 1-on-1/9-on-7 20 Spec Cat 25 7-on-7 25 Team ST-15 Pre (SP) ST-15 Post (TM)	AM—Pads (2:10) #7 15 SLED/IND/ADJ 15 IND/GRP 15 IND/GRP 15 1-on-1/9-on-7 20 Spec Cat 25 7-on-7 25 Team ST-15 Pre (SP) ST-15 Post (TM)	AM—Pads (2:10) #8 15 SLED/IND ADJ 15 IND/GRP 15 IND/GRP 15 1-on-1/9-on-7 20 Spec Cat 25 7-on-7 25 Team ST-15 Pre (SP) ST-15 Post (TM)	AM—Pads (2:10) #10 15 SLED/IND/ADJ 15 IND 15 IND/GRP 15 1-on-1/9-on-7 20 Spec Cat 25 7-on-7 25 Team ST-15 Pre (SP) ST-15 Post (TM)
		PM—Shells (1:30) #2 15 IND/ADJ 15 IND/GRP 20 7-on-7 25 Team 15 Post Practice ST-15 Pre (SP)	PM—Shells (1:30) #4 15 IND/ADJ 15 IND/GRP 20 7-on-7 25 Team 15 Post Practice ST-15 Pre (SP) ST-15 Post (SP)	PM—Shorts (1:30) #6 15 IND/ADJ 15 IND/GRP 20 7-on-7 25 Team 15 Post Practice ST-15 Pre (SP) ST-15 Post (SP)	PM—Shorts (:45) Special Teams #1 ST-15 Pre (SP)	PM—Shorts (1:30) #9 15 IND/GRP 15 IND/GRP 20 7-on-7 25 Team 15 Post Practice ST-15 Pre (SP) ST-15 Post (SP)	PM—Shorts (1:30) #11 15 IND/GRP 15 IND/GRP 20 7-on-7 25 Team 15 Post Practice ST-15 Pre (SP) ST-15 Post (TM)

Table 11-3. Continued.

	Day #1	Day #2	Day #3	Day #4 Red Zone	Day #5	Day #6 GL (7/13/88)
Offense	376-377	20-21 X Circus	Fox 2-3 D.S.O.	20-21 Scat HB Curl	200-300 Jet HB Flat	324-325 Flk Angle
	20-21 HB Read	22-23 Seattle	Draw Pass	22-23 Texas	P. 360-361 "O" X Slant	(U) P. 14-15 Lead
	22-23 Z In	78-79 HB Corner	T14-T15	22-23 Z Delay	P. HB 2-3 Cut HB Cross	(U) P. 68-69 "Y" Sneak Sprint Option
	24-25 D. Cmbk	Sweep Pass Z Option	Roll HB Corner	24-25 Dino "Y" Out	Wheel Rt/Lt	(U) Boot Rt/Lt
	P. 42-43 X(Z) Dp Over	P. 14-15 Bim X Hook	Lag Pass Y Over	(T) Fk 38-39 QB Keep	P. 68-69 Flk Post	376 Dbl Under
	2--300 Jet X Slant	24-25 "E" Sq Out	HB Fast Scrn	QB Keep FB Slide	FB Slow Screen	76 D.S.O
	22-23 Y Crs FB Fan	70-71 HB Crs FB Fan	2-3 Jet Zebra Out	Fox 2-3 X Shake	FB 14-15 Ctr	(U) FB @ 0-1
	22-23 Y Out FB Curl	2-3 Jet Flk Drive	24-25 Detroit	Fox 2-3 Flk Short Post	18-19 Bob King	(U) HB 2-3 Ctr
	54-55 Z Out	354-355 Thunder	54-55 X Arrow	22-23 Z Shallow Cross	16-17 Wk	(U) 16-17 "A" Lead
	54-55 Razor	88-89 Audible	FB 14-15 Trap	HB 6-7 Ctr	60-61 Trap	(U) 68-69 HO Solid
	HB 6-7 Wk	16-17 Power	16-17 Ctr Bluff	64-65 Ctr		(U) 92-93 Ctr
	18-19 Bob	18-19 W	(U) 68-69 Storm Toss	90-91 "O"		(U) 98-99
	30-31 Trap	FB 16-17 Bim	98-99 Boss	96-97 Basic		
	42-43 Lag	38-39 F	Z Rev Rt/Lt	X (HB) Around		
	68-69 HO	FB 40-41				
	66-67 Cor	HB 40-41				
		92-93 Ctr				
Defense	Nebraska (Swap/Omaha) Strip/Under 93	Eagle 43/Finch	Jazz	Arizona	Skin 43/93	Goal Line
		Over/Hawk Snipe	Stud/Dog 2 (Switch/Frank)	Meg/Pepper	Moscow (Bluff)	Goal Line Dbl Zeke
	Sioux 3/Special	Husky/Warrior Sam	Pro Hawk Snipe	Base 30	Hoopa Strike/ISO "Y"	Goal Line Slant
	Hoopa 2/Stay	Brave Spike Fred	Nickel 2 "E" Clamp	Pro Navajo 3/Special	Star 39	Goal Line Dbl/Gut
	Nickel 7 and 7/Wax	Pro Eagle 93/43/Finch		Nickel Dbl/Hook	Nickel 2/Wilco	Port 93
	Nickel 2/Blow and 2/Web	Nickel Zone	Nickel Navajo 2/Buck	Nickel Spider	Nickel 27/Kick	Brave/Pop Fred
		Nic Casino (Saf Dbl/Gut Whistle)	Nickel Mississippi	Nickel 5	Nickel Gap/Ohio	Sioux (Hoopa) Plugger Fred
	Nickel 2 Whip	Nic B/B and Dbl/Gut (Crs Dbl/Gut	Nickel Texas			
		Nic Box 2/Whip	Nickel Queen/Tackle 2 /Buck	Nickel Cowboy		Nickel Umbrella/Tent
						Nickel Lurk Lt/Rt

Table 11-3. Continued.

	Sunday July 24th	Monday July 25th	Tuesday July 26th	Wednesday July 27th	Thursday July 28th	Friday July 29th	Saturday July 30th
	1 Practice AM—Shorts—8:45 (1:10)						
	10:30 AM—Buffet			NFL Officials Available Thursday and Friday			
	AM—Shorts (1:10) 10 Offense 10 Defense 10 Offense 10 Offense 10 Defense ST-10	Arrive in London 11:00 AM	#12 Picture Day 11:30–Noon at Practice Field Light Workout	Practice 8 IND/ADJ 10 Def—Play Action 10 Off—Pass/Run Inst 6 Def—Nickel 6 Off—Nickel 10 Special Teams	Practice 8 IND/ADJ 10 Def—Base Blitz 10 Off—Base Blitz 6 Def—Red Zone 6 Off—Red Zone	Practice 8 IND/ADJ 10 Def—Nickel Blitz 10 Off—Nickel Aud 6 Def—Goal Line 6 Off—Goal Line 10 Special Teams	Practice #16 Practice at Stadium Review for Miami
	Leave for London 5:00 PM			Vs. Miami 15 1-on-1/9-on-7 15 Combo/3-3/Line Stnts 25 7-on-7 (OL vs. DL) 22 Team (10 Nickel) (12 Team) 10 Special Teams 10 3rd Tm Scrimmage	Vs. Miami 15 1-on-1/9-on-7 15 Combo/3-3/Line Stnts 25 7-on-7 (OL vs. DL) 33 Team (8 Goal Line) (15 Team) (10 Nickel) 10 Special Teams 10 3rd TM Scrimmage	Vs. Miami 15 1-on-1/9-on-7 15 Combo/3-3/Line Stnts 25 7-on-7 (OL vs. DL) 26 Team (8 Short Yard) (6 Prevent) (12 Team) 10 Special Teams	
				P. 330-331 "O" X Slant P. 12-13 X Hook Waggle X Out 20-21 Bingo 20-21 Bingo Spread HB G Screen FB 30-31 Tackle TR (T) 38-39 Ram HB 42-43 (T) 62-63 Ctr "O"	2-3 Jet Dbl Crs 200-300 Jet X Hitch 2-3 Jet Y Delay 324-325 Dbl Qk 22-23 Sway Sprint Rt/Lt HB Flat	374-375 Thunder 200-300 Jet 74-75 Okie 74-75 Dino (T) 376-377 (T) 22-23 Z In (U) Fox 2-3 Z Shake	
				Tusk/Rhino Fox (SY) Stud/Dog 2 Nickel Waco 2/Whip Zone Nickel Bluff Lurk Solid	Sq Lt/Rt Eagle Lt/Rt Snake Dbl/Stud Fred Nickel Baylor 2/Buck Nickel 9/Soft	"Review"	
	Day #7	Day #8	Day #9	Day #10	Day #11	Day #12	Day #13

Table 11-3. Continued.

Sunday July 31st	Monday August 1st	Tuesday August 2nd	Wednesday August 3rd	Thursday August 4th	Friday August 5th	Saturday August 6th
		1 Practice PM—Shorts—4:00 (1:00)	2 Practices AM—Shells—9:45 (2:10) PM—S.T.—2:30 (:45)	2 Practices AM—Shells—9:45 (2:10) PM—Shorts—2:45 (1:00)	1 Practice AM—Shorts—10:00 (1:00)	Pre season #1 vs. L.A. Raiders (Home) 6:00 PM
		1:00 PM—Team Lunch 6:00 PM—Dinner 6:50 PM—ST Mtg (:40) 7:30 PM—Team Mtg (2:00)	4:00 PM—Team Mtg (1:00) 6:20 PM—ST Mtg (:40) 7:00 PM—Team Mtg (:05) Night Off	6:50 PM—S.T. Mtg (:40) 7:30 PM-Team Mtg (2:00)	3:00 PM—Team Mtg (1:00) 6:50 PM—ST Mtg (:40) 7:30 PM—Team Mtg (2:00) 12:30 PM—TM Mtg (NFL Rules)	
6:00 PM American Bowl Game VS Miami Travel to USA Following Game	Arrive USA Early AM (5:30 AM)	9:00 PM-Team Curfew AM—No Practice	AM—Shells (2:10) #18 15 Sled/IND/ADJ 15 IND 15 IND/Grp 15 1-on-1/9-on-7 20 Spec Cat 25 7-on-7 25 Team ST-15 Pre (SP) ST-15 Post (TM)	AM—Shells (2:10) #19 15 Sled/IND/ADJ 15 IND 15 IND/GRP 15 1-on-1/9-on-7 20 Spec Cat 25 7-on-7 25 Team ST-15 Pre (SP) ST-15 Post (TM)	AM-Shorts (1:00) #21 Review for Raiders Mock Game ST—Situation	
		PM—Shorts (1:00) #17 10 Offense 10 Defense 10 Offense 10 Defense 10 Offense 10 Defense ST-15 Pre(SP)/15 Post	PM—Shorts (:45) Special Teams #2 ST-15 Pre (SP)	PM—Shorts (1:00) #20 10 Offense 10 Defense 10 Offense 10 Defense 10 Offense 10 Defense (TM) ST-15 Pre (SP)/15 Post	PM—No Practice	
			26-27 FB Close 26-27 FB Delay 50-51 HB Fan 76-77 X(Z) Dp Over 76-77 X Shallow Cross 76-77 X Shallow Cross HB 16-17 Bim FB 30-31 Pull HB 30-31 Pull	376-377 HB Qk PHB 2-3 D. Cmbk PHB 2-3 Dagger P. 14-15 Bim Cat Lag P X Hook P. 64-65 Ctr 'U' Cor 90-91 '0' Bounce FB Slow Draw HB 14-15 Ctr		
			Worm (PRO) Bridge (PRO) Sydney Nickel Jumbo Zone Nickel Queen/ISO	Smash Warrior Brave Pax Brave Tempe Eagle (Worm) 2/Sara Nickel Follow Casino Nickel Loaded		
Day #14	Day #15	Day #16	Day #17	Day #18	Day #19	Day #20

Table 11-3. Continued.

Sunday August 7th	Monday August 8th	Tuesday August 9th	Wednesday August 10th	Thursday August 11th	Friday August 12th	Saturday August 13th
No Practice	2 Practices AM-Shorts-8:45 (2:10) PM-S.T.-2:30 (:45)	2 Practices AM-Pads-8:45 (2:10) PM-Shorts-4:00 (1:00)	2 Practices AM-Pads-8:45 (2:10) PM-S.T.-2:30 (:45)	2 Practices AM-Shells-8:45 (1:45) PM-Shorts-3:00 (1:00)	1 Practice AM-Shorts-10:00 (1:00)	
6:00 PM-Dinner 6:30 PM-ST Mtg (1:00) 7:30 PM-Tm Mtg (2:00)	4:00 PM-Team Mtg (1:00) 6:50 PM-ST Mtg (:40) 7:30 PM-Team Mtg (2:00)	6:50 PM-ST Mtg (:40) 7:30 PM-Team Mtg (2:00)	4:00 PM-Team Mtg (1:00) 5:30 PM-Fish Derby 6:50 PM-ST Mtg (:40) Night Off	1:00 PM-NFL Security W. Welsh (1:00) 7:30 PM-Team Mtg (2:00) 7:30 PM-Team Mtg (2:00)	3:00 PM-Team Mtg (1:00) 6:50 PM-ST Mtg (:40) 1:00 PM-FBI (Dick Held)	Pre season #2 vs. Denver Broncos (Away) 6:00 PM
Players' Day Off	AM-Shorts (2:10) #22 15 Ind/Adj 15 Ind/Grp 15 Ind/Grp 15 1-On-1/9-On-7 20 Spec Cat 25 7-On-7 25 Team ST-15 Pre (SP) ST-15 Post (TM)	AM-Pads (2:10) #23 15 Sled/Ind/Adj 15 Ind/Grp 15 Ind/Grp 15 1-On-1/9-On-7 20 Spec Cat 25 7-On-7 25 Team ST-15 Pre (SP) ST-15 Post (TM)	AM-Pads (2:10) #25 15 Sled/Ind/Adj 15 Ind/Grp 15 Ind/Grp 15 1-On-1/9-On-7 20 Spec Cat 25 7-On-7 25 Team ST-15 Pre (SP) ST-15 Post (TM)	AM-Shells (1:45) #26 15 Sled/Ind/Adj 15 Ind/Grp 15 Ind/Grp 1-On-1 20 Spec Cat 20 7-On-7 vs Denvers 20 Team vs Denver ST-15 Pre (SP) ST-15 Post (TM)	AM-Shorts (1:00) #28 Review for Denver Mock Game ST-Situation	PM-No Practice
	PM-Shorts (:45) Special Teams #3 ST-15 Pre (SP)	PM-Shorts (1:00) #24 10 Offense 10 Defense 10 Defense 10 Defense 10 Defense (TM) ST-15 Pre (SP)/15 Post	PM-Shorts (:45) Special teams #4 ST-15 Pre (SP)	PM-Shorts (1:00) #27 10 Offense/Defense 10 Offense 10 Offense/Defense 10 Offense vs Denver 10 Defense vs Denver ST-15 Pre (SP)/15 Post (TM)		
Grand Opening Santa Clara New Facility		24-25 Rattle 70-71 FB Flat &Up 78-79 Flk C. Post Jet Rt/Lt Flow Pass T800-900 22-23 Scat Z In 22-23 Okie FB Hook P.66-67 Ctr X Post 358-359 Hatchet 200-300 Jet Drag Slant 20-21 Swap 'Y' Over	P. 314-315 Hitch 20-21 X Dig P.42-43 X-Y Hook S1-S2 22-23 FB Flat & UP 70-71 HB Corner 16-17 Ctr 62-63 Basic 98-99 G	"Review"		
		Hoopa Magic Freddie Smuggle Nic King Tackle 2/Whip Nickel Blast Flex/Dog Nickel Queen Bop Nickel 7 Dbl Clamp Nickel 7 'Y' Clamp	Nickel Navajo Ax/Strike Nickel Navajo Bow Nic Haley Zone/Lurk Solid			
Day #21	Day #22	Day #23	Day #24	Day #25	Day #26	Day #27

Table 11-3. Continued.

	Sunday August 14th	Monday August 15th	Tuesday August 16th	Wednesday August 17th	Thursday August 18th	Friday August 19th	Saturday August 20th
	No Practice	2 Practices AM—Shorts—8:45 (2:10) PM—ST—2:30 (:45)	2 Practices AM—Pads—8:45 (2:10) PM—Shorts—4:00 (1:00)	2 Practices AM—Pads—8:45 (2:10) PM—ST—2:30 (:45)	2 Practices AM—Shells—8:45 (1:45) PM—Shorts—4:00 (1:00)	1 Practice AM—Shorts—10:00 (1:00)	
	6:00 PM—Dinner 6:30 PM—ST Mtg (1:00) 7:30PM—TM Mtg (2:00)	4:00 PM—Team Mtg (1:00) 6:50 PM—ST Mtg (:40) 7:30 PM—Team Mtg (2:00)	6:50 PM—ST Mtg (:40) 7:30 PM—Team Mtg (2:00)	4:00 PM—Team Mtg (1:00) 6:20 PM—ST Mtg (:40) 7:30 PM—Team Mtg (:05) Night Off	6:50 PM—ST Mtg (:40) 7:30 PM—Team Mtg (2:00)	3:00 PM—Team Mtg (1:00) 6:50 PM—ST Mtg (:40) 7:30 PM—Team Mtg (2:00)	
	Players' Day Off Dinner 6:00 PM	AM—Shorts (2:10) #29 15 IND/AJD 15 IND/GRP 15 IND/GRP 15 1-on-1 20 Spec Cat 25 7-on-7 25 Team ST-15 Pre (SP) ST-15 Post (TM)	AM—Pads (2:10) #30 15 SLED/IND/AJD 15 IND/GRP 15 IND/GRP 15 1-on-1/9-on-7 20 Spec Cat 25 7-on-7 25 Team ST-15 Pre (SP) ST-15 Post (TM)	AM—Pads (2:10) #32 15 SLED/IND/AJD 15 IND/GRP 15 IND/GRP 15 1-on-1/9-on-7 20 Spec Cat 25 7-on-7 25 Team ST-15 Pre (SP) ST-15 Post (TM)	AM—Shells (1:45) #33 15 SLED/IND/AJD 15 IND/GRP 15 IND/GRP 20 Spec Cat 20 7-on-7 20 Team ST-15 Pre (SP) ST-15 Post (TM)	AM—Shorts (1:00) #35 Review for Chargers Mock Game ST—Situation	Pre season #3 vs. San Diego Chargers (Away) 6:00 PM
		PM—Shorts (:45) Special Teams #5 ST-15 Pre (SP)	PM—Shorts (1:00) #31 10 Offense 10 Defense 10 Offense 10 Offense 10 Defense (TM) ST-15 Pre (SP)/15 Post	PM—Shorts (:45) Special teams #6 ST-15 Pre (SP)	PM—Shorts (1:00) #34 10 Offense/Defense 10 Defense 10 Offense 10 Offense/Defense 10 Defense vs. Chargers 10 Defense vs. Chargers ST-15 Pre (SP)/15 Post (TM)	PM—No Practice	
			76-77 X China 78-79 HB Arrow 200-300 Jet Hb Slant Q8-Q9 2-3 Jet HB Cross 90-91 Trp 60-61 'O'	Fk Dbl Scrn 'Y' Ck Middle Fk Slow Draw 'Y' Hk 22-23 Scat 'Y' Hk P.Hb 2-3 Slow Screen Fox 2-3 Slow Screen	Run Pass 68 Run Pass 98 Triple Pass		
	Day #28	Day #29	Day #30	Day #31	Day #32	Day #33	Day #34

Table 11-3. Continued.

Sunday August 21th	Monday August 22th	Tuesday August 23th	Wednesday August 24th	Thursday August 25th	Friday August 26th	Saturday August 27th
				1:00 PM—SF Chamber Lunch		
Break Camp Retun to Santa Clara	Santa Clara	Santa Clara	Santa Clara	Santa Clara	Pre season #4 vs. Seattle Seahawks (Home)	
Day #35	Day #36	Day #37	Day #38	Day #39	Day #40	Day #41

Table 11-4. A basic schedule of how practices could be broken down.

REVISED: 14 MAY 97

PRACTICE	SITUATION	IND	9/7	1/1 3/4	SP. CAT	7 ON 7	TEAM	GROUP
#1 AM WED JULY 16 SHELLS	BASE	25	10	10	10 (1-10)	10 (1-10) 5 (2-7)	10 (1-10) 5 (2-7)	10 RUN 10 PRO
#2 AM WED JULY 16 SHELLS	BASE NICKEL	10		10	5 (3-4) 5 (3-6)	8 (1-10) 4 (3-5) 4 (3-7)	5 (1-10) 5 (3-4)	10 RUN
#3 AM THUR. JULY 17 PADS	BASE NICKEL BLITZ 2 PLAY MOVE BALL	25	10	10	5 2 PLAY 5 BLITZ 5 MB	10 (1-10) 4 (2-7) 6 (3-5)	10 (1-10) 4 (3-4) 4 MB	10 RUN 10 PRO
#4 PM THUR. JULY 17 SHORTS	SPECIAL TEAMS							
#5 AM FRI JULY 18 SHORTS	BASE NICKEL SY GL RED ZONE 2 MIN MOVE BALL	15			4 (3-1) 4 (1-10) +12 4 GL 2 2 PT	8 (1-10) 4 (3-5) 4 (1-10)+15 4 (3-4) +9	4 (1-10) 4 (2-12) 8 MB	10 RUN 10 PRO
#6 PM FRI JULY 18 PADS	SCRIMMAGE							
#7 AM SAT. JULY 19 SHORTS	MOCK GAME							
#8 AM MON. JULY 21 PADS	BASE NICKEL NIC BLITZ NO HUDDLE RED ZONE 2 MIN	15	10	10	5 (3-8) BLITZ 5 NO HUD	10 (1-10) 4)2-15) 4 (3-6) 2 (3-3)	8 BU MB 8 MB	10 RUN 10 PASS
#9 PM MON. JULY 21 SHORTS	SPECIAL TEAMS							
#10 AM TUES. JULY 22 PADS SAINTS	BASE NICKEL RED ZONE		10	10		10 (1-10) 5 (3-5) 10 (1-10) +15 5 (3-5) +15	10 (1-10) 5 (3-5) 10 (1-10) +15 5 (3-5) +15	
#10 PM TUES. JULY 22 PADS SAINTS	BASE NICKEL RED ZONE 2 MIN		10	10	10 2 MIN	10 (1-10) 5 (3-5) 10 (1-10) +12 5 (3-5) +12	10 (1-10) 5 (3-5) 10 (1-10) +15 5 (3-5) +15	
#12 AM WED. JULY 23 PADS	BASE NICKEL BLITZ NIC BLIT SY-GL MB	10			4 (3-1) 6 GL 3 BLITZ 3 NIC BLITZ	6 (1-10) 4 (3-6)	5 MB	
#13 PM WED. JULY 23 SHORTS	BASE NICKEL (SEATTLE)	10			5 (1-10) 3 (1-10)	6 (1-10) 4 (3-6)	5 (1-10) 3 (3-4)	
#14 AM THUR. JULY 24 PADS	BASE NICKEL RED ZONE SY-GL 2 MIN (SEATTLE)	10			2 (3-1) 4 (1-10) +15 4 GL 2 2 PT	5 (1-10) 4 (3-4)	4 MB	
#15 PM THUR. JULY 24 SHORTS (WALK THRU)	BASE NICKEL RED ZONE SY-GL 2 PT BACKED UP				6 (1-10) 3 (3-1) 4 (1-10 +10 3 (2-5)+5		3 (3-4) +4 4 GL 2 2 PT 3 BU	
TOTALS		120	50	60	121	180	164	90

Table 11-5. Sample training camp practice schedule.

#		1	2	3	4	5	6	7	8	9	10	11	12	13	14	15	TOTALS	
Day		Wed	Wed	Thur	Thur	Fri	Fri	Sat	Mon	Mon	Tues	Tues	Wed	Wed	Thur	Thur		**449**
Type		Shells	Shells	Pads	Shorts	Shorts	Pads	Shorts	Pads	Shorts	Pads	Pads	Pads	Shorts	Pads	Shorts		
Base	Team	20	5	24	S	12	S	M	12	S	10	10	8	13	4	6	124	**207**
	Skel	10	8	10	p	8	c	o	10	p	10	10	6	6	5		83	
2nd Long	Team	5			e	4	r	c		e							9	**22**
	Skel		5	4	c		i	k	4	c							13	
3rd Long	Team	5			i		m		8	i							13	**35**
	Skel		4	6	a		m	G	4	a			4	4			22	
3rd Med	Team			4	l	4	a	a	2	l	5	5	3	3	4		30	**54**
	Skel		4			4	g	m			5	5					24	
Short Yardage	Team				T	4	e	e		T			4		2	3	13	**13**
	Skel				e					e							0	
Goal Line	Team				a	4				a	15	15	4		4	4	16	**16**
	Skel				m					m	15	15					0	
Red Zone	Team				s	4				s	15	15			4	10	48	**86**
	Skel					8					15	15					38	
2PT						2									2	2	6	
BU									8							2	10	
Live				Blitz/ 2 Play		M.B.			Blitz/ M.B.				Blitz					

Columns 4 and 9 are labeled vertically "Special Teams"; column 6 "Scrimmage"; column 7 "Mock Game."

Table 11-6. Sample training camp meeting schedule.

1997

DATE	TIME	NEXT PRAC.	SITUATION	SUBJECTS	FILM
TUES. 7/15	8:00 PM	#1 AM 16-Jul	BASE NICKEL		
WED. 7/16	3:00 PM	#2 PM 16-Jul	BASE NICKEL		
WED 7/16	7:45 PM	#3 AM 17-Jul	BASE—NIC BLITZ 2 PLAY MOVE BALL		
THUR 7/17	5:00 PM	#5 PM 18-Jul	NFL GAME OFFICIALS		
THUR 7/17	7:45 PM	#5 PM 18-Jul	BASE—NIC RED ZONE 2 MINUTE SY—GL		
FRID. 7/18	3:00 PM	#6 PM 18-Jul	SCRIMMAGE		
SAT 7/19	8:15 AM	#7 AM 19-Jul	MOCK GAME		
SUN 7/20	7:30 PM	#8 AM 21-Jul	BASE—NIC NIC BLITZ NO HUDDLE RED ZONE 2 MIN		
MON 21 JUL	5:00 PM	#10 AM 22-Jul	BASE NICKEL RED ZONE		
MON 21 JUL	7:45 PM	#10 AM 22-Jul	BASE NICKEL RED ZONE	SAINTS	
WED 23 JUL	8:15 AM	#12 AM 23-Jul	NFL SECURITY		
WED 23 JUL	3:00 PM	#13 PM 23-Jul	BASE NICKEL	SEATTLE	
THUR. 24 JULY	8:15 AM	#14 AM 24-Jul	BASE—NIC—BLITZ RED ZONE SY—GL 2 MIN	SEATTLE	
THUR. 24 JULY	3:00 PM	#15 PM 24-Jul	BASE—NIC—BLITZ RED ZONE SY—GL 2 PT BACKED UP	SEATTLE	
THUR. 24 JULY	7:45 PM	#16 AM 25-Jul	BASE NICKEL MOVE BALL	SEATTLE	

ESTABLISHING THE PACE OF PRACTICES

It is very important that you, as the head coach, make sure that your coaches and players understand what you expect from them concerning the tempo and pacing of the team's practices. In this regard, you should remember and be sensitive to the fact that an up-tempo, fast-paced practice offers the most conducive environment for learning on the football field.

Committing to an up-tempo, fast-paced practice does not mean that such a pace must be maintained at all times. In reality, occasionally, a situation may arise when you must temporarily slow down the pace of practice in order to emphasize a particular point.

As a general rule, however, the basic pace of practice should encourage the players to exhibit a high energy level—one that "forces" them to keep up with the tempo. An example of a fast-paced practice is shown in Table 11-7.

Table 11-7. An example of a fast-paced practice.

Practice #:	1 AM	Dress:	Pads	Situations:	BASE
Date:	15-Jul-97		Shells		
Time:	8:45 AM		Shorts		

PER.	TIME	TYPE	QUARTERBACK	RECEIVERS	OFF. BACKS	TIGHT ENDS	OFF. LINE
	5	WARMUP	PAT & GO				
	10	STRETCH					PULLS
1	10	INDIVIDUAL	GET OFF (5) DROPS	RELEASE	CUT OFF	SLED	CROWTHER
2	10	INDIVIDUAL	DROPS ROUTES	TOP OF RTE SLANT	CROWTHER BALL HANDL	SLAM DRILL ZONE STEPS	POWER PULL OPEN RUBS
3	10	INDIVIDUAL	ROUTES	CURL DIG	SWING CK DOWN	PIVOT CROSS	SLIPS
4	10	CROSS GROUP	9 ON 7	BUMP REL.	9 ON 7	9 ON 7	9 ON 7
5	10	GROUP	GROUP PRO				
6	10	CROSS GROUP	1 ON 1	1 ON 1	3 ON 4	3 ON 4	PASS PRO
7	10	GROUP	GROUP RUN	STOCK BLOCK	GROUP RUN	GROUP RUN	GROUP RUN
8	10	GROUP	AIR PATTERNS				ZONE STEPS
9	10	SPECIAL CATEGORY	TEAM	10 (1-10)			
10	15	CROSS GROUP	7 ON 7	10 (1-10) 5 (2-7)			PASS PRO VS DL (STUNTS)
11	20	TEAM	TEAM	10 (1-10) 5 (2-7)			

Tables 11-8 and 11-9 illustrate the point that, by focusing on productivity, you can develop a practice format that enables you to significantly shorten the length of a practice on most occasions (e.g., from three hours to two hours or less). Not surprisingly, players tend to respond favorably to the concept of shorter practices.

Players should be made to understand, however, that having shorter practices comes at a "price." That "price" requires every player to approach every practice with a high level of focus and concentration.

The point should be emphasized to the players that because they only get a limited number of repetitions of a particular play or situation, they must make a full effort on every repetition. A "wasted" rep is a lost opportunity that will be very difficult to make up later.

An important corollary to the process of developing and implementing fast-paced practices is the fact that, as the head coach, you should have a systematic way of taking notes during every practice. Based on your observations, these notes should essentially address what your assistants are doing during practice, any questions you may have about practice, and any corrective actions you feel may have been overlooked or may need to be expanded.

Subsequently, you should follow up on the points in your practice notes with your staff in a staff meeting. Taking notes during practice is important because it is unrealistic for you to rely on your memory. Not only is it impossible to remember every observation, your memory may not provide a totally accurate account of those concerns you do recall.

> *Don't mistake activity for achievement; practice it the right way.*
>
> John Wooden
> Hall-of-Fame Basketball Coach
> UCLA

ESTABLISHING A PRACTICE FORMAT

As a general rule, the format used by NFL teams for practices involves seven distinct segments: individual warm-up, fundamentals, skill and technique work, combination and group work, the unit drill, 7-on-7 drills, and 3-on-3 drills. Although the degree to which each of these elements is addressed may vary from practice to practice, it is important to remember that each segment is a vital part of an effective practice schedule. With few exceptions, the seven segments are common to all systems and competitive levels of football.

- *Individual warm-up.* Each practice should begin with a three-to-five minute period of individual warm-ups that is directed by the position coach. This segment is usually followed by a team stretching period or a period of team calisthenics. The individual warm-up period may be supplemented with some very light agility drills that relate to the responsibilities of an individual's particular position.

- *Fundamentals.* Even though fundamentals may be perceived as too simplistic, too routine, or too boring, every player must continue to work on them. A creative position coach, however, searches for new ways to make practicing fundamentals an acceptable and relatively interesting activity to his players.

  Fundamentals should be practiced at least ten minutes a day, even in the NFL. They are typically practiced by position (e.g., offensive line, receivers, quarterbacks, etc.).

  A position coach can usually keep the tempo of the drills for developing fundamentals relatively up-beat by either injecting some form of competitiveness into the drill or by adding a time factor. For example, timing the movements of the

Table 11-8. Example of a 49ers' morning practice format.

| | | 49ers Practice No._____ | Date_____ | | AM Shorts Pads | |
| | | | Time_____ | | PM Shells | |
Per	Time (Min)	Period Type	Denny Green	Mike Holmgren	Sherman Lewis	Bobb McKittrick
1	9:00 (15)	IND	Catching Drills Blocking	Drop Progression	Bags Hit and Spin Ball Handling Fumble Scramble	Crowther Rabbit Bertha
2	9:15 (15)	IND/GRP	Patterns ————————→		Run Install C + QB	Techniques
3	9:30 (15)	IND/GRP	Group Pass Installation +C			OL Vs. DL
4	9:45 (15)	Group 1-on-1 9-on-7	1-on-1 ————————→		9-on-7 ————————→ (5) Base (5) Strip (5) Hawk	
5	10:00 (30)	Group 7-on-7 (20) Base (10) Nickel	7-on-7 ————————→			Pass Rush Vs. DL
6	10:30 (30)	Team	Team ————————→ (20) Base (10) Nickel			
7			PASSES 376-377 Drag Slant 20-21 HB Read 22-23 Z In 24-25 Dbl Comeback P. 42-43 X (Z) Deep Over		RUNS HB 6-7 WK 18-19 Bob FB 30-31 Trap HB 42-43 Lag (T) 66-67 Ctr 68-69 HO	
8			NICKEL 200-300 Jet X Slant 22-23 Y Cross FB Fan 22-23 Y Out FB Curl			
9			NAVAJO 54-55 Z Out (58-59) 54-55 Razor/Scissors (58-59)			

Table 11-9. Example of a 49ers' afternoon practice format.

| | | | 49ers Practice No._____   Date_____   AM Shorts Pads | | | |
| | | | Time_____   PM Shells | | | |

Per	Time (Min)	Period Type	Denny Green	Mike Holmgren	Sherman Lewis	Bobb McKittrick
	2:45	Warm Up				
	2:50	Stretch				
1	3:00 (15)	IND/ADJ	Blocking Catching Drills	Drops Progression Hot	2 Man Sled Pass Pro Ball Handling	Crowther Light Bag Bertha
2	3:15 (15)	IND/GRP	Patterns ———————→ Slot Passes		Run Blocks Vs. Bag	Technique
3	3:30 (20)	Group 7-on-7	7-on-7 ———————————→ (10) Base (10) Nickel			Pass Pro Vs. Rush
4	3:50 (25)	Team	Team ————————————————————→ (10) Navojo (15) Nickel [(10) Run Emphasis]			
5	4:15 (15)	Post Practice	Combo w/DB's C + QB Passes (Navajo) 54-55 Z Out (58-59) 54-55 Razor (58-59)	Pass Action Pass ————→ Ctr Pulls		

players (e.g., timing how long it takes a blocker to drive a sled ten yards; measuring how long it takes defensive players to shuffle down the attack sled; etc.) is an excellent way to enhance the players' attitude toward practicing fundamentals. It is important that each position coach is very demanding during this phase of practice and encourages the players to strive for perfection on every repetition.

- *Skill and technique work.* Usually lasting for fifteen minutes, this segment of practice is devoted to working on those specific skills that have direct application to the demands of the game. The way in which this period is managed distinguishes the "great" coaches from the "good" coaches.

The first step in this process involves having each position coach identify what skills and techniques the players need to develop to do their jobs. Next, the position coach has to decide the most effective way to teach the targeted skills and techniques.

For example, the wide receiver coach may identify twelve skills and techniques that must be mastered to play the position of wide receiver at an appropriate level. The coach then develops practical drills to enhance the teaching of these skills and techniques.

Coaches should invest a lot of time, personal research, and thoughtful inquiry when designing and implementing these drills. For example, they should consult with other coaches who have held a similar position and should ask for their opinions regarding the utility of each drill. As with all other aspects of practice, the drills must fit within the team's existing system.

Even though the position coach may be familiar with certain techniques, if those techniques are not appropriate to the system employed by the team, an assistant coach who insists on teaching those skills is wasting everyone's time and inviting conflict. The responsibility for checking to make sure that the nature of the drills used by the position coaches is compatible with the team's system lies with the head coach.

Practice without improvement is meaningless.

Chuck Knox
Former Head Football Coach
Seattle Seahawks

- *Combination (group) drills.* Compared to other kinds of drills, combination (group) drills are the most difficult type to administer. They require a number of players and can be relatively difficult to set up. Typically, combination drills are only employed in training camp.

Two basic types of combination and group drills exist—competitive and instructional. Drills which are "competitive" in nature involve bringing two groups together to work against each other. Each group attempts to achieve a specific objective—a goal that is at odds with the objective of the other group.

For example, a competitive passing drill may feature the defense working from its scheme against the offense, who is toiling from its base package. Another (somewhat more extreme) example of a competitive combination drill (sometimes referred to as a perimeter drill) is a situation where the drill is designed to give the defensive backs an opportunity to gain experience in run support and the wide receivers a chance to perform live blocking downfield. In both instances, two groups; two conflicting objectives.

A combination drill that is "instructional" in nature, on the other hand, focuses on a single objective. In an instructional combination drill, one group of players is used to "service" the needs of the other group.

Due to the heavy level of contact that may be involved and the fact that a particular combination drill can sometimes develop as many undesirable habits as good habits, only a few repetitions of this type of drill should be performed. Thus, the need for quality repetitions is critical. As a general rule of thumb, however, if a coach has a question about the value of a particular combination drill, that drill shouldn't be used.

Because of the time that may be required to set up a combination drill during a highly structured practice, it is very important that such a drill is efficiently managed. Accordingly, each drill should first be thoroughly explained to the players in the lecture room.

The drill should then be demonstrated on the field. Initially, the first few repetitions of the drill on the field should be performed at half speed. All other repetitions can be done "live" (i.e., at full speed).

Depending on the ability of a combination drill to achieve its primary objective (i.e., teach the proper skill techniques and responses), the drill can be repeated as often as desired with very little change. The key is to assess whether these drills have meaningful value to the team.

If they're designed properly and performed well, combination drills can serve a valuable role in the teaching process. On the other hand, if they don't achieve their intended purpose or if they're not executed properly, combination drills can be a complete waste of time.

- *Unit drills.* In this type of drill, two complete segments of the team are brought together to work competitively against each other or in service of each other (similar to combination drills). If they're properly administered and if they're not allowed to become so competitive that their teaching value is greatly diminished, unit drills can be invaluable.

One of the mainstay examples of a unit drill is the 9-on-7 combination drill which features nine offensive players (excluding the wide receivers) versus the front seven defenders (sometimes eight when the strong safety is included). Such a drill is a very effective way, short of a full scrimmage, to develop a team's running game.

Typically, a unit drill is carried out with a quick whistle and without tackling. Most importantly, however, unit drills must be conducted under simulated game, scrimmage conditions and must involve extensive coaching.

For example, every unit drill should be scripted so that the coaching staff can more easily evaluate the offense's execution of the play or the defense's reaction to the play as it evolves. Furthermore, coaches must not let the players get carried away emotionally during these drills.

With a veteran team, an emphasis can be placed on a specific type of play. For example, an occasional play-pass can be incorporated into the play sequence during a 9-on-7 drill to ensure a more realistic response from the defense.

A typical twelve-play sequence in a 9-on-7 drill might involve eight inside runs, two play-passes, and two 3-step drop passes. Because all kinds of run-pass combinations are possible, structuring an imaginative play sequence can enhance the enthusiasm and concentration levels of the players.

- *7-on-7 (skeleton) drills.* A form of a combination drill, a 7-on-7 drill involves the center, the quarterback, and all of the eligible pass receivers going against all of the pass coverage defenders. Using a varied cadence helps to maintain the integrity of the drill and to give both sides a realistic sense of timing.

For example, conducting the drill in this manner is essential if both sides of the ball are to practice (and retain) the discipline of responding to the center's snap of the ball. In addition, this approach to the drill requires the quarterback to realistically time his drop patterns, instead of unknowingly beginning his drop before the receivers' release.

As a general rule (particularly during training camp), defenders in 7-on-7 drills should be allowed to play the ball in the air in order to work on improving their timing (i.e., reactions, responds, etc.) and to have the coaching staff scrutinize any tendencies they might have towards fouling. Once the regular season begins, however, 7-on-7 drills are usually conducted on a non-contact basis in order to avoid any freak injury that might otherwise occur.

Situational football should be a factor in all 7-on-7 work. All players involved in the drill should be required to know what theoretical game situation they are facing in the drill. To redundantly practice 7-on-7 drills without considering specific game situations is a lost teaching opportunity for the coaching staff.

Accordingly, the coaching staff should cover various situations during 7-on-7 drills. The down-and-distance circumstance, as well as the time factor, should be indicated prior to each repetition of a drill.

During training camp, competitive move-the-ball 7-on-7 drills are an excellent method for teaching techniques and instilling proper habits. For example, if the quarterback holds the ball too long during this type of drill, the coaching staff whistles him as being sacked.

Typically, in competitive move-the-ball drills, almost every down-and-distance situation arises. As a result, different types of passes are called, and different kinds of defensive tactics are utilized.

First downs move the chains. As the ball moves, the defensive tactics change. In addition, the coach can whistle various ball placement situations for the team to work on (e.g., first-and-ten, long yardage, third-and-three, one down to make extremely long yardage, 5-yard line, red zone, goal line, backed-up, short yardage, etc.).

A form of 7-on-7 drill work for each of these situations should be included in the structured calendar of training camp. Another variation of a 7-on-7 combination drill that should be employed in training camp is the coach-on-command quarterback scramble.

In this type of drill, the coach signals the quarterback to scramble outside of the pocket, thereby forcing his receivers and the defenders to adapt to the circumstances. As a rule of thumb, if 20 passes are scheduled for a 7-on-7 drill session, at least two should involve quarterback scrambles.

- *3-on-3 drills.* Adhering to a format that we popularized with the San Francisco 49ers, 3-on-3 drills involve a situation where three linebackers work against the tight end and two running backs. These drills also include a quarterback and a center (and, on occasion, a strong safety).

3-on-3 drills are conducted by alternating groups at the same time 7-on-7 drills are being held. Usually, a 3-on-3 drill is run on the same field, just behind a 7-on-7 drill, but facing in the opposite direction.

As a result, players can be interchanged at any time between the two types of drills—especially the quarterbacks. 3-on-3 drills are designed to practice all pass patterns involving the tight end and the running backs. The linebackers cover accordingly.

Blitzing can be employed in a 3-on-3 drill to give the running backs an opportunity to be exposed to the realities of a competitive situation. Similar to 7-on-7 drills, it is very important to involve a center in the drill.

Play-passes and action passes should also be an integral part of 3-on-3 drills, in order to force the three linebackers to each make the necessary recovery. A 3-on-3 drill provides both tight ends and running backs with a substantial opportunity to develop their pass receiving skills and to practice running precision pass routes—necessary work they might not otherwise get to develop their skills.

Untutored courage is useless in the face of educated bullets.

General George S. Patton, Jr.
Commander, United States Third Army
World War II

DESIGNING AND INSTALLING THE GAME WEEK SCHEDULE

The same approach that a team uses to plan its practice schedule for training camp should be employed to plan its game week schedule. An example of how a game week schedule should be laid out is shown in Table 11-10.

As the head coach, you should keep in mind that very specific limits exist regarding the number of plays that can be efficiently practiced in a given week. Accordingly, the most appropriate way to formulate a weekly practice format is by evaluating three key factors:

- The length of a team's practice.

- How the practices are divided into specific periods (e.g., individual, groups, and team).
- What aspect of the offense or the defense is practiced in each period.

Subsequently, the total amount of time available for practice should be divided by the offensive or defensive emphasis for each given situation (e.g., red zone, third downs, etc.). Proportionally, the resultant areas of emphasis may differ slightly from the actual game calls due to the diverse nature of a given contest.

Table 11-8 illustrates a format that could be used for practices during game week. All factors considered, the weekly practice format should not change drastically as the season progresses.

A team may need to make slight adjustments to its practice format, however, in response to its needs at a particular point in the season. The needs of a team are usually determined by analyzing the team's measurable production on one or more criteria (e.g., rushing yardage, sacks, explosive play production, red-zone efficiency, interceptions, etc.).

As Table 11-11 shows, each team period is identified as a specific situation. This step enables you to isolate exactly how much time the team is spending in each area. It also helps both the coaching staff and the players to better focus on what is being called in a given situation.

Whatever particular practice structure a team employs, it should be relatively easy for you to look at that structure and determine how much time is being devoted to group or team periods and how these periods have been broken down situationally. Table 11-12 provides an example of an overview of such a detailed break-down.

The numbers in Table 11-12 represent any scripted period where the offense works against a live defense. It is important to note the interactive way the total offensive package shown in Table 11-12 is proportioned from game plan to practice structure to actual game calls.

Given the fact that the average NFL team runs approximately 63 offensive plays per game, the practice format detailed in Table 11-11 and charted in Table 11-12 provides a team with slightly more than double the offense it will likely use during a game (i.e., 129 plays practiced versus 63 plays required).

What Table 11-12 does not show are the individual and group periods where the team works on its own particular needs. "W.T." is a walk-though period which is conducted in shorts.

The relatively small number of snaps on Friday is due to two factors. First, the team uses a team period to run a live two-minute drill. In addition, the team employs a separate team period to run a semi-live "move-the-ball" drill, where the head coach starts the offense on the 30-yard line and gives them 8-10 situations to which they must react.

Table 11-10. A sample game week schedule.

MONDAY

11:00 am	Individual coaches finish viewing and grading video.
	View film as an offensive/defensive staff.
	• Written comments for each play.
	• Catalog comments by both player and play for analysis.
1:00 pm	Staff meeting.
2:00	Team meeting.
	Special teams viewing of game.
2:30	Offensive/defensive viewing of game.
	• Coordinator reviews 15-20 key plays with the entire offense, denoting major points of emphasis.
	• Break up positionally to review film.
4:15	On-field (practice).
4:45	Practice ends.
6:00	Dinner.
9:00	The running back, offensive line, and tight end coaches meet to outline basic runs and pass protection schemes for morning meeting with the coordinator.

TUESDAY   (Coaches only; players' day off)

8:00 am	Personnel report on opponent by the team's Director of Pro Personnel.
8:30	Offensive staff meets and discusses base runs and pass protections.
10:00	Offensive line coaches begin run and protection sheets, and view goal line, short-yardage, and red-zone situations. The offensive coaching staff lists base pass, play action, and action passes and specials.
11:30	Lunch, workout, miscellaneous.
2:00 pm	List nickel passes and nickel runs.
4:00	Begin scripting sheets.
5:00	Review blitz situations.
6:00	Dinner.
7:00	Finalize:
	• Script sheets.
	• Scripts and cards.
	• Scouting reports and installation slides.
9:00	Begin short yardage and goal line discussions.

Table 11-10. Continued.

WEDNESDAY

7:30 am	Staff meeting.
8:15	Quarterback meeting.

- Basic defensive profile.
- Run checks.
- Protection perimeters and concerns.

8:30	Special teams meeting.
9:00	Team meeting (5).

- Scouting report.
- Install base runs, nickel runs and protections.

9:30	The offensive line breaks off.

- Install base, play action, action and nickel passes.

10:00	Individual meetings.
11:15	Walk-through.
11:45	Lunch.
12:45 pm	Individual meetings (view video of opponent).
1:15	Meetings end.
1:30	Special teams.
2:00	Practice.
4:15	Practice ends.
5:15	Coaches review practice video.

- Finalize short yardage and goal line offense.
- Finalize red-zone offense.
- Review backed-up and four-minute offenses.
- Review script sheets and prepare cards for Thursday's practice.

THURSDAY

7:30 am	Staff meeting.
8:15	Quarterback meeting.

- Review blitz.
- Outline red-zone approach.

8:30	Special teams meeting.
9:00	Team meeting (5).

- View practice (the offensive line is separate).

9:30	Offense together—install short yardage, goal line, red zone and backed-up plans.
10:30	Individual meetings (view video of opponent).
11:15	Walk-through.
11:45	Lunch.
12:45 pm	Individual meetings (view video of opponent).

Table 11-10. Continued.

1:15	Meetings end.
1:30	Special teams.
2:00	Practice.
4:15	Practice ends.
5:00	Coaches review practice video.
	• Discuss openers.

FRIDAY

7:30 am	Staff meeting.
8:15	Quarterback meeting.
	• Discuss openers.
8:30	Special teams meeting.
9:00	Team meeting (5).
	• Review practice video (the offensive line is separate).
9:45	Offense—review the checks and alerts; review the game plan by personnel and formation.
10:00	Individual meetings.
11:30	Practice.
1:00 pm	Practice ends.
	• Finalize offensive sideline sheet.
	• List openers.

SATURDAY

9:00 am	Review practice video (the offensive line is separate).
	• Individual meetings—hand out final game plan.
10:30	Practice.
11:15	Practice ends.
6:00-8:00 pm	Check into hotel.
9:00	Special teams meetings.
9:30	Offensive/defensive meetings.
	• Review openers.
	• Use cut-ups to support opening calls.
	• View game video to give players a flavor of the game.
	• Plan and review key situations (e.g., short yardage, goal line, blitz, etc.).
10:00	Team meeting.
10:05	Snack.

Table 11-11. A sample weekly practice format.

WEDNESDAY: PRACTICE #1 (PADS)
Walk-through
Defense (10)   1-10
Offense (10)   1-10
Defense (6)   3-6
Offense (6)   3-6

Time	Minutes	Activity	
2:00 pm	5	Warm-up	
2:05	10	Stretching	
2:15	5	Individual/team	
2:20	10	Fundamentals/techniques	
2:30	10	1-on-1/9-on-7	
2:40	10	Group installation	
2:50	10	Team review	
3:00	15	Special categories	
		• Defense (8) 1-10	
		• Offense (8) 1-10	
3:15	10	Special teams	
3:25	20	7-on-7	
		• Defense (6) 1-10	Defense (4) 3-5
		• Offense (6) 1-10	Offense (4) 3-5
3:45	20	Team	
		• Defense (6) 1-10	Defense (4) 3-6
		• Offense (6) 1-10	Offense (4) 3-6

THURSDAY: PRACTICE #2 (SHELLS)
Walk-through
Defense (4)   1-10
Offense (4)   1-10
Defense (3)   3-1
Offense (3)   3-1
Defense (4)   Red zone
Offense (4)   Red zone
Defense (4)   Goal line and 2-point
Offense (4)   Goal line and 2-point
Defense (3)   Backed-up
Offense (3)   Backed-up

Table 11-11. Continued.

Time	Minutes	Activity
2:00 pm	5	Warm-up
2:05	10	Stretching
2:15	5	Individual/team
2:20	10	Fundamentals/techniques
2:30	10	Group
2:40	10	Team review
2:50	20	Special categories I

- Defense (2) 3-1   (6) Red zone   (3) Goal line   (2) 2-point
- Offense (2) 3-1   (6) Red zone   (3) Goal line   (2) 2-point

Time	Minutes	Activity
3:10	10	Special categories II

- Two-minute

Time	Minutes	Activity
3:20	10	Special teams
3:30	25	7-on-7

- Offense (4) 1-10   (4) 3-8   (4) Red zone
- Defense (4) 1-10   (4) 3-8   (4) Red zone

Time	Minutes	Activity
3:55	20	Team

- Offense (4) 1-10   (4) 3-4   (4) Red zone
- Defense (4) 1-10   (4) 3-4   (4) Red zone

FRIDAY: PRACTICE #3 (SHORTS)

Time	Minutes	Activity
11:30 am	5	Warm-up
11:35	10	Stretching
11:45	5	Individual/team
11:50	10	Group review/team review
12:00 pm	15	Special categories I

- Defense (2) 3-1   (5) Red zone   (2) Goal line   (2) 2-point
- Offense (2) 3-1   (5) Red zone   (2) Goal line   (2) 2-point

Time	Minutes	Activity
12:15	5	Special categories II

- Two-minute offense/defense

Time	Minutes	Activity
12:20	10	Special teams
12:30	20	7-on-7

- Offense (3) 1-10   (4) 3-6   (4) Red zone
- Defense (3) 1-10   (4) 3-6   (4) Red zone

Time	Minutes	Activity
12:50	10	Team

- Offense M/T/Ball
- Defense M/T/Ball

Table 11-12. A sample situational breakdown.

DAY	PERIOD	BASE	3RD LONG	3RD MED	SY	BU	RED ZONE	GL	2 PT	TOT	
WED.	W.T.	10	3	3						16	
	INSIDE	6								6	
	TEAM	8								8	
	SKEL	6		4						10	
	TEAM	6	4							10	50
THURS.	W.T.	4			3	3	4	4	2	20	
	TEAM				2		6	3	2	13	
	SKEL	4	4				4			12	
	TEAM	4		4			4			12	57
FRIDAY	TEAM				2		5	2	2	11	
	SKEL	3		4			4			11	22
TOTALS		51	11	15	7	3	27	9	6	129	
		40%	9%	12%	5%	2%	21%	7%	5%		

ESTABLISHING A SCHEDULE FOR THE HEAD COACH

The head coach should establish a weekly work schedule for himself in generally the same way that he schedules and plans the week for his staff and his players. If he does not develop a detailed schedule for himself, he risks the possibility that other projects and time-consuming situations will divert him from more legitimate priorities.

Table 11-13 gives an example of a weekly schedule for a head coach. Such a schedule should include the involvement of the head coach in any facet of the organization that either entails direct contact with the players or has a direct bearing on the game itself.

The term "involvement by the head coach" does not necessarily imply or require the head coach's participation in instructive meetings that take large blocks of time. Meetings involving the head coach should, however, be conducted in a relatively routine, consistent manner.

It is important to everyone involved in such meetings that they can count on a scheduled meeting taking place and can know what materials or subjects will be addressed at the meeting. The head coach who takes a slip-shod attitude toward these meetings runs the risk of creating a real bottle-neck within the organization.

Because his subordinates are unable to plan on any particular set schedule, they'll frequently have to adjust their own timetable of events. In the process, the players will usually wind up waiting on the head coach.

All meetings involving the head coach should be substantive (i.e., have a specific purpose). If the individual in charge of the meeting has nothing of note to cover, he can simply communicate that fact to the head coach, and the meeting can be canceled.

Regularly scheduled meetings between the head coach and his staff also provide an opportunity for each assistant coach to address a particular issue that may be of concern to him in a relatively open (i.e., an environment that is conducive to the interchange of information without a fear of being put down) atmosphere. Such a situation tends to prevent a set of circumstances where a particular staff member would feel that it would be necessary for him to go to his head coach with a problem on numerous occasions in the same day.

ESTABLISHING A POLICY ON HAZING IN TRAINING CAMP

The proper approach to establishing a policy on hazing rookies in training camp is very straightforward—simply follow the advice of the legendary Paul Brown: "There should be none of it." Rightfully so, Brown believed that any form of hazing unduly compromises a team's learning process.

In reality, rookies have a lot to do in training camp, including learning a new system and adjusting to a totally new environment (i.e., primarily the huge difference in the size, ability and experience between pro-level players and college-level players). If they're going to succeed (i.e., make the active team roster), those rookies have to give every bit of their attention to handling the relatively traumatic transition.

Any form of hazing that disrupts the ability of these rookies to focus on the tasks at hand can be counterproductive, not only to themselves, but to the team as well. Depending on the circumstances, such hazing can have more of a negative impact on some players than others.

For example, hazing typically will not prevent a high draft choice from making the team. Having invested a lot in this type of a player (i.e., money, a high draft choice, etc.), a team is usually quite reluctant to give up on the player by releasing him.

The situation is quite different, however, for those middle-round draft choices, undrafted signees, free agent pickups, and those perennial training camp players who try out for the team despite having no real chance of making the roster. These are athletes who are literally fighting for their professional lives to prove that they belong in the NFL. Hazing diminishes their chances.

Young players have far more to worry about than getting up and singing their alma mater in front of the team before dinner. Depending upon the format and the circumstances, hazing can be embarrassing, humiliating and cruel.

Unfortunately, as thoughtless as hazing may be, some veterans persist in such deplorable behavior. When given an opportunity to demean vulnerable, young rookies, those veterans who are less intelligent, who have a dysfunctional sense of reasoning, or who may view hazing as a means for wrecking any competition (for jobs) that the rookies may provide will undoubtedly surface.

Hoping to be accepted by the veterans, most of the rookies will endure these taunts, as humiliating as the insulting behavior may be. Eventually, however, some rookies will take only so much and will turn on their predators.

The key point to remember is that hazing is dehumanizing. It does nothing to bond athletes to each other. Bonding between players occurs on the field when the veterans learn to trust and respect the abilities and commitment of the rookies.

An excellent example of the negative aspects of hazing occurred recently in an NFL training camp. A first-year player actually left the team he was trying out for rather than have his head shaved.

Table 11-13. Sample training camp offensive installation and meeting schedules.

SUNDAY
3:00 pm   Meeting #1 (total time = 90 minutes)
            Bill Walsh's organizational meeting (30 minutes)
            Passes—Basic (40 minutes)
                    376-377 Drag Slant   —Brown/Blue A-C Weak/(T) Solo
                    20-21 HB Read   —Red
                    22-23 Z In   —Red
                    24-25 Dbl Comeback   —Red
                    P.42-43 X(Z) Deep Over   —Red/(T) Solo
            Runs (20 minutes)
                    HB 6-7 Weak   —Green
                    68-69 Hand Off   —(T) Solo//Brown

7:30 pm   Meeting #2 (total time = 120 minutes)
            Passes—Nickel
                    200-300 Jet X Slant   —Blue A-C Strong
                    22-23 Y Cross FB Fan   —Red/Red Slot/Red "Y" Motion
                    22-23 Y Out FB Curl   —Red/Red Slot/Red "Y" Motion
            Passes—Navajo
                    54-55 Z Out (58-59)   —Red Slot
                    54-55 Razor/Scissors (58-59)   —Red
            Runs
                    18-19 Bob   —Red//Red Close
                    FB (HB) 30-31 Trap   —Red "F" Motion ("F" Ck Motion)
                    HB 42-43 Lag   —Brown
                    66-67 Ctr   —(T) Solo//Brown

MONDAY
7:30 pm   Meeting #3 (total time = 120 minutes)
            Passes—Basic
                    20-21 X Circus   —Red
                    22-23 Seattle   —Red/(T) Solo/Red "Y" Motion
                    78-79 HB Corner FB Bag Flat   —Brown
                    Sweep Pass Z Opt   —Blue (Change)
                    P.14-15 Bim X Hook   —Red
            Passes—Nickel
                    24-25 "E" Sq Out   (E)   —Red Close "E" Motion
                    70-71 HB Cross FB Fan   —Change A-C Weak
                    2-3 Jet Flk Drive   —Blue Close

Table 11-13. Continued.

```
        Passes—Navajo
                354-355 Dbl Qk Out + (Thunder)  —Red
                88-89 Audible (Tackle Screen)    —Red
        Runs
                16-17 Power                              —Red
                18-19 W                                  —Red
                FB 16-17 Bim                             —Red/Red "Y" Motion
                38-39 F                        (T)       —(T) Solo//Brown Slot A-C Strong
                FB 40-41                                 —Red
                HB 40-41                                 —Red Ti/Red A-C Weak
                92-93 Ctr                      (U)       —(U) Blue East/Green

TUESDAY
7:30 pm     Meeting #4 (total time = 120 minutes)
            Passes—Basic
                Fox 2-3 D.S.O. (Winston)                 —Brown (Brown Slot)
                Draw Pass Flk Deep Cross                 —Blue Close/Blue "F" Short
                T14-T15                                  —Red
                Roll HB Corner                           —Blue A-C Weak/Dbl Wing
                Lag Pass "Y" Over                        —Brown
                HB Fast Screen (FB)                      —Red/(Red "F" Motion)
            Passes—Nickel
                2-3 Jet Zebra Out              (Ze)      —Dbl Wing/Dbl Wing Zebra Short
            Passes—Navajo
                24-25 Detroit                            —Red
                54-55 X Arrow Z Corner                   —Red Slot
            Runs
                FB 14-15 Trap                            —Red
                16-17 Ctr Bluff                          —Red Ti/Red "F" Ck Motion
                68-69 Storm Toss                         —Blue East
                98-99 Boss                     (U)       —Green/Green Slot
                Z Reverse Lt/Rt Fake 18-19               —Red
```

To this player, his hair was an integral part of his self-respect. Even though he had little chance of making the team as a free agent, he gave up what chance he did have rather than agree to an action he considered an assault on his sense of dignity.

Rather than receiving empathy, respect and appreciation for his valiant efforts to make the team, he was humiliated by a few thoughtless veteran players. In response, the player left camp.

The coaching staff of that particular team should have been attuned to the fact that hazing—in any form—can have a particularly negative impact on the progress of the team (especially in the ethnically diverse atmosphere of the NFL).

Under no circumstances should an athlete's career be disrupted by the sophomoric actions of a few inconsiderate individuals. The coaching staff should constantly remind everyone of the need to heed the words of Paul Brown in this regard, who said: "We're all professionals."

One of the contributing factors to the five world championships that we won in San Francisco in fifteen years (a record that some NFL followers call "dynasty-level" proportions) was the fact that we expected the 49er veterans to do everything possible to "bring along" the team's rookies. All hazing was strictly prohibited.

The issue of the veterans acting responsibly toward the rookie players was openly and directly addressed with the team and the coaching staff. Every effort was made to reinforce the fact that the team should take pride in welcoming the new players who could help the team win and who could help carry on the 49ers' winning tradition.

A coach who willingly accepts or tolerates hazing is someone who either doesn't have the understanding or the mental toughness to meet this issue head on or wants desperately to be liked by the veteran players. In either instance, such a coach is demonstrating a "lack of control"—a trait that suggests that he may not last much longer in his present position.

CHAPTER 12

PUTTING IT ALL TOGETHER

"The coach must have a definite plan in which he believes, and there must be no compromise on his part."

—Paul "Bear" Bryant
Hall-of-Fame Football Coach
University of Alabama

Finding the winning edge...

In a real sense, Grantland Rice's axiom proved out: It's how you play the game that matters, not whether you win or lose. If you do what you do well, you're eventually going to succeed without having to set the bar at some daunting height.

As always, this requires singular leadership, constant and unswerving. One person has to siphon off the pressure that failure and frustration create, and hold together people tempted to say, "My group is doing fine, but everyone else is screwing up." Everyone in an organization needs to feel connected with the concept of constant, daily improvement.

Ford can build cars of the greatest quality, but if marketing doesn't know how to sell them, that quality won't matter. When your goal is steady development rather than dramatic victories, the pieces fall into place in ways you can't initially predict. Talent rises from within, inspired by challenge.

—Bill Walsh, "Winning: The Only Thing? Sometimes the Best Way to Build a Championship Team is to Take Your Eyes off the Prize," *Forbes*, December 4, 1995.

In business, as well as in sport, a number of factors affect success. The interrelationship between these factors has been demonstrated to me on numerous occasions over the years. For example, my first two seasons taught me that even in defeat you can make progress if you have confidence, patience, a plan, and a timetable.

One of the greatest difficulties of coaching is that some people around you either do not understand what is required to get the job done or they lose their nerve. The sports pages always have instant criticisms or suggestions for quick fixes. Head coaches are under pressure from owners, fans, the media, assistant coaches, and players.

These people may feel you are moving too fast or not fast enough. The owners are often the hardest to deal with. The team is their investment; therefore, nerves and ego interfere with rationality. They need to feel you are under their thumb both when they hire you and when they fire you.

With San Francisco 49ers owner Eddie DeBartolo, Jr., I always tried to give him a written version of the plan that we had developed and were implementing. I developed an operations manual, a personnel manual, a budget manual, and an overall set of job descriptions. I outlined the job of each player and evaluated every member of the team. I also put in writing our goals and expectations for where we were and where we wanted to be.

A high degree of documentation helps owners believe their investment is in capable hands. I was fortunate; Eddie never interfered with any changes I wanted to make. In the early years, he listened to me and was enthusiastic. Unfortunately, as time went by, he did not listen quite as well.

In the face of everything, you have to be resolute about where you are going and how you plan to get there. Even though you might fail, or your plan may not develop, you can not give in to panic. Many people bring on failure by their reaction to pressure. A lot of coaches lose their nerve late in a game. When this problem occurs, players often turn on each other in an attempt to protect themselves from criticism. As soon as this situation arises, the coach is faced with people who are working against their own best interests.

The coach who has the nerve to stay with his program all the way to the bitter end is the one who will most often have the best results.

Administering the events occurring on game day, on and off the field, has become somewhat of a lost art. All too often, a comprehensive plan for handling these events and the attention to detail for implementing this plan are "lost" because the arrangements for ensuring that this plan is carried out effectively are not taken to their logical conclusion. As the head coach, you must set the example by "finishing" your preparation efforts with a well-orchestrated game plan. You must remember that an extraordinary plan is relatively useless unless the head coach can "put it all together."

"Putting it all together" requires that the head coach take specific steps to ensure that all game-day events and issues are addressed in a professional manner by either himself or his staff. Several factors must be detailed in a comprehensive game-day plan, including game-day management, game-day sequencing, communication during the game, dealing with situational circumstances during the game, and laying out the game plan.

Giving an appropriate amount of attention to each of the game day factors can have a substantial effect on the level of success achieved by a team. The "act of putting it all together" demands that no less attention be given to each game-day factor than to the individual aspects of the game itself.

One of the marks of an effective head coach is his ability to see the "big picture." In other words, he is able to identify and address all circumstances that can have an impact on his team's performance. For example, a "winning" coach establishes parameters which maximize the time his team has available for instruction.

An insightful head coach also realizes that athletes who are optimally prepared (i.e., athletes who feel they are ready for every contingency) are more relaxed and focused with regard to their specific duties and responsibilities. The moment of closure is not the time to wonder if everything is taken care of properly. Post-preparation anxiety is an unproductive and unnecessary element of stress for both players and coaches.

GAME-DAY MANAGEMENT

The well-prepared head coach establishes a situational checklist of procedures to follow when undertaking particular game-day tasks. An effective head coach does not fly by the seat of his pants. Rather, he is more like a commercial airline pilot upon whose meticulous attention to detail depends the welfare of hundreds of passengers.

One of the most common tools that a head coach employs to ensure that game-day tasks are done is the game-day checklist. Such a checklist is designed to enable the head coach or his designee to be better able to effectively manage the list of tasks or objectives that must be performed. Among the areas to be addressed and the actions to be taken that should be included in such a checklist are the following:

- Discuss the availability and operational status of the field phones with the equipment manager.
- Discuss the operational status of the Polaroid processing materials with the equipment manager.
- Discuss the availability and location of coaching materials (e.g., chalkboards, chalk, "dry ball," kicking tee, kicking net, etc.).
- Discuss the need, availability and location of the foul-weather gear and towels.
- Discuss any need for any cooling or heating apparatus at the sideline.

Play-Calling Mechanism

- Review communication mechanics with the offensive signal caller and the quarterbacks.
- Review communication mechanics with the defensive signal caller and the linebackers.

- Meet with the coordinators and restate the procedures for substituting personnel.

A general should say to himself many times a day: If the hostile army were to make an appearance in front, on my right, or on my left, what should I do? And if he is embarrassed, his arrangements are bad; there is something wrong; he must rectify the mistake.

Napoleon
Renowned General
Emperor of France

Decision-Making Process

- Meet with the quarterbacks, the coordinators and the signal callers to review the plan for clock management and the use of time outs.
- Meet with the team captains and coordinators to:
    - Review the communication process for accepting or refusing of penalties.
    - Discuss the desired option for the opening kickoff.
    - Discuss the utilization of time outs.
- Meet with the coordinators and reiterate the kicking game strategy, (e.g., punt versus field goal strategy, whom to kick to, whom not to kick to, etc.).
- Meet with the coordinators and discuss the 2-point strategy, detailing the situations when a 2-point play should be attempted.

Contingency Formula

- Discuss the plan for special considerations in the matter of clock management with the quarterbacks, the offensive coordinator, and the signal caller with regard to:
    - Leading by a small margin late in the game.
    - Leading by a large margin late in the game.
    - Trailing by a small margin late in the game.
    - Trailing by a large margin late in the game.
- Detail the guidelines for the four-minute offense with the quarterbacks, the offensive coordinator and the signal caller.
- Detail the guidelines for the two-minute offense with the quarterbacks, the offensive coordinator and the signal caller.
- Detail the guidelines for the two-minute defense with the linebackers, the defensive coordinator and the signal caller.
- Discuss special offensive circumstances (e.g., the opening series, the last three plays, etc.) with the quarterbacks, the coordinator and the signal caller.

- Discuss special defensive circumstances (e.g., the goal line defense readiness, surprise 2-point play planning, 4th-down situational planning, etc.).

- Discuss special considerations for the kicking game with the kickers and the coordinators (e.g., taking a safety, the opportunities for a fake, the degree to which the environmental conditions could affect performance, etc.).

There are only three principles of warfare—audacity, audacity, *and* AUDACITY.

> General George S. Patton, Jr.
> Commander, United States Third Army
> World War II

GAME-DAY SEQUENCING

As the head coach, you must establish a specific and structured sequence of game-day events. Miscommunicating or misunderstanding the proper sequence of game-day events can cause an undue level of distraction. The end result of such a distraction could range from the disturbance of an individual player to a loss of focus for the entire team. Early planning and adherence to the game-day management plan will prevent a disruption of game-day sequencing while allowing you to provide a supportive environment to enhance the athletes' level of mental concentration and pre-game preparation efforts.

As with any successful organizational plan, the principal features of the design may be interconnected to such a degree that the individual features become coincidental throughout the plan. To this end, the development of game-day sequencing is closely related to the head coach's efforts to develop a detailed game-day checklist.

By developing a comprehensive, systematic game-day checklist, you will help facilitate a smoother sequence of the game-day events for both your players and your staff. A detailed game-day sequence should evolve from extensive discussions and planning between you and your staff. When completed, an appropriately sequenced list of game-day actions by the head coach should include numerous steps, including:

- Organize a timetable and an itinerary for the game day, including all events involving post-game travel.

- Give the players a personal copy of the timetable and the itinerary no later than two days prior to the game.

- Post the timetable and the itinerary in the facilities at least two days prior to the game.

- Organize a detailed plan for pre-game locker room activities.
  - Provide the security personnel with the names of those individuals who are allowed access to the locker room.

- — Detail the procedures and location of "taping" opportunities.
- — Post a pre-game schedule of group sessions.
- — Post a field outline which diagrams warm-up areas and specific warm-up times.
- — Advise the assistant coaches of their assigned group meeting areas, meeting times, stretching times, and any special considerations for the pre-game ritual.
- — Meet with assistant coaches, review the warm-up routine, the game assignments and the half-time procedures.
- — Meet with team physicians to receive updated medical information.
- — Ensure that the equipment procedures are being followed and that the equipment manager is able to meet all player needs.
- — Confirm the status of the bench facilities and the field equipment with the equipment manager.
- — Meet with team captains to discuss pre-game options.

- Meet with game officials and express any concerns.
- Plan a definitive pre-game field routine which progressively meets individual, group, and team needs.
- Maintain a controlled pre-game locker room atmosphere and support it with positive statements.
- Sharpen the focus of the team on the head coach and the mission statement.
- Indicate that the team is to "take the field."
- Supervise the on-field communication, monitor the coordinators, evaluate the strategy and personnel.
- Direct the flow of the game strategy.
- Get to the locker room quickly at half-time.
- Dismiss assistant coaches to meet as independent groups (e.g., offense, defense, special teams).
- Meet with the trainer and the team physician to evaluate disposition of injured players.
- Allow the coordinators time to listen to the assistant coaches and evaluate the charts provided by press box spotters.
- Direct the position coaches when to meet with the players.
- Break up the assistant coaches' meetings in order to gather the squad.
- Listen to the input of the coordinators.
  - — Unexpected offensive strategies of opponent are identified.
  - — Unexpected defensive alignments are identified as to type, frequency, and situations used.
  - — Notable tendencies of the opponent are evaluated.
  - — Priorities for the opening series of the second half are identified.
  - — The status of any injured player is discussed and compensatory adjustments made due to any injury.

- Allow coordinators to meet with their respective groups.

- Make brief remarks to both the offensive and the defensive groups.

- Receive the report of the game official on the remaining time left in half-time.

- Address the team and lead them on the field in a timely fashion.

- Direct the flow of the game strategy.

- Take control of the post-game locker room atmosphere.
    - Allow a brief moment for emotional venting.
    - Call the team's attention to the proper perspective.
        - √ Underline the value of the victory.
        - √ Place the loss in perspective.
    - Intervene in the finger-pointing mentality.
    - Clarify the status of the team's playoff standing.
    - Set the tone for the team to address the media.

- Refrain from premature evaluations of strategy and personnel.

COMMUNICATION DURING THE GAME

As the head coach, you must set up a definite communication system that allows input from those who are critical to the decision-making process. This system must also provide a means of lateral access for those individuals so that they may communicate with one another. Important to any system of communication is a proper chain of command. Adhering to a chain of command allows for concise communication among the staff.

A chain of command is important if the information is to be delivered in a manageable and constructive manner. It should be noted that the chain of command is slightly more complex for a head coach who serves as his own offensive or defensive coordinator.

The head coach who desires to monitor the press box offensive coordinator and the press box defensive coordinator may switch back and forth between the offensive and defensive channels on his head phone. Coordinators who remain on the field are in face-to-face contact with the head coach.

The head coach must take care to restrain his emotions in the presence of an on-field coordinator. The head coach who berates a coordinator on the sidelines during a game will disturb the concentration of the coaches and possibly affect the performance of the players in a negative manner.

Effective communication during the game also requires that a systematic protocol should be established to talk to and obtain information from the team trainers and doctors. For example, a medical determination of an incapacitated player's condition must be immediately reported to the head coach. Two basic kinds of protocol are commonly employed to report a player's inability to participate in the contest.

The injury is either reported directly to the head coach by the sideline medical staff member or the information on the injury is conveyed to a designee of the coaching staff, in which case the designee immediately notifies the head coach of the player's condition.

As specified in the game-day checklist, administration of the bench facilities is crucial to maintaining order on the sideline. The head coach must be able to immediately locate an active player by walking over to a designated bench area and finding that particular player.

Accordingly, all players must be assigned by groups (e.g., offense, defense, etc.) to specific areas on the sideline. The location of these areas and who is assigned to them is a subject which should be a matter covered in the pre-game meetings.

For example, a common sideline grouping provides for an offensive line area manned by the offensive line coach, a defensive area manned by the defensive staff, a wide receiver area manned by the skill position coaches on the sideline, and a staging area for the specialty team. A typical sideline offensive staffing of a head coach who serves as offensive coordinator might include the offensive line coach, another position coach, and the signal caller.

In the press box, the tight end coach is assigned to chart the defensive fronts and tendencies while communicating with the offensive line coach on the field. The offensive line coach is responsible for the on-field blocking adjustments. He analyzes the press box information and decides on the most advantageous scheme available.

The quarterback coach in the press box charts the defensive coverages and identifies matchups on the backside wide receiver while in direct communication to the head coach who is calling the plays. If an additional coach is present on the sideline, that coach is often assigned to watch the quarterback mechanics and the backfield action. This coach reports his observations to the quarterback coach who is located in the press box.

In a system of play-calling which involves communicating manually, the signal caller's sole responsibility is to signal in the plays. He has face-to-face communication with the head coach. Using dummy callers to signal bogus information is a strategy that many head coaches employ when their teams are using a manual communication system. Dummy signalers inhibit the opponent's ability to steal the signals.

In fact, many NFL coaches currently employ a dual system of signaling in the formations while verbally communicating which play they want called. Another relatively recent NFL innovation is the helmet cam—a tool which is designed to facilitate communication between the quarterback and the offensive coordinator.

Every member of the coaching staff must focus on and be prepared to provide instantaneous information pertaining to every single aspect of the opponent's performance on the field. For example, assistant coaches should be able to immediately provide the head coach with answers in regard to the opponent's offensive point of attack and its offensive backfield execution.

In the NFL, Polaroid photographs are a particularly valuable and commonly employed tool for obtaining accurate observations of an opponent's offensive or defensive alignment in specific situations. Even this phase of the game must be practiced and refined during training camp and in the preseason games. The point to remember is that effective communication during the game can only be achieved by practicing effective communication prior to the game itself.

> *Nothing is so subject to the inconstancy of fortune as war.*
>
> Miguel de Cervantes Saavedra
> Spanish Author
> from *Don Quixote*

DEALING WITH SITUATIONAL CIRCUMSTANCES

The well-prepared head coach has a systematic plan for dealing with situations which occur during the game that deviate from the normal flow of the game. A contingency plan for dealing with situational circumstances allows the head coach to overcome an unexpected setback, as well as take advantage of an unanticipated act of providence.

A thoroughly prepared head coach devotes a sufficient amount of time considering what his team should do if it encounters unusual situations during the game. For example, among the unique circumstances that a prepared head coach should consider are the following:

- What if we fall behind by two or three touchdowns early in the game?
- What if we fall behind by two touchdowns in the 4th quarter?
- What if we are ahead by two or three touchdowns early in the game?
- What if we are ahead by two touchdowns early in the 4th quarter?
- What if the basic game plan is taken away by the opponent or by the game conditions?
- How do we take advantage of an unexpected opportunity?
- How do we respond to an opponent's unexpected opportunity?
- How do we take advantage of a noted physical mismatch?
- How do we respond to counter a disadvantageous physical mismatch?
- What can we do to revive a struggling or out-of-sync offensive unit?
- What can we do to uplift and inspire a struggling defensive unit?
- What is an effective counter strategy when the offensive unit is being overwhelmed?
- What is an effective adjustment when the defensive unit is being overwhelmed?
- How can we take advantage of an injury to a key opponent?
- What is our contingency for an injury to a key player?
- What is the best offensive strategy when enjoying a strong wind at our back?
- What is the best defensive strategy when enjoying a strong wind at our back?
- What is the best offensive strategy when facing a strong wind?
- What do we consider defensively when facing a strong wind?

- What is the best offensive strategy in a heavy rain?
- What offensive strategy will be least inhibited by poor field conditions?
- What considerations should be made with regard to the game temperature?
- What steps can be taken to ensure effective communication over the din of hostile spectators?

Successful generals make plans to fit circumstances, but do not try to create circumstances to fit plans.

General George S. Patton, Jr.
Commander, United States Third Army
World War II

LAYING OUT THE GAME PLAN

The layout of a game plan is somewhat dependent upon the personal learning style of the head coach. Personal preference and sight lines play a part in the format for the development of the game plan. Regardless of the degree to which the structure of a game plan layout is subject to personal creativity, all game plans share several basic functional features, including:

- A game plan is the result of the combined thoughts of the coaching staff.
- A game plan is an interactive tool for both players and coaches.
- A game plan must be flexible enough to facilitate minor strategy adjustments.
- A game plan facilitates the breaking of tendencies without straying from the plan.
- A game plan provides for alternative strategies that allow the coordinator to stay within the scheme.
- A game plan addresses certain special situations and allows for creativity within the scheme.
- A game plan provides for a situational response (i.e., 2nd and long, 3rd and short, etc.).
- A game plan allows for a counter to a specific strategy of the opposition (i.e., 3-4 defense, four wide receivers, 46 defense, bunch set, etc.).
- A game plan allows for specific strategies that consider field position.

The format that a head coach uses to organize and chart his game plan for a specific opponent is to a large degree subjective and based on his own personal opinion regarding how such information should be catalogued. Within the NFL, a variety of functional game-plan formats exists. Whatever the format used, however, an offensive game plan should address a number of factors including a practiced strategy for dealing with the situational, contingency, and reactive aspects of the offensive package.

As a general rule, coaches put the pertinent information concerning their game plan on either a one-page or a two-page chart which they carry with them during the game in order to have immediate access to the catalogued information. Tables 12-1 and 12-2 provide an example of a two-page chart (front page and back page) which details the dynamic elements of a comprehensive game plan.

On the front page:
- Base runs and passes—a listing of base running plays and passes grouped by type, personnel and/or formation.
- 3rd down—from the open field, a package tailored for the following down and distance situations: 3rd and short (i.e., 2 to 4 yards), 3rd and medium (i.e., 5 to 7 yards), 3rd and long (i.e., 8 to 11 yards). Also included in the 3rd down category section of the game plan are sections that allow for a plan against the nickel blitz and nickel zone defense.
- Play passes and action passes—a list of play passes and action passes.
- Red zone—plays that are normally run once a team reaches the +20 yard line (i.e., the red zone); the plays are listed for each of the areas of the red zone, progressing in 5-yard increments down to the +5 yard line with respect to the defensive tendencies of the opponent. The red-zone section of the game plan includes scripted runs and passes for 3rd down situations in all of the segments (i.e., +20 yard line, +15 yard line, +10 yard line and +5 yard line segments).
- Goal line and 2-point play—specifies available goal line plays and a 2-point play.
- Short yardage—details available plays to use in short-yardage situations, including down and distances of 3rd and 1 yard or less and 4th and 1 yard or less.

On the back page:

- Attacking fronts—lists plays to use versus a specialized defensive front, such as the 46 defense, the Navajo package, etc.
- Base blitz—outlines run plays and pass plays with audible capability that are designed for unexpected blitz situations.
- Two-minute and four-minute offense—details targeted plays from two-minute and four-minute offense package.
- Last four plays—lists the last four plays of the first half.
- Best player—lists the plays which highlight the team's best offensive player and includes the specific situational criteria to which the plays are applied.
- Base coverages—categorizes the plays with regard to type, personnel, and formation versus the basic coverages available to the defense.
- Attacking coverages—lists the plays designed to exploit a particular coverage.
- Backed up—targets the plays which are to be used when the offense is backed up against their own goal line.
- Must call—details a specific list of plays which are expected to produce big results against a particular defensive scheme.

Table 12-1. Sample game plan (front sheet).

Starters	Short Yardage	Goal Line (3-Yard Line)
1. 2. 3. 4. 5. 6. 7. 8. 9. 10. 11. 12. 13. 14. 15.	**Runs** 1. 2. 3. 4. **Passes** 1. 2. 3. 4.	**Runs** 1. 2. 3. 4. **Passes** 1. 2. 3. 4.

Base Runs	3rd and 3	+ 5-Yard Line
1. 2. 3. 4. 5. 6. 7. 8. 9. 10. 11. 12.	**Runs** 1. 2. 3. 4. **Passes** 1. 2. 3. 4.	**Runs** 1. 2. 3. 4. **Passes** 1. 2. 3. 4.

Base Passes	3rd and 6	+10-Yard Line
1. 2. 3. 4. 5. 6. 7. 8. 9. 10. 11. 12. 13. 14. 15. 16. 17. 18. 19. 20.	**Runs** 1. 2. 3. 4. **Passes** 1. 2. 3. 4.	**Runs** 1. 2. 3. 4. **Passes** 1. 2. 3. 4.

	Long Yardage	+20-Yard Line
	1. 2. 3. 4. 5. 6. 7. 8.	1. 2. 3. 4. 5. 6.

Play Passes	Action Pass	Attacking Blitz
1. 2. 3. 4. 5. 6. 7. 8.	1. 2. 3. 4. 5. 6. 7. 8.	1. 2. 3. 4. 5. 6.

Table 12-2. Sample game plan (back sheet).

Nickel	Audibles (basic to plan)	Two Minute (Three Play Sequences)
Runs 1. 2. 3. 4. **Passes** 1. 2. 3. 4. 5. 6. 7. 8. 9. 10.	1. 2. 3. 4. 5.	1. 2. 3.
		1. 2. 3.
	Four-Minute (Control Ball) Runs	1. 2. 3.
Prevent 1. 2. 3. 4.	**Runs** 1. 2. 3. 4. 5. 6. **Passes** 1. 2. 3. 4.	**Second Half Considerations** 1. 2. 3. 4. 5. 6.
Last Four Plays 1. 2. 3. 4.	**Backed Up (Inside Own 5-Yard Line) Runs** **Runs** 1. 2. 3. 4. **Passes** 1. 2. 3. 4.	**Screens** 1. 2. 3. 4.
Attacking Stunts 1. 2. 3. 4.		**Specials (Reverses, must calls, reminders, etc.)** 1. 2. 3. 4. 5.
Attacking Fronts 1. 2. 3. 4. 5. 6.	**Attacking Coverages** 1. 2. 3. 4. 5. 6.	**Notes**

- Reminders—lists personal notes with regard to opponent's tendencies, personnel, etc.
- Nickel runs—best running plays versus a defense having six defenders in the box or another defense characterized by use of nickel personnel.
- Screens and specials—a list of available screens and special plays.
- Second-half considerations—possible opening second-half plays.

"Putting it all together" requires intensive pre-game planning and a resolute commitment to follow the plan. The plan must be inclusive and comprehensive in its attention to detail. Managing the game day, sequencing the events of the game day, communicating during the game, dealing with situational circumstances during the game, and laying out the game plan are issues which the effective head coach must address in order to create an environment conducive to success for the team. An unwavering belief in developing, implementing and adhering to a well-thought out plan for game-day situations is a prerequisite for a first-class organization.

The plan was the distilled and concentrated essence of extreme daring. Jackson would take twenty-five thousand men, march the length of Hooker's front, circle around until he was due west of him, and attack his exposed right flank. The march would take the better part of the day, and to form line of battle in the trackless wilderness where Hooker's flank rested might take hours; it would be early evening before Jackson could make his fight. Until then Lee with fewer than twenty thousand men would have to confront Hooker and his eighty thousand. Indeed, merely to confront him would not be enough; he would have to pretend to be fighting an offensive battle, and the pretense would have to be convincing, because if Hooker ever found out what Jackson was up to or learned how small Lee's force really was he could destroy the Army of Northern Virginia before the sun went down.

Hooker would find out nothing, for Lee had him in his hands and was toying with him. Jackson made his march (it was discovered, but in the paralysis that had come upon his spirit Hooker was quite unable to interpret the meaning of his discovery; he concluded finally that part of Lee's army must be retreating, and he sent out a couple of divisions to prod the fugitives along). Lee gave a masterful imitation of a general who is about to open a crushing attack all along the line, and kept Hooker looking his way without inducing him to look so attentively that he could discover anything. And a little while before sundown Jackson struck Hooker's exposed flank like the crack of doom.

Bruce Catton
Pulitzer Prize-winning Author
from *This Hallowed Ground*

CHAPTER 13

STRATEGIES AND TACTICS FOR DEALING WITH A HIGHLY COMPETITIVE ADVERSARY

"The modern army commander must free himself from routine methods and show a comprehensive grip of technical matters, for he must be in a position continually to adapt his ideas of warfare to the facts and possibilities of the moment."

—Erwin Rommel
Infamous German Combat General
World War II
The Rommel Papers, ix.

Finding the winning edge...

The key to success is reaching out, extending yourself, striking, and then, if you fall, bouncing back and doing it again—being so resourceful that finally when the moment comes again, you won't hesitate. What makes this situation possible is having a plan that's broad-based enough so any number of situations may be treated as decisive moments. The main thing is to increase your chances, not live or die on one alone.

—Bill Walsh, "Carpe Diem—or the Diem After That," *Forbes*, October 25, 1993.

The accomplishments achieved by any organization are a by-product of many factors. Perhaps none is more important than the ability of the head coach to set the "tone" for success. Everyone (coaching staff and players) must be prepared to do their job properly—whatever the situation.

This point was clearly reinforced to me by "The Drive" that beat Cincinnati in the 1989 Super Bowl. "The Drive" was the culmination and embodiment of not only 10 years of work with the San Francisco 49ers, but of a lifetime of study and refinement.

Each player knew his assignment and carried it out. There was no panic, no hesitation. The players knew that they had prepared for this moment and that they possessed the abilities and the means to finish the job.

Unbeknownst to everyone, I knew that this would be my last game with the 49ers. I had decided to retire the week of the Super Bowl and was concerned about the effects of this announcement if it was made before the game. I did not want my decision to become a distraction to the players with the resultant, rampant speculation about what this would mean to the players and the organization. I even delayed the announcement for a few days after the game for the players to enjoy the accolades they so richly deserved. I did not want to divert the attention away from them with the sideshow that I knew would ensue.

Even my decision to retire involved a process that I believed in and to which I wanted to adhere. I had always worked to convince the team that no one was irreplaceable. If a player was injured or a veteran was replaced, the expectations needed to remain the same and the structure and process we had worked so hard to develop would carry us through whatever changes occurred. My whole philosophy of coaching encompassed this, and I wanted to maintain it to the end.

With this decision weighing in the back of my mind, the significance of being in the Super Bowl, trailing 16-13, with only 3:10 remaining, sitting 1st-and-10 on the eight-yard line and staring at 92 yards of turf took on an almost surreal quality. This situation would test every fiber of my experience and challenge the very core of a style and structure of play that I had spent a lifetime developing. It took every ounce of concentration I had to maintain my focus and drive out the flood of emotions and any sense of desperation that would divert my attention.

The 12-play winning drive consisted of the absolute core concepts of our system. We knew we had to execute and had enough confidence not to panic or attempt any "heroics." We would count on precision and execution. Only the last scoring play (20 HB Curl X Up) was anything close to being out of our normal sequence of our base offense. Even this play was evaluated and conceived after detailed analysis of Cincinnati's defense in this specific situation.

At this moment, you realize that coaching is not an exact science. All you can do is be as thorough with your contingency planning as possible, play the percentages, and take well-calculated risks, fully cognizant that at some point "fate" may take a hand.

The 12-play sequence of plays seemed to utilize every dimension of our offensive paradigm: the 2-minute process, the proper use of time outs, the audibling mechanism, the effective communication with the press box, the use of special motion to isolate a specific receiver, and the courage of convictions to stay within the system.

"The Drive" reflected what I love most about football: the artistry. People outside the profession sometimes find it hard to think of what we do in terms of orchestration, artistry and composition because of the brute force that is the game's nature and the finality of the competition. Yet it is this unique confluence of qualities that so captivates me and others who share this profession.

Over the years, organizations have devoted considerable time and expended substantial resources in a search for the "absolute" formula for success in the NFL. Obviously, no single "best" formula exists. If it did, every team would adopt it.

On the other hand, success in the NFL involves numerous common denominators. Perhaps, none is more important than a comprehensive plan that addresses every on-the-field and off-the-field factor that could reasonable be expected to have an impact (directly or indirectly) on the performance of the team. At the core of such a plan are offensive and defensive schemes that have been designed to enable the team's players to best utilize their skills and abilities.

DEVELOPING AN OFFENSIVE SYSTEM

If a team knows, week in and week out, that it will outman its opponent, offensive strategy and tactics are not a high priority. Unlike the collegiate level where Nebraska, Notre Dame, Florida, USC, etc. have had this advantage for years, such a set of circumstances does not exist in the NFL. As a result, the need to establish an effective offensive system is critical.

Opinions regarding what conditions are necessary components of an effective offensive system tend to vary from organization to organization. Some coaches, for example, believe that the number one priority for having a successful offense is to establish the running game. In reality, however, the logic behind such an approach is somewhat faulty.

What a team actually needs is a fully dimensional offensive system that provides it with the latitude to access whatever aspect of the offense it needs, whenever it needs it. A fully dimensional approach to offense features a balanced offense that accounts for all reasonable contingencies that can occur during the game. It provides a mechanism to address each contingency or situation as it develops.

Rather than compel a team to depend on a single dimension of offensive strategy, a fully dimensional system gives a team multiple offensive weapons. Having several options available can be particularly valuable to a team when a specific aspect of its offensive game plan is nullified by circumstances (e.g., playing conditions, the caliber of the competition, injuries to key players, etc.). In other words, if one dimension of a team's offensive arsenal is "shut down," a fully dimensional offensive system gives a team the opportunity to succeed within the existing circumstances.

A fully dimensional offense has several characteristics. At a minimum, it must be functional; it must be interactive; it must feature descriptive verbiage that facilitates communication between the coaching staff and the players; it must be flexible; and, to a degree, it must be innovative.

A team's offensive structure must be designed in such a way that it has a logical progression to it that both the coaching staff and the players understand. Not only must it be fundamentally sound conceptually, it must also be based, to a degree, on a detailed analysis of the responsibilities of each player and on a prioritized sense of appreciation regarding what skills are needed to play each position effectively.

The running game and the passing game should complement each other. The basic formations and motions employed in a team's offensive scheme must be equally functional in both phases of the game.

It is also important that a team's offensive system utilizes user-friendly language. A team's players and coaches must be able to communicate with each other quickly and effectively in pressure situations during the game.

Properly defined language is critical in a number of ways. For example, verbiage that is clear, concise, and easily understandable can enhance a player's ability to grasp and assimilate the team's offensive systems. In turn, this factor facilitates the transition of players (new and veteran) into the team's offensive structure. Similar to the system itself, the verbiage used to install, employ and manage the offensive system must be functional, concise and relevant.

A team's offensive structure must also have enough flexibility to be able to readily assimilate new players. Given the advent of free agency in the NFL in the 1990s, organizations must design their offensive systems in such a way that the systems can be adjusted or changed, as necessary, depending on the skills and abilities of the players on the team at a particular point in time.

In reality, some coaches are either unwilling or unable to recognize the fact that their team's offensive approach must be altered if the level of talent on their team is insufficient to meet the demands of their style or philosophy. Such a situation makes the already difficult decision whether to abandon a potentially productive part of the offense even more difficult.

A coach will make a serious error in judgment if he tries to force a particular play/sequence on a team that has only a minimal chance of performing it effectively, and then blames its lack of success simply on the inadequacies of his players. Every coach must remember that a system should never reduce the game to a point where the players are blamed for the failure of the system because they did not physically overwhelm the opponent.

Finally, a team must be open to change. Given the dynamic state of the NFL in the 1990s (e.g., players are bigger, faster and stronger; defensive schemes continue to evolve; etc.), a team must have an offensive system that is sufficiently innovative to keep abreast of changing circumstances. Even if a particular element of the offense has been successful in the past, no guarantee exists that it will work in the future.

One area of the offensive structure that has undergone considerable change in recent years has been the teaching progression that teams use to group and teach the skills involved in a particular offensive scheme or technique. For example, technological advances, such as the telecaster and digital video, have provided coaches with "cutting edge" tools to enhance both teaching and sequential learning.

The No-Huddle Offense

Teams employ the no-huddle offense in a variety of ways. Some teams utilize it as part of their predesigned game plan. Others use it in situations where their offense must speed up play after falling well behind as the game progressed.

Another instance in which the no-huddle offense is appropriate involves the defense. If your opponent's defensive tactics are unexpected or in the extreme (such as extensive use of high-risk blitzing), a no-huddle scheme may either reduce the number of variations a defense may employ or force the defense into automatic defensive schemes to cope with the quickened pace.

While the no-huddle offense can be utilized at anytime, it is critical that it be extensively and thoroughly practiced. As such, the scheme should be utilized on an ongoing basis in practice, throughout both minicamps and training camp.

During practice, necessary corrections and adjustments to the way the no-huddle offense is being run can be made as the players await the snap at the line of scrimmage. Such modifications can be undertaken in a relatively leisurely fashion, as opposed to rushing them.

Practicing this offensive scheme at a methodical pace simply conditions everyone to function without a huddle. This process can be speeded up or changed as desired.

For example, during practice at the team's regular (huddle) offense, everyone must be alert to the required personnel, the formation and the play called, as substitutions are being made. On a signal from a coach, the quarterback calls a code word or a phrase for the no-huddle offense (e.g., "huddle-huddle").

When I coached the 49ers, we used the phrase "Apache-Apache." As a result of this approach to practice, the no-huddle offense becomes almost second nature to a team. The team develops a "comfort zone" in using it as needed.

Utilizing a Man in Motion

Teams incorporate a man in motion as a variation in their offensive formation. Prior to the snap, an eligible receiver goes into motion to change the strength of the formation. Diagram 13-1 llustrates several examples of how a man in motion could be applied to a particular play. Using a man in motion offers several benefits, including:

- It is a fluid way for the offense to change the strength of its formation.
- It forces spontaneous adjustments by the defense.
- It improves the position of the man in motion on his release point on pass routes.
- It stretches the defense by attacking different parts of the field with multiple receivers.
- It enables the man in motion to avoid being held up by either the linebackers or defensive backs.
- It forces the defense to indicate its coverage (e.g., zone, man, blitz, etc.).
- It isolates individual defenders (i.e., the running back on the strong safety, etc.).

On the other hand, using a man in motion involves several disadvantages, including:

- During the man-in-motion process, the offensive line must stay in a set, stationary position. This circumstance is a real disadvantage because it is difficult for a player to remain in a primed state (i.e., ready to move) and be expected to hold that static position for more than a few seconds.

  This situation is particularly critical at the goal line when the defense will be exploding into the gaps while the offense is required to remain static and wait for the "motion" to be activated.

- The defense can get a sense of the snap count.

- A man in motion, because he's moving laterally, cannot explode upfield as quickly as a stationary player. This factor is a disadvantage because some plays require the receiver to sprint upfield at the snap of the ball.

- When changing the strength of the formation or the receiver relationships through the use of motion, the offense cannot be sure of what adjustments the defense will make. In reality, what the offense expected or planned on may not occur.

- The use of counter motion (i.e., the receiver checks back and forth in an attempt to confuse the defense) was relatively effective when it was initially introduced into the NFL. Some years later, however, its use has become simply cosmetic. While all of this posturing is going on, the rest of the offense has to remain in static positions, thereby losing whatever rhythm they might need.

ESTABLISHING THE RUNNING GAME

In recent years, the running game has been "reborn" in the NFL. Because most defensive linemen have been so intent on sacking the quarterback, they have sacrificed their concern with the fundamental element of "block control." As a result, they immediately commit themselves to get past the man in front of them.

As a consequence, large holes are opened between defenders who each happen to be moving in opposite directions. Requiring defenders to employ disciplined, fundamental techniques while rushing the passer has not received the proper emphasis.

The most physically demanding part of an NFL team's offense is the running game. In turn, the skills and abilities of a team's players must be the focal point of the running phase of the offense. As such, it is absolutely essential that the players be placed in a position where they can best get the job done.

Accordingly, if a team has uniquely talented people, they must be exploited. A key element in coaching is how to take full advantage of a gifted player. The head coach must determine to what extent to use a particularly talented individual before his performance suffers or the team's offense becomes too one-dimensional.

The ability to maximize the effective utilization of an outstanding ball carrier is often one of the best measures of a coach's judgment, patience and intuitive "feel"

Table 13-1. Examples of man-in-motion calls.

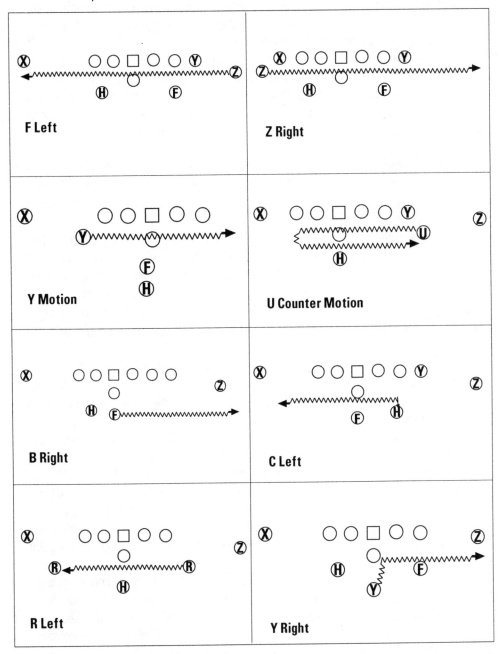

for the game. Deciding how to maintain a reasonable level of balance while simultaneously emphasizing a single player's talents calls for a head coach to possess technical knowledge, strategic insight and mature discretion.

Another key step that should be taken to ensure that the running back performs effectively is constant repetition of basic running plays. The more a running back sees the blocking on a particular play, the better the "feel" he develops about the given play.

Over the years, a number of very talented players have been extremely overused, and, in the process, have been completely worn down. Earl Campbell, an extraordinarily gifted player for the Houston Oilers, is an excellent example of an individual who was subjected to such circumstances.

Eric Dickerson, who played for the Los Angeles Rams and the Indianapolis Colts, was physically worn down (by the way he was used) to the extent that his career was measurably shortened. On the other hand, a few extraordinarily capable athletes have found themselves on teams where they were minimally utilized because their team's "system" came first and maintaining balance in the offense attack was the major priority.

What coaches have to keep in mind is the fact that some athletes have great stamina and durability. By degree, others don't. For example, neither Walter Payton nor O.J. Simpson was considered a big man, yet both could carry at least 25 times a game without being unduly physically stressed.

Two excellent examples of how great athletes should be used properly by their teams involve Dallas Cowboy players. Tom Landry demonstrated excellent judgment in the way he utilized Tony Dorsett, and Ernie Zampese has appropriately employed Emmitt Smith in the Cowboys' highly effective offensive attack.

One of the shortcomings in placing a substantial emphasis on the running game involves the fact that most teams subscribe to this approach. As a result, practically everyone on these teams is waiting for this situation to occur.

Success in these circumstances is measured by forward gains. In the meantime, the opponent is passing extensively for big chunks of yardage. Before long, the team that has a balanced offensive attack (i.e., its runs and passes are combined in approximately equal numbers) has a two-touchdown lead.

At that point, the team that has planned to dominate the line of scrimmage must either abandon or drastically alter its offensive game plan.

Although the running game is much more physically demanding than the passing game, coaches should keep in mind that the physical matchups that occur during the running game are not as likely to enable a team to overwhelmingly dominate another team. In the NFL, this statement holds particularly true because relatively few athletes are vulnerable to being physically overpowered on a regular basis.

As a consequence, as the head coach, you should not depend on a running game that relies primarily on the ability of your offense to "out-muscle" your opponent. If your players are unable to dominate the opponent physically (i.e., because of the relative physical parity of individual players in the NFL), they may become frustrated and lose confidence in the team's overall offensive plan.

Rather, a team's running game should be designed and imparted to the players in such a way that they feel the running game gives them a definitive advantage, for whatever reason. The coaching staff can take several steps to help establish the optimal conditions for success in the running game, including:

- Make effective use of formational variations.

- Utilize motion and/or shifting to force the desired defensive adjustment just prior to the snap of the ball.
- Package running plays with appropriate play action passes.
- Utilize special plays designed to take advantage of defensive commitment, intensity and aggressiveness.

An effective running game can involve several considerations. One of the most important factors is how the running game is formatted. Because football is a game of geometric relationships (relying on numbers and angles), a team should focus its efforts involving formational planning on one or more objectives, including:

- Securing a numerical advantage at the point of attack.
- Creating blocking angles that enhance the player's ability to cut off or move his opponent.
- Causing defensive hesitation in reading the play.
- Softening (slowly) support of the defensive backs.

Ultimately, developing an effective running game requires that three interrelated issues be addressed: determining the types of runs; identifying what running scheme is appropriate for the personnel on the team; and establishing a team's priorities with regard to its running scheme.

Determining the Types of Runs

A number of considerations affect the process for selecting which kind of running plays are appropriate to a team's running scheme. Three of the more important factors are the blocking scheme employed on a particular play, the degree to which misdirection plays are suitable to an offensive system, and the ability of the quarterback to run the ball.

The kinds of blocking schemes used in an offensive system have an effect on the types of plays that are included in a running game plan. Over the years, a limited number of run-blocking schemes have withstood the on-going evolution of offensive football strategy. Most of the present-day blocking schemes fall into either of two time-tested categories—man schemes and zone schemes. A fully dimensional offense incorporates some form of these two blocking schemes:

- Man schemes—schemes that take advantage of the one-on-one matchups by isolating blockers on single defenders.
- Zone schemes—schemes that require blockers to control an area of the defensive front, rather than a specific man. As a result, a blocker is able to control a defender who is moving through a particular area of control. Zone blocking schemes allow blockers for the running game to account for a more active defensive front (i.e., stunting front), as well as account for awkwardly shaded defensive alignments (e.g., the 4-3 slide front, overshifted 3-4, etc.).

An effective running game is absolutely critical in certain situations (e.g., goal line, short yardage, late stage of the game when a team who is ahead needs to keep possession of the ball and use the clock, etc.). In these instances, the base block category of moving the ball is the logical and more appropriate tool.

Employing man-on-man blocking, base-blocked plays is the universal foundation for running the football. As a rule, larger, stronger linemen with more natural capabilities are best suited for this aspect of the game.

The effectiveness of base-blocked plays was further enhanced by the efforts of Monte Clark, the renowned offensive line coach with the Miami Dolphins during their dynasty years. He developed and refined a "combo" system with two linemen who would initiate their block on a single defensive lineman. One of them would then release the linebacker.

Through the use of the blocking technique developed by Clark, Miami was able to dominate the NFL almost exclusively with its running game. In the process, Larry Csonka, Mercury Morris and Jim Kiick became premier running backs.

A critical element in a base-blocked running scheme is the tight end who serves as a "man" blocker. He must be able to effectively sustain a block against a defensive end.

Another essential element of this scheme is a fullback who can consistently take on and handle the linebacker. Many teams currently utilize an extra tight end in place of the fullback.

In a base-blocked play, the ball carrier is typically given a single defensive lineman to "break off." Upon making his first break, he then breaks off the next defender. A lead back or a pulling backside guard can also be incorporated into the play. Diagram 13-2 provides an example of a base-blocked running play.

The design of a running game plan is also influenced by the number and types of misdirection plays that are determined to be suitable for a particular running scheme. As a general rule, misdirection plays can be grouped into three categories—counter/trap plays, draws and special plays.

Diagram 13-2. An example of base-blocking protection on a running play.

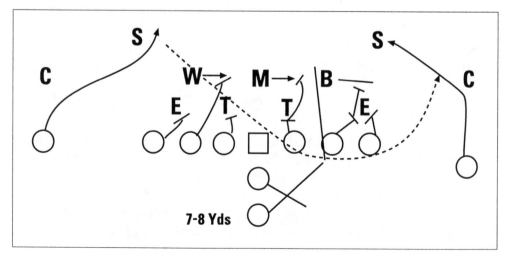

Counter/trap plays are plays that are designed to produce defensive conflict (i.e., to cause the defense to hesitate while reading a specific combination or to question what the defenders are actually seeing). Their primary purpose is to allow the offensive team to take advantage of an overly aggressive defensive charge or a conflicting defensive reaction.

A conflicting defensive response occurs when a defender properly reacts to an offensive key or play, but by doing so becomes vulnerable to a "companion" play. As such, developing and exploiting defensive conflicts can play a critical role in a running game package.

Draw plays are designed to take advantage of defensive reaction that can happen when pass rushing defenders and linebackers react to passing game keys. A draw play can be an effective counter measure to the hard upfield charge of the defensive line. Another situation in which a draw play is suitable occurs when the linebackers "bail out" upon recognizing their pass blocking keys. Using a draw play at the appropriate times may prevent the linebackers from maximizing their pass coverage drops and clogging the downfield traffic lanes.

Special plays are intended to provide tactical surprise. Sometimes referred to as "gadget plays," special plays are another method for an offensive system to develop defensive conflict. A reverse play offers an excellent example of the basic premise of most special plays, which is to have defenders overly react to the flow of the ball or the play.

The third factor affecting the ultimate makeup of a running game scheme is the degree to which a team's quarterback can run the ball. In contradiction to the long-time NFL attitude of minimizing the exposure of a quarterback to being unduly hit, more and more teams are attempting to "stretch" the capacity of their opponents' defenses by adding the quarterback into their running game plan.

Quarterbacks get involved in the running game in a variety of ways. Sometimes, the play is unplanned (i.e., the quarterback scrambles for yardage after his pass protection has broken down). Other times, the play utilizes the quarterback by design and involves almost no risk of injury (e.g., the quarterback sneak).

Still other times, the quarterbacks carry the ball on preplanned plays involving a somewhat higher degree of risk of the quarterback being injured (e.g., the quarterback bootleg, the quarterback draw). These plays are "special" plays and should be used as such. Teams should not get into a situation where such plays are essential elements of their offensive strategy.

Because a team should not expose its quarterback to defenders that anticipate he will be carrying the ball, this type of special play must have a definite element of surprise. The lower the level of surprise to the play, the higher the risk of injury to the quarterback.

In recent years, some teams have begun to factor a quarterback's running ability into their evaluative process. Depending on the type of offensive scheme a team employs, a quarterback who can run (i.e., scramble, carry the ball on special plays, etc.) will receive additional attention as a prospect.

Identifying an "Appropriate" Running Scheme

The primary prerequisite for determining what running scheme a team should employ is how well a particular scheme suits the talent level of the personnel on the team. In other words, the head coach must match the demands of a system with the abilities of his players. The head coach must also ensure that the team's system is flexible enough to accommodate any change in personnel that may make one running scheme better than another.

When deciding what running scheme to use, many teams make the mistake of trying to employ a specific play or scheme against a particular opponent solely because another team used it effectively. Unless the "borrowed" play is firmly based on principles that are compatible with the team's offensive system, a specific play or scheme which has been copied because of its success against either an opponent or the coach's own team is not likely to have sustained success.

Coaches sometimes overlook the fact that a borrowed play or scheme was successfully orchestrated by different personnel under different conditions. For example, a particular play that was effective may have been set up by a complementary play or a play action pass. Even with comparable personnel, a team may not be able to duplicate the success of a particular play without committing to the entire offensive scheme. The key point to remember is that a borrowed play or scheme is only suitable for a team if it "fits" within the philosophy and the fundamental principles of the team's existing offensive system.

The impression of the senses is stronger than the force of the ideas resulting from methodical reflection, and this goes so far that no important undertaking was ever yet carried out without the Commander having to subdue new doubts in himself at the time of commencing the execution of his work.

> Carl von Clausewitz
> Director of General War Academy
> Prussia
> from *On War*

Establishing a Team's Priorities

As the head coach, you must always identify the priorities of your team's running game when developing your game plan. The basic guideline for establishing priorities requires that the head coach apply certain doctrinal principles to the process. These fundamental precepts have served as much of the conceptual basis for offensive football since the advent of football's modern era. Among the steps that you should take to apply these principles to your team's running game are the following:

- Determine the nature of the individual physical matchups.
- Isolate the matchups which offer an advantage.

- Exploit the defensive tendencies.
- Create a numbers advantage at the point of attack.
- Create advantageous blocking angles through formation selection.
- Utilize formations that best match defensive overshifts or alignment commitments.
- Force alignment unfamiliarity upon the individual defenders through the use of shifts and motion.
- Identify any defensive vulnerability in the defender's support structure.
- Attack inherent shortcomings in the defense.
- Redirect the attack through an audible or an "over" call if the defensive alignment has made the original call inappropriate.

It is important that all weaknesses in an opponent's defense be identified. As a general rule, such weaknesses can involve personnel, strategic, or schematic considerations. Whatever the source of the weaknesses, however, a team should design its offensive strategy to attack defensive weakness and avoid strength.

As the head coach, you should keep in mind that, to a degree, your team's opponent can correct personnel and strategic weaknesses much more easily than it can deal with schematic-related problems. For example, a team that experiences performance difficulties involving a particular defender can replace that athlete or move people around.

By the same token, a team that has a defensive weakness emanating from strategic tendencies at least has the reasonable option of making appropriate strategic adjustments. An opposing coach can take note of his own tendencies and take measures to alter the tendency. If he doesn't, you must be able to recognize his strategic tendencies and ensure that your team has a system or a plan with enough flexibility to best deal with them.

On the other hand, a specific defensive scheme's tendencies are basically innate and can not be altered. It is important for you to remember that every defensive scheme (e.g., the 4-3, the 4-6, the 3-4, etc.) has one or more inherent vulnerable characteristics which can be attacked. It stands to reason that if a particular defensive scheme existed that had no schematic vulnerabilities, that scheme would likely be employed by every team. So often, it is a scheme that does not have top flight personnel at every position.

When developing a running game plan, it is also important that you should consider your own team's tendencies. Installing plays in your game plan that counter your offensive tendencies can disrupt an opposing team's defensive strategy.

It is important that you realize, however, that the presence of a strong offensive tactic is not necessarily indicative that something should be changed. A prevalent offensive proclivity that has heretofore resulted in a relatively high level of offensive production is undoubtedly a tendency you want your team to continue to demonstrate. The basic guideline is to make your opponent prove that its defense can stop your team's primary offensive instrument before you make major adjustments.

Accounting for your team's offensive tendencies can benefit your team in at least one additional way. The relatively simple act of being aware of what your opponent must stop may require alternative tactics that are not in line with your team's normal tactics. In many instances, incorporating this type of tendency breaker into your offensive system can counteract defenses designed to stop your key plays.

Another factor that should be considered when installing and implementing a running game is the "first strike" maxim. A team should always try to beat the defense to the "punch" both physically and mentally. This objective can be addressed either schematically or by the variable use of the snap count.

If the offense varies the snap count procedures it employs at the line of scrimmage (i.e., hard count, long cadence, etc.), the offensive players may gain a significant advantage. Because many NFL defenses pride themselves on "booking" the snap count procedures (i.e., anticipating their opponent's snap count) and base their entire approach accordingly (i.e., "stemming"—jumping into a slightly different defensive alignment just before the snap), an offensive team can confuse or effectively counter the defense (linemen and linebackers). In the process, the offense may gain a measure of tactical and psychological superiority.

IMPLEMENTING A PASSING GAME

Similar to its running game, a team must consider the abilities and capabilities of its skill-position players when structuring its passing game. It should also make a reasonable evaluation of the relative effectiveness of its abilities to protect the quarterback in passing situations.

In addition to the talent level of the team, designing and implementing a passing game should also involve several other considerations. Among the factors which should be addressed are the types of passes which should be incorporated, the level of precision timing that is achieved, the protection package which can be implemented, the formations and the personnel which can be utilized, how to react to specific types of coverages, passing in the red zone, and how to plan for situations when the quarterback has to move in the pocket or scramble to the outside.

Determining the "Types" of Passes

A fully dimensional passing game should include, in varying degrees, several types of passes. Not only does having several forms of passing in the passing scheme give a team a variety of offensive weapons, it also enhances the ability of the team to handle each contingency condition and situation as it occurs.

Depending upon the effectiveness of the pass rush, for example, a quarterback has a given amount of time to set up and throw a pass. That time-frame can dictate the type of pass drop the quarterback employs. As a rule, a 3-step drop, a 5-step drop, and a 7-step drop involve 0.7, 1.2, and 1.5 seconds respectively. The more intense the pass rush, the more appropriate is a decision to use a pass drop technique taking less time. This situation is an instance where an exacting form of timing is the essence of the contemporary passing game.

The abilities and skills of the team's players also affect what passes are included in a team's basic game plan and the degree to which they are utilized. The following six categories of passes are considered essential to a complete passing attack:

- The 3-step drop. This type of pass is designed to facilitate the ball control aspect of the passing game. All factors considered, a 3-step drop is the most appropriate play to use "for taking what the defense gives you." A key factor to consider when using the 3-step drop pass is how much yardage is gained relative to the number of times the play is run.

  An offensive scheme using 3-step drop passes which doesn't produce relatively significant yardage, despite numerous opportunities, may be serving the defense more than the offense. Accordingly, the coaching staff should guard against being "seduced" by the relative ease of completing 3-step drop passes.

  The three most basic pass plays that utilize the 3-step drop combination are the quick out, the slant, and the hitch. They are utilized more often as part of the audible process than made as a huddle call.

  A quick-out pass is generally successful against an "off" coverage (as opposed to a tight—"pressing"—coverage). Because of the angular nature of the route toward the sideline, the quick out route's Y.A.C. (yardage after the catch) potential is minimal. As a rule, the quick out pass yields only the yardage gained by the depth of the route (i.e., 7 yards).

  Against a pressing cornerback, the receiver typically turns a quick-out route to a fade or a go route. Depending on the coaching staff's philosophy regarding receiver routes, the fade route can occur as the result of a sight adjustment off of a quick-out route or can come about because of a pre-snap adjustment made off the quick-out route.

  A slant route pass has considerably more potential for Y.A.C. A successful slant route involves at least two elements: The quarterback must have an accurate sense of where the "window" is, and the receiver must consistently run the proper route (angle-wise). Both the slant route and the quick-out route rely on specific defensive looks and involve precise timing.

  Because fades tend to have a very low level of efficiency, a fade is a better play to check to against a team that presents multiple defensive coverage looks unless the offense is certain that it has unhindered access for the quick-out route. The fade stop has become the most popular type of fade route.

  A fade route requires the receiver to sprint upfield, while allowing the press defender to stay even or slightly ahead at a prescribed depth (i.e., 15 yards). In this route, the ball is thrown behind the receiver, who stops and catches the ball as the defender continues upfield.

  The slant is the best single route in football if practiced extensively against the numerous possible defensive responses to it. Over the years, it has been run for huge gains by the great receivers of the 49ers.

  For example, John Taylor, Jerry Rice, Dwight Clark and Freddie Solomon all made game-winning catches and runs off the slant route during San Francisco's dynasty years. I can recall John Taylor, on one occasion, catching a slant pass and going seventy-five yards for a winning touchdown late in the game.

As a result of continual practice, Joe Montana and Steve Young mastered all of the basic routes. Working with their receivers against a variety of coverages designed to ensure that their receivers had to periodically adjust their routes, these two extraordinarily talented quarterbacks were able to adapt their throws as needed.

- The 5-step drop. This type of pass normally forms the backbone of a team's timing pattern package. Designed to be thrown before the defenders have time to respond, the 5-step drop pass can be thrown utilizing three different footwork techniques: the quick 5-step drop, the big 5-step drop, and a 5-step drop plus one or two hitch steps.

When a quick 5-step drop is utilized, the quarterback throws a pass immediately off his fifth step, using a quick balance-throw action. An example of a basic quick 5-step route is the double square-out route.

Similar to the 3-step quick-out route, the double square-out route is designed to work best against a cornerback who is playing off. This route involves precision and timing between the quarterback and the receivers.

Although a receiver who runs a double square-out route is not likely to gain yardage after the catch, this route is somewhat more desirable than the 3-step quick-out route. The quick 5-step drop produces a deeper completion because the receiver runs his route at a greater depth. In the event that the defensive coverage creates a situation where the double square-out is a low percentage throw, the tight end and the running backs can serve as contingency receivers and run drop-off routes.

A pass thrown using a big 5-step drop involves the quarterback taking three big drive steps, a throttle step to slow his drop and a fifth step for balance. A third type of 5-step passing technique requires the quarterback to first execute a 5-step drop and then take one or two hitch steps before throwing. Three great quarterbacks I worked with—Ken Anderson, Dan Fouts and Joe Montana—took five big steps and threw almost the instant their right foot hit.

- The 7-step drop. This type of quarterback technique is designed to give the receiver time to maneuver before the ball is thrown. By providing the receiver with the time to take advantage of any mismatch that favors the offense between himself and either the defenders or the coverage, the 7-step drop facilitates maximum separation between the receiver and the defenders. A 7-step drop also allows a team to incorporate layered routes into its offensive attack. In addition, a 7-step drop lets the receiver make his pattern break off a double move and gives the receiver time to cross the field off a vertical push.

- The play pass. This type of pass is specifically designed to develop and take advantage of defensive conflict. A fundamentally sound play that strives to contradict the basic principles of defense, the play-pass involves getting the defensive team to initially commit to a "fake" run and then throwing a pass behind the defenders off of the fake. Three examples of the play pass are illustrated in Diagram 13-3.

Diagram 13-3. Three examples of the plays involving the play pass.

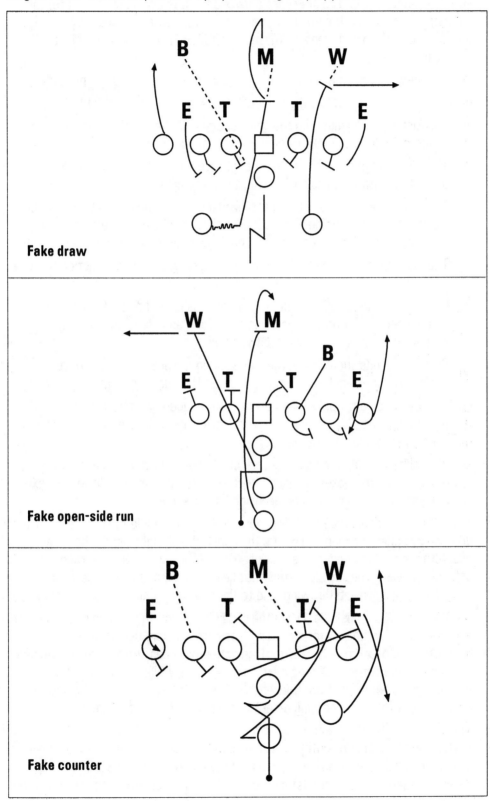

Fake draw

Fake open-side run

Fake counter

The play pass is particularly effective against defensive teams who are very active against the run. The play pass allows a team to exploit (and deflate) the intensity and zeal of a fired-up defense. In order to ensure that the play pass is designed, practiced and properly utilized, the following key elements must be addressed:

— The play-pass must appear as close to the basic running play as possible.

— Line blocking, at least at the point of attack, must simulate run blocking.

— The running backs must run the same courses as the run play, and must deliberately hold the fake through the line of scrimmage.

— The quarterback's mechanics must duplicate those of the basic run. His actions on both the pass and the run should be uniform.

— Those defenders that are being attacked must be pinpointed. They could be inside linebacker, outside linebacker, weak safety, strong safety or cornerback. The design of the play should be directed at a specific defender.

— The more successful and often used running play is the logical action from which to play-pass.

— Ball handling and faking should be practiced as part of a regular schedule, often after regular practice is completed. Here an appreciation for the intricacies of the techniques is established.

— Specific periods should be established during the practice week for team execution (for example—a 10-play period on Thursday for a Saturday game).

— Short yardage and goal line situations call for aggressive blocking below the pad level of the defensive line. Any easing up makes for easy diagnosis by linebackers and defensive backs.

— The faking back and the quarterback must know which defender they are going after. Their fakes are then directed to fool that man. A difference exists between fooling a corner and an inside linebacker, etc.

• The action-pass. This type of pass is designed to get outside the perimeter of the defense by adding a dimension where the quarterback might run the ball. The quarterback can break contain either off a play fake or by directly moving the offensive pocket. The key element is that he can shorten the distance of his throw and can achieve a throwing lane to the receiver outside the pass rusher.

Having to simultaneously deal with the possibility that the play can involve either a pass or a run by the quarterback can place extraordinary demands on a team's perimeter defense. Properly executed, an action-pass can create a severe vertical stretch in a relatively small area of the playing field, while at the same time stretching the defensive front horizontally. It stands to reason that the action-pass aspect of a team's passing attack is much more viable if the team's quarterback is highly mobile.

• The screen pass. This type of pass is designed to take advantage of an intense pass rush and defensive posturing, particularly when the offense is in a disadvantageous down-and-distance situation. It is important to note that screen passes do not have to produce substantial yardage gains to have a meaningful impact on a team's offensive package. Just the threat of throwing a screen pass on subsequent plays is often sufficient to slow down the defensive rush.

The key is to keep defensive linemen from reading the screening linemen. Many variations exist in this regard—from quick hitting past developing screens to much delayed screens off play passes. When and how linemen release takes considerable coaching and practice repetitions.

Recognizing the Need for Precision Timing

As the head coach, you must carefully monitor the timing of the passing game. The passing game should be constantly evaluated with regard to the coordinated timing between the receivers breaking into the pass window and the quarterback releasing the ball. Several factors can affect the timing of a pass pattern, including:

- The ability of the receiver to read the defensive coverages. A receiver usually has the option to break off or convert a route based upon the defender's action. As a result, the receiver must be able to properly read the coverage and decisively make the necessary route adjustments. On most inside breaking patterns, a distinct difference exists between a man and a zone defense.

- The ability of the receiver to vertically push his route to the appropriate depth. The receiver must be in top physical condition so that he consistently runs his route to the required depth. A receiver who is fatigued may unconsciously cut his route down, thereby disrupting the timing of the pass.

- The receiver must burst, then break. This burst is designed to set the defender on his heels. Typically for a route that develops down the field, the receiver bursts off the line, comes under control, bursts the last five yards and then breaks.

- The depth of the quarterback drop. The quarterback may chop his steps, when he should be driving off the line of scrimmage. This situation may be caused by several factors including fatigue, impatience, poor footwork, or an unconscious reaction to the receiver cutting down his route. The quarterback must get quick initial separation from his blockers.

- The consistency of the check-down receiver in delaying his release into his route. He must check and release in a manner which allows him to break open just as the quarterback completes his progression or scan. This action, in turn, separates him from the pass rusher. The outlet receiver should concentrate on the quarterback. He might get the ball at the last second.

- The quality of pass protection. Poor pass protection may cause the quarterback to hurry on the 5-step drops and the 7-step drops. If the receiver responds to the shortened drop of the quarterback by compressing his route as he attempts to adjust to the quarterback's quicker release of the ball, the end-result of poor pass protection may be a disruption of the precision timing needed between the quarterback and the receiver.

Quarterback Efficiency

Quarterback efficiency is the cornerstone of a fully dimensional passing attack. In order for a team to achieve continued success, its quarterback must perform at a sustained level, week in and week out.

Throughout my career as a coach, the quarterbacks on my teams have been ranked as some of the most efficient quarterbacks in their league. This situation began when I was on the staff of the Cincinnati Bengals.

My first quarterback with the Bengals, Greg Cook, led the NFL in this category. My next signal caller, Virgil Carter, was rated near the top five. Like Cook, Ken Anderson, the last quarterback I worked with while I was with Cincinnati, also led the NFL in quarterback efficiency.

During my relatively brief stay with the San Diego Chargers, Dan Fouts made dramatic improvements in his level of efficiency. When I was with Stanford, Guy Benjamin and Steve Dils led the NCAA, and Steve Stenstrom broke all PAC 10 conference records for quarterback efficiency.

In the NFL, 49er quarterbacks Joe Montana and Steve Young are both considered the most efficient passers of their era. Each has been picked as the most valuable player in the NFL and has been named as the MVP of the Super Bowl. Between the two, they have won six world championships.

Implementing a Protection Package

The caliber of a team's protection package is often the single best indicator of how comprehensive its passing scheme is. The scope and latitude of the protection schemes set the limits of the passing game package. A fully functional protection scheme allows a team to utilize the full spectrum of its passing game.

A fully functional protection scheme neutralizes the pass rush so that a team has the ability to throw "hot," flood the field with five men out, provide maximum protection with only two men out, provide solid protection to one side of the quarterback or another, and use check-down routes with the running backs. A fully functional scheme has several distinct and definite properties, including:

- Standardized blocking rules that apply to all fronts.
- Standardized blocking rule adjustments that apply to fronts which employ an overload principle (e.g., overshifted 3-4 defense).
- Adaptability for both man and zone schemes. Certain live stunts require either man or zone protection.
- Line calls that initiate gap protection when needed (e.g., against a triangular blitz from a linebacker through the "A" gap with the center and the guard covered or, on occasion, the "B" gap when the tackle is called down).
- A scheme that is designed with regard to the depth of the quarterback's drop at the line of short protection for certain 5-step drops and deep protection for a 7-step drop.

- An application to formation principles (e.g., the 7-man split-back protection, and the "79" protection which is used when the offensive team lines up in a set where the fullback is aligned behind the quarterback, etc.).

- A correlation with the "hot" principles and the "sight adjustments." An example of correlation with a "hot" principle would be the guard ignoring a delayed linebacker blitz against a one-back set because the linebacker is the "hot" read. The principle is in effect when there are too many rushers for the number of blockers. In this instance, the outside rusher should be the unblocked man.

- An adaptability that allows a team to double-team a dominant pass rusher.

A fully dimensional passing attack employs a number of different protection schemes. An offensive package that has a limited number of protection schemes may be constrained by the fact that the defense only has to design counter measures against a few isolated protection schemes.

Protection schemes must have the flexibility to allow all eligible receivers to immediately release on one extreme or offer full protection releasing only two receivers. It is also important to have the capacity to keep big men on big men. This step requires sliding off the line toward an overshift which, in turn, moves the backs to the other side. This call is made by either the center or the quarterback.

Identifying Types of Protection Schemes

Several basic types of pass protection schemes exist—drop back, play action and turn back. Each type is employed with a specific kind of pass.

In turn, there are four kinds of drop-back pass protection schemes: The quick scheme, the 7-man scheme, the 5- and 6-man scheme and the 8-man scheme. The 5-man and 6-man protections are so closely related that they are considered to be a single scheme.

- The quick scheme. This type of drop-back pass protection scheme is an aggressive scheme which utilizes man/zone principles. In this scheme, the offensive linemen must attack the pass rushers low and hard and create a "picket-line" just across the line of scrimmage.

- The 7-man scheme. Collectively, this type of drop-back pass protection scheme involves a group of three different protection schemes (e.g., split back, weak flow, and single back turnback). A 7-man scheme is employed in conjunction with plays utilizing deep progression reads. These plays do not rely on the running backs releasing to stretch the coverage.

- The 5- and 6-man scheme. This type of drop-back pass protection scheme requires the quarterback to act as the seventh man in the protection scheme. The quarterback fulfills the role of the seventh protector by dumping the ball off to a "hot" receiver.

In order to minimize the need for the quarterback to drop the ball off "hot," these types of protections will "dual read" or "fan" a lineman (man scheme) or a back (turnback scheme) to account for the sixth rusher. A "dual read" involves a technique in which the lineman/back is responsible for checking the inside linebacker first, and then the outside linebacker.

If only one defender comes, the quarterback is free to continue with his route progression. If both defenders come, the quarterback must utilize his "hot." In this manner, the defense must usually bring seven defenders in order to force a "hot" throw by the quarterback.

The "fan" protection technique is designed to turn the guard and tackle out (provided the guard is uncovered) to the two most probable rushers. However, in a 5- or 6-man "hot" scheme, this technique leaves the quarterback vulnerable to an inside "dogging" linebacker. As such, it should only be used when you can isolate a team that does not bring its inside linebackers as rushers. All factors considered, a 5- and 6-man pass protection scheme is the most complex protection procedure employed in a fully dimensional passing attack.

• The 8-man scheme. This type of drop-back pass protection scheme is characterized by keeping the running backs and the tight end in to block. An 8-man protection scheme is used predominately in a team's audible package to pick up an 8-man blitz. Although the 8-man scheme limits the number of receivers in the pattern to two, if it's properly executed it will give both wide receivers an opportunity to go deep by enabling them to break off their second cut. A deep route involving two cuts increases the probability of a "big" play over the top of the 8-man blitz. If their assigned defender does not blitz, each eligible man releases as an outlet receiver versus a zone defense.

Two other types of pass-protection schemes are designed for specific kinds of plays—play-action plays and action passes. Both protection schemes involve one of three scenarios: a hard play fake by the quarterback while he remains in the pocket; initially a play fake and then the quarterback breaks contain; and a "dash" play where the quarterback simply breaks contain.

The play-action protection is generally related to the run play being faked. The most common play-action protection scheme is a turnback or "uncovered/down" protection. In this scheme, the first "uncovered lineman" at the point of attack turns back with each lineman inside of the down block also turning back to his corresponding backside gap. The remaining playside lineman/backs and/or tight end will account for the remaining strongside defenders.

Action pass blocking is designed to isolate the end man on the line of scrimmage. Every blocker on the line of scrimmage blocks the first defensive threat aligned in the opposite direction of the quarterback's action. On dash plays, a "fan" technique is utilized on the backside, combined with a reach technique on the frontside.

With regard to play-action and action passes, every team must ensure that his quarterbacks realize that anytime they turn their backs to the defense, they are in a vulnerable position. As such, a quarterback must be allowed to audible out of more vulnerable situations.

All warfare is based upon deception.

Sun-Tzu
Chinese Military Strategist
The Art of War

Using Formations and Personnel in the Passing Game

As the head coach, you can augment and expand your team's passing structure by properly utilizing certain formations and team personnel. For example, you can use formations and motions to isolate specific matchups and to cause the defense to make adjustments that you can anticipate.

It is important that you be able to accurately predict the defensive alignment to a particular formation which your team is employing to isolate a favorable matchup. If the defense responds to the formation in a manner which you expected, then the formation is a valid method for establishing a favorable matchup. On the other hand, if the defense does not respond in the anticipated manner, the formation is not a suitable means for creating the desired matchup. More importantly, in the latter situation, such a formation (or motion) may actually be doing more harm than good if it is causing confusion in your quarterback or your receivers about what adjustments the defense will make in a particular situation.

The proper use of personnel can be another key factor affecting the level of success achieved by a team's offensive system. It is critical that a team has its best players in the game to get the job done. In turn, the suitability of these players to particular offensive alignments can have a significant impact on the offensive game plan. For example, if a team's most desirable personnel matchups can be achieved in a standard personnel alignment (i.e., two running backs, a tight end, and two wide receivers), then that team can gain an advantage on the defense in that one of the determinants that defenses typically use in making their defensive calls (i.e., down/distance and personnel) is eliminated.

In turn, if a team's personnel provide it with the flexibility to break into other formations from the standard alignment (i.e., a running back shifts out into a 3-wide receiver configuration), then the offense may be able to achieve a measurable advantage by "stretching" the defense's personnel on the field at the time further than they want to (and should) be employed. If the defense makes a substitution trying to anticipate a run or a pass from the offense's basic personnel configuration, then the offense has attained an advantage (e.g., despite the fact that the defense puts in its nickel package on a 2nd-and-long situation, the offense is able to execute a legitimate running play because its tight end and lead back are still in the game).

Resourceful substitution is another effective method for enabling the offense to dictate to the defense what the defense can do on a given down and distance—particularly, first and second down. For example, if a team can determine what adjustment (e.g., specific defenders, defensive alignment, etc.) a defense will make if certain offensive personnel are inserted into the game (e.g., three wide receivers), then, in essence, the offense can dictate what the defense is going to do.

An extensive study should be made each week to evaluate the third and fourth cornerbacks your opponent will substitute that week. The match ups between your second and third receivers and these cornerbacks can often be critical to third-down passing.

If the offense can vary its substitutions with an array of different personnel groupings (e.g., two tight ends, three wide receivers, regular, four wide receivers, etc.), the defense can be put into a position of constantly having to try to keep up with the offense's adjustments. Whatever the substitution pattern, no additional insight into the offense's intentions should be given to defense—particularly on first or second down.

Reacting to Coverages

A passing attack must have basic elements that enable the quarterbacks and the receivers to make necessary adjustments when it comes to reacting to zone versus man coverages. In the NFL in the 1990s, offensive teams cannot isolate to any high degree of certainty the basic coverage packages that are employed by the defense in a particular situation. Teams have developed multidimensional defensive schemes and go to great lengths to hide their intentions to employ a specific scheme.

A complete passing attack is well-versed in anticipating man and reacting to zone coverage. Virtually every route combination must have some identifiable sequencing for the quarterback to adjust to based on a change from the anticipated coverage.

A team's passing structure must have a distinct mechanism that allows the use of audibles to enable the quarterback to readily access different aspects of the system. This aspect is vital in order to take advantage of a particular coverage or a specific mismatch that occurs even though a team is not able to specifically isolate it in its play calling sequence due to the multidimensional nature of the defense. For example, audibling to specific "explosive plays" allows a team to take advantage of a particular vulnerability that exists in a specific coverage or defensive scheme—but one that only presents itself a few times during a game.

Passing in the Red Zone

One of the most pronounced changes that has occurred in the game over the past five years has been the attention given to developing an effective offensive strategy for scoring from the red zone. Blanket four-across zone coverage has become a popular red zone coverage scheme in the NFL, thereby making it difficult for receivers to get open in the end zone. Because of the congestion in the end zone caused by the four-across zone, the most effective red zone passing strategy is usually to throw short passes or to drop the ball off to a skilled receiver or a running back whose athleticism (i.e., the ability to run after catching a pass) offers the best opportunity to score in the red zone.

> *The unknown is the governing principle of war.*
>
> > General Ferdinand Foch, 1919
> > Commander, Allied Forces
> > World War I

Planning for Situations When the Quarterback is Forced to Scramble

Although a scrambling quarterback is usually indicative of the fact that an offensive breakdown of some sort has occurred, establishing guidelines for the quarterback to follow in this situation can salvage a positive outcome on the play. Among the guidelines to which the quarterback should adhere when he is forced to scramble are the following:

- Anticipated that one in five drop-back passes will result in a scramble. As a consequence, considerable practice time should be allotted to this aspect of the game.
- Keep his head up and look deep, scanning from deep to shallow for an open receiver. Don't waste the throw.
- Look to the near sideline for an open receiver. If every time you scramble you complete a short pass (i.e., a five- or six-yard pass), the defense is in the process of being "broken." On the other hand, if your attempts to scramble result in you being sacked, hit or having to throw the ball away, the defense will begin to dominate the offense. In turn, the offense will unravel.
- Throw a direct pass, not a leading pass, to the receiver.
- Soften the throw to offset the added velocity of a ball thrown on the run.
- Look for defenders moving on tangents toward the receivers.

When a quarterback is forced to scramble, his receivers also have additional adjustments they should make. Among the steps which a receiver should undertake if the quarterback is scrambling are the following:

- Deviate his pattern to the quarterback's line of sight when the quarterback leaves his throwing position.
- Move in the same direction as the quarterback on a plane parallel to the quarterback's scramble.

- Work back toward the line of scrimmage if the quarterback targets you between the pass defenders.

- Concentrate. Stay alert. Attack the ball if it is thrown to you.

- Slide on the horizontal plane if running a backside route.

- Remain stationary if open toward the side of the scramble (move toward the quarterback).

- Move up the sideline if you are the widest receiver on the side of the scramble.

- "Sit down" in the void between the shallow and deep defenders (move toward the quarterback).

- Work back to the line of scrimmage to screen or legally block a defender if the quarterback runs the ball.

- Scrambling to your left can be extremely dangerous. A right-handed quarterback going to his left is vulnerable because under pressure he can't get his right arm in position to throw. As he does, he is relatively helpless. During my coaching career, I personally lost three different quarterbacks to shoulder separations suffered when scrambling to their left, being hit and driven to the ground on their left shoulder. If forced to go left, the quarterback must get good clearance from his pursuers and then throw or run.

EXTREME OFFENSIVE SYSTEMS

One of the factors that must be considered when designing an offensive system is that the system must account for what its own defense will typically see from week to week. In that regard, if a team employs an extreme style of offense, its defensive unit won't get a realistic opportunity to practice against an offensive look that it might actually face.

Extreme offensive systems, such as the run and shoot on one end of the continuum and a totally conservative, "field position," ground attack team on the other end, simply do not have the necessary scope to help prepare their own defense. For example, a four-receiver team will be hard-pressed to field a defense that will be effective against the run. Conversely, a team whose offensive scheme relies heavily on running the ball and only utilizes a limited, unsophisticated passing game will field a defense that is vulnerable (all other factors considered) to a well-executed passing attack.

The blow, when struck, must to be successful be sudden and heavy.

General Robert E. Lee
Commanding General
Army of the Confederacy

REINFORCING OFFENSIVE AXIOMS

The ability of a team to maintain its offensive productivity during the course of the season involves a number of factors. The head coach should take steps to ensure that the players are aware of these factors. Among the offensive axioms the head coach should emphasize to the team and the coaching staff each year are the following:

- You must finish a pass rusher when the defender gets into trouble. Bury him.
- The quarterback must not become desperate or reckless at the end of the play when the defense is closing in on him.
- Everyone should be aware that "big" fumbles often occur at the end of "big" plays. As a result, ball carriers must protect the ball when they're fatigued and tackled.
- The offense should move explosively at the snap of the ball and beat the defense to the punch. Beating the defense to the punch (i.e., getting there first) is the essence of the offensive game.
- The ball carrier should run attack at the designated point of attack, and then slide if necessary.
- The ball carrier should carry the ball decisively. Effective blocking will enable the runner to gain the first 3-4 yards; after that point, additional yardage will be produced by the efforts of the ball carrier.
- The offensive line must have the discipline to maintain the proper fundamentals, techniques and calls while blocking. Sound communication is indispensable.
- Blockers should not open their hips to the quarterback while pass blocking. If they do, the quarterback will be sacked.
- One of the keys to effective pass protection is helping each other; players should move decisively to assist teammates when they're forced to do so. If they lose their man, they must hold and must not give up. They should look for someone else to block.
- Receivers should run their pass routes decisively as practiced. Disciplined depth and position are vital. All routes in the game must be exactly as practiced.
- Receivers should run decisively after catching the ball—whether while attempting to gain extra yardage or while making a big play. Against a zone coverage with split defenders, receivers should not stop and dodge defenders.
- Every ball carrier (whether it's a runner or a receiver) should securely hold on to the ball when hit; he should think "ball" when tackled.
- The quarterback should take a loss on plays on which he is running the ball if necessary; he must not attempt to throw "hope shot passes."
- The blocker must keep his head on the proper side of the defender while blocking.
- The running backs must employ proper blocking techniques. One of the primary keys to the running game is the blocking of the backs.

- The receiver should see the ball first, before attempting to catch it. On a timed route, as he turns his head, the receiver should look for a ball on top of him, and then trace the expected path of the ball back to the quarterback.

- No one should commit a penalty at the end of the play. Sound judgment should be used by everyone. No stupid display of toughness should be made.

- Everyone should be flexible enough during the game to make necessary adjustments in their techniques and responsibilities. This matter should be discussed and decided upon with coaches between series.

- Self-inflicted errors lead to losses and, as such, must be avoided. If you make one, forget it, learn from it and keep going.

- Mutual respect for teammates is important. This respect is related to the performance that you demand of each individual. He must perform as expected.

- Ball carriers who lose yardage on a play should not lose their poise. They should learn from what happened.

- The offense, as a whole and individually, must think clearly and efficiently. This capability is established through concentration in practice.

- Offensive players should communicate plainly and clearly with each other and the coaching staff at all times (i.e., during practices, meetings on the sideline, and while in the game).

DETERMINING THE FUTURE DYNAMICS OF OFFENSE IN THE NFL

Offenses in the NFL are constantly evolving in response to such factors as rule changes, more highly-skilled players, defensive adjustments, different priorities, etc. As a result, future dynamics of offense in the NFL may result in the following circumstances:

- Teams will huddle only when the clock is stopped.

- Teams will use single-word offensive audibles.

- The timing between the quarterback and the receiver will be more defined.

- The quarterback will receive direction from the coach at the line of scrimmage. Because the ball can be put into play at any moment, the defense must commit itself with its front and coverage.

- Substitutions will enter the game when the whistle blows and go immediately to the line of scrimmage. As they approach, the quarterback will call both the formation and the play (or the audible). The ball will then be put in play immediately.

- The quarterback will look to the sideline the instant the whistle blows on the previous play to see which personnel combination is entering the game. The designated coach indicates the formation to the quarterback and whether he should audible his own play or will receive a play call from the coach. All of these steps will occur without a huddle.

- The quarterback will have even more latitude in audibling at the line of scrimmage. His decisions will override those by the coach signaling in a play call.

- The need to protect the quarterback will be even greater because of the fact that the defenders will be larger, stronger and faster and able to hit harder. Unfortunately, it may take something catastrophic before the NFL addresses this issue.

- New systems, theories and philosophies will be developed over the years (e.g., the run and shoot offense, the 46 defense, etc.). Because much can be learned from these efforts, it is essential that each be examined closely. However, fully embracing these new ways of thinking will only lead to disappointment.

DEVELOPING A DEFENSIVE SYSTEM

Similar to its offensive system, a team should have a fully dimensional defensive system that is both functional and flexible. A functional, flexible and innovative design provides the base for a championship defense. By its nature, sound defensive football is contingency based.

The contingency factor which most often drives the defense is the field situation (e.g., down and distance, field position, etc.). Defenses must also account for circumstances which are time-related (e.g., two minutes to go at the end of half, etc.). Finally, the defensive system must be ready to respond to the reactive elements of the game (e.g., 1st down after an explosive pass, 1st down after a turnover, etc.).

Of the three elements which a defensive system must be able to address, the reactive situations are the most intense. Offenses usually are structured to maximize the yardage-gaining potential of a reactive situation. One of the characteristics of a sound defense is the fact that all defenders are fully aware of the need for sharpening their focus in reactive situations.

As the head coach, you must consider certain factors when designing, developing and implementing your team's defensive system. Among the steps that you can take to help ensure that your team has a sound defensive system are the following:

- Design a defensive system that is built around the players. As a rule, the head coach should not fall into the trap of holding to a purist philosophy or system. Find a system which fits the talents of your players. Players cannot adjust their talent level to fit the demands of the scheme. The athlete must be physically capable of performing the tasks required of him.

- Develop a defensive system which highlights the players' talents. Not only must the talent fit the system, the system must serve the talent. Incorporate elements of defensive football that allow the talent on the team to reach its fullest potential.

- Utilize simple reads. Avoid explanations to the players that involve superfluous verbiage. Keep in mind that all factors considered, an attacking defense cannot be a "thinking" defense, it should be an instinctive defense. The coaching staff must provide the defenders with simple reads and maximum quality repetitions at responding to their reads. Repetition in practice is central to developing instincts.

- Employ a defensive scheme that can maximize the ability of a team to exploit a one-on-one matchup that favors the defense. The scheme should allow the team to take advantage of an opportunistic matchup. Two examples of a defensive team addressing a particular matchup involve:

  - Using a defense that overmatches the tight end. A defensive scheme that is designed to create a favorable matchup over the tight end can produce quite an advantage.

  - Using a defense that gives a team the ability to double cover a receiver. Squat coverages and bracket coverages are examples of two of the techniques that can be built into the defensive scheme to take the offense's premier receiver out of the flow of the game.

Another primary feature of an effective defense is that it is sufficiently flexible. Because sound defensive football is situation-driven, a defensive scheme must be able to forcefully address at least five specific situations if it is to be successful. The five situations for which a team should develop a specific defensive strategy are:

- Goal line (i.e., inside the five-yard line).
- Short yardage (e.g., 3rd-and-2, or 4th-and-2, etc.).
- Long yardage (i.e., the offense must get ten or more yards in a single down).
- Prevent (i.e., extremely long situations or time-related situations).
- 3rd-and-three—the awkward possession down (i.e., the down upon which continued possession is dependent—situation that is sensitive to time, score, location on the field, etc.).

Despite the well-deserved accolades for the "West Coast Offense," much of the San Francisco 49ers' success over the years can honestly be attributed to its defense. The efforts of highly talented coaches like George Seifert, Chuck Studley, Bill McPherson, Ray Rhodes and Pete Carroll to design and direct the defenses had a major impact on the gridiron accomplishments of the 49ers.

The 49ers' defense was itself a dominating force. The attacking nature of the 49ers' defensive scheme, coupled with the sliding 4-3 philosophy on which it was based, epitomized the qualities of aggressiveness, flexibility, and simplicity. As with any successful defensive scheme, the 49ers' defense was built upon the skills of the players on a foundation of controlled movement.

Developing a great defensive system is quite similar to establishing a great offensive system. It must involve a teaching process that is properly sequenced. The defensive system must be evaluated as to its overall objectives and then partitioned into specific teaching units. The instruction of each of the units should then proceed in a concise manner that results in measurable outcomes. During the sequencing, the system should focus on addressing the contingencies which it will face during the season.

Identifying the Components of an Effective Defense

An effective defense must be sound against both the run and the pass. Among other factors on which a sound defensive scheme should be based are the following:

- Takes away what the opponent does best.
    - A critical aspect of any successful defensive game plan is to take away what the opponent does best. This step does not involve diminishing the soundness of the defense against the other features of the opponent's offense, but it may entail taking risks. Such an example must be given to the players in planning and practicing it.
- Overloads the opponent.
    - Overloading can involve many different defensive strategies. For example, an offensive team which likes to spread the field can be overloaded in two ways: either by storming the weakness of the offensive formation while risking a thin perimeter on the offense's strongside, or by blanketing the perimeter on each side of the offense and maintaining a thin inner defensive line. The principle of overloading, if applied correctly, can result in at least one very meaningful strategic advantage—it can force the offense to make an adjustment to the defense. A defensive scheme that forces numerous adjustments by the offense always has a relatively large advantage over the offense.
- Evaluates its own defensive tendencies and plans accordingly.
    - Keep in mind that the existence of defensive tendencies can have a greater impact than the presence of offensive tendencies. As a result, a team should have a fully dimensional defense that includes procedures for making immediate adjustments as needed. On the other hand, the focus of a defensive plan should not be overly influenced by an analysis of one's own defensive tendencies.
    - The primary focal point of a defensive game plan must be the opponent's capabilities, strengths and tendencies in given circumstances. Accordingly, the defensive game plan offers the defensive coordinator a menu of calls from which to choose for each situation. For example, in a first-and-ten situation, the defensive coordinator may have a choice of a "base," a "mixer," or a "stunt" call. Should the ongoing game breakdown reveal a defensive tendency in making particular calls which have allowed the offense to gain substantial yardage, a sound defense provides the defensive coordinator with the options to immediately break that tendency with a preplanned strategy.
- Develops procedures for the smooth transition of personnel.
    - A defensive scheme that is able to maintain its integrity, despite undergoing personnel changes, offers a significant advantage to the defensive team. The use of specialists can allow a defense to attack the offensive strategy in a more specific manner. Your best defenders should be in the game.

— Any time a team can retain the simplicity of its defensive scheme, yet add a degree of specificity, the defense is placed in a favorable position. For example, depending on the situation, the use of "specialists" may enable a defense to attack a particular offensive strategy in a more predetermined manner. If a specific defensive scheme allows a team to interchange its base personnel with specialists, the defense is enhanced. If any questions exist whether a key pass should be substituted, you should do so. Furthermore, you should think pass, more than run, if you have any doubts about a particular situation.

You should also consider several additional points when designing the team's defensive system. A comprehensive defensive scheme is one that is also characterized by the following features:

- Takes full advantage of the players' individual abilities. "Players" are the key to sound defense.

- Minimizes a player's shortcomings. A player should never be asked to do something of which he is not capable.

- Is able to bring immediate pressure from the outside. The defense should feature quick defenders who come off the edges.

- Allows the best hitters in the secondary to get to the ball. If at all possible, the offensive formation should not be allowed to take a key hitter out of proximity to the ball. The safeties are the defenders that are most difficult for the offense to get to.

- Is able to audible coverage versus specific formations. This aspect is a vital part of planning. It must be rehearsed continually from the first day of practice. The call should be made by the sharpest, most experienced defender.

- Is able to audible out of a blitz. Going from a blitz to a zone is excellent.

- Can protect one of the inside linebackers. Explosive movement is critical.

- Beats blockers to the point of contact (i.e., "beat them to the punch").

- Is able to isolate blockers who cannot stand up to a player with superior skills (for example, adjacent defensive linemen).

- Affords a smooth transition when substituting specialized units. This step should be practiced and rehearsed. You must demand that everyone is alert for this situation.

- Provides flexibility in pass-oriented units. Varied positions hide coverage or put the defender where he can best do the job.

- Affords the ability to double cover a specific receiver (via combinations of defenders). This situation must be clearly delineated.

- Utilizes players who have accomplished tackling skills. Does not use the following types of players: Those with tackling habits so poor that they cannot be measurably improved; those who simply can't or really won't tackle; and those who just don't quite make the stop (i.e., they can help other players make a tackle, but can't make a clean tackle by themselves).

- Utilizes players that see, move, respond and hit. This circumstance requires that the players get an appropriate number of repetitions in practice to hone their skills and their instincts. All coaching should be geared at a level that enables everyone (including the poorest learner) to assimilate the material.

- Has the total confidence of the head coach. If a problem occurs with the defense, the defense is given time to work through its difficulties (i.e., the coach would not dismantle the defense at the first signs of distress).

The Prevent Defense

The prevent defense is a defensive scheme in which the coverage philosophy is based on containment. Basically, a prevent defense is employed in two general situations.

In one, a team has a fairly comfortable lead and either wants to slow down the offense of its opponent, thereby making the other team use a lot of time when moving the ball (i.e., an "eat-the-clock" philosophy) or wants to keep its opponent from having big plays. In this instance, the team typically goes into its prevent defense with approximately four minutes left in the game.

In the other, a team has a lead of one touchdown or less and wants to keep its opponent from scoring (i.e., a "don't-let-them-score" philosophy). In this set of circumstance, the team generally uses its prevent defense with two minutes or less left in the first half of the game.

As a rule, at least one significant difference exists between a prevent defense which is used at the end of the first half and one employed at the end of the game. In the first half, a team can give up a field goal and not be overly affected. At the end of the game, it usually can't.

Any team expecting to win week after week will find itself in this defense virtually every game—often with the outcome of the game riding on its success. As such, your opponent must not know exactly what to expect from your team when it is in a prevent defense.

Personnel-wise, teams typically bring in a fifth (hence the term "nickel defense") defensive back, and sometimes a sixth, when they go into a prevent defense. Depending upon whether the defense prefers to employ a bend-but-don't-break approach or to utilize an overload coverage on the receivers, the offense can be operating against two distinctly different kinds of defensive plans.

The key factor in the success of the prevent defense is that it must be practiced extensively—beginning in training camp. Somewhat surprisingly given its critical importance, the prevent defense is, perhaps, the most poorly coached defensive category of football.

Most NFL teams only touch on their prevent defense at the end of the week—a time when most players have lost some of their concentration and are routinely finishing their Friday or even their Saturday practice. Several essential details involving the prevent defense are often neglected or fail to receive the requisite attention by coaches, including:

- The rush lanes are not coordinated, which allows the quarterback to step up between people to throw accurately downfield.

- The players do not respond to the throw downfield; convergence on the ball is critical.

- The players decide to let someone else make the play. Their tackling becomes hesitant.

- The players are not fully aware of the critical circumstances at a particular point in the game (i.e., clock, time outs, what can be given up, etc.).

DEFENSIVE AUDIBLE SYSTEM

It is critical that teams at the highest level of competition have a viable, functional system for making defensive audibles. Because of the offenses' use of multiple formations and their utilization of motion by the tight end, running backs or the flanker, the defense must be able to counter (when necessary) by changing the coverage or sliding the defensive front.

As a rule, the necessary defensive adjustments can be made at the time the initial defensive call is made. Under certain circumstances (e.g., personnel matchups, offensive tendencies against a particular defensive look, etc.), however, changing the defensive call is fully justified.

For example, if the quarterback audibles against an anticipated blitz, the defense must have the option to audible into a zone. In this regard, being able to audible is an excellent mechanism for allowing the defense to place additional tactical demands on the offense (i.e., if the offense takes a particular course of action—audible/no audible—the defense has certain options; which option does the offense want the defense to employ; what action should the offense take to counter each defensive audible; etc.).

Consequently, a team must make defensive audibling an integral part of its defensive system. As such, a defensive audible system must be installed and then practiced and rehearsed continuously. Even during those weeks when such audibling is not a basic part of the game plan, it should be touched on and reviewed.

The weak safety is the most logical signal caller for the defense. Key, codified words should be used to call defensive audibles. Steps must be undertaken to ensure that everyone on the defense is completely aware of the signals used and what those signals mean. The team should also establish and practice procedures for using "dummy" audible calls.

REINFORCING DEFENSIVE AXIOMS

Similar to the value of having the head coach take steps to ensure that his players are aware of the factors that will help the team maintain its offensive productivity over the course of the season, the head coach should assume a similar role with the defense. Among the defensive axioms that should be emphasized to the team and the coaching staff each year are the following:

- The more defenders who see the ball immediately, the better the defense.
- Everyone should be aware that "big" fumbles often occur at the end of "big" plays. For example, after an interception or a fumble recovery and a subsequent run, a defensive player—not used to handling the ball—can have it knocked loose.
- Defenders should keep their head up during play. They must "see the ball."
- The defense should move explosively at the snap of the ball and beat the offense to the punch.
- Defenders should fiercely pursue the ball carrier. They should not assume that someone else will make or finish the tackle.
- When making a tackle, a defender should get his hip across the far side of the ball carrier.
- Defenders must maintain their composure at all times; they must not lose their sense of discipline. Individuals lose their focus when their emotions get out of control. As a result, mental errors often occur in such a situation.
- After their initial charge, defensive linemen must recover to a point where they can react and adjust to changing circumstances (e.g., screen pass, play-action pass, misdirection play, scrambling quarterback, thrown ball, etc.).
- Defenders should commit themselves, and, if mistaken, should "double back." This point must be emphasized by both coaches and players. When the ball is thrown, defenders should get to it. The receiver should be hit from all sides.
- Defenders should employ the proper angle when pursuing a ball carrier downfield.
- Defender should take into account the speed of the ball carrier.
- An "astute" defender gets to know as much as possible about the opponent— particularly as the game progresses (i.e., his individual tendencies, how he blocks, how he carries the ball, how he runs his pass patterns, etc.).
- A defender must not "spend" time with a blocker unless the blocker is directly between the defender and the ball.
- A defender who is being blocked should remember that the play is just starting; a defender should play hard until the whistle blows (i.e., he never concedes the fact that he can help make the defensive stop).

SPECIAL TEAMS

Effective special teams play is critical to a team's success. Unfortunately, this phase of the game often is given too much rhetoric and not enough work or attention. As the head coach, you should consider several factors when you address special teams play, including:

- Your kicking team must have key coverage people who have good foot speed and who are strong enough to bounce off blockers.

- Ideally, your kicking team should include a talented player who is uniquely capable of beating blockers with speed and intensity that enable him to get to the kick returner before the return develops. Really successful teams often have three or four such men.

- Your punt return team must have a sure-handed punt returner who has an explosive start.

- Your kickoff team must include two physically tough return men who can take a hit and protect the ball.

- Championship-level teams are built on great return men.

- An integral part of your team's special teams play must be a well-coached, easily comprehended scheme of punt protection. This scheme should require a minimum number of "calls and adjustments."

- Your punting team must have someone who can consistently punt the ball well—particularly, the ability to place the ball inside the twenty-yard line. While this skill is frequently discussed a lot, it is seldom practiced to the extent that it becomes an "art."

- Your kickoff team must have a kicker who can get the ball to at least the five-yard line. A kickoff of the proper height and distance can be a key tactical weapon for the kicking team. This factor is frequently not given the necessary emphasis by a team. Too many teams appear to use a player in this role who may be an excellent field goal kicker but who only has poor-to-average kickoff skills.

- Your special teams unit must include a field goal kicker who is both accurate and consistent from at least thirty-five yards. This person must have the full confidence of the team.

- Your special teams unit must be coached by someone who has executive ability and command presence. This role is often the most challenging position on the staff.

Your special teams coach must possess strong organizational skills. In addition, he must be someone who is demanding, intense and energetic and must approach the job as though it were a permanent assignment.

Coaching the special teams is a coordinator position that requires that the person fulfilling this role have the full breadth of knowledge in all facets of the kicking game. Dick Vermeil, who later in his career as the head coach of the Philadelphia Eagles was named the NFL Coach of the Year, is an example of the ideal person for such a role.

Dick did a masterful job as the special teams coach for George Allen, who was the head coach of the Los Angeles Rams at the time. His determination to be the best special teams coach in football and his subsequent performance in this role started him on a path to becoming one of the truly great head coaches of his time.

The current special teams coach for the 49ers, George Stewart, is another example of someone whose skills and approach to his job reflect the ideal profile for this position. Similar to Dick, it may also someday lead to a head coaching job for him.

At times in the past, some teams have not given the special teams coaching position the attention it deserves. Instead, the job has occasionally been awarded to one of the "good guys" associated with the team—someone who may have lacked the skills to assume a "regular" staff position.

These teams then compound the error of their ways by giving only minimal assistance to their special teams coach. In the 1990s, however, NFL teams who expect to be successful simply don't have the latitude of not making their special teams unit one of their highest priorities and not providing it with all the support it needs (e.g., the services of other members of the staff).

FAULTY AND TRAGIC TACTICS

All too often, a team self-destructs in the closing minutes right up to the final seconds after making a supreme effort for the entire game. More often than not, it was a decision made by a coach that led to the stunning turn of events. Typically, the resulting circumstances have occurred because of a failure on the part of the head coach to take control of the situation in the closing minutes.

It is not necessary that the head coach makes every call, but he must dictate the overall strategy of the team and the specific tactics to be employed. He must have a mechanism in place that triggers his involvement and that establishes the consequential choices his coordinators make.

The offensive and defensive coordinators must have and deserve "direction." At this critical moment of the game, they often see the situation from a very slanted, personal point of view.

As a result, they can lose track of what it will take to win or, conversely, of the risks that they are considering that can result in a stunning loss. More often than not, some coordinators tend to have a short-term perspective in this situation and consider only their side of the ball.

Because they are often so engrossed in their play calling (offense and defense), they have to leave the "big picture" of the situation to the head coach. If, for whatever reason, they fail to account for all critical factors (e.g., the time remaining, the field position, etc.), they may find themselves focusing on elements which—while essential—are only part of the larger scope of the situation (e.g., "we must stop them"; "we've got to move the ball"; "we can't block this blitz"; "this pass should be wide open"; etc.).

For whatever reason, a number of "unbelievable" calls have been made over the years by coordinators in the final minutes of a game that have ultimately cost the head coach his job. That coordinator then has to go out and find another job, all the while counting on receiving a positive recommendation from his former head coach— an individual who has just endured the embarrassment and humiliation of being publicly ridiculed and fired, in part because of the coordinator's action (or lack thereof).

On the other hand, what happened to the head coach may have been his own fault. He may have contributed to his own demise because he didn't take control when he should have or he didn't give his trusted coordinator specific, clear instructions on how to proceed in those final dramatic moments that required his team to implement well-grounded, thoroughly considered contingency plans.

Such plans should have been discussed, conceived, indoctrinated and practiced regularly for weeks or even years. Because the coordinators are generally consumed with the call and the substitutions that are necessary at the end of the game, the head coach is much more attuned to being in control of the decision-making process at critical times late in the game.

Because the head coach is not directly involved in making calls on each play, he has the time to observe, sense, evaluate and reflect on the various developments that are occurring (i.e., he has the time to consider and analyze the situation). As such, the head coach should determine what tactics are appropriate in critical situations at the end of the game.

Several examples exist of this contemptuous situation occurring. In one recent example, the Chicago Bears had just taken a 17-13 lead in the game with less than five minutes remaining.

At that point, their opponent, the New Orleans Saints, had accumulated less than two hundred yards of total offense. Furthermore, they had not converted a single third-down into a first down the entire game. In other words, their offense was hapless.

The Bears have the Saints backed up on their own ten-yard line. Almost no chance exists that the Saints can drive the required ninety yards for a touchdown in the time remaining.

The only chance the Saints have is for a complete collapse of the Bears' defense—which up to that time has been solid—or if somehow the Bears give them the opportunity to throw a pass against a single defender. The only way the latter scenario could happen was if the Bears called an all-out blitz—which, of course, is exactly what the Bears did.

The Bears even told the Saints what they were going to do by getting up in press positions on the outside receivers. The rest is history. The Saints' quarterback dropped back; the Bears' defender tripped when his legs got tangled up with the receiver; and the receiver then caught the ball and went ninety yards for the winning touchdown.

The critical issue that must be addressed is how could that defense be called in that situation (i.e., time remaining, the score, the ineffectual offense, etc.). This type of defensive play calling is what gets head coaches fired and gives defensive coordinators a chance to sell their homes and move their families to a new city.

A second example of such a case occurred some years ago. In this situation, the New York Jets held a two-touchdown lead over the Miami Dolphins and had the ball on their own twenty-yard line with three minutes remaining in the game. Although their win-loss record for the year was very poor and they were playing an outstanding Miami team, the Jets were playing at home and were playing in an inspired manner. A great upset was in the making.

By running the ball, the Jets could have eaten up between a minute and thirty seconds and two minutes in three downs—even if they had failed to make a first down. They could also have used up at least one of Miami's two remaining time-outs.

Instead, the Jets threw three consecutive incomplete passes which took a total of fifteen seconds off the clock.

The Jets then punted to Miami with two minutes and forty-five seconds remaining on the clock. The Dolphins took the ball and drove fifty-five yards to score with one minute and fifty-five seconds remaining and with one time-out left to reduce their deficit to seven points.

The Jets could have used virtually all of the time that now remained if they had originally run the ball. Of course, as Yogi Berra is often quoted, "It isn't over till it's over."

The Jets took the ensuing kickoff back to their own twenty-five yard line. On their first play, they ran one running play that netted four yards. On the next play, with one minute and twelve seconds remaining on the clock, the Jets' quarterback threw an incomplete pass, which stopped the clock. They then threw yet another incomplete pass that took only five seconds. On fourth down, they punted with over a minute remaining.

Miami got the ball back on their own forty-yard line. With one time-out remaining, the Dolphins then drove the ball sixty yards for a touchdown, sent the game into overtime, and won.

On their last possession, the Jets had done almost everything in their power to lose the game. For one thing, they had taken less than forty seconds off the clock. In addition, their decision to throw the ball instead of running it was unbelievable from a tactical standpoint. Had the Jets run the ball, Miami would not have been able to conserve its last time-out. As a result, the Dolphins would have run out of time before they had the opportunity to score the tying touchdown.

Not surprisingly, considerable attention was given to the issue of where to place the blame for the Jets' faulty strategy in this situation. The media blamed the Jets' quarterback for throwing five incomplete passes. Up to that point the quarterback had a great game. If the Jets had only run the ball on those five plays, there is no way they could have lost. Had the Jets been able to make a first down by running the ball, their 14-point lead would have held up.

A few weeks later, the season ended, the Jets' coach was fired and his offensive coordinator got the opportunity to go job hunting. Although he was an excellent man, the Jets' head coach contributed to his own downfall. He had no plan to deal with using the clock to control the final moments of the game.

A somewhat similar situation confronted the Oakland Raiders in a recent game. The Raiders, after playing a great all-around game, lost to the Kansas City Chiefs on the final play of the game. Two actions by the Raiders contributed to their own downfall—Oakland's failure to run more time off the clock on their last possession and being in a poorly suited coverage in the last ten seconds of the game.

As a result, the Chiefs had one last shot at the end zone from the Raiders' thirty-yard line. Kansas City proceeded to win the game on a beautifully executed throw and catch. The point to remember is that Kansas City should never have had that opportunity. Mistakenly, the media blamed a Raider cornerback.

All too often, those incredible come-from-behind victories that occur in the last seconds could have been avoided if the losing team had only employed better tactics on their last possession or even their last two possessions. Teams, in time-sensitive situations, have to be able to run time off the clock. They also have to know exactly what type of defensive coverage is appropriate for a given situation.

During my years with the Cincinnati Bengals, I was responsible for calling plays from the press box. On occasion, I called plays in a critical situation without fully accounting for the circumstances. One particular set of circumstances stands out in my mind.

The Bengals had an eleven-point lead over Cleveland with approximately four minutes remaining in the game. With the ball in our possession, I called a pass play that had somewhat risky protection. The play required our running back, Essex Johnson, to block the Browns' "Turkey" Jones, a great pass rusher.

On the play, Essex had to cross the formation to get to Jones. By the time Essex got there, Jones was all over our quarterback, Kenny Anderson, who fumbled the ball when he was hit. Cleveland wound up scoring, and we ended up losing the game.

It was my call that led to the defeat. I learned my lesson, but the loss went on Paul Brown's record. Thank goodness I had Bill Johnson and Jack Donaldson to keep me in check, or Paul Brown might have had even more last-minute losses on his distinguished record.

The important point to remember is that communication between the head coach and his staff in critical situations is absolutely crucial. Such communication, however, cannot be in the form of second guessing and harassment.

Falling Prey to Initial Impressions

Frequently, what offensive and defensive coaches observe early in the game has an inordinately significant impact on their thinking from that point on in the contest. As such, their approach to deciding which strategies and tactics to employ can be affected.

For example, if an offense is frequently blitzed in the early stages of a game, from that point on, that team's offensive coordinator will likely call plays that are designed to counter blitzing defense. Correspondingly, if a defensive coordinator sees his defense give up several seven- to eight-yard gains early by a ball carrier, he may place an undue level of emphasis on trying to stop the opponent's running game for the rest of the contest.

As a coach, the key point for you to remember is that the initial impression (if it's severe) you get during a game can prey on your mind for the rest of your game. You must avoid allowing your tactical game plan to be influenced by such a psychological dimension. You must maintain your focus.

CHAPTER 14

MAKING THE "RIGHT" DECISION

"One of the main attributes a leader must have is the ability to discriminate from what is often contradictory information. In this matter, it takes a thorough understanding of the situation and of the sources of information to act effectively."

—Carl von Clausewitz
Director of General War
Academy, Prussia
On War

Finding the winning edge...

The idea of taking a chance based on gut feeling and educated guess-work begins to seem less and less credible. Admittedly, gut feelings can be overrated, but so can substituting the endless analysis of data for the instinct born of experience. General Dwight Eisenhower had to make a terribly difficult decision in the hours before D-Day, but despite break-even odds he was right. Would a computer have come to the same conclusion? I doubt the available information would have allowed it.

Information will never be less important than it is right now. With each year and each refinement in the process of collection and collation, its power will inevitably grow. But those managers best able to sift quickly through the vast debris of data—let's call it the infolanche—will be winners, while those who keep wanting more for its own sake will end up paralyzed.

—Bill Walsh, "Blinded By the Byte,"
Forbes, February 24, 1997.

The fact that one of an organization's most essential resources is the "thinking capacity" of everyone in the organization has been impressed upon me numerous times over the years. For example, in our second year in San Francisco, we were playing the New York Jets in old Shea Stadium. We had taken the lead, but very late in the fourth quarter, New York was mounting a drive that would have given them the victory.

It came down to a 4th-and-1 that, if successful, would surely have allowed them to position themselves for a game-winning field goal. They tried a toss play off the left side, and our inside linebacker, Dan Bunz, shot through his gap and tackled the ball carrier for a loss. After the game, Chuck Studley, our defensive coordinator with the 49ers, mused about the credit he was getting for the brilliant defensive call he made to save the game.

Somewhat unabashedly, Chuck observed, "I could have analyzed and schemed for months and not made a worse call based on what they did. But Dan went with his instincts, broke his assignment and made a great physical play to win the game. So much for coaching brilliance." Studley's comments overlook the fact that coaches are always seeking (through planning) to increase the percentages in their favor that "chance" plays.

Decision making involves more risk and responsibility than any other managerial activity. The work of problem analysis and evaluation can be delegated to others in the organization, but the responsibility for decision making is ultimately assigned to one individual. Choosing among various alternatives often demands courage and moral judgment, as well as intelligence. One alternative that every decision maker should always consider is the possibility the decision could be wrong.

Effective decision making is vital to the growth of any organization. In that regard, the decision-making process has received more attention from management researchers than almost any other subject. Nevertheless, in most organizations, the process is still slow, cumbersome and ineffective, if not actually nonexistent.

Decisions can range from the profound to the trivial, from the complex to the very simple. Similarly, there are many different styles of making decisions.

These styles tend to vary according to how much information is used to reach a decision, how quickly a decision is made, how likely the decision maker will stick with a decision once it's reached, and how many alternative courses of action were considered and developed as part of the process.

No one style is better or more correct than another. In fact, research has shown that, while a decision-maker usually relies on one particular style, a bit of several styles can be found in most decision-makers. As with most things in life, the key is to develop a style that best suits your own personality and the particular situation.

Regardless of your decision-making style, it is not possible to accurately predict the consequences of every one of your decisions. Each decision involves risks and uncertainties. Nevertheless, utilizing a sound process of decision making can help to reduce the level of uncertainty attendant to your decisions. Toward that end, there is a series of questions that you should address when making a decision, including:

- What difference does it make what course of action you decide to adopt?
- Do you have sufficient information to fully analyze the issue/matter under consideration?
- If you are lacking essential information, do you know how to get it?
- How critical to implementing your decision is its acceptance by those who will be affected by it?
- To what degree does the commitment of others to your decision depend on their active participation in the decision-making process?
- Is everyone affected by your decision in general agreement with its basic objective(s) (i.e., no one has a "secret" agenda concerning your decision)?
- To what degree will those who will be affected by your decision disagree over possible alternative solutions?
- Do the individuals involved in your decision have the capability to implement the decision as planned?

Another potential difficult issue involving the decision-making process is the tendency to believe that group decision making is superior because "all of us know more than any one of us knows." This situation is frequently not the case. For example, a small cohesive group, such as a coaching staff, naturally tends to maintain an "esprit de corps" by unconsciously developing a number of shared thoughts that may interfere with critical decision making.

This is not to say that group decision making cannot be productive at times. Depending upon the circumstances, participation by others can increase the acceptance of the decision by group members and can decrease the problem of persuading the group to accept the decision.

War is the province of uncertainty; three-fourths of those things upon which action in War must be calculated are hidden more or less in the clouds of great uncertainty. Here then, above all a fine and penetrating mind is called for, to search out the truth by its tact of judgment.

Carl von Clausewitz
Director of General War Academy
Prussia
from *On War*

MAKING SOUND DECISIONS

It is important to remember that individuals can improve their skills to deal with and effectively utilize the decision-making process through experience, education and practice. Among the steps that you can take to improve your decision-making ability are the following:

- Remember that not all decisions will prove to be successful even though you have based them on the best information available. No decision is irrevocable; other alternatives can be attempted. The success of the entire organization is what counts.

- Once you have decided what your decision will be, announce it so that everyone in the organization is aware of it. This step will quiet the grapevine and the rumor mill. Procrastination can be costly.

- Take into account those involved in the decision. When employees know you do this, their response to unpopular decisions is softened and their support is gained.

- Before you make a decision, try to find out what others have done in similar situations. If their decisions have resulted in success, then consider doing likewise. There is no need to "recreate the wheel" when others have found the right solutions.

- If all the necessary facts are available, make your decision. If they are not, make no decisions until the facts are available. Although getting more facts can become a delay tactic for those who don't want to make a decision, it usually is a valuable use of the decision maker's time.

- Know when not to make a decision. Research shows that when you are depressed, or feeling low, your actions tend to be aggressive and sometimes destructive; when in good spirits your behavior typically becomes more tolerant and balanced.

- Be aware that while much value exists in considering your intuitive feelings about a decision that is to be made, it is imperative that you are aware and place appropriate emphasis on your feelings, especially if they contradict the indications of all the data.

- Be careful not to become so emotionally attached to a particular decision that not even the most accurate and up-to-date information will change your mind.

- Keep your information channels unencumbered. Early warning systems from this network will provide varied views on decisions to be made.

Through the process of sound decision making, the risk of making a poor decision can be reduced significantly, even if it can never be completely eliminated. In that regard, a number of possible reasons exist for "careless" decision making, including:

- Lack of clearly defined objectives.
- Laziness.

- Complacency; resistance to change.
- Prejudiced attitudes and opinions.
- Over-reliance on past experiences.
- Copying other people's decisions.
- Impulsive reactions to events.
- Pursuit of private or irrelevant objectives.
- Noncritical pursuits of the obvious.
- Taking the easy way out.

> *An educated guess is just as accurate and far faster than compiled errors.*
>
> General George S. Patton, Jr.
> Commander, United States Third Army
> World War II

THE HEAD COACH'S RESPONSIBILITY FOR DECISION MAKING

One of the most important factors affecting the success level of a team is the ability of the head coach to make sound decisions. As the head coach, how well you approach this factor will have a substantial impact on how well your team performs on the field.

If you aspire to be a successful coach, one of the talents you must develop is decision making. As the need and opportunities for decisions arise, you must learn to get essential information, identify the alternatives which are available to you, weigh them carefully, make your decision, and follow through. While no one will expect every decision you make to be perfect, you will be expected to have a better-than-average level of success at the decision-making process.

The key feature of decision making is choice making. Choice may be exercised in a relatively simple situation, such as the selection of a starting player or the selection of an offensive play.

Choice can also be required in a somewhat complicated situation that involves conflicting goals and values, several opinions, and a substantial expenditure of time, for example, a long-range plan for the entire organization, deciding how to acquire new players (trades, free agency or the draft), etc. In either case, the primary consideration is having all the information at hand needed to make sound objective decisions.

As the head coach, you need to obtain information from a variety of sources, while being aware of the fact that much of the information that an individual receives is often faulty or biased. You must learn to rely on instinct, become aware of which people consistently offer reliable information, and create a system that systematically and expeditiously processes information.

On occasion, you must be willing to discount what may appear to be meaningful information and depend heavily on your instincts. You should keep in mind that because the process of analyzing information is not a very precise science, no one is ever able to fully master this critical task.

As a result, when you identify a core group of dependable individuals, it is important that you create an "intelligence network" and ensure that it is fully mobilized to provide useful information. They should understand what kind of information you need and be able to "pool" their reports and classify their information for your use. Not all of the information they provide to you will be useful. Some will be discarded as irrelevant, some as too tedious, and some as too simplistic.

Too much information can also lead to problems. For example, too much wholesale information can lead to either indecisiveness or not being to make the best decision under the circumstances because of the resultant tendency to overanalyze the "mountain" of available data. Indecisiveness may lead to confusion, frustration, powerlessness, and a tendency to drift. Overanalyzing, on the other hand, can impede the decision-making process, entice the staff to engage in an undue level of micro-study, and produce an errant analysis.

In the past two decades, the search for usable information has been greatly aided by technological advances in the "computer age." Computers have proven to be particularly helpful because they can instantly provide information that would not otherwise be available.

The vast potential of computers for serving as an invaluable tool has not been lost on most members of the coaching community. Their reaction lends credence to the belief that the reliance of information grows in direct proportion to the amount of information available. It stands to reason that as more powerful tools for gathering and analyzing information become available, coaches will utilize them.

Even though information is critical to success, using every bit (and byte) you can get can have negative consequences. For example, using too much information to make a decision can lead to at least three counterproductive situations:

- The sheer weight of information can be used to justify a decision.
- As information becomes the decision-maker, coaches defer decisions while they wait for one more computer printout or one more batch of crunched numbers.
- When decisions go wrong, information is used to rationalize an explanation (e.g., "I know we lost that one, but all the data indicated we couldn't miss").

The key point to remember is that information will never be *less* important than it is right now. With each passing year and each refinement in the process for collecting and collating information, the power of information will inevitably grow.

Those coaches who are best able to sift quickly and insightfully through the massive collection of available data (which can be termed an "infolanche") will be successful. On the other hand, those coaches who keep reaching and searching for even more data and even more powerful tools can end up paralyzed.

The best way to protect yourself from being buried by the "infolanche" is to make sure you have specific priorities about what information you need, when you need it, when it should be introduced into the decision-making process, and most important of all, when you have as much as necessary. At that point, a timely decision can be made.

In his book, *My American Journey*, General Colin Powell had a interesting way of quantifying the decision making process he evoked through the many pressured and sometimes life-threatening dilemmas he was confronted with in his career. He summarized his decision making philosophy as "digging up all the information you can, then go with your instincts." He goes on to observe:

> We all have a certain intuition, and the older we get, the more we trust it. When I am faced with a decision I dredge up every scrap of knowledge I can. I call in people. I phone them. I read whatever I can get my hands on. However, we do not have the luxury of collecting information indefinitely. At some point, before we can have every possible fact in hand, we have to decide. The key is not to make quick decisions, but to make timely decisions. P = 40 to 70, in which P stands for probability of success and the numbers indicate the percentage of information acquired. I don't act if I have only enough information to give me less than a 40 percent chance of being right. And I don't wait until I have enough facts to be 100 percent sure of being right, because by then it is almost always too late. I go with my gut feeling when I have acquired information somewhere in the range of 40-70 percent.

Equally important to knowing how much information you need to make a decision is knowing, how much of that information needs to be disseminated to your coaches and players. Too often, coaches will spend a great deal of time isolating a specific situation (for example, the blitzes and stunts of an upcoming opponent), then jam as many pages of blitz/dog/stunts schematics as they possibly can into the scouting report.

This approach is often overdone to the point where it is impossible for the players to sort through the "infolanche" and derive anything of specific value to them. In many cases, the coach is simply deferring his responsibility with a flood of data as though to say, "Well, I gave the players all they needed to get the job done. If we lost it certainly wasn't my fault."

At some point, prioritizing information becomes a subjective necessity. One of the primary jobs of the coaching staff is to sort through each situation, address it, and determine what information your players need. Those responsible for this process must obtain the required information, including:

- What is germane to the situation.
- What materials can be presented to the players to best help them focus and define any specific situation.
- What is your contingency plan should your opponent force alterations in the anticipated strategies.

A good example of how information can be effectively used to prepare for a particular situation might be getting ready to counter an opponent's blitz package. By mid-season, it would be almost impossible to show and prepare your team for every dog or blitz an opponent has shown thus far in the season. A recommended course of action to be properly prepared might involve the following steps:

- Determine what dogs and blitzes you can anticipate being run against you based on their tendencies against teams similar to your style of play or based on their history vs. you.

- Determine what dogs and blitzes will be picked up in your basic protections and thus need a normal amount of attention.

- Isolate those dogs or blitzes that will be the most difficult to recognize or will give your protection package the most problems, and focus on those.

- Determine what adjustments can be made on game day should the unexpected present itself. A distinct change in tactics will require an immediate adjustment. Contingencies must be in place for such an occurrence.

It is important to recognize that there is rarely one right answer. You can make a decision that is fully researched, well thought out, fundamentally sound, fully analyzed, intelligent, decisive and *wrong.* I must admit to agonizing far too much over decisions that did not work, but for which there was probably no one right answer.

For every call that was made that was well conceived, thoroughly practiced and called just at the right time, but failed because the ball was batted down or dropped, there was a parallel occurrence. An equal number of times, I made a call that was not as concise or as well-schooled and was called at the worst possible time given the defensive alignment, but was successful due to some extraordinary effort or talent by a particular player. Sound decision making enables you to reduce the amount of uncertainty in any given situation as much as possible. As a consequence, the variables you have to deal with will be reduced.

The idea of taking a risk based on logic and educated intuition may seem less and less credible in this age of instant and total information access. Admittedly, gut feelings can be overrated, but so can substituting the endless analysis of data for the instinct born of experience.

Experience has taught me that sometimes a spontaneous, instinctive decision has to be the appropriate step, simply because there is no other alternative. In the 1964 movie *Fate is the Hunter*, Rod Taylor played the pilot of a severely crippled aircraft trying to land in a total blanket of fog. In the film, Taylor informs his co-pilot that he is landing the plane, to which the co-pilot objects, "How do you know the runway is there, we can't see a thing." Taylor responded, "It has to be there, we're out of gas!"

What you come to realize is that sometimes a thing is either going to just happen, or it isn't. The old adage of "the better prepared you are the luckier you get" has merit. One of the key elements of a sound approach for preparing for all contingencies is to develop a justified comfort zone that lets you know that you have systematically and with complete detail created the best platform you can for your players and coaches to optimize their chances for success.

Having established this zone, you can then focus on the game itself, and let the winds of fortune take you where they will. This process allows you to confidently direct your concentration and application, while under the emotional pressures of game day.

CHAPTER 15

OVERCOMING THE MENTAL BARRIERS TO SUCCESS

"Now, if you're going to win any battle, you have to do one thing. You have to make the mind run the body. Never let the body tell the mind what to do."

—George S. Patton, Jr.
Commander, United States Third Army
World War II

Finding the winning edge...

When you're under pressure, the mind can play tricks on you. It's a terrible mistake to let outside forces influence you more than the pragmatic realities of the situation already are. For instance, if I'm on the sideline and the windchill factor is 10 degrees, I may decide, "Damn, it's too cold, nobody could catch a pass." So I'll depart from my plan and not call a pass, even though the players out on the field are feeling a lot warmer than I am. Better to reduce the effect of outside variables and revert to something you've practiced and practiced.

—Bill Walsh, "When Things Go Bad,"
Forbes, March 29, 1993.

Over the years, the value of focusing and concentration has been reinforced to me on a number of occasions. In 1996, for example, the San Francisco 49ers had lost much of the discipline that had been established over the past 15 years, primarily through the actions of five or six players. These players had played to TV cameras, fans and viewers through posturing, finger-pointing and inciting the crowd.

George Seifert had used every method he could to get the team back on track, but the situation called for someone outside the coaching staff who could be more critical without personalizing the remarks. I had an inkling of what was happening, but I was upstairs in the press box. George, a long-time colleague of mine, really understood the situation. The 49ers had lost games to teams they should have beaten because of a loss of focus.

Some players thought they were bigger than the team, but were actually playing very poorly. When the coach appealed for team unity, the players responded that they would always be themselves. If that meant inciting the fans and trying to intimidate the other team, so be it. George approached me for ideas on how to handle the situation. With his permission, I held a meeting with the team.

I approached the 49ers' video expert Robert Yanagi and his brother Keith about helping me put together an 8-10 minute video. I identified particular events in Wimbledon tennis, Olympic track and field, world championship boxing, and Grand Prix auto racing. Robert and Keith blended these moments into a video covering the breadth of sport and demonstrating the intense focus great champions use to handle competition where the outcome is in doubt. I wanted the stakes to be higher than those of a typical NFL game.

I spoke for five or six minutes about focus, in a very animated and demonstrative way that caught the players' attention. I also used some profanity, directed not at the players, but at their image of their opponent. Dr. Harry Edwards, a dear colleague of mine, wanted the presentation videotaped, but I didn't believe I could be myself if I was playing to a camera.

After my remarks, I showed the video. The first athlete shown was Pete Sampras in the Wimbledon finals. Winning Wimbledon can mean $20-30 million to an athlete, so the stakes are very high. Sampras never really made eye contact with his opponent; the opponent appeared to be merely an object. He served perfect, continuous aces without a hint of pleasure or displeasure other than a slight grin in the middle of competition.

His opponent exhibited the same demeanor. The stakes were too high for anything less than total concentration. The results depended completely on years of skills mastered in competition and play. Neither player engaged in gestures, finger-pointing or playing to the crowd.

The next image was Carl Lewis, just prior to his one of his Gold medal-winning long jumps. Lewis was not strutting around, challenging his opponents or playing to the crowd. Instead, he was concentrating totally on the task ahead of him. The image then changed to one of Lewis taking the baton for the anchor leg of the 4x100 relay. The players could see the concentration in his running form: knees high, arms in, head focused straight ahead. He had no time to look at his competition, to wave at them as he passed or strut over the finish line. Massive celebration occurred, but only after the race was completed.

The video then turned to boxing. Many players can identify with the intensity of this sport. The first bout shown was Julio Caesar Chavez versus Pernell Whitaker in a championship fight. Both fighters gave a slight nod to each other upon entering the ring and then brought everything into total focus, no demonstrating or posturing.

As the fighters were introduced, each had a slight smile on his face, demonstrating confidence and inner peace. I chose to show only the first round. At one point, Chavez hit Whitaker with what appeared to be a slapping blow on the hip. They touched gloves, acknowledging that the blow was unintentional and showing their professionalism.

This fight was followed by brief clips of the Ali-Frazier bout and the Ali-Norton fight in which Norton knocked Ali down and almost out and won a decision. Despite the fact that he had a broken jaw, Ali did not lose focus, even though he had to change his game plan. Though Ali was in trouble, Norton had the discipline to stick to his own plan.

Next I had chosen Grand Prix auto racing. A driver who had won several times was shown just before the race. He was not gesturing at other drivers or engaging in other theatrics. When he looked up for the final time he had a slight smile on his face. He had entered a zone of complete focus. After he won, an incredible celebration occurred.

The final clips were from the first title fight between Mike Tyson and Evander Holyfield. In what is clearly one of the greatest athletic feats of all time, Holyfield demonstrated his great boxing prowess as well as his ability to deal with the Tyson mystique. The fighters both had smiles of peace and focus as they were introduced. It was time to fight, which left no room for intimidation, demonstrations or playing to the crowd.

Coaches and players alike paid rapt attention to this presentation. They were impressed by what true focus in an athletic environment really means.

The team played very well in the ensuing weeks. Just prior to their final playoff game in Green Bay, I put together a tape of lions, leopards and cheetahs on the hunt. Once these animals zeroed in on their prey, they maintained complete focus until they either succeeded or failed. I compared their tactics and teamwork to defensive players going after the ballcarrier.

This presentation also went very well, but by the time the 49ers reached the game, the same men had reverted to their public posturing and the team was beaten convincingly. In this case, for a head coach to maintain an attitude and atmosphere among the players that is consistent with teamwork, execution, sacrifice and commitment, he must make the appropriate personnel changes.

> *Concentration is a fine antidote to anxiety. I have always felt that the sheer intensity Ben Hogan applied to the shotmaking specifics was one of his greatest assets. It left no room in his mind for negative thoughts. The busier you can keep yourself with the particulars of shot assessment and execution, the less chance your mind has to dwell on the emotional "if" and "but" factors that breed anxiety.*
>
> Jack Nicklaus
> Professional Golfer

CONCENTRATION AND FOCUS

Two of the most important factors affecting a team's performance are the capacity of the players to maintain an appropriate level of concentration and focus on the task at hand, and the capability of everyone involved (staff and players) to deal effectively with stress. Virtually every activity in which a person wants to excel requires concentration and focus. For example, if an individual wants to be successful as a football player, he must have the ability to bring all of his capacities to bear on what he is doing. Knowing what to pay attention to, how to shift his focus as needed, and how to intensify his concentration (attention) are skills essential for performing at an optimal level.

Regardless of the circumstances (e.g., the coach is deciding what play to call next in a key game; the place kicker is facing a situation where with almost no time on the clock, he must kick a field goal that will decide the game; etc.), the ability to concentrate and focus is critical. For a football player, a wandering mind can create mental lapses and cause his performance to be affected negatively. Research has shown that if an athlete is not focused 100 percent on what needs to be done, the task cannot be performed at a maximum level. For the head coach, not paying attention to what is needed and what is going on can result in confusion, poor decisions, and poor leadership.

Given the role that focus and concentration can have on both the coaching staff and the players in the athletic arena, it is critical that you (as the head coach) address the issue of how the ability to concentrate and focus can be enhanced for these individuals. A dilemma you will face in this regard involves the nature of the concept of concentration. Everyone knows what concentration is. The concept is generally understood by all, yet its meaning is quite subtle. An individual cannot concentrate on concentration; that defeats the entire process. Rather, focus and concentration must be enhanced and maintained one step at a time. Among the key steps that you can take to ensure that you and your staff remain as focused as possible are the following:

- Minimize stress factors. Stress can compromise an individual's ability to focus.
- Assimilate information being digested as the game is in progress.

- Sort through your thoughts; know what approach best deals with a particular circumstance.

- Realize that anxious, sometimes panicked, even hysterical thoughts can occur during a game.

- Decipher real, objective thoughts and how they should be considered.

- Develop the ability to discard useless information. This ability is almost as important as getting meaningful information. Often, you must sort through contradictory impressions. In that situation, you must have confidence in a preconceived plan that deals with the circumstances.

- Be aware that stress can lead to fear, which, in turn, can result in a defeatist attitude.

- Realize that stress and the intrusion of frustration can contribute to an untimely change in strategy. In reality, such a change must be a by-product of rational thought processes.

- Be cognizant of the fact that in the midst of competition, your mind must compute the legitimacy of tactical changes and alternatives.

- Realize that when the mind becomes disturbed by external factors, the first instinct is to become conservative or cautious. While caution may be the proper course of action, it should only be exercised as the result of a rational thought process—not just as an emotional response to apprehension and fear.

- Recognize that sensing and knowing when to alter tactics is at the heart of competitive focus. You must develop, acquire, and ingrain a strategical pattern that requires only simple changes that can be smoothly implemented when circumstances evolve. Any alterations made should be part of a complete contingency strategy that is understood and established prior to the competition.

- Realize that at the heart of situational and contingency preparations is the concept that strategic decisions should be made under the more clinical atmosphere in the days preceding the game. The process becomes somewhat cyclical: The more primed and focused you remain, the smoother and more timely you can deal with out-of-the ordinary circumstances.

- Recognize that the ability to accurately and effectively weigh the thoughts that cross your mind during the ebb and flow of competition is the essence of concentration.

- Realize that the ability to restrain yourself from deciding "I've got to go for it now" when things are going badly takes considerable self-control.

- Accept the fact that once you reach a point where you finally decide to switch to a "high-risk strategy" because the competition has eroded, the decision to change tactics can be very difficult (but one you must then live with).

- Avoid trying to demonstrate "style" to your opponent or the spectators at a game. Such an act can have "deadly" consequences (e.g., it can distract the coaching staff and the players, it can break down discipline, it can destroy focus, etc.).

- Develop the discipline to ward off both worry and doubt and the ability to turn to your previously established plan.

- Discipline yourself to consistently and effectively deal with the flood of emotions that occurs in stress-related environments. Just deciding to be disciplined, however, is not enough. Your mind may not respond in a manner appropriate for the circumstance. The fight-or-flight response can often feel overpowering in the harrowing moments of competition. Being disciplined, however, does not denote that you are being unnecessarily conservative or reactive. For example, fast break basketball requires discipline to be successful.

Throughout the match all I could think of was "Do it as you do in practice." I depended totally on the "game" I had established every day in practice.

> Gustavo Kuerten
> Professional Tennis Player
> Men's French Open Champion, 1997

Among the primary factors that should be considered when developing a plan to enhance the ability of your players to focus are the following:

- Realize that when an athlete is concentrating and focusing totally, he is not consciously aware of how much effort he needs to perform a particular task. He simply does it.

- Recognize the fact that an athlete's consistency of performance is established and fortified through the acquisition and development of a complete "inventory" of fundamentals. Only through constant repetition can these essential fundamentals be retained.

- Be aware of the fact that slowly but surely a player's skills are molded over time and can hold up during the heat of competition.

- Recognize the fact that players should learn and acquire fundamentals and tactics until a "condition" (i.e., the fundamentals and tactics have been fully ingrained) exists that becomes an integral part of the athletes' make-up.

- Be conscious of the fact that any conscious thoughts that an athlete expends to perform a particular task (e.g., throwing a football, hitting a tennis ball, swinging a golf club, etc.) are a distraction that interferes with the mental "flow" that has been established. In addition, all factors considered, the more advanced the skill, the more consistent the fundamentals, the less the subjective input.

- Realize that those times when a momentary lull occurs in the action is when the mind can begin to portray itself. At that point, a wide range of emotions and thoughts may occur, ranging from abject anxiety to consuming over-confidence. If an individual's mental state drifts to either extreme, that person's focus will be compromised.

- Dispel the fear that some of your players may have regarding meeting the competition. Such fear will frequently become a conscious factor as the contest progresses. For example, a player's concern about not being in physical shape may rear itself whether fatigue occurs or not.

  The resultant doubt can affect the player's confidence level, a process which, in turn, can manifest itself in caution or recklessness. An example of this latter situation would be a boxer who trains for an early-round knockout because he feels that he will not be able to go the distance with his opponent.

  Being in awe of the opposition often results in a lack of confidence and ultimately in being intimidated. The player who is mesmerized by his opponent will lose focus on "his" own game. Instead, he should focus on "his" performance and "his" execution, not the opponent.

- Consider external playing conditions, such as field, wind, heat/cold, etc., when developing a game plan. Such conditions must be accounted for (in a sense, computed) when formulating strategies. Players develop a mind set before each game. If a different game plan must be implemented because external conditions have changed drastically, the athlete must "lock-in" (and then focus) on the alternative plan—a process which can compromise his level of concentration.

- Keep in mind that verbal reference points, such as single words, to remind the athlete of the need to concentrate on specific skills or tactics during the game, are one effective way of preventing a "log jam" of thoughts during a contest.

  These terms or phrases should become part of an athlete's training in practice. They should be graphic and have a specific meaning. For example, Earl Woods implemented the code word "Sam" for his son Tiger. This code was used when the crowds around Tiger prohibited Mr. Woods from getting to Tiger to give him reassurance and help calm a stressful situation.

  The code word simply informed Tiger that his father was there and that he thought Tiger needed to pause and refocus on the task at hand. Additional examples include "get it up" to the quarterback who is throwing a pass, "toss" to an individual who is serving in tennis, "hands up" to a boxer, "reach" to a sprinter who must be reminded to extend his/her arms, etc.

  The assumption should not be made, however, that merely repeating such code words or phrases will bring about the desired results. For example, on the tennis court, we've all experienced the situation where we keep telling ourselves to "keep it in the court," only to hit it out.

- Realize that instincts and intuition which are a basic part of an athlete's make-up can make a significant difference in his performance. In reality, some individuals seem to have more of a feel for the game (i.e., a gift) than others. The term "natural" may, in fact, be somewhat of a legitimate reference for some athletes. However, those individuals who believe that they are "gifted" are courting disaster.

> *The mind games the other player uses all have the same general purpose—to disrupt your concentration. They upset your emotional equilibrium and tempo, they pull you out of your game. Instead of controlling the tempo, pace, and "attitude" of the match, you're being dictated to.*
>
> Brad Gilbert
> Professional Tennis Player
> from *Winning Ugly*

STRESS

Of all the factors which have a negative impact on an individual's level of focus and concentration, perhaps none is more important than stress. Stress is usually defined as occurring when there is a substantial difference between what is being demanded of you in a particular situation and what you perceive your capabilities are for meeting those demands (when you perceive the outcome to be important).

While stress can be either physical or mental, your body reacts to it in a very physical way. Your body experiences a biological chain reaction which is designed to return you to your natural emotional and physical state. In the process of getting a handle on stress, however, you can quickly be overwhelmed—causing you to lose focus and resulting in diminished performance and productivity. Among the factors that should be considered and the steps you should take to properly control stress are the following:

- Realize that stress is not all bad. Some individuals can be motivated by a certain amount of stress. Striving to meet a challenge (which is, by itself, stressful) can produce positive results.

- Keep your cool. The most crucial step in handling stress is to keep in mind that your reaction to a situation (e.g., a dropped pass, a missed tackle, etc.) is often the primary cause of stress, not the situation itself.

- Don't sweat the small stuff. Remind yourself regularly that you usually have a choice of whether to give in to stress or stay in control of the situation. Save your energy for dealing with the larger issues (i.e., winning).

- Visualize. Use imaging to take a short "vacation" from stress. Close your eyes and visualize yourself in a more positive, serene setting (e.g., celebrating a victory, being congratulated on a job well done, etc.). Create as many details as you can. Live the experience, however briefly. Leave your problems behind while you enter a "dreamscape" of your own making.

- Prioritize. When you're feeling overwhelmed (i.e., a defender is continually bull rushing over you), some steps (tasks) are more important than others. Mentally, make a list of all the things you need to do (e.g., move your feet, get into the proper position, keep your hands and arms up, etc.), and then perform the tasks (one at a time if appropriate) as necessary.

- Identify the causes of stress in your life. What causes you the most worry and concern? Once you know the causes, you'll be in a position to decide whether or not you can change them.

Obviously nerves reduce your effectiveness during the match as well as before the match. When I feel pressure during play there is something else I consciously do to reduce my tension. I know that nerves get worse when I think about them, when I start worrying about the consequences. I reduce that tendency by really focusing on my game plan at pressure points in the match: What am I trying to do with this serve? What am I looking to take advantage of in my opponent's shots? I stay focused on my game plan. I divert my attention away from nerves and toward the next point (where it should be anyway!). By thinking about that, I'm not thinking about nerves.

Brad Gilbert
Professional Tennis Player
from *Winning Ugly*

CHAPTER 16

STAYING ON COURSE

"Success is never final; failure is never fatal."

—Joe Paterno
Head Football Coach
Penn State University

Finding the winning edge...

One of the most misguided clichés in business is the CEO's demand, "Don't tell me all the things that can go wrong, tell me how we're going to get the job done." Though this kind of determination is an admirable and necessary trait in a highly competitive world, it misses a very important point: Things do go wrong, all the time. If you don't prepare for these serious reversals of fortune, you can easily end up being overwhelmed by them.

—Bill Walsh, "When Things Go Bad."
Forbes, March 29, 1993.

The need to remain on an even keel emotionally probably has never been more evident to me than early in my career as a head coach. In 1980, the 49ers won their first three games, including a victory over the Jets in New York City. Billboards around the Bay Area read "Roaring Back."

Then the team went on a seven-game losing streak. Our next game was a hot, sultry evening game in Miami, and a true test of character. We had to maintain our enthusiasm even as we wondered whether we would win another game that season. As the game progressed, we found ourselves trailing in the last few minutes and needing a field goal to win.

We were able to kick the field goal, but had it called back on a holding penalty. The next field goal attempt was also called back. We then completed a long pass for what should have been a first down, but came up just inches short.

I spent the five-hour flight home sitting by myself. I looked out the window so no one could see me break down. It was too much for anyone. I was emotionally, mentally and physically exhausted. I decided I would resign as soon as the season ended; I believed I had done as much as I could do and the job was just too much for me. The team needed a fresh replacement to take them to the next level. In our next game, we beat the Giants, 12-0; we then won the next two games and finished the season 6-10.

During my first two seasons, the 49ers made significant, measurable progress. We improved from 28th in the League in offense to 6th. Even in the games we lost, we were able to narrow the margin of defeat to a much more competitive point differential. We had begun to establish a standard of performance.

One of our greatest difficulties was that we did not have enough of the type of players who could make the critical difference in a game. The 1981 season was different. Excellent drafting brought us Ronnie Lott, Eric Wright and Carlton Williamson. Joe Montana and the offensive line began to show great progress in their development, and we acquired Jack Reynolds. The fact that we were able to stay on track and continue to develop during difficult seasons led to our success.

The career of a head coach can be viewed as a mosaic. It's not a by-product of any one event; rather, it's a consequence of a whole series of events. Some of these events occur simply as a factor of the passage of time. Others evolve as circumstances and situations change.

How well the head coach anticipates and handles these events can affect the performance and general well-being of his team. Dealt with properly, these occurrences can serve a productive purpose in the learning process. On the other hand, if these incidents are handled in an inadequate manner, they can become pitfalls on the road to success.

Accordingly, one of the greatest challenges facing the head coach is the need to be able to react appropriately to changing circumstances. In other words, regardless of the situation, you must be able to make a well-considered decision. The keys to making the right decision under less-than-desirable conditions are confidence, strong will, and preparation.

You must believe in yourself and your program. You must have the intestinal fortitude and commitment to remain true to your principles. And, you must be prepared to deal with the diverse array of challenging and adversarial experiences to which you will be exposed.

The variety of experiences that head coaches must deal with are stark reminders that coaching is a complex, often demanding endeavor that requires both foresight and introspection. Three of the most common kinds of experiences in this regard are those arising from seasonal situations, those attendant to different "types" of teams, and those emanating from specific game-related circumstances.

DEALING WITH SEASONAL SITUATIONS

During the course of your career as a head coach, you will be confronted by a number of situations that may require a unique sense of insight on your part, including being newly hired as the head coach, dealing with an extended losing or winning streak, sustaining success after a big season, rebounding from a poor season, handling circumstances once you leave the job, and making effective use of the off-season. Each situation may involve a different approach and level of understanding on your part.

With few exceptions, I go about my job now the same way I always have, I believe in doing things the same way. I still think the most important aspects of coaching are credibility, trust, and communication.

Marty Schottenheimer
Head Football Coach
Kansas City Chiefs
from *Game Plans for Success*

The Newly Named Coach

Once you are hired as a team's new head coach, you are thrust into a real-time learning and decision-making environment. All uncertainty must be vanquished by definitive actions. You should keep in mind that a critical part of any plan is to aggressively deal with every detail.

Initially, you need to determine what must be done if you and your team are to be competitive and successful. Next, you should define what goals must be accomplished in order to achieve success. Specific objectives should be identified (e.g., a specific number of wins the first season, reducing the number of serious injuries, acquiring an impact player at a particular position, lowering the average age of the team, etc.).

You should not establish "high-sounding" goals or set goals that are realistically impossible to reach within a relatively brief period of time. Then, you should develop a comprehensive strategy for accomplishing your objectives, including ensuring that your organization has a structure and a climate that will support your strategy. Next, you should develop short-range plans and programs that will facilitate your overall strategy.

In other words, if you're going to be the "leader," it is essential that you know which way you're going and how to get there. Having created a vision, you then must implement your tangible plan for achieving that vision. Keep in mind that it may be necessary to modify your plan as circumstances change.

As you set about developing and putting your strategic plan into action, you should consider several factors, including:

- As the head coach, you are the individual who has to see the distant point, provide guidance for both your staff and your players, and establish the momentum. The process by which you accomplish this critical leadership role is planning. A blend of expectation and patience is required.

- If you as the head coach don't know where the team is going, how can anyone associated with the team know? In addition, how can you expect to accomplish the things you set out to achieve?

- Don't be surprised (or put too much stock into the fact) that you will be told that the previous coach failed because of any number of reasons—none related to ownership or management. In all likelihood, you will also be told that the talent on last year's team was much better than generally recognized. Furthermore, you may be told that the previous coach "lost" his players (i.e., their will to follow him)—a statement that may or may not be true.

- Don't be overwhelmed by the fact that the time demands on a new head coach are particularly substantial. You may find that you have very little time for anything other than your job in the first few months in your new position. Managing your time effectively will be crucial.

An Extended Losing Streak

To a point, winning is perceived as an affirmation of the effectiveness of a team's efforts to succeed. Likewise, losing is often seen as being synonymous with failure. On the gridiron, the truth may lie somewhat between the two extremes. A team may play very well but lose to a more-talented opponent. In the same vein, a talented team can play poorly, but just well enough to win.

The major problem with losing—particularly losing continually—is that it may bring about pressures and barriers that compromise the team's efforts to win. For example, a team on a losing streak is often unable to focus on the immediate task at hand (i.e., win a game). A team in this situation frequently tends to dwell on the negative factors attendant to losing (e.g., job security, emotional turmoil, accountability, etc.).

Players on a losing team also fail to realize that there are times when failure has value as an instrument of teaching. Determining why you lost and identifying how to overcome the factors (weaknesses) that led to your loss can be a valuable learning experience. For example, most military historians would argue that more can be learned by studying an army's defeats, rather than its victories.

Another negative by-product of being mired in an extended losing streak is that it can lead to a devastating process, referred to as the "losing syndrome." This process can lead to dissension, distractions, and a singular lack of focus. You should be aware of this syndrome and do everything in your power to either keep it from establishing itself or get the best of it if it does occur. Among the factors attendant to a losing syndrome are the following:

- Some individuals associated with the team (players and staff members) may be driven to extreme levels of the survival mentality by losing continually.

- Some staff members may decide that their days with the organization are numbered. They either believe that they will probably be terminated once the season is over or feel that they don't want to be part of a "loser." Subsequently, they will spend an inordinate amount of time in their office on the phone with the door closed. As the season winds down, this practice can reach epidemic proportions.

- Some assistant coaches may look for solace with the players. They attempt to endear themselves to players whom they believe might save them by pleading their case if staff terminations occur. This scenario is particularly typical of position coaches.

    The collapse of coach-player relations can be very destructive to the welfare of the team. Through his subtle comments or his open criticism of the head coach, the assistant coach ultimately undermines the authority and respect due to the head coach. The assistant coach who fails to respond to open questioning or even ridicule of the head coach has a similar negative impact on the head coach's position.

- Staff harmony may begin to disintegrate. Such turmoil is often manifested in disharmony between the offensive and defensive units. Rarely, at least during the early stages of an extended losing streak, do both the offensive and defensive units begin to collapse (i.e., play poorly) at the same time.

    Typically, each unit is held together by a few key players whose performances make a difference. Subsequently, as one unit starts to falter performance-wise, staff members then start to turn against each other. Frequently, the players become aware of this divisive split, thereby causing a breach in the squad.

- Coaches and players may begin to lash out at one another. Their actions will be based on the misguided perception that this burst of emotion demonstrates their commitment to the team. In fact, their actions emanate from their frustration and serve almost no constructive purpose.

- Those staff members in decision-making roles—the offensive and defensive coordinators—may come under severe scrutiny from the head coach who has become frustrated and disappointed in the team's failure to win. Ultimately, the head coach cannot help but relate the decisions of unit coordinators with his team's performance.

The head coach is bound to note strategy flaws, after the fact. Criticisms by position coaches who have differences that would naturally exist in philosophy, strategy, or techniques will surface. Efforts to develop a game plan can become even more difficult because the decisions of the coordinators will now be questioned at every turn. Subsequently, this situation can breed inaction, indecision, or a diluting strategy.

- Pressure from management, initially in the form of questioning and then as second guessing, may become a major distraction. Often, the impetus of this pressure will come from the entourage surrounding management. With egos damaged and personalities embarrassed, ownership and management (though not directly involved) may begin to allow staff members to undermine the head coach.

- The media will naturally become increasingly critical as the losing streak evolves.

- A staff member may take out his frustration on the players.

- The players may receive blame publicly for the team's poor performance from anyone in the organization.

- The head coach can expect disgruntled players to begin to approach management or even ownership about their perceptions of the shortcomings of the coaches. Typically, the owner and those individuals working closely with him are the most vulnerable to the complaints of the players. Although the owner and these individuals are emotionally involved in the situation, they seldom have any real understanding of the basis for the team's continuing slide.

- The general manager may privately or secretly meet with staff members in an attempt to identify the reasons for the team's problems. The general manager should be aware of the fact that these actions are undermining the head coach. Members of the coaching staff who participate in such meetings should also be fully cognizant of the destructive nature of their actions.

- Some self-serving assistant coaches may attempt to ingratiate themselves to a sports writer. By serving as a pipeline or an "unnamed source" of information for a sports writer, these assistant coaches mistakenly believe that they will gain favor from the journalist and somehow separate themselves from the ridicule their colleagues are receiving.

Eventually, an extended losing streak may result in a losing season in which the team is virtually noncompetitive (for example, the San Francisco 49ers' 1979 season that produced a 2-14 record). Among the steps that you (as the head coach) can do to help stem the tide of a losing syndrome are the following:

- Communicate with the owner and management honestly and directly. When explanations of the situation are requested, objective rational feedback should be offered. The shortcomings and the failures of the team should be thoroughly explained. Restraint must be exercised in blaming a single player or a group of players for the losses.

- Continue to emphasize the development of the players' individual skills—regardless of whether the team is losing or winning games. Such development will translate to improvement on the field which will eventually pay dividends in the winning column.

- Maintain your level of professional ethics.

- Do everything possible not to personalize your team's loses. Exhibit an inner toughness emanating from three of the most effective survival tools—composure, patience and common sense.

- Hold regular discussions with members of your coaching staff on the potential impact of continued losing on human nature. Using examples of previous situations involving disruption and turmoil, you should review how individuals can turn against each other. These matters should be discussed both in staff meetings and on an individual basis. To a point, these discussions help prevent coaches from falling prey to losing their nerve.

- Maintain team standards. Every rule and practice that was in place before the losing streak began should continue to be followed. For example, all schedules should be retained. Furthermore, the atmosphere in meetings and on the field should be retained (i.e., the atmosphere should not become tougher or more intense, nor should it become more lax or loose).

  Humor can be used to lighten tense conditions. Keep in mind that the brunt of humor should only be directed at those coaches and players who would not be offended by its use. All teaching efforts and presentations should also remain the same. Expectations from the players should remain unchanged.

- Be careful not to label any concept or idea you are implementing as the "thing that is going to get this team back on track." If your proposed plan doesn't work and you fall into a practice of instituting a gimmick each week in an attempt to reverse your team's losing ways, the players can begin to lose faith in your abilities to truly identify the team's problems and correct them. This admonition includes the old saying, "we are going to get back to fundamentals and concentrate on basics," as being the singular answer to the team's dilemma.

  During a losing streak last season, one NFL coach made this type of "back-to-basics" speech both publicly and privately to his players. After losing another round of games, one player was prompted to observe, "Well, we've gotten back to basics and we're still losing. It must mean that we are basically and fundamentally wrong." To some, the back-to-basics mentality denotes a type of finger pointing by the coach. It insinuates that *someone* in the organization forced the head coach away from "fundamentals and basics," and that he is single-handedly going to get the team back on track. This scenario begs the question, "How did you lose control of the team in the first place?"

- Don't isolate yourself. Regardless of how poorly the team does, you must be highly visible doing your job and assisting others in doing theirs.

- Continue to test game plans. Emphasize teaching the game plan and ensuring effective communication on plans and tactics to staff members and players. It is critical that everyone involved must concentrate on the game plan. The focus must be on properly executing the game plan—not on your next opponent, the point spread, the team's chances of winning, etc. The game plan should be broken down so that every player knows (and practices) his assignment on every play.

- Don't be overly preoccupied with winning the next game. If you get consumed by the thought that one victory will somehow turn things around, you may fail to be aware of the true extent of the problems that require your attention.

- Be detail-oriented. Pay attention to every detail including teaching techniques, carrying out assignments, maintaining established organizational procedures, etc.

- Exude an upbeat attitude. This attitude should be reflected in your attention to and involvement in your duties. Showy chatter should be avoided.

- Ensure that an appropriate level of courtesy and respect is extended to all members of the coaching staff. All service-related personnel (e.g., the training staff, equipment people, field maintenance staff, etc.) must also be treated with courtesy and respect.

- Don't plead with the team to play better. Such behavior on your part can be misconstrued by players as a weakness and can compromise the "dignity" of your position.

- Avoid continually threatening or chastising your players. Eventually, your players may tune out such verbal assaults.

- Keep in mind that "simple" remedies designed to turn everything around, such as installing a new quarterback, may only serve as a temporary distraction from the trauma of continued losing. In virtually every instance, an extended losing streak crosses a broad base of shortcomings. While it may be very tempting to offer simple corrective measures, such preventative steps seldom "fix" the real problems.

- Don't retain an assistant who clearly is inadequate in his present position. The inability of the team to perform up to its capabilities and to your expectations may be due in part to shortcomings on the part of specific staff members. In that case, it would be a tragic mistake to retain an assistant who is incompetent, regardless of how long you've been associated with that individual or your loyalty to that person.

- Keep in mind that as the losses mount, the individual relationships between you and the players become critical. These relationships will be key to holding the squad together. You must, however, retain your role as the top executive. Don't forget that familiarity can be deadly.

- Deal with assistant coaches on an individual basis. On-going conversations should be held to clarify misunderstandings and clear the air. Disloyalty to some degree will be an inherent part of the losing syndrome. Staff members may experience severe disappointments in the turn of events. You shouldn't be shocked if a close personal friend among your coaching staff turns on you under the trauma of losing continuously.

- Demonstrate confidence, competence, and professionalism in all dealings with the media. At best, excessive fraternization with the media will only momentarily delay the inevitable criticism directed to you concerning the team's failures. Keep in mind that off-the-record comments from you generally serve as little more than a release mechanism for your frustration and that the media person to whom you made the comments will use them sooner or later.

- Utilize professional counseling (through an available external resource) to help you deal with the severe level of stress attendant to the situation. Typically, the head coach has no emotional support system to deal with the multiple pressures and problems he faces from all directions.

Every team is a stage setting, a place to act out the drama of our lives. When our teams excel, we win. Our best efforts, combined with those of our teammates, grow into something far greater and far more satisfying than anything we could have achieved on our own. Teams make us part of something that matters. They are the fountain from which all our rewards will ultimately flow.

Pat Riley
Head Basketball Coach
Miami Heat
from *The Winner Within*

An Extended Winning Streak

The team on an extended winning streak also presents a unique challenge. A team on a winning streak can suffer the same lack of focus as a team on an extended losing streak—obviously for a vastly differently reason.

Gordon Prange, in his acclaimed book on the battle of Midway, *Miracle at Midway,* examined one of the primary problems that can arise from winning continuously—overconfidence. Prange presents a convincing argument that the root cause of Japan's defeat at Midway was a factor which has been referred to as "victory disease."

According to Prange, "because of a long string of uninterrupted victories, the healthy self-confidence which every fighting man must feel to function had degenerated into overweening conceit and contempt for the enemy." In other words, an inferior U.S. fleet was able to overcome an overwhelmingly superior Japanese Navy because the Japanese leaders were awash with overconfidence.

The potential for a football team to be affected by the malady referred to as "victory disease" certainly exists. Overconfidence can have disastrous consequences if your players feel that their success is a reflection that they have already mastered the basic fundamentals. They may begin to ignore the attention to detail and execution that led them to success in the first place.

When combined with a lack of respect for your opponents, overconfidence can have a negative impact on your team's efforts to continue its winning ways. Accordingly, you should take specific steps to ensure that your players deal with success in an appropriate manner, including:

- Be careful not to "tighten down" on your players too far in order to prevent winning from getting away from them. You should let the players and the organization, as a whole, enjoy the moment and the euphoria that winning brings. In most instances, winning typically energizes and invigorates the team's attitude toward preparation. Misguided efforts to keep players well-grounded may sap some of the positive energy that exists within a winning environment.

- Allow your players to take pats on the back on the first two days of the work week (Monday and Tuesday), while concurrently emphasizing that the new work week will begin on Wednesday. At that point, the prior week's success becomes ancient history.

- Make your players aware of the pitfalls of becoming too receptive to all of the accolades they will receive during the season, especially from the press. Players should be made to understand that the media is equally adept at pouring it on in the good times and using the players as cannon fodder in bad times. The point should be emphasized that the difference between a pat-on-the-back and a knife-in-the-back can be as subtle as an open or a closed hand.

- Be aware that a team on a winning streak is also susceptible to experiencing a phenomenon that can best be described as "losing their nerve" once the streak ends.

   Prange discussed these circumstances in his examination of the Japanese suffering the consequences of "victory disease." In that regard, Prange concluded, "from having originally seriously underrated the enemy, the (Japanese) Combined Fleet top brass now frantically overestimated their own difficulties."

   In effect, the Japanese had lost their nerve at Midway. They lost their perspective that even though they had endured a major defeat, they were still the superior force in the Pacific. As a result, despite the fact that they had the capacity and the opportunity to continue to be on the offensive in their sphere of the world, they retreated to regroup and rethink their tactics and situation.

   Similar to the impact of "victory disease," a lack of nerve also affects football teams on occasion. Such teams endure a disappointing loss or a setback, and then lose their confidence in their ability to handle adversity. In the process, they lose the aggressive, self-confident mentality that previously gave them their competitive edge.

> *Complacency is the last hurdle any winner, any team must overcome before attaining potential greatness. Complacency is the Success Disease: it takes root when you're feeling good about who you are and what you've achieved.*
>
> Pat Riley
> Head Basketball Coach
> Miami Heat
> from *The Winner Within*

Sustaining Success After a Big Season

Being able to sustain a team's winning ways after an extraordinarily successful season (particularly after a Super Bowl win) presents its own unique set of issues that must be addressed. If you're extremely fortunate, you will find yourself in this situation.

Not surprisingly, ownership, management, coaches and players alike will experience a euphoric mental state arising from a sense of accomplishment and an enhanced level of public approval. Everyone involved with the team tends to be affected by the high visibility and the relatively high degree of notoriety resulting from the team's success.

Every reason exists to celebrate and to allow the organization as a whole to take great pride in the team's accomplishments. The achievements of the team are a positive affirmation of the sacrifices and efforts required to bring about that success. As such, the acclaim that naturally follows extraordinary success should be embraced.

Everyone in the organization should share in the team's accomplishments. Gratitude and appreciation should be shown to every individual involved with the team—from the front desk receptionist to the equipment manager. Every effort should be made to "seize the moment" by encouraging everyone involved with the organization to collectively come together to celebrate and recognize the success of the team. The expenses required to enable this gathering to occur should be perceived as worthwhile.

At some point, however, everything must return to "business as usual." All factors considered, the sooner this happens the better. While this step will not occur overnight, everyone should be expected to have refocused on the actions needed to ensure that the success of the team will be repeated in the upcoming season.

In reality, not everyone will. Herein lies the challenge for the coaching staff and management. Refocusing after the euphoria of winning the Super Bowl can be almost as challenging as raising a team up from the depths of despair. Among the factors that should be considered when developing a plan to help sustain the winning ways of a team after a successful season are the following:

- Recognize that there will be fallout from an extraordinarily successful season, particularly if the success occurred rather unexpectedly. The symptoms of such fallout will sometimes be recognizable only to the experienced or most intuitive mind.

- Realize that keeping important matters in proper perspective will be very difficult—at least initially. This situation should not be surprising, given the fact that the team has reached the pinnacle of success.

- Account for the loss of perspective (and the resulting lack of attention to meaningful matters) by developing a plan to ensure that staff members return to the mode of operation that produced the team's success this past season. Do not assume that anyone else involved with the team will effectively deal with this issue.

- Expect the media to give a great deal of attention to the problems of repeating. The press will offer numerous examples of teams which failed to repeat their successes; complete and usually valid scenarios of how difficult it is to repeat successes will also be described in detail by the media.

- Be cognizant of the fact that almost everyone will be aware of the problems of repeating and will talk about how to avoid the dreaded fall. Collectively, these individuals will pledge to maintain their commitment to excellence. You should document and use these proclamations to hold both staff and players accountable for their assurance to do whatever it takes for the team to be successful.

- Expect, however, that many of the individuals involved with the team will become preoccupied with the need for more acclaim and more attention. In fact, some individuals will become consumed by the wish for more personal recognition.

- Expect your assistant coaches to be in demand from other organizations. This situation is part of the price of success. Not surprisingly, your coaches will want more lucrative contracts and more security. You may lose some key personnel. In addition, other members of the organization may feel that they have not received enough credit for the team's success.

  In the NFL, there have been a number of instances where second-level management personnel (e.g., scouts, personnel directors, assistant coaches, etc.) have contacted the owner after a team has had a "great" year in a back-door attempt to let the owner know that they were responsible for the team's success.

- Realize that your schedule may become very crowded. In turn, you may expect a sizable bonus or demand a new contract. Eventually, you may lose focus regarding what's important.

- Don't be surprised if ownership becomes a "national figure." In the process, the owner will become even more quotable than before. Don't be surprised if ownership may be inclined to take much of the credit for the team's success.

- Expect some players to be no-shows at mini-camps. In defense of such lamentable behavior, the agents who represent these no-shows will demand that their clients' contracts be renegotiated or will claim their clients' absences were due to prior commitments. Eventually, there may even be no-shows as the preseason camp gets underway.

- Anticipate that the lives and careers of some of your players will be affected in various negative ways, including:
  - Some of your players will embark on a journey of substance abuse (e.g., drugs, excessive alcohol consumption, etc.), as a result of new acquaintances drawn to the players by the players' sudden affluence.
  - Some players will lose perspective on financial matters. Expecting that more and more money will come their way, these players will spend beyond their means.
  - Some players will demand a new contract. Their demands will be reinforced by their agents who will be quick to point out that their client was the "key to victory." Some agents will insist that their clients' contracts be renegotiated to bring them up to the level of other players in the League. Often, the agents will take their demands public.
  - Some players will not adhere to their prescribed off-season conditioning program. This lackadaisical attitude will usually affect those players who tend to gain weight the most (e.g., big linemen).
  - Some of the players who become free agents will be offered substantially more lucrative contracts by other teams. You should expect to lose a few players whom you perceived as being totally loyal to the team.

The coaching staff is often susceptible to the same type of problems as the players. Accordingly, your coaching staff may have to deal with several critical issues, including:

- The staff's effort to prepare for the upcoming season may not adhere to the same level of detail it did the previous season due to an attitude that subcribes to the belief, "we'll just do what we did last year."
- The staff will have considerably more demands on their time during the off-season. For example, they'll be invited to speak at more clinics and seminars. As a result, they'll be on the road more. They'll also be besieged by coaches who want to meet with them to tap their "insights into success."
- The staff may experience disruptive turmoil arising from those staff members who feel that their contributions to the team's success are unappreciated or from those who are jealous of professional opportunities being given to other staff members—but not to them.

Two fundamental lessons of war experience are—never to check momentum; never to resume mere pushing.

B.H. Liddell Hart
Military Tactician and Historian

As the head coach, you should undertake specific actions to counteract the negative factors that may arise from your team's extraordinary success. Among the steps that you can take are the following:

- Be demanding. Inform the squad that they will continue to be held to high standards and that you will continue to expect (and demand) nothing less than their best performance at all times.

- Stimulate and reenergize the squad. Do everything possible to retain the positive chemistry of the team. Replace lost free agents with comparably or more talented players. Keep in mind that new players, if chosen properly, can add "new vitality" to the team. By the same token, don't overlook the fact that a player who doesn't "fit in" may disrupt team chemistry.

- Use the energy and enthusiasm that is generated by winning to help solidify the gains made by the team. This step will require more contact with the squad than the coaching staff has had previously. At the very least, the players must see that the organization is continuing to refine and extend its effort to sustain the success the team has experienced.

- Hold numerous meetings with the team. Conduct these meetings in a variety of forums (e.g., the entire team, individually by position, and separate offensive, defensive and special teams units). Schedule these meetings at appropriate times and in appropriate settings. Emphasizing honesty, find as many suitable ways as possible to get your basic points and message across. Explain to your players what steps must be taken to sustain the momentum of the team, including what will be expected and required of each player.

- Refocus the staff by covering in detail why and how each game was won in the just completed, championship season. Subsequently, thoroughly address the shortcomings of the team and the areas that need improvement prior to the next season. An objective analysis of the team's strengths and weaknesses can help bring the staff back to reality.

- Require each of your position coaches to conduct a comprehensive evaluation of each of the players for which he is responsible. Have video tapes prepared that illustrate both outstanding and poor performances by each player. Keep in mind that the sobering effect of his play being closely reviewed will often motivate a player to rededicate his efforts to excel and to work on those skill-areas which need improvement.

- Orchestrate your practices to address specific situations. All factors considered, the more specific the application, the more your players will be able to find a reason to focus. For example, you can increase the likelihood that your players will focus on "how to get better" by identifying specific steps that they can take to bring about a higher level of efficiency.

- Meet with each player several times to discuss what you will expect from that player next season. Although your conversation will include positive feedback regarding the player's personal contribution to the winning season just concluded, the primary focus of your meetings with each player will be to exhort that player to keep improving his individual skill level.

- Don't be so overconfident that you feel you should change what your team is doing in order to elevate your team's game by incorporating new plays or defenses that are counterproductive to the approach that enabled your team to be successful in the first place. Keep in mind that straying very far from your current approach may, in fact, become a step backward.

- Devote a substantial amount of time to studying your team's system and your opponents' systems. The more you understand your system and how your system can be applied to counter the efforts of your opponents, the more effective and efficient your system becomes. As a consequence, your system will evolve naturally over time.

- Keep in mind that "hard" decisions on personnel matters may be forthcoming. It may become necessary for some players who have helped make a difference in the just concluded championship season to be released or traded. Such actions (particularly in the midst of victory celebrations) are brutal, but—on occasion—entirely necessary.

- Ensure that you give an appropriate amount of attention to the upcoming draft. Over the years, it has not been uncommon for a Super Bowl team to become somewhat "reckless" with the ensuing draft. Unfortunately, the euphoria that typically accompanies extraordinary success and the attendant notoriety and recognition that results from playing in the Super Bowl can turn the head of many of the individuals associated with the team, particularly scouts and personnel directors.

- Address the issue of how to deal with the media. Remind players and organizational personnel that every remark they make will be "quotable." Any remark, even one offered in a humorous vein, can come back to haunt the individual and the team. Furthermore, too much pontificating will be tough to live down as the next season progresses. Don't allow team personnel to talk "too much" and damage the image of the club.

- Do everything possible to ensure that everyone associated with the team maintains an appropriate level of focus on the job. Take a positive firm approach to guarantee individual compliance with stated responsibilities, goals and expectations.

Rebounding from a Poor Season

Handling a team that had a poor season the previous year also places particular demands on a head coach. In responding to these demands, you must resist the inevitable tendency to simply make bold proclamations or grandiose statements about how things are going to be different. Your players will be looking for tangible evidence that next season will be different (e.g., the return of a key player who was lost to injury the previous year, the addition of a key player via a trade or free agency, etc.). If such evidence does not exist, you should consider several steps, including:

- Reenergize your efforts to evaluate all aspects of team operations, including your assistant coaches, all individual players, and the offensive and defensive schemes used by the team.

- Incorporate changes in the offensive and defensive schemes employed by the team if you decide that making a fundamental modification in one of those plans will benefit the team.

- Let the players know the key areas of change and how they are going to impact on the upcoming season.

- Replace those assistant coaches who are not making the contributions expected of them.

- Make those player personnel moves which will improve the team. Such actions should be consistent with your short-range and long-range plans for the team.

- Make sure that everyone associated with the team understands what will be expected of him during the upcoming season and maintains the proper focus regarding his responsibilities.

The Coach Who Leaves the Job

In reality, job turnover is relatively high in the NFL for head coaches. Every year, a number of teams find themselves in circumstances where they hire a new head coach. In most instances, a team usually changes head coaches in an attempt (however misguided or on the mark) to give its program a "new" start. On a rare occasion, a team will be forced to hire a new head coach because the former head coach has decided to give up coaching. Not surprisingly, either circumstance can be somewhat traumatic for the head coach who leaves the job.

Getting fired. Being terminated is never a pleasant experience for the head coach. Being fired is a very public display that ownership is holding you accountable for the failure of the team to meet ownership's expectations. Given human nature, when you're fired, it's likely that you will experience a wide array of conflicting emotions—anger, hurt, bewilderment, betrayal, rejection, disappointment (at being unable to complete the "task" for which you were hired), etc.

The key will be to deal with these feelings in a professional manner. The point to remember is that being fired means that you're out of work. If you plan to stay in coaching, it is obviously not in your best interests to say or do anything that will have a negative impact on your future job opportunities in coaching.

Another aspect of getting fired that you should deal with is to remember that while in most instances there is certainly an element of truth to the old axiom that coaches "are hired to be fired," there are certain actions on your part that can expedite the likelihood that you will lose your job. *Among the steps that you can take that will put you on the path of losing your head coaching job are the following:*

- Exhibit patience, more patience, paralyzing patience. In reality, patience is not always a virtue. The belief that sooner or later things will work out, instead of taking a proactive approach to changing the situation, can be viewed as condoning incompetence (a stepping stone to failure).

- Engage in delegating, more delegating, massive delegating. Turning key decisions over to others and assuming things will get done properly can be a fatal error in judgment.

- Take action in a tedious, overly cautious, slow-moving manner. In reality, effective leaders (head coaches) are take-charge individuals who are able to make decisions decisively and quickly.

- Hold (and act on) false beliefs concerning the way a particular group of certain athletes will react to a certain situation or a specific leadership style. Such a mind-set will have disastrous consequences on your ability to relate to your players and to get them to play to the maximum of their capabilities.

  Effective coaches are very sensitive to the fact that all players are individuals—each with unique needs and interests. A successful coach is aware of the strengths and weaknesses of his players and "manages" them as individuals (i.e., "different strokes for different folks").

- Attempt to patronize, neutralize and charm the media. At best, such efforts are a waste of time. (Note: A comprehensive discussion of how to work with the media is presented in Chapter 17.)

- Become close friends with individual players. Some head coaches want to be a buddy with their players off the field and serve as their "leader" on the field. In reality, it's an either/or situation. You can be a buddy or a leader to players—not both. When you are around the people you coach, the situation requires a professional, business-like relationship.

- Spend an excessive amount of time socializing with ownership in the misbelief that somehow the two of you are bonding. While you can be friendly with ownership, on the whole, your relationship with ownership should reflect both a professional demeanor and a detached level of decorum.

- Fail to continue to evaluate the performance of those individuals who have been longtime members of your coaching staff—especially those staff members who have become "dominant fixtures" over time. An effective head coach should never take the performance of his staff for granted. On an on-going basis, you must ensure that every assistant coach knows what his job is, knows how to do his job, and does it.

- Fail to actively participate in efforts to evaluate and acquire players. Given the fact that you will be held directly accountable for your player's accomplishments on the field (or lack thereof), it is critical that you play an active role in deciding who will be on the team. Failure to do so is both foolish and a major abdication of your responsibilities as a head coach.

- Trust others to carry out duties that are fundamentally yours. While staff members can be valuable resources in an organization, the bottom line is that it is unreasonable to assume that everyone who works for you will be completely loyal only to you. Effective coaches understand that, in a successful organization, everything begins and ends with top management. In order for an organization to work effectively, the head coach must be accountable (i.e., "the buck stops here").

- Attempt to find ways to get out from under the pressure of the position. Like it or not, coaching is a stressful profession. The pressure of serving as the head coach only multiplies the stressful demands placed on the individual. Spending time looking for ways to lessen the pressure can be counterproductive.

  At the least, such an approach can cause you to lose sight of your primary objective (build a winning team). Instead of focusing on coaching, you dissipate your time and energies on getting rid of the unwanted "pressure." In reality, you should consider stress in a more positive light—one that views pressure as a natural by-product of the challenges inherent in coaching.

- Promote an atmosphere that is routine and comfortable in the misbelief that the work environment should be "fun." The only feature of an effective organization that could be considered "routine," however, is its never-ending commitment to excellence. While a positive work environment is certainly desirable, the steps needed for a dynamic organization to continue to grow and evolve have little to do with a "fun" environment. Literally speaking, success is a by-product of systematic efforts to achieve and maintain high standards of performance. A routine and comfortable atmosphere is more apt to lead to overconfidence and internal acceptance of the status quo.

Making a Career Change. As a point of fact, life after football can be an extremely traumatic experience for the head coach who decides to give up coaching. Among the factors that can have a negative impact on a former head coach's emotional state (i.e., mental health) are the following:

- The loss of significant recognition that has been a major part of his life.
- The loss of status of being an insider to the interworkings of the NFL. Although there are aspects of the day-to-day environment of the NFL the head coach disdains, he has learned to live with and appreciate his work habitat.
- After leaving the job, the fraternal relationships and mutual appreciation with coaches and players are no longer part of his life.
- The frustration that arises over his inability to utilize his professional knowledge and insights. To the former head coach, his professional knowledge and insights subsequently have no place in his life. At this point in time, such professional acumen appears to be wasted.
- A vacuum has replaced the head coach's daily routine. No matter how arduous or fatiguing his daily routine was, his established schedule was a very basic

ingredient of his life. It often becomes very difficult for a former head coach to fill up the vacuum that has occurred. Even the absence of such basic tasks as going down to work every day and coming home can create an emotional void.

- The former head coach misses the excitement of his work—the games themselves, the thrill of victory, etc. The euphoric feel of victory is all too elusive.

- The former head coach grieves the loss of a major thrust of his life (i.e., not being included). Such grief is counterbalanced to a degree by his sense of celebration over the conclusion of his former professional life (i.e., he grieves and celebrates at the same time).

- The former head coach is unsettled by the fact that his life has gone from one extreme to another. Before leaving his job, his life was consumed by coaching. Coaching demands a total commitment (time, energy, etc.) from an individual. For a coach, virtually everything else must become of secondary importance. The job takes him to extremes—emotionally, intellectually, and physically. Not surprisingly, most individuals can only handle such demands for so many years.

- Some head coaches, however, hold on to their positions for too many years. In the process, they become ceremonial leaders of their teams, rather than full participants as head coaches. They delude themselves into believing that their continued involvement will make a difference with their teams.

  They stay longer than their ability to exert direction and leadership. Historically, very little has been accomplished during those years when a head coach should have moved into another phase of his life.

- It is important to remember, however, that a head coach of relatively advanced age can be of real value to an organization—even as a titular head. He just can't legitimately fulfill the same role he once held. Rather, if such an individual were to choose to remain in the head coaching role, he must employ top coordinators and an experienced staff (which, in essence, assume some of his responsibilities).

  For example, while George Halas and Paul "Bear" Bryant had retained the title of head coach late in their professional careers, they had delegated virtually all of the planning and decision-making to others. Paul Brown, founder and former head coach of the Cincinnati Bengals, is another example of a head coach who had to make adjustments late in his career. Every year, he would reflect on whether to continue as the Bengal's head coach. In turn, he would delegate more responsibility to his staff. All factors considered, Brown's efforts had mixed results.

The former head coach learns who his real friends are almost from the moment he steps away from his position as the team's "leader." Many individuals who previously were considered friends will act and behave in a manner contrary to friendship (e.g., individuals who previously gave the former head coach credit for the team's accomplishments will now attribute those achievements to someone else).

Off-season

The "off-season" is anything but. This period is a critical time to accomplish specific functions of your organization and team. Accordingly, it is vital that you bring the same attention to detail and specific structuring to your objectives in the off-season as you do to your practice structure and game planning during the regular season.

The off-season used to be a time when coaches could ease up on their schedule a little and address special projects, work with new players and get some needed time off. With the increased demands that many clubs put on their coaches with regard to the evaluation of both college talent and free agent pro personnel, the way the head coach and his coaching staff must approach the off-season has changed drastically.

First and foremost, the need for systematic planning of the off-season program has become acutely obvious. Specific criteria and a set of detailed objectives for each of the key areas that should be addressed during the off-season must be established. Otherwise, you may get to the end of the off-season period and find that the organization has not accomplished as much as you had hoped—a situation which will severely hinder your team's ability to effectively handle the challenges posed by the upcoming regular season.

Among the steps that you should take to ensure that your team's off-season program is productive are the following:

- Set up a detailed calendar of critical dates and deadlines for you and your staff during the off-season. Initially, this schedule should include those specific dates relating to the evaluation of college and pro-level personnel, including the various college all-star games, the NFL's combine workouts, the period when NFL free agency begins and ends, the days for visiting college campuses and working out potential draft choices, NFL draft days, and specific days prior to the draft when the staff meets to share player evaluations and to compile player rankings for the draft (these meetings are typically held twice a month leading up to the draft and daily the two weeks preceding the draft).

- Identify specific time periods your staff can plan on having off as vacation. This allocation of time off is essential. The effectiveness of coaches, like players, can be negatively impacted if these individuals do not have the opportunity to get away from the pressures of the game and relax for awhile during the off-season.

    Regardless of a staff member's passion for the game, he will (all factors considered) be better prepared to organize his time and efforts and to accomplish his coaching responsibilities if he takes time off to "recharge his batteries"—mentally and physically. If he doesn't take time off, the wear and tear he has experienced may or may not manifest itself during the off-season. If it doesn't, it will certainly be noticeable, however, during the season when the energy level of your assistant coaches will erode prematurely.

- Keep in mind that it is not necessary to give your staff a substantial block of time off that will leave them with an insufficient amount of time to get their work done. It is important, however, to schedule your staff's time off well ahead of time so that they can make plans to use this time wisely (e.g., family vacation plans, etc.).

- Schedule times for staff meetings to review pertinent team issues and to identify steps for addressing those issues (e.g., system analysis, player evaluation, incorporating new players into the system, off-season conditioning, etc.).

- Establish an environment in which your veteran players are challenged to refine and improve those skills and techniques that are crucial for success. Getting your existing players—particularly those who have been with you for a long period of time—to commit themselves fully to an off-season improvement program can be a formidable task. Unfortunately, not every NFL player has the work ethic of Jerry Rice.

- Ensure that every player who has an injury or a medical condition that needs to be rehabilitated receives appropriate treatment. It is essential that such treatment be coordinated with and conducted under the supervision of your medical and athletic training staff. This advice also holds true for players who do not live in the city where they play.

  All rehab efforts conducted by outside personnel must be closely coordinated with your medical staff. In addition, steps should be taken to make certain that any conditioning efforts that a player engages in are not counterproductive to his rehabilitation program and do not expose him to further risk of injury (i.e., your team's conditioning coach should coordinate his programs with your medical and athletic training staffs).

- Ensure that every player has a complete understanding of what is expected of him in the off-season. For example, a specific set of conditioning objectives and how those objectives should be met should be developed for each player.

  Your coaching staff should work closely with the team's conditioning coaches to make sure that whatever conditioning goals and programs are established for the players are consistent with the objectives you have determined for the team. In the event that a player is training off-site (i.e., because he lives in another town), his training program must be coordinated with your conditioning coaches. Your staff must make sure that anyone who trains your athletes understands and adheres to your priorities and training program guidelines.

- Take steps to assimilate new players (physically and mentally) into your team's system. Given the constant turnover in personnel due to free agency, off-season workout sessions are more critical than ever. One of the essential keys to making free agency work for your team is how readily and effectively you can absorb newly signed players into your system.

  "Life" in the NFL used to be relatively static in that a team would have a base core of players who would remain with it for a number of years. Such a situation facilitated communication between coaches and players because a majority of the team was familiar with the team's way of operating. Previously, if one or two players were added to the team, it was fairly simple to assimilate them into the system because it was relatively easy to focus on their particular needs.

In the free-agent era of the NFL, however, it is not uncommon for a team's offense or defense to have three or four new faces in the lineup (not just backups, but front-line starters). As a consequence, it is critical that a team do everything possible in the off-season to absorb these new players into its system in order to provide as much continuity as possible going into the upcoming season.

- Evaluate your team's personnel immediately after the season as a prelude to identifying your team's needs in the free-agent market. Keep in mind that sometimes it can be very time consuming to be as thorough as you would like with regard to assessing your players beyond rating your players versus those available in free agency. Among the steps that your staff can take to evaluate each individual player are the following:
    - Identify those skills through which a player should be graded and establish a standardization of what levels make up those grades.
    - Review each grade and any comments given to each player on every play during the season. It is vital to determine if an athlete is having a reoccurring problem with the same concept. This step will give the staff a chance to emphasize to the athlete his deficiencies on that particular aspect of the play/sequence. Of equal importance is the fact that if problems with a particular play/series are recurring with more than one player, it may indicate that the dynamics of the play/series have not been adequately communicated to the team.
    - Indicate each player's contribution to the team and how the staff perceives that player's role in the upcoming season.
    - Project what the team's expectations are for each player for a three-year period.
    - Make a video of each player's 10 best plays and 10 worst plays from the past season, illustrating the athlete's most accomplished skills and those most in need of improvement.
- Evaluate your team's system. Every play and series from each of your games during the recently completed season should be evaluated to determine its effectiveness and whether is should continue to be part of your team's overall system.

Given the extensive demands on your staff's time in the off-season, it is often extremely difficult to coordinate everyone's schedule to conduct a comprehensive system review when the entire staff can meet together to analyze the relevant materials. As a result, your coordinators need to assign specific tasks to the assistant coaches (both individually and in groups). This step will enable a wider range of areas to be covered within the existing time constraints. The system review should be performed for all runs, protections, individual routes and route combinations.

The same review and methodology should be applied to critique and analyze each of the situational and contingency offensive plays used and if these plays need to be revised (in any way) for the upcoming season. In order to accomplish this step, a viable measuring tool to compare each aspect of the offense in these situations should be developed. Whatever form the system evaluation takes, it should include the following features:

- A system of rating the efficiency of each play and series should be developed to quantify the success for that play versus other series in your system and against its success in previous years.
- A determination of the particular skills needed to execute the play/series.
- A determination of the reason the play/series was or was not successful (e.g., talent level, execution, defense, etc.).
- A determination of whether your present talent level is capable of executing this play/series.
- A determination of the future of the play for the coming season.
- Cutups of the 10 best examples of why the play worked and 10 of why it didn't work.

- Establish a procedure for rating each play and series. The following points should be considered when developing such a procedure:

  - Keep in mind that one of the most "difficult" football-related aspects to quantify is the relative level of success or efficiency of a particular play or series. In numerous instances, for example, the simple measures of "yards gained per attempt" or "completion percentage" do not accurately convey the true value of a specific play or series.

  - Several data bases exist (e.g., the NFL, the Elias Sports Bureau, Stats Inc., etc.) that provide teams with access to the multitude of statistics that chart the relationship between the teams in the league with regard to interactive measures of production (e.g., turnover ratio, third-down conversion, red zone efficiency, yards after the catch, etc.).

  - In conjunction with the existing data base, each team needs, however, to develop a way to measure the relative effectiveness of its plays and series solely within the reference frame of itself. Although such a mechanism would be totally subjective, its subjectivity could be tempered somewhat by the experience-based judgments of your coaching staff.

    For example, one of the last things you would want to do is to discard a play or series in which you have faith just because a set of "arbitrary" numbers doesn't add up right. By the same token, you don't want to retain a play or series that is not providing the necessary level of production.

  - One possible type of play-rating measure that could be used within a team's total offensive system involves a variation of the formula the NFL uses to rate quarterbacks. While the NFL's rating system doesn't appear to be either particularly meaningful or applicable with regard to quantifying the abilities of quarterbacks, the mathematical ratios yielded by the NFL's formula (with some additional input) can be used to provide a basis for assessing the relative effectiveness of a specific play or series.

    For example, the NFL's formula for rating quarterbacks could be adjusted by factoring in sacks (refer to Table 15-1). The adjusted measure could then be used as a benchmark to assess the value of a particular play or series (i.e., how effective a specific protection scheme or route combination is relative to other protection schemes or route combinations that your team employs). The higher the number, the more effective the play.

HANDLING DIFFERENT TYPES OF TEAMS

As a head coach, the type of team you will be coaching will tend to vary somewhat over time. Each type of team will present a specific challenge to your skills and abilities and may require unique insights on your part for dealing with those challenges. Among the diverse types of teams which you may find yourself coaching are inexperienced teams, down-and-out teams, talented teams, and teams with high expectations.

Inexperienced Team

Although an inexperienced team can provide a real challenge to a head coach, it also can be quite gratifying. Because such a team has a preponderance of younger players, this type of team is often very receptive to learning—a situation which can be very enriching for the coach who enjoys his role as a teacher. Among the factors which you should consider if you have an inexperienced team are the following:

- Check (and recheck) your level of preparation and teaching progression constantly to make sure that you haven't assumed anything. Keep in mind that even the most obvious of situations may catch an inexperienced player (or team) off guard.

- Be aware that your responsibility for a squad is at its highest with an inexperienced team because younger players will tend to rely on you for every possible detail (e.g., down to where to park at the airport for team trips).

- Be as clear and to the point as possible when communicating with young or inexperienced players. Don't rely on subtlety. Such players may miss the point you are attempting to make.

A good general not only sees the way to victory; he knows when victory is beyond him.

Polybius
Greek Historian
125 B.C.

Down-and-Out Team

One of the most difficult scenarios a coach can face is how to handle a team which has no chance to make the playoffs. In professional football, a team can take on a wholly different profile once the players realize that they have been eliminated from

Table 15-1. The NFL's quarterback rating formula and an adjustment for quarterback sacks.

NFL's Formula

Step #1:   (# of completions ÷ # of passing attempts minus 30% x 100) multiplied by 0.05

Step #2:   (total # of yards ÷ # of passing attempts minus 3) multiplied by 0.25

Step #3:   (total # of touchdown passes thrown ÷ # passing attempts x 100) multiplied by 0.20

Step #4:   (2.375 minus the # of interceptions thrown ÷ the # of passing attempts x 100) multiplied by 0.25

Step #5:   The NFL's quarterback rating is the sum of the calculations produced by steps #1-#4, which is then divided by 6

Sack Adjustment

Step #6:   The amount resulting from the calculation of (2.375 minus the # of quarterback sacks ÷ the # of passes thrown x 100) multiplied by 0.25 is added to the NFL's quarterback rating aggregate. This collective number is then divided by 7.

---

the playoffs. It is important to remember that even a relatively untalented team will hold some hope for postseason participation until it has been mathematically excluded.

Regardless of the circumstances, once a team's playoff aspirations are finished, the problems and challenges facing the head coach are expanded. Among the steps that you should take if you find yourself in this situation are the following:

- Watch for telltale signs that either your staff or the players have packed it in (e.g., players are often late for meetings, coaches spend an excessive amount of time behind closed doors, individuals exhibit general body language in meetings that indicates they lack focus, etc.). If this is the case, take appropriate actions to refocus the team and your staff.

- Establish a number of sub-goals that will bring some sense of purpose to the team for the remainder of the season. These sub-goals should be focused on several levels—team, group, and individual. For example, even though the team won't be in the playoffs, the team could be given specific situational goals (e.g., being in the top ten in the league in total offense or defense, leading the league in 3rd down conversions, not allowing a punt or a kick-off to be returned for a score, etc.).

By the same token, group goals could be established for a particular position (e.g., quarterback sacks by the defensive linemen, minimize the number of fumbles by the offensive backs, interceptions by the secondary, etc.). Of the three levels, individual goals may be the easiest to "sell" to the players because of the potential for directly benefiting the individuals involved. Doing well (e.g., being selected to the Pro Bowl, achieving contract incentives, establishing a personal or team record, etc.) can have a positive impact in a number of areas, including free agency, future contract negotiations, the amount of playing time, etc.

- Appeal to the players' sense of professionalism. Such an appeal can occasionally be an effective way of refocusing the motivational level of the players. You can also remind the players of how enjoyable the role of being a spoiler can be.

Far better it is to dare mighty things, to win glorious triumphs, even though checkered by failure, than to take rank with those poor spirits who neither enjoy nor suffer much, because they live in the gray twilight that knows not victory nor defeat.

Theodore Roosevelt
26th President of the United States

Talented Team

Serving as the head coach of a talented team has its own unique set of demanding circumstances. At a minimum, the players on a talented team often have to be driven constantly to "live up" to their full potential. In addition, because expectations are usually very high for such a team, care must be taken to ensure that the players do not begin to set unrealistic goals. Among the steps that you can take to be better prepared to properly handle a talented team are the following:

- Realize that your team may have a couple of key players that aren't quite as talented as the other players on the team. This situation is particularly true in the age of free agency. The financial outlay to augment a relatively talented team that may be on the verge of breaking into the upper echelon of the league (or is even poised for a Super Bowl run) may have created a scenario whereby the organization has had to "fill in" a couple of areas on the team with personnel who fit the salary cap.

- Keep in mind that the financial division that often exists on a team between the "haves" and the "have-nots" can lead to a substantial amount of finger pointing when the team hits the inevitable bump in the road. All factors considered, such a situation is probably best handled at the individual level. At a minimum, you should make sure that the talented players are reminded of the responsibilities that having talent brings and ensure that these athletes understand and accept their role with the team as a whole.

- Be careful that you don't confuse the difference between talent and skill. Sometimes the two go hand-in-hand, while other times they don't. For example, a player can often be able to play effectively on sheer physical ability, even though he lacks the necessary fundamentals and skills. It is the responsibility of the coaching staff to convince a talented player that his God-given abilities can be enhanced by developing and adhering to a proven set of fundamentals.

A Team With High Expectations

Coaching a team with high expectations can be a demanding experience. On one hand, the expectations can be totally unrealistic—a scenario which virtually guarantees that the head coach will "fail." On the other hand, the expectations can be so high (even if they are reasonably realistic) that they create an environment where the pressures to succeed are extraordinarily intense. Among the steps that you should take when coaching a team with high expectations are the following:

* Identify who has placed the expectations on the team. For example, the fans, the media, and (in some cases) ownership will often view matters from a peripheral level and will place arbitrary (i.e., unrealistic) expectations on a team.
* Attempt to establish within the organization (and eventually with the fans of the team) what the realistic expectations should be for the team based on the facts and your considered judgment. Inform the organization of the "obstacles" the team is facing on its journey to success and the plan for overcoming each of those obstacles.
* Don't lower the expectations of a team just to keep the pressure off yourself. Your staff and your players expect and will appreciate honesty in your dealings with them.
* Keep your goals and expectations realistic and attainable. Adhere to the S.M.A.R.T. acronym with regard to establishing goals and expectations (*S*pecific-*M*easurable-*A*ttainable-*R*ealistic-*T*imely).

DEALING WITH INDIVIDUAL GAME CIRCUMSTANCES

Although it may be argued that every game, in and of itself, is a test of a head coach's capacity to lead, some individual game circumstances offer particular challenges. Among those situations which may involve additional attention and planning are key games, games when your team is either a big underdog or a lopsided favorite, games after a huge win, road games, games when key personnel are injured, and preseason games.

Key Games

All factors considered, each game may have a different level of significance to you and your team. Accordingly, given the divergent priorities that you may place on games, you have to decide what approach you will take to each game.

One of the primary keys to preparing for a critical regular season game involves distinguishing the significance of this game without totally devaluing the normal regular season game. Obviously, you do not want to place so much significance on a single game that regardless of whether the team is successful or not in that game, the team loses several subsequent games while rebounding from the emotional roller coaster attendant to the critical game.

Coaching in the playoffs or a championship game involves a whole new set of circumstances that have to be addressed. The immediacy and urgency of the game is obvious to the players. It is important for them to recognize that the mode and tempo of preparation by the team remains the same.

The team should be handled during the week in such a way that any excitement generated during the week does not detract from the efforts to prepare for the game and does not cause the team to peak too early. Keep in mind that any additional distractions (e.g., extra demands for the time by the media, requests by family and friends, etc.) can impede your plans, especially for a young or inexperienced team.

The need to deal effectively with distractions will multiply many times when the key game involves preparing for and playing in the Super Bowl. Teams who have participated in this "very public arena" state almost unequivocally that relatively little gets accomplished (football-wise) the week before the game. As a result, the efforts the week preceding the week of the game are critical with regard to internalizing and installing the game plan.

Among the steps that you can take to ensure that your team is properly prepared for a key game are the following:

- Keep in mind that a simple, clean game plan is best.
- Depend and count on what got your team to the key game (e.g., system, program, schemes, etc.).
- Plan on utilizing only those plays that have been previously used successfully.
- Make your practices crisp and shorter.
- Ensure that your players have "fresh" legs for the game.
- Base your game plan on a four-game study, instead of three games, of your opponent.
- Keep in mind that over the course of the season, too many games can dilute the tendency and willingness of your staff to spend sufficient time studying your opponent.
- Have your administrative assistant review all available videotapes of your opponent to determine what special plays, blitzes, out-of-the-ordinary plays, etc. your opponent uses.
- Have your assistant coaches review videotapes of earlier games late in the week to verify the game plan.
- Keep in mind that while it may be appropriate for you to vary the formations you plan to employ, you are not sure of the adjustments your opponent will make in response to those variations.
- Work on execution; allow your players to make mistakes.

- Give your players something that looks out of the ordinary as a change of pace, but is actually basic (i.e., make the change-up "cosmetic," rather than fundamental).

- Don't distract your players with new "secret" weapons.

- Ensure that your players feel that with regard to preparation, it's business as usual. Brief work on fundamental skills and techniques should continue.

- Devote one day of practice to light contact work (in pads).

- Don't attempt to be overly inspirational; rather, be distinct and specific on what it will take to win the game. Explain in detail, but not too tediously, how the game plan will be installed.

- Don't disrupt the continuity of your special teams. However, if some of your starters are the best coverage people in the kicking game and have had a reasonable amount of practice, be prepared to use them late in the game.

- Keep interview periods with the media as brief as possible; do only what the NFL requires in this area.

- Review all contingency plans in a classroom setting with the players; give those plans most likely to be used field work.

- Stress the need for privacy with the squad with regard to plans and preparation. Although the players will receive a considerable amount of public attention, such attention will be very distracting.

- Install 80 percent of your game plan in the first week if you have two weeks to prepare for the game (especially for the Super Bowl). Several factors make such a schedule appropriate. For example, the inevitable media crush will make it very difficult to have continuity in your practice schedule as the game approaches.

  Your team will be meeting and practicing at another site. You may be in a different time zone than you usually are, resulting in practicing and eating at unfamiliar times. In addition, the distractions are immense. As a result, virtually all of the planning and decision making should be done early in the first week.

  The players can be given an extra day off to partially recover from the long season, while the staff meets to develop the game plan. The two week period allows for four additional days of field work (Thursday, Friday, Saturday, and Sunday). At that point, the team then travels to the site of the game. In the final week before the game, all practices should last no more than 90 minutes, with the final two days of practice limited to 60 minutes of light work.

Another example of a type of a key game in which you may be involved is the postseason bowl game. Such a bowl game can involve either NFL players (the Pro Bowl) or collegiate-level players who have used up their eligibility (e.g., the East-West game, Senior Bowl, Blue-Gray game, etc.). All factors considered, coaching in one of these games is usually a relatively enjoyable experience. Not only do you have the opportunity to coach players who are generally recognized as being very talented, you also get to work in a relaxed and open environment.

In these bowl games, it is important that you are able to put a functional system together in a relatively short period of time that can be assimilated quickly and allows the players to communicate easily with each other. You should anticipate and be comfortable with the fact that a great deal of improvising will occur during this type of game.

Coaching in postseason bowl games involving collegiate players involves additional factors that should be considered. For example, one of your primary focuses in this type of game will be to evaluate the skills and pro potential of the players who will be much younger and less experienced. Finally, if the coaching staff for the game has been assembled from several different teams, the efforts involved in working with assistant coaches from other teams may be somewhat distracting (particularly in the short time frame for a bowl game).

Games as a Big Underdog or a Lopsided Favorite

Coaching a team which has to play a game as a big underdog or a lopsided favorite requires that you address several factors, including:

- Do everything possible to refocus the players for the immediate task at hand.
- Keep in mind that diverting the attention of the players to any of the perceived circumstances for this situation has no meaningful value. The operative word in this instance is "perceived."
- Ensure that the players understand that on many occasions the favorite/ underdog role is determined by a group of individuals who have a separate agenda.
- Do not allow the players to let the agenda of others affect their preparation for the game.

Games After a Huge Win

Coaching a team which has a game after a huge win may necessitate that you consider several issues, including:

- Keep in mind that getting players to refocus their attention while they are constantly getting pats on the back may be difficult.
- Give the players enough time to enjoy their big win, but also give them a specific timetable regarding when they need to stop celebrating and get back to their normal work routine.
- Understand that a huge win can exert an emotional toll on the physical aspect of your team. As a result, you must make sure that your players are doing the things necessary to recuperate from such a disruption (e.g., you may have to give your players a little more rest than usual).

The Last Second Loss

A catastrophic loss can take a team into shock. For example, early in 1997 season, the Oakland Raiders—after playing an excellent game—lost on the last play of the game to the Kansas City Chiefs on a thirty-yard pass that should never have been completed.

The loss resulted from the complete failure of one defensive back to do his job properly and, possibly, by the design of the defense. In reality, because one or two individuals failed on a single play, the entire team suffered an unbelievable loss. The Raiders put forth an outstanding team effort for almost sixty minutes, only to give the game away in the last seconds.

Just a day later, a similar fate stunned the Philadelphia Eagles. Ray Rhodes' Eagles lost on the last play of the game to the Dallas Cowboys when the holder bobbled the ball on a Philadelphia field-goal attempt from the five-yard line.

Up to the point of the ill-fated misplay, the Eagles had played a magnificent game. Initially, they dominated the Cowboys. They then fell behind, before driving the length of the field in the last thirty seconds of the game, only to botch the potentially winning field goal.

Last-second losses are devastating experiences for everyone involved, but especially for the head coach whose emotions are firmly tied to the travails of his team. Almost every coach has experienced this type of shocking tragedy. I certainly did, having been on both ends of the emotional roller coaster (i.e., unbelievable victories on one hand and shattering losses on the other).

As such, the head coach must suddenly handle the responsibility that has been thrust into his lap concerning the last-second loss. He must respond, as appropriate, to the team, the ownership, the fans, and the media.

As the head coach, you should consider taking several steps when dealing with a last-second loss, including:

- Allow the team to be by themselves for a brief period immediately following the game to cope with their sense of distraught mourning and frustration. At this moment, having privacy is important to them. Take a few moments to collect your thoughts and gather your wits before meeting with the team.

- Make sure that you don't meet with the team too soon, or they may not hear a word you say.

- Consider the alternative approaches that you can employ with them in this situation.

- Try to minimize (hopefully, avoid) any temptation you may have to lash out at those individuals whose actions were directly responsible for the loss. Because of your emotional state, you could be mistaken about whose fault it was.

- Regroup the entire squad as soon as possible.

- Eliminate, as much as possible, any anger the players might be directing at those individuals being blamed for the team's defeat.

- Connect everyone to the loss, because in a very real sense, each player could have failed to perform as assigned on a given play that could have made a difference in the outcome of the game.

- Be aware of the fact that these games happen every so often—hopefully, only once every few years.

- Firmly address the fact that under extreme duress, players can turn on each other.
- Remind the players that in sports, there are no guarantees. Sometimes, bad things occur.
- At this point, focus on positive factors.
- Recognize the great sacrifices made. The intense play, and the outstanding performances that occurred during the game.
- Emphasize instances and examples of toughness, resiliency, and resourcefulness.
- Direct the anger of the players to the next opponent.
- While the players should be mad, upset and disgusted concerning the loss, do not allow them to whine or feel sorry for themselves.
- Don't allow the players to blame others for the loss for more than just a few minutes.
- Make sure that everyone understands if staff members were part of the breakdown that led to the loss (which they often are). These staff members should go unnamed.
- Be a pillar of strength and resolve once you gather your emotions.
- Channel your reaction to the loss as being upset, disturbed and riled, yet under complete control of your faculties (as opposed to allowing yourself to being perceived as "philosophical" towards the situation).

How you handle yourself personally in this traumatic situation can help establish you as a true leader. In this regard, your collective actions should reflect the following factors:

- Don't whine.
- Don't say "why me."
- Don't expect sympathy.
- Don't keep accepting condolences.
- Don't blame the officials.
- Don't lock out the media (although you should allow everyone time to regain their composure before meeting them).
- Don't blame the team.

If the player who was obviously responsible for the team's loss couldn't handle the pressure (i.e., he cracked under the strain and failed to do his job) or completely lost his sense of discipline, you should consider sending a strong message to the squad by releasing that player immediately if he is otherwise replaceable. Such an act on your part establishes the fact that you have standards and high expectations of everyone.

Furthermore, it also makes a statement that you will not tolerate a stupid, gutless performance. Such a judgment on your part should not be reached as the result of a single error or mistake by a player, but rather on your objective, considered determination that the offending player will, in all likelihood, continue to fail to meet your competitive standards. Although you might be wrong in a particular instance, you should not accept a substandard level of competitive poise.

If the player is released, no need exists for any public (or even private) revelation of why you took such an action. Everyone will know. Although releasing such a player is somewhat ruthless, it does demonstrate the indisputable reality that when all but a few players make the extreme sacrifice, those who won't, don't or aren't up to it are expendable.

Road Games

One of the primary hallmarks of a good team is that it is able to play well on the road. Among the steps that you can take to help your team to be better prepared to win on the road are the following:

- Make sure that your players understand that a road trip is a business trip and that their focus and attention should reflect that fact.

- Prepare your players to deal with the unexpected distractions of playing on the road (e.g. late planes and buses, poor hotel food, uncomfortable beds, being away from your family, the change in game-day routine, etc.).

- Remove as many difficulties and distractions attendant to playing a road game as you can. Keep in mind, however, that your players must take it upon themselves to handle road games in a professional manner.

- Get your players to feed on the hostile environment in which the road game will be played (i.e., they should thrive on the negative energy and combative atmosphere they will encounter in cities like New York, Philadelphia, Buffalo, Oakland, and Chicago).

- Do everything possible to prepare your players to handle the environmental conditions they will face on the road (e.g., the altitude in Denver, the heat in Phoenix, the winter cold in outdoor stadiums, etc.). The one type of stadium-related distractions that you can at least partially prepare for is the noise that you will often encounter in most of the dome stadiums. For example, the use of a noise (crowd) simulator during practice can help your players and your staff develop the ability to focus through such a distraction.

Nothing in life just happens. It isn't enough to believe in something; you have to have the stamina to meet obstacles and overcome them, to struggle.

Golda Meir
Prime Minister of Israel
1969-74
from *My Life*

Games When Key Personnel Are Injured

Although injuries are an inevitable part of the game, a team must be prepared to play games when key players are injured. Among the actions that you can take to help your team deal with this situation are the following:

• Do everything feasible to enable your players to deal effectively with the emotional trauma resulting from losing a key player because of an injury.

• Do not let your players succumb to the impulse to panic when key players are lost to injuries.

• Provide extra support to those players who are expected to raise their level of play and pick up the mantle of leadership to fill any void created by the loss of key players who suffer injuries.

• Make each non-starting player understand the importance of his role as a backup player and the urgency that will exist if (and when) he is pressed into duty.

• Make sure that your players understand that the team's expectations for success will not change (i.e., be lowered) simply because one or more key players are lost to injuries.

Preseason Games

Preseason games usually involve a set of priorities that normally do not exist in regular season games. Evaluating players, trying out new schemes and systems, getting players in game-condition, and avoiding injuries are among the primary objectives which are frequently attributed to preseason games.

Not surprisingly, it is critical that coaches recognize the importance of the preseason and plan accordingly. Among the steps that you can take to ensure that your team's preseason period is productive and the factors that you should consider when developing plans for the preseason are the following:

• Establish a prioritized list of what objectives you expect to accomplish in each preseason game and collectively over the course of the four (or five) preseason games. Keep in mind that because of the nature of football games, it is difficult (at best) to precisely anticipate what will happen.

As a consequence, all of your goals may not be met in each game. If for any reason they're not, you must be prepared to adjust your plans for ensuing preseason games to meet the team's needs as appropriate. Because so much must be accomplished in the preseason, the team should closely adhere to all plans and schedules as much as possible.

• Play an instrumental role in ensuring that your staff holds to "game commitments." Keep in mind the potential environment in which preseason games are conducted. For example, in the heat of competition, the natural instinct of everyone involved is to try to win—win at all costs. In particular, coordinators can get so "into the game" that all that matters to them is "stopping people" or "moving the ball."

Subsequently, position coaches may want to substitute as planned, only to be turned down by the coordinator. In another situation, the special teams coach may hesitate in substituting because each kicking situation seems critical. As a consequence, members of your staff may find themselves postponing called for substitutions or disregarding the game plan in order to have the best chance of winning.

If left unchecked, everything is postponed until the "second half," or the "next game." Such a situation illustrates why the head coach must make everyone understand what he expects to be accomplished in each preseason game. You must never let yourself forget that egos are involved. No one likes losing; even preseason losses are tough to swallow.

- Get as complete a look as possible at those individuals who are competing for a spot on the team. Try to assess their ability to perform as many requisite skills and techniques as feasible. Try to evaluate them in individual match-ups with other athletes who are at the same comparable level of development.

  Keep in mind that it's not the amount of playing time that's so important; it's the quality of performance during the time spent playing. For example, a wide receiver can play a full thirty minutes without having a ball thrown to him. By the same token, a defensive lineman may not have an opportunity for an actual pass-rush situation, yet play almost an entire half.

  Accordingly, it may be up to the coaching staff to orchestrate specific "calls" to create a situation that provides a player with an opportunity to demonstrate his ability to perform particular skills or techniques. For example, even if your team's defensive signal caller does not feel that a situation warrants a "blitz" call, if you want to see an outside linebacker rush the passer, such a call must be made.

- Make sure that your younger players gain experience. Players who have been in back-up roles need "game exposure." These players must "hone" their skills because they have seen relatively little playing time during the regular season. The back-up quarterback is an excellent example of such a player. As a rule of thumb, these back-up players should see action relatively early in the game.

- Exert every effort to minimize the chances that one of your players will be injured—particularly the team's starters. Although no absolute method of protecting players from injury exists, thorough planning can play a significant role in this regard. For example, when the starters are in the game, plays with a relatively high risk of injury should not be called. In addition, player fatigue levels can be controlled.

  Keep in mind that the length of time a player is actually on the field has a greater impact on his fatigue levels than does the number of quarters he plays. Probably the most compelling measure to control fatigue is to limit the number of plays an individual is on the field.

- Be aware of the fact that your team's substitution pattern can also affect injury rates. For example, having a veteran player reenter a preseason game after he has played his allotted time (or participated in his prescribed number of plays) can be dangerous. While such a situation can't always be avoided, the combination of the general fatigue that results from training camp with sitting on the bench for an extended period of time and cooling off and then being recalled into the game can leave a veteran player (particularly an older one) vulnerable to injury.

Furthermore, because veteran players often gear themselves (psychologically) to play for so many minutes or plays in a preseason game, the player may not exhibit his normal level of intensity when he's reinserted back into the game. All factors considered, anyone who's not "going full speed" is more susceptible to being injured.

- Make sure that when your starting quarterback is in the game, he has the best pass protection unit available. Immeasurable losses of starting quarterbacks frequently occur in the preseason because of such factors as excessive blitzing by the defenses, a breakdown in pass protection, the fact the most teams frequently don't have their entire starting offensive line on the field at any given point in time, the lack of adequate rules to protect quarterbacks in certain situations, etc.

  The serious injuries suffered by Mark Brunell (Jacksonville Jaguars) and Kerry Collins (Carolina Panthers) in 1997 preseason games illustrate two examples of injuries which occurred from not adequately dealing with such factors. Collins had his jaw broken in two places when hit by a blitzing linebacker. Brunell incurred a knee injury when he was hit below the knee (after he had thrown the ball).

  For years the NFL has been trying unsuccessfully to legislate a rule prohibiting hitting a quarterback at knee level or below. One additional step that can be taken in this regard is to reach an agreement with your opponent's coaching staff to limit the level of "hitting" on each others' quarterbacks. Some teams will concur in such a request, while others will not.

- Don't forget that quarterbacks are particularly vulnerable in preseason games. Teams have those players who are fighting to survive the final roster cut who will do anything to make the team, including trying to put the opposing quarterback out of the game. An assault on quarterbacks may come from several sources (e.g., an individual fighting for a starting role, a veteran doing everything possible to keep his job, a rookie or free agent who is trying to make the squad, etc.).

- Make sure that a variety of special teams combinations is used in the game. Without such a commitment, it may be too easy to stick to the special teams units normally used. For example, a team may have a good prospect assigned to its back-up punt unit. While it may be important to see how this player performs in a coverage situation, the head coach may decide that a particular set of circumstances when his team is punting are too critical to risk using this player.

  As a result, not only does the staff never see this player perform in a coverage situation, the player doesn't get the invaluable experience of protecting and covering in a critical point in the game. Your staff must remember that regardless of whether the preseason game is won or lost, the most important factor is to "see" this player in action.

- Plan your play calling even more extensively than you do for a regular reason game. Such an approach should be followed not because you are overly committed to winning the preseason game, but because every play call offers an excellent opportunity to evaluate essential elements of your program (e.g., individual personnel, specific blocking combinations, pass routes, etc.).

  Any variation, adjustment, or new technique should be given a "shake down." All new plays should be tested, put on video for teaching purposes, evaluated, and the results documented.

- Even though they typically don't get too much playing time in preseason games, make sure your starting quarterback and his receivers get a lot of work together (i.e., be able to anticipate each other's actions, moves, routes, etc.) during training camp in 7-on-7 team play.

- Integrate veteran free agents who have joined the team into the line-up to ensure that they have the opportunity to play alongside their new teammates. It is critical that lines of communication between a free agent and his teammates be fully developed in the preseason. The experience gained on the line of scrimmage, as well as exposure to the positive atmosphere which occurs by being in the competitive arena with his new teammates, must be acquired in the preseason.

  The preseason offers an invaluable opportunity to determine how the newly acquired player measures up to your expectations of him. In reality, he may have strengths or shortcomings that you have not anticipated.

- Synchronize your base offense and defense during the preseason. While scrimmaging against other teams and practice can help, nothing can facilitate getting your offensive and defensive schemes in tune like a "game."

  The preseason is a time when your offense gets into rhythm and refines its ability to execute. As the preseason proceeds, your "starters" should play enough (i.e., the first half) to ensure that your offense and defense are ready for the regular season. Play selection is critical for the offense.

- Make sure that your medical staff (athletic trainers and team physicians) is extremely alert for any signs of undue fatigue or undue risk of injury among regular squad members. For example, play should be stopped immediately if any indication exists that a player has pulled a muscle. The point should be stressed that training camp often heightens the fatigue level of players—a situation which increases the possibility of a muscle injury (e.g., pull, strain, etc.) occurring.

- Don't allow your staff to lose valuable opportunities for evaluation and analysis by permitting your coordinators to spend time on developing a particular game plan for a specific preseason opponent. The distraction inherent in such a game plan can cause everyone to lose sight of the primary goals to be achieved during the preseason, including improvement in team execution, team technical enhancement, and, most importantly, the development of personnel.

- Keep in mind that it is the primary responsibility of the head coach to closely manage the game and assure that all plans are implemented. Toward that end, you should make sure that your assistant coaches make all substitutions as planned, regardless of the situation, unless you dictate a change in plans.

You should also make sure that the specific plays which your staff has decided should be run for particular players are actually called. In addition, you should limit your first units to a twenty-play maximum during a game. Individual players should be inserted into the game for specific reasons (e.g., a running back selected in the draft could be sent into the game to run a specific play or a series of plays).

- Consider using alternative criteria for deciding how much playing time an athlete gets, including:

  — Player competes until he has completed what the staff has planned for him.

  — A player or a unit takes part in a specific number of plays.

  — A unit completes a preplanned series of plays (e.g., the offensive line performs all twenty scripted plays).

  — A unit takes part in a predetermined number of plays regardless of the situation.

  — The units play by quarters. Although this method is the simplest approach, it does not offer a likely means for everything planned to be accomplished.

  — The units alternate playing time. For example, the first team offense plays the first and third quarters, while the offensive back-ups play the second and fourth quarters. Such an approach will force the first unit to stay in the game (physically and mentally), be briefed at half-time, warm-up, and be prepared to return and execute. While this method may offer certain benefits, it does heighten the risk of injury.

  — Different combinations can be utilized. For example, the first defensive line can play with the second team linebackers, etc. This approach can offer several benefits to the coach, including that unanticipated shortcomings and strengths of specific players can be revealed, one group or the other may face additional pressure which may cause them to rise up to meet new challenges, it can serve as an excellent evaluation tool, etc.

    One of the best combinations that can be employed is inserting a back up player into the regular lineup to get experience. Such a move allows that player to be ready in case he's called upon instead of you being forced to juggle your lineup if someone is injured.

  — Individual players can be interjected into the game who have an opportunity to "produce" with a solid supporting cast. These athletes are individuals who may play an important role with the team in the future.

  — Solid, durable "camp" players can be used to fill in during preseason. Such an approach can offer specific advantages to the team because these players can serve as capable replacements for starters or regular squad members who have been held out for one reason or another. While "camp" players typically love to play, they normally have relatively little chance of making the team. Accordingly, these individuals are often signed to serve just as practice players and to play in preseason games as needed.

— No individual should be played without a specific reason. If that player suffers a real or a "phantom" injury, he could take the team to litigation.

- Make sure that you take enough time to thoroughly plan for each preseason game. The tendency is to slack-off on planning. With the heavy schedule imposed in training camp, a preseason game offers some relief from the 16-hour days the staff usually faces during the regular season.

  To ensure that adequate planning occurs, a basic format for the game plan for the preseason game should be developed that includes a comprehensive outline of each element to be addressed. At that point, a step-by-step plan should be formalized. A philosophy that focuses on the objectives to be accomplished during the preseason games should be established and adhered to while finalizing the game plan. The staff should hold a series of four one-hour meetings to discuss and review the game plan in the three days preceding the game and the day of the game.

- Hold two mock games in training camp, each lasting approximately 45 minutes. These games should be played in shorts without contact. Officials should be used to run the game (e.g., clock, chains, etc.). All factors considered, the officials involved in these sessions tend to be grateful for the opportunity to work on their "full team officiating mechanics."

  Game-day procedures should be established and refined during these sessions (e.g., substitutions, play calling, bench procedures, etc.). The offense goes against the defense, with the officials whistling the ball dead after each play (gain). The officials should be instructed to make (fictitious) calls that incur penalties.

  Appropriate substitutions should be made. "Shock" substitutions can also be made to keep everyone alert. Special teams are also employed. The only element of the game that is not utilized is an opposing special team. Return men are used when coverage teams are employed. A punter or a kicker is used when the return teams are deployed. The head coach should orchestrate the game, making sure that every situation comes up. Every form of down-and-distance should occur during these mock games.

  You should signal the referee what situation you want. Every possible offensive combination of personnel can be utilized. The defensive coaches can counter the offense with their own personnel combinations. At the discretion of the coaching staff, both units can encounter a variety of game circumstances, including short yardage, goal line, long yardage, red zone, backed up, nickel, and prevent situations. These mock games offer the team a meaningful "shake down" test of its game management organization to get the season started.

- Prohibit hazing in training camp. Hazing serves no positive purpose. The San Francisco 49ers, for example, have never encouraged or allowed hazing.

- Rest the older players the week of the last preseason game.

- Keep the preseason games in perspective—particularly the last scheduled one. While instances may occur when it becomes important (for whatever reason) to win a preseason game, it certainly must not be the final preseason game, with League play beginning the next week. The playing time of your starters should be limited.

  On occasion, a more complete game plan may be necessary. While full, regular season-like participation may be appropriate in your opinion, the temptation to open your offense up and show "everything" must be avoided. Keep in mind that in the history of the NFL, a few teams have lost every preseason game, yet have gone on to have outstanding regular seasons. There should be some point in the preseason (typically the third game) when your starting units are in sync and are functioning smoothly. From a standpoint of team development, this point is the critical stage of the training camp (i.e., preseason) cycle.

PART V

THE
BUSINESS

CHAPTER 17

WORKING WITH THE MEDIA

"The press, in effect, has to decide what is fair and what is not. It has to discipline itself. I see both sides of the issue, but I do not believe that the line between the two is nearly as fuzzy as some people suggest."

—Arthur Ashe
Tennis Legend
Days of Grace

Finding the winning edge...

On occasion, the relationship between a high-profile executive and the media not only appears to be somewhat hostile, but in fact is adversarial. Nevertheless, it is critical that the executive in charge conduct all dealings with the media in a professional and responsible manner. By developing a rapport with members of the media and respecting their roles as professionals, you are able to work to create a reservoir of respect that can earn you a measure of understanding during tough times and that may even assist you in getting through a crisis situation. Moreover, you will be able to establish a forum where you can enhance the likelihood that "your side of the story" will be heard in both good times and bad times. The key point to remember is to never mislead, fabricate or be coy with the media.

—Bill Walsh
Personal Interview
July 11, 1997

Over the years, I have had numerous opportunities to work with the media. In 1982, I had a particularly impressionable experience involving the media. It all started the year earlier when San Francisco became one of the surprising teams of the 1981 season. The team changed the course of its history with a shocking 45-14 victory over the Dallas Cowboys at Candlestick Park. The score might have been even higher if we had continued to utilize our passing attack. The year before, we had been defeated 59-17 in Dallas. At that time, one of the features of Monday Night Football was highlights of the previous weeks game. San Francisco had never been in a Monday night highlight, even as a losing team. So the next week, the entire 49ers staff stopped its work to watch the highlights and see how the team's destruction of Dallas would be framed. To our surprise, the game was not even mentioned. We learned that Dallas was to be the featured team on the next Monday night's broadcast, and therefore, to ensure that they would be a real attraction, their loss to San Francisco was not mentioned.

During my press conference on Tuesday, being as impetuous and foolish as I was in exalting my victory, I was asked about my team not being featured on the highlights. I responded with an intelligent, thoughtful tirade against network "elitists" who put promoting a game over providing the public with highlights. The media asked more questions and I gave more answers. The course of action was honest and direct, but definitely not in my professional best interest. The only purpose it served was stirring up the people at ABC.

The 49ers went on to win the Super Bowl that year, and I become a somewhat notable football personality. In March of 1982, I met Howard Cosell for the first time at a large cocktail party gathering. Howard was at the height of his career, more demonstrative and vocal than any other sports broadcaster. Some people appreciated him and some didn't, but they all knew of him. Assuming I would be well-received, I stepped through the crowd to introduce myself. The hundreds of people looking on were as stunned as I was by Howard's prolonged, vitriolic attack on me. He compared me to a variety of villains depicted throughout history. "Who are you, sir, to confront someone like me or the people I represent? You are nobody. You are nothing."

I was unable to offer a civilized response. I retreated into the crowd, embarrassed for myself and also for Howard. Everyone had stopped and turned to watch the confrontation. I had learned a valuable lesson. I allowed a few days to pass and wrote a long, thoughtful letter to Howard explaining my position and stating that I did not hold him responsible, but rather the management and production staffs.

Within a few days, I received an eloquent, conciliatory letter from Howard, in which he spoke warmly about me and congratulated San Francisco on its great achievement. I wrote back, thanking him for his letter. At Howard's invitation, I met him for dinner at one of San Francisco's finest restaurants on the Saturday prior to our first Monday night game in 1982. I was unable to match Howard martini for martini, but we had a marvelous dinner and great conversation. From that point on, Howard championed me and I spoke of him with reverence and respect. I wrote him a long personal letter shortly before his death addressing his greatness and achievements. Following his death, I received a long reply from his daughter.

In 1981, I demonstrated my immaturity and lack of experience by allowing my impetuousness and the euphoria of being successful to lead to the arrogance which caused me to "take on the network." My initial meeting with Howard Cosell gave me an insight into the importance of not making enemies. In this case, I was able to undo the damage by conceding the error on my part that had led Howard to make an inaccurate judgment.

Of all the factors with which a head coach must be concerned, perhaps none is more demanding and obtrusive than having to deal with the media. Many of the difficulties attendant to dealing with the media can be attributed to the multidimensional nature of the media.

Although "the media" is a term which is frequently used in a singular sense, as if it were really a person or a particular medium, that's not the case. Rather, "the media" is a descriptive designation which collectively represents a wide variety of medium venues and personalities.

The term "media," for example, includes two broad groups of medium types which are categorized according to how the information is disseminated—print media (e.g., newspapers, magazines, etc.) versus electronic-based media (e.g., radio, television, the internet, etc.). The media can be further classified into various geographical levels according to what audience a particular medium is attempting to serve (e.g., local, national, or international). Such a classification can become a problem when, at any given time, the head coach finds himself interacting with one specific media type from three different areas—for example, newspaper reporters.

The kinds of individuals who work in the different types and levels of media also vary. Over time, the head coach will be exposed to a diverse array of personnel, ranging from thoughtful, serious professional journalists to individuals who prefer to subordinate content and ethics for tabloid-sized sound bites designed to entertain or inflame their audiences regardless of the consequences.

CONFLICTING PRIORITIES

Without question, one of the most difficult aspects of dealing with the media is the fact that each of the various types of media tends to have its own distinct set of needs and priorities. In turn, the needs and priorities of one type of medium not only may be different from those of the head coach, but also may conflict with those of other types of media.

The local beat writer, for example, has a decidedly different job and perspective than does the local columnist. As an individual with whom you interact on a continual basis, the local beat writer must rely on a certain familiarity with you and your players in order to do his job.

A columnist, on the other hand, may write something about you periodically without having ever talked with you once the entire season. In reality, some columnists can be the most frustrating to deal with because they feel that their position gives them a certain level of autonomy. Accordingly, under the guise of "personal opinion," they use whatever leeway is necessary to "mold" their information to fit the point they want to make. Simply stated, they may not bother to let the facts get in the way of what they perceive as a good story.

It is interesting to note that often these two specific groups of writers, even though they may write for the same paper, don't always see the same event through the same viewpoint. One experienced beat writer once told me:

> The columnists write checks we beat writers can't cash. They may write a story based on speculation or their opinion. My editor then gets on me about it because I don't have anything on this particular story. Although the columnist's "speculation or opinion" is wrong, I'm caught chasing down a story that doesn't exist—one I didn't even initiate in the first place. Concurrently, the columnist simply moves on to his next speculative venture.

Complicating the potential for confusion and conflict even further is the fact that both of these local types of writers may have distinctly different priorities and viewpoints than their national counterpart.

The radio and television media has yet another set of perspectives compared to those of the "pencil press." For example, the nature of the electronic media requires a very different type of response from the head coach who is asked to answer a particular question. A response that would otherwise be comprehensive and well thought out if it were for the written media will not be appropriate for the 30-second sound bite environment in which television and radio operate.

In reality, any listing of the possible areas of conflict in priorities between (and within) the various types of the media would be virtually endless. The point you must constantly keep in mind when dealing with the media is that these conflicts exist and that your media-related actions should be conducted accordingly. Fortunately, you can undertake specific steps to enhance the likelihood that your experiences with the media will be positive, rather than counterproductive.

BE PREPARED

No single step you take will serve you better than to be prepared. In both press and broadcast interviews, you need to know what you want to say and use whatever questions you are asked to say it. Such a mandate requires ongoing planning on your part.

You should not assume that you can match "wits" with the media—particularly print reporters. You should not assume that your intellect will match theirs in a free-for-all session of questioning. They have had professional training and experience in how to ask probing and penetrating questions concerning your thoughts on specific matters and issues. As such you need to be prepared. Media preparation can be correlated somewhat to developing an effective game plan (refer to Chapter 10). You need both a defensive and an offensive game plan.

Your defensive game plan should come first. You should anticipate what questions you may be asked. Rest assured, if there is one question you dread being asked, that question will be forthcoming. Fortunately, anticipating an interviewer's questions beforehand doesn't require a degree in advanced insight—just some foresight and thoughtful deliberation on your part.

Once you have identified what questions may be asked, you should decide beforehand how you will answer each query. Depending on the relative importance of each question in your mind, you should delineate which salient points you wish to make when responding to a particular request for information.

Once your defensive game plan has been defined, you should then formulate an offensive game plan. An offensive game plan involves taking steps to ensure that whatever points you want to make during an interview are, in fact, made. You should keep in mind that an interview is essentially a conversation, as opposed to a media-version of the Spanish Inquisition. During an interview, you must be prepared to appropriately take the (offensive) initiative whenever the opportunity arises.

The primary difference between the two approaches is fairly obvious. Whereas defense is essentially response-oriented, offense proactively attempts to dictate the dissemination of specific information. Once you come to the devastating realization that a reporter's words can be used to deceive, as well as reveal, you'll be grateful to have both game plans at your disposal.

Similar to football, going from offense to defense during an interview requires an exchange. In the conversational dynamics of an interview situation, this exchange occurs when you bridge a question from an interviewer and seize the initiative (i.e., offense). In other words, a bridge gets you from where you are in a discussion to where you want to be. Effective bridging requires a non-contrived connecting phrase, clause, or sentence that serves as a preface to the point you really want to address.

For example, in response to a question about why your team played so poorly, you might answer with either "let me put that matter in a slightly different perspective" or "at this point, it may be more beneficial to consider the larger issue." You would then be able to "bridge" to the point you want to address without appearing to be too evasive. Two men who were unequalled in their capacity to make statements in their team's best interests while responding to almost unrelated questions were Al Davis and Carmen Policy.

Put your own ego aside. Don't be concerned with people writing about what a great coach you are. Make the team the focus. If the team wins, you have done your job. I did not need any more satisfaction than that.

Bud Grant
Hall-of-Fame Football Coach
Minnesota Vikings
from *Game Plans for Success*

PRESS CONFERENCE

Although the head coach may deal with the media in a variety of situations, there are two major media-related events in which he (by the nature of his job) must participate—press conferences and broadcast interviews. Press conferences (i.e., a meeting of the press en masse) can be stressful experiences, depending upon the circumstances. Usually, they involve an opening statement by the head coach, followed by a question-and-answer session.

More often than not, the question-and-answer period is the primary focal point of a press conference. If you want to maximize the benefits of holding a press conference, while concurrently minimizing any detrimental side-effects, you should consider the following guidelines:

- Start the press conference on time. Limit any grace period for waiting for late arrivals by members of the *third estate* to ten minutes or less. A failure to be punctual is an affront to those who are.

- Provide a copy of the complete text of your prepared remarks if such a service is both appropriate and expected in a particular situation.

- Find ways to respond in your answer—regardless of how impertinent the questions may seem—to make the points you want to make (i.e., use the bridging technique). Ira Miller, an award-winning NFL sports writer for the *San Francisco Chronicle*, sometimes asked me a question, which was, in fact, a statement that could not be answered. If you encounter such a "dreaded question," you should dissect the statement and answer each point as if it were a distinct question.

- Have the individual who asked the question repeat the question if necessary. Such a step can accomplish at least two things—help clarify the question in your mind and give you time to consider your answer.

- Maintain steady eye contact with each person as that individual asks a question. If a question is relatively friendly or easy, continue eye contact with the individual throughout your response. That action may prompt a follow-up query from the same person (who has already been identified as being user-friendly from your perspective).

   By the same token, if you receive an unfriendly or even hostile question, you should look to the other side of the meeting room as you complete your answer. Often, this technique on your part will lead to two things—both positive. One, it prevents you from noticing that your previous antagonist wants to ask another question. Second, it may prompt a question from someone more friendly to your point of view.

- Ask yourself those questions which (for whatever reason) no one else has bothered to ask but you feel need to be answered. For example, after responding to a question from the audience, and before you acknowledge someone else, you might say: "One of the basic questions I'm certain you are concerned about is. . ." and then go about answering it before continuing.

BROADCAST INTERVIEW

The second primary type of media event in which the head coach is often asked to participate is the broadcast interview. The nuances of a broadcast interview vary somewhat according to whether the interview is being conducted on radio or television.

Unlike radio, where what you say and how you say it are preeminent factors, television often places an inordinate amount of emphasis on style over substance. In other words, to a point, it is as equally (if not more so) as important to look good while you're saying something as it is to say the right thing. On television, appearances often count for more than reality.

Among the points you should consider when participating in a broadcast interview are the following:

- Be yourself. If you put on airs or act in an unnatural way (for you), your audience will notice—particularly on television.

- Back up your statements with relevant, crisp examples whenever possible.

- Don't lose control of the interview. Don't let the interviewer manipulate you into surrendering your dignity or your autonomy as a guest on the broadcast.

- Don't forget that while a broadcast interview is structured, it doesn't have legal ground rules. In other words, you can decide what questioning will be too out-of-bounds for you to answer. Obviously, misleading, irrelevant, or immaterial questions should not go unchallenged by you.

- Keep in mind that you can stray somewhat from the line of questioning. If you feel it is appropriate, you can change the subject of the question and direct your remarks to something in which the audience has an interest in your opinion.

BEING SMART

While you unfortunately don't have the power to control all of the aspects of your dealings with the media, you certainly have control over your own actions. The more appropriate your actions, the less likely your media dealings will be adverse to your needs and expectations. Among the guidelines you should consider are the following:

- Set and adhere to specific time constraints in personal interviews (e.g., 5-10-15 minutes, etc.). Let the media know why your interview will have a time limit. For example, you have another appointment, a staff meeting, etc.

- Have an understanding of the subject which will be covered in one-on-one interviews. Whenever necessary, bring the dialogue between you and the interviewer back into focus.

- Keep in mind that it never pays to be confrontational. Be calm. Soften hard questions with your responses. Control your emotions—the interviewer may know how to trigger them.

- Don't forget that while honest, direct responses are important, you are not required to provide distinct personal feelings, strategies or contingencies.

- Have specific information at hand or available. Back up assertions with facts, statistics, and even relevant personal experiences. Be careful of making careless observations using unsubstantiated numbers or names.

- Change or shift the subject if you are asked a provocative question (i.e., answering another question is one possible step you can take).

- Don't forget that humor can be reported as sober, serious remarks. Any humor you use should be far afield of serious exchange. While light, engaging humor can naturally soften intense, critical exchanges, its use can be a double-edged sword.

- Don't expound, as a general rule, on a particular subject outside a straight-forward response. Pontificating often results in overstatement and careless observations. Keep in mind that the media will seldom forget or overlook such comments.

- Don't repeat a negative question. If you do, it then can be (mistakenly) reported as having been initiated by you. It can also serve as an admission of something to which you don't want to be associated.

- Carefully consider the medium when pressed for comments on volatile social or political views. For example, you could leave yourself very vulnerable if you attempt to comment on the lack of progress on a particular social issue in the NFL in a 30-second sound bite. Be careful of observing or remarking on significant issues outside the venue of your team.

- Don't expect members of the media to understand or appreciate the emotional or mental state of mind you may be in after a game. Because you may be emotionally exhausted, your responses may not seem rational. In reality, they may not be. You should not expect the collective media to be sympathetic.

- Don't be afraid to question a reporter's story if you feel the story is inaccurate. Such questioning should occur only after you have personally read the piece—not as the result of second-hand information. In your interaction with the reporter, you should be direct, but not confrontational. Finally, you should not assume the reporter intentionally made a mistake or had a specific agenda. The inaccuracy may have been just that—a mistake.

- Never assume the reporter is either knowledgeable or knows nothing about the subject the individual is writing about. For example, some men mistakenly believe that women don't know the basic rudiments of football. In fact, many female sports writers have an extensive football knowledge.

- Avoid the loaded statement. In these times of shock journalism, some journalists will deliberately insert an inflammatory adverb into a question that will turn the question into two issues. For example, the word "deservedly" in the statement, "Given the *deservedly* low regard in which (insert the name of an NFL city) is held, why would anyone want to coach there?" Do you focus on the word "deservedly," address the primary question, or bridge to your own point?

The key is to defuse the insult clearly and go on to your next point in such a determined manner that further attention is not given to the journalist's disparaging remark. You can respond to the statement in a parallel way, but not directly.

- Keep in mind that you're allowed to change your views and opinions. Don't be trapped by someone who recalls that twenty years ago you stated a differing point of view. While consistency is certainly admirable in most instances, your views don't have to be irrevocably transcribed into the permanent record after you first publicly uttered them.

  You're allowed to change your mind, grow, become aware of additional information, etc. The flexibility you exhibit in changing your views can be perceived as a demonstration of the fact that you've become more mature and experienced. As such, it can be seen as a virtue of sound leadership.

- Don't attack an absent party. Most people are offended by someone who disparages an individual who is not present to defend himself. If you are presented with a question asking you about a derogatory comment someone allegedly made about you or your program, simply defer your answer until you have seen the exact quote, context and all, or you have spoken to that person about the remarks.

- Be positive. Demonstrate energy and enthusiasm. It is human nature to prefer someone who is bullish (optimistic) rather than bearish (pessimistic). Keep in mind that things can be better is the flip side of things could get worse.

- Know your stuff. Giving an incorrect response—no matter how insignificant the issue—can undermine your credibility. Not knowing why your coordinators made particular decisions or what they were actually attempting to do strategy-wise can result in direct contradiction if you attempt to respond to questions about these issues.

- Keep in mind that the term "on the record" means different things to different people. As a general rule, don't ever forget that if you know something you don't want to see in newspapers, don't talk about it. "Off-the-record" usually means you won't see your comments for a week. "Strictly off-the-record," on the other hand, involves two weeks, while "strictly confidential" may mean that your remarks won't show up for a month or two.

- Make your comments relatively easy to understand. If you want to make a point about a shovel, don't ramble on about a portable, manually operated earth relocator. While football can involve incredibly complex and technical issues, it's far more meaningful to discuss it in easy-to-understand terms.

- Keep your ego in check. An ego that is so inflated that you eventually become "consumed" by your own notoriety will bring on unwanted episodes of humiliation.

- Learn to live with the fact that as the head coach, you will sometimes be the brunt of remarks about you professionally and personally that can be stupid, cruel, inane, inaccurate, and off-the-wall. Typically, they will come from inexperienced radio or television color commentators who have virtually no understanding of the stress that you're under or what it takes to deal with the myriad of problems you face.

You must learn to live with the situation. It's an unfortunate fact that some of the commentators currently analyzing football games on radio and television lack the insight and the competence to do so in a professional manner. Perhaps, worst of all are those radio and sports talk show hosts whose style often appears to involve seeing just how bizarre and irreverent they can get away with being on the air. As a coach, it is critical that you learn to coexist with such madness.

- Keep in mind that the media may recklessly criticize and ridicule you or your decisions. They may completely change their position in 48 hours. As such, you must not allow your emotions to rise and fall with the media's level of hysteria.

  By the same token, you must not let yourself be affected if the crowd reacts in a negative manner during the game. It is only natural when your team is performing poorly that the crowd will be disappointed and frustrated. Some of that frustration may be manifested vocally (i.e., boos, catcalls, derisive comments, etc.). You must maintain your poise and focus.

PREPARING FOR THE INEVITABLE

No matter what your record; no matter how well chronicled your accomplishments; no matter how much everyone (the media, fans, etc.) seems to like you; at some point, as the head coach, you will be put "on the bubble" and a "Death Watch" for your firing will begin. The cycle begins and ends hundreds of times around the country each year.

Literally thousands of men and women have experienced it. It is not unique to any coach, or any sport, although it certainly feels that way if you are the one going through it. Because it is an inherent feature of the job, coaches must come to grips with this aspect of the profession. Accordingly, you should understand this inevitable reality like any other area of your contingency planning for life.

The basis for the "Death Watch" is quite simple: losing games. Organizations with a history of winning and having high expectations each season may not be able to tolerate anything short of winning at least one playoff game. It truly doesn't matter that logical and legitimate factors have contributed to the team not living up to its expectations (e.g., injuries, inexperience, individual poor performances, etc.). While poor or inconsistent play on the part of the quarterback position may be at the center of the problem (as it often is), you should not expect the media or fans to care. The final result is the only barometer they are capable of understanding.

The media, sensing the coach is struggling, will quite naturally begin the process of building a case based on the relatively poor results the coach's team achieved on the field. The coach who has maintained a positive working relationship with the press typically will be given a little more time and may even be treated with a little more dignity. Nevertheless, the process will continue to evolve.

Most often, a single, prominent columnist will set this death watch cycle into motion. Blending fact with conjecture, this columnist typically begins the process slowly. Eventually, a collective media fascination occurs with this often-repeated scenario.

As others in the media begin to take a position attendant to various arguments for either disavowing or advancing the process, some may be supportive if only to create an environment for open debate and more stories. Most of the media will carefully straddle the issue until a more definitive outcome can be determined. Then, these same fence straddlers will simply stand on their conviction that they had called it right from the beginning regardless of which way it turns out.

Often, the very attributes the media hailed the coach for, when things were going well, are the very same ones they will use to focus on as the reason for his downfall. For example, Don Coryell established the San Diego Chargers with one of the most feared offensive arsenals ever to take the field.

His easy manner with the players and reputation as a "players coach" was often acclaimed as the reason for the Chargers' on-the-field success. Subsequently, however, when factors contributed to a lessening of San Diego's winning ways, the media was quick to label the same coaching style as being too soft and lacking authority.

As the death watch cycle begins to take shape, the head coach can make a number of all too common mistakes (all of which should be avoided), including:

- Engaging in an ongoing ridicule of the team. Comments such as: "They don't understand what it takes"; "They just haven't learned how to win"; etc. never help.

- Trying to reach and influence the players through the media. Comments such as: "I believe in these men"; "They're a great bunch of guys"; "Believe me they're playing their hearts out"; while well-intended are inherently hollow.

- Offering blind support for an embattled player. Comments such as: "I believe in him"; "We're going to make this work"; "He is human"; are usually transparent and become redundant.

- Asking the press and public for more time by promising things will get better next year. If such comments are repeatedly made, they can be perceived as a "plea." Subsequently, the media may view them as a "weakness" on your part.

- Unknowingly displaying out-of-control emotions. All factors considered, neither the press nor the public will respond well to such a display. In fact, most see it as a sign of weakness. While being animated is fine and being upset (to a point) is acceptable, emotions such as rage or melancholy are demeaning. Keeping his temperament within reasonable boundaries is extremely important to the head coach—even in such dire circumstances.

- Socializing excessively with ownership. The head coach can never reverse the process by heavy socializing with ownership. Eventually, the owner will do what has to be done. Although it may be difficult, the owner will make changes in the head coaching position if they are necessary. The head coach should remember that most owners will respect professionalism above all else. Head coaches have been known to cultivate and count on this relationship. In reality, it never really helps.

- Insinuating that a coordinator is at fault in an attempt to try and gain some time. Certainly addressing staff shortcomings, as part of an honest evaluation of the staff, has its place. It is highly unprofessional and unethical, however, to use an assistant as an available scapegoat. If you continue to lay blame for lack of success on one of your assistants, even if by inference, the media will view it as an excuse.

- Taking his case to every available public channel. Although a coach may want to use every avenue to "plead his case" to the public, he should avoid all talk show question-and-answer formats. It is relatively well documented that shows of this nature have very small demographics with regard to those who call in to respond.

  Typically, these callers represent a very small percentage of the population. These individuals usually have a set agenda and are less interested in the response than they are in hearing their own criticisms or questions. In addition, it is important to remember that everything a coach says on a talk show is quotable.

The disappointment and dissension began to be focused— undeservedly so—on the head coach, Paul Westhead. The players were in pain. They wanted that pain salved, and they talked themselves into believing he was its source. He wasn't. Our team's problems all came from inside.

> Pat Riley
> Head Basketball Coach
> Miami Heat
> from *The Winner Within*

As the death watch cycle evolves, a number of counterproductive circumstances commonly occur which the head coach should anticipate and should guard against, including:

- Players will be quoted, especially those who are relatively uninformed. Some players will become the self-proclaimed spokesmen for the squad. Although most of these individuals will be sincere and honest, even their well-intended remarks to the press will usually have an adverse impact on the situation. Furthermore, most of these individuals will typically tend to oversimplify the situation (i.e., they insinuate that some of their teammates "aren't going all out").

- The owner may volunteer antagonistic remarks to the press, either carelessly, honestly or vindictively. Whatever the situation, the coach must stay cool. To a point, the emotions the owner feels are understandable. After all, it's the owner's team. It is the owner's money.

  On the other hand, if the lines of communication are open between the head coach and the owner, contentious issues should be discussed privately. Even when the owner tries to do the right thing by "backing the coach 100%," there is often a collective assumption throughout the profession of "that coach is in trouble." In reality, an overstatement of support can appear to be a "death knell." While supportive remarks can be helpful, they should not appear to be too guarded or excessively unrealistic.

- Members of the management team may become sources (usually unnamed) for the media. Obviously, unnamed sources within an organization can play a destructive role. This practice is not uncommon. The coach should discuss the situation on an ongoing basis with members of management, including the personnel staff. Without appearing desperate, the coach should confront those who are exhibiting disloyalty. Honest, direct exchanges with the collective staff will hopefully embarrass and prevent individuals from succumbing to this human frailty.

At the same time, the coach should be careful not to succumb to overt paranoia. Given the circumstances, it would be understandable to comprehend the basis for such a psychological state on your part. In these instances, the traditional one-liner, "Just because you're paranoid, doesn't mean that they are not really after you," certainly has some merit.

During the death watch cycle, it is ill-advised for a coach to read the newspapers or listen to talk shows. If you must read the paper, you should not pore over the newspaper in great detail. All factors considered, it is best to have a member of the administration staff (preferably a member of the public relations department) create a set of newspaper clippings, highlighting those matters the head coach should be aware of or needs to address, including:

- Inaccurate stories. On occasion, the media may want to only meet with part of the team, an action which may allow them to "frame" a story or an opinion.

- Stories that personally attack a player or a member of the staff. Built solely on subjective opinion, these stories are often vindictive.

- Quotes from players or staff members that are inconsistent with and potentially divisive to the overall attitude of the team. In reality, differences in semantics exist which can "distort" the message for some.

You should keep in mind you don't want to "shoot the messenger." This situation is an instance where a good PR director can be extremely helpful to the head coach. By being a source of information and counsel to the head coach, the PR director can help address any situation that may come up.

A responsible PR director will aggressively protect the head coach and confront any gross inaccuracies that will inevitably come up as part of the vast array of materials that are generated in a "death watch" environment. The PR director should permit no inaccuracy to go unchallenged. An excellent example of an outstanding PR director in the NFL is Rodney Knox of the San Francisco 49ers.

Finally, in the stressful period of the death watch cycle, it is critical that the coach maintain a normal exercise routine. The benefits of exercise are immeasurable. Not only does exercise tend to dissipate the chemicals which build up in your body during periods of excessive stress, it also improves your ability to think (i.e., cognitive functions).

If you don't exercise regularly, you are vulnerable to being worn down physically and mentally. In addition, you are more likely to lose control of your emotions at an inopportune time. By enabling you to divert your focus and concentration to other activities (e.g., working out, tennis, jogging, etc.), exercise affords you a break from your stressful circumstances and gives you an opportunity to regroup mentally and physically.

MAKING THE MOST OF THE SITUATION

The relationship you have with the media will depend upon several factors, some of which will be beyond your control. Optimistically, a majority of your dealings with the media will be reasonably positive. As a general rule, most members of the media are men and women who experience disappointments, triumphs, and frustrations, not unlike you. Keep in mind, however, that the nature of their job is somewhat in conflict with yours. Their priorities will not always be the same as your priorities.

As such, at times, you may have an adversarial relationship with them. Hopefully, you won't have to work with reporters who harbor an attitude of "the bigger the coaches are, the harder they fall, and the more rewarding it is to topple them." The point to remember is that you must learn to coexist with the media.

Over the years, a number of NFL coaches have learned this lesson and learned it well. Extremely intelligent and self-confident individuals such as Marv Levy, Mike Shanahan, and Joe Gibbs have forged an excellent working relationship with the media based on honest, straight-to-the-point dealings. The key is to be prepared to deal with the media—whatever relationships or circumstances exist. Louis Pasteur once wrote, "Chance favors the prepared man." As such, don't leave anything to chance when interacting with the media.

CHAPTER 18

FOCUSING ON FINANCIAL MATTERS

"You can never overpay a good player. You can only overpay a bad one. I don't mind paying a good player $200,000. What I mind is paying a $20,000 player $22,000."

—Art Rooney
Hall-of-Fame Football Owner
Pittsburgh Steelers, 1933-87

Finding the winning edge...

Your highly-paid star bombs? Don't let the economics of a bad hire cloud your reasoning. A smart manager worries more about fixing the problem than about disguising it to save face. In sports this may require the very public benching of a celebrity. In business, it may mean turning over some of the key responsibilities of a major player to someone else, possibly someone lower on the totem pole. Not the least of a manager's diplomatic tasks is to make the situation clear to the person taking on the star's responsibilities—covering a larger sales territory, for instance, or assuming the direction of an important R&D project—while the star continues to make more money. Once again, there's no way to pretend that this is fair, but you can pretty safely predict that sooner or later the situation will be resolved, and you'll be able to give credit (and compensation) where it's due.

—Bill Walsh, "How to Manage Super-stars," *Forbes,* June 7, 1993.

The significance of sound financial management cannot be overestimated in any company or corporation. When I joined the San Francisco organization, for example, the 49ers had the lowest season ticket base in the NFL. After the first season, I began working to market season tickets.

We advertised on billboards and in newspapers in an attempt to persuade fans to purchase tickets. We even tied a ribbon to every unused seat in Candlestick Park and held "Pick-A-Seat-Day," complete with games, music and food for the attendees. We worked the entire day and only sold seven tickets. I purchased three more myself so we could get to double digits for the day.

The true bottom line is the quality of your product, not how you package it. From that point on, I spent very little time on promotion, instead focusing my efforts on winning on Sundays. Our 1981 home game versus Dallas was the 49ers' first sellout in many years, and games have been sold out ever since. Having a good product on the field is critical to that type of success, and should be the focal point of everyone's attentions.

Some people would give credit for the 49ers' on-field success to owner Eddie DeBartolo's money. This philosophy may hold a bit of truth, but in fact, the year we won our first Super Bowl (1981), we were not the highest paid team in the NFL. The team's standard of performance must be the point, not money. The organization must take care to spend its money wisely.

Over the years, San Francisco has become one of the highest-paid NFL teams, but there is no true correlation between success on the field and high salaries. Sound financial management is critical to an organization. Appropriate use of funds, the chemistry of the team, standard of performance, efficiency and the team's execution combine to form the essence of success.

Football may be a game, but the NFL is a business. As a result, every head coach must, at some point, deal with the reality of his team's financial state. To expect financial matters to simply work themselves out would be naive at best, and disastrous at worst.

From a head coach's perspective, a team's approach to financial issues tends to give rise to two primary concerns. First, it is critical that the team's available financial resources are allocated in the most effective and efficient manner possible. From a financial perspective, the focal point needs to be to assure that the organization acquires the tools needed to develop a successful program and, ultimately, win championships.

Second, it is essential that current financial decisions do not negatively impact the team's long-range plans. Collectively, financial issues tend to involve at least two distinct areas where the head coach must be involved: dealing with the team's chief financial officer (CFO) and understanding (and responding to) the NFL's salary cap.

Every time I call it a game you call it a business, and every time I call it a business you call it a game.

John Matuszak
Former NFL Player
Oakland Raiders

DEALING WITH THE CFO

The team's CFO is ultimately responsible for all of the team's financial functions, including accounting, data processing, taxes, expenditures and income. The CFO may oversee these functions personally, but in an organization as large as an NFL franchise, it is more likely that the CFO will be assisted by various controllers and treasurers who supervise the business and accounting staff. As a general rule, the financial management staff of a team has three main functions:

1.   Planning for the team's financial needs. This step involves formulating a financial plan, then evaluating the plan after it has been put into action and making changes when necessary. The financial planning process should include establishing objectives (both short-term and long-term), budgeting and identifying sources of funds.

2.   Acquiring sufficient funds at the appropriate times to keep the company moving forward. These funds may come from a variety of sources, classified as positive cash flow, retained earnings or outside financing.

3.   Deciding how and where to spend the funds on hand.

When dealing with your team's chief financial officer, you should remember that you and the CFO may have different short-term concerns, even though your long-term goals may be the same. On one hand, you may be focused primarily on on-the-field matters (e.g., team performance, the development of individual players, injuries, offensive and defensive game plans, the upcoming opponent, etc.). On the other hand, the CFO may (by nature of the position) be concentrating essentially on fiscal issues (e.g., aligning a team's financial priorities with the organization's objectives, securing and managing the necessary resources, etc.).

Despite having different priorities on occasion, the positions of the head coach and the CFO are inextricably connected. The team's performance affects the financial resources available to the CFO, and the organization's finances impact the human resources available to the head coach. When interacting with the CFO, it is important to keep in mind that the CFO has a myriad of responsibilities which must be dealt with on a daily basis, including:

• Calculate and manage numbers continuously.

• Require complete, ongoing, updated knowledge of each contract and its ramifications.

- Stretch formulas to help with what the team needs.

- Work to be fully informed, knowledgeable, and current on the present fiscal formulas and equations utilized across the NFL.

- Understand and study past financial projections for the team's future.

- Acquire a working knowledge of the circumstances facing every other NFL franchise, including their financial officers, their philosophy and their formula for meeting their salary cap requirements.

- Utilize financial and accounting tables as established. Check for accuracy and remain alert for alternative methods to become more efficient.

- Be familiar with league appraisals and various NFL resources.

- Require complete confidentiality from all financial and business staff members. Monitor confidentiality and security continually.

- Know the disposition and allocation of every dollar.

- Calculate and project future revenue sources accurately using available information.

- Be able to access any essential information source regarding financial matters within minutes.

- Work with the head coach to ensure that everything is being done to provide the team with the tools it needs to win.

- Develop a loss scenario for various contingencies if requested by the head coach or upper management (i.e., what is the worst that can happen?).

In the NFL, several unique demands are placed on a CFO. For example, the CFO must be conversant with League projections of resources and know the disposition and allocation of every dollar due to the organization. It is also important for the CFO to be aware of the circumstances facing other NFL teams.

Perhaps the most unique challenge facing the CFO of an NFL franchise is dealing with the budgetary restraints imposed by the NFL salary cap. The implementation of the cap has had a substantial impact on the role of the financial officer. For example, the CFO must have a detailed knowledge of the terms and ramifications of each player's contract and be constantly managing the numbers to work to the team's best advantage. In this regard, the CFO must avoid being unduly influenced by the coaching staff, support personnel, media members and even the team's CEO when exploring various options or the feasibility of different contract alternatives.

UNDERSTANDING THE NFL SALARY CAP

No part of the game is less understood, yet has a greater impact on professional football currently, than the NFL's salary cap. In 1993, the NFL adopted the current system of free agency. In an attempt to implement this new policy and yet maintain the competitive balance within the League, the salary cap was established. The basis of the salary cap was that each team would have to abide by a "budget" for salaries established by League-mandated (and court-approved) guidelines.

The salary cap is another example of the NFL practice of attempting to establish league-wide policies and rules that focus on the concept of "common good." This practice is frequently referred to as the "League Think" principle. The basis of the "League Think" principle was put forth by then-NFL commissioner Pete Rozelle in late 1960. Rozelle advocated that the NFL should sell its collective television rights as a single package and share its broadcast revenues equally among all franchises.

Rozelle surmised that if each franchise were left to fend for itself financially, particularly in regard to television, the ensuing division into rich and poor teams would give a few big market franchises enormous advantages as television revenues grew. Eventually, Rozelle concluded, this division would result in a corresponding imbalance on the field, thereby lessening the League's marketability as a whole.

Thirty-three years later, the advent of player free agency had a major impact on the way that NFL teams did business. Many in management perceived free agency as a quick-fix method for correcting personnel mistakes, while a majority of the players viewed the free agency process as a way to share more in the revenue they generated for their teams. Most owners, however, realized that a mechanism was needed to ensure relative balance (i.e., the "League Think" rule mentality) among the teams in their efforts to acquire free agents. The instrument that was mutually agreed upon by the NFL Players Association and the NFL Management Council was the NFL salary cap. Literally speaking, the cap defined how much an NFL team could spend on salaries.

In its purest theoretical form, the NFL's salary cap has three main elements:

1. Using the defined gross revenues (DGR), made up primarily of ticket sales, TV and radio revenues, the players are paid (via the salary cap) a specific percentage (62-63 percent) of the profits of the DGR; the better the League does the bigger the financial pie to be divided among the players.

2. Establishing a salary cap allows the small-market teams , which cannot generate the same excluded defined gross revenues (EDGR) as the large-market teams, to stay relatively competitive economically. EDGR are those moneys generated by outside sponsorship, stadium suite sales, concession and parking revenues and, to a certain degree, NFL Properties.

3. The cap keeps the more economically viable franchises from stockpiling an excessive number of talented players. Instead, the salary cap increases the likelihood that the talent level will be somewhat available to other teams.

With these elements in mind, each NFL team is then given the latitude to spend its cap dollars the most efficient way it can. The graph below, "Distribution by Position," provides an example of the way a team might allocate its funds by position. Although the funds can be divided in any number of ways, this example is fairly indicative of how a team might allocate its funds in any given year.

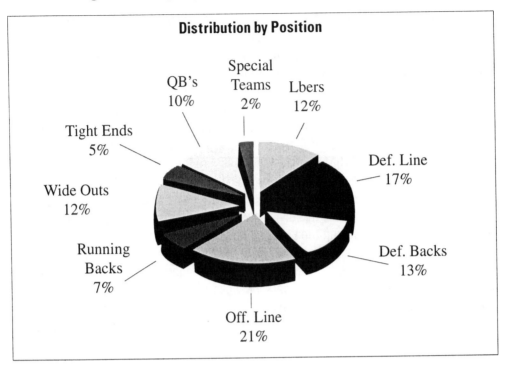

Distribution by Position

- Special Teams 2%
- QB's 10%
- Lbers 12%
- Tight Ends 5%
- Def. Line 17%
- Wide Outs 12%
- Running Backs 7%
- Def. Backs 13%
- Off. Line 21%

Because the salary cap is still in its relative infancy, it is too early to judge its effectiveness. On one hand, many NFL players feel they still have not reaped the total benefits of free agency; while, on the other hand, virtually every NFL team has experienced some form of a bust in its free agent acquisitions.

The fact that both sides have openly criticized the salary cap at one point or another indicates it is apparently doing its job. The reality of the situation is that the salary cap has both positive and negative features. Over time, as teams have more experience with dealing with the cap, a more accurate assessment of its utility can be made.

When practical application branched off from theory, as is usually the case, the EDGR proved to be far more of a factor than was originally anticipated. The ability of a team like the Dallas Cowboys, for example, to generate $30-40 million more in excluded defined revenues than smaller-market teams could in such cities as Buffalo, Minneapolis or Indianapolis has drastic implications for the "League Think" mentality. As a result, the NFL is left with an ever-increasing number of teams threatening to leave their respective cities unless they, too, can be promised increased off-field revenues.

Another area on which the salary cap impacts is making personnel decisions. Teams no longer have the latitude to build their squads regardless of financial factors. As a result, salary-cap decisions often outweigh personnel decisions.

While scouts and coaches may find the players, the NFL's "capologists" make the financial decision to determine the amount of relative risk. As a consequence, one of the primary tasks facing an NFL team in today's environment is to provide a platform to lure the best athletes to their organizations without exceeding the salary ceiling, which is set at a little over $41 million per team for the 1997 season.

The value and notoriety of these "capologists" has increased to the point where their hirings are being listed in the transaction section of the sports pages. At some point in the not so distant future, it may not be too outlandish to imagine that the Indianapolis Colts have traded two linebackers and a wide receiver to Jacksonville for their "capologist" and an accountant to be named later. Not surprisingly, the worth of an extraordinarily competent capologist is considerable. For most NFL teams, the CFO or general manager serves as the capologist.

Not that long ago, a head coach could not have told you what the players on his own team were making. Today, every NFL head coach gets a daily printout of what every player in the league is making. In personnel meetings, to a great extent, the focus has shifted from the abilities of the players to their cap numbers and what the team can afford.

When the head coach tells his offensive line coach to find a guard, one of the first questions that has to be addressed is, "Are we looking for a $1 million guard or a $500,000 guard?" Terms such as "fixed salary," "value investing" and "incremental upgrades" have become a part of the coaching lexicon in the age of the free agency process.

An example of a "capologist's" creativity in financial dealings arising from salary cap considerations is illustrated in the Denver Broncos' restructuring of quarterback John Elway's contract:

- Elway was scheduled to make $4.2 million in salary during 1997. For NFL accounting purposes, his team also had to count $1.1 million from his previous signing bonus. Accordingly, Elway's total 1997 charge against the cap would be $5.3 million.

- Elway will now receive $565,000 in salary during 1997, a $2.26 million signing bonus that will be pro-rated over five years (at $452,000 annually) for cap purposes and a $1.1 million roster bonus in March 1998.

- The team must still count $1.1 million from Elway's previous signing bonus against the 1997 salary cap.

- Elway's new charge against the Broncos' 1997 cap figure is now slightly over $2.1 million, thereby clearing $3.2 million for Denver's 1997 cap total and deferring it into future cap years.

Similar to Elway, many NFL players have shown they are willing to work with their organizations in restructuring their contracts in hopes of surrounding themselves with more talented teammates. In all honesty, such restructuring is not a totally selfless act since a revised contract will usually pay the player the same dollars over time.

Renegotiating a player's contract to make more money available for the cap is a viable but costly adjustment for a team. Typically, a renegotiated contract means that a player will receive the same money, but spread out over a longer period of time.

Renegotiating also involves some risk for the player. Unlike the National Basketball Association and Major League Baseball, very few player contracts in the NFL are guaranteed. As a result, if a player is lured to a team with a big signing bonus up front, or if he is a veteran with a relatively sizable contract, he runs the risk in future years of being cut by that club in the weeks leading up to training camp if the team decides (for whatever reason) that he is not worth his cap now. Releasing a player after June 1 allows clubs to count some of the pro-rated money against the following year's cap, which in theory should always be a little higher.

Accordingly, the time between the 1st of June and the start of training camp is often a period when a number of other veterans are still looking to sign on with teams. Subsequently, some of these veteran players end up signing for substantially less than they would otherwise have received under their previous contracts.

Like the federal government, a natural tendency for some NFL teams is to push up their (cap-related) debt in future years, while dealing with the more immediate concern of clearing room for the salary cap this year. Some clubs take this approach in anticipation of increased revenues (via an enhanced network television contract) and, subsequently, a larger cap in the future. Given that the NFL's television contract expires after the 1997 season, most NFL owners anticipate that bidding for the new rights could be quite lucrative.

One of the by-products of the cap is the need for players to realistically assess their value in the open market, particularly second-tier athletes. This assessment has proven to be very costly for some players, especially for older veterans and injured players. For every example of a player profiting by venturing into the open market because of the "insulting initial offer" from his original club, there seems to be another who ends up playing for considerably less than what his former club was willing to pay.

One aspect of the cap that is a major concern for all parties is the disproportionate amount of funds being committed to a smaller and smaller group of

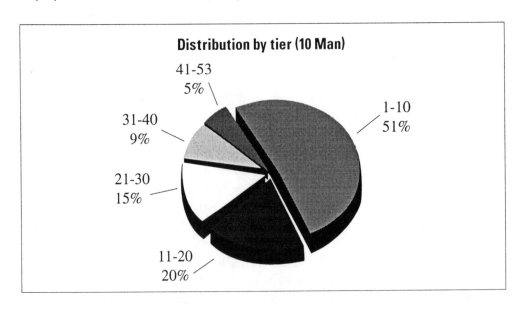

Distribution by tier (10 Man)

41-53
5%

31-40
9%

21-30
15%

11-20
20%

1-10
51%

players. In 1996, for example, NFL teams spent more than half their money on ten players. The "Distribution by Tier (10-Man)" graph illustrates the average distribution of cap money on a typical NFL team. If the players are tiered in ten-man groups, based on top to bottom salaries, this graph illustrates an example of an NFL team where the top ten players account for 51 percent of the total cap allotment of $41 million.

Although these top players represent a high percentage of the total cap expenditure, the "Players Bracketing by Salary" graph shows they make up, on average, about 20 to 25 percent of the total roster. The bulk of the players on this particular team are making less than $500,000 a year. One of the teams closest to an

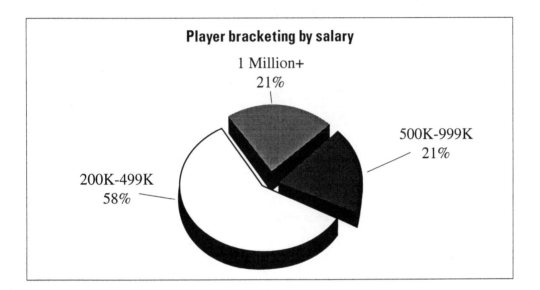

even split between the stars and the rank and file in 1996 was Minnesota.

One trend that seems to have evolved is for teams to maintain their core of players rather than selling out to free agency. While nearly 45 percent of unrestricted free agents joined new clubs in 1995, that figure fell below 12 percent in 1997.

Like the NCAA rolling back football scholarship allotments to 25 per year, the cap has proven its effectiveness in keeping teams from stockpiling talent, especially at the quarterback position. It is not likely that players such as Scott Mitchell, Mark Brunell, Elvis Grbac and Ty Detmer would have so readily left their initial clubs had the teams been able to accommodate them outside the salary cap.

Free agency has also resulted in the need for NFL teams to put together a comprehensive plan for attracting free agents. In fact, some individuals feel that free agency has taken on similar properties to the recruiting process in the college ranks.

Certainly, each organization has a well-developed process for exposing the free-agent athlete to the positive features offered by a team, and indeed for wining and dining an athlete on his visits to the club. More than one NFL player, however, has summed up the process best when they said, "Don't kid yourself. The players change teams for one reason—money."

Without question, the NFL salary cap will continue to evolve in the future. Several proposals are currently in the offing—on both sides of the bargaining table—between the Players Association and the owners. Among the changes being considered are those involving the number of years needed to be a free agent (currently five, or four with a capped year) and a plan for redistributing the amount of money to incoming rookies. Regardless of whatever salary cap format exists, a team's need for personnel who understand how to properly apply the cap to the organization's particular situation will continue to be critical.

APPENDICES

APPENDIX A

SELECTED REFERENCES

Anderson, Ken. (1984). *The art of quarterbacking.* New York: Linden Press.

Ashe, Arthur. (1993). *Days of grace: A memoir.* New York: Alfred A. Knopf.

Bannon, Joseph J., & James A. Busser. (1992). *Problem solving* (3rd ed.). Champaign, IL: Sagamore Publishing.

Bothwell, Lin. (1983). *The art of leadership.* New York: Prentice Hall Press.

Bryant, Paul W. (1960). *Building a championship football team.* Englewood Cliffs, NJ: Prentice Hall Press.

Catton, Bruce. (1956). *This hallowed ground: The story of the union side of the Civil War.* Garden City, NY: Doubleday.

de Cervantes Saavedra, Miguel. (1991). *Adventures of Don Quixote.* New York: Knopf.

Didinger, Ray. (Ed.). (1995). *Game plans for success: Winning strategies for business and life from ten top NFL head coaches.* Boston: Little, Brown and Company.

Driver, Michael J., Brousseau, Kenneth R., & Hunsaker, Phillip L. (1990). *The dynamic decision-maker.* New York: Harper & Row, Publishers.

Ellis, William D., & Colonel Thomas Cunningham, Jr. (1974) *Clarke of St. Vith: The sergeants' general.* Cleveland, OH: Dillon Liederbach.

Fallows, James. (1996). *Breaking the news: How the media undermine American democracy.* New York: Pantheon Books.

Fraser, David. (1993). *Knight's cross: A life of field marshal Erwin Rommel.* New York: HarperCollins.

Fuller, J.F.C. (1993). *The decisive battles of the western world.* Stevenage, Herts, United Kingdom: Spa Books.

Gilbert, Brad. (1993). *Winning ugly: Mental warfare in tennis—tales from the tour and lessons from the master.* Secaucus, NJ: Carol Publishing Group.

Hitler's generals. (1989). New York: Grove Weidenfeld.

Hesselbein, Francis, et al (editors). (1997). *The organization of the future.* San Francisco, CA: Jossey—Bass Publishers.

Janis, I.L. (1983). *Groupthink: Psychological studies of policy decisions and fiascoes* (2nd ed.). Boston: Houghton-Mifflin.

Kurtz, Howard. (1996). *Hot air: All talk all the time.* New York: Times Books.

Landry, Tom. (1990). *Tom Landry, an autobiography.* Grand Rapids, MI: Zondervan Books.

Lombardi, Vince. (1963). *Run to daylight!* Englewood Cliffs, NJ: Prentice-Hall.

Meir, Golda. (1975). *My life.* New York: Putnam.

Overy, Richard. (1995). *Why the Allies won.* New York: W.W. Norton and Company.

Parcells, Bill. (1995). *Finding a way to win: The principles of leadership, teamwork, and motivation.* New York: Doubleday.

Patton, George S. (1947). *War as I knew it.* Boston: Houghton-Mifflin.

Powell, Colin. (1995). *My American journey: An autobiography.* New York: Random House.

Prange, Gordon. (1982). *Miracle at Midway.* New York: McGraw Hill.

Rapaport, Richard. (1993, January-February). To build a winning team: An interview with head coach Bill Walsh. *Harvard Business Review,* 111-120.

Riley, Pat. (1993). *The winner within: A life plan for team players.* New York: Putnam's Sons.

Rommel, Erwin. (1953). *The Rommel papers.* New York: Harcourt, Brace.

Shultz, George P. (1993). *Turmoil and triumph: My years as secretary of state.* New York: C. Scribner's Sons.

Sun-Tzu. (1963). *The art of war.* Oxford: Oxford University Press.

VanDerveer, Tara. (1997). *Shooting from the outside: How a coach and her Olympic team transformed women's basketball.* New York: Avon Books.

von Clausewitz, Carl. (1974). *On war.* Princeton: Princeton University Press.

Vroom, V.H., & Yetton, P.W. (1973). *Leadership and decision making.* Pittsburgh: University of Pittsburgh Press.

Walsh, Bill. (1995, June 5). Beware of the crisis lovers. *Forbes,* A17.

_____. (1997, February 24). Blinded by the byte. *Forbes,* S22.

_____. (1993, October 25). Carpe diem—or the diem after that. *Forbes,* S17.

_____. (1994, October 10). The case for kudos. *Forbes,* S17.

_____. (1994, June 6). Go ahead—kick the tripod. *Forbes,* S18.

_____. (1996, August 26). Holy macro: Delegating requires a sure touch: Too little and you become a figurehead, too much and you squelch creativity. *Forbes,* S30.

_____. (1996, October 7). Home sweet huddle. *Forbes,* S26.

_____. (1993, June 7). How to manage superstars. *Forbes,* S17.

_____. (1995, February 27). Information, please! *Forbes,* S19.

_____. (1996, April 8). Insecurity complex: Managers must figure out new ways to generate staff loyalty when pink slips are in the air. *Forbes,* S18.

_____. (1994, December 5). Let 'em see you sweat. *Forbes,* 15.

_____. (1994, August 29). Managing for the big idea. *Forbes,* S19.

_____. (1993, September 13). Succeeding despite success. *Forbes,* S17.

_____. (1994, February 28). Surviving a high-speed blowout. *Forbes,* S21.

_____. (1995, April 10). Two cheers for pissed off. *Forbes,* S17.

_____. (1996, February 26). What price glory? Walking the line between ruthless and toothless. *Forbes,* S16.

_____. (1994, April 11). When good isn't good enough. *Forbes,* S19.

_____. (1996, June 3). When past perfect isn't (achieving back-to-back success). *Forbes,* S18.

_____. (1993, March 29). When things go bad. *Forbes,* S13.

_____. (1995, December 4). Winning: The only thing? Sometimes the best way to build a championship team is to take your eyes off the prize. *Forbes,* S17.

_____. (1997, April 7). Young Turks at the gate. *Forbes,* S14.

_____, & Dickey, Glenn. (1990). *Building a champion: On football and the making of the 49ers.* New York: St. Martin's Press.

Yeager, Chuck. (1985). *Yeager, an autobiography.* Boston: G.K. Hall.

SAMPLE EMPLOYEE LECTURES

COACHES GENERAL MEETING LECTURE #1

Why you are employed by San Francisco:

- Intelligence.
- Compatibility.
- Expression/teaching ability.
- Honesty; character.
- You are capable of being the best in the business at your specialty.

What is expected of you:

- Dedication to being or becoming the best in the business at your chosen specialty.
- Open exchange with everyone.
- Contribution to the club—providing the best possible instruction and technical expertise to the squad.
- Loyalty to yourself, the squad, the staff, the organization, and me.
- If a request is made, either carry it out or question it immediately.
- Be honest with the organization regarding expenses.
- Be honest with me, and be thorough and detailed when completing your assignments.
- Exhibit "class" in your general demeanor (e.g., attire, speech, social exchange).
- Treatment of other employees of the organization (e.g., staff, secretaries, training room staff, etc.).
- Be inquisitive and show an interest in all facets of your work (e.g., technical, scouting, organizational, personnel, etc.).
- Concern for your family.
- Be honest, prudent, mature, confidential, non-quotable, and positive in your dealings with the media; do not exhibit bravado or be concerned with yourself.

- Keep all technical and personnel aspects of our football system confidential.
- We must all work to maintain the appropriate atmosphere involving players, the locker room, social interaction, the staff, and public relations.
- Be punctual.
- Make me aware of your hours if they are not routine. Inform me of travel, absenteeism, and unexpected considerations.
- Keep the office orderly.
- If you have a problem, approach me confidentially.
- Be willing to make decisions and live with them; be willing to change. Be aware of the "point of no return."
- Do not be embarrassed to take free time.
- Keep legible, accurate, up-to-date files and records.
- My staff and I are all equals.
- Be aware of NFL deadlines, procedures, and policies.
- Assert yourself to get the job done with other employees, if necessary.
- Accept differences; avoid arguments between staff members and other employees.
- Remember that you represent the 49er organization, not just your coaching group.

Considerations to avoid:
- Making private deals (e.g., cars, tickets, income, influence, gifts, entertainment, etc.) without consulting me.
- Discussions of salary.
- Excessive familiarity with players.
- Lack of respect for other employees.
- Mistreating or ignoring the media.
- Lack of respect for or loyalty to ownership, even in jest.
- Overreacting to player demands, moods, or requests.
- Public lack of respect for 49er players (e.g., calling them dumb, slow, etc.).
- Misuse of 49er expenses.
- Heavy public drinking.
- Eccentricities that attract attention.
- Making commitments involving the 49ers without consulting management.
- Hinting to the players regarding confidential management decisions or policies.
- Gossiping in-house or with other staffs.
- Special treatment of me (e.g., opening doors, getting coffee, etc.).

Immediate considerations:

- Home and family:
  - Keep John McVay and me abreast of events.
  - Travel plans.
  - Club assistance.
- Living expenses while in Redwood City.
- Family assistance when moving (e.g., house hunting).
- Moving expenses:
  - Trips home in conjunction with club business.
  - While waiting for a home or furniture.
- Automobiles.
- Work calendar for February, March, and April.
- Office setup.
- Secretarial setup.
- Telephone procedure.
- Pay and benefit schedule (Keith Simon).

COACHES GENERAL MEETING LECTURE #2

- Expect action to be taken against any conduct contrary to the expectations of the 49er organization.
- Become acquainted with all squad members, not just those with whom you associate frequently.
- Maintain the "49er line" on all squad regulations and standards; all coaches should have the same basic attitude.
- Avoid confidential and personal exchanges with players (e.g., concerning teammates, etc.).
- Avoid public confrontations with players and other coaches—speak about it later.
- Coaches should be "seen" in the locker room, dorms, etc. The players do not have a "private sanctum" (i.e., the back of the plane, etc.).
- Do not go beyond an explanation to the head coach in public; it is important for him to maintain his position.
- Maintain security of 49er notebooks, films, or reports.
- Avoid leaving confidential material where someone (e.g., writers, squad members, visitors, coaches) could see or examine it.
- When I begin to speak, I expect everyone's immediate attention. I will occasionally "interfere" with your work with squad members. Do not be sensitive or "thin-skinned." Do not sulk if you are "outvoted." Make changes only after a great deal of planning and deliberation.
- Do not try to get the "last word" in a disagreement or discussion.

- Do not perpetuate something that "isn't right."
- Offense vs. defense—avoid personal antagonism with players.
- You may have to adjust if your roommate's living habits are different from your own.
- Game plan and playbook should be returned by players.

COACHES PRE-TRAINING CAMP MEETING LECTURE #3

- It is important to convey loyalty to me in all communication with others; competitors, agents, and the media will pick up on any problems.
- Expect me to act on any conduct contrary to the expectations of the 49er organization.
- Make an effort to associate and communicate with all squad members. Build team strength and loyalty and work to integrate the squad.
- All 49er standards must be maintained; do not be lax in enforcing them.
- Don't be a "soft touch" as a coach.
- Avoid confidential and personal relationships with players. Don't try to be a counselor or become too close to any single player. Do not discuss players with their teammates.
- Avoid public confrontation with a player or another coach.
- Be visible in the locker room, dorm, and training room. Don't allow the players to develop any sanctuaries where you feel uncomfortable.
- Don't go beyond an explanation to me in public; I can not allow my position to be compromised.
- All 49er materials must be accounted for and treated with respect. Security of film and written materials is essential—don't leave confidential material on your desk or where anyone can see it.
- When I am talking, I expect everyone's immediate attention. Protocol must be followed.
- Don't be "thin-skinned" when I say something to you. If things don't go the way you planned, don't sulk.
- Don't have the "last word" in any disagreement with me.
- Don't perpetuate a misjudgment; be analytical and open to change.
- Avoid becoming annoyed in offensive/defensive practice competition.
- Be flexible regarding others' lifestyles and feelings.
- Avoid gossiping with players.
- If you have differences with a player or another coach, rectify them immediately— do not let them linger.
- Be punctual, but don't expect me to be.
- Introduce any friends who visit camp.

- All game plans must be returned and accounted for.
- Be specific when coaching and teaching; do not talk and say nothing of importance. Positives are much more effective than negatives (e.g., "Let's try this"; "How about this way instead"; etc.). Use an example of a great player doing something in a preferred way.
- Finish each drill strong; do not allow effort or intensity to wane.
- Allow only the minimum of talking on the field. Keep players moving; don't keep others waiting.
- Store up some of your observations; do not attempt to critique every repetition.
- Use first names whenever you can.
- Take care not to criticize the same player too often.
- Do not avoid any player; talk to the players who will not make it.
- Stress movement in all phases of play—players should be explosive.
- Players must produce; you must do whatever it takes as a coach to get a player to reach his potential.
- Be flexible in motivating players; treat players as individuals.
- Remember that players expect and thrive on regimentation, good organization, and emphasis on movement and explosiveness in all activities.
- Teaching can be done in many ways; use any method necessary to get the job done. Find the best way to reach the player (e.g., film, lecture, demonstration, watching another player do it correctly, etc.).
- Do not become territorial and become sensitive to suggestions or criticisms of your coaching area.
- I may suggest "bizarre" concepts in various areas to provoke thought; accept this approach.
- I want to get input from all coaches—I will listen to you and consider your opinion.
- Expect me to coach less on the field. I am assuming a broader role and becoming less involved in detail work.
- Do not become concerned about the team atmosphere and take matters into your own hands—leave it to me to develop and maintain the team climate.

COACHES PRE-TRAINING CAMP MEETING LECTURE #4

- Do not develop your own "domain" and become stubborn or sensitive.
- Want and expect Dean—W position.
- Report all gratuities.
- I will try to provoke thought—do not assume that I am irrational.
- I want your input, but do not feel like you are "saving me." I may alternate between pro and con positions.
- Decisions have generally been good ones. Everyone's opinions have been considered.

- Master plan:
  - Deal with situations.
  - Improvement.
  - Deal with multi-faceted problems.
  - Consider definitive moves.
- Be willing to discuss situations, even if you feel they can be dealt with quickly on a yes-no basis.

COACHES PRE-TRAINING CAMP MEETING LECTURE #5

Press Relations:
- Technical information.
- When discussing mistakes, never mention names.
- Avoid failure as a phase of the game.
- Player limitations.
- Player comparison; NFL comparisons.
- Limit conversations.
- Remarks on competition.
- Other contests.
- Source of information.
- Treat everyone the same way.
- Assistant coach in public relations.
- Give credit.

COACHES TRAINING CAMP MEETING LECTURE #6

- Avoid long personal phone calls at camp.
- Dress for coaches will be a standard 49er coaching uniform.
- Make sure you have shoes with cleats for demonstration purposes.
- Coaches are responsible for their own conduct as well as working hours during training camp.
- Avoid socializing with the media. Don't talk to them too long.
- Know our waiver procedure. Assistant coaches are involved when we are waiving a specific position player. "Do not commit yourself to specifically helping waived players in the future unless you are willing to accept the time, responsibility and effort it entails."
- Training room cleanliness—make sure that conference rooms, meeting rooms, film rooms, and your own personal room are kept clean at all times.
- Coach and player relationships—do not socialize with players during camp. Avoid frequenting the same local establishments where players might relax.

- Be careful of the types of relationships you have with players' parents, family, friends, and agents.
- Do not give players extra favors.
- Show the same dignity and respect to all players, regardless of ability.
- Know and understand my role as head coach and treat me the way I expect to be treated. Be aware that I will use various forms of motivation during practice sessions. Be alert for my methods and do not be offended by my efforts to help motivate players in different ways.
- When talking to friends who coach for other teams, make certain you are not specific about any aspect of our football program (e.g., personnel, organizational procedures, specific techniques, etc.). "Don't give someone else an edge by mistake."
- Each coach is responsible to go to every meal (he does not have to eat) unless he is otherwise cleared by the head coach.
- Billie Matthews will outline the procedure regarding the loan of our players to our visiting coaches.

COACHES TRAINING CAMP MEETING LECTURE #7

- Don't "coach" unless you say something specific.
- If you are not certain of what you are saying, do not say anything.
- It is important to remain positive. Begin with a positive, then state the negative.
- Use phrases such as "Let's try this"; "Do more of this"; or "Think about this."
- Point out that a specific player performed a technique or skill in a certain way.
- Finish every drill and play strong.
- Watch the schedule and be alert for changes. Do not skip any given drill period.
- Minimize the occurrence of everyone waiting while you talk to or coach one person.
- Store up some of your observations and relate them to players later.
- Only one person should be talking.
- Be enthusiastic—use first names.
- Allow players their dignity—do not criticize only the poorest players. Never show contempt for any player.
- Don't avoid players who do not have a chance of making it.
- Stress movement.
- It is most important for the players to produce and reach their top physical potential. Do whatever it takes to get a player to that level. Be flexible in motivating, communicating with, and "reaching" the athlete.

GENERAL EMPLOYEE MEETING LECTURE #1

- Part of result.
- Pride in organization.
- Not a 9-to-5 job.
- Feel responsibility.
- Cannot be routine.
- Everyone has a role and expectations.
- Clean up and decor; ours is a small facility that must be kept orderly; there is a place for everything; everything should be neat at end of day—particularly your desk.
- Locker room; shoes; equipment; pictures.
- Training room.
- Weight room and outdoor area.
- Doorway.
- Yearly salary adjustment—February—June—increase—fair—equitable.
- Robert Yanagi—new video program.
- Mo Fowell and Bob Cusick are responsible for the operation of luxury suites.
- Give-away items (e.g., shirts, jackets, etc.).
- Confidentiality.
- Compatibility is vital.
- Communication.
- Detailed job profile of each person (in two weeks).
- Business during business hours.
- Private matters—own business, drugs, alcohol, etc.
- Reminder—Mr. DeBartolo is a priority.
- Accommodating to public.
- Must not indulge people, business, or public.

GENERAL EMPLOYEE MEETING LECTURE #2

- Not a great crusade. You should not be consumed with emotion. There is no reason for the dramatic.
- With public, you cannot appear to be bored, lax or indifferent.
- Be punctual, alert, and anticipating.
- Public/community relations should always be positive and genial.
- Must control gossip and general criticism.
- Must have an interest and a feeling for the team or should release for more day-to-day type work.
- Within my power to establish employees.

- Neatness (e.g., desk, office, hall, etc.) is important, for example, cardboard boxes.
- Care for facilities.
- Responsible for own desk and supplies.
- Prompt hours, must have a willingness to complete task before departing.
- Confidentiality of 49er business.
- Communicate with others (e.g., administrative, coaches, Bill, etc.),
- Telephone systems; avoid lengthy private calls; semi-business conversations.
- Visitors in building or at camp.
- Productivity vs. idleness.
- Meeting of deadlines and unavoidable rushes.
- Accepting direction pleasantly and without personal sensitivity.
- Be rather "tough-skinned." Don't let anyone get you down or sulk when offended.
- Don't worry when others appear to be doing less.
- You will be included; you should feel part of it.
- Ownership relations.
- Security.
- Eventful position; more demanding; rewarding—"something happening."
- Fraternization and socializing.
- Special treatment of athletes; avoid compromising or making concessions.
- Proper forms for business office.
- If you have questions or doubts, you should settle them. Have confidence, patience and trust in the team's administration.

SECRETARIAL STAFF LECTURE #1

- New season.
- Intensely competitive business.
- The organization sets the standards, not the employees.
- You should be somewhat casual and relaxed at work. You should not, however, be familiar, a laugh a minute, mad cap, entertaining person on the job.
- Just having a light hearted, open atmosphere is not doing the job. Achieving such a work environment is not an accomplishment.
- An effective, sustained, consistent job commitment and responsibility is the required, expected response.
- Any relationship you may have with players is not the basis for employment.
- Nor is the "one big happy family" atmosphere a justification for employment.
- Standards of excellence are priority. Specific, required work hours are established.
- A strong work ethic is fundamental.
- Proper dress and appearance is fundamental to your position and reflects a certain sophistication or lack of it.

- Full—alert—responsive day is expected. If you're not completely focused on doing your job, you're not meeting your responsibilities.
- Lunch hour is either a social event or a cocktail party; it should last no more than one hour.
- Because nothing is said, don't be misled by our notice, reaction or approval.
- Be orderly, neat and organized. Maintaining an uncluttered appearance of your desk and the office facility is important.
- One basic justification for our existence—highly competitive team. Winning—losing. Extremely efficient administration and support—group performance.
- This is not civil service or even big corporate business. We exist to support and field a football team. In other words, we don't "exist for the sake of existing"; we are not "maintaining" something.
- Each year is an entity in itself. It's not "business as usual." It's not "routine."
- Complete projects in a timely manner; reduce procrastination; meet deadlines.
- The more day-to-day routine people we have, the more pressure on the others.
- It isn't a case of "let Bill do it."
- Bill isn't a good, swell, fun, understanding, gentle, father-figure, loving person. If anything in those areas is ever demonstrated, it's a luxury. Such behavior does not in any way figure in our success.
- Your job is not justified on social association. If you're to find satisfaction, it must be in your work and your performance. You should value your accomplishments.
- You should take pride in your contribution, in our success and in the respect we have in our community, nationally and in football circles.
- As we function well as an organization, we can then take pride in each other.
- Social "pecking orders" had better not show themselves. Such social in-groups affect our ability to function as an organization. Your likes and dislikes cannot be a factor in your behavior or job performance.
- Respect the position and the status of all other employees and individuals involved with the team (e.g., doctors, attorneys, etc.).

SECRETARIAL POINTS LECTURE #2

- Be poised.
- Maintain a businesslike atmosphere at all times.
- Be efficient.
- Do not be too familiar.
- Be demanding, yet even-handed.
- Motivate people to do things; don't use fear.
- Be aware of my moods.
- Can't act as though inaccessible to other employees, players or coaches.

- Can't reflect my feelings in dealing with people.
- Be constructive.

DEPARTMENTAL HEADS GUIDELINES LECTURE

- Avoid familiarity with players; do not socialize with them. It is best if we can remain apart and aloof from the players and still maintain a solid working relationship.
- Do not volunteer opinions of players' abilities unless you're asked by Bill Walsh or John McVay.
- Confidentiality in critical matters (e.g., your work, salary, private lives of players and staff, player evaluations, etc.) is essential. Do not indicate or even hint to players of confidential management decisions or policies.
- Be sure everyone in your department is working well together. We must not allow any disagreement to go unresolved.
- What you hear here, leave it here (e.g., public remarks, effect on NFL, pro sports, 49ers, our people, etc.).
- All of your dealings with the press and the media should be honest, prudent, mature, confidential, non-quotable and positive, with no bravado and little self. Confidential materials must not be exposed to the media. Do not conduct business in front of writers.
- The 49ers have *one* central voice—Bill Walsh. Do not become a "club spokesman." In particular, avoid making remarks that concern matters that are outside of your sphere of responsibility. Keep a low profile and a non-visible role.
- Avoid generally damaging gossip by you or your spouse. Do not presume to pass judgment on others. Your private life is your own business, except alcohol.
- Do not become condescending in your comments regarding doctors, trainers, players, coaches, scouts, secretaries and other members of the administrative staff. Employee relations, from top to bottom, should be businesslike and cordial. Maintain high expectations of their performance. Avoid confrontations.
- Semi-business expenses on your part should involve considerable thought.

SAMPLE JOB DESCRIPTION OUTLINES

EXECUTIVE VICE PRESIDENT FOR FOOTBALL OPERATIONS

Major areas of responsibility:

- To direct and supervise overall 49er football operations as designated by Edward J. DeBartolo, Jr., and in coordination with Carmen Policy.

- To focus effort, energy and expertise in furthering the short- and long-range goals of the 49er organization. Continue to maintain and work to improve the 49ers' high standards of football-related performance.

- To oversee the planning and implementation of effective personnel strategy dealing with the college draft, trades, acquisitions and signings. This role would be closely coordinated and planned with John McVay, George Seifert, the scouting staff and the coaching staff.

- Study, coordinate and plan trade opportunities within the NFL framework. Through interchange with Edward J. DeBartolo, Jr., and Carmen Policy, initiate these trades.

- Coordinate the scouting staff and coaching staff in preparation, final planning and in direct participation in the yearly college draft.

- Plan and coordinate with John McVay and Carmen Policy the strategy in contract negotiations with players and agents. This format would also include contract negotiations and salary scheduling with all employees.

- To act in concert with Carmen Policy in assuring the short- and long-term interests of the 49er franchise, at all League meetings, and subsequent dialogue and voting. To represent the San Francisco 49ers at League meetings and in other business, as directed by Edward J. DeBartolo, Jr., and Carmen Policy.

- To provide counsel and advice, as needed by head coach, his staff, and members of the management team. Would be actively available to assist the coaching staff, as well as the head coach, with opinions and expertise.

- To create an atmosphere that best enhances individual initiative and freedom of action by the head coach and other staff employees. This atmosphere is developed in conjunction with carrying out their specific stated responsibilities.

- To provide a definite structure in which individual members of the management team can make independent decisions with confidence and support. Delegate responsibilities through a continuous monitoring and evaluating process.

- Foster a decision-making process based on objective analysis of the available facts, history and projections. This would be characterized by a "what's right," rather than "who's right," attitude.

- Oversee and monitor the maintenance and utilization of the Marie P. DeBartolo Sports Centre. Work in conjunction with John McVay and Norb Hecker in this ongoing process.

- Communicate directly, on an ongoing basis, with Edward J. DeBartolo, Jr., the general and specific plans and progress regarding 49er activities. To seek input and feedback on overall planning strategy and performance. Document all business activities of importance for further use, confirmation, and any legal activities.

- To schedule regular meetings with the management team in the following areas:
  - Development of present squad.
  - Acquisition of free agents.
  - Potential trades.
  - College draft.
  - Cost strategy.
  - Interchange and communication within the organization.
  - Franchise goals and fiscal planning.

- Continue to develop functional expertise of all employees in the pursuance of their assigned duties.

- Communicate directly with Carmen Policy and Keith Simon on all financial considerations related to football operations. Interact with the business sector of the organization on all salary and operating expenses.

GEORGE SEIFERT—HEAD COACH

Major areas of responsibility:
- Skill development. To develop, in conjunction with the coaching staff, all fundamentals and skills required to consistently perform as a competing member of the National Football League.

- Coordinate all phases of game. To coordinate and orchestrate the development of offense, defense, and special teams. This would include preparing the team for all contingencies that may occur during a game.

- Personnel placement. Placement of personnel best suited for individual positions and playing roles. The consequent ongoing development of individual players to increase their effectiveness as to designated roles. This selection will be made through consultation with Bill Walsh.

- Practice preparation. Coordinate, direct, and monitor the overall day-to-day operation of the team and coaching staff. Organize, plan, and coordinate all 49er practice schedules. This will include mini camp, summer camp, and seasonal sessions.

- Game planning. Research, develop, and finalize all game planning. This would include preparing the team through scouting reports, classroom preparation, and on-the-field practice.

- Coaching staff. Manage and direct the planning and teaching of the coaching staff. Oversee a continuous development of their expertise related to the 49er system of football. Measure and monitor their performance. Coordinate and integrate their efforts with the support staff.

- Communication with management. Establish and maintain effective communication and liaison between the coaching staff and the management team.

- Organizational philosophy. To implement and maintain the 49er organizational philosophy and operating format as instituted by Ed DeBartolo and Bill Walsh.

- Player protection. To ensure the utmost safety and well-being of 49er personnel during practice sessions and when participating in games. This process should be established in concert with procedures set forth by team doctors, trainer, and 49er management. Support and reinforce and implement all decisions made by the medical staff.

- Media dealings. To develop and maintain strategies and relationships with the media (i.e., television, radio, and newspapers) which direct themselves to the best interests of the total 49er organization. Candor, prudence, and foresight in this continuing interaction are vital. Directness, clarity, and honesty should be used as guidelines.

- Off-field demeanor. Demonstrate insight, sensitivity, and responsiveness to the "off-field" demeanor of players, coaches, and support staff when they are not involved in formal 49er business.

- 49er image. Maintain an environment that effectively blends club requirements and standards of demeanor with individual personalities. Stress discretion and good judgment by players and coaches when dealing with the press and in other public-oriented situations. The image of the 49er organization will be maintained and enhanced at all times.

- Ethics. Maintain professional ethics and personal integrity in relationships and dealings with other NFL organizations. Responsible for any breach of club confidentiality or ethics in dealing with other NFL staff members by any member of the assistant coaching staff.

- Scouting. Work in conjunction with Bill Walsh and the scouting department as to the utilization of coaches for college scouting and evaluation. This would include necessary preparation for the yearly college draft. Also coordinate with Bill Walsh individual NFL player evaluations by coaching staff related to potential trades or signings.

- Fiscal. To adhere to essential business and financial guidelines and directives as set forth by club management. This is related to a responsibility for fiscal matters related to head coaching responsibilities (i.e., discretion and foresight in exchanging on player's salaries and financial matters of the 49er franchise).

- Accessibility. As requested, be prepared to critique player performances, team development, and post-game analysis. Participate with 49er ownership and management regarding short- and long-term planning, specific goals and objectives.

- NFL constitution. A working knowledge of the NFL constitution and bylaws (refer to Article IX, Prohibited Conduct, pages 24-19) is essential and any infraction that may occur is to be reported immediately to San Francisco 49er management.

- Outside commitments. Association or involvement in external personal business ventures should be communicated to and approved by management. This would include radio, television shows, and commercials.

- Staff selection and evaluation. The head coach will be directly responsible for evaluation and selection process of coaching staff. His decision will be subject to reasonable approval from Ed DeBartolo and Bill Walsh. Termination would be subject to the same process and not be unreasonably withheld. The head coach can expect support and accommodation in this area.

JOHN E. MCVAY—VICE PRESIDENT FOR FOOTBALL ADMINISTRATION

Major goals:

- Effectively raise the talent level of the San Francisco 49ers by assisting in the conducting of the NFL college draft, compiling trades with other teams, claiming players from the NFL waiver system, and signing free agent players.

- Effectively conduct the day-to-day business activities of the 49ers as they relate to the NFL office, and interact with the other NFL franchises.

- Effectively negotiate player contracts within the guidelines prescribed by the NFL and the 49ers.

Major areas of responsibility and measures of effectiveness:

1. Talent acquisition.

2. Effective office management—scouts, trainers, doctors, personnel department, equipment men, video department, administrative assistant staff.

3. NFL waiver procedures—rules.

4. Contract negotiations.

5. Administrative support to the head coach and the assistant coaches.

6. Liaison with Management Council.

7. Overall administration of training camp.

8. Radio—TV contracts—assist Carmen Policy.

9. Interact with business operations.

10. Charitable contributions.

11. Substance abuse program.

12. Personal growth.

AREA #1

Acquisition of talent for the San Francisco 49ers professional football team.

Talent for NFL teams is acquired in four general ways:

- The NFL college draft.
- Trades with other NFL teams.
- Claiming players from the NFL waiver wire system.
- Through signing free agent players.

In order to prepare the 49ers to make proper decisions in theses areas, we rely upon our College Scouting Department and our Pro Personnel Department.

Measures of effectiveness:

- Effective use of the college draft as evidenced by 50 percent of each year's draft making the roster annually.
- Increase in the number of victories each year as a result of improved player acquisition.
- Effective development of, and implementation of, a professional personnel (active pro players) rating and evaluation system.
- Maintenance of an effective atmosphere and relationship with other NFL teams to foster possible trade(s) of players and a spirit of cooperation.

AREA #2

Effective management of personnel under his direction.

Among the personnel under his direction are scouts, doctors, trainers, personnel staff, video staff, equipment staff, administrative assistants and related secretaries, etc.—including providing administrative support for the people involved, and creating an atmosphere in which these people can grow professionally to achieve self-satisfaction and, consequently, be of greater value to the 49er organization.

The 49ers' in-house training, as far as the development of our personnel, consists of on-the-job training, attendance at outside seminars, and the advancement of capable staff members within the organization.

This office is also responsible to anticipate the non-player personnel movement that occurs because of attrition or other reasons that would create job vacancies within our organization. Therefore, it is necessary to hire people or interview candidates who would be integrated quickly and effectively into our current structure.

Measures of effectiveness:

- Professional growth of scouts and office staff, training department, and support staff.
- All office personnel are proficient in carrying out defined procedures.
- Work with Bill Walsh in overall administration tasks as defined on organizational chart.
- Selection, assignment and training of new office personnel in cooperation with Keith Simon.

AREA #3

Effective utilization of the NFL waiver procedures and the Player-Management Council Collective Bargaining Agreement.

The NFL Personnel Department circulates daily to all member clubs a list of players waived (cut or released) and players newly signed by various clubs, the movement of players from the active roster to Injured Reserve or a variety of other reserve categories. An understanding of the Collective Bargaining Agreement, its application to the players' rights, and the rights and responsibilities of the various clubs is a necessary function of the office.

Measures of effectiveness:

- NFL procedure satisfactorily completed within the prescribed guidelines and time limitations.
- Compliance with Collective Bargaining Agreement and the elimination of unfavorable arbitration decisions.
- Effective use of NFL waiver procedure in supplementing player talent pool.

AREA #4

Effective negotiation of NFL player contracts.

Beginning in 1979, every effort was made to take the various players of the 49ers and to build a salary integrity scale. The idea is to pay the higher salaries to our most productive football players. There are approximately 20 squad members whose contracts must be negotiated on an annual basis. In addition, there are 10 to 14 drafted players whose contracts are to be negotiated. Beyond this, every club will sign approximately 40 free agents and these contracts are negotiated. All major contracts are reviewed with Keith Simon from our business office and Carmen Policy to determine the impact on our salary structure. In the majority of contracts with which we deal, the player is represented by a player agent.

Measures of effectiveness:

- Completing contracts within the 49ers' Salary Integrity Scale.
- Maintain ongoing trust relationships with player representatives (agents).
- Work with Keith Simon and Carmen Policy in overall impact of player contracts.

AREA #5

Administrative support to head coach, George Seifert, and Executive Vice President, Bill Walsh.

There is a variety of assignments that needs administrative attention, such as the activities of the trainers and the doctors as related to player movement from injured reserve to the active squad. Reviewing the expense of major equipment and maintaining a high level of efficiency in the medical department.

The coaches are utilized from time to time as consultants in evaluating personnel for the College Scouting Department, and also for the Pro Personnel Department.

Measures of effectiveness:

- Supervise and direct the activities of the trainers and equipment men.
- Provide support and direction for assistant coaches in non-coaching assignments—scouting, etc.

AREA #6

Liaison with NFL Management Council.

The Management Council acts on behalf of all teams in interpreting the effects of the Collective Bargaining Agreement, and in an advisory capacity to member clubs. Grievance hearings are prepared in cooperation with the Management Council, and decisions rendered by various arbitrators are distributed. These are interpreted by Management Council for the benefit of member clubs.

Management Council represents member clubs' positions, and the National Football League Players' Association represents the players' position on various subjects.

Measures of effectiveness:

- Effective use of advice and opinions from Management Council relating to legal matters surrounding the League.
- An understanding of the Collective Bargaining Agreement, its application to player rights and responsibilities of the various member clubs.

AREA #7

Overall administration of training camp.

The selection of the training camp site and the proper cooperation of the university in question is essential to a positive training camp experience. San Jose State University, a public institution, and Santa Clara University, a private institution, and currently Sierra College, have served as training camp sites for the past several years for the 49ers. Training camp costs have recently escalated greatly. Currently, R.C. Owens is acting as Training Camp Director under the direct supervision of the business office and this office.

Measures of effectiveness:

- Work with, and direct, Training Camp Director in establishing an effective training camp.
- Administrative support in the effective operations of training camp.

AREA #8

Radio-TV contracts.

Assist, as needed, Carmen Policy in negotiations for broadcast rights with our local radio and television stations.

AREA #9

Interaction with Keith Simon, Vice President of Business Operations and Chief Financial Officer.

Continue to cooperatively work with Keith Simon in assignment, training, and evaluation of new and present personnel. Work to maintain an effective atmosphere of intra-departmental cooperation and communication for the overall good of the franchise in cooperation with Edward J. DeBartolo, Jr., Executive Vice President Carmen Policy, Executive Vice President Bill Walsh, and Vice President Keith Simon.

AREA #10

Charitable contributions.

Community affairs donations to be coordinated through the 49er legal counsel to determine if the political expense is justified.

AREA #11

Substance abuse program.

Work with Dr. Klint, Chris Shannon, and the NFL (Dr. Forest Tennant) in effectively operating a program of education, supervision, testing and follow-up of substance abuse problems involving players and other employees.

AREA #12

Personal development effectiveness.

In order to expand effectiveness with the organization, there must exist a willingness to consult with the NFL and the Management Council to keep abreast of current flow of information through the reading of communiqués from these two offices. In addition, attending outside seminars (Management Council seminar—negotiating skills). Finally, to enlarge the area of responsibility of a willingness to accept additional duties and responsibilities as directed by Edward J. DeBartolo, Jr.

Measures of effectiveness:

- An upgrading of skills, knowledge and effectiveness to such a degree to assure the attainment of the major goals.
- Attend one major training program and NFL meeting every six months.
- Enlarging effective area of responsibility as evidenced by accepted added duties and responsibilities.

ALLAN WEBB—DIRECTOR OF PRO PERSONNEL

Major goals:

- To upgrade level of the San Francisco 49ers through effective ongoing study and evaluation of all NFL players (offensive, defensive, and specialists) for direct purpose of trade, waiver claim, or free agent signing.
- Evaluate top Canadian Football League and players from any new pro football league for free agent signing.
- To effectively negotiate player contracts within the guidelines prescribed by the NFL and the 49ers' salary schedule.

Major areas of responsibility and measures of effectiveness:

1. Talent study and evaluation.
2. NFL waiver procedure.
3. Contact with NFL player personnel directors and pro scouts.
4. Utilization of IBM computer system.
5. Contract negotiations.
6. Coordinating with interdepartmental offices regarding free agent players.
7. Special projects.

AREA #1

Talent study and evaluation.

- Provide ongoing reports and grades on every NFL player by viewing film and game evaluation with special emphasis on the NFC Western Division.
- Report strengths and weaknesses of NFL team groups (offensive line, defensive line, etc.) and rate.
- Evaluate the 49er players in training camp and during the season.
- Utilize comparisons of 49ers' players in ratings.
- Knowledge of our needs by contact with President and head coach Bill Walsh and General Manager John McVay.

- Maintain notebook for Bill Walsh and John McVay—containing NFL team depth charts, strengths, weaknesses, needs, and performance grades of each individual and group. Also include up-to-date stats.
- Provide ongoing reports and grades on top CFL players and players from any new pro football league through film, game evaluation, and personal contacts within the respective leagues.
- Update John McVay's pro personnel board daily (injured reserve also).
- Formulate and update in-season "disaster" list daily.
- Contact free agent players expressing our interest in a "disaster" situation upon their release.
- Conduct free agent tryouts in-season (weekly) and off-season.
- Utilize the evaluation talents of Neal Dahlen.
- Continue utilization of the assistant coaches in evaluating the opponent (his position players) we will face from week to week, using a "short" form. This evaluation should be completed by Tuesday following the game. This provides the Pro Personnel Department an additional objective opinion on a player whom we might acquire via trade or claim to improve our team.

AREA #2

NFL waiver procedure.

Study waiver wire daily and advise John McVay and Bill Walsh of players who we might claim to improve the 49ers or use in a "disaster" situation.

AREA #3

Contact with NFL player personnel directors and pro scouts.

Maintain ongoing contact with NFL personnel directors and pro scouts for the purpose of needs, trades, cooperation, and general working relationships, also with (un)employed assistant coaches in regard to players they have coached.

AREA #4

Utilization of IBM computer system

- Utilize current IBM system for storing and retrieving information on all NFL players, active and inactive.
- Maintain current individual profile including specifics, moves, injuries, and comments.
- Prepare annual list for Coach Walsh and John McVay. Rate in order of excellence by position.
- Rate teams by division and conference (NFC first).
- Suggest to John McVay and Bill Walsh improvements in the present system.

AREA #5

Contract negotiations.

- Work with John McVay on completing player contracts within the 49ers' salary scale (free agents, draftees, and vets).
- Maintain ongoing contact and trust relationships with player agents.

AREA #6

Coordinating with interdepartmental offices regarding free agent players.

Interface with the Business Office and the General Manager's secretary in regard to free agent players' travel and lodging. Communicate with the Public Relations Department regarding free agent tryout player biographies.

AREA #7

Special projects.

- Make available time to respond and complete "special" projects for Coach Walsh and John McVay.
- Maintain and update "unemployed" college and NFL coaches list with home telephone number and biography (utilized by Bill Walsh for assistant coach selection).
- Continue present draft choice visitation itinerary program in terms of being responsible for the contact check list.

TONY RAZZANO—DIRECTOR OF COLLEGE SCOUTING

Major goal:
- To effectively provide personal and related information on all college senior professional football prospects for the San Francisco 49ers. In addition, similar information is afforded on the professional level.

Major areas of responsibility and measures of effectiveness:
1. Talent acquisition.
2. Coordinate and direct our college scouting staff.
3. NFL waiver procedure as directed.
4. Training camp—player information—college and pro.
5. Coordinate college player personnel information with all our coaches.
6. Cooperate with all aspects of the 49er football organization.
7. Maintain the physical plant and decor of the 49er scouting room.

AREA #1

Talent acquisition.

Assist John McVay in the acquisition of talent for the San Francisco 49ers professional football team. This step includes college and professional personnel.

Performance standards:

- Effective use of the college draft.
  - Charged with ranking the players by position according to ability. Also ranking all players according to ability.
  - Physically prepare the draft room (i.e., space for doctors, trainers, computers and computer technicians; space and phones for coaches who are scheduled on an hourly basis to man our open line to New York; space for our six scouts; space for binders and other paperwork; etc.) These and other items are necessary in preparing for a good draft.
- Improve 49er talent to increase the number of victories each year.
- Aid John McVay and Allan Webb in the development and implementation of pro personnel (active pro players). Also rate and evaluate system.
- Aid in establishing and maintaining an effective relationship with other NFL teams to foster trades, etc. Give opinion on trade possibilities when requested.

AREA #2

Coordinate and direct our college scouting staff.

Performance standards:

- Work with our scouts to ensure consistent good work within our department.
- Our department has been a very effective entity to the 49er organization. I feel it is superior to Blesto, National, and the Buffalo/Dallas/Seattle/San Francisco combines I've experienced.
- Prepare and organize all scouting meetings. Responsibilities at these meetings vary:
  - Scouting seminars; this is generally a refresher course for all scouts on all aspects of scouting as listed below.
  - Physicals given to prospects in conjunction with all NFL teams once a year; individual physicals given to a few select players in Redwood City.
  - Interviewing all our scouts on upcoming college talent.
  - Properly completing all the different college player report forms; review different categories.
  - Review and practice our method of weighing, measuring, testing and timing players.
  - Study both college and pro films as a group and discuss methods of evaluating personnel and determining our needs as a team.

AREA #3

NFL waiver procedure as directed.

Effective use of the NFL waiver procedures.

Performance standard:

- Provide information to John McVay and other pro personnel staff when requested on all players involved in the waiver procedure to affect a good margin of return to the 49ers in upgrading our football player talent.

AREA #4

Training camp—player information, college and pro.

Performance standards:

- Provide information on any or all players available.
- Constantly evaluate our players on field.
- Meetings with our scouts Billy Atkins, Michael Lombardi, Ernie Plank, Neil Schmidt, Bob Whitman, and Billy Wilson during this camp period. Most of our work during this period involves a continuous reviewing, revising, scheduling, and general preparation for the fall scouting season. Scouts are also assigned college prospects from the board in areas by position to read and report on in summary form.
- Assist in hosting college coaches during their period in camp. Also assist any and all other community or out of town persons.

AREA #5

Coordinate college player personnel information with all our coaches.

Performance standard:

- Familiarize and assist our coaches with the college talent available for the draft. Each coach is to have as much knowledge as possible about college prospects at the position or positions he is responsible for. They submit reports on all prospects they see. Extra time is afforded to those new coaches in familiarizing them with our scouting procedures.

AREA #6

Cooperate with all aspects of the 49er football organization.

Performance standard:

- To maintain a good and wholesome stability among all members of the 49er organization.

AREA #7

Maintain the physical plant and decor of the 49er scouting room.

Performance standards:

- Continue to keep the office organized and effectively utilize the limited space available for current and past scouting reports.
- Maintain the magnetic boards to reflect the current group of draft eligible college prospects for use by both scouts and coaches.
- All of the scouting supplies, past records, and college media guide files located in the storeroom are to be kept neat and accessible.

NEAL DAHLEN—FOOTBALL OPERATIONS

Major areas of responsibility:

(Estimated percentage of time required)

1. Defensive coaching support (30%).
2. Pro personnel (25%).
3. Football administration (25%)(Walsh).
4. Research and development (5%)(Walsh).
5. Practice operations (15%).
6. Local level political and community involvement.

AREA #1

Defensive coaching support.

- Film analysis and the charting of the opponent's offense to produce a computer-generated scouting report. Based on the statistical print-out, a supplemental report is developed that includes formation "Hit Charts." Both reports are used for defensive planning and player information.
- Develop a thorough understanding of the opponent's personnel and strategic tendencies in order to be a competent source of information for the defensive coaching staff.
- Work with the defensive coordinator during games—recording our calls, studying and charting the opponent's offense, and communication with the coaches on the field.

AREA #2

Pro personnel.

- Player procurement for future need.
  - Locate, evaluate, and acquire the free agent players required to rebuild our roster each year.
- Operation of the "Emergency List" process.
  - Maintain a current listing of the best available players at each position.

- — Bring players in for tryouts and physical examinations.
- Player procurement for immediate need.
  - — Acquire the best player available in emergency situations (this step includes arranging transportation, contract negotiations, etc.).
- Liaison with coaching staff.
  - — Tryouts.
  - — Provide depth charts, rosters, pertinent information as requested.

AREA #3

Football administration.

- Performance of assignments or projects requested by Bill Walsh or John McVay.
- Assist Norb Hecker with mini-camp, schedules, etc.
- Liaison with Keith Simon regarding facilities, equipment and special coaching requests.
- Training camp administration.
- Administrative role per Bill Walsh.

AREA #4

Research and development.

- Special assignments related to innovation and change. For example:
  - — Coordinate the conversion from film to video tape.
  - — Work with architect and 49er employees in the designing of a new facility.
  - — Study the NFL rules changes each year.
  - — Make suggestions to the head coach for his consideration.
- Documentation of the football related activities of the President-head coach. For example:
  - — Video taping of offensive teaching and lectures.
  - — Notes of meetings where policies are established in either coaching or administration.

AREA #5

Practice operations.

- Be present at each practice to handle administrative or operational matters as they occur.
- Fields—liaison with maintenance services.
- Liaison with Keith Simon for practice needs in away game situations.

AREA #6

Political and community involvement—local level.

KEITH A. SIMON—VICE PRESIDENT FOR BUSINESS OPERATIONS AND CHIEF FINANCIAL OFFICER

Major areas of responsibility:
1. Owner assistance.
2. Business operations.
3. Football operation support.
4. Financial.
5. Administration.

AREA #1

Owner assistance.

- Coordinate rooms and transportation as required.
- Supervise maintenance of Sharon Heights condominium.
- Coordinate game day requirements and office assistance.
- Provide financial analysis on various projects.
- Be available for special projects.

AREA #2

Business operations.

Administer and support all non-football operations.

- Stadium operations—Murlan Fowell.
- Ticket office—Ken Dargel.
- Marketing—Laurie Welling.
- Business office—Keith Simon/Mel Frear.
- Legal—Carmen Policy/Ed Alvarez and John Ottoboni.
- Public relations—Jerry Walker/Rodney Knox.
- Coordinate public relations activities and operation with Bill Walsh and John McVay.
- Office administration and maintenance.
- Coordinate office activities and maintenance with Norb Hecker and assist John McVay with any field maintenance requirements.

AREA #3

Football operation support.

- Team travel arrangements and coordination with John McVay, Bill Walsh, and George Seifert.
- Provide financial support for player contract negotiations.

AREA #4

Financial.

- Provide budgets and financial statements.
- Oversee accounting operations, controls, and procedures.
- Cost saving recommendations.

AREA #5

Administration.

- Legal coordination: workers' compensation, player grievance, general.
- Record maintenance.
- Coordinate computer applications.
- Supervise pension plans, insurance coverage and investments.
- Office supervision and policies.

NORB HECKER—EXECUTIVE ADMINISTRATOR

Major areas of responsibility:

AREA #1

Liaison with the DeBartolo Corporation for specific requirements and requests.

- Specifically daily correspondence with Lou Zarlenga related to facility needs, requirements, budget, internal, external operations. Liaison with Lou Zarlenga with general contractor and subcontractors.
- Liaison with Bob Cusick, DeBartolo Corporation, on related matters.
- Liaison with Dennis Moritz (project manager) on related matters for Marie P. DeBartolo Sports Centre.
- Liaison with Blair Spangler (interior design) on related matters for Marie P. DeBartolo Sports Centre.

AREA #2

Maintain and operate Marie P. DeBartolo Sports Centre.

- Daily operation of facility.
  - — Approval of all expenditures and purchase order requests.
  - — Liaison with security operation of building.
  - — Liaison with Reliable Maintenance Company on interior and exterior upkeep of building and landscape grounds.
- Daily schedules of building maintenance manager and the landscape and athletic fields superintendent.

AREA #3

Administrative assistant to Bill Walsh.

- Liaison with coaches, trainers, equipment department.
- Coordinate and implement social activities for coaches and 49er personnel.

AREA #4

Liaison with the DeBartolo Corporation related to individual needs (recreational, other).

AREA #5

Specific scouting—collegiate/professional; assignments as directed by Bill Walsh.

- To do fall scouting of west coast schools.

AREA #6

Liaison with NFL; general business with John McVay.

- Game officials.

AREA #7

Administration of training camp with R.C. Owens as director.

- Oversee daily operations of training camp.
- Coordinate and implement social activities of training camp.
- Coordinate and run fish derby with sponsors.

AREA #8

Administration of mini-camp at Santa Clara working with Neal Dahlen.

- Coordinate and implement all travel, hotel and transportation for camps.

AREA #9

Liaison with city and county of Santa Clara.

AREA #10

Liaison with businesses—Santa Clara and area.

AREA #11

Liaison with Candlestick Park—fields/structural.

AREA #12

Travel coordinator with Keith Simon.

- Help to coordinate and implement airline, bus travel on all road travel.
- Help to coordinate and implement meals, hotels and stadium facility needs on all road travel.

AREA #13

Special project research.

AREA #14

Alumni relations with R.C. Owens.

AREA #15

Computer/inventory system.

R.C. OWENS—EXECUTIVE ASSISTANT

Major goal:

To advance quickly to a higher level of authority and responsibility in the scope of his employment with the 49ers, based on personal skills and job duties with a clear understanding from management in relation to other jobs.

Major areas of responsibility:

1. Administration in Santa Clara.
2. Director of training camp.
3. Special assignments for Bill Walsh.
4. Speakers Bureau—via the public relations department.
5. Special assignments for George Seifert.
6. Game day assignments.
7. Santa Clara county community affairs.
8. 49er coaches and players liaison.
9. Player payroll; game day tickets.
10. Coordinate alumni affairs (for home and away games).
11. 49er booster clubs.
12. Special promotions.
13. Special assignments.

AREA #1

Administration in Santa Clara.

- Perform as directed by Bill Walsh, John McVay, Keith Simon, George Seifert or coaches on a day-to-day basis related to 49er matters. Confer with department heads in communicating 49er desires if necessary,
- Be available to assist night before game needs at hotel, or otherwise.
- Have the ability to interpret and perform administrative requests.
- Always be available to undertake major responsibilities and/or work requests (a.m. or p.m.).
- Develop required communication (verbal and written correspondence) as related to job functions.
- Direct all correspondence in relation to job duties in office, or when in travel status.
- Prepare supplemental materials in relation to job scope.
- Perform secretarial duties (i.e., respond to correspondence in relation to job duties, and type pertinent information when necessary. Ensure daily work flow is completed).

AREA #2

Director of training camp.

- Develop an accurate assessment of all needs in a clear and concise manner in advance of opening date of camp.
- Undertake responsibilities that rest heavily in campus communications and business integrity.
- Distribute all materials which are helpful to administrative department heads, coaches, and players in camp area.
- Develop system and procedures regarding meal times for entire administrative staff.
- Update changes in rooming assignments.
- Escort necessary 49er "special" guests on campus.
- Arrange "special" autograph sessions at conclusion of most practice sessions when time permits (e.g., Big Brothers/Big Sisters, Boys Clubs, schools, Special Olympic youngsters, etc.).
- Make approximately 15-20 public appearances during summer camp.
- Be aware that the 49ers training camp is under close supervision of the director and assistant director of training camp.
- Assess daily camp needs.
- Direct, as deemed necessary, the schedule for 49er personnel who will relocate from Santa Clara to Rocklin, California.

- Ensure that the transformation runs smoothly during the summer training camp period.
- Locate hotel accommodation sites and coordinate NFL officials.
- Arrange "special" meals for administrative officials of 49ers' requests.
- Assign security personnel to proper campus area for special practice situations.
- Hire personnel to staff summer camp.
- Sign contracts subsequently, when thoroughly reviewed by 49er Business Manager (e.g., contracts for business office equipment, office machines, rental equipment).
- Implement all matters which center around summer training camp in advance, and for the duration of camp.
- Arrange and coordinate meetings with campus personnel at college campus location in advance for all 49er requested needs (this step involves the entire 49er organization—the owner, Executive Vice Presidents, Vice Presidents, administrative staff, coaches, and secretarial).
- Represent 49ers at the contract signing site with the Sierra College Board of Directors.
- Be present at meetings in order to have a keen knowledge and awareness of all 49er administrative requests.
- Be responsible for purchase orders and requisitions relating to training camp.
- Tactfully handle the stressful "waiver cycle."
- Be responsible for disbursement of player(s) per diem, and personnel payroll checks.
- Assume total responsibility for ensuring transportation, whether commercial or private air carrier, to connecting site or for medical care.
- Coordinate all camp travel arrangements.
- Ensure that the aforementioned training camp procedures have all been resolved by the time of the training camp "phase-out."
- Supervise the work of training camp secretaries, including:
  - Prepare requisitions and order office supplies as requested. Perform any related function as required by department heads. Daily petty cash report update. Type for seven office executives in camp. Make hotel and travel reservations. Type all training camp information in administrative office. Handle all telephone calls, fax machine information, emergency matters. Office hours 7 a.m. to 10 p.m. seven days per week. Disseminate information as deemed necessary from executive office.
  - Coaches' office and all player dorms (two secretaries daily and weekends). Type all coaches' information regarding daily practice schedules. Computer input and retrieval. Operate telephones, office machines, fax machine equipment. Order supplies, initiate purchase orders. Make travel

arrangements for head coach, administrative staff, scouts and players as deemed necessary. Arrange cleaning and laundry service with off-campus client services. Coordinate office and dorm furniture rentals where necessary. Log and file mail. Compute weekly hours worked by hourly employees, as deemed necessary by 49ers' Santa Clara Business Office. Direct staff members to coordinate "courier service" for camp from Santa Clara daily to Rocklin and return. Direct staff members to coordinate office equipment "move" to training camp, and return.

AREA #3

Special assignments for Bill Walsh.

- Coordinate requests made by Bill Walsh.
- Handle assignments in Santa Clara, or while in travel status with the team.
- Coordinate with John McVay and other departments as deemed necessary in Santa Clara or Candlestick Park.
- Provide a direct communication link between Bill Walsh, John McVay and Keith Simon as directed.
- Coordinate personal assignments upon request by Bill Walsh.
- Provide various backup relief as needed.
- Confer with management and others for clear understanding of the working relationships and skills and work requirements in relation to the designated assignment.
- Serve as Bill Walsh's liaison in the past and present on personal matters in relation to a 49er player who might justify disciplinary action.
- Attend special meetings as requested by Bill Walsh, John McVay and Keith Simon and communicate 49ers' posture.
- Properly handle those assignments that require the ability to accurately summarize the results of the particular undertaking in a clear and concise manner.
- Be able to make the appropriate decision in Bill Walsh's behalf, when given an assignment.
- Clearly justify the approach and manner which were best taken for the assignments given at any time by Bill Walsh.
- Call on resources, through golf and tennis tournaments, to open otherwise closed doors.
- Help the needs of the 49ers in the community.
- Act as a 49er speaker and/or representative at meetings, banquets, tournaments, etc.
- Assist department heads or host invited 49ers clients to Santa Clara on the NFL's annual draft day.

- Be available to attend executive NFL meetings upon request, to document on behalf of Bill Walsh. Review and cooperate with other NFL team executives on selected topics to enhance 49ers' awareness in related areas.
- Visit children's hospitals upon request, around the Bay Area.
- Hand out 49er souvenirs to children. Coordinate the attendance of handicapped and terminally ill patients at a 49er home game with family members.

AREA #4

Speakers Bureau—via Public Relations Department.

- Serve as a key speaker in the Speakers Bureau for a limited number of appearances and $50.00 per appearance.
- Coordinate with the Public Relations Department aspirations and key communications to 49er fans through Speakers Bureau appearances upon request.
- Maintain a log of all personal appearances for the club.
- Write letters regarding requests for "speakers."
- Schedule coaches' appearances through Bureau.
- Make approximately 30-35 appearances during the calendar year with the 49er highlight film (Note: Because the highlight film in the Bureau gives exposure of the 49er football, additional season ticket holders or game ticket buyers may be attracted).
- Develop a base of communication, constantly strengthening the image of the 49ers.
- As a speaker, utilize the 49er highlight film within a radius of the advertising market of the 49ers. Interpret 49er philosophy via the Bureau.
- Treat each appearance positively.
- Conduct proper question and answer periods at meetings to protect the 49er organization's image.
- Even if the highlight film is unavailable, give the speech anyway.

AREA #5

Special assignments for George Seifert (head coach).

- Ensure that all request are completed in a timely manner in Santa Clara and at summer camp in Rocklin, as well as other areas, as deemed necessary.

AREA #6

Game day assignments.

- Pre-game locker room security. One hour prior to game time no admittance to locker room, other than coaches and players. Also coordinate official game time with game day officials and head coach. Two minute warning, pre-game, in dressing room for half-time, two minute warning between head coach and officials.

- Post-game coaches' wives meeting and reception room. Host, arrange and set up hospitality room following game. Review weekly invoice and verify audit in concert with Business Office all expense incurred on a game-to-game basis.

- Super Bowl season. Go to the Super Bowl site one week to ten days in advance of the team to arrange hotels and day-to-day operations prior to arrival of team's plane (i.e., fulfill owner's requests; help families and business clients, teams guests; etc.). Arrange restaurant reservations, no more than ten in number. Distribute information on a daily basis, keeping Super Bowl party abreast of ongoing activities which have been previously arranged.

- Items requested: Ensure telephone network, desk. One secretary, telephone lines, and office supplies for Super Bowl operation office base. Coordinate buses for Super Bowl traveling party. Host 49er cocktail party, game day brunch, private modeling show. Obtain all room assignments, coordinate with staff members. Coordinate with hotel managers, as well as hotel staff on the arrivals of 49er guests, as deemed necessary. Responsible for hotel check out of entire traveling party's return to home base. Review invoices and audit bills in concert with 49er Business offices, all expense incurred at hotel sites during Super Bowl week. Under close supervision, advise bus drivers of itinerary to ensure that hotel departure coincides with plane departure.

AREA #7

Santa Clara county community affairs.

- Community involvement in American Red Cross, Big Brothers/Big Sisters, ALS, YMCA and others.
- Recruit 49er alumni when necessary.
- Work with the Public Relations Department in other areas of involvement.

AREA #8

49er coaches and players liaison.

- Assist players as relates to (rental agencies), locating vacant apartments for rental and/or leasing cars, as well as apartment furniture.
- Assist and coordinate 49er business office player requests.
- Provide 49er staff and players with information regarding "drive-away" service agencies.
- Develop job resumes if deemed necessary on behalf of the players.
- Assist players in finding employment for themselves or for their significant others.

AREA #9

Player payroll; game day tickets.

- Disseminate pay forms, insurance forms per Business Office requests.
- If deemed necessary and they're available, issue game tickets to administrative staff, coaches and players.

AREA #10

Coordinate alumni affairs for home and away games.

- Contact alumni who travel with team to all away games.
- Advise all departments of who is traveling with the team (i.e., 49er guests, raffle ticket winners, highest bidders at charity auctions).
- Serve as the 49er dinner host of alumni on road games.
- Keep updated address list for alumni contact purposes.
- Make the following arrangements: alumni day brunch, buses to game, coordinate two complimentary tickets for alumni to 49er games, Highway Patrol and City Police caravan escort arrangement to Candlestick Park, etc.
- Coordinate all relevant projects with Michael Olmstead, 49ers Entertainment Director (e.g., the alumni pre-game show; the alumni day half-time activities, etc.).
- Arrange and coordinate food caterer, music, magician, invitational letters and 49er highlight film, concerning alumni picnics.
- Coordinate special parking requests, special game day tickets, handle stadium club guest's arrangements.
- Assist San Francisco Chapter on NFL and Alumni Affairs.

AREA #11

49er booster clubs.

- Serve periodically as master of ceremonies at club functions.
- Show 49er highlight film.
- Introduce 49er players.

AREA #12

Special promotions.

- Provide assistance for implementation and development of special promotion and community activities.

AREA #13

Special assignments.

- Be available for special assignments, as directed, from the Edward J. DeBartolo Corporation, Bill Walsh, John McVay and Keith Simon.

JERRY WALKER—DIRECTOR OF PUBLIC RELATIONS

Major goal:

To make the San Francisco 49ers recognizable as the National Football League's most highly visible, public relations club, an organization of immense image achieved through its football successes and its cooperation with the news media, the League, and the fans.

Major areas of responsibility and measures of effectiveness:

1. Press relations.
2. Publicity.
3. Publications.
4. Promotions.
5. Photography.
6. Public relations.
7. Press box and other game-day duties.
8. Player appearances and other public gatherings.
9. Advancing.
10. Personal growth, department supervision and NFL Office Liaison for NFL Films, broadcast affairs.

AREA #1

Press relations.

Establish and provide liaison contact between 49ers and members of the local and national media.

- Develop relationships with members of the media.
- Entertain the press corps during the week in advance of a road game, during the season, and occasionally during the off season.
- Include media on invite list for special events.
- Service media needs during all personal visits to office and stadium.
- Coordinate press travel and lodging for all 49ers' road trips.
- Coordinate interviews, press conferences, conference calls for media.
- Supply media with photographs, statistics, features, etc.

AREA #2

Publicity.

Develop a constant flow of 49ers information to the media outlets in the San Francisco bay area and throughout the country, all the while keeping the reputation of the 49ers organization utmost in mind.

- Arrange all press interviews.
- Arrange all press conferences.
- Arrange weekly conference to opposing coach.
- Create story ideas of the positive nature for media use.
- Write feature stories for media use.

AREA #3

Publications.

Oversee the writing, editing, lay-out, and proofreading for all of the team's publications, including:

- Media guide (press book).
- Game day magazine (10 issues and playoffs).
- Preseason prospectus.
- 49ers' yearbook.
- News releases.
- Credentials (10 home games and playoffs).
- Calendar.
- Advertising rate card and brochure.
- Ticket brochure.
- Posters, schedules, etc.
- Christmas cards.
- Business cards.
- Any (and all) other printed materials from/by/about the 49ers.

AREA #4

Promotions.

To plan and organize as many promotions as possible each year in an effort to gain more interest and fame for the team, create goodwill for the team toward its fans, and create added income for the club. All the while, keep the reputation of the 49ers organization utmost in mind.

- Attract paid support for annual club flyers, brochures, and other publications.
- Establish give-a-ways for home game fans (10 games and playoffs).
- Express promotional themes in 49ers' publications.
- Establish a speakers bureau and players' appearances system.
- Gain advertising support to pay for year-round hand-outs to fans.
- Identify those money-making ideas that will also promote the 49ers.

AREA #5

Photography.

Work with team photographers (and sometimes outside photogs) in shooting assignments and all photo projects, including:

- Picture orders.
- Photo file maintenance.

- Interior photo decorating projects for the 49ers' offices.
- Selection of art for publications.
- Team pictures.
- Staff pictures.

AREA #6

Public relations.

Although everything we do has an impact on the 49ers' public relations, the following are some of the key areas:

- Make personal appearances at public and private gatherings.
- Handle phone and mail requests from the public.
- Handle auction item and donation requests.
- Oversee the areas of statistics and research.
- Work in conjunction with NFL Films to produce an annual highlight film to encourage season ticket sales, promote the team to the fans, and give players and staff a tool to supplement their speaking engagements.

AREA #7

Press box and other game-day duties.

Handle the supervision of the press box and assist other 49ers and NFL officials in the timely execution of all game day functions.

- Accommodate media on all game-day needs (seating, information, research, interviews, etc.)
- Serve as general "fire fighter" for any problems that arise with media, team, scoreboard, lights, clock, stats, etc.
- Assist game officials and electronic media with game-day logistics.
- Assist stats crew, PA, message board operators, etc.
- Help fulfill the needs of the visiting club.

AREA #8

Player appearances and other public gatherings.

Oversee the coordination of scheduling all player and staff appearances and public functions with which the 49ers are involved (supply materials in such situations, put together speeches for players and staff, etc.).

AREA #9

Advancing.

- Travel to the city in which the 49ers will play during the week of a road game and set up hotel, promote the game with the local media, speak to local clubs, radio and TV shows and print media about the game and the 49ers.

- Try to make the 49ers' visit go as smoothly as possible, especially those aspects involving meals and rooms.

AREA #10

Personal growth, department supervision and NFL Office Liaison

The goal in this situation is to have continual improvement in overall knowledge of this profession, which is reflected in improved performances by the 49ers' Public Relations Department. This objective can be enhanced on a day-to-day basis, as well as a yearly basis, by undertaking the following steps:

- Continued attendance and participation in all office and team functions and meetings, along with daily work assignments.
- Continued attendance and participation in all annual NFL meetings, for example, the annual NFL Public Relations Directors meeting. Continue to serve on any national panels (e.g., the NFL PR Directors' Special Projects Committee).
- Taking on additional work assignments with an attitude of "whatever it takes" to be successful as an organization, an NFL franchise, a Public Relations Department and a PR Director. Do whatever needs to be done to help the 49ers win the world championship each season.
- Maintaining constant communication with the NFL office and all other teams in all areas of responsibility (e.g., NFL Films, broadcast affairs, etc.).

RODNEY KNOX—PUBLICATIONS COORDINATOR

Major goal:

To perform as a liaison between the team and the public in general, and the media specifically; provide information and communication that will enhance the perception of the San Francisco 49ers football organization.

Major areas of responsibility:

1. Publications.
2. Media relations.
3. Advancing.
4. Day-of-game coordination.
5. Community contact.
6. Special projects.
7. Personal growth.

AREA #1

Publications.

- Media guide.

- Game day magazine.
- Prospectus.
- News releases.
- Weekly updated player biographies.
- Press box notes.
- Scoreboard and public address announcements.
- General fan mail correspondence.
- Composition of special correspondence.
- Speech writing for players.
- Team yearbook.

AREA #2

Media relations.

- Setting up interviews.
- Conducting conference calls.
- Creating story ideas for media use.
- Writing feature stories.
- Handling national requests (TV networks, NFL Films, etc.).

AREA #3

Advancing.

- Ready all the sleeping, meeting, and function rooms for the team.
- Contact the local media to brief and promote 49ers.
- Contact with general public through luncheons, radio talk shows, fan club meetings.

AREA #4

Day-of-game coordination.

- Accommodate media on all game day needs (seating, statistical information, reference source, etc.).
- Serve as a general "fire fighter" for any problems that arise with media, team, or other game day staffers.
- Assist game officials with timely procedure of game-day functions.
- Aid electronic media with game day logistics.

AREA #5

Community contact.

- Work with charitable and support groups to promote team (Kidney Foundation, Children's Hospital, etc.).

- Serve as a volunteer in Big Brothers/Big Sisters of San Francisco.
- Serve on the board of directors of "Champs Foundation" (established by members of the team).

AREA #6

Special projects.

- Handling requests of other departments within the organization.
- Coordination of the players' off-season appearances (when directly requested by group).
- Media fishing derby.
- Solicitation of sponsors for advertising in publications.

AREA #7

Personal growth.

- Taking on additional learning tasks to help improve quality of work (computer schooling, video work).
- Attending seminars on sports administration.

KENNETH DARGEL—TICKET MANAGER

Major goal:
To efficiently administer all functions of the Ticket Department of the San Francisco 49ers and to continue our reputation as one of the better ticket operations in the NFL.

Major areas of responsibility:
1. Season ticket sales.
2. Individual game ticket sales.
3. Customer relations.
4. Financial accountability.
5. Community orientation.
6. Management and staff relations.
7. Working area.
8. Equipment and inventories.
9. Income generation.
10. Box office statements and supporting documentation.

Measures of effectiveness:
- To conduct orderly season ticket sales to continuing and new customers on a fair and equitable basis in accordance with policy measures in effect or forthcoming.

- Ethics. Maintain professional ethics and personal integrity in relationships and dealings with other NFL organizations. Responsible for any breach of club confidentiality or ethics in dealing with other NFL staff members by any member of the assistant coaching staff.

- Scouting. Work in conjunction with Bill Walsh and the scouting department as to the utilization of coaches for college scouting and evaluation. This would include necessary preparation for the yearly college draft. Also coordinate with Bill Walsh individual NFL player evaluations by coaching staff related to potential trades or signings.

- Fiscal. To adhere to essential business and financial guidelines and directives as set forth by club management. This is related to a responsibility for fiscal matters related to head coaching responsibilities (i.e., discretion and foresight in exchanging on player's salaries and financial matters of the 49er franchise).

- Accessibility. As requested, be prepared to critique player performances, team development, and post-game analysis. Participate with 49er ownership and management regarding short- and long-term planning, specific goals and objectives.

- NFL constitution. A working knowledge of the NFL constitution and bylaws (refer to Article IX, Prohibited Conduct, pages 24-29) is essential and any infraction that may occur is to be reported immediately to San Francisco 49er management.

- Outside commitments. Association or involvement in external personal business ventures should be communicated to and approved by management. This would include radio, television shows, and commercials.

- Staff selection and evaluation. The head coach will be directly responsible for evaluation and selection process of coaching staff. His decision will be subject to reasonable approval from Ed DeBartolo and Bill Walsh. Termination would be subject to the same process and not be unreasonably withheld. The head coach can expect support and accommodation in this area.

JOHN E. MCVAY—VICE PRESIDENT FOR FOOTBALL ADMINISTRATION

Major goals:
- Effectively raise the talent level of the San Francisco 49ers by assisting in the conducting of the NFL college draft, compiling trades with other teams, claiming players from the NFL waiver system, and signing free agent players.
- Effectively conduct the day-to-day business activities of the 49ers as they relate to the NFL office, and interact with the other NFL franchises.
- Effectively negotiate player contracts within the guidelines prescribed by the NFL and the 49ers.

Major areas of responsibility and measures of effectiveness:
1. Talent acquisition.

- To supervise printing of tickets in-house and to ensure the improbability of "leakage" of blank stock or overprint of tickets.

- To arrange and supervise the packaging, sorting, weighing and delivery of season tickets by the U.S. Postal Service for ultimate delivery to customers in accordance with prevailing U.S. Postal regulations.

- To supervise collection and accounting for all funds from sale of season tickets and to ensure proper banking procedures of such funds. This step includes initiation of collection procedures on "bad checks" in conjunction with the Business Office.

AREA #2

Individual game ticket sales.

- To arrange for inventory controls of all available tickets (after season sales) and to ensure financial accountability for sale of all such tickets. This step includes supervision of assignment of tickets to electronic outlets, mail order sales, across-the-counter sales and day-of-game sales at stadium.

- Ensure procurement of adequate qualified help both for advance ticket sales and day-of-game ticket sales and to provide adequate instruction to all employees to assure proper performance of their duties in accordance with stated aims and procedures.

- Supervise collection, balancing and accounting for all funds from sale of individual game tickets.

- Prepare the weekly ticket sales report to the Owner which is included in the Accounting Department's weekly financial report.

AREA #3

Customer relations.

In many respects, the public relations aspects of this position may be one of the most important responsibilities of the Ticket Manager. There are few other departments within an NFL franchise which have as much direct contact with the public as the Ticket Department. Fair and honest relations with the buying or inquiring public can create a positive market where a suspicious or wary market might otherwise develop.

AREA #4

Financial accountability.

The Ticket Manager is responsible for administering procedures to ensure prompt and accurate deposit of all ticket sales monies. Cooperation with the Business Manager is essential to facilitate money management and cash flow. As the Ticket Office is presently a detached entity, close communication is necessary between the Business Manger and the Ticket Manager.

AREA #5

Community orientation.

It is the responsibility of the Ticket Manger, as well as all department head level personnel, to constantly represent the 49er ownership and management as "involved" citizens of the community. It is the stated aim of our Owner to participate with "worthy cause" groups by issuing complimentary tickets, within the guidelines set forth in the constitution and by-laws of the NFL, to such groups whenever possible and to determine to the best of our ability which groups should receive such tickets.

AREA #6

Management and staff relations.

The Ticket Manager is responsible for seeing that his staff cooperates to the fullest with all other staff and management personnel in matters concerning the allocation of tickets within the limits of sound box office procedures. It is also his responsibility to curb any potential abuses of ticket allocations and to make other members of management and/or ownership aware of such abuses, should they occur.

AREA #7

Working area.

The Ticket Manager, in conjunction with the Business Manager, should be responsible for the proper janitorial services rendered at the Ticket Office and related spaces at Candlestick Park (i.e., 3Com Stadium). A presentable professional appearance of the Ticket Office is necessary for a proper public reaction to our operation.

AREA #8

Equipment and inventories.

Relatively sophisticated computer equipment is installed and in operation in the Ticket Office. Service contracts are in force to protect and maintain this equipment; however, certain supervision is necessary to make sure all systems are functioning properly. It is necessary to keep in step with the state of the art so that whenever new or improved equipment becomes available, evaluations can be made concerning the desirability of acquiring any new equipment.

Maintaining sufficient inventories of supplies and projections of future needs is the responsibility of the Ticket Manager. Purchasing such supplies is generally most economical if done in bulk lots (e.g. envelopes, invoices, etc.). The task should be delegated to an assistant.

AREA #9

Income generation.

It would be unfair to state that the Ticket Manager or Ticket Office Staff is responsible for any increased sales. On a public relations basis, it is important that the

Ticket Manager and his staff be held accountable for any behavior which could cause loss of income such as desultory or insulting actions which would result in cancellations of ticket purchases.

AREA #10

Box office statements and supporting documentation.

Box office statements and supporting documents must be completed on the day of the game and submitted to the NFL Office and for use internally to account for ticket sales. These are completed by the Ticket Manager, and must be cross checked for balancing purposes.

Progress report and projections:

- We are at our optimum season ticket sales with a waiting list consisting of approximately 11,000 new season tickets requested and approximately 7,000 season tickets requested by existing ticket holders.

- We have continued to acquire sponsors for most of our Ticket Office mailings which help defray our costs for envelopes and tickets which are our major expense.

- The Ticket Office is working closely with architects and designers with respect to the expansion and renovation of Candlestick Park. We will attempt to inconvenience season ticket holders as little as possible with regard to relocating seating.

MURLAN C. FOWELL—DIRECTOR OF STADIUM OPERATIONS

Major areas of responsibility:

1. Supervision of game day operations:
   - Parking:
   - Administration.
     - √ Billing
     - √ Collection
     - √ Public relations
   - Operation.
     - √ Coordinate outside contractors
     - √ Supplement staffing
     - √ Security
   - Concessions.
   - Security.
   - Supervise ushers and people.
2. Supervision of suite operations (refer to next section).

MURLAN C. FOWELL—LUXURY SUITE MANAGER

Major goals:

- Effectively execute the operational responsibilities of the Luxury Suites Office. Establish and maintain consistent communication with the suite holders and the 49er Administrative Offices. Provide all suite holders with VIP service at all times.

- Develop sales referrals for phases II & III by maintaining close contact with suite holders and guests. Pursue contacts made by interested parties to our office, secure deposits and establish a priority waiting list in an effort to pre-sell all suites.

Major areas of responsibility:

1. Supervision of suite operations.
2. Inspection of suites during baseball season.
3. Maintenance of suites during football season.
4. Coordinate marketing and sales of phases II & III suites.
5. Administration of contracts, rules and regulations.
6. Collection of rents, deposits and accounts receivable from suite services.
7. Architectural and construction liaison for the 49ers between the city and the DeBartolo Corporation.
8. Develop and maintain rapport with suite holders.
9. Administer parking and food and beverage concessions as they become available.
10. Prepare and submit budget for administrative staffing and concession operations.
11. Provide updated sales and status reports for areas of responsibility.
12. Coordinate suite services with outside contractors as required (i.e., Stevens).
13. Hire, train, and supervise temporary personnel for suite operations on game day.
14. Supervise suite operations on game day.
15. Community affairs—San Francisco Recreation and Park Department.
16. Candlestick Park (3Com Stadium)—regular liaison.
17. Personal growth.

AREA #1

Supervision of suite operations.

- Effectively manage and supervise day-to-day operations of the Luxury Suite Office and Staff.

- Analyze administrative needs, establish and implement systems, controls, and staffing as required.

- Through effective management, create a professional work environment in which staff personnel can be proud of their accomplishments, producing effective results for the 49er organization.

AREA #2

Inspection of suites during the baseball season.

- Develop and implement inspection and reporting system designed to notify interested parties as to damages and cleanliness standards established by the San Francisco Giants organization.
- Report results to the City and conduct follow-up to ensure proper repairs and maintenance is conducted. Ensure that inspections are done immediately following each break in Giants' home games.

AREA #3

Maintenance of suites during the football season.

- Establish a maintenance program for the football season to include: warehouse facilities, spare parts inventory, subcontractors, and maintenance personnel, in order to timely effect repairs and reduce suite holder complaints and inconvenience.
- Hire and supervise a janitorial contractor for clean-up of suites after each event.

AREA #4

Coordinate marketing and sales of phases II & III suites.

- Develop sales referrals for open suites in phases II & III.
- Meet with prospective suite holders; show them through existing suites; explain contractual obligations; services available; benefits; amenities; etc., in a effort to close suites prior to availability.
- Maintain informational files as to prospective suite holders' needs and match up those that are willing to share suites. This step will give us an additional level of potential licensees.

AREA #5

Administration of contacts, rules, and regulations.

- Create informational documents establishing rules and regulations for suite holders. Instruct staff on how to handle complaints and supervise administration of rules.
- Maintain up-to-date files on each suite to include contracts, correspondence, and inquiries from suite holders.
- Conduct effective follow-up to maintain standards set forth by the Luxury Suite Office.

AREA #6

Collection of rents, deposits and accounts receivable from suite service.

- Establish a billing system for all accounts receivable and conduct effective follow-up to ensure all monies due are collected in a timely manner.
- Establish an ordering system for services available with enough lead time to ensure proper stocking and delivery of food to suites to accomplish a timely and professional service.
- Supervise all service to suite holders and personally be involved with any and all problems and resolve them immediately.

AREA #7

Architectural and construction liaison for the 49ers between the City and the DeBartolo Corporation.

- Follow-up on architects and contractors and report the status of progress weekly to the 49ers and the DeBartolo Corporation.
- Maintain contact with city offices and report any needs or problems that may arise that would affect the 49ers' position regarding the luxury suites.

AREA #8

Develop and maintain rapport with suite holders.

- Maintain close contact with suite holders on game day and establish positive rapport to minimize any problems that may arise.
- Cultivate guests as potential suite holders and provide top level service to all.
- Conduct effective follow-up after each game and implement correspondence to suite holders notifying them as to disposition of requests, problems, etc.

AREA #9

Administer parking and food & beverage concessions as they become available.

- Develop a full understanding of concession operations prior to the contracts coming due.
- Analyze our abilities to operate and/or negotiate new contracts with existing concessionaires.
- Administer concession operations once we assume responsibilities or enter into new agreements.

Area #10

Prepare and submit budgets for administrative staffing and concession operations.

- Prepare budgets for each area within overall responsibility and group together into a masterbudget and submit to 49er Administrative office.

- Administer all operational areas within budget limitations and maximize profitability for 49er organization.

AREA #11

Prepare updated sales and status reports for areas of responsibility.

- Maintain consistent up-to-date communications with all concerned parties.
- Prepare a weekly sales report which clearly outlines all activity during the preceding week. Prepare a weekly status report which updates construction and any relevant activities.

AREA #12

Coordinate suite services with outside contractors as required.

- Coordinate services required with any outside contractors, such as Stevens, regarding Food and Beverage operations. This step will be ideal training for either a potential takeover of concession operations or an improved ability to negotiate a contract with the existing contractor.
- Interview and negotiate with other vendors as needed to provide necessary services to the suite holders.

AREA #13

Hire, train, and supervise temporary personnel for suite operations on game day.

- Establish needs of luxury suites on game day.
- Hire and train all temporary personnel to provide the level of service required. Areas of responsibility that will require temporary workers will include but not be limited to: supervisors and hostesses, bartenders, maintenance, and food and beverage service personnel.
- Coordinate with Keith Simon any crossover between stadium ushers and suite personnel.
- Work closely with usher supervisors to maintain continuity between different groups of employees, unions, etc.

AREA #14

Supervise suite operations on game day.

- Maintain a highly visible active posture on game day.
- Work closely with all supervisors and other personnel and resolve problems quickly and effectively.
- Maintain a high state of morale and energy levels to maximize efficiency resulting in superior service to suite holders.
- Establish a communication system between all key personnel and maximize reaction time for any and all problems.

- Check closely with as many suites as possible during the game and collect feedback on the overall operation from the suite holder's perspective.

AREA #15

Community affairs—San Francisco Recreation and Park Department.

- Continuing communication and informal presentations with the San Francisco Recreation and Park Commission.

AREA #16

Candlestick Park—regular liaison.

- Regular attention to Candlestick Park facilities and maintenance, including luxury suites.

Area #17

Personal growth.

- Expand knowledge of stadium operation in order to function efficiently and effectively as more responsibilities occur.
- Develop rapport with other stadium personnel and maintain communication in an effort to stay current with stadium operations.
- Attend seminars regarding stadium management and visit other stadiums to develop an overview of concession and luxury suite operations.
- Learn computer operations through outside classes in order to maximize efficiency of my office.
- Enlarge area of responsibility by accepting additional duties as directed by the General Manager.

GENERIC JOB DESCRIPTIONS

AREA SCOUT (COLLEGE)

Basic qualifications for the position:

- Has a full knowledge and understanding of the written requirements (e.g. forms, reports, deadlines, etc.) for the position.
- Has completed thorough training and preparation in club procedures and operational guidelines.
- Has a working knowledge of the assigned area and a familiarity with the assigned universities.
- Has an understanding of each position and the key evaluation features for each position (e.g. linebacker, cornerback, offensive lineman, etc.).
- Is proficient in testing and measuring as required by the club.

- Is proficient in operating a home computer system.

Basic responsibilities of the position:

- Utilize the head coach, assistant coaches, trainer, team physician, football secretaries and others as evaluation resources.

- Develop a yearly schedule that includes spring and fall practice and assigned all-star games. This schedule should be detailed, including travel, lodging, practice schedules and appointments as they are set.

- Utilize club process in evaluating video at universities.

- Wears professional attire, as designated by club.

- Is well-versed in the interview process, mental personality profiles, and is able to conduct the desired performance and written tests.

- Work in conjunction with the Director of College Scouting on special "projects" and collaborates with fellow scouts in "cross" evaluations.

- Maintain complete confidentiality in the scouting process.

- Avoid lengthy distractions with contemporaries while doing business.

- Interact with the team's coaching staff as part of the final step in the evaluation process; solicit their imput and involvement in the evaluative report.

- Be fully prepared at designated club meetings (i.e., be able to provide whatever information is requested and be able to provide a subjective evaluation of each candidate).

- Work with the video technician in preparing a tape of each suitable candidate which can be utilized by coaches and management.

- Work with the team's strength coach regarding his requirements as part of a complete file on each player.

- Participate in the evaluation of the current squad in both mini-camps and early training camp, as well as in evaluations of college free agents, veteran free agents and requested "vested" free agents.

- Participate in evaluating ratings after one year.

- Follow current NFL players from his assigned area as they join and leave other teams and prepare to respond on them.

- Keep in mind that sophomore and junior evaluative ratings can become crucial as athletes decide whether to declare for the NFL draft; as such considerable work is required with the top underclassmen.

HEAD ATHLETIC TRAINER

The individual in this position is responsible for formulating and coordinating a "total" athletic training operation for the organization. Typically, this operation includes the head trainer, the assistant trainers, the physiotherapists, and those individuals who are involved in the general, rehabilitative, preventive and specialized duties as required.

Basic responsibilities of the position:

- Establish priorities for the training department related to seriousness of the injury and the prescribed treatment.
- Maintain a professional atmosphere in the training quarters and among the staff.
- Indoctrinate and train the new staff and familiarize them with the team's operational practices and policies.
- Guarantee professional certification of the staff.
- Organize a continuing education program for the staff, constantly updating the entire staff's approach to training, conditioning and rehabilitation.
- Establish a budget for all supplies and equipment, as required by management or the business office.
- Coordinate with the team's doctors/specialists.
- Establish a working relationship with hospitals and ensure that the team's emergency needs can be met.
- Coordinate with the rehabilitation specialists.
- Coordinate with the team's doctors for individual and squad physicals.
- Schedule appointments with medical specialists, as required.
- Maintain the athletic training facility (i.e., headquarters, training camp, etc.).
- Purchase supplies and equipment.
- Delegate and define the responsibilities of the training staff.
- Report to the head coach and/or management as appropriate.
- Serve as personal liaison with assistant coaches.
- Provide daily updates to the coaching staff in the training camp.
- Serve as a resource for the coaching staff and management in player evaluations (physically and otherwise).
- Be on the field during games and practices to provide athletic training services as required.
- Establish procedures and policies for responding to injuries on the field during both practices and games.
- Tape and otherwise attend to the athletic training needs of the players to prepare them for practices and games
- Stay abreast of the newest athletic training techniques.
- Develop rehab and preventive plans and programs for individual players.
- Maintain a complete, updated history of each consequential injury.
- Monitor each injury rehab.

- Establish and continue to refine injury preventive programs.
- Establish emergency procedures.
- Act as a contact with college trainers in preparing for the NFL's collegiate draft.
- Prepare a complete file on free agent players as directed by management.
- Direct the transport of training supplies for training camp and all home and away games.
- Establish an athletic training staff "hotline" that is available 24 hours a day to both players and the coaching staff.
- Establish procedures and a timetable for contacting a player's family when a consequential injury occurs (as agreed upon by coach and management).

LEGAL COUNSEL

Basic responsibilities of the position:
- Oversee and coordinate all legal actions involving the organization.
- Provide professional advice on all organizational legal matters and concerns of employees and players.
- Develop a projection of and a plan for handling short- and long-term legal issues that the organization should address, particularly those dictated by ownership and CEO.
- Maintain absolute confidentiality in all legal matters involving the organization.
- Act as a conduit with the League office with regard to its dictates and covenants.

DIRECTOR OF RESEARCH AND DEVELOPMENT

The individual in this position is responsible for managing the computer applications attendant to coaching, game analysis, player personnel analysis, and computerized video editing. In most NFL organizations, this individual is also in charge of the team's physical conditioning and training staff.

All factors considered, the individual hired for this position should have at least three years of football coaching experience. He should also have a proven record of developing useful computer applications within a football environment. As a rule, hiring preference should be given to a person with a graduate degree, teaching experience, and relevant coursework in research methodology, statistical analysis, and scientific writing skills.

Basic responsibilities of the position:
- Develop and produce weekly scouting reports, video editing, and NFL compliance reports.

- Develop and produce ad hoc research, applications and reports within the organization's football operations as requested by management, coaches and staff.
- Assist other staff members in learning and developing computer applications within the team's football operations.
- Identify, evaluate and recommend new applications and technologies to improve football operations.

DIRECTOR OF MARKETING

Basic responsibilities of the position:

- Coordinate and promote all sales and promotion activities involving tickets, suites, and merchandise.
- Coordinate and promote all personal appearances (by players, coaches, and staff) and special events (e.g., charitable events, etc.)
- Coordinate and promote half-time shows and programs.
- Serve as a liaison with NFL Properties and League marketing personnel.

DIRECTOR OF MEDIA RELATIONS

Basic responsibilities of the position:

- Serve as a liaison with the written and electronic media:
  - Facilitate interviews.
  - Provide credentials.
  - Establish storylines that are in the best interest of the club.
- Orchestrate crisis and announcement events.
- Must keep organization and players' best interest in mind.
- Must not give into any disruptive agenda the media might have (i.e., negative finger-pointing).
- Must be very aggressive in confronting inaccurate or false reporting.
- Act as liaison with League media personnel.
- Coordinate internal media needs.
- Help to educate all members of the organization who interact with media.
- Coordinate all organizational publications.
- Serve as an advance agent for the team's road games:
  - Oversee travel arrangements.

- Promote the game with local media and fans.
- Coordinate player interviews with local media.

EQUIPMENT DIRECTOR

Basic responsibilities of the position:
- Oversees the procurement and maintenance of all equipment.
- Coordinate all shipping of equipment-related materials.

FACILITY DIRECTOR

Basic responsibilities of the position:
- Direct the activities of the maintenance group for the facility.
- Supervise the groundskeeper.

DIRECTOR OF SECURITY

Basic responsibilities of the position:
- Oversee all security measures for the facility and playing venue.
- Establish a network in the community for security concerns of the players and coaches.
  - Establish protocol with local law enforcement agencies.
- Coordinate and oversee all security measures with regard to travel.
- Establish a complete security protocol for training camp.
- Serve as a liaison with League security personnel.
- Provide assistance to both players and coaches with regard to background checks of prospective business associates.

SAMPLE SCHEDULE OF
SUPPLEMENTAL DUTIES

George Seifert. (Basic assignment: defensive coordinator.)
Supplemental assignments:

- Defensive playbooks.
- Scouting report supervision (defense).
- Ongoing evaluation of defensive personnel.
- Fellowship coaches.
- Computer—training camp practices.

Bill McPherson. (Basic assignment: linebackers coach.)
Supplemental assignments:

- Defensive video tape (with Tom Hart).
- Locker rooms (with Ray)—camp and Santa Clara.
- Liaison with Msg. Armstrong.
- Workouts of squad candidates during the year.
- Computer—statistical analysis for defense.

Mike Holmgren. (Basic assignment: quarterback development.)
Supplemental assignments:

- Offensive computer (with Bobb).
- Offensive playbook (with Bobb).
- Workouts of squad candidates during the year.
- Video training cut-up tapes (with Denny).
- Yearly passing game composite (with Denny).
- Computer—mini-camp formats, regular season practice plans.

Dennis Green. (Basic assignment: wide receivers and tight ends coach.)
Supplemental assignments:

- Off-season practice organization.
- Video training cut-up tapes.
- Yearly passing game composite.
- Workouts of squad candidates during the year.
- Computer—training camp.

Sherman Lewis. (Basic assignment: running backs coach.)
Supplemental assignments:

- Offensive scouting report.
- Buses—roster check.
- Assist Ray with planes.
- Workouts of squad candidates during the year.
- Computer—scouting reports file.

Bobb McKittrick. (Basic assignment: offensive line coach.)
Supplemental assignments:

- Offensive computer (with Mike).
- Offensive scouting report (assist Sherman).
- NFL rules and regulations—by-laws and constitution.
- Research and development (field equipment).
- Offensive playbook (with Mike).
- Offensive cut-ups (video tape).
- Workouts of squad candidates during the year.
- Computer—statistical analysis (offense) file.

Lynn Stiles. (Basic assignment: special teams coach.)
Supplemental assignments:

- Player fines.
- Rule books.
- Player equipment liaison (with Bronco).
- Computer—statistical analysis (special teams), player personnel liaison.

Ray Rhodes. (Basic assignment: defensive backs coach.)
Supplemental assignments:

- Player finance program (with Keith).
- Planes—roster check (with Sherman).
- Assist Sherman with buses and roster check.
- Locker rooms (with McPherson)—camp and Santa Clara.

- Workouts of squad candidates during the year.
- Computer—mini-camp formats—regular season practice plans.

Fred vonAppen. (Basic responsibility: defensive line coach.)
Supplemental assignments:
- Video exchange liaison with Robby.
- Daily practice video—photography.
- Assist Neal with visiting coaches.
- Visual aid equipment.
- Video exchange (with Robby).
- Workouts of squad candidates during the year.

Tom Hart. (Basic assignment: assistant defensive line coach.)
Supplemental assignments:
- College scouting.
- Player try-outs (defense).
- Preparation for draft.
- Player relations counseling.
- Materials, equipment and supplies (defense).
- Meeting rooms (staff/defense).
- Workouts of squad candidates during the year.
- Defense video tapes (with McPherson).

Jerry Attaway. (Basic assignment: weight training.)
Supplemental assignments:
- Scouting—physical checks/injuries (draft—pro).
- Research and development—current trends in physical training field.
- Nutritional needs—training camp and regular season.
- Off-season physical programs.
- Staff computer specialist.
- Monitor training camp food service.
- Team meals on the road (with Keith).

Norb Hecker. (Basic assignment: executive administrator.)
Supplemental assignments:
- Liaison with NFL—general business with John McVay.
- In charge of training camp—with R.C. as Director.
- Administrator of mini-camps—with Neal Dahlen.
- Liaison with city and county of Santa Clara.
- Local business—liaison.

- Liaison with Candlestick—fields/structural.
- Travel coordinator with Keith Simon.
- Special project research.
- Alumni relations with R.C. Owens.
- Computer/inventory system.

Neal Dahlen. (Basic assignment: Director of Football Operations.)
Supplemental assignments:
- Research and development.
- Mini-camp—assist Norb.
- Liaison with Norb—fields.
- Coaches meetings, schedules, communications.
- Weekly highlight tape.
- Liaison with Keith—facilities and services for football operation.
- Field security personnel and procedures (training camp).
- Visiting coaches (with Fred).
- Video/audio—visual coaching needs (liaison with Robby).
- Field equipment needs (liaison with Bronco).
- On-field work incentives.
- Liaison with Bill on team functions, meals/social functions.
- Fellowship coaches.
- Coordinate Polaroid services.
- Bed check (hotels).
- Medical/trainers liaison.
- Bed check rotation (coaches schedule—training camp).
- Liaison with Jerry Attaway.
- Practice arrangements outside of Santa Clara.
- Coordinate football-related computer services.

SAMPLE TEAM LECTURES

SQUAD LECTURE #1
(mini camp)

1. Introduction:
   - coaches—trainers—etc.
2. Atmosphere:
   - conditioning
   - system
   - exchange—players—coaches
3. Be punctual.
4. Please don't destroy self in drills.
5. Everyone—equal chance.
6. Opportunity will come—some may have to have patience.
7. Observe veterans—learn from them.
8. Conditioning vital—pay price—invest your career—existence to championship excellence.
9. We have two months.
10. Every team—talented.
11. How well we function as a unit—together—system—skills coordinated.
12. I may not be acquainted with everyone. Don't be concerned—I'm involved with overall operation now—we will become acquainted.
13. Conditioning—knowledge—then you can demonstrate your abilities—become expert in condition nutrition.
14. Cooperate with managers.

15. Hard work as team—brings mutual trust.
16. Don't talk yourself out of making team.
17. Earn—specialization:
    • special teams—nickel—short yardage—etc.
18. Everyone—optimistic at this point.
19. Toughest class you've had—never been so motivated.
20. Same basis of competition as you faced in high school—college. "Not simply a business."

SQUAD LECTURE #2
(rookie training camp)
1. We want to get a solid start in a three-day "crash program of football." That will be repeated when the veterans arrive. It is important for us to find out how much that you can learn and retain in this period.
2. Stamina and durability are vital qualities for which we will be looking.
3. Our style of football requires "special qualities"—hitting, flawless execution, etc.
4. We expect to win—we are not building.
5. As you practice, you must not play with "desperation"—you must show poise. (Don't sacrifice your body.)
6. Punctuality is essential.
7. Use good judgment in your personal behavior during camp. Avoid drugs and alcohol.
8. Treat the college and community with full respect.
9. Study your material—don't short-change yourself.
10. Don't worry about the performance of other players.
11. Observe veteran players—learn from them
12. Look like a professional—keep your shirttail in, don't sit on your helmet, keep track of your equipment—don't leave it lying around.
13. Wear all of your protective equipment (prevent injury).
14. Program regular study time into your daily schedule.
15. Don't grab shirts in drills; it can cause injuries.

SQUAD LECTURE #3
(training camp)
Initial Squad meeting
1. It is vital you show respect to all 49er employed personnel, regardless of their responsibility.
2. Reminder to sign in for every meal—no exceptions.

3. Be on time for all scheduled events.

4. Dorm reminders—don't interfere with another man's life style. Don't impose your life style on others—be considerate.

5. Show respect for others—don't push it to the limits.

6. No gambling in the rooms—it leads to problems.

7. Telephone set up in dorm—sign up on an individual basis. Reminder of emergency number. Check with front desk.

8. Parking outlined—when, where and how. Lock cars at all times.

9. Attire—clothing code outlined. Shirts with sleeves.

10. Dining manners—use common sense and think of the other fellow. Use judgment in volume of talk.

11. Minimize the amount of food taken back to the dorms.

12. Use good judgment in taking care of your valuables. Don't tempt the person with the problem.

13. No liquor in your rooms.

14. Visitors check in through your position coach.

15. Be careful of the casual acquaintances.

16. Avoid smoking in rooms.

17. Keep clear of vulgar language in public.

18. Respect the facilities which will be our home for some two months in duration.

19. Show class in public to people that hang around the camp.

20. Show respect for the fans that want to interact with players around camp.

21. Keep appointments with sports writers and when you have scheduled interviews.

22. Police the locker room and make it as livable as possible.

23. Outlined Bronco's role as equipment man.

24. Take care of your field equipment and seek help if you are not satisfied.

25. Cooperate with the trainers and avail yourself of their care.

26. Know the taping schedule. Rookies tape first. Be prompt for treatment. Training room is not a meeting place.

27. Laundry facilities in the dormitory.

28. Off campus recreation—avoid frequenting the same hangouts. No downtown difficulties—show class at all times.

29. Think respectfully of your teammates at all times.

30. Covered fine list put out in their individual playbooks.

31. We, as professional club, will levy fines and hold to them when necessary.

32. Critique of physical testing that took place in demonstrating the level of individual preparation.

33. You will find the staff to reinforce certain coaching points—we will habitually repeat verbally certain vital concepts.

34. We are in a business proposition but it runs far deeper than that—emotion, fellowship, sacrifice.

35. Don't be selfish—people can't respect someone who is selfish.

36. Thrive on the details of your job on our football team. Take great pride in your technical and physical expertise.

37. We must thrive to have your best year—if we reach that goal collectively, we will be successful.

38. Performance, big plays—we must have those from individual players.

39. Everybody is given the same level of respect from the 49er organization. You are a 49er and not a tryout candidate. Remember you have the responsibility of being a 49er.

40. Mutual respect of teammates is critically important.

41. 49er football is just that; it is not a platform for politics, religion, geography. Keep our business strictly football. Each man has a right to privacy.

SQUAD LECTURE #4

1. Atmosphere:
    - businesslike—professional
    - attention—study—personal development
    - respect for team—teammates
    - thrive on skills—techniques
    - develop individual performance
    - teaching—learning combination (coach/player)
    - everyone is considered—given same respect by coaches and management

2. Teammates:
    - mutual respect—as pro athlete, competitor, and person
    - honest competition between dedicated, highly motivated athletes
    - no hazing or harassing
    - no taunting of opposing position (i.e., offensive/defensive line)
    - communicate in developing other position (i.e., WR vs. DB)
    - don't force your values on others

3. Goals:
    - team coordination—timing—development
    - selection of best athletes for 49ers and their particular position
    - individual skill development and specialization

- prepare for opponent—tactics—methods
- develop 49er system—fundamentals—skills
- develop ability to communicate under stress (between coaches and players)

4. Pulling for someone to make it—different option than coaches:
   - best attacking team
   - best late game poise
   - in sync—no error
   - big turnover ratio
   - score touchdowns
   - deal with situations
   - special teams

5. SF 49ers—NFL profession or career is not a platform for:
   - politics
   - religious beliefs
   - geographic preference
   - racial or ethnic preference
   - fraternal or other personal affiliations
   - a source for sales or business ventures

SQUAD LECTURE #5
(standard of performance)

1. You have a stake—investment in regard to time spent.
2. First minute and last minute must be identical regardless of score—situation—seasonal circumstances.
3. Opponent should be considered as object rather than personality.
4. Take pride in execution and the victories will follow.
5. Prepare decisively and specifically. Must be prepared for all circumstances—have poise and confidence for all game situations.
6. Can't let up—be confused—disoriented.
7. Standard of play cannot vary according to opponent—i.e., Seattle/New York Giants.
8. Standard of play cannot vary according to who is in game—regulars/backups.
9. If we win—we are not going to talk—i.e., San Diego vs. Cardinals.
10. Only prerequisite is a field—not concern over weather—playing surface—travel—opponent's record. Best atmosphere will be completely silent crowd when we are on the road.
11. Don't concern yourself over teammate's failure:

- don't lose concentration because of previous failure on previous play
- no frustration because of continuing lack of results—examples
- score not a factor—can reverse itself quickly—examples

12. Outside influences (friends, family, business associates, fans) affecting your attitudes and state of mind.

13. Agents spreading dissatisfaction with your financial arrangements.

14. Comparing so-called contracts and commitments with other player (they will exaggerate between 20-40%).

15. Protect against—"I was great in 1981"—"Just watch me now"—"I have a reputation to live up to"—"I must make the 'Big Play' or 'Big Hit.'"

16. Execute—decisive—explode—courses—movement.

17. Skill—best at each position.

18. Perform—think clearly under pressure.

19. Concentrate—each play by itself.

20. Lean—as game progresses.

21. Discipline—total unit cohesive—together.

22. Detail—every aspect of skill—responsibility.

23. Study—your position.

24. Patience—early—late—season—drive.

25. Confidence—yourself—team—coach.

26. Recovery—after disappointment—defeat—score.

27. Pressure opponent—continuous.

28. From start to finish—game—play—season.

29. Flexibility—adjustability—during game—weather—stadium.

30. Mutual respect—look teammate in eye—he too is committed.

31. Simply can't make self-inflicted errors—late hits—offsides—etc. We do not have a margin for error.

32. Set a high standard of play individually and collectively each week.

33. Don't expect someone to get you ready to play—prepare yourself.

34. Common things in NFL:
    - everybody hits at this level
    - everybody competes
    - every team is eager to play early
    - every team knows their business

35. Our philosophy:
    - we will handle big losses and wins

- can you deal with setbacks
- we must be patient when we play
- poise is vital to success
- concentrate on detailing your football
- master more skills and have better knowledge than the other guy
- communicate with fellow players and with the coaches
- each week is a new season

36. What we look for individually:
    - concentrate on each play
    - all you remember is how you did

37. Don't be awed by anyone.

38. Don't be consumed by the competition.

39. Don't be distracted by outside problems.

40. Be ready when the opportunity appears.

41. Don't think of your opponent as a personality.

42. The goals of our training camp:
    - be the best attacking team in football
    - must be the best late in the game—poise is critical in the league
    - must fit together and be in sync as a team—coordinated
    - must increase our positive turnover ratio
    - must score touchdowns—not be a field-goal team
    - must practice situational football
    - must improve our level of special teams—special teams are vital to our success
    - while we are here, we must make decisions on personnel and formulate a roster of the best people.
    - we need the big play player—who concentrates and preps for situations

SQUAD LECTURE #6
(coaches' job—role)

1. Utilize personnel. Quite willing to specialize.
2. Style—best suited for our athletes.
3. Style—best suited for our NFL competition.
4. Willing to commit to best calculated chance of "winning"—will not hope to win if opponent "gives us the game." May mean we could bomb out.
5. Will commit skills—method system—specifically spelled out.
6. Responsible for any/all minorities.
7. Not a fool.

8. If anything, I'm too "sensitive" for club.

9. Much of coaching is giving a man a chance to perform.

10. Personal association—relationship:

    - individual in nature—regardless of role played by coach or player
    - not democratic yet everyone treated with same dignity
    - team development more important than personal feelings and sensitivities
    - coach will not react to every little show of emotion—personal dissatisfaction
    - SF system—"not searching for the best way"—we already know it
    - every minute accounted for—hours, minutes, drills, skills, group work
    - team situation—time—score—field position—down and distance—etc.

11. Authority:

    - head coach—role
    - specific assignment—difference in direction between coaches—remind coaches must not have contradiction or confusion
    - must have honest—open—clarified—mature man-to-man relationship

12. Head coach:

    - maximum protection of field
    - maximum care—assistance—treatment of injuries
    - actions prior, during and after game in dealing with press and public must be put in best interest of team—club—NFL
    - actions in private life identical to that expected of players regarding questionable associations—unacceptable social behavior
    - integrity—honest in all dealings
    - accepting responsibility for group's performance—not using squad members—circumstances as a scapegoat or excuse for failure—inadequacies
    - confidentiality with papers—private lives—contacts—future—inadequacies
    - cannot sacrifice one player—career—performance for personal reasons or to enhance coach's reputation
    - must not pit one player against another in public competition
    - individual squad members—their unique place—existence
    - the minority whether it be religious—ethnic—economic—social—sexual
    - competence—professionally:
        - decisive—live with decisions
        - technical—concept
        - under duress
        - best interests of present

13. Will not get excited with early success or disappointment.

SQUAD LECTURE #7

1. Those players who are fighting to make the team must concentrate to the fullest. They must not be distracted by anything.
2. Movement is the key to success—"get there first and knock the hell out of the guy when he arrives!"
3. Correct your mistakes—but move—never hesitate or stop!
4. Offense requires discipline—run your courses— they will come to you.
5. When handling the ball, you must be decisive.
6. Special teams note: in coverage you must maintain lane integrity.
7. Use your eyes—be aware and alert to everything.
8. Special teams play is vital:
   - last five players on the roster will be retained due to special value
   - don't overlook the importance of special teams' preparation and performance

SQUAD LECTURE #8

1. Conditioning is the key—best physical condition of your career—minor pulls early in the season will be the biggest distraction on the practice field.
2. Drugs—their continued use will destroy this team and you personally—it erodes the foundation of mutual trust and confidence we have built.
3. Mental condition—clear mind—ability to concentrate—vital.
4. Begin with wrong state of mind—we never break it.
5. We are not going to play ourselves into shape.
6. Assume you are on the squad—same status.
7. Don't pay attention to your status in the newspapers.
8. Physical risk taking—your career is at stake.

SQUAD LECTURE #9
(following championship season)

1. Tremendous—concerted sustained effort in 1981.
2. Our progress—e.g., development has never been rivaled or equaled.
3. Can take great pride in accomplishment—became champions in greatest team athletic competition in history.
4. We believed in each other—depended upon each other—respected each other. We had great confidence in each other and appreciated the role each of us played.
5. We're talented, confident, proud champions. We have key veterans, outstanding youth.
6. Now—as champions—we must meet the challenge of the 1982 season. Many teams will improve—some will fade—all will respect us—the good ones will want to take us.

7. What must we do to continue as champions? What will it take? First, does it mean anything to you? If so, let's examine the forces working for us—and those working against us.

SQUAD LECTURE #10
(forces that can work against us—that are capable of eroding or even destroying us)

1. Relieved—relaxed—"we will turn it on when we have to."
2. Self-satisfied—cocky—arrogant. "We're the greatest"—lose respect for opponent.
3. Think we can win with "status quo"—simply do what we did last year.
4. Let down in dedication—preparation—conditioning—mental—psychological readiness.
5. Outside interests that detract from football:
    - appearances
    - activities to gain from 1981
    - business—jobs that take time—thought—at the sacrifice of football
6. Financial dealings that compromise—distract—from concentration. Forced to disrupt life to deal with it.
7. Paranoia about salary. Rumors about other salaries—"what you should be getting"—allowing this to affect feeling about team—organization.
8. Drugs—physical state, self image, financial loss, self destruction.
9. Willingness—temptation to "ease up just a little."

SQUAD LECTURE #11
(substance abuse)

1. On premises
2. Police—law enforcement:
    - they're looking to make big hit
    - are aware of normal trafficking
    - approach employers
    - more prevalent—consequently more police involvement
3. Public more sensitive to problem:
    - will take more critical position
    - will gossip—draw conclusions
    - rumors will persist—some justified—others not justified
4. When involved—who do you deal and associate with. What kind of people deal in drugs. To get to drugs—what kind of people do you come into contact with. There's bound to be a "rub off":

- People talk—use your name—use your money

5. Women—swingers—"high rollers"—hang around—meet young players—pull them down—have nothing to lose.

6. Best effort—how it can be eroded—diminished. Can you see yourself as a champion—can you reach your full potential.

7. Now—if you have a drug habit—forget reaching your potential—reaching your goals.

8. Now—you can't reach your potential—without teammates.

9. Scenery people have no stake in your life—career—teammates.

10. Impact of drugs:
    - financial
    - rest
    - nutrition
    - self-image
    - play

11. Outlined the law enforcement agency's approach toward drug dealing and usage.

12. Drug abuse can haunt you the rest of your natural life.

13. Drugs widespread in our society and within the framework of the NFL.

14. Fortunately, players are becoming more aware of the long-term ramifications of drug abuse.

15. Drug use and abuse generally destroy nutritional foundation. Users don't eat right or sleep right.

16. Discussed the financial ramifications of being involved with drugs.

17. Don't trade a future lifetime for a few pleasant todays.

18. Beware because a crackdown is in motion.

19. Be careful who you socialize with—change your scenery.

20. Impossible to reach full potential when you abuse your body.

21. Seek help if needed—agencies and policies were outlined.

SQUAD LECTURE #12
(championship season after dismal following season)

1. Everyone went in different directions:
   - lifestyle
   - exaggerated importance
   - each profiting in his own way
   - example—basketball fiasco—appearance
   - personalities—show biz in nature

- paranoid—salaries—greed—unrealistic demands—expectations

2. Willingness to physically pay price—hitting.

3. Loss of discipline—conviction in what we are doing.

4. Fundamentals—no concentration.

5. Discipline—depending on each other lost.

6. Leadership—fail to deal with players—not meeting expectations of others.

7. So "busy" with other life—failed to give football what they should.

8. Lacked simple things:

   - rest
   - nutrition
   - distracting interests—problems
   - preoccupied socially

9. Some individuals—almost hopeless. We like them as people—just can't rededicate to 49ers. May need completely new atmosphere.

10. Took too much for granted with football career. Talk a good game—failed to sacrifice.

11. Eliminate—totally mystery traveler—no phone—no whereabouts.

SAMPLE SCOUTING WORKOUT CRITERIA FOR SELECTED POSITIONS

WORKOUT CRITERIA: QUARTERBACKS

- Required personnel: Another quarterback, hopefully a present squad member, to demonstrate and make comparison.

- Throw a timed pass (e.g., qk out; square out; slant). Use a 3-5 step drop.

- Throw a pivot, hook, slant pass, holding on right foot. Use a 3-5 step drop.

- Drill ball between the defenders—hooking pattern—basic cross pattern. Use a 5-step drop.

- Throw short (e.g. HB-FB curl) with wrist; employ a high release.

- Shallow cross; extreme angle off 7-step cross.

- Throw "hot" receiver technique to the tight end. Shoot. Running back—wide—curl—Texas.

- Throw go-fly pattern, 40 yds. downfield off a 5-step (hitch-no hitch) and 7-step drop.

- Throw over defender, 20 yds. downfield (e.g., comeback—deep over—seam post deep cross).

- Sprint—roll action, setting up and throwing on move.

- Utilize drop (3-5-7)—lateral movement in pocket on coaches' signals. Emphasize mechanics—agility—touch.

- Mobility—scramble—throw. Schedule at end of practice when athlete is somewhat fatigued. Signal QB out of pocket after 3-5-7-step drop. Receivers stationary rather than moving.

- Check out play pass proficiency.

- Functional intelligence evaluation.

- Communicative skills evaluation.

- Leadership qualities.

- Present physical condition (e.g., stamina, endurance, etc.).
- Physical examination.
- Agent—ramifications.

WORKOUT CRITERIA: RUNNING BACKS

- Required personnel: A quarterback, a center and another running back, hopefully, one currently on the squad for comparison and demonstration.
- Stretch and warm up. Catch assorted passes thrown softly. Check out his ability to catch on the move. Note flaws in technique.
- Receive handoff and execute inside run break off a bag held by the coach.
- Take pitchout and break off bag held by the coach.
- Receive the handoff while breaking inside or outside off the block of the other back or the pulling guard. Kick out or logged. In this instance, the action does not need to be live—it is simulated.
- Take handoff on sweep action. Stretch then cut off the block of the pulling lineman or the lead back. Coach can act as defender. This action is simulated—not live.
- Take assorted handoffs utilized in the team's offensive system (e.g., draw, etc.).
- Run required pass routes, alternating short and deep with rest between repetitions. Catch the ball, breaking outside. Inside, straight upfield.
- Instruct back on routes. Check out his ability to comprehend your instructions and his skills. If a coverage man is available, use him to shadow the back.
- On the two-man sled, have the back perform two repetitions with each shoulder. Utilize the other back on sled with him. Make comparison between the skills of the two backs.
- Active blocking vs. a shield or a bag. Check out his balance, shocking power and his technique. His blocking technique should include pass protection—lead—power—cut.
- Run deep routes, throwing the ball deep down the field. Check body control while he's fatigued.
- Speed test (prior to or following the workout).
- Agility and vertical jump tests (before or following the workout).
- Strength testing.
- Functional intelligence evaluation.
- Communicative skills evaluation.
- Present physical condition (e.g., stamina, endurance, etc.)
- Previous injuries; history of injury.

- Physical examination.
- Agent—ramifications.

WORKOUT CRITERIA: WIDE RECEIVERS

- Personnel required: A quarterback, center (if possible), other receivers—hopefully currently on the roster for comparison—and a defensive back to shadow the receiver.
- Warm up. Catch softly thrown balls at various angles.
- Three-step routes (e.g., hitch—quick out—slant—fade).
- Five-step routes (e.g., square out, 12-yd square in, hook, seam post, etc.). Check out his adjustments to coverages.
- Shallow crossing routes; read coverage.
- Seven-step routes (e.g., come back, dig, circle out, deep over, deep cross, etc.).
- Releases versus press coverage and versus rotating corner.
- Double-move routes (off 3-5-7 step drops).
- Work selected routes against shadowing press corner.
- Speed tests (before or following the workout).
- During workout, evaluate:
  - Acceleration
  - Hands—full range of adjustment
  - Body control—agility when catching
  - Change of direction
  - Skill—technique in running routes
  - Ability to adapt to new system—different coaching of routes—reads.
- Identify role he would play with our team (i.e., who he would compete against, etc.)
- Speed test (before or following the workout).
- Strength test.
- Functional intelligence evaluation.
- Communication skills evaluation.
- Present physical condition (e.g., stamina, endurance, etc.).
- History of injury; present medical condition.
- Physical examination.
- Agent—ramifications.

WORKOUT CRITERIA: OFFENSIVE LINEMEN

- Required personnel: Offensive lineman for comparison and demonstration, hopefully currently a member of the squad; a defensive lineman.
- Defensive player instructed to make specific moves (example—pass rush).
- Against a line stunt, pick-up after an explanation.
- Establish priorities (role needed).
- Pass protection (vs. defender).
- Base blocking (one-on-one).
- Plug—slip (vs. big bag).
- Trap—short—long—fold (vs. bag).
- Pull outside—(guard courses).
- Pull and lead through the hole (vs. bag).
- Angle block down (vs. bag).
- Reach block—man outside—scramble (vs. bag).
- Specific agility drills.
- Strength test.
- Long snap history.
- Experience in playing multiple positions.
- Present physical condition (e.g., stamina, endurance, etc.).
- History of injuries.
- Functional speed test (before or following the workout).
- Functional intelligence evaluation.
- Communicative skills evaluation.
- Personal inventory (conversation and question format).
- Complete history of injuries.
- Determination of how soon he will be able to play.
- Physical examination.
- Agent—ramifications.

WORKOUT CRITERIA: TIGHT ENDS

- Personnel required: A quarterback, a center (if possible), a defensive coverage man, a lineman or linebacker for blocking purposes, and another tight end for comparative purposes.

- Vertical jump and other agility tests.
- Warm up. Receiving ball that is softly thrown. Ball delivered at varying angles.
- Speed test (before or following the workout).
- Strength test (before or following the workout).
- Run basic patterns (e.g., shoot, slant, basic cross, shallow cross, stick, hook, corner, seam, sail, corner, out, etc.).
- Check out his adjustments to coverages on all routes.
- Angle block (turn out and drive) against the big bag.
- Block against a hand-held bag on a linebacker head up, hooking him and turning him out.
- On the two-man sled, have the tight end perform two reps with each shoulder; conduct exercise in combination with the other tight end.
- Check out his releases versus the linebacker, as he is running routes.
- Catch deep balls (versus seams and corners).
- Evaluate:
    - Strength, girth, ballast as a blocker.
    - Agility blocking moving blocker (hand-held shield).
    - Power—explosiveness while blocking the big bag (vs. defensive lineman).
    - Hands—ability to adjust.
    - Body control when going for ball (i.e., his ability to turn, leap, concentrate on ball, etc.)
    - Skill and technique in running routes.
    - Ability to assimilate new system.
- Functional intelligence evaluation.
- Communicative skills evaluation.
- Present physical condition (e.g., stamina, endurance, etc.).
- History of injuries.
- Physical examination.
- Agent—ramifications.

SAMPLE BASE PLAY SCHEMATICS

BASE RUNS: INSIDE ZONE

94-95 (STRONG)

A man-blocking play that may break anywhere from bouncing outside the TE and cutting back as far as the backside T's block.

Blocking Rules:

All linemen and TE covered by a down lineman block man; all linemen covered by a LB use a "Plug" to block the DL/ILB toward the call. "Plug" any gap D-linemen. The TE should block the outside man on the LOS versus a "9" look. The offside G & T should "Slip" block if appropriate.

BB —Block the end man on the LOS to the back side of the play.

BC —Take the hand-off aiming for the "B" gap, but anticipate making a cutback move.

X —Block the safety to your side.

Z —Block the safety to your side.

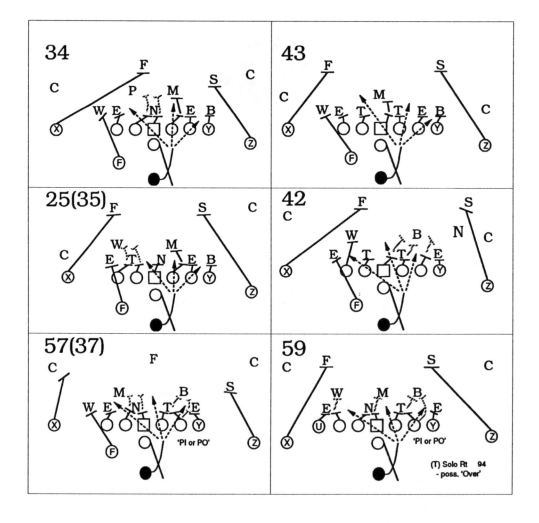

BASE RUNS: INSIDE ZONE

94-95 (WEAK)

A man-blocking play that may break anywhere from bouncing outside the hole to cutting back as far as outside the TE.

Blocking Rules:

All linemen covered by a down lineman will block man; all linemen covered by a LB will "Plug" block the DL/ILB toward the call. "Plug" any gap D-linemen. The onside T should block the outside man on the LOS versus a "5" look. The offside T and TE should "Slip" block if appropriate.

BB —Block the end man on the LOS to the front side of the play.

BC —Take the hand-off aiming for the "B" gap, but anticipate making a cutback move.

X —Block the safety to your side.

Z —Block the safety to your side.

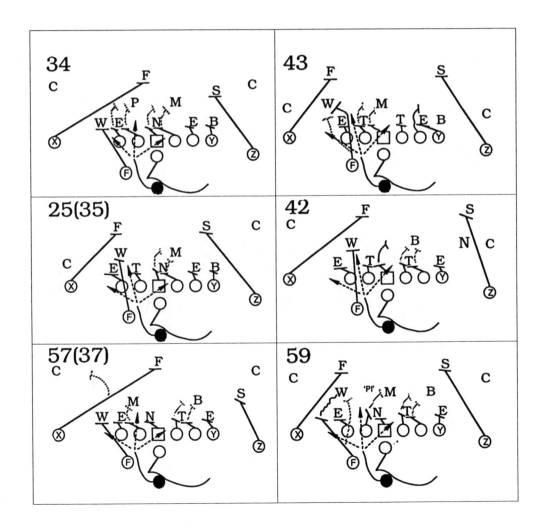

BASE RUNS: OUTSIDE ZONE

69-68 HO

A man-blocking play that may break from the sideline to the backside of the center.

Blocking Rules:

All linemen covered by a down lineman should "Hook" their man (perhaps front side of a slip); all linemen covered by a LB either "Slip" onside or "cutoff" the LB as appropriate. Versus a "5" look, the onside T should cut off the bubble LB only if there is NO doubt about having enough lead angle to get him; otherwise he should reach and cut the outside man on the LOS. The offside T and TE should "Slip" block if appropriate.

The halfback should "Bob" block the outside man on the LOS; if the tackle reaches and cuts that man continue for the scrapping ILB. The "X" (or "Z" in Solo) receiver should block the first force to that side. If a TE is onside, he should hook the man covering him. The outside slip technique with the "T" should be used versus a "7" look.

X   —Block first force.

Z   —Block the safety.

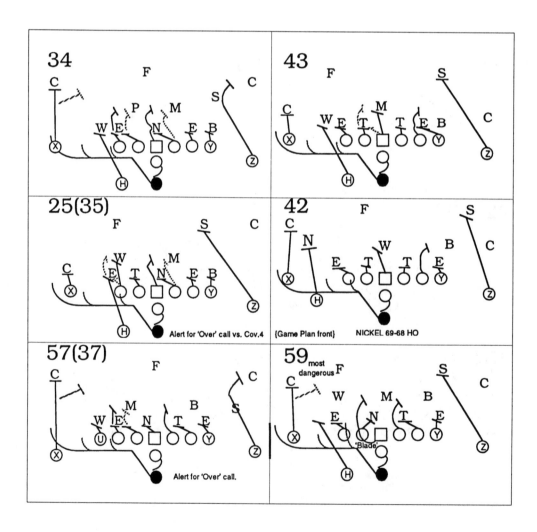

BASE RUNS: INSIDE MAN

FOX 2-3 RUN

TE —Block the man over you. Alert *"RO," " TO,"* "Ink," or "9."

O-line: Block Fox 2-3 pass protection assignments EXCEPT:

T   —If T covered by LB, Alert *"RO," " TO,"* "Ink," or "9."

G

C   }
OG }   Possible fold vs. *Even* front with no MLB over C.
OT }

FB —Vs. *Base* defenses: block MLB. Vs. *Nickel:* block 1st LB from C to call side.

HB —Slide over the top, take the hand-off and start over G.

X   —Block the safety your side.

Z   —Block SS to your side unless Nickel, then block the corner.

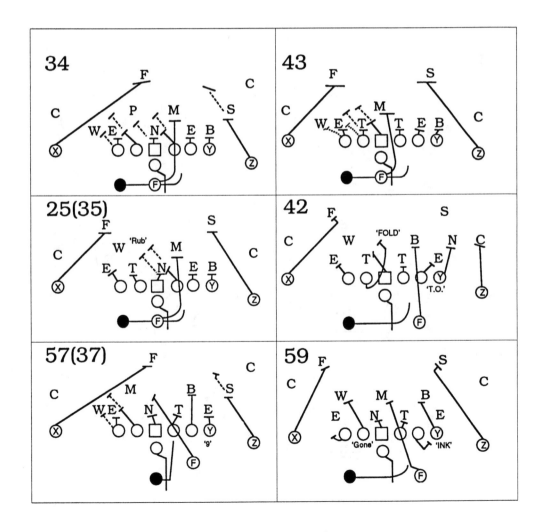

BASE RUNS: OUTSIDE MAN

98-99 "H"

TE —Man ("Hook"), possible "B" block.

T —Man, possible "B" block. Block down versus "7" look. (Area block w/FB by game plan.)

G —Pull on sweep course, blocking 1st force.

C —*Even front:* Reach onside DT or block MLB; *Odd front:* Man or "Slip" with OG.

OG —Man or "Slip" with C or OT. "If" when C & G are covered.

OT —Cutoff, "Sift," or "Slip" with OG.

FB —Search and destroy ILB; be alert for run through by LB. (Area block w/T by game plan.)

BC —Stretch to outside and stay on hip of frontside guard until you have to cut inside; then pick up backside guard.

X —Block the safety

Z —Block the corner playside; Vs. corner rotation: release outside 2nd block the safety.

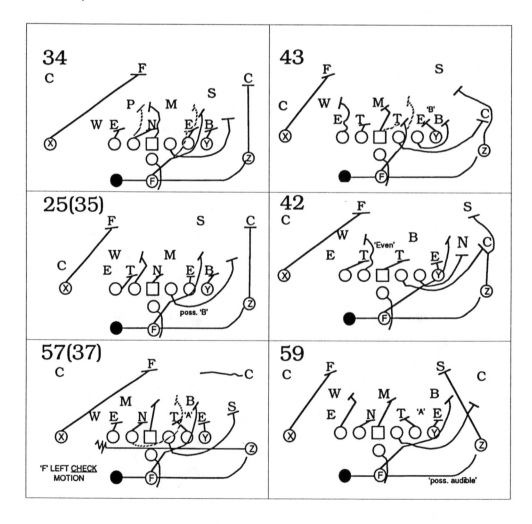

BASE RUNS: DRAW

FB 40-41   Basic draw blocking—Man, DL or LB over you Or:

TE —Possible "Slip; with T. Alert to "TO," "RO," "9" and "Ink."

T —Possible "Drug" with G or "Slip" with TE.

G —Basic draw blocking: Alert for "If" around C. Possible "Drug" with T.

C —Man, DL or LB over: Not there LB to call.

OG —Alert for "If" around C. Possible "plug" with T. ("Gut" with OT by game plan.).

OT —Block DE.

HB —Block WLB.

BC —Read the guard box. Run to daylight.

X —Block the safeties if possible

Z —Block the safeties if possible

** For one back, we will call Nickel 40-41.

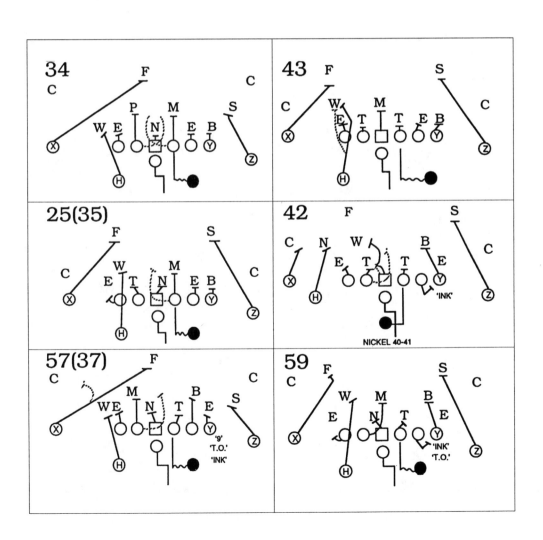

PROTECTION: 7-MAN SPLIT BACK

24 (25) PROTECTIONS OR 324 (325)* PROTECTIONS

Offensive Line:

—Basic man protection—possible "open," "snuggle" or "gap" calls.

—Vs. nickel, the uncovered lineman has the call side LB ("stay," "slide," "elephant," "L.A."/"Raider").

—Navajo—Basic Navajo protection. Alert for gap situation.

—"Open" away from call vs. 3-man line; "No open" vs. 4-man line.

FB —Outside LB, alert for "bag," "open," "gap," "elephant," and "score" calls. Vs. Nickel: check 2nd LB to call side. Release routes could change weekly.

HB —Outside LB alert for "bag," "open," "gap," and "elephant" calls. Release routes could change weekly.

* In 324 (325) the line never "opens" away from the call due to the 3-step drop by the QB. RB's have "B" & "W."

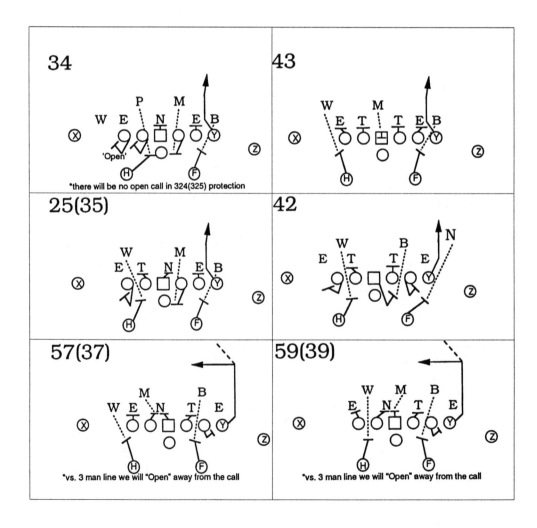

PROTECTION: 7-MAN WK FLOW

74 (75) PROTECTIONS OR 374 (375)* PROTECTIONS

Offensive Line:

- —Basic man protection—possible "open" or "gap" calls.
- —Vs. nickel, the uncovered lineman has the call side LB ("Stay," "slide," "L.A."/ "Raider").
- —"Open" away from call vs. 3-man line.

TE —Slow protection, possible "tuf" call. Alert personnel group—"Tiger"=free release (see diagram vs. 59 front).

FB —Block "Whip" alert for "open," "gap" calls. Vs. nickel, check 1st LB/DB away from the call.

HB —Free release and run appropriate route.

*In 374 (375), the line never opens away from the call due to the 3-step drop by the QB. FB has "Whip."

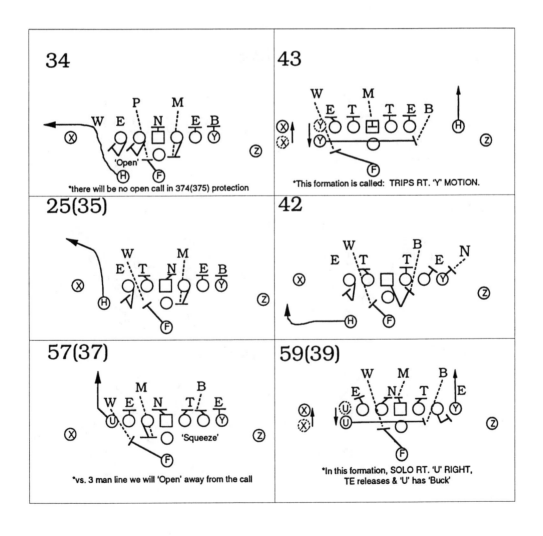

34

'Open'

*there will be no open call in 374(375) protection

43

*This formation is called: TRIPS RT. 'Y' MOTION.

25(35)

42

57(37)

'Squeeze'

*vs. 3 man line we will 'Open' away from the call

59(39)

*In this formation, SOLO RT. 'U' RIGHT, TE releases & 'U' has 'Buck'

PROTECTION: 6 MAN

22 (23) PROTECTIONS OR 322 (323)* PROTECTIONS

Offensive Line:

—Double read by call side G vs. 34 front. Alert for "tuf" call.

—1st LB to call side vs. even and over shift fronts ("stay," "slide," "snuggle," "L.A."/"Raider," "L-R").

—Possible "gap" or "Lucky/Ringo" calls.

—NAVAJO. Navajo open protection; alert for gap situation.

—"Open" away from call vs. 3-man line.

FB —Free release to side of tight end and run appropriate route.

HB —Block "Whip"—alert for "bag," "open" and "gap" calls. (Vs. 3-man line you have "P.")

* In 322 (323), the line never "opens" away from the call due to the 3-step drop. HB has "Whip."

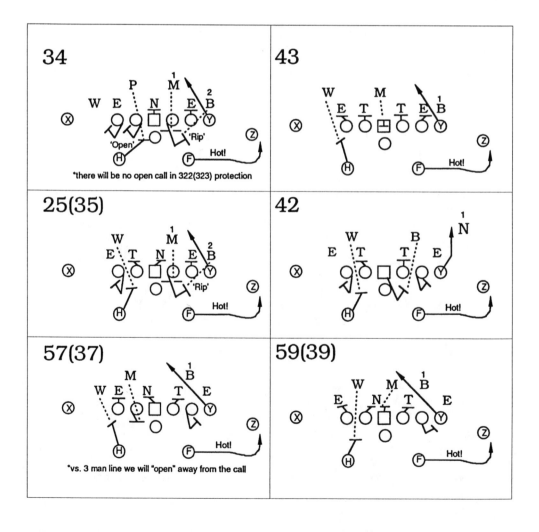

PROTECTION: 6-MAN TURNBACK

2 (3) JET PROTECTIONS OR 200 (300) JET PROTECTIONS

Offensive Line: (Alert for "*Tom*" or "*Base*" calls)

—Slide away from the call.

—Backside guard may "open," "in" or "out."

—Use "L.A."/"Raider" or "L-R" protection when appropriate.

—"Base" call will be made vs. "B" & "M" blitz or 34 fronts.

—Alert for "Gap," "Ringo/Lucky" calls.

FB —Double read for two blitzers to the call side. Alert for "*Tom*" or "*Base*" calls. Also read offside ILB when C & G are covered (51 & 57 Fronts). Alert to check SS vs. the blitz.

HB —Free release and run appropriate route.

* This is also Fox 2-3 Protection for the line.

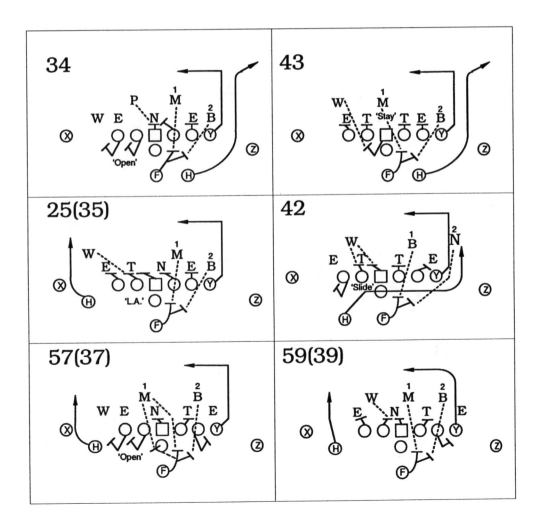

PROTECTION: 8-MAN SPLIT FLOW

28 (29) PROTECTIONS OR 328 (329) PROTECTIONS

Designed as a protection for a 4-man blitz coming from the strong side. This is usually called when a SS blitzes from the TE side.

Offensive Line:

   —Basic man protection.

   —Vs. Nickel: uncovered lineman has weakside ILB ("stay," "slide," "elephant," "L.A."/"Raider").

   —Better called vs. "Odd" front blitzes.

   —"Open" away from the call vs. 3-man line; "no open" vs. 4-man line.

TE —Blocks "Slow" Protection.

FB —Block SS blitz. Vs. Nickel: check 2nd LB/DB.

HB —Outside LB, alert for "bag," "open," and "gap" calls (like 24-25).

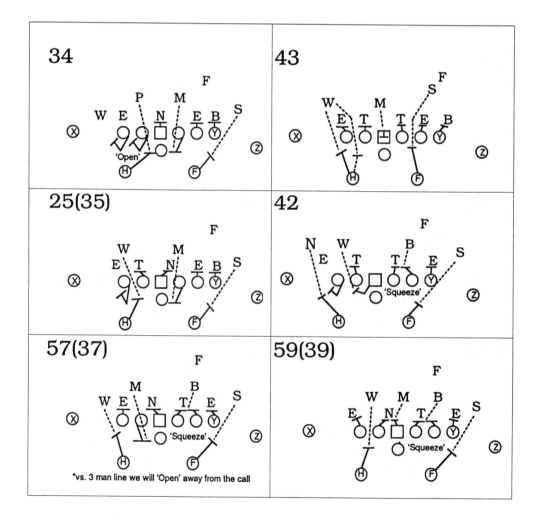

PROTECTION: 8-MAN WK FLOW

78 (79) PROTECTIONS OR 378 (379) PROTECTIONS

Designed as an audible for FS blitz that is threatening weak.

Offensive Line:

   —Base protection.

TE —"Slow" protection

FB —Block FS (may switch I and O with guard) or 1st blitzer away from call.

HB —Block outside (2nd) blitzer.

* This protection is used more out of a "Brown" set.

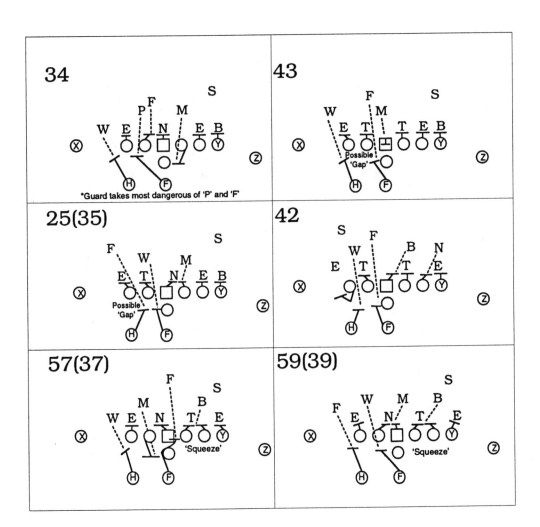

3-STEP ROUTES

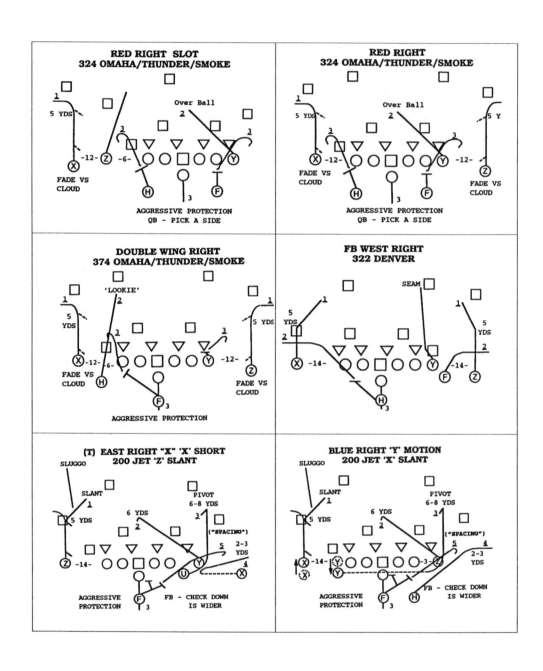

RED RIGHT SLOT
324 OMAHA/THUNDER/SMOKE

Over Ball
FADE VS CLOUD
AGGRESSIVE PROTECTION
QB - PICK A SIDE

RED RIGHT
324 OMAHA/THUNDER/SMOKE

Over Ball
FADE VS CLOUD
FADE VS CLOUD
AGGRESSIVE PROTECTION
QB - PICK A SIDE

DOUBLE WING RIGHT
374 OMAHA/THUNDER/SMOKE

'LOOKIE'
FADE VS CLOUD
FADE VS CLOUD
AGGRESSIVE PROTECTION

FB WEST RIGHT
322 DENVER

SEAM

(T) EAST RIGHT "X" 'X' SHORT
200 JET 'Z' SLANT

SLUGGO
SLANT
PIVOT 6-8 YDS
("SPACING")
AGGRESSIVE PROTECTION
FB - CHECK DOWN IS WIDER

BLUE RIGHT 'Y' MOTION
200 JET 'X' SLANT

SLUGGO
SLANT
PIVOT 6-8 YDS
("SPACING")
AGGRESSIVE PROTECTION
FB - CHECK DOWN IS WIDER

5-STEP ROUTES

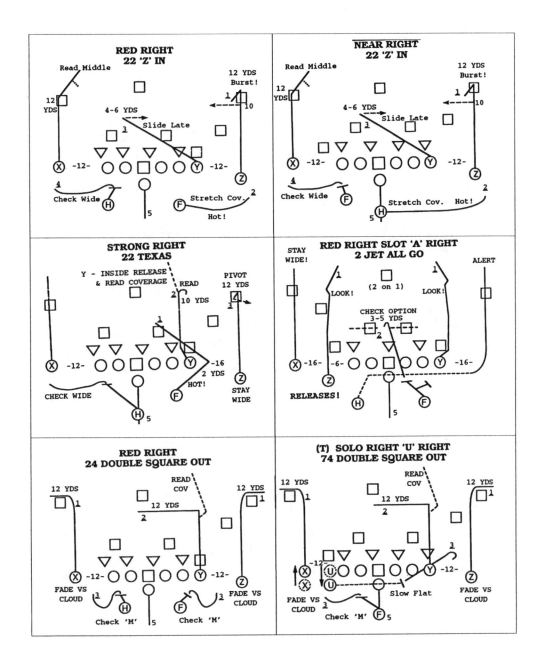

RED RIGHT 22 'Z' IN

NEAR RIGHT 22 'Z' IN

STRONG RIGHT 22 TEXAS

RED RIGHT SLOT 'A' RIGHT 2 JET ALL GO

RED RIGHT 24 DOUBLE SQUARE OUT

(T) SOLO RIGHT 'U' RIGHT 74 DOUBLE SQUARE OUT

7-STEP ROUTES

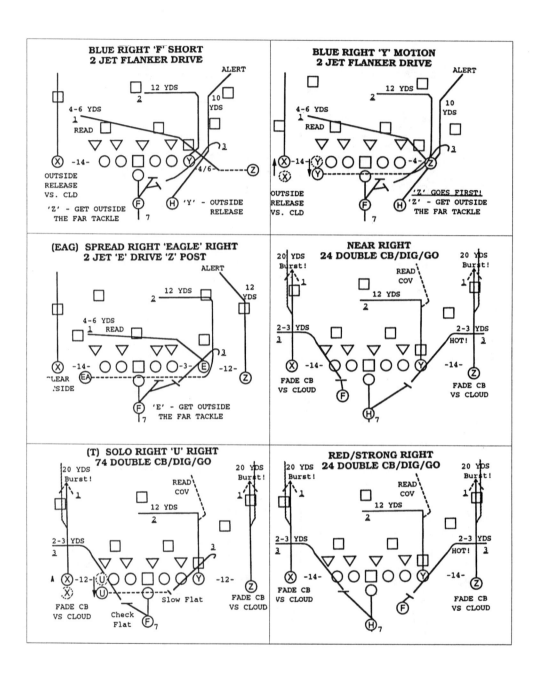

PLAY/ACTION PASS

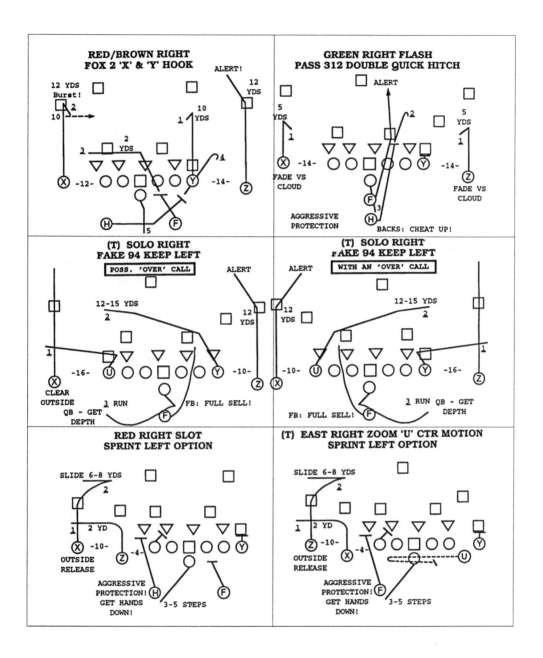

SAMPLE CLASSIC PLAY SCHEMATICS

INSIDE RUNS

Wide Trap Play

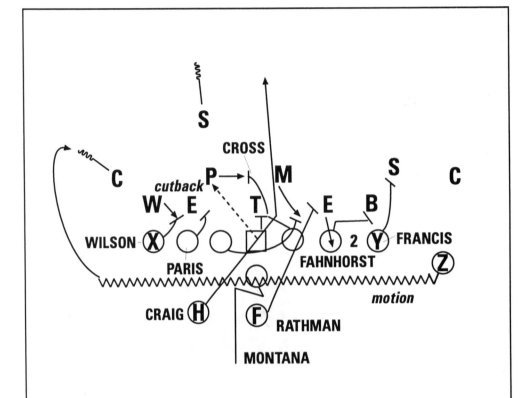

This inside run was designed as an offshoot of a play originally designed to run against a 4-3 defense. The fullback, Tom Rathman, trapped the defensive end. The backside guard, Guy McIntyre, pulled and trapped the filling inside linebacker. The center, Fred Quillan, and right guard Randy Cross double-teamed, picking off the backside linebacker. The right tackle, Harris Barton, set up the defensive end, then turned out on the linebacker. The running back, Roger Craig, read the pulling guard. He cut underneath that defender's block or cut back behind the nose tackle if he moved. The backside tackle, Bubba Paris, had to cut off his man. A tight X receiver was preferable for this play because he could cut off an inside blitzing weak linebacker.

Trap Play

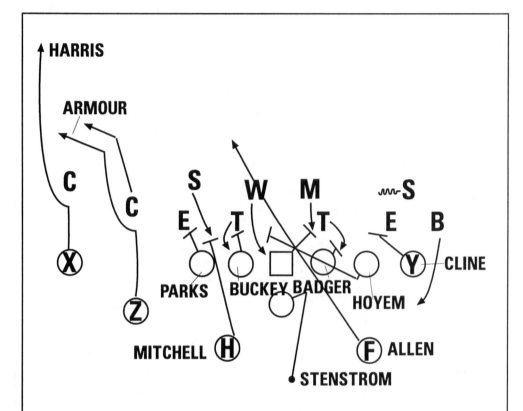

This play was an audible trap versus the 44 split dog, but it can be very effective against any inside gap dog. The tackle ran an inside-out course. Both guards turned out. The center blocked back. The fullback read the tackle's block. This step required a great deal of practice. The fullback had to see the defensive look, the audible, and the full-speed course off the tackle numerous times in order to read the blocks effectively.

Trap Play

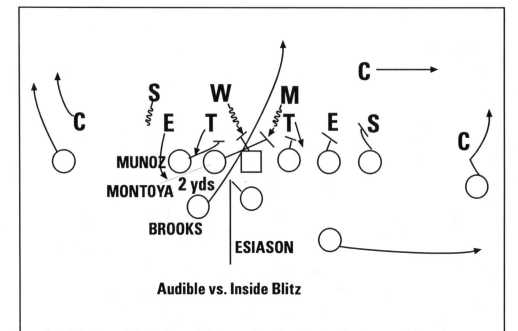

Audible vs. Inside Blitz

Sam Wyche originated a guard trap when the 44 split dog type of blitz was diagnosed. He moved his backup very close to the line of scrimmage as though to pick up the blitz. He even pointed to a man as though to pick him up. Instead, he was given the ball on a quick trap.

Counter Play

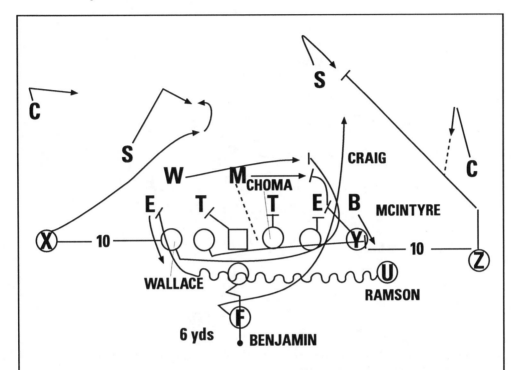

This counter action was popularized by Joe Gibbs during the Redskins dynasty
years. With John Riggins behind a great offensive line, this play became the
most potent running play of its time. The onside tight end and tackle had to
"move" the defensive end and be ready to "rub off" on a pursuing linebacker.
The center had to cut off penetration by the defensive tackle. The pulling guard
and tackle ran full-speed courses. That guard trapped or logged the first
unblocked man. The tackle read the guard's block, leading inside if the guard
trapped or outside if he logged. The fullback also read. He cut inside the guard
and outside the tackle unless all three slid to the outside. A seal on the backside was critical to cut off pursuit.

Counter Play

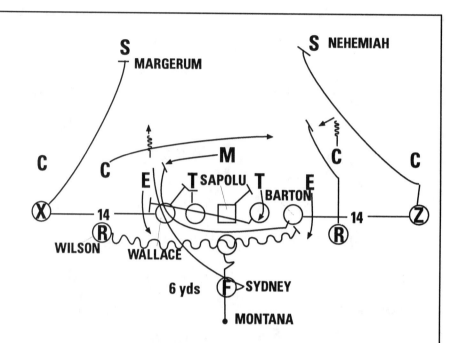

This play used the same counter action as the previous play. In this instance, it was run to the open side. This play was ideally suited for pass rush schemes in which the defensive end came upfield. The center had the critical block. Jesse Sapolu did an outstanding job for the 49ers. Steve Wallace and Guy McIntyre did a "double and rub" on the defensive tackle and the linebacker. A change in the defensive front might force the pulling tackle to stay and seal. This play had major problems with line stunts or blitzing. The quarterback had to be prepared to audible to the other side or to a pass if the anticipated front was not faced. In an optimal situation, the backside defensive end would come upfield before pursuing. In this case, the backside seal was not always necessary.

Draw Play

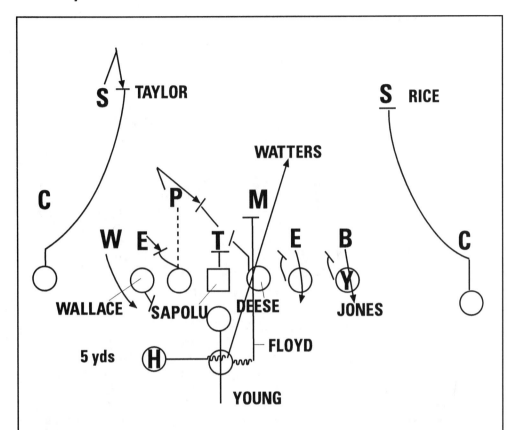

This play was a semi-draw that fit together well with the accompanying play pass. The fullback William Floyd led on the middle backer. Both backs delayed slightly, allowing the backers to begin dropping in coverage. The front guard and center "double and rubbed" on the nose tackle and "plugger" backer. The right tackle got inside out on his defensive end. The left guard was alert for the plugger dog, then turned out. Other blocking combinations could also be employed. The right guard and the tackle could turn out and the tight end could release. In that case, the ball carrier would break off the center's block. Versus an even front the fullback had the middle backer. The center would then block back in combination with the left guard. This play is most popular from the I formation.

OUTSIDE RUNS

Wide Sweep

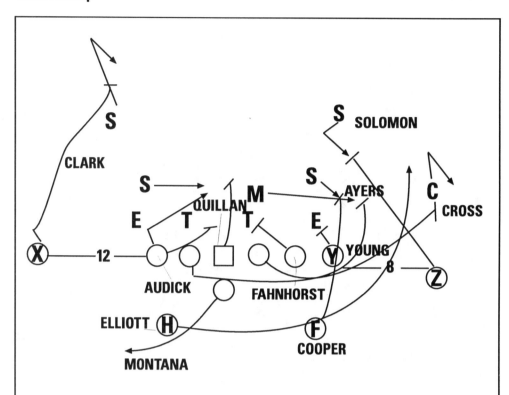

This sweep play gained much notoriety when it became a key element in the final drive that defeated Dallas for the NFC Championship. It was set up to block their famed nickel defense. Dallas was playing for the pass and the 49ers were sweeping. Both of San Francisco's guards did a beautiful job of running excellent courses and cutting down their assigned defenders. Keith Fahnhorst and Charle Young cut off their pass rushers. Lenvil Elliot read his blockers perfectly, cutting inside off the block of Randy Cross. Everyone ran full-speed courses and let the defenders come to them. If a strong safety is on the line of scrimmage, the quarterback should use an audible.

Wide Sweep

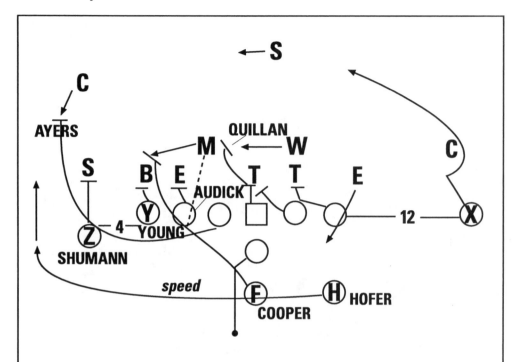

This play was a "speed sweep" designed to get outside before the defense could respond. It is diagrammed here with a "close flanker." This alignment cut off penetration by the strong safety. The tight end, Charle Young, and left tackle Dan Audick had to sustain contact. A dominating blocker such as Young at tight end was critical to making this play work. If the tight end could hook his man without allowing penetration, the play had a good start. The pulling guard was responsible for the first unblocked man. He ran a full-speed course, cutting down the defender. With a wide flanker the guard was responsible for the safety. With a close flanker, he was responsible for the cornerback. The fullback, Earl Cooper, had the inside linebacker. He followed the linebacker and cut him down as he entered the line of scrimmage. The running back Paul Hofer sprinted, got on the guard's hip, and broke off his block. This play was a foot race to the sideline. If he was cut off, the running back broke back inside the block. Versus an even front, the fullback may be assigned the defensive tackle.

Pitch Play (Weak Side Toss)

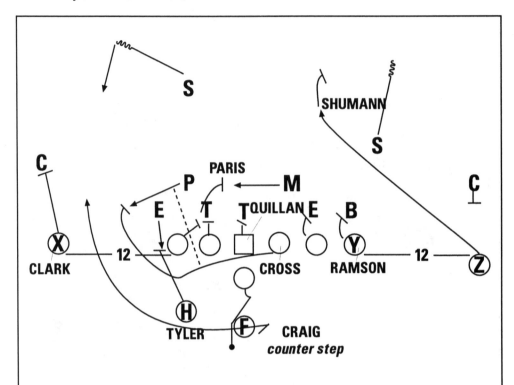

This play was popularized by the Pittsburgh Steelers during their dynasty years. Rocky Bleier cut down the defensive end, with Franco Harris counter-stepping. Harris took the ball and broke off the block of the pulling guard. San Francisco utilized Wendell Tyler, a great blocker, at halfback and Roger Craig, a ball carrier much like Franco. The pulling guard ran a course behind the block of the halfback. The ball carrier broke off the guard's block. The left tackle blocking inside combined with the pulling guard brought the defensive end inside to play for a trap. The halfback had to hit the end thigh-high on the outside leg, cutting him down. If the defense lined up two men on the line of scrimmage outside the tackle, the quarterback went to an audible.

Pitch Play (Weak Side Toss)

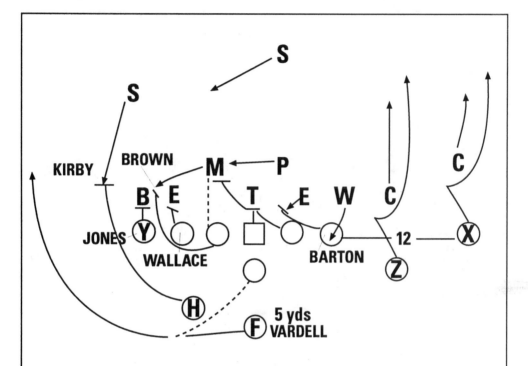

This simple toss play might be the best utility run in football. The tight end and
tackle had to sustain contact. The backside "slip" blocks by the center, guard,
and tackle were critical. The halfback Terry Kirby ran a course and cut down the
safety. The left guard was responsible for the inside linebacker. He either fired
out and cut him or, more likely, pulled around, cutting him down as he pursued.
Fullback Tommy Vardell, at a depth of five yards, started laterally, stretching the
defense. He wanted to go outside, but if the tight end, Brent Jones, had to widen
with his man, Vardell cut inside him. The left tackle, Steve Wallace, had to
sustain contact. This play was excellent in short yardage or goal line situations.
When facing an even front, the center and guard combined on the defensive
tackle and middle linebacker. This play may be the best run in football against the
blitz. It is an excellent way to get outside an attacking defense. This blocking
scheme is also most popular utilizing a handoff.

Toss Play

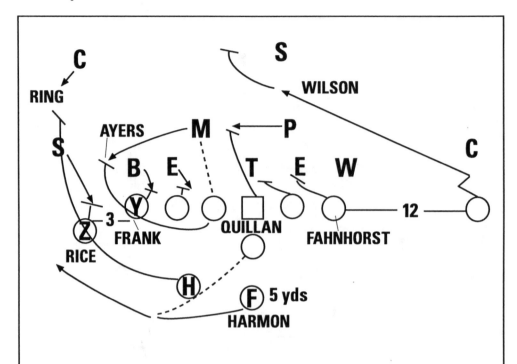

In this play, the "close flanker" (2- or 3-yard split) could cut off the blitzing safety. He could also be used to seal off a linebacker blitzing outside the tight end. Jerry Rice was an outstanding blocker for this assigment. A tight end can also be employed as the flanker.

Toss Play

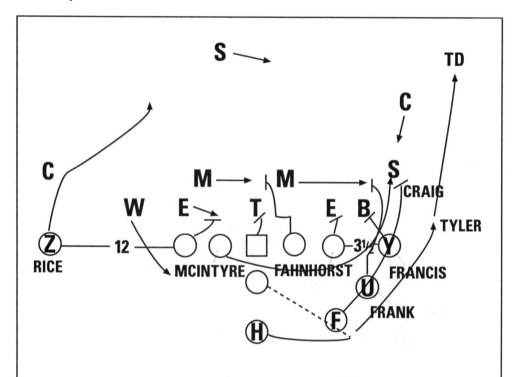

This combination was conceived by Blanton Collier with the Cleveland Browns.
The backfield was Jim Brown and Bobby Mitchell. Cincinnati, Stanford, and San
Francisco all employed it as a change-up. On one afternoon, Darrin Nelson gained
over 100 yards on this play, running into the short side of the field. The players
involved in this diagram broke the great New Orleans defense. Wendell Tyler
went 35 yards for a touchdown. The key block came from right tackle Keith
Fahnhorst. He had to hook, or at least sustain contact with the defensive end.
The U, Y, and tackle had to combine calls to account for the defensive end,
outside linebacker, and inside linebacker. Francis blocked down on the linebacker. John Frank worked around him to pick off the inside backer. The fullback
ran a course to cut down the safety.

PASS PLAYS

Versus Two-Deep Coverage

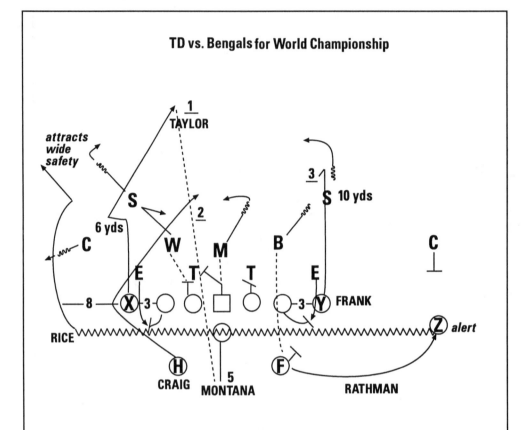

TD vs. Bengals for World Championship

This red zone play was designed to break a four-deep combination that double-covered both wide receivers. The flanker in motion forced quick adjustments by the linebackers. The "curling" halfback, Roger Craig, held both linebackers. Jerry Rice attracted the weak safety, and the tight end, John Frank, held the other safety. John Taylor split three yards, released upfield, and at six yards made an out move designed to deceive the weak side linebacker dropping into coverage on him. Taylor then broke back upfield, inside the safety. A throwing lane opened and Joe drilled the ball to him in the back of the end zone.

Versus Two-Deep Coverage

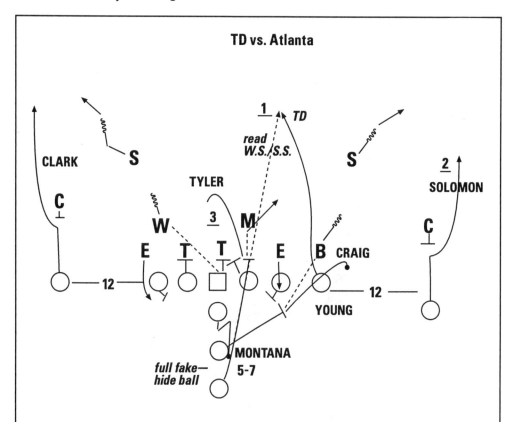

TD vs. Atlanta

This play was an excellent play pass versus the double rotating zone. The fake was designed to hold the middle linebacker, allowing the tight end, Charle Young, to slip by him into the middle. As he released, Young read the safeties. If they both rotated he went straight into the middle, catching the ball approximately 25 yards deep. If a safety stayed in the middle, Young hooked at 14 yards depth. The outside receivers ran fade patterns outside the respective cornerbacks. They had to force the safeties to rotate to them. Comebacks or deep hooks (digs) might be the original call, with routes turning into fades versus rotation. The backs had to "sell" the run, check their backers, and then become outlets. The halfback got the ball if the middle linebacker ran with the tight end. Montana did a great job of faking and read the safeties. When he saw no double rotation, he looked to the individual patterns of his outside receivers, then Young hooking, and finally Wendell Tyler "over the ball."

Versus Two Deep

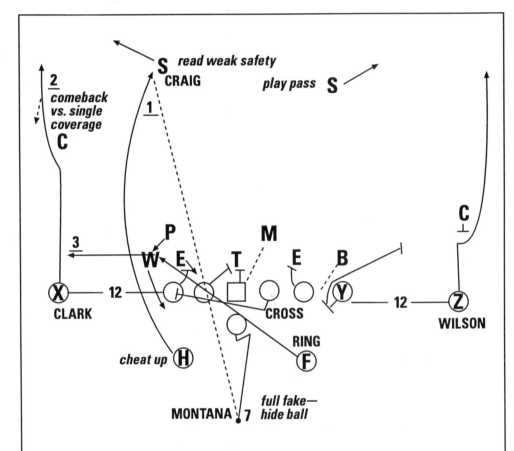

This action was designed to split a double-rotation zone. The play fake with a pulling guard completely "sold" the run. This action pulled the linebackers into the line of scrimmage, opening a big hole in the coverage. If the weak safety stayed in the middle, Montana looked for Clark on a comeback, and then the faking fullback in the flat. This pattern was used by Mike Shanahan to score the first of many touchdowns in Super Bowl XXIX. In that instance, the pass was thrown by Steve Young to Ricky Watters.

Two Deep

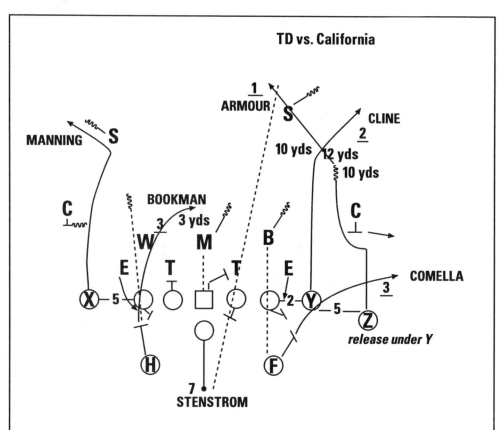

TD vs. California

This play was designed specifically for double rotation. The split end, Brian Manning, and the tight end, Tony Cline, ran corner patterns to take both safeties to the outside. The release of both of these men was vital. The flanker, Justin Armour, aligned himself five yards outside the tight end, three yards deep. He allowed Cline to release upfield ahead of him, and he stayed inside the rotating cornerback. When Cline broke to the corner, Armour hesitated slightly, then cut underneath him to the middle. The quarterback looked first to the strong safety, then the weak safety. If both rotated, he looked into the middle for the flanker. If the safeties did not rotate far enough, the corner patterns might open. In that case the halfback became the key outlet.

Two Deep

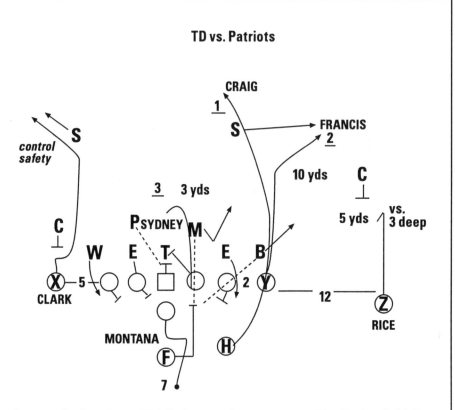

This play was designed specifically for two-deep coverage. The flanker held the cornerback up. The tight end, Russ Francis, went to the corner. Roger Craig released outside, then broke into the middle underneath Francis. The quarterback faked a draw to hold the middle linebacker as he read both safeties. The fullback had a tough job. He checked for the middle and strong side linebackers as he faked, then set down over the ball as the outlet. Faced with a coverage other than two-deep, Montana looked immediately to Jerry Rice, then Harry Sydney.

Versus Two Deep

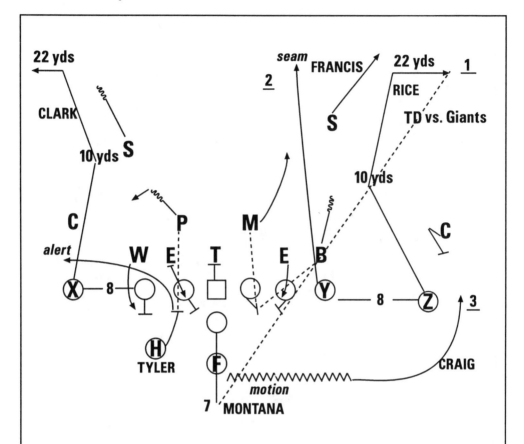

This combination was designed to attack a two-deep zone. The tight end, Russ Francis, released straight upfield into the seam between the rotating safeties. If one of the safeties remained in the middle, Russ hooked at 14 yards. Roger Craig, at fullback, was sent in quick motion and ran a wide flare to attract the rotating cornerback. Jerry Rice released inside and drove at the strong safety to hold him. He then broke out at approximately 22 yards. Montana dropped the ball over the cornerbacks' heads, pulling Rice to the outside away from the safety. Dwight Clark, a split end, ran the same pattern as Rice, pulling his safety to the outside. The pressure was on the strong safety, forcing him to either commit to the tight end or cover the flanker. The fullback forcing the cornerback to rotate and the clean release of the tight end were critical to this play.

Versus Four Across Coverage (Red-Zone Route)

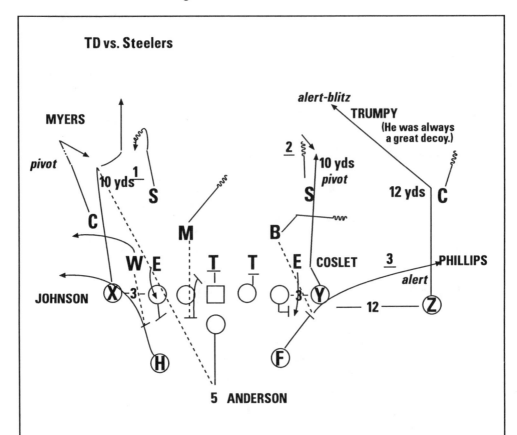

This play was run from the 20-yard line. The defense was using a tight four-deep coverage to double team both outside receivers. The X and Y receivers released upfield, splitting defenders. They pivoted at 10 yards. Ken Anderson hit Chip Myers before the corner and weak safety could recover. The quarterback took five big steps and threw the instant his right foot hit. The timing had to be perfect, which required practice.

Four Across Coverage

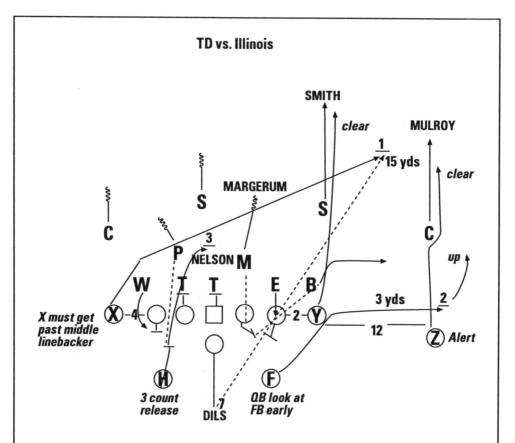

TD vs. Illinois

The prevalent coverage in the late 1990's is four-deep zone with the defensive backs bracketing wide receivers. In this instance, both the tight end and the flanker drove their defenders deep. This step was critical to the pattern's success. Ken Margerum, the split X end, took a four-yard split, crossing the field to a 15-yard depth. He had to get past the middle linebacker, who might have been an obstacle. The fullback had to attract the strong side linebacker, opening a big hole in the coverage behind him. This pattern was a specialized one; if the quarterback did not get this coverage he had to be prepared to look to the fullback and then the halfback.

Four Across Coverage

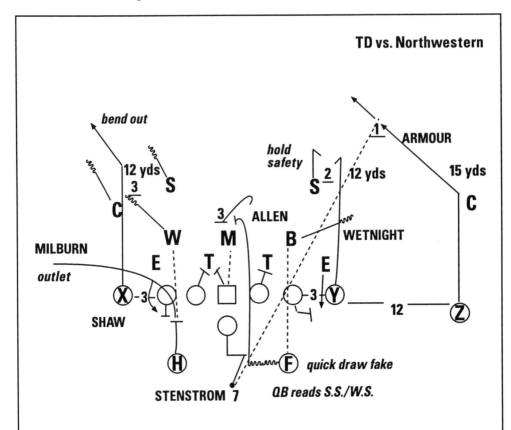

This play was also designed for four-deep coverage. Pivot hooks coupled with a good draw fake by the fullback held the safeties isolating the flanker on the corner. A 15-yard break point for Z behind the strong safety was critical. This step required an advantageous match-up for the flanker. This pattern was specialized; consequently, the quarterback had to be prepared to throw the pivot hooks, then look to the fullback versus a free safety coverage.

Four Across Coverage

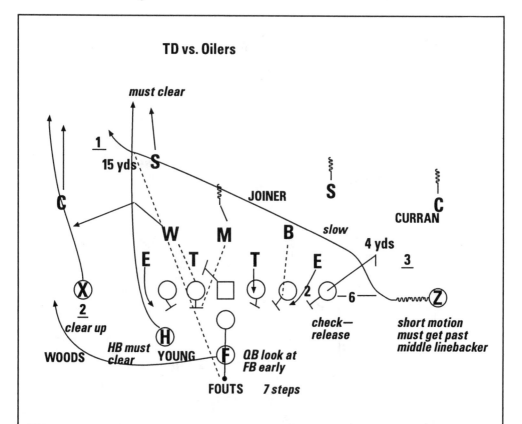

This play was designed for four-deep coverage. In this instance the halfback and split end cleared for the crossing flanker. The halfback had to be in a position to release cleanly up the field. A double wing position was best. The position required an active athlete. The flanker had to negotiate the middle linebacker. The swinging fullback had to attract the weak side linebacker. Dan Fouts looks to the fullback then finds Charlie Joiner.

Four Across Coverage

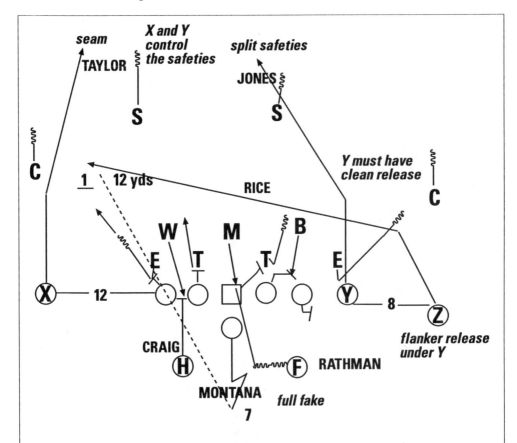

The faking between Montana and fullback Tom Rathman is critical. Rathman must keep his pads down; Montana must hide the ball. The offensive linemen should not allow space between themselves and the defensive men opposite them. The halfback must attack his blitzer. The flanker works behind the dropping defensive linemen who are held at the line by the fake.

Man Coverage (Red-Zone Route)

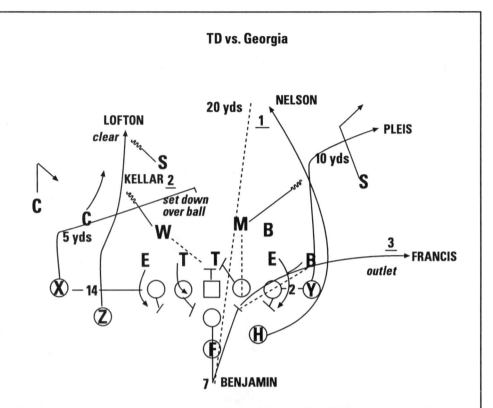

TD vs. Georgia

The line of scrimmage for this play was the 20-yard line. The defense double-covered great receiver James Lofton with the cornerback and weak safety. The tight end released outside, breaking to the corner against the strong safety. Darrin Nelson released just outside the tight end, then broke into the middle, catching the ball 20 to 25 yards deep. The quarterback read the weak safety as he looked toward Lofton. If the safety "bit," the ball would go to the halfback. If the safety stayed in the middle, X would get the ball setting down over the middle. If the strong safety was aligned "head up" on the tight end, the quarterback would look for the first, then the halfback.

Man Coverage

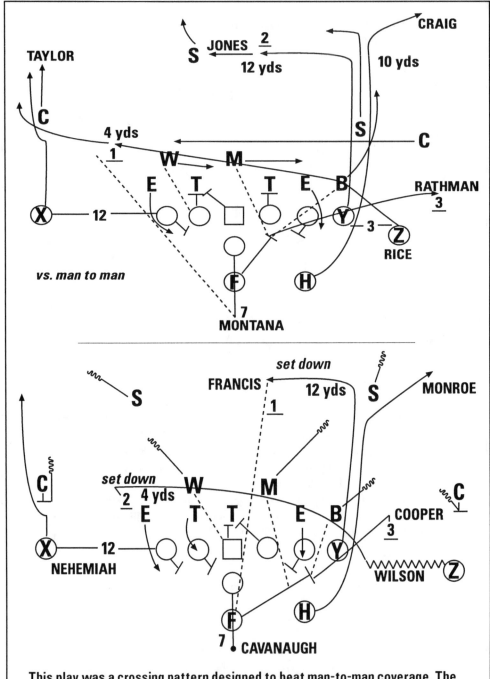

This play was a crossing pattern designed to beat man-to-man coverage. The flanker (Z) released under the tight end (Y). If the halfback was covered by a linebacker, he could be the primary receiver. If the flanker and tight end were covered, they kept going. If the defenders were dropping back, the flanker and tight end set down. They did not look at the quarterback until they had made their decision and committed to it.

Man Coverage

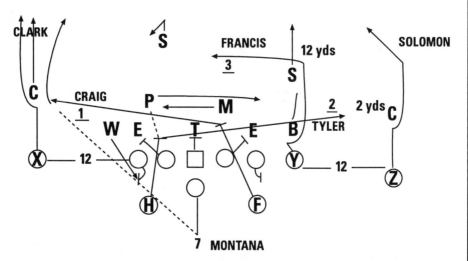

TD vs. Miami—Super Bowl

This pass combination took full advantage of man-to-man coverage that had the linebackers covering the backs. The offensive linemen "open" blocked to create release lanes for the backs. The backs were responsible for the inside linebackers. If the linebackers penetrated across the line, the backs stayed with them. If the backs met the linebackers at or beyond the line of scrimmage, then the backs would bounce off of the linebackers and release. The backs simply outran the backers. The tight end became the primary receiver if the inside linebackers blitzed. Joe Montana looked first to Roger Craig, then to Tyler, and finally to Francis.

Man Coverage

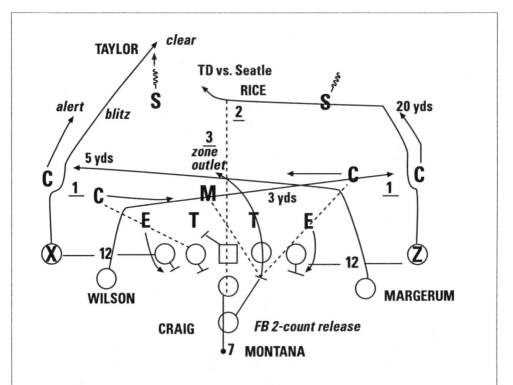

This four-receiver combination is designed to first beat man-to-man coverage underneath. The quarterback concentrates to his right at the snap of the ball. If the corner "dogs", he looks to Margerum "hot". If not, he looks to Wilson first, then quickly to Margerum. At that point, Rice will be breaking open in the middle. No free safety, the quarterback looks to Taylor on the post. Rathman is the outlet receiver vs. zone. Against zone coverage, both shallow crossing receivers would set down over each other's respective original position. The most important requirement for Montana is to look precisely from one receiver to the next. The first one open, he should hit. He should not leave the progression.

Man Coverage

TD vs. Dallas

We scored on this combination pass play the first time we used it. From 30 yards out, Dwight Clark made a double move on Everson Walls for a touchdown. On the play, Jerry Rice breaks across the face of the weak safety, pulling him up and distracting him. This situation gives Dwight the whole side of the field. As the man in motion, Wendell Tyler widens the strong safety. If the weak safety doesn't bite, Joe Montana hits Jerry. If Jerry is covered, Joe looks quickly to Russ Francis on a shallow cross. Roger Craig is the outlet receiver.

Blitz Route (Versus Man Coverage)

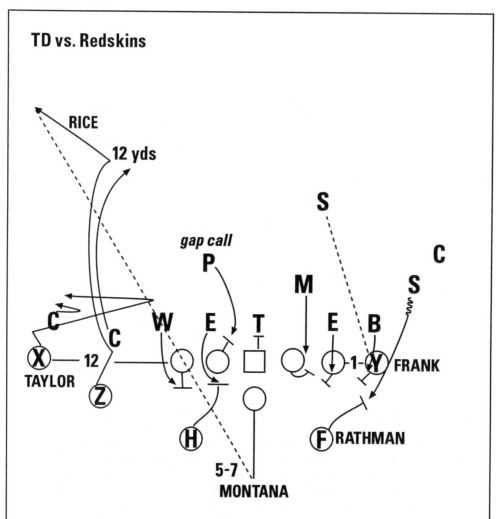

TD vs. Redskins

This play was an audible versus a double press on X and Z. Jerry Rice started inside and jumped outside, getting a jump on the cornerback. At 10-12 yards he bent in, then broke to the outside, catching the ball at 25 yards. John Taylor started inside, the slid back out. This "arrow" route held the cornerback. Against zone coverage, Taylor set down. This play was an audible pass designed to pick up eight pass rushers. Against a zone the halfback, fullback, and tight end released as outlets. The quarterback threw outside, letting the flanker run to the ball. If the quarterback read the zone, he held the ball and then dropped it off to the outlets.

Blitz Route (Versus Man Coverage)

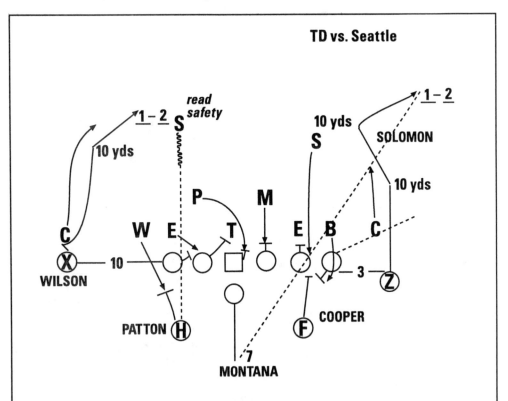

TD vs. Seattle

This play was an audible versus an eight-man pass rush. In this instance Freddie Solomon reduced his split to three to five yards. He then released outside into the corner. The split end, Mike Wilson, got inside his cornerback and broke to the post. Joe Montana read the weak safety. If the safety crowded the line of scrimmage, Joe looked to the post. If not, he immediately looked to Solomon. The other eligible receivers released late as outlets versus a zone.

Blitz Route (Versus Man Coverage)

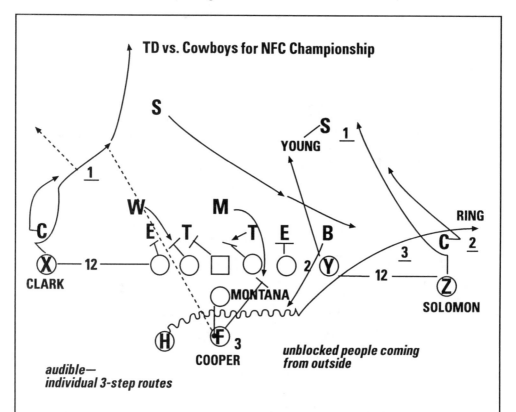

TD vs. Cowboys for NFC Championship

audible—
individual 3-step routes

unblocked people coming
from outside

This play was a blitz-oriented call. The idea was to isolate the split end, Dwight Clark, on his cornerback. It was Clark's job to inside his man and break up the field. The halfback, Billy Ring, was sent in motion to the strong side to force the defense to commit itself. If the weak safety or linebacker followed Ring, a hole was opened for Clark. The flanker and tight end released inside. If Clark could not get free, Montana looked first back to Solomon, then to tight end Charlie Young. Montana also had to be alert if the defense failed to cover Ring. This play was a three-step drop pattern. The guards had to be prepared to call "gap" to protect their gaps against a blitz. Clark could also be signaled to run a "Colorado," which started as a slant and then broke to the corner.

Blitz Route (Versus Zone Coverage)

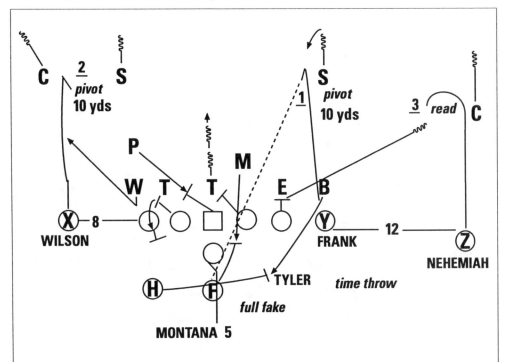

Timing is vital in this play that is employed against a zone-blitz. The play fake is designed to hold dropping defensive linemen momentarily. The ball should be faked and thrown before they can get adequate coverage depth. Offensive linemen make contact and sustain it as long as possible. The running backs attack the blitzers.

Blitz Route

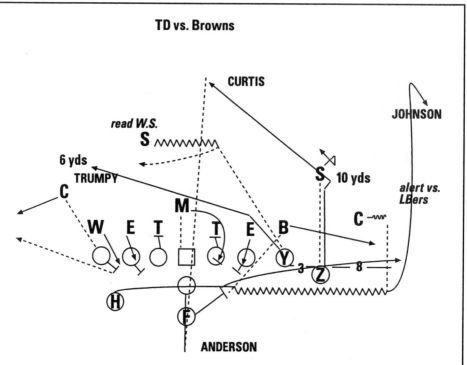

TD vs. Browns

This short post variation was designed to beat the blitz if a team "slid" its coverage. The strong safety ended up covering the flanker. The weak safety covered the tight end. If the weak safety ran with the halfback, the flanker had an open area in the middle of the field. Versus a zone the tight end set down and became the primary receiver. This was an excellent red zone play.

Blitz Route

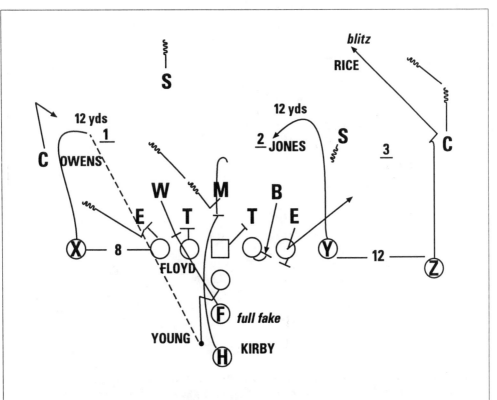

A full fake, timed throw. The quarterback hides the ball for an instant. The tailback keeps his pads down. The fullback attacks the blitzer. No space is left between the blockers and the defenders. All passes must be perfectly timed. Young throws as his left foot hits the ground.

Play Pass

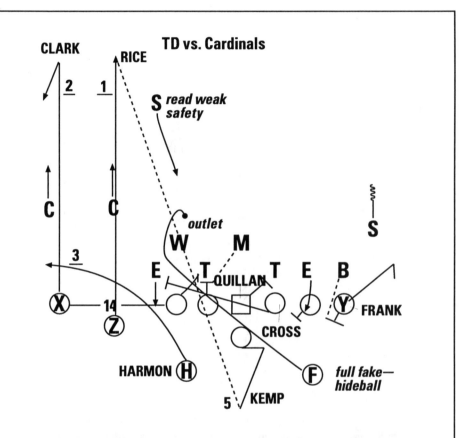

This trap action was staged to pull an aggressive weak safety to the line of scrimmage. This strategy should only be used when a team is facing a weak safety who has a history of flying up to make a hit. Jeff Kemp, an excellent deep passer filling in for Montana, hit Jerry Rice on this pattern four times for touchdowns. Guard Randy Cross had to locate the defensive end and adjust to his course; he had to be sure not to pull up early.

Play-Action Pass

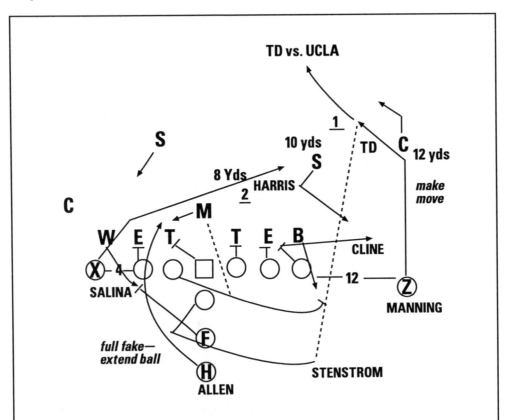

This action was designed to completely sell the base block "reach" play. Both backs had to "sell" the run. The quarterback, Steve Strenstrom, held the ball out to the running back, Ethan Allen. He then broke to his right behind the pulling guard. Strenstrom immediately looked to tight end Tony Cline, who stepped down simulating a block to the inside and then released into the flat. The split end, Mark Harris was split four yards. He released inside on a shallow crossing pattern that took him 12 yards deep. The flanker, Brian Manning, broke to the post. Strenstrom looked to the safeties. If they had been fooled or were out of position, he pulled up and went to Manning. The quarterback would audible out of this play if four men were threatening to the tight end side. On 3rd and 3 or in short yardage, Cline becomes the primary.

Play-Action Pass

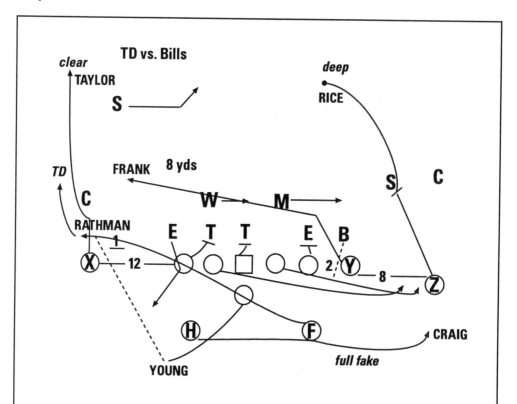

TD vs. Bills

This play committed virtually everyone to selling a sweep. Guards pulled. The halfback, Roger Craig, sold the sweep. Fullback Tom Rathman slid inside the unblocked defensive end into the flat. The tight end, John Frank, released inside as though to block and run a cross. Young made a quick fake on the move. He outran the defensive end and dropped the ball to Rathman or Jones. If this play was well-executed, the linebackers were pursuing the halfback and guards. This play was excellent for short yardage or in the red zone. We designed this play in the mid-seventies while we were with the Bengals. The first time it was used Booby Clark went 50 yards against the Raiders.

BILL WALSH COACHING LINEAGE

A number of extraordinarily talented coaches have worked with or for Bill Walsh over the duration of his coaching career. Many of these people have subsequently gone on to attain very responsible positions in the coaching profession, including those individuals listed below.

NFL Head Coaches (in alphabetical order)

- Pete Carroll (Head Coach, New England Patriots).
  - Worked for George Seifert and worked with Bill Walsh in San Francisco.
- Bruce Coslet (Head Coach, Cincinnati Bengals).
  - Played for Bill Walsh in Cincinnati and coached with him in San Francisco.
- Tony Dungy (Head Coach, Tampa Bay Buccaneers).
  - Played for Bill Walsh in San Francisco and coached for Denny Green with the Minnesota Vikings.
- Denny Green (Head Coach, Minnesota Vikings).
  - Worked with Bill Walsh at both Stanford and San Francisco.
- Mike Holmgren (Head Coach, Green Bay Packers).
  - Worked with Bill Walsh at San Francisco.
- Steve Mariucci (Head Coach, San Francisco 49ers).
  - Worked with Mike Holmgren in Green Bay.
- Ray Rhodes (Head Coach, Philadelphia Eagles).
  - Coached and played for Bill Walsh in San Francisco.
- Mike Shanahan (Head Coach, Denver Broncos).
  - Worked for George Seifert in San Francisco.
- George Seifert (Former Head Coach, San Francisco 49ers).
  - Coached for Bill Walsh at both Stanford and San Francisco.
- Dick Vermeil (Head Coach, St. Louis Rams).
  - Worked with Bill Walsh at Stanford.

- Mike White (Former Head Coach, Oakland Raiders).
  - Worked with Bill Walsh at both San Francisco and Stanford.
- Sam Wyche (Former Head Coach, Cincinnati Bengals and Tampa Bay Buccaneers).
  - Played for Bill Walsh at Cincinnati and coached with him in San Francisco.

NFL Coordinators

- Ken Anderson (Offensive Coordinator, Cincinnati Bengals).
  - Played for Bill Walsh at Cincinnati.
- Brian Billick (Offensive Coordinator, Minnesota Vikings).
  - Worked with Bill Walsh in San Francisco and with Denny Green at Stanford and Minnesota.
- Matt Cavanaugh (Offensive Coordinator, Chicago Bears).
  - Worked with Bill Walsh in San Francisco.
- Jon Gruden (Offensive Coordinator, Philadelphia Eagles).
  - Worked with Mike Holmgren and Ray Rhodes in San Francisco and Green Bay.
- Paul Hackett (Offensive Coordinator, Kansas City Chiefs).
  - Worked with Bill Walsh in San Francisco.
- Gary Kubiak (Offensive Coordinator, Denver Broncos).
  - Worked in San Francisco with George Seifert and Mike Shanahan.
- Sherman Lewis (Offensive Coordinator, Green Bay Packers).
  - Worked with Bill Walsh in San Francisco.

College Head Coaches

- Tom Holmoe (Head Coach, University of California-Berkeley).
  - Played for and coached with Bill Walsh in San Francisco.
- Terry Shea (Head Coach, Rutgers University).
  - Worked with Bill Walsh at Stanford.
- Fred vonAppen (Head Coach, University of Hawaii).
  - Worked with Bill Walsh in San Francisco.
- Tyrone Willingham (Head Coach, Stanford University).
  - Worked for Bill Walsh in San Francisco (as a member of the 49ers' minority intern program) and with Denny Green at both Stanford and Minnesota.

APPENDIX J

INDEX